KT-210-057

Provence & the Côte d'Azur

Nicola Williams, Fran Parnell

Contents

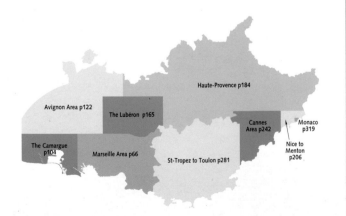

Haute-Provence p184

Avignon Area p122

The Lubéron p165

The Camargue p104

Marseille Area p66

St-Tropez to Toulon p281

Cannes Area p242

Monaco p319

Nice to Menton p206

Destination Provence & the Côte d'Azur

There's much more to Provence than *pétanque,* pastis and pretty villages tumbling down hilltops. Roughly wedged between meaty Marseille, with its rough-cut neighbourhoods and edgy art scene, and megalomaniacal Monte Carlo, with its slick Hong Kong–style skyline, this sunny spot screams action, glamour and just a hint of the ridiculous.

Travellers with a fascination for the ancient can gorge on Roman arches, aqueducts and amphitheatres. A resplendent papal palace, vineyards and an orgy of hues and scents to drink and savour – almond blossoms and asparagus, cherries, melons, lavender fields and pig-ugly truffles – are other heady treats. In the wild-west Camargue, cowboys herd cattle, Roma blaze flamenco and James Bond wannabes gallop on beaches and pedal round salt-pans beneath flamingo-filled skies. Paragliding, climbing, mountain biking and hot-dogging Europe's largest canyon top off the 'don't miss' thrills and spills list.

The Côte d'Azur is a legend in its own time. Renoirs, Matisses and Picassos in and around Nice, Cannes and St-Tropez lure tourists by the millions – as does Grace Kelly's Monaco, the chestnut-studded Massif des Maures, the rocky-red Estérel and Alpine foothills that plummet precipitously into the Med east of Nice. Cats on leads, dogs in handbags and prima donnas dusting sand from toes with shaving brushes are madcap sights to savour on this frenetic coastal strip.

Then there's Mont Ventoux, the Provençal king that rules this action-packed kingdom with stone-capped peaks atop barren, sun-baked slopes. The mistral adds a bitter bite to the air, while the sun bequeaths a warmth and intensity of light absolutely unknown elsewhere in Europe.

Tell anyone you're off to Provence and the Côte d'Azur and a kaleidoscope of quintessential images flashes by: sipping **pastis** (p58); chinking champagne glasses in a port-side café or ogling yachts in sexy **St-Tropez** (p283); rubbing shoulders with stars and window-shopping in **Cannes** (p245); sauntering along Nice's **promenade des Anglais** (p211); watching the **changing of the guard** (p324) at the palace or sharks at Prince Albert's **Musée Océanographique** (p324) in Monaco; or simply frolicking at a **festival** (p341). Inland there are **villages perchés** galore to visit in the **Lubéron** (p174) and **northern Var** (p295); stone-capped **Mont Ventoux** (p143) to scale; the **Nice–Digne-les-Bains mountain railway** (p194) to ride; and the green-watered **Gorges du Verdon** (p186) to canoe along.

Laze on the beach (p218)

Join in a game of *pétanque* (p29)

BILL WASSMAN

Stroll through a lavender field (p144)

BILL WAS

JON DAVISON

Explore Europe's largest Gothic palace, the Palais des Papes (p126) in Avignon

STEVE DAVEY

Marvel at the Roman Pont du Gard (p162), north of Nîmes

Stroll through the Villa et Jardins Ephrussi de Rothschild (p230), St-Jean-Cap Ferrat

DAN HERRICK

HIGHLIGHTS Art & Architecture

There's no escaping the region's extraordinary art heritage. Be it Vincent van Gogh in **Arles** (p108) and **St-Rémy de Provence** (p151), Matisse in **Nice** (p208) and **Vence** (p265), Picasso in **Vallauris** (p255) and **Antibes** (p256), Cézanne in **Aix-en-Provence** (p95) or Renoir in **Cagnes-sur-Mer** (p262), there are famous footsteps galore to follow. Notable modern art collections are showcased in **Marseille** (p75), **Nice** (p214), **Nîmes** (p160), **St-Tropez** (p285), **St-Paul de Vence** (p264) and **Mouans-Sartoux** (p268); **Aix-en-Provence** (p98) stars Vasarely, and **Biot** (p262) Fernard Léger. Architectural greats include the *belle époque* **Salle Garnier** (p331) and **casino** (p326) in Monaco; and Le Corbusier's radical creations in **Marseille** (p79) and **Cap Martin-Roquebrune** (p232).

Thrills and spills are abundant in Provence and the Côte d'Azur outdoors. In Marseille **dive** (p78) with fish around its **offshore islands** (p77) and **Les Calanques** (p89), or explore a subterranean shipwreck off the **Presqu'île du Giens** (p309). Galloping like a cowboy along sandy beaches gets the blood pumping in the wild-west **Camargue** (p107), and the Avignon area conjures up **Mont Ventoux** (p143) with its legendary **cycle climb** (p39) and grassy slopes to **ski** (p40). Take a **hot-air balloon flight** (p37) over the Lubéron before hitting the wild child of Provence: be it **hot-dogging** (p187) in the Gorges du Verdon, rock climbing or **via ferrata** (p204), **skiing** (p198), **ice-diving** (p199) or soaring with the region's vultures on a **paragliding course** (p191) in St-André-les-Alpes, Haute-Provence stuns.

Kayak the beautiful Verdon River in Castellane (p187)

BILL BACHMANN

CHRISTER FREDRIKSSON

Break the pace with some gentle cycling (p38)

Hike through the unspoilt Parc National du Mercantour (p197)

HUGH

JEAN-BERNARD CARILLET

Discover the wealth of flora and fauna of Les Calanques (p89)

MICHAEL GEBICKI

Visit one of the region's many vineyards (p57)

Revel in the amazing colours of Roussillon (p171)

DAVID TOMLINSON

HIGHLIGHTS Natural Beauty

Stunning scapes abound: the **Digne-les-Bains mountain railway** (p194) and **Le Train des Alpilles** (p114) from Fontvielle to Arles are great ways to gulp down loads of breathtaking scenery with minimum effort. Walking around **Mont Ventoux** (p145), the **Dentelles de Montmirail** (p141), a **Haute-Provence peak** (p202), the petroglyph-rich **Vallée des Merveilles** (p202), Mary Magdelene's **Massif de la Ste-Baume** (p93) or around the **Gorges du Verdon** (p186) is rewarded tenfold.

The Lubéron's rainbow of colours – **ochre rock formations** (p172) in Rustrel, **lavender fields** (p177) around Lagarde d'Apt, **silver bories** (p171) near Gordes – is dazzling. Seaside beauties include the islands of **Îles d'Hyères** (p301); **Cap Martin** (p232) and **Cap d'Ail** (p231); and Menton's **belle époque gardens** (p239).

Kick off that moveable feast of gastronomic highlights with a **pastis aperitif** (p85) in Marseille, a **chestnut liqueur** (p298) in Collobrières or an **amandine liqueur** (p195) in Forcalquier. As a starter, take a **cantaloupe melon** (p178) from Cavaillon doused in **muscat** (p142) from Beaumes de Venise, or something with **black truffles** (p140) from the Enclave des Papes. Main course contenders include **tellines** (p121) from the Golfe de Beauduc, **bull-meat stew** (p118) in the Camargue, **fish flambéed in pastis** (p83) at the Vallon des Auffes or a *tian* starring olives from **Nyons** (p141). Next comes **goats' cheese wrapped in chestnut leaves** (p196) from Banon, followed by **tarte Tropézienne** (p290) in St-Tropez.

DIANA MAYFIELD

Sample Provençal wine (p57)

Try authentic bouillabaisse (p83) in Marseille

GREG

GREG ELMS

Taste Vallée des Baux olive oil (p55)

Getting Started

Planning a trip to the region is as straightforward or as tricky as you make it: razz around Riviera hot spots in July and August and you need to book everything months in advance to make it affordable. But hop south to Marseille for an autumnal city break and planning time hovers close to zero. Travelling with children and/or on a budget is manageable and fun.

WHEN TO GO

Not in hot-and-bothered July and August when holiday-makers hog the region, clogging up roads and hotels and making life in the blistering heat unbearable.

See Climate Charts (p337) for more information.

May and June are the best times, followed by September and October. Spring is a cocktail of flowering poppy fields and almond trees. In September vines sag with plump red grapes, pumpkin fields glow orange and the first olives turn black in van Gogh's silver-branched olive groves. The *vendange* (grape harvest) starts around 15 September, followed by the *cueillette des olives* (olive harvest) from 15 November through to early January.

If you ski (p42), late December to March is for you. Lavender fields blaze purple (see The Perfume of Provence, p144) for two or three weeks any time between late June and mid-July.

COSTS & MONEY

Accommodation will be your biggest expense: count on €60 a night for a mid-range hotel double with bathroom. Hostel-sleeping, bread-and-cheese-eating backpackers can survive on €35 a day; those opting for mid-range hotels, restaurants and museums will spend upwards of €70.

LONELY PLANET INDEX

Litre of petrol €1.15

Litre bottle of Evian/Perrier mineral water €0.35/0.75

Cheap/expensive bottle of wine €4/a small fortune

Souvenir T-shirt €15

Ice cream (two-scoop cone) €3.50

TRAVEL LITERATURE

High Season in Nice (Robert Kanigel) 'How one French Riviera town has seduced travellers for 2000 years' is the tag line of this fascinating portrait of Nice.

Everybody Was So Young (Amanda Vaill) Beautiful evocation of an American couple and their glam set of literary friends (F Scott Fitzgerald, Hemingway, Cole Porter, Picasso etc) on the Côte d'Azur in the jazzy 1920s.

The Olive Farm (Carol Drinkwater) One of a spate of travelogues by a Brit who settles in Provence. This one, by a British TV actress, makes wholesome-if-predictable beach reading.

An Orderly Man and **A Short Walk from Harrods** (Dirk Bogarde) British film icon renovates his farmhouse in 1960s Provence.

The Hairdressers of St-Tropez (Rupert Everett) Comedy of hairdressers and talking dogs that kicks off on St-Tropez's Pampelonne Beach in 2042.

HOW MUCH?

Filled baguette €4

Croissant and *café au lait* €3

Local/foreign newspaper €1/3

Ten-minute taxi ride €15

Metro, tram or city bus ticket €1.20 to €1.40

For books on history and society, see the History and Culture chapters.

DON'T LEAVE HOME WITHOUT ...

- Valid travel insurance (p342), ID card or passport and visa (p348) if required
- Driving licence, car documents and car insurance (p358)
- Sunglasses, hat, mosquito repellent, a few clothes pegs and binoculars
- An insatiable appetite, a pleasure-seeking palate (p54) and a thirst for good wine (p57)
- Your sea legs (p42)

TOP FIVES & TENS

DESIGNER SLEEPS

Contemporary design dominates these stunning sleeping creations.

- Hôtel Hi, Nice (p221)
- Hôtel Le Corbusier, Marseille (see the boxed text, p79)
- Chambre de Séjour avec Vue, Saignon (see the boxed text, p180)
- Palm Beach Marseille, Marseille (p82)
- Hôtel Les Ateliers de l'Image, St-Rémy de Provence (see the boxed text, p153)

DRAMATIC DRIVES

Kill your speed, watch the road and watch out for killer views.

- Rte des Crêtes, Cassis to La Ciotat (see the boxed text, p91)
- Col de Canadel, Corniche des Maures (p301)
- The D36B from south of Arles to Salin de Giraud (p119) with detour to Beauduc (see boxed text, p121), then D36D to Plage de Piémanson, Southeastern Camargue (p120)
- The D39 from Collobrières to Gonfaron, Massif des Maures (p298)
- Moyenne Corniche, Nice to Beausoleil (p232)
- Grand Corniche, Nice to Roquebrune (p233)
- Col de l'Espigouler, Gémenos to Plan d'Aups (see A Pilgrim's Detour, p93)
- Formula One Grand Prix circuit, Monaco (see the boxed text, p331)
- Europe's highest mountain pass, the Col de Restefond la Bonette, Vallée de la Tinée (p200)
- Rte des Crêtes and Corniche Sublime, Gorges du Verdon (p186)

FESTIVALS & EVENTS

Legendary fêtes are a dime a dozen. See p341 for regional festivals and regional chapters for city festivals.

- Carnaval de Nice (Nice), February (p219)
- Pélerinage des Gitans (Stes-Maries de la Mer), May and October (p115)
- Fête des Gardians (Arles), May (see A Bullish Affair, p116)
- Cannes International Film Festival (Cannes), May (see the boxed text, p247)
- Formula One Grand Prix (Monaco), May (see the boxed text, p331)
- Fête de la Transhumance (St-Rémy de Provence), June (p151)
- Les Nuits du Théâtre Antique (Orange), June to August (p136)
- Festival d'Aix-en-Provence (Aix-en-Provence), July (p99)
- Festival d'Avignon and Festival Off (Avignon), July (p129)
- Festival de Lacoste (Lacoste), July (p175)

INTERNET RESOURCES

AngloINFO Riviera (www.angloinfo.com) Life on the Côte d'Azur in English; lots of pre-departure planning links.

Avignon & Provence (www.avignon-et-provence.com) Discerning accommodation and dining guide for mid-range travellers.

Comité Régional de Tourisme Provence-Alpes-Côte d'Azur (www.crt-paca.fr) Regional tourist board website.

Lonely Planet (www.lonelyplanet.com) Notes and posts on travel in Provence, plus Thorn Tree bulletin board.

Provence Web (www.provenceweb.fr) Online tourist guide.

Provence Beyond (www.beyond.fr) Online tourist guide.

TER-SNCF.com (www.ter-sncf.com/paca) Regional train tickets, fares and schedules.

Itineraries
CLASSIC ROUTES

BEST OF THE REGION
Two weeks / Nice to Avignon

There's no better place to kick off a whistle-stop tour than **Nice** (p208), the French Riviera queen. Visit its **museums** (p214), amble along **promenade des Anglais** (p211), splash out on **beach activities** (p218) and get lost in **Vieux Nice** (p210). On day three, train it to **Monaco** (p319). Don't miss the changing of the guards at the **Palais du Prince** (p324), Prince Albert's **Musée Océanographique** (p324) and **Monte Carlo Casino** (p326).

Then head west along the coast, stopping in **Antibes** (p256), **Cannes** (p245) or **Grasse** (p268) with its sweet-smelling perfume industry, depending on your interests. Then it's west again to oh-so-elegant **Aix-en-Provence** (p95) with its **Provençal markets** (p100) and chic **café life** (p97). To get here, either follow the coast via **St-Tropez** (p283) and its pretty **presqu'île** (p283) – with a boat excursion to the **Îles d'Hyères** (p303) and the **Massif des Maures** (p298) – or head inland past the action-packed **Gorges du Verdon** (p186), prime **whitewater sports** (p44) territory.

Devote week two to greener depths, entering the **Parc Naturel Régional du Lubéron** (see the boxed text, p169) at its southern foot near the Romanesque **Abbaye de Silvacane** (p180). Explore **Bonnieux** (p174), **Ménerbes** (p176), **Gordes** (p171) and other hilltop villages by car or **pedal power** (see the boxed text, p38). See red in **Roussillon** (p171) or **Rustrel** (p172), lavender in **Lagarde d'Apt** (see the boxed text, p177), then whizz up and down **Mont Ventoux** (p143) en route to the Friday morning market in **Carpentras** (p148). Not yet breathless? Finish the fortnight with papal **Avignon** (p124).

From Nice to Avignon, with a few short detours along the way, is a relaxed 550km, taking in the very best of Provence and the Côte d'Azur. The trip can be done in a whirlwind fortnight, but definitely merits as much time as you can give it.

HILLTOP VILLAGES

One week / Èze to Les Baux de Provence

Èze (p232) and **Roquebrune** (p233) are great excuses to motor along the **Moyenne Corniche** (p232) and **Grande Corniche** (p233) from Nice. A footpath links **Gorbio** (p240) with **Ste-Agnès** (p240), Europe's highest seaside village. **Beau Séjour** (p241) in Gorbio is a memorable lunch-time spot.

Spend another day wiggling up, down and around the **Arrière-Pays Niçois** (p234): untouched **Peille** (p235), eagle's-nest **Peillon** (p235), **Contes** (p234) with its still-functioning olive-oil mill, flower-filled **Tourrette-Levens** (p234) and photogenic **Coaraze** (p235) are all worth the hike. Chic **St-Paul de Vence** (p263), with legendary lunch-time spot **La Colombe d'Or** (p264), is a hilltop classic.

Follow this week-long 650km tour to delve into the nooks and crannies of one of Provence's greatest attractions: medieval *villages perchés* on and off the beaten tourist track. Bring your camera and a hearty appetite for lunches to remember.

Alternatively, whizz west to the orgy of villages atop hills around St-Tropez: **La Garde Freinet** (p300), **Grimaud** (p294), **Gassin** (p292) and **Ramatuelle** (p292). To get here, go off the beaten track via **Callas** (p295), **Châteaudouble** (p296), **Tourtour** (p296) and **Les Arcs-sur-Argens** (p297).

Devote the second half of the week to the Lubéron. Start with chateau-clad **Ansouis** (p182), cinematic **Vaugines** (p181) and cute **Cucuron** (p181). Shop at the Friday morning market in **Lourmarin** (p181) then head to **Bonnieux** (p174), **Lacoste** (p175), **Ménerbes** (p176) and ruined **Oppède le Vieux** (p176). From Bonnieux detour east to **Auribeau** (p182), feasting in **Sivergues** (see Author's Choice, p181) and sleeping in **Saignon** (see Author's Choice, p180).

Two quintessential villages form the final leg: approach **Gordes** (p171) from the south for a full frontal of it tumbling down the hillside and lunch in peace at the **Mas de Tourteron** (p174), then brace yourself for busy **Les Baux de Provence** (p153).

*MEDITERRANEAN
SEA*

CITY BREAK

Four days / Nîmes & Marseille

Fly into Nîmes-Arles-Camargue airport, pick up a car and hit **Nîmes** (p157), a Roman giant of a city with its mighty **amphitheatre** (p159). Time it right and you could catch a bullfight during one of the city's three big **férias** (p160). Fight or no fight, find out about bullish culture at the **Musée des Cultures Taurines** (p160). Lunch with views atop Norman Foster's **Carré d'Art** (p159), then saunter around place de la Maison Carrée with its **Roman temple** (p159), and the **old town** (p157). Mid-afternoon, stop for a drink and a couple of **caladons** (p162) in an outdoor **café** (p161).

On day two take a trip to the **Pont du Gard** (p162) or the Camargue. For the former, take gear to swim or **canoe** (p163) beneath the aqueduct, sturdy shoes to walk along the **Mémoires de Garrigue** (p163) and a picnic of **brandade de Nîmes** (see Shopping, p162) and local produce from **Les Halles** (p161). A circular drive to the **Camargue** (p104) takes in **Aigues-Mortes** (p118), flamingos at the **Parc Ornithologique du Pont de Gau** (p107) and bull ribs for lunch in **Stes-Maries de la Mer** (p117), returning via **Arles** (p108).

Speed east on day three to **Marseille** (p69), taking in its **Vieux Port** (p71) and offshore **islands** (p77) in the morning, followed by a **bouillabaisse** (see Tasty Tip, p83) lunch and **coastal stroll** (p76). Devote the last day to **Les Calanques** (p89).

Four days gives you just enough time to squeeze in the very best of two of Provence's most fascinating – and contrasting – cities. That said, there's no reason why you can't devote a long weekend to one or the other, or stretch out the two-city 360km trip into a week instead.

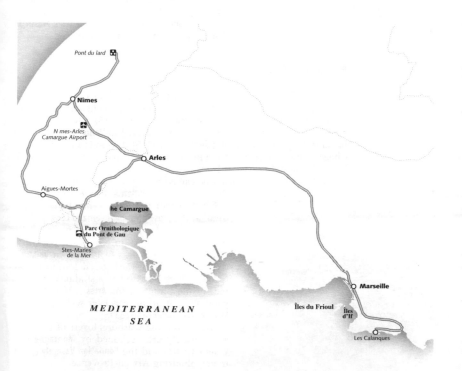

TAILORED TRIPS

NATURAL WONDERS

Kick off a green adventure of natural marvels in the mountains of **Haute-Provence** (p184). Riding the **Nice–Digne-les-Bains mountain railway** (see the boxed text, p194) as far as Puget-Théniers, and lunching on hearty Haute-Provence fodder at Auberge des Acacias, is a scenic way to arrive.

Once in the **Parc National du Mercantour** (p197), must-sees made to make you feel small include **Europe's highest mountain pass** (p197) and **largest Alpine lake** (p199); the **Vallée de l'Ubaye** (p197) with its wild white waters, perfect

for rafting; the deep-red **Gorges de Dalius** (p200) and **Gorges du Cians** (p200); the sublime clifftop views at the end of a **walking trail** (p200) near Guillaumes; the moonscape **Vallée des Merveilles** (p202); and the frenzy of wildlife seen on **walks** (p202) with local mountain guides.

Venturing west, the fossil deposits around **Barles** (p192) are spectacular – as is the **Gorges du Verdon** (p186), the penitent monks at **Les Mées** (p195), and stone-capped **Mont Ventoux** (p143). Coastal quarters cook up the unique wetland of the **Camargue** (p104); **Les Calanques** (p89); **France's highest cliff** (see Naturally Beautiful, p91); a clutch of **idyllic islands** (p303); and the red-rock **Massif de l'Estérel** (p272), best seen as the sun sets.

ARTISTS IN PROVENCE

With its designer chapels and avant-garde art museums, the region is a living art museum: on the Côte d'Azur, Matisse hung out and died in **Nice** (p208), home to his grave and the **Musée Matisse** (p215), where dozens of his works can be viewed. During WWII he fled to **Vence** (p265), where he later designed the **Chapelle du Rosaire** (p265). Ukrainian painter Marc Chagall, whose work also has a museum of its own in Nice, spent his life in nearby **St-Paul de Vence** (p263).

The **Menton** (p236) of Jean Cocteau is an easy day trip from Nice. Other episodes from the artist's life come alive in **Villefranche-sur-Mer** (p228).

Northeast of Cannes, Fernand Léger fans drool at the **Musée National Fernand Léger** (p262) in Biot. From here, tie in a trip north to the **Musée Renoir** (p263) in Cagnes-sur-Mer or south to see the works of Picasso in **Vallauris** (p255). Should it be the latter, detour to **Antibes** (p258), where Picasso had a studio. Van Gogh meanwhile plumped for **Arles** (p108) to live, paint and cut off his ear, later seeking help in **St-Rémy de Provence** (p151).

Away from the seashore, lovers of Cézanne and Vasarely are beckoned by **Montagne Ste-Victoire** (p103) and the **Fondation Vasarely** (p98) in neighbouring Aix-en-Provence.

GREAT GARDENS

Provence is a gardener's paradise, as a stroll through **Menton's Top Five Gardens** (p239), a stunning collection of horticultural treasures, attests: Jardin Botanique Exotique du Val Rahmeh, created in 1905; Spanish-inspired Jardin Fontana Rosa; Jardin de la Villa Maria Serena, where the temperature never falls below 5°C; the English-inspired 1920s winter garden at La Serre de la Madone; and the Jardins des Colombières. Thousands of cactus and succulent varieties sprout in Monaco's **Jardin Exotique** (p327).

Equally sumptuous is the *belle époque* creation at St-Jean-Cap Ferrat's **Villa et Jardins Ephrussi de Rothschild** (p230). To re-create an ancient Greek garden was the drive behind the 1902 gardens at the **Villa Grecque Kérylos** (p231), Beaulieu-sur-Mer. Two decades on, American artists became green-fingered eccentrics at **Château de la Napoule** (p272), Mandelieu-La Napoule, while Edith Wharton tended green matters at the **Villa Noailles** (p311) in Hyères. **Domaine du Rayol** (p301), just south of Le Rayol, is another legendary Riviera garden.

Inland, medieval garden design takes shape at Mane's **Prieuré de Salagon** (p196). Herbs are the focus of Lourmarin's **Ferme de Gerbaud** (p181), and figs grow like crazy at **Les Figuières du Mas de Luquet** (p156), Graveson. Gardens with an unusual twist include the **Jardin de l'Alchimiste** (p155), Eygalières; the **Jardin des Neuf Damoiselles** (see An Oddity Detour, p139), Vaison-la-Romaine; **Le Potager d'un Curieux** (see A Curious Detour, p182) near Saignon; and Lauris' **Jardin Conservatoire de Plantes Tinctoriales** (p179).

The Authors

NICOLA WILLIAMS
Coordinating Author; Marseille Area; The Camargue; Avignon Area; The Lubéron

For Nicola, a Lyon-based journalist, it is an easy three-hour train hop to Marseille, from where she has spent endless years eating her way around the region. (Sivergues' Ferme Auberge Le Castelas is still the most memorable.) Nicola wrote the 1st edition of *Provence & the Côte d'Azur* in 1999 and has worked on many other Lonely Planet titles since, including *The Loire* and *France*.

My Provence & the Côte d'Azur

For me, the region means food (p54), art (p45), architecture (p47) and an extraordinarily varied landscape that ensures a new find with every visit. Mood depending, the frenetic pace of the Côte d'Azur – the Nice beach buzz (p218), the high-life restaurant-bars of Monaco (p329), the feisty Cap Ferrat cicadas (see Love Song, p33) – thrills. Other times, give me a *chambre d'hôte* (B&B) in the middle of nowhere (Au Pied du Lubéron, Bonnieux; p174) or something a tad different (Chambre de Séjour avec Vue, Saignon; see Author's Choice, p180); a natural landscape to explore – the Camargue (p104), the Massif des Maures (p298) – and I'm sand-girl happy. Top tips? Eat on a farm (see Author's Choice, p181), watch the sun set over the Massif de l'Estérel (p272) and follow Le Corbusier from Marseille to Cap Martin-Roquebrune (see the boxed text, p49).

FRAN PARNELL
Haute-Provence; Nice to Menton; Cannes Area; St-Tropez to Toulon; Monaco; Transport

Fran's love of Provence and its romantic literary heritage was born while studying Medieval French at Cambridge University. Having pottered round France on a tiny canal boat, it was also an experience to visit St-Tropez and learn how to boat in style.

Snapshot

Fat cat Provence and the Côte d'Azur has a right to be smug: its Mediterranean coastline – built up as it might be – is lush, lovely and tourist-laden. Its climate is enviably mild. And its most buzzing, biggest city, brazen Marseille, stands proud as a diamond with oh-so-elegant and aloof Aix-en-Provence as France's largest urban conglomeration after Paris and Lyon.

Tourism rakes in the primary income of this wealthy, healthy and bright region. That said, the 2003 season witnessed a drop in the number of foreigners visiting these sun-drenched parts. 'Is the French Riviera of Bardot (see BB, p286) and Beckham (see Riviera High Life, p28) fame finally losing some of its sex appeal?', shouted critics. 'No way' was the determined response from local hoteliers, who cited a rollercoaster of unfortunate world and domestic events – the terrorist attacks of 9/11, the US-led invasion of Iraq, a tumbling dollar, ferocious forest fires (p34), flash floods (p26) and the sabotage of the region's premier cultural festival by striking artists (p26) – as the reason why a good many Americans, Brits and others simply stayed away that summer.

Information technology – source of the region's secondary income – booms. Nowhere is the power of this pulsating industry better felt than in Sophia Antipolis, a 2300-hectare techno-pole established near Cannes in 1969 as a launch pad for piloting advanced technology. Today Europe's premier hi-tech and science park employs 25,000 people split across 1250-odd companies, contributing in part to the region's standing as second only to Paris in job creation and business growth.

Creating more jobs remains top priority nonetheless for local government: unemployment in the Provence-Alpes-Côte d'Azur (PACA) *région* was 11.7% in mid-2004; a drop of 0.3% on the previous year but still a fair whack higher than the national unemployment rate (8.8%).

Unemployment is particularly marked among Provence's substantial immigrant community (see p30), for whom daily life is by no means a bed of roses. About 20% of immigrant men work in agriculture or construction, but unemployment in multicultural ranks remains around 12% higher than the regional average. The national government's ban of the Islamic headscarf (along with Jewish skullcaps, Sikh turbans, crucifixes and other religious symbols) in French schools in 2004 did little to appease an already disgruntled ethnic population. The law, as Marie-Josée Roig (France's minister for the family and Avignon city's mayor) explained to a UN committee for child rights, might well be intended to place schoolchildren on an equal footing in the republican French classroom. But for many Muslims – a couple of thousand of whom took to the streets of Marseille in protest – the law is merely confirmation that the French state is really not prepared to fully integrate Muslims into French society.

It was in the turquoise depths of the Mediterranean between Marseille and Cassis that the book was closed on one of aviation's greatest mysteries: in 2004 a local diver uncovered the wreckage of the plane of Antoine de Saint-Exupéry, thus identifying the spot where the legendary author of one of the world's most enchanting tales, *Le Petit Prince* (The Little Prince), plunged to his death in July 1944.

FAST FACTS

Population: 4.5 million

Area: 31,399 sq km

GDP: €95.7 billion

GDP growth: 0.5%

Unemployment: 11.7%

Population density: 144 people per sq km

Largest cities: Marseille, Nice & Toulon

Percentage of *résidences secondaires* (second homes): 17.2% of all homes

History

PREHISTORIC MAN

Provence was inhabited from an exceptionally early age and has a bounty of prehistoric sights to prove it. In Monaco the Grottes de l'Observatoire (p327) showcase brilliant prehistoric rock scratchings, carved one million years ago and among the world's oldest. Around 400,000 BC, prehistoric man settled in Terra Amata (present-day Nice): the archaeological site's Musée de Paléontologie Humaine de Terra Amata (p216) explores prehistoric man and his movements at this time.

Neanderthal hunters occupied the Mediterranean coast during the Middle Palaeolithic period (about 90,000 to 40,000 BC), living in caves. Provence's leading prehistory museum, the Musée de la Préhistoire des Gorges de Verdon (p190) in Quinson, runs visits to one such cave, the Grotte de la Baume Bonne (p190).

Modern man arrived with creative flair in 30,000 BC. The ornate wall paintings of bison, seals, ibex and other animals inside the decorated Grotte Cosquer in the Calanque de Sormiou (p89), near Marseille, date to 20,000 BC.

The Neolithic period (about 6000 to 4500 years ago) witnessed the earliest domestication of sheep and the cultivation of lands. The first dwellings to be built (around 3500 BC) were *bories:* learn about life inside these one- or two-storey beehive-shaped huts at the Village des Bories (p171) near Gordes.

The star of Provence's prehistoric show is the collection of 30,000 Bronze Age petroglyphs decorating Mont Bégo in the Vallée des Merveilles (p202). Marked walking trails lead to the rock drawings, dated between 1800 and 1500 BC.

> For a highly detailed and fascinating study of the Gauls in Provence and the *oppidum* they built at Entremont, go to www.entremont.culture.gouv.fr.

GREEKS TO ROMANS

Massalia (Marseille) was colonised around 600 BC by Greeks from Phocaea in Asia Minor; from the 4th century BC they established more trading posts along the coast: at Antipolis (Antibes), Olbia (Hyères), Athenopolis (St-Tropez), Nikaia (Nice), Monoïkos (Monaco) and Glanum (near St-Rémy de Provence). With them, the Greeks brought olives and grapevines.

While Hellenic civilisation was developing on the coast, the Celts penetrated northern Provence. They mingled with ancient Ligurians to create a Celto-Ligurian stronghold around Entremont, its influence extending as far south as Draguignan.

In 125 BC the Romans helped the Greeks defend Massalia against invading Celto-Ligurians from Entremont. Their subsequent victory marked the start of the Gallo-Roman era and the creation of Provincia Gallia Transalpina, the first Roman *provincia* (province), from which the name Provence is derived.

THE GALLO-ROMANS

Provincia Gallia Transalpina, which quickly became Provincia Narbonensis, embraced all of southern France from the Alps to the Mediterranean Sea and as far west as the Pyrenees. In 122 BC the Romans destroyed

TIMELINE	c90,000–30,000 BC	600 BC
	Neanderthal hunters occupy the Mediterranean coast; around 30,000 BC Cro-Magnons start decorating their caves	The Greeks colonise Massalia and establish trading posts along the coast, bringing olives and grapevines

the Ligurian capital of Entremont and established the Roman stronghold of Aquae Sextiae Salluviorum (Aix-en-Provence) at its foot.

During this period the Romans built roads to secure the route between Italy and Spain. The Via Aurelia linked Rome to Fréjus, Aix-en-Provence, Arles and Nîmes; the northbound Via Agrippa followed the River Rhône from Arles to Avignon, Orange and Lyons; and the Via Domitia linked the Alps with the Pyrenees by way of Sisteron, the Lubéron, Beaucaire and Nîmes. Vestiges of these roads – the Pont Julien (p174) from 3 BC at Bonnieux and an arch (p178) in Cavaillon – remain.

The Roman influence on Provence was tremendous, though it was only after Julius Caesar's conquest of Gaul (58–51 BC) and its consequent integration into the Roman Empire that the region flourished. Massalia, which had retained its independence following the creation of Provincia, was incorporated by Caesar in 49 BC. In 14 BC the still-rebellious Ligurians were defeated by Augustus, who built a monument at La Turbie (p233) in 6 BC to celebrate. Arelate (Arles) became the chosen regional capital.

Under the emperor Augustus, vast amphitheatres were built at Arelate (p109), Nemausus (Nîmes; p159), Forum Julii (Fréjus; p277) and Vasio Vocontiorum (Vaison-la-Romaine; p138). Triumphal arches were raised at Arausio (Orange; p136), Cabelio (Cavaillon; p178), Carpentorate (Carpentras; p146) and Glanum (p151), and a series of aqueducts were constructed. The 275m-long Pont du Gard (p162), with its impressive multimedia museum, was part of a 50km-long system of canals built around 19 BC by Agrippa, Augustus' deputy, to bring water from Uzès to Nîmes. All these ancient public buildings remain exceptionally well preserved and lure sightseers year-round.

The end of the 3rd century saw the reorganisation of the Roman Empire. Provincia Narbonensis was split into two provinces in AD 284. The land on the right bank of the Rhône (Languedoc-Roussillon today) remained Narbonensis, and the land on the left bank (today's Provence) became Provincia Viennoise. Christianity penetrated the region and was adopted by the Romans.

DID YOU KNOW?

Provençal legend says Christianity was brought to the region by Mary Magdalene, Mary Jacob and Mary Salome who sailed into Stes-Maries de la Mer in AD 40.

MEDIEVAL PROVENCE

After the collapse of the Roman Empire in AD 476, Provence was invaded by various Germanic tribes: the Visigoths (West Goths, from the Danube delta region in Transylvania), the Ostrogoths (East Goths, from the Black Sea region) and the Burgundians of Scandinavian origin. In the 6th century it was ceded to the Germanic Franks.

In the early 9th century the Saracens (an umbrella term adopted locally to describe Muslim invaders such as Turks, Moors and Arabs) emerged as a warrior force to be reckoned with. Attacks along the Maures coast, Niçois hinterland and more northern Alps persuaded villagers to take refuge in the hills. Many of Provence's perched, hilltop villages (see p12) date from this chaotic period. In AD 974 the Saracen fortress at La Garde Freinet was defeated by William the Liberator (Guillaume Le Libérateur), count of Arles, who consequently extended his feudal control over the entire region, marking a return of peace and unity to Provence, which became a marquisate. In 1032 it joined the Holy Roman Empire.

125–6 BC	AD 5th to 9th centuries
Romans create Provincia Gallia Transalpina, from which Provence gets its name; Provence joins Roman Empire	Roman Empire collapses and Germanic tribes invade Provence; Franks encourage villagers to move uphill to avert Saracen attacks

The marquisate of Provence was later split in two: the north fell to the counts of Toulouse from 1125 and the Catalan counts of Barcelona gained control of the southern part, which stretched from the River Rhône to the River Durance and from the Alps to the sea. This became the county of Provence (Comté de Provence). Raymond Bérenger V (1209–45) was the first Catalan count to reside permanently in Aix (the capital since 1186). In 1229 he conquered Nice and in 1232 he founded Barcelonnette. After Bérenger's death the county passed to the House of Anjou, under which it enjoyed great prosperity.

THE POPES

In 1274 Comtat Venaissin (Carpentras and its Vaucluse hinterland) was ceded to Pope Gregory X in Rome. In 1309 French-born Clement V (r 1305–14) moved the papal headquarters from feud-riven Rome to Avignon. A tour of the Papal palace (p126) illustrates how resplendent a period this was for the city, which hosted nine pontiffs between 1309 and 1376.

The death of Pope Gregory XI led to the Great Schism (1378–1417), during which rival popes resided at Rome and Avignon and spent most of their energies denouncing and excommunicating each other. Even after the schism was settled and a pope established in Rome, Avignon and the Comtat Venaissin remained under papal rule until 1792.

The arts in Provence (p45) flourished. A university was established in Avignon as early as 1303, followed by a university in Aix a century on. In 1327 Italian poet Petrarch (1304–74) encountered his muse, Laura: visit Fontaine de Vaucluse's Musée Pétrarque (p150) for the full story. During the reign of Good King René, king of Naples (1434–80), French became the courtly language.

FRENCH PROVENCE

In 1481 René's successor, his nephew Charles III, died heirless and Provence was ceded to Louis XI of France. In 1486 the state of Aix ratified Provence's union with France and the centralist policies of the French kings saw the region's autonomy greatly reduced. Aix Parliament, a French administrative body, was created in 1501.

This new addition to the French kingdom did not include Nice, Barcelonnette, Puget-Théniers and the hinterlands of these towns which, in 1388, had become incorporated into the lands of the House of Savoy. The County of Nice, with Nice as its capital, did not become part of French Provence until 1860.

A period of instability ensued, as a visit to the synagogue in Carpentras (p146) testifies: Jews living in French Provence fled to ghettos in Carpentras, Pernes-les-Fontaines, L'Isle-sur-la-Sorgue, Cavaillon or Avignon – all were part of the pontifical enclave of Comtat Venaissin, where papal protection remained assured until 1570.

An early victim of the Reformation that swept Europe in the 1530s and the consequent Wars of Religion (1562–98) was the Lubéron. In April 1545 the population of 11 Waldensian (Vaudois) villages in the Lubéron were massacred (see the boxed text, p179). Numerous clashes followed between the staunchly Catholic Comtat Venaissin and its Huguenot (Protestant) neighbours to the north around Orange.

974	1309-76
William the Liberator extends his feudal control over Provence, which becomes a marquisate and joins the Holy Roman Empire	The Holy See moves from feud-riven Rome to Avignon; nine pontiffs head the Roman Catholic church from the city

In 1580 the plague immobilised the region. Treatments first used by the prophetic Nostradamus (1503–66) in St-Rémy de Provence were administered to plague victims. The Edict of Nantes in 1598 (which recognised Protestant control of certain areas, including Lourmarin in the Lubéron) brought an uneasy peace to the region – until its revocation by Louis XIV in 1685. Full-scale persecution of Protestants ensued. Visit Aigues-Mortes's Tour de Constance (p118) and Château d'If (p77) to see where Huguenots were killed or imprisoned.

The close of the century was marked by the French Revolution in 1789: as the National Guard from Marseille marched north to defend the Revolution, a merry tune composed in Strasbourg several months earlier for the war against Prussia – *Chant de Guerre de l'Armée du Rhin* (War Song of the Rhine Army) – sprung from their lips. France's stirring national anthem, *La Marseillaise*, was born.

LA ROUTE NAPOLÉON

Provence was divided into three *départements* in 1790: Var, Bouches du Rhône and the Basse-Alpes. Two years later papal Avignon and Comtat Venaissin were annexed by France, making way for the creation of Vaucluse.

In 1793 the Armée du Midi marched into Nice and declared it French territory. France also captured Monaco, until now a recognised independent state ruled by the Grimaldi family (see the boxed text, p324). When Toulon was besieged by the English, it was thanks to the efforts of a dashing young Corsican general named Napoleon Bonaparte (Napoleon I) that France recaptured it.

The Reign of Terror that swept through France between September 1793 and July 1794 saw religious freedoms revoked, churches desecrated and cathedrals turned into 'Temples of Reason'. In the secrecy of their homes, people handcrafted thumbnail-sized, biblical figurines, hence the inglorious creation of the *santon* (see Little Saints, p102).

In 1814 France lost the territories it had seized in 1793. The County of Nice was ceded to Victor Emmanuel I, king of Sardinia. It remained under Sardinian protectorship until 1860, when an agreement between Napoleon III and the House of Savoy helped drive the Austrians from northern Italy, prompting France to repossess Savoy and the area around Nice. In Monaco the Treaty of Paris restored the rights of the Grimaldi royal family; from 1817 until 1860 the principality also fell under the protection of the Sardinian king.

Meanwhile the Allied restoration of the House of Bourbon to the French throne at the Congress of Vienna (1814–15), following Napoleon I's abdication and exile to Elba, was rudely interrupted by the return of the emperor. Following his escape from Elba in 1815, Napoleon landed at Golfe-Juan on 1 March with a 1200-strong army. He proceeded northwards, passing through Cannes, Grasse, Castellane, Digne-les-Bains and Sisteron en route to his triumphal return to Paris on 20 May. Unfortunately Napoleon's glorious 'Hundred Days' back in power ended with the Battle of Waterloo and his return to exile. He died in 1821.

During the revolutions of 1848, French revolutionaries adopted as their own the red, white and blue tricolour of Martigues (p92) near Marseille. This became France's national flag.

Gérard Depardieu, Leonardo DiCaprio and Jeremy Irons star in the Hollywood box office hit *The Man in the Iron Mask*, a modern adaptation of the 'iron mask' mystery that occurred on the Île Ste-Marguerite near Cannes in the late 17th century.

Bone up on current events in the Provence-Alpes-Côte d'Azur region at www.cr-paca.fr (in French), or with its web TV arm www.lawebtv .cr-paca.fr (in French).

1481	1539
Good King René's successor dies heirless and Provence falls to Louis XI of France	French (rather than Provençal) is made the official administrative language of Provence

---

THE SKY-BLUE COAST

The Côte d'Azur (literally 'Azure Coast') gained its name from a 19th-century guidebook.

La Côte d'Azur, published in 1887, was the work of Stéphane Liégeard (1830–1925), a lawyer-cum–aspiring poet from Burgundy who lived in Cannes. The guide covered the coast from Menton to Hyères and was an instant hit.

Its title, a reflection of the coast's clear blue cloudless skies, became the hottest buzz word in town. And it never tired. The Côte d'Azur is known as the French Riviera by most Anglophones.

THE BELLE ÉPOQUE

The Second Empire (1852–70) brought to the region a revival in all things Provençal, a movement spearheaded by Maillane-born poet Frédéric Mistral; the house museum in his home town (see p156) looks at his life. Rapid economic growth was another hallmark: Nice, which had become part of France in 1860, was among Europe's first cities to have a purely tourist-based economy. Between 1860 and 1911 it was Europe's fastest-growing city. In the Victorian period the city became particularly popular with the English aristocracy, who followed their queen's example of wintering in mild Nice. European royalty followed soon after. The train line reached Toulon in 1856, followed by Nice and Draguignan, and in 1864 work started on a coastal road from Nice to Monaco. The Nice Opera House (p224) and the neoclassical Justice Palace (p210) were built in fine Second Empire architectural style.

In neighbouring Monaco the Grimaldi family gave up its claim over its former territories of Menton and Roquebrune in 1861 (under Monégasque rule until 1848) in exchange for France's recognition of its status as an independent principality. Four years later Monte Carlo Casino – a stunning place, still operational, that should not be missed (see Loser Risks All, p326) – opened and Monaco leapt from being Europe's poorest state to one of its richest.

Côte d'Azur: Inventing the French Riviera by Mary Blume looks at the glamorous rise and fall of the Côte d'Azur.

The Third Republic ushered in the glittering *belle époque* with Art Nouveau architecture, a whole field of artistic 'isms' including impressionism, and advances in science and engineering. Wealthy French, English, American and Russian tourists and tuberculosis sufferers (for whom the only cure was sunlight and sea air) discovered the coast. The intensity and clarity of the region's colours and light appealed to many painters (see p45). And in 1887 the first guidebook to the French coast was published; see The Sky-Blue Coast (above).

WWI & THE ROARING 1920S

No blood was spilled on southern French soil during WWI. Soldiers were conscripted from the region, however, and the human losses included two out of every 10 Frenchmen between 20 and 45 years of age. With its primarily tourist-based economy, the Côte d'Azur recovered quickly from the post-war financial crisis that lingered in France's more industrial north.

The Côte d'Azur sparkled as an avant-garde centre in the 1920s and 1930s, with artists pushing into the new fields of cubism and surrealism, Le Corbusier rewriting the architectural textbook and foreign writers

1790–92	1860
Provence is divided into three *départements;* Papal Avignon and Comtat Venaissin are annexed by France and Vaucluse is mapped	The County of Nice becomes part of French Provence; European royalty winter in Nice, Europe's fastest-growing city

attracted by the coast's liberal atmosphere: Ernest Hemingway, F Scott Fitzgerald, Aldous Huxley, Katherine Mansfield, DH Lawrence and Thomas Mann were among the scores to seek solace in the sun. Guests at Somerset Maugham's villa on Cap Ferrat included innumerable literary names, from TS Eliot and Arnold Bennett to Noël Coward, Evelyn Waugh and Ian Fleming.

Nightlife gained a reputation for being cutting edge, with everything from jazz clubs to striptease. Rail and road access to the south improved: the railway line between Digne-les-Bains and Nice was completed and in 1922 the luxurious *Train Bleu* made its first run from Calais, via Paris, to the coast. The train only had 1st-class carriages and was quickly dubbed the 'train to paradise'.

The roaring 1920s hailed the start of the summer season on the Côte d'Azur. Outdoor swimming pools were built, seashores were cleared of seaweed to uncover sandy beaches, and sunbathing sprang into fashion after a bronzed Coco Chanel appeared on the coast in 1923, draped over the arm of the duke of Westminster. France lifted its ban on gambling, prompting the first casino to open on the coast in the Palais de la Méditerranée (today a hotel; p211) on Nice's promenade des Anglais in 1927. The first Formula One Grand Prix (see the boxed text, p331) sped around Monaco in 1929, while the early 1930s saw wide pyjama-style beach trousers and the opening of a nudist colony on Île du Levant. With the advent of paid holidays for all French workers in 1936, even more tourists flocked to the region. Second- and 3rd-class seating was added to the *Train Bleu,* which had begun running daily in 1929.

Edith Wharton and the French Riviera by Philippe Collas portrays – with both pictures and words – the French Riviera at its most glamorous.

WWII

With the onset of war, the Côte d'Azur's glory days turned grey. Depression set in and on 3 September 1939 France and Britain declared war on Germany. But following the armistice treaty agreed with Hitler on 22 June 1940, southern France fell into the 'free' Vichy France zone, although Menton and the Vallée de Roya were occupied by Italians. The Côte d'Azur – particularly Nice – immediately became a safe haven from war-torn occupied France; by 1942 some 43,000 Jews had descended on the coast to seek refuge. Monaco remained neutral for the duration of WWII.

On 11 November 1942 Nazi Germany invaded Vichy France. Provence was at war. At Toulon 73 ships, cruisers, destroyers and submarines – the major part of the French fleet – were scuttled by their crews to prevent the Germans seizing them. Almost immediately, Toulon was overcome by the Germans and Nice was occupied by the Italians. In January 1943 the Marseille quarter of Le Panier was razed, its 40,000 inhabitants being given less than a day's notice to pack up and leave. Those who didn't were sent to Nazi concentration camps.

Two months after D-Day, on 15 August 1944, Allied forces landed on the southern coast. They arrived at beaches – all open for bronzing and bathing today – along the Côte d'Azur, including Le Dramont near St-Raphaël, Cavalaire, Pampelonne and the St-Tropez peninsula. St-Tropez and Provence's hinterland were almost immediately liberated, but it was only after five days of heavy fighting that Allied troops freed Marseille on

A detailed history of WWII with Nazi leader biographies and a Holocaust timeline with over 150 images make www.historyplace.com stand out.

1920s	1939–45
The Côte d'Azur sparkles as Europe's avant-garde centre	Nazi Germany occupies France and the Vichy regime is established; Provence is liberated two months after D-Day

28 August (three days after the liberation of Paris). Toulon was liberated on 26 August, a week after French troops first attacked the port.

Italian-occupied areas in the Vallée de Roya were only returned to France in 1947.

DID YOU KNOW?

The Resistance movement, particularly strong in Provence, was known in the region as *maquis* after the Provençal scrub in which it hid.

MODERN PROVENCE

The first international film festival (see Starring at Cannes, p247) at Cannes in 1946 heralded the return to party madness. The coast's intellectuals reopened their abandoned seaside villas, and Picasso set up studio in Golfe-Juan. The 1950s and 1960s saw a succession of society events: the fairy-tale marriage of a Grimaldi prince to Hollywood film legend Grace Kelly in 1956; Vadim's filming of *Et Dieu Créa la Femme* (And God Created Woman) with Brigitte Bardot in St-Tropez the same year; the creation of the bikini (see the boxed text, below); the advent of topless sunbathing (and consequent nipple-covering with bottle tops to prevent arrest for indecent exposure); and Miles Davis, Ella Fitzgerald and Ray Charles appearing at the 1961 Juan-les-Pins jazz festival.

Dip into the history of glitzy Monaco and its celeb line-up with *Once Upon a Time: Behind the Fairy Tale of Princess Grace and Prince Rainier* by J Randy Taraborelli.

In 1962 the French colony of Algeria negotiated its independence with President Charles de Gaulle. During this time some 750,000 *pieds noirs* (literally 'black feet', as Algerian-born French people are known in France) flooded into France, many settling in large urban centres like Marseille and Toulon.

Rapid industrialisation marked the 1960s. A string of five hydroelectric plants was constructed on the banks of the River Durance and in 1964 Électricité de France (EDF), the French electricity company, dug a canal from Manosque to the Étang de Berre. The following year construction work began on a 100-sq-km petrochemical zone and an industrial port at Fos-sur-Mer, southern Europe's most important. The first metro line opened in Marseille in 1977 and TGV high-speed trains reached the city in 1981.

From the 1970s mainstream tourism started making inroads into Provence's rural heart. While a concrete marina was being constructed at Villeneuve-Lourbet-Plage (west of Nice), the region's first purpose-built ski resort popped up inland at Isola 2000. The small flow of foreigners that had trickled into Provence backwaters to buy crumbling old *mas* (Provençal farmhouses) at dirt-cheap prices in the late 1970s was an uncontrollable torrent by the 1980s. By the turn of the new millennium, the region was welcoming nine million tourists annually.

THE BIRTH OF THE BIKINI

Almost called *atome* (French for atom) rather than bikini after its pinprick size, the scanty little two-piece bathing suit was the 1946 creation of Cannes fashion designer Jacques Heim and automotive engineer Louis Réard.

Top-and-bottom swimsuits had existed for centuries, but it was the French duo who plumped for the name bikini – after Bikini, an atoll in the Marshall Islands chosen by the US in 1946 as a testing ground for atomic bombs.

Once wrapped around the curvaceous buttocks of 1950s sex-bomb Brigitte Bardot on St-Tropez's Plage de Pampelonne, there was no looking back. The bikini was born.

1946	1956
The first international film festival opens at Cannes	Prince Rainier of Monaco weds his fairy-tale princess, Hollywood film legend Grace Kelly

THE TREATY OF NICE

No pan-European agreement has been more influential on the future map of Europe than the Treaty of Nice, a landmark treaty thrashed out by the-then–15 EU member states in the seaside city of Nice in late December 2000. Enforced from February 2003, the treaty laid the foundations for EU enlargement starting in 2004, determined the institutions necessary for its smooth running and – not without controversy – established a new system of voting in the Council of Ministers for the 25 EU countries from 1 November 2004.

Corruption cast a shady cloud over France's hot south in the 1980s and early 1990s. Nice's mayor, the corrupt right-wing Jacques Médecin (son of another former mayor, Jean Médecin, who ruled Nice for 38 years), was twice found guilty of income-tax evasion during his 24-year mayorship (1966–90). In 1990 King Jacques – as the flamboyant mayor was dubbed – fled to Uruguay, following which he was convicted *in absentia* of the misuse of public funds (including accepting four million francs in bribes and stealing two million francs from the Nice opera). Médecin was extradited in 1994 and imprisoned in Grenoble where he served two years of a 3½-year sentence. Upon being released the ex-mayor, who died in 1998 aged 70, returned to Uruguay to sell hand-painted T-shirts.

Get the complete low-down on regional politics in the prefecture with www.paca.pref.gouv.fr (in French).

During 1994 Yann Piat became the only member of France's National Assembly (parliament) since WWII to be assassinated while in office. Following her public denunciation of the Riviera Mafia, the French *député* (member of parliament) was shot in her Hyères constituency. Her assassins, dubbed the 'baby killers' by the press after their conviction in 1998, were local Mafia kingpins barely in their 20s.

THE FN

In the mid-1990s blatant corruption, coupled with economic recession and growing unemployment, fuelled the rise of the extreme-right Front National (FN). Nowhere else in France did the xenophobic party gain such a stronghold as in Provence, where the FN stormed to victory in municipal elections in Toulon, Orange and Marignane in 1995, and Vitrolles in 1997.

DID YOU KNOW?

Paris-Île de France aside, Provence is the most touristic region in France: it lures 12.5% of all French tourists and 14.8% of those who come to France from abroad.

Yet the FN, led by racist demagogue Jean Marie Le Pen, never made any real headway in the national arena. Party support for the FN rose from 1% in 1981 to 15% – a level it has pretty much stayed at ever since – in the 1995 presidential elections, yet the FN never secured any seats in the National Assembly. And despite gaining 15.5% of votes in regional elections in 1998 and 14.7% in 2004, the FN never succeeded in securing the presidency of the Provence-Alpes-Côte d'Azur *région* (see p343).

A deadly blow was dealt to the FN in 1998 when second-in-command Bruno Mégret split from Le Pen to create his own breakaway faction. In subsequent European parliamentary elections in 1999, Le Pen and the FN won just 5.7% of the national vote (enough to secure just five of the 87 French parliamentary seats), while Mégret's splinter group, the Mouvement National Républicain (MNR) party, trailed with 3.28% (and no seats). This was in contrast to the Socialists, Rassemblement pour la

1962	2000
Algeria negotiates its independence with French president Charles de Gaulle	European leaders meet in Nice to thrash out future EU expansion

République (RPR), communists and extreme left who won the backing of 21.95%, 12.7%, 6.8% and 5.2% of the electorate, respectively.

The next blow came in 2000 when Le Pen was suspended from the European Parliament after physically assaulting a Socialist politician three years previously. A year later the extreme right lost the mayorship of Toulon. Extreme-right mayors Jacques Bompard (FN) and Daniel Simonpiéri (MNR) clung onto Orange and Marignane, but in Vitrolles elections were declared invalid, only for the last bastion of MNR power to be smashed to smithereens by left-wing candidate Guy Obino in repeat elections the next year.

Le Pen's incredible success in the first round of presidential elections in 2002 – he landed 16.86% of votes – shocked the nation and the world. More than one million protestors took to the streets across France in the days preceding the second round of voting in which the FN politician was up against incumbent president Jacques Chirac. Fortunately 80% of the electorate turned out to vote (compared to 41.41% in the first round) and Chirac won by a massive majority.

Never to be defeated, Le Pen pulled out his final trump card – his blonde daughter, Marine (dubbed 'the clone' because of the uncanny likeness to her father). Despite accusations of nepotism following her appointment as party vice-chairman at the FN party congress in Nice in 2003, Marine Le Pen stoically pushed forth in her drive to inject youthful zest into an otherwise ageing party (Jean Marie Le Pen is in his seventies), and was rewarded with relative success in the 2004 European elections.

NEWFOUND OPTIMISM

Nowhere was the newfound optimism sweeping through France at the start of the new millennium more pronounced than in multicultural Marseille, France's third-largest city that, since the victory by the French team in the 1998 football World Cup and Euro 2000 (see p29), has been at the cutting edge of hip-hop, rap and football.

France's sea-blue south sped into the 21st century with the opening of the high-speed TGV Méditerranée railway line (see p355) and a booming information technology sector (p17). In Marseille, Euroméditerranée laid the foundations for a massive 15-year rejuvenation project in the port city (see Docklands, p74); while the arrival by sea of the world's largest floating dike in Monaco promised to double the capacity of the already thriving port. The €2 million purchase of a vast 19th-century estate near Bargemon (p295) by the Beckhams (footballer David and ex-Spice Girl Victoria) was mere confirmation that the Côte d'Azur had not lost its legendary sexy edge.

Flash floods devastated northwestern Provence in September 2002, killing 26. A year later floodwaters rose again, this time in Avignon, Arles and other Rhône Valley cities, where five died and thousands lost their homes after the river burst its banks. The floods topped off a year which had seen the legendary Festival d'Avignon – Europe's premier cultural event with an annual revenue of €15 million – paralysed by striking artists, furious at government proposals to tighten the unemployment benefit for arts workers.

DID YOU KNOW?

Fearing heir to the Monaco throne, Prince Albert, will die childless, the principality's National Council passed a succession law in 2002 keeping the crown in Grimaldi hands, heir or no heir.

Tune into the hub of France's hi-tech information technology sector, the Parc International de Sophia-Antipolis, at www.sophia-antipolis.net/uk/.

2001	2004
The high-speed TGV Méditerranée railway line puts Marseille just three hours away from Paris by train	The National Assembly bans overtly religious symbols, including the Islamic headscarf and Jewish skullcap, in state schools

The Culture

REGIONAL IDENTITY

While Parisians systematically slam every city other than their own, so people in Provence perceive the oh-so-cold north – that is, anything north of Avignon, capital included – as far less attractive than their own sunlit region. For them, Provence is bathed in a golden glow year-round. Come the big chill of the mistral in autumn and winter, true Provençaux are barely bitten by the unbearable cold, unlike their foreign neighbours who shut the shutters tight, curl up by the fire – and still shiver in their sleep. Unless you're born and bred in Provence, you have little hope of ever adjusting to the mistral's menacing climes, as any true Provençaux will very proudly point out.

Provençaux are staunchly proud of their natural treasures and rich cultural heritage. Most have an equally staunch loyalty to the hamlet, village, town or city where they live. The rough-and-tumble Marseillais are famed throughout France for their blatant exaggerations and imaginative fancies – such as the tale about the sardine that blocked Marseille port. The Niçois, by contrast, are more Latin in outlook and temperament, sharing a common zest for the good life with their Italian neighbours. Monégasques in Monaco tend to dress on the flashy side, while St-Tropez's colourful community is clearly split between bronzed-year-round glamour queens and reborn hippies. Wild gesticulations, passionate cheek kissing (three is generally the limit) and fervent handshaking are an integral part of Provençal daily life, regardless of geographical location. Food and wine (see p54) are likewise serious preoccupations across the board.

Prouvènço (Provençal in French), the region's mother tongue, can no longer be deemed a fair expression of regional identity, given the vast majority of born-and-bred Provençaux don't read, let alone speak, the language of their ancestors.

When travelling in Monaco, do not mention the Revolution – or refer to Monaco as a part of France. Monégasques will explain that their principality is a distinctly separate country with its own strong history, culture and traditions. Listen to what they have to say and respect their patch of land.

Delve into local Provençal culture and bone up on useful Prouvènço phrases with Lou pourtau de la culturo prouvençalo (the portal of Provençal culture) at http://prouvenco .presso.free.fr (in French).

Hone into Anglophone life on the Riviera with AngloINFO Riviera at http://riviera.angloinfo .com.

LIFESTYLE

Daily life for the cherry farmer near Apt, the unemployed immigrant in Marseille (see p30) or the inhabitants of the isolated farmhouse – snowed in for weeks in winter – in the wild Vallée du Haut-Verdon is a far cry from the legendary razzmatazz of Riviera high life (see the boxed text, p28). The average hourly wage is – after all – €8.50.

That said, life for the majority is comfortable (Provence is one of France's wealthiest regions). Then Prime Minister Lionel Jospin slashed the standard French working week from 39 to 35 hours in 2000 (applicable to employers of more than 20 from 2002), making most people rich overnight in playtime: the 35-hour work week and five weeks annual holiday plus every religious holiday in the book are very much honoured in this lunch-driven neck of the woods where everything – work included – revolves around the kitchen table.

With a long-standing tradition of renting rather than buying (38% of households rent the property they live in), home ownership is low. Almost 20% of privately owned homes are *résidences secondaires* (second

---

RIVIERA HIGH LIFE

From the giddy days of the *belle époque* to the start of the summer season during the avant-garde 1920s, the Côte d'Azur has long shone as Europe's most glamorous holiday spot: the Beckhams own a 15-bedroom mansion in Bargemon, their old pal Elton John lives next door on Mont Boron near Nice, BB has called St-Tropez home since her heyday, and Tina Turner, Leonardo DiCaprio, Claudia Schiffer and Bono of U2 are seasonal residents.

Hidden behind high stone walls it might be, but celebrity high life on the Riviera can still be peeped on, be it during a sunlit stroll between luxurious villas on Cap Martin and Cap Ferrat, over an apéritif at St-Tropez's yacht-filled Vieux Port, where millionaire yachtsmen pay €90,000 a week to moor, or in Monaco, where pleasure boats have helicopter pads.

Legendary places to eat, sleep and spend a small fortune alongside the rich and famous include Hôtel de Paris (p329), Louis XV (see Author's Choice, p329) and Bar & Boeuf (p330) in Monaco; La Colombe d'Or (p264) in St-Paul de Vence; Hôtel du Cap Eden Roc (p260) in Cap d'Antibes; the Hôtel Martinez (p250) and Carlton InterContinental (p250) in Cannes; and La Voile Rouge (p285), Hôtel Byblos (p289) and Spoon Byblos (p290) in St-Tropez. Bars and clubs so hot that even celebrities go there include Le Club 55 (p285), VIP Room (p291) and La Bodega du Papagayo (p291) in St-Tropez; and Palm Square (p251), Living Room (p252), Le Loft (p252) and others in Cannes' so-called *carré magique* (magic square).

For a peep into different houses in Provence and the lifestyles led inside them, invest in two photography-driven coffee-table books: *Provence Interiors* edited by Lisa Lovett-Smith and Angelika Muthesius, and Johanna Thornycroft's *The Provençal House*.

homes owned mainly by people living and working in other parts of France); Brits and Germans top the 'foreigner' charts of those owning a Provençal pleasure pad. Meanwhile, as 'outsiders' buy up the region traditional community life is changing (dying?) as village post offices, *boulangeries* (bakeries) and so on – unable to earn a livelihood in villages only partly inhabited for much of the year – are being forced to shut.

For the select few who live in Monaco, the lifestyle is more formal, a jacket and tie being the uniform at most cultural events.

POPULATION

Busy Bouches du Rhône (see p343), with Marseille at its portside helm, is jam-packed with 40% of the region's population. Another 15% inhabit the three interior *départements*, the largest and most rural being 6925-sq-km Alpes de Haute-Provence, where just 3% of people live. Population density in this remote neck of the woods remains astonishingly low – 20 people per sq km (compared to 361 per sq km in Bouches du Rhône and 107 people per sq km nationally).

Provence emerged as one of France's most buoyant regions in the last decade, with people flocking from traditional population strongholds such as Paris and the northeast to Provence and the Côte d'Azur where work opportunities are rife. If the trend continues, the regional population could rise by 30% in the next 30 years.

DID YOU KNOW?

Just 10% of mayors in the Provence-Alpes-Côte d'Azur *région* are women. Of the 15,000-odd municipal and 120-odd regional councillors, 36% and 25% respectively are female.

While France's overall population is ageing in keeping with European trends (by 2050 one in three people will be aged 60 or more), the population on the dynamic Mediterranean coast remains young and active, thanks to ever-increasing work opportunities. That said, the population of much of the interior (and even pockets of the coast) reflects national trends.

See p30 for a snapshot of the region's foreign population.

SPORT

Be it bullfighting in the southwest, deemed both a sport and a passionate celebration of Provençal tradition by those who partake in it (see the boxed text, p116), or motor racing in Monaco, sport in Provence is dramatic and entertaining. The Monaco Grand Prix (see the boxed text, p331) in May, the most glamorous race on the Formula One (F1) calendar, is the only race of its kind to see F1 speed machines tear around regular town streets rather than a racetrack. For motorcycle enthusiasts there is the Circuit du Castellet (see p318), owned by French industrialist Paul Ricard since the 1970s and sold to F1 tycoon Bernie Ecclestone in the late 1990s. Cycling is another great passion – and more accessible to boot. Sports enthusiasts keen to give it a go should see p38.

Football

Football has long been the region's stronghold sport, with Marseille standing at the heart of French football. During France's greatest sporting moments – the 1998 World Cup (which it hosted and won) and subsequent victory in Euro 2000 – it was Marseille-born midfielder of North African origin Zinedine Zidane (b 1972), with his goal-scoring headers and extraordinary footwork, who emerged the true champion. Zidane's subsequent transfer from Juventus (Italy) to Real Madrid (Spain) in 2001–02 was worth a mind-blowing €75.1 million and turned him into the world's most expensive football player. His humble Marseillais grin has since been used to advertise everything from Adidas sports gear to Volvic mineral water and Christian Dior fashion.

At club level, Olympique de Marseilles (OM) was national champion for four consecutive years between 1989 and 1992, and in 1991 became the first French team to win the European Champions League. In keeping with national trends, though (which have seen France win no major title in recent years), OM has won nothing since. This is due in part to the exodus of the best French players to better-paid clubs abroad: Arsenal manager Arsène Wenger and star striker Thierry Henry both began their careers with the region's other strong club, AS Monaco (ASM). That said, 2004 saw former ASM goalkeeper Fabian Barthez (who won the English Premier League championship with Manchester United in 2001 and 2003) transfer to OM. To see him in action and visit OM's home ground, see the boxed text (p86).

Pétanque

Despite its quintessential image of a bunch of old men throwing balls on a dusty patch of gravel beneath trees, Provence's national pastime is in fact a serious sport with its own world championships and a museum (p256) to prove it.

Pétanque (Provençal *boules*) was invented in La Ciotat, near Marseille, in 1910 when arthritis-crippled Jules Le Noir could no longer take the running strides prior to aiming demanded by the *longue boule* game. The local champion thus stood with his feet firmly on the ground – a style that became known as *pieds tanqués* (Provençal for 'tied feet', from which '*pétanque*' emerged).

Big dates on the *pétanque* calendar include France's largest tournament, La Marseillaise, held each year in Parc Borély in Marseille in early July; and the annual celebrity tournament organised in Avignon on the banks of the River Rhône.

Nautical Jousting

Joutes nautiques is typical only to southern France. Spurred on by bands and a captive audience, participants (usually male and traditionally dressed in white) knock each other into the water from rival boats with 2.60m-long lances. The jouster stands balanced at the tip of a *tintaine*, a

DID YOU KNOW?

People in Provence live a tad longer than elsewhere in France: men live to an average age of 76 (compared to 75 nationally) and women to 83 (compared to 82 nationally).

Duck, dive, dribble, defend and shoot with the world's most expensive football player at www .zidane.fr.

Sit back, put your feet up and watch one of the world's great car rallies, the Rallye Automobile Monte-Carlo, with Walt Disney and his loveable VW Beetle in the classic 1970s film *Herbie Goes to Monte Carlo*.

PÉTANQUE

Should you wish to partake in *pétanque,* here is what you need to know.

Two to six people, split into two teams, can play. Each player has three solid metal *boules,* weighing 650g to 800g and stamped with the hallmark of a licensed *boule* maker. Initials, a name or a family coat of arms can be crafted on to made-to-measure *boules.* The earliest *boules,* scrapped in 1930, comprised a wooden ball studded with hundreds of hammered-in steel nails.

Each team takes it in turn to aim a *boule* at a tiny wooden ball called a *cochonnet* (jack), the idea being to land the *boule* as close as possible to it. The team with the closest *boule* wins the round; points are allocated by totting up how many *boules* the winner's team has closest to the marker (one point for each *boule).* The first to notch up 13 wins the match.

The team throwing the *cochonnet* (initially decided by a coin toss) has to throw it from a small circle, 30cm to 50cm in diameter, scratched in the gravel. It must be hurled 6m to 10m away. Each player aiming a *boule* must likewise stand in this circle, with both feet planted firmly on the ground. At the end of a round, a new circle is drawn around the *cochonnet,* determining the spot where the next round will start.

Underarm throwing is compulsory. Beyond that, players can dribble the *boule* along the ground (known as *pointer,* literally 'to point') or hurl it high in the air in the hope of it landing smack-bang on top of an opponent's *boule,* sending it flying out of position. This flamboyant tactic, called *tirer* (literally 'to shoot'), can turn an entire game around in seconds.

Throughout matches *boules* are polished with a soft white cloth. Players unable to stoop to pick up their *boules* can lift them up with a magnet attached to a piece of string.

---

wooden gangplank protruding from the wooden boat where the rest of his team members spur him on.

The sport is particularly strong in St-Raphaël, where the annual jousting championships (p275) are invariably held. In the Vaucluse, river jousters set L'Isle-sur-la-Sorgue ablaze with colour on 14 and 26 July.

Keep abreast with cultural affairs in the region with www.culture.gouv.fr/paca (in French).

MULTICULTURALISM

Immigrants form around 9.5% (430,000) of the regional population, a constant since 1975 when France implemented its first immigration law. The largest foreign communities are European (31.4%), Algerian (19%), Moroccan (19%), Tunisian (13.8%) and Turkish (1.7%). The vast majority of this ethnic community do have French citizenship, which is subject to various administrative requirements rather than being conferred at birth.

The Algerian community originates from the 1950s and 1960s, when over one million French settlers returned to metropolitan France from Algeria, other parts of Africa and Indochina. At the same time millions of non-French immigrants from these places were welcomed as much-needed manpower. A 1974 law banning all new foreign workers ended large-scale immigration.

Racial tensions are fuelled by the Front National (FN; see p25), whose leader makes no bones about his party's antiforeigner stance. The French republican code, meanwhile, does little to accommodate a multicultural society. While the government's banning of the Islamic headscarf, Jewish skullcap, Sikh turban, crucifix and other religious symbols in French schools was meant to place all schoolchildren on an equal footing, Muslims slammed it as intolerant and yet more proof that the French state is not prepared to properly integrate them into French society.

Marseille in particular has sizable Muslim and Jewish populations, a big chunk of which live in depressed city suburbs (unemployment among immigrants is 12% higher than the regional average). In 2002 one of Marseille's 14 synagogues was burnt down in an anti-Semitic attack.

Immerse yourself in a fascinating portrait of a hilltop village and its Provençal culture and customs from 1945 to the present with *Provençal Trilogy* by Evelyn Watts.

RELIGION

Countrywide, 80% of people identify themselves as Catholic, although few attend Mass. Catholicism is the official state religion in neighbouring Monaco, which marks a number of religious feasts with public holidays. Protestants account for less than 2% of today's population.

Many of France's four to five million nominally Muslim residents live in the south of France, comprising the second-largest religious group. France's Jewish community – the largest in Europe – numbers 650,000, some 80,000 of which live in Marseille (p30). There are synagogues in Avignon, Marseille, Cavaillon and Carpentras.

Environment

THE LAND

Provence and the Côte d'Azur – an elongated oval in southeast France – is bordered by the southern Alps to the northeast, which form a natural frontier with Italy, and by the River Rhône to the west. The Grand Rhône (east) and Petit Rhône (west) form the delta of the Rhône, a triangular alluvial plain called the Camargue.

The Mediterranean washes the region's southern boundary – a 250-odd kilometre coastline (the Côte d'Azur in French, the French Riviera in English) stretching from Marseille to Menton on the French-Italian border. Offshore lie several islands: the Îles du Frioul (Marseille), the Îles des Embiez (Toulon) and the Îles de Lérins (Cannes). The most southern, the Îles d'Hyères (Hyères), are inhabited. A chain of calcareous rocks, known as the Calanques, forms the coastline around Marseille and France's highest cliff (406m) crowns Cap Canaille in nearby Cassis.

Three mountain ranges cut off the coast from the region's vast interior: the Massif de l'Estérel is formed from red volcanic rock; the Massif des Maures is limestone; and the foothills of the Alps kiss the Niçois hinterland immediately north of Nice.

The interior is dominated by hills and mountains, peaking with stone-capped Mont Ventoux (1912m) in the northwest and the southern Alps in the northeast. Lower-lying ranges (west to east) include the Alpilles, Montagne Ste-Victoire, Massif Ste-Baume, the Vaucluse hills and the Lubéron. Further east is the Gorges du Verdon, Europe's largest and most spectacular canyon.

WILDLIFE

Provence boasts a rich variety of flora and fauna: the Parc National du Mercantour alone is home to 2000 of the 4200 flora species known to France.

Animals

The Camargue (p104) is prime wildlife-watching terrain, home to over 400 land and water birds including the kingfisher, bee-eater, stork, shelduck, white egret, purple heron and more than 160 migratory species. It also shelters 10% of the world's greater flamingo population and a large native horse and bull population (see p116).

DID YOU KNOW?

Europe's highest mountain pass, the Col de Restefond la Bonette (2802m), strides through the Vallée de l'Ubaye in the Parc National du Mercantour.

Discover the crucial role played by the land, its soil and geological make-up on one of the region's best known products in *Terroir: Role of Geology, Climate and Culture in the Making of French Wine* by James Wilson (with a foreword by Hugh Johnson).

THE MUD-EATING MISTRAL

Folklore claims it drives people crazy. Its namesake, Provençal poet Frédéric Mistral, cursed it, while peasants in their dried-out fields dubbed the damaging wind *mange fange* (*manjo fango* in Provençal), meaning 'mud eater'.

The mistral, a cold, dry northwesterly wind, whips across Provence for several days at a time. Its furious gusts, reaching over 100km/h, destroy crops, rip off roofs, dry the land and drive tempers round the bend. It chills the bones for 100 days a year and is at its fiercest in winter and spring.

The mistral's intense and relentless rage is caused by high atmospheric pressure over central France, between the Alps and the Pyrenees, which is then blown southwards through the funnel of the narrow Rhône Valley to an area of low pressure over the Mediterranean Sea. On the upside, skies are blue and clear of clouds when the mistral is in town. A soaking of rain in July, followed by a healthy dose of sun and mistral in August, followed by more showers and more mistral in early September works wonders for the grape harvest.

LOVE SONG

The frenzied buzz that serenades sunny days in Provence's hot south is, in fact, *cigales* (cicadas) on the pull.

Cicadas are transparent-winged insects, most common in tropical or temperate climes. The male cicada courts when the temperature is above 25°C in the shade. Its shrill love song is produced with tymbals, vibrating music-making plates attached to the abdomen. Female cicadas do not sing.

The life span of a cicada is three to 17 years, all but four to six weeks of which is spent underground. Upon emerging from the soil to embark on its adult life, the cicada attaches itself to a tree, where it immediately begins its mating rituals. It dies just weeks later.

The island of Port-Cros (p306) is an important autumn stopover for migratory birds. The puffin, ash-grey shearwater and yelkouan shearwater are among the many species to spot in its diverse seabird population.

Nowhere do more mammals romp than in Parc National du Mercantour (p197), home to 8000 chamois (mountain antelopes) with their dark-striped heads, 1100 *bouquetin* (Alpine ibex), and the mouflon, which hangs out on stony sunlit scree slopes in the mountains. At higher altitudes the alpine chough – a type of crow with black plumage, red feet and a yellow beak (that appears white from a distance) – can be seen. Other treats include the ermine, the green lizard, the viper, the very rare Alexanor butterfly and 19 of Europe's 29 bat species. Look for the rock ptarmigan – a chicken-like species around since the Ice Age which moults several times a year to ensure a foolproof camouflage for every season (several shades of brown in summer, white in winter) – on rocky slopes and in alpine meadows above 2000m.

Wildlife enthusiasts keen to follow in the footsteps of local naturalists or pick up a guide on the region's fauna should get in touch with the Conservatoire Etudes des Écosystèmes de Provence, with an informative website at www.espaces-naturels-provence.com (in French).

ENDANGERED SPECIES

The Hermann's tortoise, once indigenous to Mediterranean Europe, is now found only in the Massif des Maures (and Corsica), and forest fires threaten to further diminish its population. Learn more about the yellow-and-black creature at Gonfaron's Village des Tortues (see the boxed text, p301).

The Bonnelli eagle can be seen in Les Calanques (p89), and 40 pairs of golden eagles nest in the Parc National du Mercantour (p197). The buzzard, the short-toed eagle and the golden eagle also prey here. The griffon vulture, as well as the bearded vulture with its unsavoury bone-breaking habits and awe-inspiring wing span of 3m, only remain in the wild thanks to reintroduction programmes instigated in protected areas such as the Gorges du Verdon and the Parc National du Mercantour; see Vulture Culture (p192).

The Parc National de Port-Cros (p306) safeguards the monk seal, a 3m-long mammal that lives in warm Mediterranean waters but is in danger of extinction due to its natural food supply (of plaice, mackerel and flounder) being gobbled up by intensive fishing and pollution.

An estimated 30 wolves roam in the Parc National du Mercantour – to the horror of the mouflon (on which its preys) and sheep farmers. Dogs, corrals and sound machines are effective alternatives to more murderous means of getting rid of this unwanted predator, although one wolf was deliberately shot in 2004; see Of Wolves & Men (p198).

DID YOU KNOW?

Of the 39,000 insect species identified in France, 10,000 creep and crawl around the Parc National du Mercantour.

Plants

Take a springtime stroll along any of the 600km of walking trails in the Parc National du Mercantour (p197) and you'll see dozens of different

Gardens in Provence by Louisa Jones not only captures the region's most beautiful, fascinating and unique horticultural creations on camera; it also lists plants typical to the region, explains when and where the green-fingered can see what, and so on.

species in bloom. Particularly enchanting are the 63 types of orchids, 30 endemic plants and 200 rare species: wild blueberry bushes, rhododendrons, fuchsias and geraniums are abundant.

Rare or threatened species visible during coastal walks in the Parc National du Port-Cros (p306) include the *ail petit moly,* a type of garlic that sprouts in early autumn, flowers in January and lingers until spring – look for six white petals. The powis castle artemisia, typical to stony, sun-baked soils, is identified by its lacy, silver-grey leaves and small yellow flowers. Jupiter's beard, a clover-like plant resistant to sea spray, thrives on the coastline where it breaks out in a riot of small white flowers in spring. Dozens more native flowers can be seen in the region's great gardens (see p14).

Forest covers 40% of the region, the most heavily forested areas – predominantly oak and pine – being northeastern Provence and the Var. Cork oak and chestnut trees dominate the Massif des Maures; maritime, Aleppo and umbrella pines provide shade along the coast; and plane trees stud village squares. The olive tree was brought by the Greeks in the 4th century BC, and the palm tree arrived with the English in the 19th century, as did the mimosa, eucalyptus and other succulents imported from Australia.

DID YOU KNOW?

Lemon and orange trees, typical only to the hot coast, have been grown since the Middle Ages.

Maquis is a form of vegetation whose low, dense shrubs provide many of the spices used in Provençal cooking. Garrigue, typified by aromatic Mediterranean plants such as juniper, broom and fern, grows on predominantly chalky soil.

NATIONAL & REGIONAL PARKS

Two national parks fully protect 2.6% of the region and another 16% is protected to a lesser degree by three regional parks *(parcs naturals régionaux).* Nature reserves *(réserves naturelles),* some managed by the Conservatoire du Littoral (see High-Factor Protection by the Sea, p36), offer protection of sorts, as do the three Unesco-backed *réserves de biosphère* (biosphere reserves) – the Camargue, Lubéron and Mont Ventoux.

While the central zones of national parks are uninhabited and fully protected by legislation (dogs, vehicles and hunting are banned and camping is restricted), the ecosystems they protect spill into populated peripheral zones in which tourism and other invariably environmentally unfriendly activities run riot.

Parks and reserves strive to maintain – and improve – local ecosystems: in the Parc Régional Marin de la Côte Bleue, artificial reefs were submerged in the sea in the 1980s to encourage sea life to grow and prevent illegal fishing.

For more factual and practical information on the region's national and regional parks, take an electronic walk on the wild side (with Flash Player, preferably) at www.parcsnation aux-fr.com and www .parcs-naturels-region aux.tm.fr.

ENVIRONMENTAL ISSUES

Forest fires are the hottest issue: 3000 fires destroy 150 sq km of forest a year on average, eight out of 10 being caused by careless day-trippers or arsonists seeking to get licences to build on the damaged lands. While a concerted fire-prevention effort by local authorities in the 1990s paid off in the early years of the new millennium (the number of forest fires fell by 45% between 1999 and 2000 and subsequently remained low), it was back to square one in 2003 when a freakishly hot summer sparked off the worst fires for 15 years, destroying vast tracts of land (250 sq km in all) and killing seven people: in less than 24 hours in the Massif des Maures alone, 100 sq km of pine forest and garrigue between Fréjus and Ste-Maxime was burnt to cinders, 1500 firefighters battling in vain against flames that spread 3km/h. 'An ecological massacre' was the reac-

Park	Features	Activities	Best Time to Visit	Page Ref
Parc National du Mercantour (1979; 685 sq km)	majestic 3000m-plus peaks, uninhabited valleys; mouflon, chamois, ibex, wolves, eagles & vultures	skiing (alpine), whitewater sports, mountain biking, walking & donkey trekking	spring, summer & winter	p197
Parc National de Port-Cros (1963; 7 sq km plus 13 sq km of water)	island marine park; puffins, shearwaters & migratory birds	snorkelling, bird-watching, swimming, gentle strolling & sunbathing	summer (water activities) & autumn (bird-watching)	p306
Parc Naturel Régional du Verdon (1997; 1769.6 sq km)	Europe's most spectacular canyon, five green-water lakes & pre-alpine massifs; griffon vultures	whitewater sports, swimming, horse riding, walking & cycling	summer	p186
Parc Naturel Régional du Lubéron (1977; 1650 sq km)	hilltop villages & limestone gorges; eagles, Egyptian vultures & European greater horned owls	walking, cycling, rock climbing & paragliding	spring, late summer & autumn	p169
Parc Naturel Régional de Camargue (1970; 863 sq km)	paddy fields, saltpans & marshes; horses, bulls, boars, flamingos, egrets & herons	horse riding, cycling, bird-watching, botany & walking	spring & autumn	p106
Parc Régional Marin de la Côte Bleue (1983; 2.95 sq km)	marine reserve protecting Cap Couronne & surrounding waters; marine flora & fauna	guided snorkelling expeditions & boat tours	spring & summer	p93
Réserve Géologique de Haute-Provence (1900 sq km)	geological reserve; 185-million-year-old fossilised ichthyosaur skeleton & fossils from 300-million-year-old tropical forests	geology & walking	year-round	p192
Réserve de Biosphère du Mont Ventoux (1990; 810 sq km)	1912m-high mountain; 60 rare flora species, Lebanese cedars, mouflon & chamois	cycling, walking, skiing & snowboarding	spring & summer (cycling & walking), winter (skiing)	p143

tion of French interior minister Nicholas Sarkozy when he visited the region. Only 8.5% of forests in Provence are protected; 70% of them are privately owned.

It was during the same heatwave that the French government, to the disgust of environmentalists, allowed some of its 19 nuclear power plants (responsible for generating 80% of the country's electricity) to discharge reactor-cooling water into rivers at higher temperatures than normal. The controversial emergency measure was taken to prevent power shortages.

The main victim of the country's hydroelectric programme are rivers, dammed to produce electricity and thereby creating vast recreational

---

HIGH-FACTOR PROTECTION BY THE SEA

Precious pockets of the coast fall within the realm of the **Conservatoire du Littoral** (Coastal Protection Agency; ☎ 05 46 84 72 50; www.conservatoire-du-littoral.fr; Corderie Royale, BP 13 7, F-1 7306 Rochefort Cedex), an association that acquires threatened natural areas by the sea to restore, rejuvenate and protect.

Among the Conservatoire's rich pageant of *espaces naturels protégés* (protected natural areas) are the Archipel de Riou (p78), a cluster of uninhabited limestone islands offshore from Marseille sheltering 30% of France's cory's shearwater population; a twinset of wildlife-rich capes (Cap Lardier and Cap Taillat; p286) on the St-Tropez peninsula; the former salt marshes on La Capte in Hyères (p309); the Corniche des Maures (p301), with the beautiful gardens of the Domaine du Rayol (p301) as its next-door neighbour; and several soggy chunks of the Camargue (p106).

Find out more about the region's role in the world quest to develop fusion power at www.iter.org and www.iter.gouv.fr.

Interested in protecting the Calanques? Find out how you can with the Union Calanques Littoral at www.echodes calanques.com.

lakes like Lac de Ste-Croix, Lac de Castillon and Lac de Chaudanne around the Gorges du Verdon. Lip service was paid to an alternative means of producing power in 2002 when the first wind turbine (32V) started turning at Port-St-Louis du Rhône.

Ironically, the region could be home to the world's first thermonuclear experimental reactor: Cadarache, at the confluence of the Verdon and Durance rivers, is the European candidate for an international US$5 billion engineering project between the EU, the US and Japan (among others) that could revolutionise world power production. The decision on where this cleaner, new-generation reactor will be sited – Cadarache in Provence or Rokkashomura in Japan – is expected to be made by the end of 2004. Unlike conventional nuclear power plants, fusion reactors produce energy through the fusion of light atom nuclei and produce dramatically less radioactive waste. The plant would start generating fusion power in 2014.

Northwest of Marseille, a large area of the Crau plain – France's last remaining steppe – has been devoured by industrial development. Oil refineries dominate the southern and eastern shores of the Étang de Berre. Equally hazardous to the environment are the millions of tourists that descend on the region. Marine pollution from tourist boats threaten fragile ecosystems on Port-Cros, the Calanques and so on. In 2004 a Marseille diving club collected 50 cubic metres of litter from the Calanques during its annual Opération Calanques Propres.

Marine life is being choked by *Caulerpa taxifolia*, a bright-green seaweed that starves native flora of sunlight (thus starving the fish who feed on the flora). Originating in the Pacific, the 'killer algae' was first found in Mediterranean beneath the Musée Océanographique in Monaco in 1984. Today it covers a vast and uncontrollable expanse between Toulon and Menton.

BLUE FLAG BEACHES

No green label says more about the state of a beach than the **Blue Flag** (www.blueflag.org), a recommendation of quality awarded to clean, safe and well-maintained beaches, ports and marinas Europe-wide. Clean bathing water, sanitary facilities and litter bins are among criteria needed to fly a Blue Flag.

Beaches clean enough to do so for the 2004 season (beaches are re-assessed seasonally) included those in Antibes, Cap d'Ail, Ste-Maxime, Six Four les Plages, La Londe les Maures, Hyères, La Croix Valmer and Le Lavandou. Of the 92 beaches in Bouches du Rhône, just seven – in Port de Bouc, Fos-sur-Mer and Martigues – scored a blue flag.

Beaches in Marseille, Nice and St-Tropez haven't been flagged for years.

Provence & the Côte d'Azur Outdoors

This thrill-rich land of sea and mountains offers a wealth of outdoor pursuits, guaranteed to appease both the feistiest and laziest of appetites.

ASTRONOMY

With its fine clear nights, Provence is an obvious place to watch stars in dark skies. Observatories welcoming stargazers include the Observatoire de Haute-Provence (p196), a national research centre in St-Michel l'Observatoire, west of Manosque, and the nearby Centre d'Astronomie (p196); the Observatoire de Nice (p233) in La Trinité and nearby Astrorama (p233), both east of Nice; and the Observatoire de la Côte d'Azur (see A Starry Detour, p266), north of Grasse.

For young astronomers the Parc d'Astronomie, du Soleil et du Cosmos (p129) near Avignon enthrals.

Stuck for something to do with the kids? Want to search for an activity by age and/or interest? Log into Provence en Famille for the complete run-down on everything to do *en famille* (as a family) at www.provence-enfamille .com (in French).

BALLOONING

Hot-air balloon flights last one to 1½ hours (count three to four hours in all for getting to/from the launch pad, inflating the balloon and so on) and cost €200 per person (€230 with champagne picnic). Operators:

Hot-Air Ballooning (☎ 04 90 05 76 77; montgolfiere@infonie.fr; Le Mas Fourniguière, Joucas) Just outside Gordes; flights in the Avignon area.

La Provence en Ballon (☎ 04 90 95 53 28; www.provence-en-ballon.com; Traverse Castel Mouisson, Barbentane) Near Avignon.

Les Montgolfières du Sud (☎ 04 66 37 28 02; www.sudmontgolfiere.com in French; 64 rue Sigalon, Uzès) Float around the Pont du Gard from this base in neighbouring Languedoc.

A wealth of information on outdoor activities in the entire region is listed on the website of the regional tourist board at www.crt-paca.fr.

BIRD-WATCHING

The spectacular Camargue delta (p105) – where clouds of pink flamingos are a common sight – and the Parc National du Mercantour (p197), with its majestic birds of prey, lure ornithologists like crazy. The national **Ligue pour la Protection des Oiseaux** (LPO; League for the Protection of Birds; www.lpo.fr in French) has a regional branch, **LPO PACA** (☎ 04 94 12 79 52; paca@lpo.fr; Villa La Paix, rond-point Beauregard, F-83400 Hyères), which organises guided bird-watching expeditions (€2.50 per person), and can tell you where to spot what and put you in touch with LPO-affiliated bird-watching groups in the region.

DIVING & SNORKELLING

The coastline and its offshore islands – Porquerolles and Embiez particularly – offer enticing diving opportunities. Experienced divers enjoy the waters around Hyères and the Presqu'île du Giens, where the sea beds

---

DAREDEVIL CALL

The brave, daring and fearless can leap off Europe's highest bridge (182m) in the Gorges du Verdon (p186) or from a sweet 80m-high equivalent in the red-rock Gorges de Dalius (p200), near Guillaumes in the Vallée de la Tinée. *Saut en 'élastique* (bungee jumping) costs €60 to €95 and is generally only organised on weekends. Daredevils don't need to book; just turn up at the designated spot. See the respective sections in the Haute-Provence regional chapter for details.

CYCLING

Pedalling Provence is tremendously popular. Bar the barren slopes of Mont Ventoux in the Vaucluse, the region has few killing hills to climb, making it ideal two-wheeling territory for professionals and amateurs, adults and kids, alike. On the coast the noisy motorway is never far away, making cycling a less tranquil affair: two-wheelers on a budget often base themselves in Nice, from where they take a train along the coast each morning with their bicycles, to avoid the trauma of cycling out of the city. Some GR trails (see p43) are open to mountain bikes, although those keen to pedal the region's roughest mountain terrain should hit Haute-Provence.

Road and mountain bikes can be easily hired for around €15 a day including helmet, puncture-repair kit and suggested itineraries. Many rental outlets, especially on the coast and in the Lubéron, have tandems (€20 to €30 per day), children's bikes (€10 per day), toddler seats (€3 per day) and two-seater trailers (*remorques* or *carrioles;* €5 to €12.50 per day) to tow little kids and babies along. Some deliver to your door for free. Rental outlets are listed under Getting Around in the respective regional chapters.

Both on- and off-road cycling itineraries of various lengths and difficulties, compiled by local experts, can be picked up at most tourist offices. The **Conseil Général du Var** (www.cg83.fr in French) publishes an excellent cycling *topoguide* for the St-Tropez to Toulon area containing 22 detailed itineraries. For Nice, its coastal climes and hinterland, *Rando VTT: Guide RandOxygène*, published by the **Conseil Général des Alpes-Maritimes** (www.cg06.fr in French), maps out 30 cycling routes ranging from a gentle 7km (1½ hours) to a sportful 22km (four hours). And for the Avignon area, there are the 13 routes suggested by the Vaucluse *département* (www.vaucluse.fr in French) in its *VTT: Loisirs de Plein Air* booklet. These free guides (French only) can all be ordered online.

Otherwise, the **Ligue Provence Alpes de Cyclotourisme** (☎ 04 90 29 64 80; http://perso.wanadoo.fr/cyclo-provence-alpes in French; Hôtel de Ville, Espace Acampado, BP 27, F-84220 Piolenc) publishes a clutch of excellent French-only guides, some free; while Didier-Richard publishes *Les Guides VTT* series of cyclists' *topoguides*, sold in bookshops. Outside France, Lonely Planet's *Cycling France* details six cycling itineraries in the region.

Tip-top cycling spots and itineraries:

Le Lubéron en Vélo

Nearest towns Apt & Cavaillon   **Difficulty** easy to hard
Information Maison du Parc ☎ 04 90 04 42 00, Vélo Loisir en Lubéron ☎ 04 92 79 05 82; www.parcduluberon.fr (in French), www.veloloisirluberon.com

Cyclists can cross the Parc Naturel Régional du Lubéron by following a circular 230km-long itinerary. Roads – steep in places – have little traffic and saunter up, down and around photogenic hilltop villages, vineyards, olive groves, lavender fields and fruit farms. The northern route pedals cyclists 111km from Forcalquier to Cavaillon via Apt, Bonnieux, Lacoste and Ménerbes; the southern route links the two towns by way of Lourmarin, Vaugines, Cucuron and Manosque.

Those who enjoy a stiff climb should tackle the northern route east to west (signposted with white markers). Freewheelers should opt for the easier westbound route, which is marked by orange signs. For day-trippers in Cavaillon, the 40km round trip to Ménerbes makes for an exhilarating bike ride.

Information boards posted along both routes provide details on accommodation, eating and sightseeing. Mountain Bike Lubéron (p175) in Bonnieux is the only rental outlet in the area to stock kids' trailers.

Les Ocres en Vélo

Nearest town Apt   **Difficulty** easy
Information Maison du Parc ☎ 04 90 04 42 00, Vélo Loisir en Lubéron ☎ 04 92 79 05 82; www.parcduluberon.fr (in French), www.veloloisirluberon.com

This colourful itinerary forms a 50km circular route around the land of Lubéron ochre (see the boxed text, p172), linking rocky-red Roussillon with Villars (north), Rustrel (east), Apt (south) and Gargas (west). The route can be followed in either direction; green signs mark the westbound way from Apt and ochre markers flag its eastbound counterpart.

Le Pays de Forcalquier et Montagne de Lure en Vélo

Nearest town Forcalquier   **Difficulty** easy to hard
Information ☎ 04 92 75 10 02; www.velopaysforcalquier.com (in French)
The rough-cut plains of rough 'n' ready Haute-Provence star on the agenda of this mountainous-in-parts, 78km-long route which can be followed in either direction from Forcalquier; ochre signs mark the eastbound route, blue the west, and brown the 6km *boucle* (loop) that can be picked up in Lurs. Villages passed en route include Aubenas les Alpes, St-Michel de l'Observatoire and Mane.

Île de Porquerolles

Only town Porquerolles   **Difficulty** easy
Information ☎ 04 94 58 33 76; www.porquerolles.com
The only means of transport on the national park–protected island of Porquerolles – bar one's feet – is bicycle. Sights are few and distances between beaches are small, making it a hot cycling choice for families happy to spend the day sauntering about by pedal power. In all, 70km of unpaved biking trails zigzag across the island and there are 10 rental companies; some provide picnic hampers (€13.50 per person) for cyclists.

Toulon–St-Raphaël

Nearest towns Toulon, Hyères & Cavalaire-sur-Mer   **Difficulty** dead easy
Information ☎ 04 94 18 53 00, 04 94 01 84 50, 04 94 01 92 10; www.cg83.fr (in French)
Between 1905 and 1949 a steam train (poetically named *le macaron* after a local almond cake containing pine kernels extracted from the same pine cones that fuelled the locomotive) huffed and puffed its way between Toulon and St-Raphaël. Today the same 102km-long coastal stretch is covered by a smooth-as-silk two-lane cycling path *(piste cyclable)* instead. In 2004 the track was still being built, but the 18.5km section linking Toulon with Hyères via Cap de Carqueiranne (great lunch-time spot; see Author's Choice, p312) was finished, as were sections around Cavalaire-sur-Mer and St-Tropez.

Mont Ventoux

Nearest towns Malaucène & Sault   **Difficulty** killer hard
Information ☎ 04 90 65 22 59, 04 90 64 01 21; www.lemontventoux.net (in French)
Many cyclists who make it to the summit of Provence's cycling great – the mighty Mont Ventoux – are inspired by the British world-champion cyclist Tommy Simpson (1937–67), who suffered a fatal heart attack on the mountain during the 1967 Tour de France. A roadside memorial to Tommy Simpson can be found 1km east of the summit. The epitaph on the stone tablet reads 'There is no mountain too high'. The road ascent from Chalet Reynard on the westbound D974 to the summit is six painful kilometres but a good many cycling enthusiasts only pedal part of the road, just to see how hard it is!

Tourist offices have information on guided bike rides on the mountain, including night descents by road and daytime mountain-bike descents.

Brevet des 7 Cols Ubayens

Nearest towns Barcelonnette   **Difficulty** very hard
Information ☎ 04 92 81 03 68; www.ubaye.com
The seven cols – Allos (2250m), Restefond la Bonette (2802m), Larche (1991m), Vars (2109m), Cayolle (2326m), Pontis (1301m) and St-Jean (1333m) – linking the remote Vallée de l'Ubaye in Haute-Provence with civilisation form the region's most challenging bike rides. The series of loop rides from Barcelonnette involves 207km of power-pedalling and can only be done May to September when the passes aren't blocked by snow. Cyclists who do all seven get a medal (to prove it, participants have to punch a special card in punch-machines installed on each mountain pass). Local tourist offices sell a map of the route (€6.10).

are graced with numerous shipwrecks. Military WWII wrecks can be explored from St-Raphaël.

The region's most spectacular dives are in and around Marseille: in the Rade de Marseille (a bay with a far-from-flat bottom), along Les Calanques and around the port city's offshore islands (p78). Henri Cosquer, famed for his discovery of prehistoric paintings in a cave around the Calanques, runs his own diving school in Cassis (see p91).

The diving season generally runs mid-March to mid-November. Irrespective of who you are – a first-timer about to embark on a *baptême de plongée* or a highly experienced diver – you will need to show a medical certificate. You should automatically be covered by the diving school's own insurance, but check. A baptism/explorative dive costs €55/45 including full equipment hire, and a seven-dive diving course is around €300/450 without/with equipment hire.

Children can have fun discovering marine life with a clutch of underwater nature trails designed especially for amateur snorkellers and the young-at-heart: there are trails at Domaine du Rayol (p301) on the Corniche des Maures and on Île de Port-Cros (p307), and park authorities on Cap Couronne near Marseille organise one-hour guided snorkelling sessions in the Parc Régional Marin de la Côte Bleue (p97).

Diving shops and clubs are listed in the relevant regional chapters.

HORSE RIDING

With its famous cowboys, cream-coloured horses and vast sandy beaches just made for galloping along, the Camargue (see A Bullish Affair, p116) is the obvious spot to saddle up. Elsewhere, tourist offices have lists of stables and riding centres where you can ride, and the national **Fédération Française des Relais d'Etape de Tourisme Équestre** (☎ 03 86 20 08 04; www .chevalfrance.org in French; Mairie, F-58800 Corbigny) arranges riding itineraries and accommodation.

ICE DIVING

Diving James-Bond wannabes who find themselves high and dry in Provence in winter can always plunge into the chilly but extraordinarily crystal-clear depths of an ice-topped lake. See An Icy Detour (p199) for the full ice-diving lowdown.

GRASS-SKIING

Come the melting snow of spring, off go the sleek snow skis and on go the grass-skis which – for those not familiar with this fringe sport, invented in Germany in the 1960s to help Alpine skiers train year-round – resemble short clunky skis with a caterpillar tread like a bulldozer.

Prime spots in France for *le ski sur herbe* (grass-skiing) are the Mont Serein ski station (p145) on Mont Ventoux's gentle slopes, and La Foux d'Allos and Sauze in Haute-Provence. Ski and boot hire costs around €15 a day and a one-day drag-lift pass is €15. The season – July and August in the main – is super short and face-first wipe outs can be frequent and brutal. As with other types of skiing, grass-skiing has its own world championship, world cup and European cup. For more information see http://grass-ski.alpesprovence.net.

NATURISM

Nudist spots – an *aire naturiste*, not to be confused with an *aire naturelle* which is a primitive farm camp site – range from small rural camp sites to large chalet villages with cinemas, tennis courts and shops. Most open

---

MELLOW OUT

Lavender and algae baths, shiatsu massages, Mediterranean mudpacks and a host of other self-pampering pleasures soothe and rejuvenate weary feet and souls at a handful of spas.

A super-soak in a bubbling thermal bath laced with essential lavender oil at Les Thermes de Digne-les-Bains (see p193) costs €20.

Thermes Sextius (p98), a Roman spa in Aix-en-Provence, hits the spot with Zen massages (€35 to €94), Camargue-salt skin scrubs (€47) and dozens of other mellow-out treatments.

Aromatherapy, *oshiboris* (Japanese hot towels) and shiatsu prove a potent cocktail at the Shiseido Spa at Le Mas Candille (p268) in Mougins, near Cannes. Surrounded by Japanese gardens and all things Zen, the spa practises the Qi method; test it out with a 45-minute body polish (€75), 30-minute quick tension release (€55), ultimate pampering day (€335) or men-only energising antistress day (€305).

At Monaco's Les Thermes Marins de Monte Carlo (see p328), the region's most exclusive and luxurious spa, the truly decadent can splurge on everything from a Monte Carlo diamond massage – a body scrub with diamond powder, followed by a rose-scented massage and cream (€398 for 90 minutes) – to a more humble, good old-fashioned shave (€40).

April to October; visitors need an International Naturist Federation (INF) *passeport naturiste*, available at naturist centres.

The coastline between Le Lavandou and the St-Tropez peninsula is well endowed with nudist beaches. Héliopolis on Île du Levant – an oddball island off the coast between Le Lavandou and Hyères, 90% of which is occupied by the French military – is the region's only genuine nudist colony. It dates from the 1930s and can be easily visited on a day trip by boat.

The **Fédération Française de Naturisme** (☎ 08 92 69 32 82; www.ffn-naturisme.com in French; 5 rue Regnault, F-93500 Pantin) can tell you precisely where in Provence you can roam in the buff.

PARAGLIDING

St-André-les-Alpes (p191), 20km north of Castellane in Haute-Provence, is the French capital of *parapente* (paragliding). If the thermals are good – as in St-André – you can stay up for hours, peacefully circling the area and enjoying breathtaking aerial views. Paragliding schools in St-André and St-Dalmas-Valdeblore (p201) typically charge €370/460 in low/high season for a five-day initiation course and €55/80 for a 10-/20-minute tandem flight (with instructor) for those who'd rather not brave it alone.

In the Lubéron paragliders can soar with the birds over Provence's very own russet-red Colorado in Rustrel (p172).

QUADING

Racing around by quad, wind in face, is an exhilarating way of exploring the great outdoors. Mont Ventoux and the Alpilles are hot quad spots; see p145 for details.

ROCK CLIMBING & VIA FERRATA

The Gorges du Verdon, the *calanques* around Marseille, the lacy Dentelles de Montmirail in the Vaucluse, Buoux in the Lubéron and the Vallée des Merveilles in the Parc National du Mercantour are but a handful of the region's *sites d'escalade* (climbing sites). Most tourist offices and branches of Club Alpin Français (CAF; listed in the regional chapters) stock lists of spots to climb, guides and climbing schools, including local authority **Améthyste** (☎ 04 90 74 05 92; http://amethyste1901.free.fr in French; La Baume, Buoux), a top-notch Lubéron-based climbing club.

Via Ferrata: A Complete Guide to France by Philipe Poulet is precisely what its title says it is – a bible for anyone intending to haul themselves up rocks in Haute-Provence.

There are four heart-thumping *via ferrata* (a type of rock climbing using pre-attached cables) courses in Haute-Provence; see p204 for details and locations.

ROLLERBLADING

Rollerblading (in-line skating) is a tiptop way to cruise around town – and be seen. A set can be hired in any of the larger cities as well as most resorts on the Côte d'Azur for around €10 to €20 per day. Nice's promenade des Anglais, La Croisette in Cannes and Marseille's La Canebière and Marseille Skatepark (p78) are chic spots to blade.

Hundreds of Rollerbladers meet each week for a police-escorted evening blade around town in Avignon, Marseille and Nice; see Activities in those city sections for details. Nice Roller Attitude (p218) runs Rollerblading hockey and acrobatic courses.

Rollerblading is forbidden in Monaco.

SAILING & SEA SPORTS

Sailing is big business on the French Riviera: Antibes, Cannes, Mandelieu-La Napoule and St-Raphaël as well as Marseille are large water-sports centres where non-boat owners can hire a set of sails. Tourist offices have a list of sailing centres *(stations violes)* that rent gear and run courses. Count on paying around €35 per hour to rent a catamaran, and €40 for a one-hour sailing lesson.

Other sea sports readily available on the beach include windsurfing (around €30 per hour to rent a board), water-skiing (around €20 per hour), jet-skiing (around €50 for 30 minutes) and rides from the back of a boat in a parachute (€40/55 for one/two people for a 10-minute ride) or hair-raising rubber ring (€20 per person for a 10-minute ride).

Surfing the waves with a kite has yet to really take off on the French Riviera – although there is no saying what the next season will bring. Meantime, kite-surfers can ride the best winds on a board propelled 'n' powered by a kite with **Air'X Kite** (☎ 06 60 41 87 34; www.airxkite.com; Centre Nautique, St-Laurent du Var; ☽ Mar-Nov), a 'travelling' kite-surfing school that surfs around St-Laurent du Var, St-Raphaël and Fréjus. It runs one-/three-day kite-surfing courses for €110/320 including equipment hire, and takes accomplished kite-surfers out to sea (by boat) for €30 a day.

In Marseille, paddling the open sea in a sea-kayak as the sun sets is particularly memorable; see p78 for details.

To get a marine weather forecast before setting sail, call ☎ 3250 or visit www.meteo.fr/marine (in French).

SKIING & SNOWBOARDING

Haute-Provence's few ski resorts are low-key, with little of the glitz and glamour attached to the Alps' better-known resorts. They are best suited to beginners and intermediates and are marginally cheaper than their northern neighbours.

Resorts include the larger Pra Loup (1500m) and La Foux d'Allos (1800m), which share 230km of downhill pistes and 110km of cross-country trails; the pinprick sister resorts of Le Sauze (1400m) and Super-Sauze (1700m) in the Vallée de l'Ubaye, which tend to attract domestic tourists; and Barcelonnette (1300m), a small town surrounded by a sprinkling of tiny hillside villages. Isola 2000 (2450m) is the largest of the resorts – and the ugliest.

These resorts – all in the Parc National du Mercantour (p197) – open for the ski season from December to March/April/May (depending on

Should boating be your thing, then *A Spell in Wild France* (1992) by Bill and Laurel Cooper – a portrait of the highs and lows of life on a boat moored near Aigues-Mortes in Camargue cowboy land – will entertain.

For everything you need to know to hit the snow-packed slopes, surf www.skifrance.com.

the snow conditions), and for a short period in July and August for summer walkers. Buying a package is the cheapest way to ski. For information on ski passes, ski hire and so on, see the relevant sections in the Parc National du Mercantour section.

Mont Ventoux offers limited downhill and cross-country skiing; **Chalet Reynard** (www.chalet-reynard.com in French) in Bédoin and **Mont Serein** (www.stationdu montserein.com) are the two ski stations. See p145 for details.

WALKING

The region is crisscrossed by a maze of *sentiers balisés* (marked walking paths) and *sentiers de grande randonnée* (long-distance paths with alphanumeric names beginning 'GR'). Some of the latter are many hundreds of kilometres long, including the GR5, which goes from the Netherlands through Belgium, Luxembourg and the spectacular Alpine scenery of eastern France before ending up in Nice. The GR4 (which crosses the Dentelles de Montmirail before climbing up the northern face of Mont Ventoux and winding east to the Gorges du Verdon), GR6 and their various diversions all traverse the region too. Provence's most spectacular trail, the GR9, takes walkers to most of the area's ranges, including Mont du Vaucluse and Montagne du Lubéron.

No permits are needed but there are restrictions on where you can camp, especially in the Parc National du Mercantour. Between 1 July and 15 September paths in heavily forested areas – such as the section of the GR98 that follows the Calanques between Cap Croisette (immediately south of Marseille) and Cassis – are closed due to the high risk of forest fire. The GR51 crossing the Massif des Maures, paths in the Montagne de Ste-Victoire east of Aix-en-Provence and numerous trails in Haute-Provence are likewise closed.

Many walking guides – predominantly in French – cover the region. The *Guides RandOxygène* walking guides published by the Conseil Général des Alpes-Maritimes (Alpes-Maritimes General Council) are outstanding. The guides detail 60 walks of varying lengths – for seaside amblers to serious walkers – in the Alpes-Maritimes *département*: *Rando Haut-Pays* covers the Parc National du Mercantour, *Rando Moyen-Pays* tackles the hilltop villages north of Nice and *Rando Pays Côtier* features invigorating coastal walks. Incredibly, the glossy 80-page guides are free at tourist offices and their contents – minus the maps – can be viewed online at www.cg06.fr (in French).

Practically every tourist office takes bookings for short two- to three-hour guided nature walks in their areas; many are organised by the local branch of the Office National des Forêts (ONF, National Forests Office) or by a local

DID YOU KNOW?

The local Manosque-based branch (☎ 04 92 70 54 54) of Handi Cap Évasion (☎ 04 78 22 71 02; chemin de la Creuzette, F-69220 Fontaines sur Soânes) organises nature walks for travellers with disabilities (including those in wheelchairs).

English-language walking guides include Lonely Planet's *Walking in France*; *Walking in Provence* by Janette Norton; and the excellent *Walks in Provence: Lubéron Regional Nature Park*, a topoguide by the Fédération Française de Randonnée Pédestre.

WALKING WITH A FARMER

To really get to grips with the lay of the land, sign up for an *itineraire paysan* (farmer's itinerary): an innovative two- to three-hour walk led by a local farmer across his land. Walks are thematic and take nature-lovers through fruit orchards and Alpine pastures, past beehives, along canals, around goat farms and in search of black diamonds (truffles).

These *itineraires paysans* take place on farms and agricultural land in Haute-Provence (including the area around Manosque in the Lubéron). They cost €7/3 for adults/six to 16 years and must be booked directly with the farmer at least 24 hours in advance. A calendar of walks is online at www.itineraires-paysans.com. Alternatively, contact the **Centre Permanent d'Initiatives pour l'Environnement Alpes de Provence** (☎ 04 92 87 58 81; www.cpie04.com in French; Château de Drouille, F-04100 Manosque).

TOP TEN ACTIVITY TOURS FROM ABROAD

Most cycling- and walking-tour operators lighten the load by taking charge of transporting baggage by minibus between hotels. Tours take in hilltop villages and other sights en route.

Andante on Foot (☎ 01722-713813; www.andanteonfoot.co.uk; The Old Barn, Old Rd, Alderbury, Salisbury, SP5 3AR, UK) You book your own low-budget airline flight to/from Nice and let Andante on Foot do the rest, ie organise 11km to 17km (four to eight hours) a day of scenic walking from the hilltop villages of the Roya Valley to *belle époque* Menton, seven night's B&B accommodation, six picnic lunches and luggage transfer, costing UK£565.

ATG Oxford (☎ 01865-315678; www.atg-oxford.co.uk; 69-71 Banbury Rd, Oxford OX2 6PJ, UK) Independent walking holidays, including an eight-day 'painters and gardens of Provence' trip (UK£1995 excluding flights) and an eight-day Lubéron tour (UK £495/675 for standard/superior accommodation).

Erna Low – Body and Soul Holidays (☎ 020-7594 0290; www.bodyandsoulholidays.com; 9 Reece Mews, London SW7 3HE, UK) Mellow out (see the boxed text, p41) with a four-night re-mineralising programme on St-Jean-Cap Ferrat (UK£590 to UK£1085 per person including accommodation and flights) or a three-night pampering stopover at Mougins' Sheiseido Spa (UK£570 to UK£740 per person).

European Riding Holidays (☎ 01653-617930; www.europeanridingholidays.co.uk; c/o Inntravel, Nr Castle Howard, York YO60 7JU, UK) Riding holidays in the Lubéron and Haute-Provence.

Europeds (☎ 800-321 9552, 831-646 4920; www.europeds.com; 761 Lighthouse Ave, Monterey, CA 93940, USA) Cycling, walking and hiking tours by this California-based Europe specialist; pay US$2695 for a seven-day 'Provence Loops' cycling holiday.

Explore Worldwide (☎ 01252-760000; www.explore.co.uk; 1 Frederick St, Aldershot, Hants GU11 1LQ, UK) Eight-day walking tour in Haute-Provence by the UK's adventure specialists costs upwards of UK£499.

Golf Holidays Abroad (☎ 020-8644 9229; www.golfinfrance.f9.co.uk; 362 Sutton Common Rd, Sutton, Surrey SM3 9PL, UK) Take your pick from one of 20-odd different golf courses in southern France.

Headwater (☎ 01606-720033; www.headwater-holidays.co.uk; The Old School House, Chester Rd, Castle, Northwich, Cheshire CW8 1LE, UK) Seven- to 11-day walking, cycling and gastronomic tours in the Lubéron, northern Var and on the coast; nine-day gastronomic cycling adventures.

Susi Madron's Cycling for Softies (☎ 01612-488282; www.cycling-for-softies.co.uk; 2 & 4 Birch Polygon, Rusholme Manchester M14 5HX, UK) The 'soft' approach to cycling Provence: seven- to 14-day tours of the Camargue or Lubéron, catering to all cycling abilities.

Top Yacht (☎ 01243-520950; www.top-yacht.com; Southgate, Chichester, West Sussex PO19 8DN, UK) Charter a yacht with or without a professional skipper and sail from Bormes-les-Mimosas to the Îles d'Hyères. Weekly rates start at UK£952/2023 a week for two-/five-cabin yacht.

---

mountain guide. Several companies, both within and outside the region, organise longer treks; see Top 10 Activity Tours from Abroad (above).

WHITEWATER SPORTS

Between April and September Haute-Provence promises thrills and spills galore with its exquisite whitewater rafting, canoeing, kayaking, canyoning (scaling waterfalls and rivers with ropes), hot-dogging (bombing in an inflatable canoe), hydrospeed (bombing on a bodyboard) and water-rambling (navigating rivers on a mountain bike) opportunities. The Rivers Verdon, Vésubie, Roya and Ubaye are easily the region's most dramatic waters; leading centres where you can sign up for guided half- and full-day expeditions are Castellane (for the Gorges du Verdon), St-Martin-Vésubie (for the Vésubie descent), Breil-sur-Roya (for the Vallée de la Roya) and Barcelonnette (for the Vallée de l'Ubaye). Expect to pay around €50/75 for a half-/full-day group expedition with guide. Full details are listed in the Haute-Provence chapter.

The less intrepid, in search of peace rather than pumping adrenalin, can canoe beneath the Pont du Gard (see p162), along the bird-life-laden Camargue waterways (see p107) or along the River Sorgue from Fontaine de Vaucluse to L'Isle-sur-la-Sorgue (see Canoeing, p149).

The Arts in Provence & the Côte d'Azur

The region is a living art space. Be it tracing the steps of some of the 19th and 20th centuries' greatest artists (see p14) or catching a contemporary happening at a Marseillais tobacco factory–turned-cutting-edge art space, the Provence portfolio covers the whole spectrum of periods and styles.

PAINTING
Papal Pleasures to Rococo Silliness

In the 14th century Sienese, French and Spanish artists working at the papal court in Avignon created an influential style of mural painting, examples of which can be seen in the city's Palais des Papes (p126) – or rather on postcards featuring the paintings that once adorned the palace's now very bare interior.

While the rest of France found itself preoccupied with the Hundred Years' War, art flourished in Nice county, where the School of Nice emerged, led by Louis Bréa. View his works at Nice's Église Notre Dame (p217) and Menton's Palais Carnolès, which houses a Musée des Beaux-Arts (p237). In the Vallée de la Roya, meanwhile, a pair of artists from northern Italy set to work on what has since been dubbed the 'Sistine Chapel of the southern Alps' (p203).

Blindman's bluff, stolen kisses and other courtly frivolities were the focus of Enlightenment artists. One of the most influential was Avignon-born Joseph Vernet (1714–89), who left a landscape series depicting French ports, including Toulon. Rococo influences brushed the landscapes of Jean-Honoré Fragonard (1732–1806), whose playful and often licentious scenes immortalised his native Grasse and captured the silliness of the rococo spirit. His villa (p270), containing many of his works, can be visited.

The elevated style of Nice-born Carle van Loo (1705–65) represented rococo's more serious 'grand style'; good examples hang in the Musée des Beaux-Arts (p216) in Nice and Avignon's Musée Calvet (p127).

19th Century

The strong empathy with nature expressed in watercolour by François Marius Granet (1775–1849), a born-and-bred Aix-en-Provence artist, was a trademark of early-19th-century Provençal painters.

Landscape painting further evolved under Gustave Courbet (1819–77), a prominent member of the Paris Commune, who was a frequent visitor to southern France where he taught Provençal realist Paul Guigou (1834–71). A native of Villars in the Vaucluse, Guigou painted the Durance plains overdrenched in bright sunlight.

Provence's astonishing intensity of light drew the impressionists, among them Alfred Sisley, Camille Pissarro, Berthe Morisot and Pierre-Auguste Renoir (1841–1919). Renoir lived in Cagnes-sur-Mer from 1903 until his death. Many of his works are displayed in the Musée Renoir (p263), his former home and studio, in Cagnes-sur-Mer.

Paul Cézanne (1839–1906), celebrated for his still-life and landscape works, spent his entire life in Aix-en-Provence and painted numerous canvases in and around the fountain city; the tourist-office trail (p98) traces what he painted where.

Southern France was also immortalised by Paul Gauguin (1848–1904), who spent much time in Arles. While there, Gauguin worked for a time with Dutch artist Vincent van Gogh (1854–90), who spent most of his painting life in Paris and Arles. A brilliant and innovative artist, van Gogh produced haunting self-portraits and landscapes, in which colour assumes an expressive and emotive quality. Unfortunately, van Gogh's talent was largely unrecognised during his lifetime. He was confined to an asylum in St-Rémy de Provence and eventually committed suicide. He painted his most famous works, *Sunflowers* and *Van Gogh's Chair* (1888), in Arles. Van Gogh's later technique, exhibited in works dating from his St-Rémy period such as *Starry Night* and *Olive Trees* (1889), foreshadowed pointillism.

Pointillism was developed by Georges Seurat (1859–91), who applied paint in small dots or with uniform brush strokes of unmixed colour. His most devout pupil was Paul Signac (1863–1935), who settled in St-Tropez from 1892. Part of the Musée de l'Annonciade (p285) in St-Tropez is devoted to pointillist works and includes *Étude pour le Chenal de Gravelines* (Study for the Channel at Gravelines) painted by Seurat in 1890, as well as numerous works by Signac. Many depict St-Tropez or Marseille.

20th Century

It was on the Côte d'Azur that leading fauvist exponent Henri Matisse (1869–1954) spent his most creative years, lapping up the sunlight and vivacity of the coast in and around Nice. While in St-Tropez with Signac, Matisse began sketches that produced *Luxe, Calme et Volupté* (Luxury, Calm and Tranquillity). Pointillism's signature uniform brush strokes were still evident, but were also intermingled with splashes of violent colour. His subsequent painting, *La Gitane* (1906) – displayed in St-Tropez's Musée de l'Annonciade (p285) – is the embodiment of fauvism.

Cubism was launched in 1907 by Spanish prodigy Pablo Picasso (1881–1973), for whom Provence had a tremendous importance: he spent most of his creative life here. As demonstrated in his pioneering *Les Demoiselles d'Avignon,* cubism deconstructed the subject into a system of intersecting planes and presented various aspects of it simultaneously. The collage, incorporating bits of cloth, wood, string, newspaper and anything lying around, was a cubist speciality.

After WWI the School of Paris was formed by a group of expressionists, mostly foreign, such as Marc Chagall (1887–1985), who was born in Vitebsk (present-day Belarus) but lived in France from 1922 and spent his last few years in St-Paul de Vence; his grave can be visited at the town's cemetery (p264). The largest collection of his works is at the Musée National Message Biblique Marc Chagall (p215) in Nice. It was at La Colombe d'Or (p264) in St-Paul de Vence that Chagall, Picasso and others ate and slept in exchange for a canvas or two in the 1920s. Dining here today is tantamount to dining in a precious art museum.

With the onset of WWII many artists left, and although some later returned, the region never regained its old magnetism. Picasso moved permanently to the Côte d'Azur, settling first in Golfe-Juan, then Vallauris and finally Mougins, where he died. In 1946 he set up his studio in Antibes' Château Grimaldi (p258) and later painted a chapel, now the Musée National Picasso at Château Musée De Vallauris (p255) in Vallauris.

The other great artist of this period was former fauvist Matisse, who lived in Nice from 1917 until his death. He also decorated a chapel (p265). His bold and colourful works culminated in his familiar blue-and-white cut-out montages, which he completed in the early 1950s. See these and others at Nice's Musée Matisse (p215).

Essential art-driven reads include *Artists and their Museums on the Riviera* by Barbara Freed, and Jacques Lartigue's *Riviera,* with its stunning collection of black-and-white photographs of the coast taken by the local photographer from the 1920s to 1960s.

DID YOU KNOW?

Fauvism took its name from the slur of a critic who compared the exhibitors at the 1905 Salon d'Automme in Paris with *fauves* (wildcats) because of their radical use of intensely bright colours.

The 1960s ushered in new realists Arman, Yves Klein and César (see p51), all well represented in the Musée d'Art Moderne et d'Art Contemporain (p214), Nice. Suddenly, art was generated from recycled trash, dirty crockery, crushed cars and scrap metal. In 1960 Nice-born Klein (1928–1962) produced *Anthropométrie de l'Époque Bleue*, a series of blue imprints made by two naked women (covered from head to toe in blue paint) rolling around on a white canvas – in front of an orchestra of violins and an audience in evening dress. Nice-born Arman (b 1928) became known for his trash-can portraits, made by framing the litter found in the subject's trash bin. Another influential realist from the School of Nice was Martial Rayasse, born in Golfe-Juan in 1936, and renowned for pioneering the use of neon in art. Most notable is his 1964 portrait of *Nissa Bella* (Beautiful Nice) – a flashing blue heart on a human face.

Another influential artist was Hungarian-born Victor Vasarely (1908–97). In Gordes from 1948, the avant-gardist turned his attention to geometrical forms, juxtaposed in contrasting colours to create shifting perspectives. Forty-two works by Vasarely are displayed in the Fondation Vasarely – designed and funded by the artist himself (see p49) – in Aix-en-Provence.

The 1970s supports-surfaces movement focused on deconstructing the traditional concept of a painting and transforming one of its structural components – such as the frame or canvas – into a work of art instead. The Groupe 70, specific to Nice, expressed an intellectual agitation, typical to Vivien Isnard's 1987 *Sans Titre* (Without Title) and Louis Chacallis' *Tension* (1978).

In the 1990s bold paintings of naked angels brought world fame to Arles-born Louis Feraud (1921–99), an artist and couturier who dressed Brigitte Bardot and Ingrid Bergman in the 1950s.

Keep up-to-date and clued-up on the very latest in the regional art scene with the indispensable and inspirational www.art-en-provence .com (in French).

www.documentsdar tistes.org showcases the works of dozens of visual artists, up-and-coming or already established, in southern France.

ARCHITECTURE
Prehistoric to Villages Perchés

See remnants of stone megaliths at the Musée d'Archéologie Méditerranéenne (p74) in Marseille, Monaco's Musée d'Anthropologie Préhistorique (p327) and Quinson's Musée de la Préhistoire des Gorges du Verdon (p190). Numerous petroglyphs are evident in the Vallée des Merveilles (p202) and examples of the region's earliest habitats – beehive-shaped huts built from dry limestone called *bories* – can be seen near Gordes (see p171).

The architectural legacy left by the Romans is impressive: look no further than the mighty Pont du Gard aqueduct (p162), the colossal amphitheatres at Nîmes (p159) and Arles (p109), the theatres at Orange (p136) and Fréjus (p277), Nîmes' Maison Carrée (p159) and the triumphal arches at Orange (p136) and Carpentras (p146) to see their architectural brilliance.

Bar the octagonal 5th-century baptistry (p277) that can be visited in Fréjus, few churches constructed between the 5th and 10th centuries remain. The region does, however, have dozens of *villages perchés* (hilltop

---

THE WASH HOUSE

Until the 19th century the women of the village used them to wash their clothes in. Today, the most common use for these empty stone basins, covered with a stone roof and found in most old villages, is to host art exhibitions. *Lavoirs* (wash houses) in St-Tropez and Mougins are regular art hosts.

villages) that cropped up from the 10th century as villagers on the plains moved atop rocky crags to better defend themselves against Saracen attacks; see p12 for a classic hilltop-village itinerary.

Romanesque to Renaissance

A religious revival in the 11th century ushered in Romanesque architecture, so-called because of the Gallo-Roman architectural elements it adopted. Round arches, heavy walls with few windows and a lack of ornamentation were characteristics of this style, Provence's most famous examples being the 12th-century abbeys in Sénanque (p172), Le Thoronet (p297) and Silvacane (p180). You can visit all three.

Fortress-like sacred buildings also marked this era, as the majestic Chartreuse de la Verne (p299), the older monastery on Île St-Honorat (p254) and the church at Stes-Maries de la Mer (see p114) demonstrate. The exceptional dimensions of Digne-les-Bains cathedral (p192) are typical of the late Provençal-Romanesque style.

Provence's most important examples of Gothic architecture are Avignon's Palais des Papes (p126), the Chartruese du Val de Bénédiction (p134) in Villeneuve-lès-Avignon and Carpentras' Cathédrale St-Siffrein (p146). When visiting, look for ribbed vaults carved with great precision, pointed arches, slender verticals, chapels along the nave and chancel, refined decoration and large stained-glass windows.

The French Renaissance scarcely touched the region – unlike mighty citadel architect Sébastien Le Prestre de Vauban (1633–1707), who thundered in with his star-shaped Fort Carré in Antibes (p258), hilltop Entrevaux (see Along the Mountain Railway, p194), Château de Sisteron (p195) at Sisteron and constructions at Toulon (p313).

'Nice is exceptionally well endowed with *belle époque* chocolate-box creations'

Classical to Contemporary

Classical architecture fused with painting and sculpture from the end of the 16th to late 18th centuries to create stunning baroque structures with interiors of great subtlety, refinement and elegance: Chapelle de la Miséricorde (p211) in Nice, Menton's Italianate Basilique St-Michel Archange (p236) and Marseille's Centre de la Vieille Charité (p71) are classics.

Neoclassicism came into its own under Napoleon III, who used it to embody the grandeur of imperial France. Both the Palais de Justice (p210) and Palais Masséna, which houses the Musée d'Art et d'Histoire (p216), in Nice demonstrate the renewed interest in classical forms that neoclassicism exhibited. The true showcase of this era, though, is 1878 Monte Carlo Casino (p326), designed by French architect Charles Garnier (1825–98). In 1887 Garnier, together with Gustave Eiffel (1832–1923) of tower fame, who lived in Beaulieu-sur-Mer, came up with the Observatoire de Nice (p233). Elegant Aix-en-Provence's fountains and *hôtels particuliers* (private residences) date from this period; as do the intricate wrought-iron campaniles.

The *belle époque* heralded a fantastical eclecticism of decorative stucco friezes, trompe l'oeil paintings, glittering wall mosaics, brightly coloured Moorish minarets and Turkish towers. In short, anything went. Nice is exceptionally well endowed with these chocolate-box creations.

The stark, 1920s concrete-and-glass Villa Noailles (p311) in Hyères is an expression of the cubist movement that gained momentum in the interwar period. Examples of surrealist interiors designed by Jean Cocteau (see p53), who lived in Menton at this time, include Menton's Salles des Mariages (p236), Chapelle St-Pierre (p228) in Villefranche-sur-Mer and Cap d'Ail's amphitheatre (p231).

TRAILING LE CORBUSIER

Track down Le Corbusier in Marseille (where he built the ground-breaking Unité d'Habitation), Cap Martin (where he had a studio) and Roquebrune (where he's buried).

Swiss-born, it was the latter part of his life that saw Charles Édouard Jeanneret (1887–1965), alias Le Corbusier, turn to southern France for inspiration. Of all his architectural achievements, it was the mammoth concrete apartment block he designed in Marseille that was the most revolutionary – and controversial. Built between 1947 and 1952 as a low-cost housing project, the Unité d'Habitation saw 337 apartments arranged inside an elongated block on stilts. Apartments were built in 23 different configurations, and everything needed for functional living, including a school and gym, was on site.

Considered a coup by architects worldwide, the apartment block – or rather, its façade, communal corridors and rooftop terrace – has been protected as a historical monument since 1986. Apartments on the 7th and 8th floors function as a hotel (see Author's Choice, p79), and the rest are private, home to 1400 people.

Le Corbusier frequently visited the coast from the 1930s, often staying with his architect friends, Irish Eileen Gray and Romanian-born Jean Badovici, in their 1920s seaside villa, E-1027, on Cap Martin. In 1938 Le Corbusier painted a trio of wall frescoes in E-1027, one of which featured three entangled women and offended Gray (a proclaimed lesbian) so much that she broke off her friendship with the architect and moved to Menton.

After WWII Le Corbusier befriended Thomas Rebutato who ran L'Étoile de Mer, a neighbouring shack restaurant. He bought a plot of land from Rebutato and in 1951 came up with Le Cabanon, a one-room wooden cabin containing everything needed for holiday living in 13 sq metres. He gave this experiment in minimalist habitation to his wife, Monégasque model Yvonne Gallis (whom he wed in 1930), as a birthday present and it remained their summer home until 1965 when Le Corbusier suffered a fatal heart attack while swimming in the sea.

Future plans for Le Cabanon will see the site developed as a museum and architectural research centre, incorporating the cabin, L'Étoile de Mer (still owned by the Rebutato family) and E-1027 (inhabited by squatters from 1990 until 1999). The coastal footpath promenade Le Corbusier leads from Roquebrune-Cap Martin train station to the site; exit the station and bear left along the *sentier littoral* (coastal path; signposted 'Plage de Carnolés').

Le Corbusier is buried with his wife, who died in 1957, in section J of Roquebrune cemetery. His grave (which he designed before his death) is adorned by a cactus and the epitaph, painted in Le Corbusier's cursive hand on a small yellow, red and blue ceramic tile: *ici repose Charles Édouard Jeanneret (1887-1965)*.

Le Corbusier – France's most celebrated 20th-century architect – spent a great deal of time on the Côte d'Azur, rewriting the architectural stylebook here. For the complete Le Corbusier tour see the boxed text (above).

Aix-en-Provence's Fondation Vasarely (p98), designed by Victor Vasarely (1908–97), was an architectural coup when unveiled in 1976. Its 14 giant monumental hexagons reflected what he had already achieved in art: the creation of optical illusion and changing perspective through the juxtaposition of geometrical shapes and colours. This 'father of Op Art' went on to design the town hall in La Seyne-sur-Mer, near Toulon, and the stained-glass windows inside Port Grimaud's church (p293). The single most influential period in his career was spent in Gordes (p171).

Steel meets glass at the Carrée d'Art (1993; p159) in Nîmes, designed by British architect Sir Norman Foster, who also came up with Quinson's Musée de la Préhistoire des Gorges du Verdon (p190). Nîmes also sports a bus stop on av Carnot designed by Philippe Starck (b 1949), a contemporary French designer who redesigned Nîmes' coat of arms and teamed up with French chef Alain Ducasse to design the interior of the upmarket Monaco restaurant, Bar & Boeuf (p330).

For a fascinating look at E-1027, Eileen Gray, Le Corbusier et al in words and images see www .e1027.com.

Other great examples of contemporary architecture include Monaco's glass-and-steel Grimaldi Forum (2000; p326), two-thirds of which sits beneath sea level, and Nice's Musée d'Art Moderne et d'Art Contemporain (1990; p214) and Fondation Maeght (1964). The holiday village of Port Grimaud (1969; p293) was the conception of François Spoerry (1912–99), subsequent architect of Port Liberty in New York.

Nothing competes with the lime-green building designed by Swiss-based architects Annette Gigon and Mike Guyer to 'complement' the neighbouring 16th-century chateau museum in Mouans-Sartoux (p268).

CINEMA

Posing for the camera in Cannes at the foot of the red-carpeted steps (see Starring at Cannes, p247) where many a silver-screen star has stood is a must for film buffs – as is a peep at Eden Théâtre (p92), the world's oldest cinema, in La Ciotat.

With its spectacular light and subtle shadows, southern France was inspirational to cinema: the world's first motion picture by the Lumière brothers premiered in Château Lumière in La Ciotat in September 1895. The series of two-minute reels, entitled *L'Arrivée d'un Train en Gare de La Ciotat* (The Arrival of a Train at La Ciotat Station), made the audience leap out of their seats as the steam train rocketed forward. In March 1899 the brothers opened Eden Théâtre (currently being restored) on La Ciotat's seafront.

French film flourished in the 1920s, Nice being catapulted to stardom by Hollywood director Rex Ingram, who bought the city's Victorine film studios in 1925 and transformed them overnight into the hub of European filmmaking.

A big name was Aubagne-born writer Marcel Pagnol, whose career kicked off in 1931 with *Marius,* the first part of his *Fanny* trilogy portraying pre-war Marseille. Pagnol filmed *La Femme du Boulanger* (The Baker's Wife; 1938) in Castellet (see A Lavender Detour, p177). These films launched the career of France's earliest silver-screen heroes, Toulon-born comic actor Raimu, alias Jules Auguste César Muraire (1883–1946), and 'horse face' Fernandel (1903–71), an honorary citizen of Carry-le-Rouet where he summered most years. Throughout his career Pagnol stuck to depicting what he knew best: Provence and its ordinary people.

Portraits of ordinary people dominated film until the 1950s when surrealist Jean Cocteau (1889–1963) eschewed realism in two masterpieces of cinematic fantasy: *La Belle et la Bête* (Beauty and the Beast; 1945) and *Orphée* (Orpheus; 1950). Both starred the beautiful blonde-haired Vallauris-born actor Jean Marais (1914–98), who met Cocteau in 1937 and remained his lover until Cocteau's death in 1963. Find out more about the filmmaker at the Musée Jean Cocteau (p236), the town where Cocteau is buried.

Nouvelle Vague (New Wave) directors made films without big budgets, extravagant sets or big-name stars. Roger Vadim's *Et Dieu Créa la Femme* (And God Created Woman; 1956) – an internationally acclaimed portrayal of the amorality of modern youth – brought sudden stardom to Brigitte Bardot (see the boxed text, p286) and St-Tropez.

A clutch of French classics filmed in the region followed, among them François Truffaut's *Les Mistons* (1958), filmed exclusively in Nîmes; Jacques Démy's *La Baie des Anges* (The Bay of Angels; 1962); Henri Decoin's *Masque de Fer* (Iron Mask; 1962), parts of which were filmed in Sospel; Rohmer's *La Collectionneuse* (The Collectors; 1966), again shot in St-Tropez; and the first in the series of Jean Girault's celebrated *Le Gendarme de St-Tropez* (1964, see the boxed text, p291). In 1972 François

Truffaut filmed part of *La Nuit Américaine* (The American Night; 1972) in the Victorine studios, the Niçois hinterland and the Vésubie Valley.

Foreign directors also flocked to the sunlit Riviera: Hitchcock's suspense thriller *La Main au Collet* (To Catch a Thief; 1956), starring Cary Grant and Grace Kelly; John Frankenheimer's *French Connection 2*; and Disney's lovable *Herbie goes to Monte Carlo* (1977), starring Herbie the Volkswagen Beetle, were all shot here.

Generous state subsidies to filmmakers focused on costume dramas and 'heritage movies' in the 1980s, prompting a renewed interest in Pagnol's great Provençal classics. Parts of Claude Berri's *Jean de Florette* and *Manon des Sources* were shot in the Massif de la Ste-Baume (see A Pilgrim's Detour, p93). In 1990 Yves Robert directed film versions of Pagnol's autobiographical novels *La Gloire de Mon Père* (My Father's Glory) and *Le Château de Ma Mère* (My Mother's Castle). Big-name stars, slick production values and a strong sense of nostalgia were dominant motifs of the 1998 Hollywood box office hit *The Man in the Iron Mask* – an adaptation of the 'iron mask' mystery that occurred on the Île Ste-Marguerite near Cannes in the late 17th century – starring Gérard Depardieu, Leonardo DiCaprio and Jeremy Irons.

To see the region from a funnier perspective, watch the Marseille comedy *Taxi 3* (2003), filmed and set in Marseille. Norman Jewison's *The Statement* (2004), starring Michael Caine, was shot on location in Marseille and in the tiny Var village of Ste-Anne d'Evenos, northwest of Toulon.

Film stars congregate on the Côte d'Azur once a year for an orgy of glitz and glamour at the *Festiva International du Film*, the French film industry's main annual event (see Starring at Cannes, p247). In 2004 three new film studios – one with a 17m-high ceiling, making it among the biggest sets in Europe – opened in Marseille's La Friche le Belle de Mai.

SCULPTURE

At the end of the 11th century, sculptors decorated the portals, capitals, altars and fonts of Romanesque churches, illustrating Bible stories and the lives of the saints for the illiterate. Two centuries on, sculpture spread from the central portal to the whole façade, paving the way for Marseille-born sculptor Pierre Puget (1620–94). Puget introduced the idea of adorning ship sterns with elaborate ornamentation, and was among the first to experiment with atlantes (the use of figures of men instead of columns to support an entablature). The anguished figures supporting the balcony of honour at the old city hall on quai Constradt in Toulon are a celebrated example.

Marseille also produced César, alias César Baldaccini (1921–98). Greatly inspired by Michelangelo (a replica of his David stands in Marseille today) and Picasso (one of the first to use scrap metal as a medium), César started out using wrought-iron and scrap metals but later graduated to pliable plastics. From 1960 he used crushed motor cars as a medium, compressing no less than 23 cars between 1960 and 1989: see the result at Nice's Musée d'Art Moderne et d'Art Contemporain (p214) and Marseille's Musée d'Art Contemporain (p75).

LITERATURE
Courtly Love to Sadism

Lyric poems of courtly love, written solely in Occitan *langue d'oc* by troubadours, dominated medieval Provençal literature.

Provençal life featured in the works of Italian poet Petrarch (1304–74), exiled to Avignon in 1327 where he met Laura, to whom he dedicated

Searching for a location to shoot your next Hollywood hit? Keen to read more about the local film and TV industry? Flick through cinematic history and current affairs with the South of France Film Commission at www .filmvar.org.

DID YOU KNOW?

It was César who created the little statue handed to actors at the Césars – the French cinema awards named after the Marseillais sculptor no less.

François Ozon's *The Swimming Pool*, quickly dubbed by the critics 'the summer's sexiest mystery', sees a dispirited middle-aged English novelist seeking repose and inspiration in the Lubéron at the summer house of her publisher – only for the latter's high-spirited, very sexy and very French daughter to show up.

his life's works. Petrarch lived in Fontaine de Vaucluse from 1337 to 1353, where he composed his song book *Canzonière* and wrote poems and letters about local shepherds, fishermen he met on the banks of the Sorgue and his pioneering ascent up Mont Ventoux. The village's Musée Pétrarque (p150) tells his life story.

Bellaud de la Bellaudière (1533–88), a native of Grasse, wrote *Oeuvres et Rîmes* in Occitan. The literary landmark is a book of 160 sonnets drawing on influences by Petrarch and French epic writer Rabelais.

In 1555 philosopher and visionary writer Nostradamus (1503–66), from St-Rémy de Provence, published (in Latin) his prophetic *Centuries* in Salon de Provence, where he lived until his death (from gout, as he had predicted). Find out why the papal authorities banned his work as blasphemous at Salon de Provence's Maison de Nostradamus (p94).

The 17th *grand siècle* yielded Nicolas Saboly's the *Noëls Provençaux*, poems encapsulating a nativity scene. The pious tone was representative of the strait-laced fervour that dominated baroque Provençal literature – hence the utter outrage at the sexually explicit works of Marquis de Sade (see Sadism, p175).

Mistral to Mayle

The 19th century witnessed a revival in Provençal literature, thanks to Frédéric Mistral (1830–1914). A native of Maillane, Mistral's passion for Provence and its culture, history and language was awakened by his Avignon tutor Joseph Roumanille (1818–91), who published *Li Margarideto* in 1847. In 1851 Mistral started work on his most momentous work, *Mirèio*. Three years later Le Félibrige was founded by seven young Provençal poets who pledged to revive Provençal and codify the language's orthography.

Mistral's epic poem *Mirèio* – the story of a beauty who flees to Stes-Maries de la Mer when her parents forbid her to marry her true love, only to die of a broken heart on the beach – was published in 1859. A succession of poems followed, all in Provençal and depicting a facet of Provence. Between 1878 and 1886 Mistral's most influential work on Provençal culture was published, the monumental *Trésor du Félibrige*. The 1890s saw Le Félibrige popularise his work with the opening of a museum in Arles (the Museon Arlaten; p111) and the publication of the *L'Aïoli* journal.

Another outstanding Provençal writer was Nîmes-born Alphonse Daudet (1840–97) who wrote *Lettres de Mon Moulin* (Letters from My Windmill; 1869) from a windmill, a replica of which can be visited, in Fontvieille (p155). Daudet is best remembered for his comic novels evoking small-town Tarascon through the eyes of his anti-hero Tartarin. The *Tartarin de Tarascon* trilogy was published between 1872 and 1890.

Parisian novelist Émile Zola (1840–1902) lived in Aix-en-Provence from the age of three to 18. Zola aimed to convert novel writing from an art to a science by the application of experimentation – a theory that, though naive, produced powerful works. Aix-en-Provence is evoked in *La Conquête de Plassans* (1874), and his friendship with Cézanne is the focus of *L'Oeuvre* (The Masterpiece; 1886).

Early-20th-century Provençal literature is dominated by writers depicting their homeland. Jean Giono (1895–1970) from Manosque blended myth with reality in novels that remain a celebration of the Provençal Alps and their people. Aubagne-born writer/filmmaker Marcel Pagnol (1895–1974) spent his life in and around Marseille, where he wrote novels and screen adaptations.

The surrealism that played a vital force in French literature until WWII is evident in the works of Jean Cocteau (1889–1963), the French poet, dramatist and filmmaker. Cocteau ran away from home to the Côte d'Azur at the age of 15, then returned to settle there from 1924 and is buried in Menton. His work – in his prose, on the cinematic set and in the chapels and other buildings he decorated (see p48) – captures the spirit of the surrealist movement: the fascination with dreams, divination and all manifestations of 'the marvellous'. His best-known novel, *Les Enfants Terribles* (1955), portrays the intellectual rebellion of the post-war era.

During WWII Roussillon served as a refuge to playwright Samuel Beckett, who stayed until April 1945 and wrote *Watt* (not published until after *Waiting for Godot* in 1953) there. Colette (1873–1954), who thoroughly enjoyed tweaking the nose of conventional readers with titillating novels that detailed the amorous exploits of such heroines as the schoolgirl Claudine, lived in St-Tropez from 1927 until 1938. *La Naissance du Jour* evokes an unspoilt St-Tropez.

The post-WWII years saw the existentialist literary movement develop around Jean-Paul Sartre (1905–80), Simone de Beauvoir (1908–86) and Albert Camus (1913–60). The latter moved to Lourmarin in the Lubéron (where he is buried; see p181) in 1957, and started his unfinished autobiographical novel *Le Premier Homme* (The First Man) there. The manuscript was found in the car wreckage when the Algerian-born writer – son of an illiterate mother – died in a car accident three years later.

The British novelist and travel writer Lawrence Durrell (1912–90) settled in Somières, near Nîmes, and dedicated the last 33 years of his literary career to writing about Provençal life. Other notable figures who settled in the region in the latter part of their careers include Dirk Bogarde, James Baldwin, Anthony Burgess and Peter Mayle.

The Fly-Truffler by Gustaf Sobin is both unusual and captivating. A philosophical novel, it tells the tale of a professor of the Provençal language and his insatiable appetite for truffles.

MUSIC

Immigrant life in the Marseillais *banlieue* (suburbs) finds expression in the hip-hop lyrics of rapping legend IAM, France's best-known rap group whose smash-hit first album in 1991, *...de la Planète Mars* ('...from Planet Mars', Mars being short for Marseille), nudged rap into the mainstream.

In world music Cheb Khaled, Cheb Aïssa and Cheb Mami – all from the same multicultural portside city – have contributed hugely to the development of Algerian rai. Ahmed Whaby, pioneer of Oran music and dubbed the world's most beautiful Arab voice, was born in Marseille in 1921 to a Spanish mother and Algerian father.

DANCE

The *farandole* is a Provençal dance, danced at the close of village festivals in and around Arles since the Middle Ages. Men and women take their partner by the hand or remain linked with a cord or handkerchief as they briskly jig, accompanied by a tambourine and *galoubet* (shrill flute with three holes).

In classical ballet France led the way until the 19th century, when the centre for innovation shifted to Russia. France's leading talent, Marius Petipa (1818–1910), a native of Marseille, moved to St Petersburg in 1847, where he mixed French dance tradition with Slavic sensibilities to create *La Bayadère* (1877), *Le Lac des Cygnes* (Swan Lake; 1895) and other masterpieces.

The rising star of contemporary dance is Aix-en-Provence; see Dance in Aix (p101).

DID YOU KNOW?

It was in Nice that icon of modern dance Isadora Duncan (1878–1927), Paris resident from 1900, died. Duncan's neck was broken in a freak motoring accident on the Riviera when the customary scarf that trailed behind her got caught in the car wheels.

Food & Drink

Food and drink – a feast of an affair in this part of France – wangles its way in to the most seemingly unrelated of conversations. And not without good cause: Provençal cuisine is reputed the world over and is a reason in itself to holiday here. Lazing over a long lunch with friends, feeling so full three hours later you wouldn't even dream of moving all afternoon, is a Provençal experience not to be taken lightly.

Yet the secret of Provençal cuisine lies not in elaborate preparation techniques or state-of-the-art presentation but in the use of fresh ingredients produced locally. Some traditions are upheld everywhere – oodles of olive oil, garlic and invariably tomatoes: any dish described as *à la Provençal* involves garlic-seasoned tomatoes.

The Provence Cookbook by Patricia Wells is the recipe-book bible for anyone keen to try their hand at Provençal cooking.

Regional culinary differences have their roots in sheer geography, which sees fishermen return with the catch of the day in seafaring Marseille and along the coast; herds of bulls grazing (yes, they are eaten) and paddy fields in the Camargue; lambs in the Alpilles; black truffles in the Vaucluse; and cheese made from cows' milk in alpine pastures. The Italianate influence tasted in Niçois cooking is a legacy of Savoy rule.

STAPLES & SPECIALITIES

Be it in a premier market town or a backwater village, walk through its Provençal market and you'll be struck by the abundance of different fruits and vegetables. Staples like onions, aubergines (eggplant) and courgettes (summer squash or zucchini) are stewed alongside green peppers, garlic and various aromatic herbs to produce that perennial Provençal favourite, ratatouille.

Artichokes, another typical vegetable, are eaten young and can be stuffed with a salted pork, onion and herb mix, then baked, to become *petits légumes farcis* (little stuffed vegetables); stuffed courgette flowers make an enchanting variation. Most vegetables that grow under the Provençal sun can be thrown into a *tian* (vegetable-and-rice gratin) or eaten as crudités, that is, chopped up and served raw with *anchoïade* (a strong, anchovy paste laced with garlic and olive oil), *tapenade* (an olive-based dip seasoned with garlic, capers, anchovies and olive oil) or *brandade de morue* (a don't-mess-with-me mix of crushed salt cod, olive oil and garlic), and an apéritif.

Garlic gives a distinctive Provençal kick to strong-tasting sauces, traditionally served to complement soups and fish dishes. *Soupe au pistou* is a vegetable, three- or four-bean and basil soup, always served with *pistou*, a basil, garlic and olive-oil sauce that you stir into the soup to spice it up, or spread on pieces of toast. *Soupe de poisson* (fish soup) likewise comes with crisp toast, a garlic clove and a pot of pink *rouille* (a garlic mayonnaise with breadcrumbs and crushed chilli peppers, hence its colour). Rub the garlic over the toast, spread the *rouille* on top, bite it and breathe fire.

Herbs

Provençal cooking uses a titillating array of aromatic herbs and plants, a legacy of the heavily scented garrigue (herbal scrub) that grows with vigour in the region. While the classic herbal mix of dried basil, thyme and rosemary seasons dishes throughout Europe, culinary creations in the region rely more on fresh herbs: fresh basil lends its pea-green colour and strong fragrance to *pistou* (but is used dried to flavour *soupe au pistou*).

Sage, traditionally an antiseptic, is another *pistou* ingredient, while aromatic rosemary – a common Mediterranean shrub – flavours meat dishes. Chervil leaves are used in omelettes and meat dishes, and tarragon's tender young shoots flavour delicate sauces accompanying seafood.

Particularly rife is the sensual aniseed scent of the bulbous fennel. While its leaves are picked in spring and finely chopped for use in fish dishes and marinades, its potent seeds (plucked at summer's end) form the basis of several herbal liqueurs including pastis (see The Milk of Provence, p58) and the 50% alcohol by volume Lérina liqueur made by monks on Île St-Honorat (see p254). Equally distinctive to Provençal cuisine is the use of lavender – only its green leaves are used in the kitchen.

Olives & Olive Oil

Succulent, sun-baked black olives – born from clusters of white flowers that blossom on knotty trees in May and June – are harvested from mid-November to January. Olives destined for the oil press are not picked until December; 5kg produces 1L of oil. Olive oils from northern Vaucluse around Nyons, the Vallée des Baux and the Alpilles have their own *appellation d'origine contrôlée* (AOC). *Oléiculteurs* (olive growers) in these regions have to comply to a rigid set of rules in order to have their bottles of oil stamped with the quality-guaranteed AOC mark.

Olive oil is tasted in the same way one samples wine. It can have various degrees of sweetness or acidity, and can be clear or slightly murky (which means the oil has not been filtered). A bottle of olive oil should be kept out of direct sunlight and consumed within six months of opening.

The secret behind many a Provençal dish, olive oil is also a key ingredient for *socca*, a traditional chickpea-flour pancake cooked up in and around Nice.

Truffles

Provence's most luxurious culinary product is the truffle, a fungus *(Tuber melanosporum)* that takes root underground at the foot of a tree, usually in symbiosis with the roots of an elm or oak tree. As precious as gold dust, these 'black diamonds' are snouted out in modest amounts in the Vaucluse, especially around Carpentras, Vaison-la-Romaine and in the Enclave des Papes. For an in-depth look at truffle culture see the boxed text (p140).

Sweets

Lavender and thyme flavour milk-based dishes such as *crème brûlée* as well as jams and honey. Anise and orange blossoms give *navettes* (canoe-shaped biscuits from Marseille) and *fougassettes* (sweet bread) their distinctive flavours. A secret 60 different Mont Ventoux herbs are used to make the

DID YOU KNOW?

In medieval Provence rosemary was said to possess magical powers which, if eaten regularly, ensured eternal youth.

Learn more about *oléiculture* (olive culture) at www.olivierdeprovence .com and www.oleiculture.com (in French).

DID YOU KNOW?

It is a waste of a decent olive oil to use it in cooking; when heated above 80°C it loses some of its taste.

SHOPPING FOR OLIVE OIL

The best place to buy *huile d'olive* (olive oil) is direct from the *moulin* (mill), ideally after the December harvest, from January through to Easter. Sold in glass bottles or plastic containers, it costs around €18 per litre and *dégustation* is an integral part of buying; millers pour a drop of oil onto a plastic spoon for you to taste.

Some mills are listed in the regional chapters; tourist offices also have lists. Otherwise, try markets or upmarket olive-oil shops like Oliviers & Co (Cannes, St-Tropez and Valbonne), Le Comptoir des Oliviers (Aix-en-Provence) and Olive: Les Huiles du Monde (St-Rémy de Provence and Les Baux de Provence).

TOP TEN EATS

The 'best' in the conventional sense they might not be, but we followed our stomachs around the region to nose out – several hundred meals later – this tasty cross section of taste-bud ticklers.

- Les Abeilles (see the boxed text, p143) – quintessential hilltop village dining in Sablet
- Zé and César Place (see the boxed text, p84) – designer chic at Marseille's Vieux Port
- Chez Marc et Mireille (see A Fishy Detour, p121) – edge-of-the-world seafood in Beauduc
- Ferme Auberge Le Castelas (see the boxed text, p181) – farmhouse feast in Sivergues
- Le Valbergan (see the boxed text, p201) – cockle-warming mountain fodder with views in Valberg
- L'Oursinade (see the boxed text, p312) –clifftop bouillabaisse on Cap de Carqueiranne
- Spoon Byblos (p290) and Bar & Boeuf (p330) – Ducasse dining in St-Tropez and Monaco
- Chez René Socca (see the boxed text, p223) – scrum for *socca* (a traditional chickpea-flour pancake) in Nice
- La Ferme de Mougins (p268) – classy gastronomy in rural Mougins
- Stars 'n' Bars (p330) – brash blast of Americana in blue-blooded Monaco

liqueur which laces *papalines d'Avignon* (pink liqueur-laced chocolate balls). Almonds are turned into *gâteaux secs aux amandes* (snappy almond biscuits) around Nîmes; into *calissons* (almond biscuit frosted with icing sugar) in Aix-en-Provence; and into black honey nougat everywhere.

Nice and Apt excel at *fruits confits* (crystallised or glazed fruits); see them made in Apt (p167) and Pont du Loup (p266). *Berlingots* are hard caramels originating in Carpentras, and *tarte Tropézienne* is a cream-filled sandwich cake from St-Tropez. Massif des Maures desserts star *glace aux marrons glacés* (chestnut ice cream) or *crème de marrons* (chestnut cream). A popular dessert in the Vaucluse is cantaloupe melon from Carpentras doused in Muscat de Beaumes de Venise, a sweet dessert wine made in a village nearby.

Delve behind the scenes of the region's truffle culture with Dominique and Eric Jaumard at www .truffes-ventoux.com.

Regional Dishes

The king of regional dishes is bouillabaisse. Essentially a pungent fish stew, this legendary yellow-orange dish has been brewed by Marseillais for centuries and involves at least four kinds of fresh fish cooked in a rockfish stock (broth) along with onions, tomatoes, garlic, saffron (hence its colour), parsley, bay leaves, thyme and other herbs. Its name is derived from the French *bouillir* (to boil) and *baisser* (to lower, as in a flame), reflecting the cooking method required: bring it to the boil, let it bubble ferociously for 15 minutes, then serve it: the *bouillon* (broth) first as a soup, followed by the fish flesh as a main course.

The Magic of the Truffle: The Favourite Recipes of Christian Étienne with a preface by Daniel Boulud takes an insider's look at what must be Provence's ugliest – and most treasured – culinary product.

No two cooks serve up an identical bouillabaisse, the debate about which fresh fish constitute a true bouillabaisse being endless. Shell fish, including *langouste* (crayfish) or *langoustine* (small saltwater lobster), is thrown into a bog-standard bouillabaisse to make a *bouillabaisse royale,* while the Toulonnais throw potatoes in. *Bourride* is a cheaper version of bouillabaisse; it contains no saffron, features cheaper white-fleshed fish, and is served with aïoli (a garlic mayonnaise) instead of pink *rouille*.

Aïoli is smeared over many a fish dish as well as *aïoli Provençal complet,* a plate of vegetables (including artichokes), boiled potatoes, a boiled egg and *coquillages* (small shellfish), all of which are dunked into the pot of aïoli accompanying them. *Supions frits* (squid pan-fried with fresh garlic and parsley) is another Marseillais dish. In fishing ports west of the port city, the orange roe of *oursins* (sea urchins) is scooped out with a spoon, like a soft-boiled egg, and eaten. The iodine-infused yellow flesh of clam-like *violets* (sea squirts) tastes like the sea.

It is a bullish affair (see the boxed text, p116) in the Camargue where *guardianne de taureau* (bull-meat stew) and *saucission d'Arles* (air-dried bull sausage) are specialities. *Pieds et paquets* (literally 'feet and pack-ages'), common to the Alpilles, are sheep's feet wrapped in tripe and cooked with wine and tomatoes. *Banon* is a type of chèvre (goat cheese) or *brebis* (sheep cheese), wrapped in a chestnut leaf, from Haute-Provence.

DRINKS

From the dazzling pea-green *sirop de menthe* (mint syrup diluted with water) sipped through straws on café pavement terraces to fruity apéritifs downed at dusk and the chateaux-aged wine spat *in situ*, drinking in Provence is a treat.

Coffee, the usual way to end a meal, is served espresso-style – short, black and strong – unless you specify otherwise: *café crème* is an espresso with steamed milk or cream and *café au lait* is hot milk with a dash of coffee. Tea comes in the form of an empty cup and a teabag (no milk).

Apéritifs & Digestifs

Savouring a pre-dinner drink is one of the region's great sensual delights. Pastis (see The Milk of Provence, p58) is the quintessential Provençal drink, closely followed by a crisp, chilled Côtes de Provence rosé (see p58). Beaumes de Venise, a sweet muscat wine, is a popular aperitif in northern Vaucluse. *Amandine* (an almond liqueur) and *rinquinquin de pêche* (a peach liqueur mixed with chilled white wine), distilled at the Distillerie Domaine de Haute-Provence in Forcalquier, feature on drinks menus in the Lubéron and Haute-Provence. *Liqueur de châtaignes* (chestnut liqueur) is mixed with white wine in the Massif des Maures to make another sweet choice.

Round off a feast with a marc (a fiery spirit distilled from grape skins and pulp left over from the wine-making process) or eau de vie (the generic name for brandies distilled from the region's bounty of fruits). Those with sweeter tooths will lap up Reverend Father Gaucher's Elixir (yellow chartreuse blended from 30 aromatic herbs in Tarascon) or La Farigoule (a thyme liqueur).

Wine

Provençal wines are by no means France's most sought after, but their making and tasting is an art and tradition which bears its own unique and tasty trademark. Each AOC is stamped by a common trait: an exception-ally cold mistral wind and an equally exceptional, hot ripening sun.

Wine can be bought direct from the *domaine* (wine-growing estate) of the *producteur* (wine producer) or *vigneron* (wine grower). Most offer *dégustation*, allowing you to sample two or three vintages with no

Author of the best-known piece of travel literature on Provence returns with a vengeance to eat his way around the whole of France: *French Lessons: Adventures with Knife, Fork and Corkscrew* by Peter Mayle takes in St-Tropez and other southern spots from a purely gastronomic angle.

If you're a gourmet on wheels keen to track down cyclist-friendly places to eat and shop in Provence, *Pedalling through Provence Cookbook* by Sarah Leah Chase and Linda Montgomery is the book for you.

DID YOU KNOW?

Pastis 51 is called such after the year in which it was launched – 1951. It just happens to also spell out the ideal ratio of water to pastis.

PLAIN OLD WATER

Tap water is safe to drink, but the water spouting from fountains that tout a sign reading *eau non potable* (non-drinking water) isn't. In restaurants, order *une carafe d'eau* (a jug of tap water) if you don't want to pay €5 to €10 for a bottle of *plate* (still) or *gazeuse* (fizzy) mineral water.

THE MILK OF PROVENCE

When in Provence, do as the Provençaux do: drink pastis. The aniseed-flavoured alcoholic drink is a classic apéritif in the region, although it can be drunk any time of day.

Amber-coloured in the bottle, it turns milky white when mixed with water. Bars and cafés serve it straight, allowing you to add the water (roughly five parts water to one part pastis). It's best drunk in the sun and on the rocks.

A dash of *sirop de menthe* (mint syrup diluted with water) transforms a regular pastis into a *perroquet* (literally 'parrot'). A *tomate* (tomato) is tarted up with one part grenadine, while the sweet Mauresque is dressed with *orgeat,* an orange and almond syrup.

Pastis was invented in 1932 in Marseille by industrialist Paul Ricard (1909-97). The earliest aniseed liqueur to hit the market was absinthe, a dangerous and potent liqueur distilled with wormwood oil that, from the early 1800s, was manufactured in France by Henri-Louis Pernod. The drink – which boasted an astonishing 72% alcohol content – was banned in 1915, paving the way for Ricard's 45% alcohol pastis and other harmless (except for the alcohol) aniseed and liquorice liqueurs, such as the modern-day Pernod. Leading pastis brands are Pastis 51 and Ricard, both owned by the Ricard empire (in addition to Pernod, taken over by Ricard in 1974). Taste these and others at Marseille's Maison du Pastis (p87).

obligation to buy. Purchasing just a couple of bottles or several boxes (six or 12 bottles per box) is equally acceptable. Lists of estates and *caves* (wine cellars) are available from most tourist offices and *maisons des vins* (wine houses) in Avignon (see p127), Les Arcs-sur-Argens (see p297) and elsewhere.

Rare is the meal in Provence served without a carafe or bottle of wine on the table.

DID YOU KNOW?

Châteauneuf du Pape was the first wine in France to be granted its own AOC in 1929; exceptional vintages are 1988–90, 1995 and 1997.

CÔTES DU RHÔNE

The most renowned vintage is Châteauneuf du Pape (see p135), a full-bodied red wine bequeathed to Provence by the Avignon popes who planted the vineyards 10km south of Orange. It is one of the many diverse wines in the respected Côtes du Rhône appellation, which dates from 1937.

Châteauneuf du Pape reds are strong (minimum alcohol content 12.5%) and well-structured masters in their field. Whites account for 7% of total annual production. Châteauneuf du Pape wine growers, obliged to pick their grapes by hand, say it is the *galets* (large smooth, yellowish stones) covering their vineyards that distinguish them from others. Both whites and reds can be drunk young (two to three years) or old (seven years or more). Irrespective of age, whites should be served at 12°C; reds at 16°C to 18°C.

DID YOU KNOW?

Most wine-producing areas have a wine co-operative where you can fill up with local *vin de table* (table wine) for €2 or so per litre; take your own container with you.

The Tavel rosé is another popular Rhône Valley *grand cru* (literally 'great growth'). The vineyards around the Dentelles de Montmirail, some 15km east of Orange, produce notable red and rosé Gigondas, and the sweet dessert wine, Muscat de Beaumes de Venise.

CÔTES DE PROVENCE

The 18 hectares of vineyards sandwiched between Nice and Aix-en-Provence produce red, rosé and white Côtes de Provence, France's sixth largest appellation, dating from 1977. The *terroir* (land) ranges from sandy coastal soils around St-Tropez to chalky soils covering subalpine slopes around Les Arcs-sur-Argens.

The appellation is the largest in Provence, with an annual production of 100 million bottles; 75% are rosé. Côtes de Provence rosé is drunk young and served at a crisp 8° to 10°C. Reds drunk young should be served at 14° to 16°C, while older red *vins de garde* – a traditional accompaniment to game, sauced meats and cheese – are best drunk at 16° to 18°C.

Côtes de Provence whites, a golden friend to fish, should be chilled to 8°C.

DID YOU KNOW?

More than half of all the rosé wine made in France comes from Provence.

OTHERS

Six other pocket-sized appellations are dotted along or near the coast: Bandol, Cassis, Coteaux Varois, Coteaux d'Aix-en-Provence, Bellet and Palette. Of these, Bandol is the most respected, known for its deep-flavoured reds produced from the dark-berried *mourvèdre* grape, which needs oodles of sun to ripen (hence its rarity). In neighbouring Cassis, crisp whites (75% of its production) are drunk with gusto.

Those who like a dry rosé should try Coteaux d'Aix-en-Provence. Palette, east of Aix, is just 20 hectares, dates from 1948 and produces well-structured reds from its old vines. Four of every five Palette bottles come from Château Simone. Wines from the Bellet AOC are rare outside Nice.

Vast areas of the region's interior are carpeted with Côtes du Ventoux (6900 hectares established in 1973) and Côtes du Lubéron (3500 hectares dating from 1988) vineyards.

Visit the Comité Interprofessionnel des Vins Côtes de Provence and learn all about Côtes de Provence wine at www.cotes-de-provence.fr.

CELEBRATIONS

Food itself is a reason to celebrate: practically every harvest (grapes, olives, cherries, chestnuts, melons, lemons and so on) is honoured with its own festival. The start of the grape harvest is celebrated with particular gusto in Nîmes, where a spectacular three-day bullfighting festival fills the Roman amphitheatre. During Arles' week-long Fête des Prémices du Riz at the start of the rice harvest in mid-September, a young girl is crowned rice ambassadress.

Countrywide, christenings and weddings see guests receive *dragées*, porcelain-smooth sugared almonds tinted pink for a girl, blue for a boy and white for a bride. Another national tradition very much alive, the *jour des rois*, marks Epiphany on 6 January and sees people flock to the patisserie to buy a *galette des rois* (literally 'kings' cake'), a puff-pastry cake filled with frangipane cream and topped with a paper gold crown. Whoever gets the so-called *fève* (literally a 'bean' – which it was in the old days, but a plastic figurine these days) in their slice of cake is crowned king or queen.

Christmas in Provence sees families rush home after Mass on Christmas Eve for Caleno vo Careno, a traditional feast of 13 desserts symbolising Jesus and the 12 apostles. Among the culinary delights are *pompe à huile* (leavened cake baked in olive oil and flavoured with orange blossom), sweet black-and-white nougat (home-made from honey and almonds), nuts and an assortment of dried and fresh fruits.

From olive fairs in Nyons to melon madness in Cavaillon, read all about Provence's most legendary and least-known food festivals and celebrations in *La France Gourmande: Four Seasons of Fêtes and Foires* by Maroln Charpentier.

TOP FIVE FOOD FESTS

- Messe de la Truffe (Truffle Mass; Richerenches), January (see Black Diamonds, p140)
- Fête des Citrons (Lemon Festival; Menton), February (p238)
- Fête de la Cerise (Cherry Festival; Apt), June (p167)
- Fête du Melon (Melon Festival; Cavaillon), July (p178)
- Fête de la Châtaigne (Chestnut Festival; Collobrières), October (p299)

WHERE TO EAT & DRINK

Dining à la Provençal can mean spending anything from €10 in a village bistro to upwards of €75 at a multistarred gastronomic temple. Irrespective of price range, a *carte* (menu) is usually pinned up outside, allowing for a price and dish check.

The most authentic places to eat are invariably in tiny hamlets off the beaten track – living proof that locals will drive any distance for a good meal. These places often tout just one *menu* (two- or three- course meal at a set price) with *vin compris* (wine included), serve a flow of chunky cut bread with your meal, and the patron (owner) is usually the chef.

Standard opening hours for eating places are listed on p336 and on the Quick Reference page on the inside back cover; those deviating from these are listed in the regional chapters.

Fermes Auberges & Chateaux

Feasting on home-made food on a wine-producing estate or working farm (*ferme auberge*) is a great way to dine, especially for kid-laden families or those seeking a long slow meal. Typical Provençal cuisine and pace is guaranteed; portions are giant-sized enough to appease the feistiest of appetites; dining is often around shared tables; and there's plenty of space (not to mention animals to admire) for children to run around. A *menu*, comprising four courses and often wine too, costs between €20 and €40 a head.

Maisons des vins have lists of chateaux where you can eat; Gîtes de France (p336) have farm details.

> Search by product, establishment or village to track down a tasty of choice of fabulous and authentic *fromageries* (cheese shops), farmhouse kitchens and so on with the annual *Guide Gantié Provence & Côte d'Azur* at www.guide gantie.com (in French).

Cafés

Cafés are the hub of village life, and many double as the local bar and bistro. Most serve croissant-and-coffee breakfasts (see p62) and lunchtime baguettes filled with cheese (around €4) or charcuterie (cold meat). Some have terraces hidden out the back where you can dine in the shade of overhead vines.

In towns, cafés on grand boulevards or chic spots like the Vieux Port in St-Tropez charge more than a place fronting a quiet side street. In fine café tradition Aix-en-Provence's Les Deux Garçons (p100), the region's most famous café, hikes up its prices after 10pm.

Quick Eats

Though people may snack between meals, they certainly don't relish the types of street food popular elsewhere; hot-dogs stands and noodle carts are not for them. On the coast crepe makers and ice-cream and *beignet* (doughnut) stalls are rife in seaside resorts, but in inland villages and towns people simply nip into a café for a sandwich, or a *salon de thé* (tea room) or patisserie for a slice of something sweet to munch sitting down or on the move.

> Find out which villages and towns in Provence are deemed *sites remarquables du goût* (remarkable sites of taste) and why at www .sitesremarquablesdug out.com (in French).

Self-Catering

When shopping, do as the locals do: buy fresh local produce from the weekly market (market days are listed at the start of regional chapters). They are always in the morning (from around 7am to noon or 1pm) and – if a *marché paysan* (farmers market) or *marché bio* (organic market) – sell produce grown without the aid of pesticides, chemical fertilisers etc. Staple products include fruit and vegetables, olives, olive oil, bunches or woven plaits of *aïl* (garlic), marinated olives and dried herbs in stubby coarse sacks.

TOP FIVE SPECIALIST FOOD MARKETS

- Farmers Market, Apt (Tuesday April to December)
- Fresh Fish Market, quai des Belges, Marseille (mornings year-round)
- Garlic Market, cours Belsunce, Marseille (daily June and July)
- Melon Market, Cavaillon (mornings May to September)
- Truffle Market, Richerenches (Saturday November to March)

Markets aside, buying a baked-that-hour baguette or loaf of *pain aux olives* (olive bread) in the local *boulangerie* (bakery), a *tarte aux fruits* (fruit tart) in the patisserie, cheese in the *fromagerie* (cheese shop), the catch of the day in the *poissonnerie* (fishmongers) and cold meats, seafood salads and so on in the charcuterie (delicatessen) can be more expensive – but is definitely more satisfying – than shopping in a supermarket.

Those needing shedloads of beer, bottled water etc will, of course, do no better than Monoprix or one of the *hypermarchés* (Leclerc, Inter-marché etc) that skirt larger towns.

In The Provence of Alain Ducasse by Alain Ducasse, Provence's most modern chef takes readers on a tour of his Provence, divulging his favourite markets and the best places to shop, taste and buy wine, to take an apéritif and so on. Addresses aside, there are also a few recipes.

VEGETARIANS & VEGANS

In a country where *viande* (meat) once meant 'food' too, it comes as no mean surprise that vegetarians and vegans are not catered for particularly well, if at all: vegetarian restaurants are nonexistent, as are vegetarian *menus*. That said, vegetables form the backbone of many typical Provençal dishes, meaning non-meat eaters won't starve (even if it does mean compiling a full meal from a selection of starters); while *produits biologiques* (organic products) are all the rage nowadays, even among carnivores.

Strict vegetarians should note that most cheeses in France are made with *lactosérum* (rennet), an enzyme derived from the stomach of a calf or young goat, and that some red wines are clarified with the albumin of egg whites. Vegetarian wine (clarified using a chemical substitute or not at all) is impossible to find in the region, but *le vin bio* (organic wine) – made from grapes grown without the aid of chemical fertilisers and pesticides and often bottled in recycled glass – is becoming increasingly popular.

Enjoy a culinary tour of the region's markets with Markets of Provence: A Culinary Tour of Southern France by Ruthanne Long.

DINING WITH KIDS

Children are generally welcomed in eating establishments, despite the lack of facilities that suggests otherwise. Highchairs are rare and the *menu enfant* (children's *menu*) that ventures away from the €5 to €8 realm of *boeuf haché* (minced beef), *frites* (fries) and *glace* (ice cream) is an exception. That said, *menus* geared to smaller appetites are increasing, with several upmarket places touting *menus* in the €15 range for pint-sized gourmets. For parents with toddlers who can't sit still, *fermes auberges* (see p60) are an attractive option.

Breastfeeding in public is not frowned upon. The choice of baby food, infant formulas, soy and cows' milk and the like is as great in French supermarkets as it is back home; larger pharmacies also sell these products. For grizzly babies cutting teeth, there's nothing better to shut them up than the knobbly end of a baguette!

See p337 for more kid-oriented tips.

Find out what's cooking with the region's most modern chef, and the world's first chef to score six sparkling Michelin stars to boot, at www .alain-ducasse.com.

HABITS & CUSTOMS

People think, dream and live food, most people's day being geared around satisfying their insatiable appetite for dining well.

Three square meals – *petit dejeuner* (breakfast), *dejeuner* (lunch) and *diner* (dinner) – are the order of the day. Breakfast is a croissant or chunk of baguette with butter and home-made jam, and is accompanied by a strong black coffee, *café au lait* or – in the case of children – *chocolat chaud* (hot chocolate).

Lunch is the traditional main meal. It starts at noon, continues well into the afternoon, and entails eating excessive amounts that will leave you vowing never to eat that much again – until tomorrow. It always kicks off with an apéritif (see p57), and lunch without wine is an oddity.

Most restaurants serve a *plat du jour* (dish of the day) or *formule* (fixed main course plus starter or dessert) at lunch time as well as three- and four-course *menus*. The latter offer better value than ordering à la carte; most include an entrée (starter), *plat* (main course) and *fromage* (cheese) or dessert. Many top-end restaurants serve an *amuse-bouche* (complimentary morsel of something very delicious) between the starter and main course; some also serve a sweet equivalent before dessert, plus petit fours (bite-sized biscuits) with coffee.

Lunch is a convivial affair with few airs and graces beyond a *bon appétite* said to dining companions before tucking in. Some restaurants in larger towns and illustrious addresses regionwide get crowded, so it's best to book. Few accept reservations for more than one seating, allowing ample time to linger over coffee and digestif (see p57).

Using the same knife and fork for your starter and main course is common in many *fermes auberges* and bistros. Don't be surprised either if, at the end of the meal, the waiter adds up your *addition* (bill) on the paper tablecloth. Many such places don't accept credit cards. Asking for *une carafe d'eau* (a jug of tap water) in any type of restaurant is perfectly acceptable.

Santé (cheers!) is the toast used for alcoholic drinks and requires everyone at the table to raise a full glass and chink it lightly against those of their fellow drinkers.

DID YOU KNOW?

Margarine-based croissants can be identified by their almost touching tips; buttery ones have their tips facing outwards.

DID YOU KNOW?

Many restaurants only serve *aïoli Provençal complet* one day of the week (invariably Friday).

COOKING COURSES

At Home with Patricia Wells (www.patriciawells.com; c/o Judith Jones, 708 Sandown Place, Raleigh NC 27615, USA) Five-day courses with Patricia Wells, the only wholly foreign cook considered to have truly embraced the soul of Provençal cooking. Courses cost US$3500 (excluding accommodation) and take place in Wells' 18th-century farmhouse kitchen near Vaison-la-Romaine.

DON'T...

- express so much as a mild dislike of *pieds et paquets* (sheep tripe), *testicules de mouton* (sheep testicles) or other regional speciality – unless you want to offend.

- skip lunch or decline a *dégustation* (wine-tasting) session – cardinal sins in the Provençal book.

- bother trying to balance your bread on your main-course plate (side plates are often not provided); sprinkling the table with crumbs is acceptable.

- ask for ice cubes to drop into warm wine, or tomato sauce (ketchup)/mayonnaise to douse over food.

- order anything other than *un café* (espresso) to end your meal.

École de Cuisine du Soleil (☎ 04 93 75 78 24; www.moulin-mougins.com; Notre Dame de Vie, F-06250 Mougins) Thematic sessions (2½ hours) with well-known Provençal chef Alain Llorca cost €56/255 for one/five sessions.

Hostellerie de Crillon le Brave (☎ 04 90 65 61 61; www.crillonlebrave.com; place de l'Église, F-84410 Crillon le Brave) Five-day courses in October and November with French chef Philippe Monti; €2100 to €2900 per person per week, including hotel accommodation.

Jean-Jacques Prévôt (☎ 04 90 71 39 43; www.restaurant-prevot.com in French; 353 av de Verdun, Cavaillon) Half-day sessions for €110/100 with/without a market visit with Provence's melon-mad chef.

Le Marmiton (Map p128-9; ☎ 04 90 85 93 93; www.la-mirande.fr in French; Hôtel de la Mirande, 4 place de la Mirande, F-84000 Avignon) Morning/afternoon/evening classes for €75/100/120 in the *atelier de cuisine* of Avignon's loveliest hotel.

Le Moulin de Lourmarin (☎ 04 90 68 06 69; www.moulindelourmarin.com in French; Lourmarin) Thematic one-day cooking courses with France's youngest Michelin-starred chef for €230, including gourmet lunch.

Mas de Cornud (Map p152; ☎ 04 90 92 39 32; www.mascornud.com; rte de Mas Blanc, F-31210 St-Rémy de Provence) Morning classes (€130), wine-tasting sessions (from €170) and week-long thematic courses (from €2700 with accommodation) in a four-star, 18th-century farmhouse.

Learn how to make bouillabaisse, *bourride* etc with *Cooking in Provence: Over 70 Timeless Recipes* by French cuisine expert Alex MacKay. The photography is particularly enticing.

EAT YOUR WORDS
Useful Phrases

I'd like to reserve a table.
J'aimerais resérver une table.   zhay·mer·ray ray·zair·vay ewn ta·bler

A table for two, please.
Une table pour deux, s'il vous plaît.   ewn ta·bler poor der seel voo play

Do you have a menu in English?
Est-ce que vous avez la carte en anglais?   es·ker voo a·vay la kart on ong·glay

Could you recommend something?
Est-ce que vous pouvez recommender   es·ker voo poo·vay re·ko·mon·day
quelque chose?   kel·ker shoz

I'd like a local speciality.
J'aimerais une spécialité régionale.   zhay·mer·ray ewn spay·sya·lee·tay ray·zhyo·nal

I'd like the set menu.
Je prends le menu.   zher pron ler mer·new

I'd like today's special.
Je voudrais avoir le plat du jour.   zher voo·dray a·vwar ler pla doo zhoor

I'm a vegetarian.
Je suis végétarien/végétarienne. (m/f)   zher swee vay·zhay·ta·ryun/vay·zhay·ta·ryen

I don't eat meat/fish/seafood.
Je ne mange pas de viande/poisson/   je ne monzh pa de vee·and/pwa·so/
fruits de mer.   fwee·de·mair

I'd like to order the ...
Je voudrais commander ...   zher voo·dray ko·mon·day

Is service included in the bill?
Est-ce que le service est inclu?   es·ker ler sair·vees ay un·klew

The bill, please.
La note, s'il vous plaît.   la not seel voo play

Food Glossary
STARTERS
anchoïade (on·sho·yad) – anchovy puree laced with garlic and olive oil
assiette anglaise (a·syet ong·glayz) – plate of cold mixed meats and sausages
assiette de crudités (a·syet de krew·dee·tay) – plate of raw vegetables with dressings
banon à la feuille (ba·no a la fer·yer) – goat cheese dipped in eau de vie and wrapped in a chestnut leaf

bouillon (boo·yon) – broth or stock
bourride (boo·reed) – fish soup; often eaten as a main course
brandade de morue (bron·dad der mo·rew) – mix of crushed salted cod, olive oil
    and garlic
brebis (brer·bee) – sheep's milk dairy product
fromage de chèvre (fro·mazh der shev·rer) – goat cheese (also called *brousse*)
pissala (pee·sa·la) – Niçois paste mixed from pureed anchovies
pissaladière (pee·sa·la·dyair) – anchovy, onion and black olive 'pizza' from Nice
soupe au pistou (soop o pees·too) – vegetable soup made with basil and garlic
soupe de poisson (soop der pwa·son) – fish soup
tapenade (ta·per·nad) – sharp, olive-based dip
tomme arlesienne (tom ar·ler·syen) – moulded goat cheese from Arles

MEAT, CHICKEN & POULTRY

agneau (a·nyo) – lamb
boeuf (berf) – beef
boeuf haché (berf ha·shay) – minced beef
canard (ka·nar) – duck
chèvre (shev·rer) – goat
chevreau (sher·vro) – kid (baby goat)
daube de boeuf à la Provençale (dob der berf a la pro·von·sal) – beef stew
entrecôte (on·trer·cot) – rib steak
épaule d'agneau (e·pol da·nyo) – shoulder of lamb
estouffade de boeuf (es·too·fad der berf) – Carmargais beef stew with tomatoes
    and olives
filet (fee·lay) – tenderloin
jambon (zham·bon) – ham
lardon (lar·don) – pieces of chopped bacon
pieds de porc (pyay der pork) – pig trotters
pieds et paquets (pyay ay pa·kay) – sheep tripe; literally 'feet and packages'
poulet (poo·lay) – chicken
saucisson d'Arles (so·see·son darl) – sausage made from pork, beef, wine and spices
taureau de Camargue (to·ro der ka·marg) – Camargais beef

FISH & SEAFOOD

aïoli Provençale complet (a·ee·o·lee pro·von·sal kom·play) – shellfish, vegetables, boiled
    egg and aïoli
anchois (on·shwa) – anchovy
coquillage (ko·kee·lazh) – shellfish
coquille St-Jacques (ko·keel san zhak) – scallop
crevette grise (kre·vet grees) – shrimp
crevette rose (kre·vet ros) – prawn
fruits de mer (frwee der mair) – seafood
gambas (gom·ba) – king prawns
homard (o·mar) – lobster
langouste (lang·goost) – crayfish
langoustine (lang·goos·teen) – small saltwater 'lobster'
oursin (oor·san) – sea urchin
paella (pa·ay·a) – rice dish with saffron, vegetables and shellfish
palourde (pa·loord) – clam
rouget (roo·zhay) – red mullet
stockfish (*estocaficada* in Niçois) (es·to·ka·fee·ka·da) – dried salt fish soaked in water for four to
    five days, stewed for two hours with onion, tomato and white wine, then laced with anchovies
    and black olives

VEGETABLES, HERBS & SPICES

aïl (ai) – garlic
artichaut (ar·tee·sho) – artichoke
asperge (a·spairzh) – asparagus
basilic (ba·see·leek) – basil
blette de Nice (blet der nees) – white beet
cèpe (sep) – cepe (boletus mushroom)
estragon (es·tra·zhon) – tarragon
fleur de courgette (fler der coor·zhet) – courgette flower
légumes farcis (lay·goom far·see) – stuffed vegetables
mesclun (mes·kloo) – Niçois mix of lettuce
ratatouille (ra·ta·too·yer) – casserole of aubergines, tomatoes, peppers and garlic
riz de Camargue (reez der ka·marg) – Camargais rice
romarin (ro·ma·ran) – rosemary
salade Niçoise (sa·lad nee·swa) – green salad featuring tuna, egg and anchovy
thym (teem) – thyme
tian (tyan) – vegetable-and-rice gratin served in a dish called a *tian*
tourta de bléa (toor·ta de blay·a) – Niçois white beetroot and pine-kernel pie
truffe (troof) – black truffle

SAUCES

aïoli (ay·o·lee) – garlicky sauce to accompany bouillabaisse
huile d'olive (weel do·leev) – olive oil
pistou (pees·too) – pesto (pounded mix of basil, hard cheese, olive oil and garlic)
Provençale (pro·von·sal) – tomato, garlic, herb and olive-oil dressing or sauce
rouille (roo·yer) – aïoli-based sauce spiced with chilli pepper; served with *bourride*
vinaigrette (vun·ay·gret) – salad dressing made with oil, vinegar, mustard and garlic

BREAD & SWEETS

chichi freggi (shee·shee·fre·gee) – sugar-coated doughnuts from around Marseille
fougasse (foo·gas) – elongated Niçois bread stuffed with olives, chopped bacon or anchovies
fougassette (foo·gas·set) – brioche perfumed with orange flower
gâteaux secs aux amandes (ga·to sek o a·mond) – crisp almond biscuits
michettes (mee·shet) – Niçois bread stuffed with cheese, olives, anchovies and onions
navettes (na·vet) – canoe-shaped, orange-blossom-flavoured biscuits from Marseille
pain aux noix (pan o nwa) – walnut bread
pain aux raisins (pan o ray·son) – sultana bread
pan-bagnat (pan·ba·nya) – Niçois bread soaked in olive oil and filled with anchovy, olives and
    green peppers
panisses (pa·nees) – chickpea flour patties from in and around Marseille
socca (so·ka) – Niçois chickpea flour and olive-oil pancake

Marseille Area

CONTENTS

The urban geography and atmosphere of rough-and-tumble Marseille, utterly atypical of Provence, are a function of the diversity of its inhabitants, many of whom are immigrants (or their children and grandchildren) from Greece, Italy, Armenia, Spain, North Africa, West Africa and Indochina.

Speak to any cynic and they'll tell you the port city's 'centre' sits 15-odd kilometres north in well-to-do Aix (pronounced like the letter 'x') -en-Provence, where Marseille's wealthy live in luxurious mansions amid a harmonious fusion of majestic public squares and mossy, century-old fountains. In the 19th century Montagne Ste-Victoire, on Aix's eastern edge, was immortalised on canvas by the city's most famous son, Cézanne.

Dramatic coastline skirts Marseille's southern tip: from Callelongue, on the true city outskirts, a dramatic succession of sharp-ridged, overhanging rocks called Les Calanques (literally 'rocky inlets') plunge south to sweet Cassis, with its wealthy vineyards, and La Ciotat, known for its shipyards and cinematic history.

Head west and the landscape becomes an eyesore. Rapid industrialisation has polluted the water and encroached upon the land surrounding the Étang de Berre, a salty, 6m-deep pool which – with a surface area of 155.3 sq km and volume of 900 million cubic metres – is Europe's largest brine lake.

Salon de Provence, 10km north of the Étang de Berre and 37km west of Aix-en-Provence, marks the boundary between the soft green and purple hues of affluent Pays d'Aix (literally 'Aix Country') and the savage cut of the barren Crau plains in the lower Rhône Valley.

HIGHLIGHTS

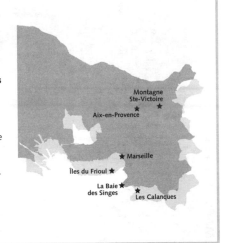

- Eye the day's catch at Marseille's **fish market** (p85), visit the **docklands** (p74) and sail to the **Îles du Frioul** (p77)

- Explore **Les Calanques** (p89) on foot or with a snorkel; lunch at **La Baie des Singes** (p84)

- Follow Cézanne around **Aix-en-Provence** (p98) and **Montagne Ste-Victoire** (p103)

- Eat your way around Marseille: pastis at the **Vieux Port** (p85), *supions frits* at **Pizzeria Étienne** (p83), **bouillabaisse** (p83) by the beach or fish flambéed in pastis at the **Vallon des Auffes** (p83)

- Make a **pilgrim's detour** (p93) to see where Mary Magdalene retreated at the end of her life

Montagne Ste-Victoire
Aix-en-Provence
Marseille
Îles du Frioul
La Baie des Singes
Les Calanques

MARSEILLE AREA

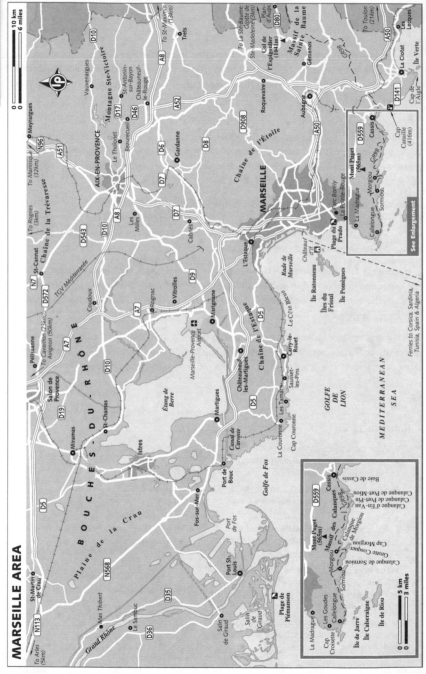

MARSEILLE

pop 798,430

Cosmopolitan Marseille (Marseilles in English) is Provence's largest city, and the second-largest city in France. Slammed in the 1980s and early 1990s as a hell hole of organised crime and racial tension, new-millennium Marseille flaunts a different appeal: with its cutting-edge music scene, warehouses-turned-nightclubs, cultural centres and art museums, the port city is a happening place to be. Tell anyone in France you're off to La Canebière and they'll know instantly where you mean.

Visitors who enjoy exploring on foot will be rewarded with more sights, sounds, smells and big-city commotion than anywhere else in the region. Its seaport remains the most important in France, and is the third-largest port in Europe, while high-speed rail tracks put Marseille just three hours away from Paris by train.

Provençal writer Marcel Pagnol (p52) was born in Aubagne, 16km east of Marseille. Senegalese novelist Sembène Ousmane, who portrayed his life as a black docker and African ghetto inhabitant in *Le Docker Noir* (The Black Docker; 1956), is another 20th-century literary figure to find inspiration in rough-cut Marseille. In the realm of popular culture, the best-known contemporary product 'made in Marseille' is footballer Zinedine Zidane – the world's most expensive player to boot.

HISTORY

Massalia was founded by Greek mariners around 600 BC. The city backed Pompey the Great in the 1st century BC, prompting Caesar's forces to capture the city in 49 BC and exact revenge by confiscating its fleet and directing Roman trade elsewhere.

Calamity struck in 1720 when the plague killed more than half of the city's 90,000 inhabitants. Under French rule the Marseillais, after whom the French national anthem is named (see p21), gained the rebellious reputation that has stuck with them ever since.

Colonial trade saw Marseille prosper in the 19th century: commerce with North Africa soared after the French occupation of Algeria in 1830 and the opening of the Suez Canal in 1869 further expanded maritime opportunities. During WWII the city was heavily bombed.

An economic downturn bred poverty, delinquency and unemployment (as high as 30% in some quarters) in the 1990s. Extreme-right politicians (see p25) rode the wave of discontent to win mayorships in Vitrolles and Marignane, two Marseillais suburbs, and morale remained low until 1998 when a Marseillais footballer struck gold for France (see p26).

ORIENTATION

Marseille's legendary main boulevard, La Canebière, stretches east from the Vieux Port (old port), the hub of tourist life. A few blocks away sits cours Julien, a village-like square with a water garden, palm trees, a kids' playground and a plethora of eating and drinking places.

From the central Gare St-Charles (St-Charles train station), north of La Canebière at the northern end of blvd d'Athènes, it is a 10-minute walk or two-minute metro ride to the Vieux Port. Shuttlebuses link Marseille airport, 28km northwest, with the station. The ferry terminal is west of place de la Joliette, again a 10-minute walk or two-minute metro ride to the Vieux Port.

Marseille is split into 16 arrondissements (districts).

Maps

The tourist office distributes a free and decent city map. Otherwise, bookshops sell the Blay-Foldex *Plan de Ville Marseille* (€4.75).

INFORMATION
Bookshops

Librairie de la Bourse (Map pp80–1; ☎ 04 91 33 63 06; 8 rue Paradis, 1er; metro Vieux Port) Unbeatable range of maps and guides.

Librairie Maritime et Outremer (Map pp80–1; ☎ 04 91 54 79 26; 26 quai de Rive Neuve, 1er; metro Vieux Port) Seafaring books, maps and guides.

GASTRONOMIC SHOP

Marseille and Aix-en-Provence have daily food markets; see p85 and p100 for details. Morning market days elsewhere:
Tuesday La Ciotat
Wednesday Cassis, Salon de Provence
Friday Cassis

MARSEILLE AREA

MARSEILLE IN ...

Two Days

Stroll around the **Vieux Port** (p71), taking in the **fish market** (p85) and the cross-port **ferry boat** (p88). Then delve into **Le Panier** (opposite). After a **bouillabaisse** (see Tasty Tip, p83) lunch, ride **Le Grand Tour** (p79) to the **Basilique Notre Dame de la Garde** (p75) for an unforgettable panorama.

Dedicate day two to a **coastal walk** (p76), stopping for **lunch by the beach** (p84) and – depending on your interests – visiting the **Stade Velodrome** (see OM, p86), **Musée d'Art Contemporain** (p75), **Parc Borély** (p77) or Le Corbusier's **Unité d'Habitation** (see Author's Choice, p79) in the afternoon. Come dark, get your glad rags on and dance the night away beneath stars at **La Maronnaise** (p86) on Cap Croisette.

Four Days

In addition to the two-day itinerary, spend a day on the **Îles du Frioul** (p77). Come dusk, energise tired limbs with a tapas-accompanied tasting of the local firewater at **L'Heure Verte** (p85) and adjoining **La Maison du Pastis** (p87). On the fourth day venture to **L'Estaque** (p93) with its painters' trail; **Cassis** (p90) with its busy market and tasty **vineyards** (p91); or the **calanques** (p89) for some dramatic walking, **snorkelling** or **diving** (p78).

One Week

In addition to the four-day itinerary, plan a Sunday outing to Marseille's Moroccan-style **Marché aux Puces** (p87) and book a thematic **guided tour** (p78).

Maison de la Presse (Map pp80-1; 29 quai des Belges, 1er; metro Vieux Port) English-language newspapers, magazines and local guides.

Emergency

Police headquarters (Préfecture de Police; Map pp72-3; ☎ 04 91 39 80 00; place de la Préfecture, 1er; metro Estrangin-Préfecture; ⏰ 24hr)

Internet Access

Esc@lia (Map pp80-1; ☎ 04 91 91 65 10; 3 rue Coutelleine, 1er; metro Vieux Port; first 15 min €1, then per min 6.6 centimes; ⏰ 11.30am-7.30pm Mon-Sat, 3.30-7.30pm Sun)
Info Café (Map pp80-1; ☎ 04 91 33 74 98; 1 quai de Rive Neuve, 1er; metro Vieux Port; 30/60 min €2/3.80; ⏰ 9am-10pm Mon-Sat, 2.30-7.30pm Sun)

Internet Resources

Mairie-marseille (www.mairie-marseille.fr in French) Official city website.
Marseille-tourisme (www.marseille-tourisme.com) Tourist office website.
Webcity Marseille (http://marseille.webcity.fr in French) City guide with a particularly strong nightlife section.

Laundry

La Savonnerie (Map pp80-1; 5 rue Breteuil, 1er; metro Vieux Port; ⏰ 6.30am-8pm) A 7/10kg load costs €3.50/5.

Left Luggage

Gare St-Charles (Consignes; Map pp80-1; small/medium/large locker €3.50/6/8; ⏰ 7.30am-midnight)

Media

Mars Magazine Hip *The Face*–style 'magazine of the Marseillais' with short but sharp dining and nightlife city guide (€5, published quarterly).

Medical Services

A list of pharmacies open at night and/or on Sunday is pinned outside the tourist office.
Hôpital de la Timone (off Map pp72-3; ☎ 04 91 49 91 91, 04 91 38 60 00; 264 rue St-Pierre, 5e; metro La Timone) Just over a kilometre southeast of place Jean Jaurès.

Money

Several banks and exchange bureaus dot La Canebière, 1er.
Canebière Change (Map pp80-1; ☎ 04 91 13 71 26; 39 La Canebière, 1er; metro Vieux Port) Amex agent.

Post

Central Post Office (Map pp80-1; 1 place de l'Hôtel des Postes, 1er; metro Colbert)

Tourist Information

Comité Départemental du Tourisme (Map pp72-3; ☎ 04 91 13 84 13; www.visitprovence.com;

Le Montesquieu bldg, 13 rue Roux de Brignoles, 6e; metro Estrangin-Préfecture) Tourist information on the Bouches-du-Rhône *département* (department).
Main Tourist Office (Map pp80-1; ☎ 04 91 13 89 00; accueil@marseille-tourisme.com; 4 La Canebière, 1er; metro Vieux Port; ☼ 9am-7.30pm Mon-Sat, 10am-6pm Sun Jul-Sep, 9am-7pm Mon-Sat, 10am-5pm Sun Oct-Jun)
Tourist Office Annexe (Map pp80-1; ☎ 04 91 50 59 18; Gare St-Charles, 1er; metro Gare St-Charles; ☼ 10am-noon & 1-5pm Mon-Fri)

Travel Agencies
Voyages Wasteels (Map pp80-1; ☎ 04 95 09 30 60; marseille@wasteels.fr; 67 La Canebière, 1er; metro Noailles; ☼ 9am-12.30pm & 2-6pm Mon-Fri, 9.30am-12.30pm Sat)

DANGERS & ANNOYANCES
It is by no means a dangerous city, but be vigilant and keep your wits about you. *Never* leave anything valuable in a parked car and keep your wallet well away from pickpocketing fingers. At night avoid walking alone in the Belsunce area. Day and night, motorists should keep their doors locked, especially when stationary at a red traffic light.

SIGHTS
Marseille grew around the Vieux Port, where ships have docked for at least 26 centuries. The main commercial docks were transferred to the Joliette area on the coast north of here in the 1840s, but the old port remains a thriving harbour for fishing boats and pleasure yachts, and is the hub of tourist life.

Around the Vieux Port
VIEUX PORT & LE PANIER
At the **Vieux Port** (Map pp80-1), the harbour entrance is guarded by **Fort St-Nicolas** (Map pp72-3) on the southern side and, across the water, **Fort St-Jean** (Map pp72-3), founded in the 13th century by the Knights Hospitaller of St John of Jerusalem. In 2008 a national Musée des Civilisations de l'Europe et de la Méditerranée (Museum of European and Mediterranean Civilisations) will open inside the latter as part of Marseille Euroméditerranée (see the boxed text, p74).

Marseille's 17th-century **town hall** (Map pp80-1; quai du Port) dominates the port's northern quay. The Musée des Docks Romains (p74) and Musée du Vieux Marseille (p74) are a two-minute walk from here, as is the trendy **Le Panier** (literally 'the basket'; Map pp80-1) quarter, the historic 'Montmartre of Marseille' which slinks uphill from the quayside with pretty **place des Moulins** and museum-clad Centre de la Vieille Charité (p71) at its heart.

BELSUNCE & LA PLEINE
La Canebière (Map pp80-1) – from the Provençal word *canebe*, meaning 'hemp', after the city's traditional rope industry – stretches northeast from the old port to sq Léon Blum (metro Vieux Port or Noailles).

The quarter bounded by La Canebière, cours Belsunce and rue d'Aix, rue Bernard du Bois and blvd d'Athènes is **Belsunce** (Map pp80-1), a poorer neighbourhood slowly being rehabilitated. The **public library** (Map pp80-1) on cours Belsunce was the legendary Alcazar music hall from 1857 until 1964.

North lies the central train station area and La Friche la Belle de Mai (see the boxed text, p74), the hub of Marseille's underground arts scene . Aubagne-born Marcel Pagnol (1895–1974) spent his childhood at 52 rue Terrusse in **La Pleine** (Map pp72–3); his footsteps can be traced with a city tour.

Museums
CENTRE DE LA VIEILLE CHARITÉ
The **Centre de la Vieille Charité** (Old Charity Cultural Centre; Map pp80-1; ☎ 04 91 14 58 80; 2 rue de la Charité, 2e; metro Joliette) is built around Provence's most impressive baroque church, designed by Marseillais architect Pierre Puget. Before restoration it was a barracks, a soldiers' rest home and, later, low-cost housing for people who lost their homes during WWII.

TOP FIVE CITY PANORAMAS

- The old port seen from a ferry boat (p88)
- Château d'If and the Îles du Frioul seen from corniche Président John F Kennedy (p76)
- The Notre Dame de la Garde (p75) panorama
- The harbour views (old port and new ferry terminal) from Jardin du Pharo (p76)
- Sunset over the harbour seen from a kayak out at sea (p78)

MARSEILLE

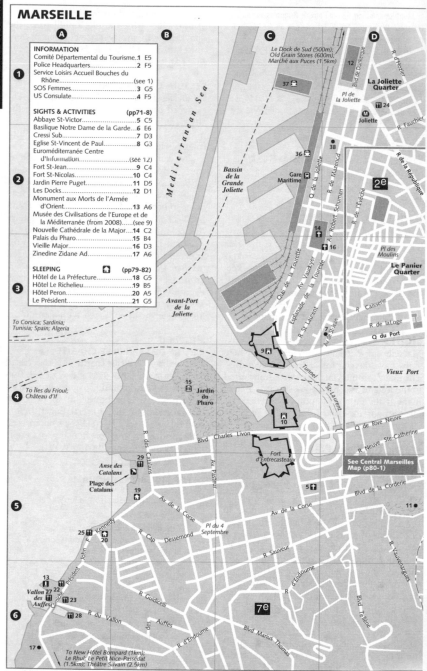

INFORMATION
Comité Départemental du Tourisme..1 E5
Police Headquarters.........................2 F5
Service Loisirs Accueil Bouches du
Rhône..................................(see 1)
SOS Femmes...............................3 G5
US Consulate..............................4 F5

SIGHTS & ACTIVITIES (pp71-8)
Abbaye St-Victor...........................5 C5
Basilique Notre Dame de la Garde..6 E6
Cressi Sub..................................7 D3
Eglise St-Vincent de Paul...............8 G3
Euroméditerranée Centre
d'Information........................(see 12)
Fort St-Jean..............................9 C4
Fort St-Nicolas.........................10 C4
Jardin Pierre Puget.....................11 D5
Les Docks...............................12 D1
Monument aux Morts de l'Armée
d'Orient...............................13 A6
Musée des Civilisations de l'Europe et de
la Méditerranée (from 2008)......(see 9)
Nouvelle Cathédrale de la Major...14 C2
Palais du Pharo.........................15 B4
Vieille Major............................16 D3
Zinedine Zidane Ad.....................17 A6

SLEEPING (pp79-82)
Hôtel de La Préfecture.................18 G5
Hôtel Le Richelieu.....................19 B5
Hôtel Peron.............................20 A5
Le Président............................21 G5

To Corsica; Sardinia;
Tunisia; Spain; Algeria

To Îles du Frioul;
Château d'If

Mediterranean Sea

Le Dock de Sud (500m);
Old Grain Stores (600m);
Marché aux Puces (1.5km)

La Joliette
Quarter

Joliette

Bassin
de la
Grande
Joliette

Gare
Maritime

2e

Pl des
Moulins

Le Panier
Quarter

Pl de
la Joliette

Quai de la Joliette

Av. Robert Schuman

R. de Mazenod

R. de l'Evêché

R. Fauchier

R. d'Hozier

Blvd de Dunkerque

R. de la République

Avant-Port
de la
Joliette

Esplanade de la Tourette

Quai de la Tourette

Av. Vaudoyer

R. St Laurent

Tunnel

R. St Laurent

Av. de Saint Jean

R. Caisserie

R. de laLoge

Q. du Port

Vieux Port

Jardin
du
Pharo

Blvd Charles Livon

Fort
d'Entrecasteaux

Q. de Rive Neuve

R. Neuve Ste-Catherine

Blvd de la Corderie

See Central Marseilles
Map (p80-1)

Anse des
Catalans

Plage des
Catalans

R. des Catalans

Av. de la Corse

Av. Pasteur

Av. de la Corse

Av. du Président John F. Kennedy

R. Cap Dessemond

Pl du 4
Septembre

R. Sauveur

R. d'Endoume

R. Vauvenargues

Vallon
des
Auffes

R. Guidicelli

R. du Vallon

des Auffes

R. d'Endoume

R. d'Endoume

Blvd Tellène

Blvd Marius Thomas

7e

To New Hôtel Bompard (1km);
Le Rhul; Le Petit Nice-Passédat
(1.5km); Théâtre Silvain (2.5km)

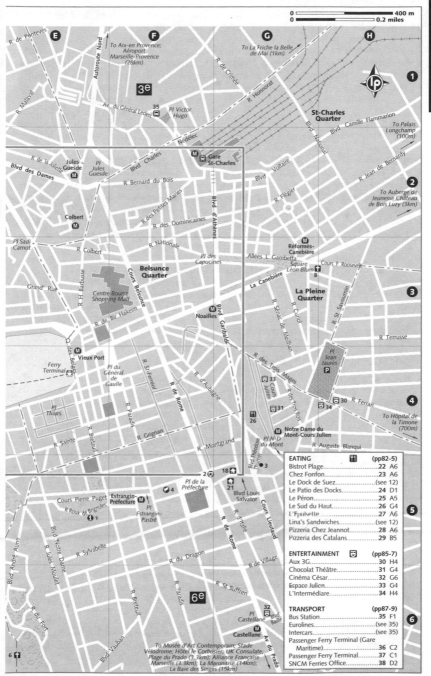

EATING 🍴 (pp82-5)
Bistrot Plage.................................22 A6
Chez Fonfon................................23 A6
Le Dock de Suez....................(see 12)
Le Patio des Docks.....................24 D1
Le Péron.....................................25 A5
Le Sud du Haut..........................26 G4
L'Épuisette................................27 A6
Lina's Sandwiches................(see 12)
Pizzeria Chez Jeannot.................28 A6
Pizzeria des Catalans..................29 B5

ENTERTAINMENT 🎭 (pp85-7)
Aux 3G......................................30 H4
Chocolat Théâtre........................31 G4
Cinéma César.............................32 G6
Espace Julien..............................33 G4
L'Intermédiare............................34 H4

TRANSPORT (pp87-9)
Bus Station.................................35 F1
Eurolines.............................(see 35)
Intercars............................(see 35)
Passenger Ferry Terminal (Gare
    Maritime)...............................36 C2
Passenger Ferry Terminal............37 C1
SNCM Ferries Office....................38 D2

Its courtyard arcade houses a **Musée d'Archéologie Méditerranéenne** (Museum of Mediterranean Archaeology; adult/10-18 yrs €2/1; 11am-6pm Tue-Sun Jul-Sep, 10am-5pm Tue-Sun Oct-Jun) and a **Musée des Arts Africains, Océaniens & Amérindiens** (Museum of African, Oceanic & American-Indian Art; adult/10-18 yrs €2/1; 11am-6pm Tue-Sun Jul-Sep, 10am-5pm Tue-Sun Oct-Jun).

MUSÉE CANTINI

Inside a 17th-century *hôtel particulier* (private mansion), the **Musée Cantini** (Cantini Museum; Map pp80-1; ☎ 04 91 54 77 75, 19 rue Grignan, 6e; metro Estrangin-Préfecture; adult/10-16 yrs €3/1.50; 10am-5pm Tue-Sun Oct-May, 11am-6pm Tue-Sun Jun-Sep) has a collection of 17th- and 18th-century Provençal ceramics, rotating contemporary art exhibitions and a centre dedicated to 21st-century works.

MUSÉE D'HISTOIRE DE MARSEILLE

Roman-history buffs should visit this **history museum** (Map pp80-1; ☎ 04 91 90 42 22; ground fl, Centre Bourse, 1er; metro Vieux Port; adult/10-16 yrs €2/1; noon-7pm Mon-Sat), on the ground floor of the Centre Bourse shopping centre. Exhibits include the remains of a merchant vessel that plied the waters of the Mediterranean in the early 3rd century. The 19m-long timbers, which include five different kinds of wood, show evidence of having been repeatedly repaired. To preserve the soaked and decaying wood, the whole thing was freeze-dried right where it now sits – hidden behind glass in a very dimly lit room.

Roman ruins can be seen outside the museum in the **Jardin des Vestiges** (Garden of Ruins; rue Henri Barbusse, 1er; metro Vieux Port; admission free).

MUSÉE DES DOCKS ROMAINS

At the **Musée des Docks Romains** (Roman Docks Museum; Map pp80-1; ☎ 04 91 91 24 62; place Vivaux, 2e; metro Vieux Port; adult/10-16 yrs €2/1; 10am-5pm Tue-Sun Oct-May, 11am-6pm Tue-Sun Jun-Sep), 1st-century Roman structures are displayed. The huge jars on display could hold up to 2000L of wine or oil.

MUSÉE DU VIEUX MARSEILLE

All things traditional to old Marseille – like *santons* (p102), Marseillais tarot cards etc – can be seen in the **Musée du Vieux Marseille** (Museum of Old Marseille; Map pp80-1; ☎ 04 91 55 28 68; 2 rue de la Prison, 2e; metro Vieux Port), inside the

---

DOCKLANDS

Nowhere is the sparkling rejuvenation of the city's notoriously tatty squats and districts more explicit than in **Marseille Euroméditerranée**, a 15-year project (1996–2010) which will see €3.05 billion poured into Marseille's docklands (La Joliette quarter) and central train station area (St-Charles quarter).

Unemployment in these two districts (population 30,000) currently stands at 25.77% (it was 30% in 2002). By 2010 Euroméditerranée will have created 15,000 to 20,000 new jobs, 4000 homes and 800,000 sq metres of commercial real estate. The two districts' green recreational areas will double in size.

At the docklands, offices and a couple of trendy restaurants are up and running in **Les Docks** (Map pp72-3; 10 place de la Joliette), a former warehouse and the project showcase. At the time of writing it was expected that by 2005 the old grain silos on quai d'Arenc will house a 2000-seat cinema, business centre and panoramic restaurant with stunning island views; and in 2008 Fort St-Jean will house a **Musée des Civilisations de l'Europe et de la Méditerranée** (Map pp72-3; Museum of European and Mediterranean Civilisations), which will replace – much to many people's horror – the National Museum of Arts and Popular Traditions, in Paris since 1937.

The St-Charles quarter is to be the site of a new **Grand Halle** (Grand Hall), designed by French architect Jean-Marie Duthilleul, at the central train station and a state-of-the-art home for the country's first national **Internet school**. In the nearby Belle de Mai district, **La Friche la Belle de Mai** (off Map pp72-3; ☎ 04 95 04 95 04; www.lafriche.org in French; 23 rue Guibal), former tobacco factory and sugar-refining plant, houses theatrical and artists' workshops, cinema studios (see p51), a couple of radio stations, multimedia displays and exhibition halls.

For more information visit **Euroméditerranée Centre d'Informations** (Map pp72-3; ☎ 0 800 111 114; www.euromediterranee.fr; Atrium 103, Les Docks, 10 place de la Joliette, 2e; metro Joliette; 10am-1pm & 2-6pm Mon-Thu, 10am-1pm & 2-5pm Fri).

Maison Diamantée. The façade of the 16th-century town house, built in 1570 for a wealthy trader, is covered in diamond-shaped cut stones, hence its name.

MUSÉE DE LA MODE

Glitz and glamour dresses the **Musée de la Mode** (Fashion Design Museum; Map pp80-1; ☎ 04 91 56 59 57; 11 La Canebière, 1er; metro Vieux Port; adult/10-16 yrs €3/1.50; ⏰ 11am-6pm Tue-Sun), dedicated to fashion trends since 1945. Among the 4000-odd items displayed are original Chanel designs, many worn by Madame herself.

MUSÉE DE LA MARINE ET DE L'ÉCONOMIE

The colonnaded Chamber of Commerce (also known as the Palais de la Bourse), built between 1854 and 1860, houses a **Musée de la Marine et de l'Économie** (Naval & Economy Museum; Map pp80-1; ☎ 04 91 39 33 33; 9 La Canebiére, 1er; metro Vieux Port; adult/under 12 yrs €2/free; ⏰ 10am-6pm Tue-Sun).

PALAIS LONGCHAMP

Constructed in the 1860s, the colonnaded **Palais Longchamp** (off Map pp72-3; blvd Philippon, 4e; metro Cinq Avenues Longchamp) was designed in part to disguise a water tower built at the terminus of an aqueduct from the River Durance. Prehistoric Provence is captured in its **Musée d'Histoire Naturelle** (Natural History Museum; ☎ 04 91 14 59 50; adult/10-16 yrs €3/1.50; ⏰ 10am-5pm Tue-Sun Oct-May, 11am-6pm Tue-Sun Jun-Sep).

MUSÉE D'ART CONTEMPORAIN

Marseille's **Musée d'Art Contemporain** (Museum of Contemporary Art; MAC; off Map pp72-3; ☎ 04 91 25 01 07; 69 blvd de Haïfa, 8e; adult/10-16 yrs €3/1.50; ⏰ 10am-5pm Tue-Sun Oct-May, 11am-6pm Tue-Sun Jun-Sep) displays works by Christo, Nice new realists Ben and Klein, pop artist Andy Warhol and the city's very own César (see p51).

Take bus No 44 from the rond-point du Prado (Prado roundabout) metro stop to the place Bonnefons stop, from where it is a short walk along av de Hambourg to rond-point Pierre Guerre, easily recognisable by a giant metal thumb – César's doing – that sticks up from the middle of the roundabout.

Churches & Cathedrals
BASILIQUE NOTRE DAME DE LA GARDE

This enormous Roman-Byzantine **basilica** (Map p72-3; place Colonel Edon, 6e) is not to be missed if you like overwrought 19th-century

CITY PASS MARSEILLE

For dedicated sightseers this city pass is just the ticket. It costs €16/23 for one/two consecutive days and covers admission to 14 city museums, unlimited use of public transport, a city tour (p78), a boat trip to Île d'If and admission to the island's chateau (p77), a ride on the two tourist trains (p79), a bilingual French-English city guide and a clutch of discounts. It's available from tourist offices.

architecture. The hike up to the church, 1km south of the Vieux Port atop the city's highest point at 162m, is a stiff 30-minute walk – albeit a walk rewarded with stunning panoramic views.

The domed basilica – ornamented with all manner of marble, mosaics, murals and gilded objects – was erected between 1853 and 1864. The bell tower is topped by a 9.7m-tall gilded statue of the Virgin Mary, traditional protector of the city, on a 12m-high pedestal. The great bell inside is 2.5m high and weighs a hefty 8.3 tonnes (the clapper alone weighs 387kg). Bullet marks from Marseille's Battle of Liberation (15–25 August 1944) scar the cathedral's northern wall.

Bus No 60 links the Vieux Port with the basilica.

NOUVELLE CATHÉDRALE DE LA MAJOR

A frenzy of cupolas, towers and turrets tops Roman-Byzantine **Nouvelle Cathédrale de la Major** (New Cathedral of the Major; Map pp72-3; place de la Major, 2e; metro Joliette). Built between 1852 and 1893, the structure is enormous: 140m long and 60m high. It dwarfs the little that remains of the neighbouring old cathedral, **Vieille Major** (Map pp72-3; closed to visitors), from the 11th century.

ABBAYE ST-VICTOR

The twin tombs of 4th-century martyrs and a 3rd-century sarcophagus are among the sacred objects inside imposing Romanesque 12th-century **Abbaye St-Victor** (Map pp72-3; 3 rue de l'Abbaye, 7e; metro Vieux Port), set on a hill above the Vieux Port. The annual Pélerinage de la Chandeleur and Marseille's annual sacred music festival also happen here (see p79).

MARSEILLE AREA

The Coast

A seaside stroll along **corniche Président John F Kennedy**, 7e – Marseille's main coast road built in 1848 and enlarged in the 1960s – reveals a very different side of the city. It begins 200m southwest of **Jardin du Pharo**, with its imperial **Palais du Pharo** (Map pp72–3) congress centre built by Napoleon III,

and continues south past the small and busy **Plage des Catalans** – which resembles a scene from *Baywatch* with its bronzed, bikini-clad volleyball players – to **Vallon des Auffes** (Map pp72–3). The village nestled around the picture-postcard cove and fishing harbour is filled with traditional *cabanons* (seaside cabins), built by fishermen to store tackle and

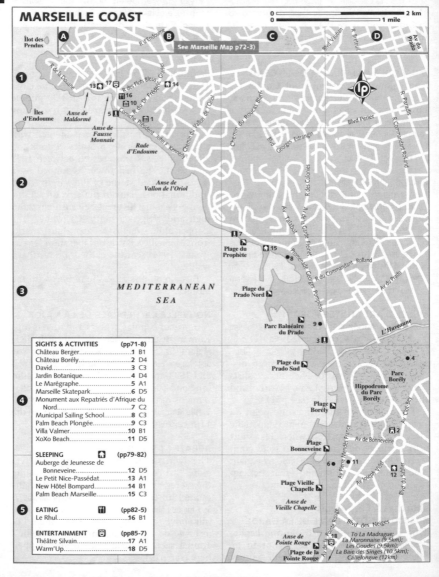

MARSEILLE COAST

See Marseille Map p72-3

SIGHTS & ACTIVITIES	(pp71–8)
Château Berger	1 B1
Château Borély	2 D4
David	3 C3
Jardin Botanique	4 D4
Le Marégraphe	5 A1
Marseille Skatepark	6 D5
Monument aux Rapatriés d'Afrique du Nord	7 C2
Municipal Sailing School	8 C3
Palm Beach Plongée	9 C3
Villa Valmer	10 B1
XoXo Beach	11 D5

SLEEPING	(pp79–82)
Auberge de Jeunesse de Bonneveine	12 D5
Le Petit Nice-Passédat	13 A1
New Hôtel Bompard	14 B1
Palm Beach Marseille	15 C3

EATING	(pp82–5)
Le Rhul	16 B1

ENTERTAINMENT	(pp85–7)
Théâtre Silvain	17 A1
Warm'Up	18 D5

cook traditional Sunday bouillabaisse. A narrow staircase (behind the bus stop) leads from corniche Président John F Kennedy to the harbour. The pinprick island, naked bar an obelisk, is Îlot des Pendus (below). On the road above stands the 1922 **Monument aux Morts de l'Armée d'Orient** (Map pp72–3), a WWI memorial statue. Further south is local hero **Zinedine Zidane** (Map pp72–3), plastered in gigantic Adidas-ad form on the side of 82B corniche Président John F Kennedy; in front there are sea-facing benches, a telescope and a fine café terrace.

Villa Valmer (Map p76; ☎ 04 91 31 32 49; 275 corniche Président John F Kennedy; admission free; ☒ gardens 8am-7pm, villa closed to public), with its potent garden-cocktail of pistachio, palm and pine trees, is one of the few bourgeoisie villas built along the coast during the Second Empire to survive. Opposite, **Le Marégraphe** (Map p76; closed to visitors) measures elevations in France. **Château Berger** (Map p76; 281 corniche Président John F Kennedy) – today a luxurious seawater therapy spa – is another beautiful architectural example from this period.

A short walk away is the **Monument aux Repatriés d'Afrique du Nord** (Map p76), an enormous propeller sculpted in bronze by César in 1971 to honour those who returned from North Africa. South of the **municipal sailing school** (Map p76), in front of the body-packed Prado beaches (p78) on the intersection of av du Prado and promenade Georges Pompidou, stands Marseille's best-endowed landmark: **David** (Map p76), by Jules Cantini, a 1903 marble lookalike of Michelangelo's masterpiece.

Across the street, **Parc Borély** (Map p76; ☎ 04 91 76 59 38; av du Parc Borély) encompasses a **lake**, **jardin botanique** (botanical garden) and 18th-century art-exhibition host **Château Borély** (Map p76; ☎ 04 91 25 26 34; 134 av Clot Bey; various admission & opening hr).

Promenade Georges Pompidou continues south to **La Pointe-Rouge, La Madrague, Callelongue** and **Les Goudes**, the latter two being harbour villages on Cap Croisette from where the breathtaking *calanques* (p89) can be accessed on foot. Bus No 19 from the rond-point du Prado metro stop runs along promenade Georges Pompidou to La Madrague; from La Madrague bus No 20 continues to Callelongue.

Along almost its entire length corniche Président John F Kennedy, and its continuation promenade Georges Pompidou, is served by bus No 83, which goes to the Vieux Port (quai des Belges) and the rond-point du Prado metro stop on av du Prado. From the rond-point du Prado, blvd Michelet leads south to Olympique de Marseille's stade vélodrome (see the boxed text, p86), home ground to the football club since 1937, and Le Corbusier's Hôtel Le Corbusier (see Author's Choice, p79).

ÎLE D'IF

The main reason to make the scenic, 20-minute voyage to this rocky 30,000-sq-metre island is to visit **Château d'If** (Map p68; ☎ 04 91 59 02 30; adult/under 18 yrs €4.60/free, 1st Sun of month everyone free; ☒ 9.30am-6.30pm May-Sep, 9.30am-5.30pm Tue-Sun Oct-Mar, 9.30am-5.30pm Apr), the 16th-century fortress-turned-prison made famous by Dumas' classic work *Le Comte de Monte Cristo*. Among the people incarcerated here were hundreds of Protestants, revolutionary hero Mirabeau (who served a stint here in 1774 for failing to pay debts), some 1848 revolutionaries and the 1871 Communards. Castle aside, the island is barren.

Boats run by **GACM** (Map pp80-1; ☎ 04 91 55 50 09; www.answeb.net/gacm in French; 1 quai des Belges, 1er; metro Vieux Port; return fare €10; hourly 9am-7pm) depart from outside the GACM office at the Vieux Port.

OTHER ISLANDS

Ratonneau and **Pomègues**, each about 2.5km long and – together with Île d'If – known collectively as the **Îles du Frioul**, are a few hundred metres west of If. From the 17th to the 19th centuries the two barren white limestone islands were used to quarantine suspected plague and cholera sufferers. Today they shelter sea birds, rare plants, fortifications used by German troops during WWII, the ruins of an old quarantine hospital and a fort.

Pinprick **Îlot des Pendus** and **Îlot Debagy** are the smallest islands visible from Marseille. Pendus (literally 'the hanged') remembers the 12 hostages taken here by Alphonse d'Aragon in 1442 with an obelisk marking the spot where the gallows were. Debagy is recognisable by the fortress-like building that dominates its 3566 sq metres. It was built in the 19th century for a wealthy jeweller and hosts private receptions today.

The **Archipel de Riou**, four uninhabited islands and several *ilots* (small islands) off the tip of Cap Croisette, shelters sea birds galore including 30% of France's Cory's shearwater population. The entire archipelago (off limits to visitors) is protected by the Conservatoire du Littoral (see High-Factor Protection by the Sea, p36). **Île Tiboulen de Maïre** (23,000 sq metres) and **Île Maïre** (280,000 sq metres), just 125m from the shore, are a snorkeller's haven.

Further out to sea, **Île de Planier** (20,000 sq metres) has been lit by a lighthouse since medieval times. The current 70m-tall structure, built anew after WWII, was manned manually until 1992.

GACM boats sail to the Îles du Frioul (return €10, €15 with a stop on Île d'If; hourly 6.45am to 8.30pm) in 30 minutes. None of the other islands can be visited, but you can sail around them: **AVP Location** (☎ 04 91 91 86 77; 96 quai du Port, 2e; metro Vieux Port) rents boats and yachts of all shapes and sizes.

ACTIVITIES

Scout out walking and mountain-bike trails with outdoor enthusiasts at the **Club Alpin Français** (CAF; Map pp80-1; ☎ 04 91 54 36 94; http://cafmarseille.free.fr in French; 12 rue Fort Notre Dame, 1er; metro Vieux Port; ☺ 10am-1pm & 4-6pm Mon, 10am-1pm & 4-8pm Thu).

Watching the sun set over the harbour from a kayak is memorable; the tourist office organises sunset **sea-kayaking** adventures at 7pm on Saturday, mid-May to early September (€35 for three hours).

Beaches

The closest beach to the centre is **Plage des Catalans** (Map pp72-3; 3 rue des Catalans; ☺ 8.30am-6.30pm Jun-Sep), a small sandy public beach with beach-volleyball courts, beachside terrace huts to rent (€4) and a pizzeria (p85). Near the **Vallon des Auffes** (Map pp72–3), sunbathers spread out on wooden decks built atop the rocky seafront, climbing down short ladders to dip in the sea. Further south, **Plage du Prophète** is favoured by families for its shallow waters.

Marseille's main beach area is the part-sandy, part-shingle 1km-long **Parc Balnéaire du Prado** (Map p76; ☎ 04 91 29 30 40), 5km south of the centre and split into five beaches (north to south): **Plage du Prado Nord** (also called Plage du Petit Roucas Blanc), **Plage**

du Prado Sud (also called Plage de David), **Plage Borély**, **Plage Bonneveine** and **Plage Vieille Chapelle**. These beaches have public toilets, showers, first-aid posts with coastguards and free lockers to safeguard valuables. Prado du Nord and Sud are wheelchair accessible; Prado du Nord and Borély have a children's playground; and café-clad Borély and Bonneveine have sun-loungers/parasols to rent (€10/4 per day). Sandy **Plage de la Pointe Rouge**, further south again, is hot with windsurfers, surfers and water-skiers.

To get to all these beaches, take bus No 83 (No 583 at night) from quai des Belges to the Plage David or La Plage stop; or bus No 19 or No 72 from the rond-point du Prado metro stop. On foot, follow corniche Président John F Kennedy.

Diving & Snorkelling

The *calanques* (p89) and the islands (p76) offer spectacular diving and snorkelling. Hire equipment from **Cressi Sub** (Map pp72-3; ☎ 04 91 90 95 74; 11 av de St-Jean, 1er; metro Vieux Port) or **Palm Beach Plongée** (Map p76; ☎ 04 91 22 10 38; www.airdive-provence.com; Hôtel Concorde Palm Beach, 2 promenade de la Plage, 8e). Both schools organise baptism, regular and night dives (€40 to €55) and snorkelling expeditions (€23). Mid-June to mid-September, half-day baptism dives (€41) can be booked through the tourist office.

Rollerblading

The bowl at **Marseille Skatepark** (Map p76; www.marseilleskatepark.fr.st; av Pierre Mendès, 8e) is legendary on the international skating circuit. To get to the beachfront park, take bus No 19 from rond-point du Prado to the Vieille Chapelle stop (in front of Plage Vieille Chapelle). Hire blades opposite for €3.80/7.60/12 per hour/half-day/day from surf shop **XoXo Beach** (Map p76; ☎ 04 91 25 15 39; 197 av Pierre Mendès France, 8e; ☺ 10am-7pm).

Several hundred bladers meet at 9.15pm on Friday outside the **Stade Vélodrome** (off Map pp72-3; 3 blvd Michelet, 8e; metro rond-point du Prado) for a police-escorted, 12km-long blade run organised by **Marseille en Roller** (MER; ☎ 06 26 50 34 76; www.marseilleenroller.com). At the stadium, look for the guys in the orange bibs.

TOURS

The tourist office runs guided tours (€6.50), many thematic (in the footsteps of novelist Alexandre Dumas, Art Deco architecture and so on). July to mid-September, it organises nocturnal Vieux Port tours at 9.30pm on Friday. All tours must be booked in advance.

The tourist office also sells tickets for **Histobus** (☎ 04 91 10 54 71), a three-hour city tour (adult/child €11/4.60) by bus run by **Régie des Transports de Marseille** (RTM; www.rtm .fr in French). It departs at 2.30pm on Sunday, July to September, from the Vieux Port.

Le Grand Tour (☎ 04 91 91 05 82; s-mt@wanadoo .fr; one-/two-day pass adult €16/19, 4-11 yrs €8/8) tours Marseille from the top of an open double-decker bus. The tour (with English audio-guide commentary) takes 1½ hours, but pass holders can hop on and off as they please, using stops at 16 strategic points (Vieux Port, Parc Borély, place aux Huiles etc). Bus drivers and tourist offices sell the pass.

With **Les Petits Trains** (☎ 04 91 40 17 75; train tour13@aol.com; quai du Port, 1er; metro Vieux Port; adult/child €5/3; ☷ 10am-12.20pm & 1.40-6.20pm Apr-Oct, shorter hr Nov-Mar), the prime sights can be viewed aboard an electric train. Tours last an hour and head along the coast or up to Notre Dame de la Garde.

As well as boats to/from the islands (see p77), GACM runs half-day boat trips (€25) in July and August from the old port to the *calanques* (p89).

FESTIVALS & EVENTS

Each year on 2 February the statue of the Black Virgin inside the Abbaye St-Victor (p75) is carried through the streets in a candle-lit procession during the **Pèlerinage de la Chandeleur** (Candlemas Pilgrimage). The **Carnaval de Marseille** – a street carnival with decorated floats – follows in March, and Plage du Prado hosts the **beach volleyball world championships** in July.

July's **Festival de Marseille** (www.festivaldemar seille.com in French) brings three weeks of contemporary international dance, theatre, music and art to various venues. In July and August the **Ciné Plein Air festival** brings films (in French) to open-air venues around town; look for posters or ask at the tourist office. Admission is free.

October's month-long **Festival des Chants Sacrés en Méditerranée** brings sacred music concerts to Marseillais churches; while the **Fête de l'Assomption** on 15 August honours the city's traditional protector with a Mass in the Nouvelle Cathédrale de la Major (p75) and a procession through Le Panier.

October's month-long **Fiesta des Suds**, held at the Docks des Suds (p86) each October, is a celebration of world music.

SLEEPING

The tourist office runs a last-minute **hotel reservation service** (☎ 0 826 886 826), allowing you to book a hotel room for that evening.

Budget
HOSTELS
Auberge de Jeunesse de Bonneveine (Map p76; ☎ 04 91 17 63 30; marseille-bonneveine@fuaj.org; impasse du Docteur Bonfils, 8e; dm incl breakfast 1st/subsequent night €13.90/11.90, d per person incl breakfast 1st/subsequent night €15.90/13.90; ☷ mid-Jan–mid-Dec) An HI card is obligatory at this hostel, 4.5km south of the centre, which handily rents bikes (€13/day). Take bus No 44 from the rond-point du Prado metro stop and get off at the place Bonnefons stop.

Auberge de Jeunesse Château de Bois Luzy (off Map p72-3; ☎ /fax 04 91 49 06 18; allées des Primevères, 12e; dm €11.40, breakfast €3.20; ☷ reception 7.30am-noon & 5-10.30pm Jan–mid-Dec) Venture 4.5km east to find this grandiose chateau atop a hill with Marseille Bay views. A hostelling card is mandatory. Take bus No 6 from near the Réformés-Canebière metro stop or bus No 8 from La Canebière.

AUTHOR'S CHOICE

Hôtel Le Corbusier (off Map pp72-3; ☎ 04 91 16 78 00; www.hotellecorbusier.com; 280 blvd Michelet; d with shower €40, small/large d with shower & toilet €50/80, 2–4-person studio with balcony & sea views €90, baby cot €10; P ☘) Frequented mainly by architects and architecture fiends, this fabulous concrete block was the creation of celebrated architect Le Corbusier (p49) and is by far the hottest choice for travellers into all things design. Deemed massively innovative when built in the early 1950s as part of Le Corbusier's Unité d'Habitation, the ugly 337-apartment block on stilts continues to fascinate with its original apartments that can be visited, rooftop swimming pool and jogging track. To get here, take the metro or bus No 83 from the Vieux Port to rond-point du Prado, or bus No 21 from the Vieux Port to the 'Le Corbusier' stop.

MARSEILLE AREA

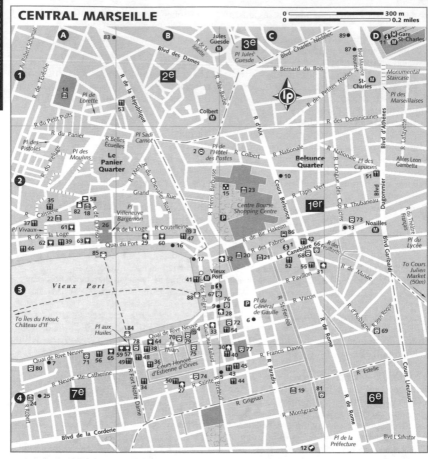

CENTRAL MARSEILLE

HOTELS

Hôtel de la Préfecture (Map pp72-3; ☎ 04 91 54 31
60; fax 04 91 54 24 95; 9 blvd Louis Salvator, 6e; metro
Estrangin-Préfecture; d with shower €29, with shower &
toilet €32; ℗ ✕) Don't get too excited: 'parking' at this budget hotel translates as nab-
bing one of the handful of spaces on the
street outside. Inside, staff are friendly and
rooms are clean and modern.

Le Président (Map pp72-3; ☎ 04 91 48 67 29; fax
04 91 94 24 44; 12 blvd Louis Salvator, 6e; metro Estrangin-
Préfecture; d/tr with shower & toilet €35/50; ✕) Opposite Hôtel de la Préfecture, the President
comes a close second in terms of price-
quality ratio and standards of cleanliness.

South of La Canebière, there's several
rock-bottom hotels on rue Sénac de Meil-
han, rue Mazagran, rue du Théâtre Français
and around place du Lycée (all near metro
Réformés-Canebière, 1er). To the west, rue
des Feuillants (metro Noailles) has some
one-star hotels.

Mid-Range
Looking straight out to sea:

Hôtel Le Richelieu (Map pp72-3; ☎ 04 91 31 01
92; hotelmer@club-internet.fr; 52 corniche Président John
F Kennedy, 7e; s €56, d €56-73, tr €68, ste €86-92; ℗)
Breakfast on a sea-facing terrace is the highlight of this friendly two-star place, built into
the rocks near Plage des Catalans. Its suites
have terraces to die for and those with kids
can rent a cot for €6. Road-facing rooms can
be noisy. Parking costs €10 a night.

Hôtel Péron (Map pp72-3; ☎ 04 91 31 01 41; http://hotel-peron.com; 119 corniche Président John F Kennedy, 7e; s/d with shared toilet €33/60.50, d with shower & toilet €69.50; P) Despite its weathered appearance, seaside Hôtel Péron touts decent two-star rooms and has been run by the same family for three generations. Bus No 83 from quai des Belges stops a suitcase-drag away.

In the heart of urban action:

Hôtel Relax (Map pp80-1; ☎ 04 91 33 15 87; fax 04 91 55 63 57; 4 rue Corneille, 1er; metro Vieux Port; d with courtyard/opera views €55/60; ✸) Neighbouring the opera house, this old-fashioned gem might be small but its rooms are spick and span, its geranium-filled flower boxes are a picture in summer, and the owners could not run the place with more pride or smiles.

Etap Hôtel (Map pp80-1; ☎ 04 91 54 73 73; 46 rue Sainte, 7e; metro Vieux Port; s/d/tr €46/50/50; P ✸) It might be part of a chain, but its location in an old building overlooking cours Honoré d'Estienne d'Orves – Marseille's loveliest café-clad square – makes its rooms a steal. The spacious wood-beamed rooms in the sea galley captain's house are the most atmospheric.

Hôtel St-Louis (Map pp80-1; ☎ 04 91 54 02 74; www.hotel-st-louis.com; 2 rue des Récollettes, 1er; metro Noailles; s/d/tr from €32/42/57) St-Louis is elegant and pretty-in-pink with its wrought-iron balconies, and is located stumbling distance from the old port in the hub of Marseille's shopping district.

Hôtel Hermes (Map pp80-1; ☎ 04 96 11 63 63; hotel.hermes@wanadoo.fr; 2 rue de la Bonneterie, 1er; metro Vieux Port; s/d from €45/67; P ✕ ✸) Right on the quayside, Hôtel Hermes is bright, cheerful and good value. The roof terrace and the honeymoon-room balcony have terrific views over the harbour. Nearby secure parking costs €6.

Tonic Hôtel (Map pp80-1; ☎ 04 91 55 67 46; www.tonichotel.com; 43 quai des Belges, 1er; metro Vieux Port; s/d/tr €90/115/140, with port views €115/140/160; ✸) Yet another well-restored old building at the Vieux Port houses this handsome, three-star portside pad. Pets can kip with their owner for an extra €5 a night.

Hôtel Alizé (Map pp80-1; ☎ 04 91 33 66 97; www.alize-hotel.com in French; 35 quai des Belges, 1er; metro Vieux Port; s/d €58/63, with port views €75/80; ✸) Hotel Alizé is an atmospheric and elegant pile, wedged between cafés and touting a bird's-eye view of the old-port comings and goings. Cheaper rooms at the back overlook a patio.

MARSEILLE AREA

New Hôtel Vieux Port (Map pp80-1; ☎ 04 91 99 23 23; marseillevieuxport@new-hotel.com; 3bis rue Reine Elisabeth, 1er; metro Vieux Port; s/d €110/125, ste from €125; 🔀) Overlooking the bustling old port, this renovated complex contains 47 modern rooms furnished with stylish understatement in a variety of subtle ethnic styles. The priciest tout a terrace to watch the boats bobbing in the harbour.

Le Rhul (Map p76; ☎ 04 91 52 01 77; www.bouillabaissemarseille.com; 269 corniche Président John F Kennedy, 7e; d from €95; P 🔀) Known as much for its bouillabaisse (see Tasty Tip, opposite) as for its three-star rooms overlooking the sea, Le Rhul is one of the old boys of the Marseille hotel scene.

Top End

Palm Beach Marseille (Map p76; ☎ 04 91 16 19 00; h3485@accor-hotels.com; 200 corniche Président John F Kennedy, 7e; s/d/ste from €189/210/375; P ✕ 🔀 📃 🖳) Le Corbusier was clearly an influencing factor behind the designer who came up with this stunning interior. A geometric concrete façade hides a contemporary interior of glass, light and designer furniture. Rooms are less bold.

Le Petit Nice-Passédat (Map p76; ☎ 04 91 59 25 92; www.petitnice-passedat.com; Anse de Maldormé, 7e; d low/high season from €190/260, ste/loft from €390/610; P ✕ 🔀 📃 🖳) Built atop rocks above a little cove, Marseille's most sought-after hotel falls under the prestigious Relais & Châteaux parasol and sports a dozen rooms, all with sea views. Heated water from the sea fills its pool.

New Hôtel Bompard (Map p76; ☎ 04 91 99 22 22; marseillebompard@new-hotel.com; 2 rue des Flots Bleues, 7e; s/d €91/108, Mas des Genêts s/d €170/200; P ✕ 🔀 📃 🖳) Part of a chain it might be but the Bompard, just off corniche Président John F Kennedy, cooks up good sea breezes, a flowery park and multistarred rooms with gadgets galore. Four rooms are inside Mas de Genêts, an even more luxurious house in the grounds.

EATING
Vieux Port & Around   Map pp80–1

Cafés and touristy restaurants plaster the old port quays; those on northern quai du Port are more original than those on southern quai de Rive Neuve. From the latter, place Thiars and cours Honoré d'Estienne d'Orves, packed with eating and drinking places, stretch south. Neighbouring place aux Huiles is equally restaurant-laden.

Chez Madie Les Galinettes (☎ 04 91 90 40 87; 138 quai du Port, 1er; metro Vieux Port; lunch menu €15, dinner menus €22 & €27; ☾ lunch & dinner Mon-Sat) If it's traditional *pieds et paquets* (sheep tripe, literally 'feet and packages'), *rougets au pistou* (mullet in basil sauce) or another hearty regional speciality you're after, this is your place. Locals love it.

La Lucciola (☎ 04 91 91 84 56; 184 quai du Port, 1er; metro Vieux Port; mains €10-15; ☾ lunch & dinner) Eat pasta, meal-sized *assiettes* (salad platters) and *gambas* (king prawns) in various guises at this casual but chic Italian-inspired place.

Lemon Grass (☎ 04 91 33 97 65; 10 rue Fort Notre Dame, 7e; metro Vieux Port; menus €27, €35 & €49; ☾ lunch & dinner Mon-Sat) World cuisine is the name of the game at this refined choice, where the culinarily adventurous can wrap their tongue around fresh tuna rolls with mint and coriander, or *bouillabaisse de Bangkok* made with coconut milk and lemon grass.

Bistro Gambas (☎ 04 91 33 26 44; 29 place aux Huiles, 1er; metro Vieux Port; menus from €17.50; ☾ lunch & dinner Mon-Sat) Those with a fetish for lip-smacking, finger-licking prawns should hit this *gambas* joint. Its *menu crevettes à volonté* (€17.50) is a bottomless *menu*, allowing you to eat as many prawns as your tummy can take.

Bistrot à Vin (☎ 04 91 54 02 20; 17 rue Sainte, 1er; metro Vieux Port; mains around €12; ☾ lunch & dinner Mon-Fri, dinner Sat) Local Marseillais cram into this tiny little wine bar at lunchtime to feast on giant-sized salads guaranteed to please and fill. The *assiette garrigue* – a mix of warm goat cheese, dried ham, fresh figs and melon – is a refreshing change. Come night, operagoers enjoy this bistro.

La Comedia (☎ 04 91 54 99 78; 21 rue Sainte, 1er; metro Vieux Port; lunch/dinner menu €12.50/24; ☾ lunch & dinner Tue-Sat, dinner Sun) *Gastronomie* and lounge is what this chic and highly sought-after modern restaurant cooks up – and with great panache too. Food is strictly creative Mediterranean and the décor is red, white and minimalist.

Toinou (☎ 04 91 33 14 94; 3 cours St-Louis, 1er; metro Noailles; ☾ lunch & dinner) The Marseille reference for *dégustation coquillages* (tasting shellfish), Toinou runs a stall where you can taste on the move and a brasserie-style restaurant where you can sit down and feast on sea urchins, sea squirts, oysters, whelks and magnificent seafood platters.

TASTY TIP

No trip to Marseille is complete without tasting bouillabaisse (pronounced bwee-ya-bess), a traditional fish stew. Although many touristy restaurants advertise the signature dish for as little as €15, an authentic bouillabaisse – evident from the manner in which it is served and its fresh fish content – costs €40 to €50 per person.

Authentic bouillabaisse restaurants don't dish up the stew to solo diners (minimum two people). Many demand that you order the dish 24 hours in advance – a sure sign of freshness. Among the 16-odd places to have signed the Charte de la Bouillabaisse Marseillaise – a charter aimed at safeguarding the century-old culinary creation – are Marseille's most legendary bouillabaisse restaurants (advance reservations are essential at all four):

L'Épuisette (Map pp72-3; ☎ 04 91 52 17 82; rue du Vallon des Auffes, 7e; menus €43, €63 & €90; ☼ lunch & dinner Tue-Sat) A concrete-and-glass edifice perched on a rock looking out to sea.

Chez Fonfon (Map pp72-3; ☎ 04 91 52 14 38; 140 rue du Vallon des Auffes; menus €35 & €50; ☼ lunch & dinner Tue-Sat, dinner Mon) Overlooking a quaint harbour, where adventurous diners can also try fish flambéed in pastis.

Le Miramar (Map pp80-1; ☎ 04 91 91 10 40; 12 quai du Port, 1er; metro Vieux Port; ☼ lunch & dinner Tue-Sat) Portside.

Le Rhul (Map p76; ☎ 04 91 52 54 54; 269 corniche Président John F Kennedy, 7e; no menus, bouillabaisse for two people €79; ☼ lunch & dinner)

For more about bouillabaisse see p56.

504 Restaurant Familial (☎ 04 91 33 57 74; 34 place aux Huiles, 1er; metro Vieux Port; tajines/couscous from €13.50/12; ☼ lunch & dinner Tue-Sat, dinner Mon) For something different, eat smoked aubergines in garlic, *tajines* (slow-cooked meat and vegetable stew), lamb brochettes, couscous and the like in a colourful and exotically furnished interior. The delicately spiced *méchoui* (half a shoulder of lamb) is particularly mouth watering.

Les Arcenaulx (☎ 04 91 59 80 30; 25 cours Honoré d'Estienne d'Orves, 1er; metro Vieux Port; menus €28.50 & €49.50; ☼ closed Sun & Mon Jul & Aug) Dine amid historic splendour in the city's most elegant restaurant-cum–*salon de thé* (tea room), which is wrapped around an interior courtyard.

La Casertane (☎ 04 91 54 98 51; 71 rue Francis Davso, 1er; metro Vieux Port; pasta €8; ☼ 9am-7.30pm Mon-Sat) One of Marseille's best Italian *épiceries* (grocers) has traded on its well-earned reputation to cook up some splendidly tasty morsels to eat in.

Chez Vincent (☎ 04 91 33 96 78; 25 rue des Glandèves, 1er; metro Vieux Port; mains around €10; ☼ lunch & dinner Mon-Sat) Vincent's Place is small, simple and ruled with a heart of gold by Rose – chef, patron and legendary grandmother of this Marseillais establishment. Her *soupe au pistou* (vegetable, bean and basil soup; €12) is like no other.

Restaurant O'Stop (☎ 04 91 33 85 34; place de l'Opéra, 1er; metro Vieux Port; menu €9; ☼ 24hr) Opposite the opera house, this simple bar-cum-bistro is by no means stunning on the culinary front but it does deserve something of a mention for serving decent munchies around the clock.

Le Panier

On, or just off, rue de la République are Vietnamese and Chinese restaurants worth a nibble.

Pizzaria Étienne (Map pp80-1; 43 rue de Lorette, 2e; metro Colbert; meals around €25; ☼ lunch & dinner Mon-Sat) Evocative of the real Marseille, Pizzaria Étienne has been run by the same family since the 1940s and is famed for its *supions frits* (pan-fried squid with garlic and parsley) and juicy *pavé de boeuf* (beef steak). From rue de la République, cut down passage de Lorette and walk up the staircase. Étienne has no telephone (so no advance reservations) and doesn't accept credit cards.

Bobolivo (Map pp80-1; ☎ 04 91 90 20 68; 29 rue Caisserie, 2e; metro Vieux Port; starters/mains around €9/15; ☼ 8-11pm Tue-Sat Sep-Jul) Known about town as an unpretentious, good-value spot, Bobolivo (after Bob, the patron) cooks up treat-yourself dishes (fresh-from-the-sea *noix de St-Jacques* and so on) on a delightful summertime terrace.

Le Panier's western fringe flows into the commercial port area (metro Joliette, 8e), where the 'London docks–feel' complex, Les Docks, touts several places to eat, including the voluminous **Le Dock de Suez** (Map pp72-3; ☎ 04 91 56 07 56; 10 place de la Joliette, 2e; metro Joliette; starters/mains €8/14, plat du jour €10.50; ⏲ lunch & dinner Mon-Fri).

Cours Julien

This bohemian patch of town is lined with restaurants offering a tantalising variety of French and ethnic cuisines. Rue des Trois Mages cooks up Greek, Indian, Lebanese and Spanish. By day the elongated tree-studded square buzzes with family activity. Come dusk, the tone is less jolly.

Le Sud du Haut (Map pp72-3; ☎ 04 91 92 66 64; 80 cours Julien, 6e; metro Notre Dame du Mont-Cours Julien; mains around €10; ⏲ lunch & dinner Wed-Sat) A colourful, sky-topped terrace is the main draw of this cheery, brightly painted restaurant with eclectic interior and sun-inspired food.

By the Beach   Map pp72–3

If you want to dine with sand between your toes, try the multitude of beach cafés, restaurants and bars overlooking Plage Borély and Plage Bonneveine.

More elegant dining with sea views can be had at one of Marseille's legendary bouillabaisse restaurants (see the boxed text, Tasty Tip, p83).

AUTHOR'S CHOICE FOR ...

Breakfast

Le Pain Quotidien (Map pp80-1; ☎ 04 91 33 55 00; 18 place aux Huiles, 1er; metro Vieux Port; breakfast menus €5.60-7.80; ⏲ 8am-6.30pm) Kick-start the day with fresh bio bread, croissants, home-made jams (including the sweetest, most finger-licking chocolate spread), a hard-boiled egg and more.

Lunch inside

Le Patio des Docks (Map pp72-3; ☎ 04 91 91 94 57; 114 rue de la République, 2e; metro Joliette; buffet lunch €9.80, sushi menus €12.50-28; ⏲ noon-2.30pm Mon-Fri) This renovated glass-topped car park sports startling industrial décor, contemporary art exhibitions, urban feel, cutting-edge sushi bar and eat-as-much-as-your-tummy-can-take buffet lunch. From 2005 it should be open evenings too.

Lunch on the rocks

La Baie des Singes (The Bay of Monkeys; off Map p76; ☎ 04 91 73 68 87; Cap Croisette; ⏲ lunch & dinner Apr-Sep) This place is well worth the trip for its stunning location on a cape, 15km south of the centre. From Les Goudes follow the signs to Cap Croisette, park in the car park and walk 500m along the narrow path through rocks to the seaside restaurant. Eat seafood over prime views of Île Maïre, then collapse on a comfy deck chair on sun-drenched rocks. To get here by boat call ☎ 06 66 42 71 70.

Vegetarians

Ardamone (Map pp80-1; ☎ 04 91 90 18 09; www.ardamone.com; 28 rue Caisserie, 2e; metro Vieux Port; lunch menu €11, dinner menus €15-20; ⏲ lunch & dinner Wed-Sat, lunch Tue & Sun) Marseille's only *bio resto* is a safe bet for noncarnivores and carnivores alike. Gluten-free dishes, vegetable apéritifs and a couple of vegan dishes are included on the strictly organic menu.

Dinner

Take your pick from two chic and appealing, contemporary haunts.

Zé (Map pp80-1; ☎ 04 91 55 08 15; 19 quai de Rive Neuve, 1er; metro Vieux Port; menu €28; ⏲ lunch & dinner) Style-oozing vast windows overlook the port; *zé bon menus*.

César Place (Map pp80-1; ☎ 04 91 33 25 22; 21 place aux Huiles, 1er; metro Vieux Port; lunch/dinner menu €20/32.50; ⏲ lunch & dinner) The creative chef makes no bones about the intensely passionate love affair he has with food.

Other popular restaurants:

Le Péron (☎ 04 91 52 15 22; 56 corniche Président John F Kennedy, 7e; menu €43, starters/mains/desserts €16/27/10; ☺ lunch & dinner) One of the hottest places ever since it opened, this chic London-feel place sports a *très moderne* nautical wood-decking interior, a terrace hanging over the sea and an inventive menu to match.

Pizzeria Chez Jeannot (☎ 04 91 52 11 28; 129 rue du Vallon des Auffes, 7e; pizza/pasta from €6/9; ☺ lunch & dinner Tue-Sun) Not pricey and always packed thanks to its great harbour location, Jeannot serves salads, pasta, oysters and shellfish as well as pizza.

Seaside spots where you can wear your bikini:

Pizzeria des Catalans (☎ 04 91 52 37 82; 3 rue des Catalans, 7e; small/large pizzas from €7.80/11.50; ☺ lunch & dinner) Enviable terrace next to the beach-volleyball courts on Plage des Catalans.

Bistrot Plage (☎ 04 91 31 80 32; 60 corniche Président John F Kennedy, 7e; mains around €12; ☺ lunch & dinner Mon-Sun) Adjoining a private beach beneath the Vallon des Auffes WWI memorial. It's open until 2am Friday and Saturday.

Self-Catering

Marseille's most aromatic markets are its daily **fresh fish market** (Map pp80-1; quai des Belges, 1er; metro Vieux Port; ☺ 8am-noon), at the old port, and **garlic market** (Map pp80-1; cours Belsunce, 1er; metro Vieux Port). Fruit, vegetables, fish and dried products are sold at the **Marché des Capucins** (Map pp80-1; place des Capucins, 1er; metro Noailles; ☺ 8am-7pm) and the morning market on **place de la Joliette** (Map pp72-3; place de la Joliette, 2e; metro Joliette; ☺ Mon-Fri).

Monoprix (Map pp80-1; 36 La Canebière, 1er; metro Noailles; ☺ 8.30am-8.30pm Mon-Sat) is a central supermarket.

DRINKING

L'Heure Verte (The Green Hour; Map pp80-1; ☎ 04 91 90 12 73; 106 quai du Port, 1er; metro Vieux Port, pastis from €2; ☺ 10am-10pm Mon & Tue, 10am-2am Wed-Sun, shorter hr low season) Discover all there is to know about pastis (see The Milk of Provence, p58) at this unusual bar-cum-bistro a temple to the fiery Provençal spirit – which serves tapas dishes (€10 for 5 tapas) to help ease digestion.

Cup of Tea (Map pp80-1; ☎ 04 91 90 84 02; 1 rue Caisserie, 2e; metro Vieux Port) If it's a nice homy cup of Earl Grey or English breakfast drunk in peace you fancy, then this stylish bookshop-

café at the foot of Le Panier is the place to plop yourself down.

Le Crystal (Map pp80-1; ☎ 04 91 91 57 96; 148 quai du Port, 2e; metro Vieux Port; ☺ to 2am) The Crystal, decked out 1950s style complete with red banquet seats, is a lovely place to lounge.

La Caravelle (Map pp80-1; ☎ 04 91 90 36 64; 34 quai du Port, 2e; metro Vieux Port; ☺ to 2am) Hidden on the 1st floor of the Hôtel Bellevue, this gem of a trendsetter hosts jazz concerts, cooks up an awesome Sunday-morning brunch and is prime apéritif-quaffing territory.

La Fabrique (Map pp80-1; ☎ 04 91 91 40 48; 3 place Jules Verne, 2e; metro Vieux Port; ☺ 7.30pm-2am Thu & Fri, 1pm-2am Sat & Sun) Hidden behind Marseille's quayside town hall, this hip bar-cum-restaurant has retro sofa seating to lounge on, board games to lose track of time with and brunch to while away the weekend. The bar is concrete.

Quai de Rive Neuve is lined with places to drink and be merry well into the wee hours: **O'Malleys** (Map pp80-1; 9 quai de Rive Neuve, 1er; metro Vieux Port) and the **Shamrock** (Map pp80-1; 17 quai de Rive Neuve, 7e; metro Vieux Port) are Irish pubs; Pagnol drank at the **Bar de la Marine** (Map pp80-1; 15 quai de Rive Neuve, 7e; metro Vieux Port); and **Exit Café** (Map pp80-1; 12 quai de Rive Neuve, 7e; metro Vieux Port) buzzes with a young crowd.

ENTERTAINMENT

What's on where is listed in *Agenda*, a free monthly listing magazine available at the **Espace Culture** (Map pp80-1; ☎ 04 96 11 04 60; www.espaceculture.net in French; 42 La Canebière, 1er; metro

Vieux Port; 10am-6.45pm Mon-Sat) and the tourist office. Buy event tickets in the latter or at ticket desks in **FNAC** (Map pp80-1; ☎ 04 91 39 94 00; Centre Bourse, 1er; metro Vieux Port) and **Virgin Megastore** (Map pp80-1; ☎ 04 91 55 84 11; 75 rue St-Ferréol, 6e; metro Estrangin-Préfecture).

The entire cultural spectrum – from theatre, ballet and contemporary music to installation and video art – is embraced with vigour at La Friche la Belle de Mai (see Docklands, p74), a cutting-edge cultural centre.

Nightclubs

Le Trolleybus (Map pp80-1; ☎ 04 91 54 30 45; www .letrolley.com in French; 24 quai de Rive Neuve, 7e; metro Vieux Port; 11pm-6am Thu-Sat) DJs spin everything from soul, groove and house to tech-house and acid jazz at this Marseillais institution, inside an 18th-century warehouse. Early evening drinkers can play *pétanque* over an apéritif.

Warm'Up (Map p76; ☎ 04 96 14 06 30; www.warm up-marseille.fr in French; 83 av de la Pointe Rouge & 8 blvd Mireille Jouran Barry, 8e; admission free-€10; bar & club 7 or 8pm-1 or 2am Tue-Sat, pool from 11am Sat & Sun) This vast industrial space near Plage de la Pointe Rouge is much more than a supertrendy club-cum-disco. Learn to salsa or rock'n'roll here, laze by the pool with cocktail in hand, or gaze out to sea over an apéritif on its roof terrace.

Metal Café (Map pp80-1; ☎ 04 91 54 03 03; 20 rue Fortia, 1er; metro Vieux Port; admission €5; Thu-Sun) This downtown 'in' choice sits at the foot of the staircase linking cours Honoré d'Estienne d'Orves with rue Sainte. Look for the steely grey door.

La Maronnaise (off Map p76; ☎ 04 91 73 98 58, 04 91 72 42 65; rte de la Maronnaise, 8e; admission €10; 11pm-5am Wed-Sun mid-Apr–mid-Oct) Those in the know have heard of this fabulous seaside venue well before setting foot in Marseille. To dance to hip beats with trendy Marseillais beneath the stars, follow the coastal road to Les Goudes on Cap Croisette, 10km south of the Prado beaches.

Fashionable disco-clubs around the old port:

Millenium (Map pp80-1; ☎ 04 91 41 38 85; 38 rue St-Saëns, 1er; metro Vieux Port; admission incl drink €20; midnight-6am Thu-Sat) Strict dress code.

Le Passe Temps (Map pp80-1; 6 rue Fortia, 1er; metro Vieux Port; 11pm-5am Wed-Sat) Small & intimate.

Pourquoi (Map pp80-1; 1 rue Fortia, 1er; metro Vieux Port; 11pm-6am)

Live Music

Docks des Suds (☎ 04 91 99 00 00, 0 825 833 833; www .dock-des-suds.org in French; 12 rue Urbain V, 2e; various admission prices; variable depending on concerts/events) Marseille's cutting-edge, hip-hop, top-of-the-pops live-music venue, near the com-

---

OM

Olympique de Marseille (OM) is not just another football team. It's an institution backed by a city full of fans who sing *'Nous sommes les Marseillais! Et nous allons gagner!'* ('We are the Marseillais! And we will win!').

Guided tours of OM's home ground, the **Stade Vélodrome** (off Map pp72-3; 3 blvd Michelet, 8e; metro rond-point du Prado), kick off from the stadium six times daily Monday to Saturday in July and August only. One-hour tours cost €6.50; reserve at the tourist office.

Built in 1930, the stadium can seat up to 60,000 screaming spectators. Within the stadium complex is the **Musée-Boutique de l'OM** (☎ 04 91 71 46 00; admission free; 2.30-7pm Mon-Sat), a museum-shop that unravels the history of the club from its creation in 1899 and sells the club's pale-blue-and-white colours. If the latter is closed, try **Virage Sud** (☎ 04 91 77 15 28; 46 blvd Michelet; 9.30am-noon & 2-6.30pm Mon-Sat), opposite the stadium.

In town, match tickets, shirts, scarves and other OM paraphernalia are sold at OM's **Boutique Officielle** (Map pp80-1; ☎ 04 91 33 52 28; 44 La Canebière, 1er; metro Noailles; 10am-7pm Mon-Sat) and **Café OM** (Map pp80-1; ☎ 04 91 33 80 33; 3 quai des Belges, 1er; metro Vieux Port; to midnight), the club café-cum-bar where supporters who fail to score a ticket can be found during matches staring agog at one of several TV screens.

OM has an official website with online boutique at www.olympiquedemarseille.com (in French) and is the second club in the world (after Manchester United's MUTV) to have its own TV channel (www.omnet-web.com/tv.html in French) that fans can pay to watch. OMTV broadcasts four hours a day (5pm to 9pm) on Canal Satellite.

mercial port. Host to, among other things, the prestigious Fiesta des Suds (see p79).

Espace Julien (Map pp72–3; ☎ 04 91 24 34 10; 39 cours Julien, 6e; metro Notre Dame du Mont-Cours Julien; admission free–€15; variable) Marseille's leading venue hosts rock concerts, opérock, alternative theatre, reggae, hip-hop, Afro-groove and other cutting-edge entertainment.

L'Intermédiaire (Map pp72–3; ☎ 04 91 47 01 25; 63 place Jean Jaurès, 6e; metro Notre Dame du Mont-Cours Julien; admission free; 6.30pm-2am Mon-Sat) Friendly, vibrant and invariably packed, the Intermediary has been around for 15-odd years and showcases everything from cover bands to blues and up-and-coming, rising-star local acts.

Pelle Mêle (Map pp80–1; ☎ 04 91 54 85 26; 8 place aux Huiles, 1er; metro Vieux Port; admission €2; 5pm-2am Tue-Sat) Jazz bistro with live bands from 10pm.

La Machine à Coudre (Map pp80–1; ☎ 04 91 55 62 65; 6 rue Jean Roque, 1er; metro Noailles) Funk, punk, blues and rap in a small street off the southern end of blvd Garibaldi.

Gay & Lesbian Venues

Gay spots include **L'Énigme** (Map pp80–1; ☎ 04 91 33 79 20; 22 rue Beauvau, 1er; metro Vieux Port; 7pm-4am), easily spotted by the signature rainbow flag outside; and nearby **MP Bar** (Map pp80–1; ☎ 04 91 33 64 79; 10 rue Beauvau, 1er; metro Vieux Port; 6pm-2am). Men are a rare breed at **Aux 3G** (Map pp72–3; ☎ 04 91 48 76 36; 3 rue St-Pierre, 5e; metro Notre Dame du Mont-Cours Julien; 6.30pm-midnight Thu & Sun, 6.30pm-2am Fri & Sat), Marseille's lesbian haunt.

Opera, Ballet & Classical Music

Opéra de Marseille (Map pp80–1; ☎ 04 91 55 11 10; http://opera.mairie-marseille.fr in French; 2 rue Molière, 1er; metro Vieux Port; tickets €8-35) Housed in an Art Deco building built in 1921; enter on place Ernest Reyer.

Théâtre Silvain (Map p76; corniche Président John F Kennedy, 7e) In June and July performances are staged beneath the stars at the Théâtre Silvain, an open-air amphitheatre midway between Plage des Catalans and Plage du Prophète.

Theatre

Théâtre National de Marseille (Map pp80–1; ☎ 04 96 17 80 00; www.theatre-lacriee.com in French; 30 quai de Rive Neuve, 7e; metro Vieux Port) Mainstream dramas are staged in Marseille's old fish-auction house, built in 1909.

Alternative performance venues include three pocket-sized places in the **Passage des Arts** (Map pp80–1; 16 quai de Rive Neuve, 7e; metro Vieux Port):

Théâtre Off (Map pp80–1; ☎ 04 91 33 12 92)
Le Quai du Rire (Map pp80–1; ☎ 04 91 54 95 00) A café-theatre where you eat and be entertained.
Théâtre Badaboum (Map pp80–1; ☎ 04 91 54 40 71)

There's also comedy theatre–restaurant **Chocolat Théâtre** (Map pp72–3; ☎ 04 91 42 19 29; www.chocolattheatre.com in French; 59 cours Julien, 6e; metro Notre Dame du Mont-Cours Julien).

Cinema

Les Variétés (Map pp80–1; ☎ 04 96 11 61 61; cesar varietes@wanadoo.fr; 37 rue Vincent Scotto, 1er; metro Noailles) and **Cinéma César** (Map pp72–3; ☎ 04 91 37 12 80; 4 place Castellane, 6e; metro Castellane) screen foreign films in their original language.

SHOPPING

La Maison du Pastis (Map pp80–1; ☎ 04 91 90 86 77; 108 quai du Port) Shop for Provence's local firewater at Marseille's House of Pastis, run by the same guys as the adjoining L'Heure Verte (p85). In all, the portside bottle shop sells 65 varieties of pastis and the more wicked and wild absinthe.

Marché aux Puces (off Map pp72–3; av du Cap Pinède, 15e; 9am-7pm Sun) Marseille's premier market, north of the centre. Live chickens killed to order and African carved animals are among the colourful sights you encounter at the indoor and outdoor stalls. Take bus No 35 or No 70 from rue des Fabres (in front of Espace Infos RTM).

Cours Julien (Map pp72–3; 6e; metro Notre Dame du Mont-Cours Julien) Hosts various morning markets: fresh flowers on Wednesday and Saturday, antique books alternate Saturdays, and stamps or antique books on Sunday.

Shop for Marseillais soaps at **Savon de Marseille** (Map pp80–1; ☎ 04 91 56 20 94; 1 rue Caisserie, 2e; metro Colbert or Vieux Port).

GETTING THERE & AWAY
Air

Aéroport Marseille-Provence (Marseille-Provence airport; ☎ 04 42 14 14 14; www.marseille.aeroport.fr) is in Marignane, 28km northwest of Marseille.

Boat

From two terminals at Marseille's **passenger ferry terminal** (Gare Maritime; Map pp72–3; ☎ 04 91 39

45 66; 23 place de la Joliette & blvd des Dames, 2e; metro Joliette), **SNCM** (Map pp72-3; ☎ 0 891 701 801; www .sncm.fr; 61 blvd des Dames, 2e; metro Joliette; ☒ 8am-6pm Mon-Fri, 8.30am-noon & 2-5.30pm Sat) operates ferries to/from Corsica, Sardinia, Tunisia and Algeria. **Algérie Ferries** (Map pp80-1; ☎ 04 91 90 89 28; 29 blvd des Dames, 2e; metro Joliette; ☒ 9-11.45am & 1-4.45pm Mon-Fri) operates boats to/from Algeria.

For more information about boat travel to and from Marseille see p355.

Bus

Most buses use the **bus station** (Map pp72-3; ☎ 04 91 08 16 40; 3 place Victor Hugo, 3e; metro Gare St-Charles) next to the train station, but some services to/from Bandol, La Ciotat and Cassis use the stop on **place Castellane** (Map pp72-3; ☎ 04 91 79 81 82; 6e; metro Castellane), south of the centre. Bus drivers sell tickets.

There are buses to/from Aix-en-Provence (€4.20, 35 minutes via the A51 *autoroute*/one hour via the N8, every 15 minutes). Nice-based **Phocéens Cars** (in Nice ☎ 04 93 85 66 61) operates regular services between Marseille and Nice (€23.50, 2¾ hours, up to three daily).

Year-round services going to/from Digne-les-Bains (€14.10, 2¼ hours) and ski-season buses to/from Pra-Loup (€25.50, 4½ hours) via Barcelonnette (€22.50, four hours) are operated by the Gap-based **Société des Cars Alpes Littoral** (SCAL; ☎ 04 92 51 06 05).

Other services include two to four buses daily to/from Cassis (€3.30, 1¼ hours), La Ciotat (€4.10, one hour to 1½ hours), Carpentras (€11.70, two hours), Cavaillon (€11.70, one hour) and Avignon (€15.24, two hours).

International routes are covered by **Euro-lines** (☎ 04 91 50 57 55) and **Intercars** (☎ 04 91 50 08 66), both at Marseille bus station.

Car & Motorcycle

Car rental agencies:
Avis (Map pp80-1; ☎ 04 91 64 71 00; Gare St-Charles, 1er) Desk in train-station building.
Europcar (Map pp80-1; ☎ 04 91 99 09 32; 7 blvd Maurice Bourdet, 1er)
Hertz (Map pp80-1; ☎ 04 91 14 04 24; 21 blvd Maurice Bourdet, 1er)

Train

From **Gare St-Charles** (Map pp80-1; metro Gare St-Charles, 1er), Marseille's central passenger train station, there are direct services to/from Aix-en-Provence (€6.10, 30 minutes, 16 to 24 daily); Avignon centre (€15.90, one hour, hourly); Nîmes (€20.50, 1¼ hours, 12 daily) via Arles (€11.90, 50 minutes); Orange (€18.90, 1½ hours, 10 daily) and others.

Over two dozen trains a day chug east along the coast on the Marseille–Vintimille (Ventimiglia in English) line, linking Marseille with Toulon (€9.70, 45 minutes to one hour), Cannes (€22.80, two hours), Antibes (€26.10, 2¼ hours), Nice (€27.30, 2½ hours), Monaco (€29.20, three hours) and Menton (€29.60, 3¼ hours). The Marseille–Hyères train (€12, 1¼ hours, four daily) stops at Cassis, La Ciotat, Bandol, Ollioules, Sanary-sur-Mer and Toulon.

For trains to other parts of France and Europe see p353.

GETTING AROUND
To/From the Airport
Shuttle buses (☎ 04 91 50 59 34) link Aéroport Marseille-Provence with Marseille's St-Charles train station (adult/six to 10 years €8.50/5). Buses to the airport leave from in front of the St-Charles train station's main entrance approximately every 20 minutes between 5.30am and 9.50pm. Journey time is 25 minutes.

Bicycle
Motorists parked with Vinci Park (below) can pick up a bicycle for free to pedal around town. **Tandem** (Map p76; ☎ 04 91 22 64 80; 6 av du Parc Borély) rents wheels near the beach.

Boat
A ferry yo-yos between the town hall on quai du Port and place aux Huiles on quai de Rive Neuve 8am to 6.30pm daily. An adult single/return fare costs €0.50/0.80 (under seven years free). Sailing time is three minutes. Tickets are available on the ferry.

Car & Motorcycle
Dead-central underground car parks run by **Vinci Park** (www.vincipark.com in French):
Bourse (Map pp80-1; rue Reine Elisabeth, 1er; metro Vieux Port; 1/24hr €1.70/12) Underneath the shopping centre.
De Gaulle (Map pp80-1; 22 place du Général de Gaulle, 1er; metro Vieux Port; 1/24hr €1.90/14; ☒ 24hr) Just off La Canebière.

MARSEILLE AREA

Public Transport

Marseille's two metro lines (Métro 1 and Métro 2), tramline and bus network are operated by RTM. Services run from around 5am to 9pm, after which metro and tram routes are covered every 15 minutes until 12.30am by surface bus Nos M1 and M2, and tramway No 68; stops are marked with fluorescent green signs reading *métro en bus.* Most 'Fluobus' night buses begin their runs in front of the **Espace Infos RTM** (Map pp80-1; ☎ 04 91 91 92 10; 6 rue des Fabres, 1er; metro Vieux Port; ⊙ 8.30am-6pm Mon-Fri, 9am-12.30pm & 2-5.30pm Sat).

A ticket for a solo/double trip costs €1.60/3.20, a 12-journeys-in-seven-days card is €10.30 and a one-day pass allowing unlimited travel is €4.50. Tickets can be used on any combination of metro, bus and tram for one hour after they've been time-stamped (aboard buses or in blue ticket distributors at tram stops and metro stations).

Taxi

Marseille Taxi (☎ 04 91 02 20 20)
Radio Taxi France (☎ 04 91 85 80 00)
Taxi Blanc Bleu (☎ 04 91 51 50 00)

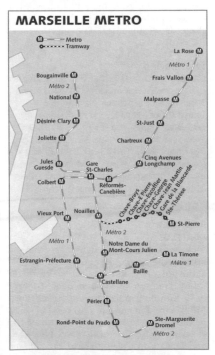

AROUND MARSEILLE

Built up as it might be, the coast around Marseille proffers a cluster of beautiful rocky inlets and coves, some superb snorkelling, delicious wines and a couple of the region's most stunning roads – guaranteed to make your heart lurch.

LES CALANQUES

Since 1975 this 20km strip of coast, and the inland Massif des Calanques covering 500 sq km, has been protected. Despite its barren landscape, the massif shelters an extraordinary wealth of flora and fauna – including 900 plant species, of which 15 are protected, such as the dwarf red behen, Marseille astragalus and tartonraire sparrow wort. The Bonnelli eagle is a frequent visitor to Les Calanques, which also shelters Europe's largest lizard and longest snake – the eyed lizard (60cm) and the Montpellier snake (2m) – in its darker cracks and crevices.

Les Calanques offers ample walking opportunities, including the coastal GR98, which leads south from the Marseille suburb of La Madrague to Callelongue on Cap Croisette, and then east along the coast to Cassis. Count on 11 to 12 hours at least to walk this 28km stretch. For bus information from Marseille to Callelongue see p77.

Boat excursions to the *calanques* leave from Marseille (see p78), Cassis (see p90) and La Ciotat in the Marseille area and from Bandol (p317) and Sanary-sur-Mer (p317) further east.

Sormiou & Morgiou

Sormiou, the largest *calanque,* hit the headlines in October 1991 when Henri Cosquer, a diver from Cassis (see p91), discovered an underwater cave. Its interior was adorned with prehistoric wall paintings from around 20,000 BC. The only access was a narrow, 150m-long passage, 36m underwater. Named the **Grotte Cosquer**, the cave is a historical monument and closed to the public. Many more are believed to exist.

To get here by car from place Louis Bonnefon (next to Château Borély) in Marseille, follow the southbound av de Hambourg past César's thumb on rond-point Pierre Guerre to chemin de Sormiou. From the end of this road, the rte du Feu forest track (a 45-minute

NO ENTRY

The threat of forest fire to the semiarid flora skirting Marseille's limestone coastline prompts the Office National des Forêts (National Forests Office) to close the *calanques* each year from 1 July until the second Saturday in September. The entire massif interior is off limits when winds blow 80km/h or more. At other times walkers can usually only access footpaths between 6am and 11am. (In 2004 it was so dry that access was restricted to 9am to 11am.) Anyone found ignoring these strict 'No Entry' rules is fined €150 on the spot.

walk) leads to Sormiou's small fishing port and beach. By bus, take No 23 from the rondpoint du Prado metro stop to La Cayolle stop, from where it is a 3km walk to Sormiou.

Sormiou and Morgiou are separated by Cap Morgiou. **Calanque de Morgiou** nestles on the eastern side of the cape. From av de Hambourg, follow the Morgiou road signs past Marseille's infamous prison in Les Beaumettes. Morgiou beach is one hour's walk from the car park. By bus, take No 23 and continue past La Cayolle. Get off at the Morgiou-Beauvallon bus stop.

En-Vau, Port-Pin & Port-Miou

Continuing east along the stone sculptured coast you come to **Calanque d'En-Vau** which, with its emerald waters encased by cliffs occasionally studded with dangling rope-clad climbers, is the most photographed *calanque*. Its entrance is guarded by the **Doigt de Dieu** (literally 'God's Finger'), a giant rock pinnacle, and its beach is pebbly. En-Vau is accessible by foot. There is a marked three-hour trail starting from the car park on the Col de la Gardiole (south off the D559), 5km west from Cassis on a wiggly dirt road into Forêt de la Gardiole. Approaching from the east, it is a good 1½-hour walk on the GR98 from Port-Miou. En route you pass the neighbouring **Calanque de Port-Pin**, a 30-minute walk from Port-Miou. In summer boats sail from Cassis to En-Vau.

Calanque de Port-Miou, immediately west of Cassis, is one of the few inlets accessible by car; the tourist office in Cassis distributes free maps featuring the three *calanques* plus the various walking trails that lead to them.

CASSIS

pop 8070

Sweet Cassis is known for its white wines, of which Provençal poet Frédéric Mistral wrote 'the bee does not have a sweeter honey, it shines like an untroubled diamond'. Quality aside, the neat picture postcard of Cassis' terraced vineyards, which climb up the slopes in little steps against a magnificent backdrop of sea and cliffs, can hardly be disputed.

Cassis (pronounced 'ca-see') has nothing to do with the blackcurrant liqueur (pronounced 'ca-sees') that is mixed with white wine to create a kir apéritif.

Orientation

Cassis train station is 3.5km east of the centre on av de la Gare. Buses stop at rondpoint du Pressoir, five minutes' walk along av du Professeur René Leriche and rue de l'Arène to the port. The old town surrounds the port. Its 14th-century chateau, now privately owned and closed to visitors, peers down on the port from a rocky outcrop. Quai St-Pierre, from where boat trips depart, runs alongside the port to the beach, the sandy Plage de la Grande Mer. Pebbly Plage de Bestouan is 700m northwest of the port.

Information

Côté C@ssis (☎ 04 42 01 10 64; www.cote-cassis.fr.st in French; 9 rue Victor Authemann; ☽ 9.15am-12.30pm & 3-7pm) Wash (clothes) and surf (the Internet).

Tourist Office (☎ 08 92 25 98 92; www.cassis.fr; quai des Moulins; ☽ 9am-7pm Mon-Fri, 9.30am-12.30pm & 3-6pm Sat & Sun Jul & Aug, 9am-12.30pm & 2-6.30pm Mon-Fri, 9.30am-12.30pm & 3-6pm Sat, 10am-noon Sun Jun & Sep, slightly shorter hr Oct-Apr) In Oustaou Calendal, a reconstruction of the portside casino where fortunes were won and lost following its opening in 1951.

Activities

BOATING

Tickets for the 15-odd daily boats that sail around the *calanques* year-round are sold at the portside **kiosk** (☎ 04 42 01 90 83; www.cassis -calanques.com; sq Gilbert Savon) on quai St-Pierre. A 45-minute trip to three *calanques* (Port-Miou, Port-Pin and En-Vau) costs €11/6.50 per adult/two to 10 years; a 65-minute trip covering these three *calanques* plus Oule and Devanson Calanques is €13/9.50; and a 1½-hour trip covering seven *calanques* (including Morgiou) costs €16/12.50. You can't pay by credit card.

In addition to the circular boat trips, you can disembark at En-Vau (return adult/two to 10 years €15/12), spend a couple of hours on the beach, and return to Cassis on a later boat. The walk from the boat to the beach is a 200m scramble across rocks, not recommended for young children.

Boats of all shapes and sizes can be hired from **Loca'Bato** (☎ 04 42 01 27 04; impasse du Grand Carnot).

DIVING
Diving expeditions are organised by the **Cassis Services Plongée** (☎ 04 42 01 89 16; www.cassis-services-plongee.fr; 3 rue Michel Arnaud), a school run by Henri Cosquer (see p89), who leads everything from baptism/regular dives (€55/45 including equipment) to night dives and shipwreck expeditions.

WINE TASTING
There is no better time to taste the local *vin* than at the annual **Fête des Vendanges et du Vin Cassis**, which marks the grape harvest on the first Sunday in September. Failing that, you can visit one of the 14 wine-producing estates that produce the Cassis appellation (AOC); the tourist office has a list and suggested itineraries. Cassis white is particularly fine drunk with sea urchins (see p93).

NATURALLY BEAUTIFUL

One of Europe's highest maritime cliffs, the imposing 416m-high **Cap Canaille**, dominates the southwest side of **Baie de Cassis** (Cassis Bay). The hollow peak of the rocky limestone cape hides **Grotte des Espagnols** (Spaniards' Cave), a fantastic cave (closed to visitors) filled with a magical assortment of stalactites and stalagmites. From the cliff there are magnificent views of Cassis and **Mt Puget** (565m), the highest peak in the Massif des Calanques.

An equally awesome panorama unfolds as you drive along the well-maintained but more-wiggly-than-wiggly **rte des Crêtes** (literally 'road of crests') that leads 16km from Cassis, along the top of its cliff-caked coastline, to La Ciotat.

Sleeping & Eating
Le Jardin d'Émile (☎ 04 42 01 80 55; www.lejardin demile.fr; d €100-130, menus €25 & €37; P ⚡) Set beneath trees opposite Plage de Bestouan, Emily's Garden has seven classy rooms, some with sea views and some with garden views, and a chef who brews a delicious bouillabaisse (around €40); it must be ordered in advance.

La Bastidaine (☎ 04 42 98 83 09; www.labastidaine.com; 6b av des Albizzi; B&B €69-89, evening meal €22; P ⚡) Should a centuries-old wine grower's house be your preference, then this delightful four-room *chambre d'hôte* (B&B), 1.5km from the centre, will charm your socks off. Better still, the hosts cook up enticing evening meals accompanied by local Cassis wine.

Auberge de Jeunesse (☎ 04 42 01 02 72; dm with/without HI card €8.70/11.60; ⏰ reception 8-10am & 5-9pm Mar-Dec) Isolated in the heart of the Massif des Calanques, 4km west of Cassis centre, this 60-bed hostel has no running water (hence no showers), relies on the sun and wind for its electricity, is one hour's walk from the nearest road – and you have to bring your own food. By car, follow the signs off the D559 from Marseille, park in Port-Miou, then follow the trail from av des Calanques. Families note: kids aged under seven aren't allowed to stay here.

Getting There & Around
Cassis is on the Bandol–Marseille (five daily) and La Ciotat–Aix-en-Provence (three to 12 daily) bus routes; see www.lepilote.com (in French) for schedules.

Cassis train station is on the Marseille–Hyères rail line and there are regular daily trains in both directions including to/from La Ciotat (€2.10, six minutes), Bandol (€4.20, 18 minutes), Marseille (€4.50, 22 minutes) and Toulon (€6.50, 30 minutes).

Bus Nos 2, 3 and 4 link Cassis train station with the town centre (€1.30, 10 minutes, at least hourly).

LA CIOTAT
pop 30,620
The rusty old cranes cranked up over the once-prosperous naval shipyards of La Ciotat, 16km east of Cassis, lost their gleam long ago. La Ciotat's quaint old port – a favourite of Georges Braque (1892–1963), who painted it several times – faces the

now-defunct yards and the rocky 155m-high **Bec d'Aigle** (literally 'eagle's beak') on Cap de l'Aigle rises above them. The whole ensemble, protected by the Parc Marin de La Ciotat, is best viewed from **Île Verte** (Green Island), a minuscule island offshore from the cape's southeastern tip, which can be visited by boat.

La Ciotat **tourist office** (☎ 04 42 08 61 32; www .laciotatourisme.com in French; blvd Anatole France; ☯ 9am-8pm Mon-Fri, 10am-1pm Sun, shorter hr low season) sits on the headland separating the old port from the yacht-filled pleasure port and La Ciotat's wide sandy beaches.

Maritime history is not the only topic covered in the **Musée du Vieux Ciotat** (☎ 04 42 71 40 99; 1 quai Ganteaume; adult/child €3.20/1.60; ☯ 4-7pm Wed-Mon Jun-Sep, 3-6pm Wed-Mon Oct-May). The history museum also tells the tale of bowls player Jules Le Noir, who invented Provence's favourite game (see p30), and of the pioneering Lumière brothers, who chose La Ciotat to shoot the world's first motion picture (see p50).

The history of that film – *L'Arrivée d'un Train en Gare de La Ciotat* (The Arrival of a Train at La Ciotat Station) – comes to life at the **Espace Simon-Lumière** (☎ 04 42 71 61 70; 20 rue du Maréchal Foch; admission free; ☯ 3-6pm Tue-Sat), an exhibition hall dedicated to filmography and the Swiss-born film icon Michel Simon (1895–1975), who lived in La Ciotat. On the seafront, film buffs can see the world's oldest cinema, the **Eden Théâtre** (blvd Georges Clemenceau), currently being restored, where the Lumières screened many films from 1899.

The old port quays host a **market** (food, clothes, baskets etc) on Tuesday mornings and an evening **arts and crafts market** on Saturdays, late June to early September.

Getting There & Around

From La Ciotat train station, a 5km trek from the centre, there are trains on the Marseille–Hyères line (see p91).

The **bus station** (☎ 04 42 08 90 90; blvd Anatole France) adjoins the tourist office. **Ciotàbus** (☎ 04 42 08 41 05, 0 800 199 413; ☯ 9am-12.30pm & 1.30-7pm Mon-Fri, 8.45am-12.30pm & 1.30-7pm Sat), at the bus station, doles out bus information. Online go to www.lepilote.com (in French).

In season, kid-friendly, feet-kind **Les Petits Trains des Lumières** (☎ 06 60 51 23 17; adult/under 12 yrs €6/3) departs hourly from in front of the tourist office for a 45-minute tour of town.

Electric trains follow two different routes along the coast.

Boats (☎ 04 42 83 11 44, 06 63 59 16 35; adult/under 10 yrs return €7/3; ☯ departures hourly 9am-noon & 2-6pm May, Jun & Sep, every 30 min 9am-7pm Jul & Aug) to Île Verte arrive and depart from quai Général de Gaulle at the old port. On weekends a boat departs at 7am for fishermen; book in advance.

AUBAGNE
pop 43,083

Marcel Pagnol's home town lies on the easternmost fringe of Marseille, 14km inland. Although the writer moved to Marseille proper when he was two, he evoked 19th-century Aubagne's brick-and-tile factories in many of his works. A guided tour run by the **tourist office** (☎ 04 42 03 49 98; www.aubagne .com/tourisme; av Antide Boyur; ☯ 9am-noon & 2-6pm Mon-Sat) follows his trail.

The primary reason to visit this otherwise unmomentous town is for its **Biennale de l'Art Santonnier** (see Little Saints, p102) or neighbouring **Massif de la Ste-Baume** (see A Pilgrim's Detour, opposite).

ÉTANG DE BERRE

Some 24 million tons (30% of French production) of petrol a year are processed at oil refineries in the port area around the waters of the Étang de Berre. **Marignane** (pop 34,238), on its southeastern shore, is dominated by Marseille-Provence airport. **Istres**, on the western shore of the Étang de Berre, is known for its military airport, here since 1914.

This vast industrial landscape can be scowled at from the ruins of an 11th-century Saracen tower, bizarrely perched on top of a rock in **Vitrolles** (pop 37,087). Across the waters, the Canal de Caronte links the fishing port of **Martigues** (pop 44,256), on the southwestern corner of the Étang de Berre, with Golfe de Fos in the Mediterranean. It is from Martigues that the French flag originates. Martigues' **tourist office** (☎ 04 42 42 31 10; ot.martigues@visitprovence.com; 2 quai Paul Doumer) has more information.

Unattractive **Fos-sur-Mer** (pop 14,732) sits at the helm of this industrial heartland, where the Solomat-Merex industrial waste processing plant, a Shell oil refinery, Total-FinaElf's chlorine and sodium works, and the distillation site of petroleum magnate Esso can all be found. The **tourist office** (☎ 04

42 47 71 96; place de l'Hôtel de Ville; ⊗ 8.30am-noon & 1.30-5pm Mon-Fri, 8.30am-noon Sat) arranges lake tours with industrial views.

Pockets of crystal-clear water still exist thanks to the **Chaîne de l'Estaque**, an uninhabitable massif that forms a natural blockade between the industrial Étang de Berre and the Mediterranean. The rocky limestone coastal stretch on the protected southern side of the massif from Cap Couronne to Marseille is known **La Côte Bleue** (the Blue Coast).

Cap Couronne & Carry-le-Rouet

From Martigues the D5 leads 10km south to **Cap Couronne**, a sandy cape that draws plenty of Marseillais at weekends. The waters around it, rich in marine life, are protected by the **Parc Régional Marin de la Côte Bleue** (☎ 04 42 45 45 07, 06 83 09 38 42; http://perso.wanadoo.fr/parc marin in French), marked out with yellow buoys topped with St-Andrew's Crosses. In July and August the park authority organises one-hour **snorkelling** sessions (free), open to anyone aged eight or over, aimed at discovering marine fauna and flora.

A unique gastronomic delight – *oursins* (sea urchins) – can be sampled in **Carry-le-Rouet** (population 6107), a harbour town favoured by French comic actor Fernandel in the 1930s. The prickly little creatures can only be caught between September and April; fishing for them in summer when they reproduce is forbidden.

Each year, on the first three Sundays of February, Carry-le-Rouet celebrates **L'Oursinade**, a sea-urchin festival which sees a giant open-air picnic spill across the old-port quays. Restaurants and hotels set up stalls selling urchins, allowing everyone to taste the delicacy around shared tables. The so-called *châtaignes de mer* (sea chestnuts) are best served with chilled Cassis white wine. For more details contact the **tourist office** (☎ 04 42 13 20 36; www.carry-lerouet.com in French; av Aristide Briand; ⊗ 10am-noon & 2-5pm Tue-Sat).

L'Estaque

Lying 17km east of Carry-le-Rouet is **L'Estaque**, a once-untouched fishing village butting onto Marseille's northern suburbs which, like St-Tropez, lured artists from the impressionist, Fauvist and cubist movements; Marseille's tourist office has information on the fascinating artists' trails that follow in the footsteps of Renoir, Cézanne, Dufy and Braque around L'Estaque.

A PILGRIM'S DETOUR

From Aubagne follow the eastbound D2 for 5km to **Gémenos**. In the village stay on the D2, following the signs for 'Vallée St-Pons & La Ste-Baume'. Should you be hungry for coffee or lunch, stop at **Le Moulin de Gémenos** (☎ 04 42 32 22 26; rte de St-Pons; menu €16; ⊗ lunch Tue-Fri & Sun), a rambling stone mill hidden behind trees on the eastern fringe of the village. Then continue past Gémenos' outdoor **Théâtre de Verdure** (☎ 04 42 32 89 00; rte de St-Pons), where the annual **Les Arts Verts** world music festival is held from June to mid-August, for a couple of kilometres.

The going now gets green and dramatic, the smooth tarmac road wiggling uphill through the **Parc Départemental de St-Pons**, whose dry scrubby terrain is protected by the same fire regulations as Les Calanques'. After 8km, just as the sea pops up on the horizon, the road narrows and loses its smooth surface. A kilometre and several hairpins later, the road markings return for the final 2km climb to the **Col de l'Espigouler** (725m), a mountain pass with dramatic coastline views.

The winding descent down is dominated by the **Massif de la Ste-Baume**, a hulk of a mountain with rolling ridged sides and a 12km-long shelf-like top. After a couple of kilometres the breathtaking vistas disappear and signs of habitation start to appear. At the D45a/D2 junction, continue on the D2 through **Plan d 'Aups** (2km) to **La Ste-Baume** (8km), home to the **Ecomusée de la Ste-Baume** (☎ 04 42 62 56 46; ⊗ 9am-noon & 2-6pm mid-Apr–Oct, 1.30-5.30pm Nov–mid-Apr), where local flora, fauna and geology can be discovered; and the **Hôtellerie de la Ste-Baume** (☎ 04 42 04 54 85; dm/s/d/tr €9/18.50/25/33, breakfast/picnic/dinner €3.50/8/12; P), where pilgrims stay. From here a 40-minute path through forest leads to the **Grotte de Ste-Madeleine** (950m), a cave in the mountain where Mary Magdalene is said to have spent the last years of her life. Daily mass is celebrated here at 10.30am. Before entering take in the breathtaking panorama of Provence: Montagne Ste-Victoire, Mont Ventoux and the alps.

Snacks, just made for munching during a water's-edge stroll, are *chichi frégi* (sugar-coated doughnuts) and *panisses* (chickpeaflour cakes). Kiosks around the harbour sell both.

Getting There & Away

Bus No 34 links Marseille's bus station with Martigues (€6, one hour, hourly). A couple of buses a day continue to Fos-sur-Mer.

From Marseille more than a dozen daily trains (less in winter) trundle along La Côte Bleue stopping at L'Estaque (€2.10, 8 minutes), Carry-le-Rouet (€4.30, 25 minutes), La Couronne (€5.70, 35 minutes) and Port de Bouc (€7.20, 55 minutes), from where the train line heads inland to Miramas (€7.90, 1¼ hours), on the northern shore of the Étang de Berre.

SALON DE PROVENCE
pop 38,137

Salon de Provence, about 15km north of the Étang de Berre and 35km west of Aix, is known for its olive oil and *savon de Marseille* (Marseille soap) industry. Medieval Salon served as the residence of the Arles archbishops, and the philosopher Nostradamus (1503–66) lived and died here.

Since 1936 France's military flying school, the École de l'Air et École Militaire de l'Air, has been stationed here, although it is practically impossible to catch the Patrouille Aérienne de France – France's equivalent of the UK's Red Arrows – in action. The school is closed to the public and France's aerial acrobatic showmasters are invariably on tour; ask at the **tourist office** (☎ 04 90 56 27 60; 56 cours Gimon; ⊙ 9.30am-12.30pm & 2-6pm Mon-Sat) for an update.

Sights

A giant, moss-covered mushroom of a fountain, **Fontaine Moussue** (place Crousillat), dominates Salon's prettiest square, which is tucked outside the walled old city opposite the **Tour de l'Horloge** (clock tower; 1626).

Inside the pedestrian Vieille Ville (old city), rue de l'Horloge leads to place de l'Ancienne Halle, a large square from which rue Nostradamus leads to the **Maison de Nostradamus** (☎ 04 90 56 64 31; 11 rue Nostradamus; adult/

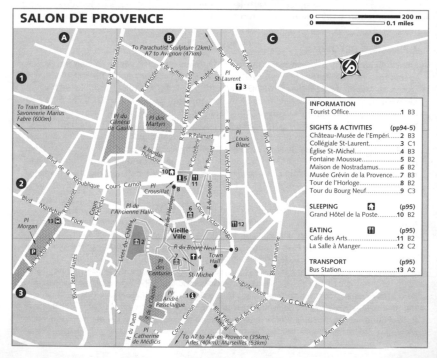

SALON DE PROVENCE

0 ——— 200 m
0 ——— 0.1 miles

To Parachutist Sculpture (2km);
A7 to Avignon (47km)

To Train Station;
Savonnerie Marius
Fabre (600m)

To A7 to Aix-en-Provence (35km);
Arles (40km); Marseilles (53km)

INFORMATION	
Tourist Office...........................1 B3	

SIGHTS & ACTIVITIES	(pp94-5)
Château-Musée de l'Empéri......2 B3	
Collégiale St-Laurent................3 C1	
Église St-Michel.......................4 B3	
Fontaine Moussue....................5 B2	
Maison de Nostradamus...........6 B2	
Musée Grévin de la Provence....7 B3	
Tour de l'Horloge.....................8 B2	
Tour du Bourg Neuf..................9 C3	

SLEEPING	(p95)
Grand Hôtel de la Poste...........10 B2	

EATING	(p95)
Café des Arts.........................11 B2	
La Salle à Manger...................12 C2	

TRANSPORT	(p95)
Bus Station...........................13 A2	

under 7 yrs €3.05/2.30; ☺ 9am-noon & 2-6pm Mon-Fri, 2-6pm Sat & Sun). The philosopher lived here from 1547 until his death in 1566. He is buried in a side chapel inside **Collégiale St-Laurent** (place St-Laurent), an imposing church built in 1344.

From the southern end of place del' Ancienne Halle, steps lead to the **Château-Musée de l'Empéri** (☎ 04 90 56 22 36; place du Château; adult/7-18 yrs €3.05/2.30; ☺ 10am-noon & 2-6pm Wed-Mon Dec-May, Sep & Oct, 10am-6pm Wed-Mon Jul & Aug), home to the archbishops of Arles from the 9th to the 18th centuries. Some 30 of its spacious medieval halls are filled with over 10,000 exhibits dedicated to French military history up to WWI.

Local lore and legend is unravelled with 54 life-size waxworks at the **Musée Grévin de la Provence** (☎ 04 90 56 36 30; m-grevin@salon-de .provence.org; place des Centuries; adult/7-18 yrs €3.05/2.30; ☺ 9am-noon & 2-6pm Mon & Wed-Fri, 2-6pm Sat & Sun). A combination ticket for the Musée Grévin and Maison de Nostradamus costs €5.35/3.05 per adult/seven to 18 years.

Tour du Bourg Neuf, at the eastern end of rue du Bourg Neuf, is part of the fortified ramparts built around the city in the 12th century. In the 13th century, young women wanting to conceive venerated the statue of the Black Virgin tucked in the gate. A rare treat is the solemn **Gregorian chants** sung at Sunday Mass (9am) in the 13th-century **Église St-Michel** (place St-Michel) on the first and third Sunday of the month, September to June.

One of Salon's two remaining *savonneries* (soap factories), the **Savonnerie Marius Fabre** (☎ 04 90 53 24 77; www.marius-fabre.fr; 148 av Paul Borret; adult/15-18 yrs €3.85/1.95; ☺ guided tours 10.30am Mon & Thu), can be toured. The factory produces 100 tonnes of soap a year. Exit the train station, turn right along av Émile Zola, left along blvd Maréchal Foch, then right onto av Paul Borret.

The **parachutist sculpture**, 2km from Salon de Provence on the northbound N538 (N7), is a memorial to French Resistance leader Jean Moulin (1899–1943), who landed here in 1942 – a year before his arrest and death at the hands of the Gestapo – to rally together organised Resistance in southern France.

Sleeping & Eating

Grand Hôtel de la Poste (☎ 04 90 56 01 94; 1 rue des Frères J & R Kennedy; d with shower/shower & toilet €34/40) This serviceable town-house hotel overlooks the Tour de l'Horloge, present-ing guests in some rooms with a nice wet, mossy outlook.

La Salle à Manger (☎ 04 90 56 28 01; 6 rue du Maréchal Joffre; 2-course lunch/dinner menu €15/23; ☺ lunch & dinner Tue-Sat) The Dining Room is a 19th-century *hôtel particulier* wrapped around a secret garden where diners sip apéritifs accompanied by a lavender dip. The icing on the cake is the choice of 40 desserts; for a typical taste of Provence take the thyme, lavender and rosemary sorbet.

Café des Arts (☎ 04 90 56 00 07; place des Arts; lunch formule €13.50; ☺ lunch & dinner) With a terrace overlooking Salon's famous fountain, this bistro is a busy lunch spot. Meats are grilled *au feu de bois* (over a wood fire) and come with a tasty choice of *tapenade* (olive-based dip), onion chutney or *pistou* (basil, garlic and olive oil).

Getting There & Away

From the **bus station** (☎ 04 90 56 50 98; cnr blvd Maréchal Foch & blvd Victor Joly) there are daily services to/from Aix-en-Provence (€4.90, 35 minutes, up to 12 daily) and Arles (€4.90, 1¼ hours, eight daily Monday to Saturday, two a day Sunday).

The **train station** (av Émile Zola) is a 1km-walk from town. There are eight or so trains a day to/from Marseille (€9.30, 1½ hours) and Avignon (€8.10, 40 minutes).

PAYS D'AIX

What with the awe and esteem in which elegant Aix is held, not to mention the gastronomically and artistically rich pageant of land surrounding the city, Pays d'Aix – meaning 'Aix country' – really is top dog of this Marseillais region.

AIX-EN-PROVENCE

pop 134,222 / elevation 206m

Snooty Aix is jolly lucky that it wasn't called Sex, given its wet origins as a military camp under the name Aquae Sextiae (the Waters of Sextius), settled in 123 BC on the site of thermal springs which still flow. Under the enlightened King René (1409–80) the city peaked as a centre of art and learning. Home to the University of Aix-Marseille, it remains an academic centre.

Aix's graceful squares and avenues are studded with 200-odd elegant *hôtels*

MARSEILLE AREA

AIX-EN-PROVENCE

0 — 200 m
0 — 0.1 miles

INFORMATION
Book in Bar..................................1 C5
Hub Lot Cybercafé.......................2 C3
L'Agence......................................3 B5
Laundrette...................................4 D4
Laundrette...................................5 A4
Laundrette...................................6 A4
Laundrette...................................7 C3
Maison de la Nature et de
    l'Environnement.......................8 B5
Net Games...................................9 B4
Paradox.....................................10 A5
Police..11 A5
Post Office..................................12 A5
Tourist Office..............................13 B5

SIGHTS & ACTIVITIES   (pp97-8)
Cathédrale St-Sauveur................14 B2
Église St-Jean de Malte...............15 D5
Fontaine d'Eau Thermale.............16 C5
Fontaine de la Rotonde...............17 C4
Fontaine du Roi René...................18 C4

Former University
    Building.................................19 B3
Galerie d'Art du Conseil Général des
    Bouches du Rhône...................20 B5
Musée d'Histoire Naturelle...........21 C4
Musée des Tapisseries.................22 B2
Musée du Vieil Aix......................23 B4
Musée Granet.............................24 D5
Musée Paul Arbaud.....................25 C5
Palais de Justice.........................26 C4
Pavillon de Vendôme...................27 A3
Pétanque Pitch...........................28 C6
Thermes Sextius.........................29 A3

SLEEPING   (p99)
Grand Hôtel Nègre Coste..............30 C4
Hôtel Cardinal............................31 C5
Hôtel Cardinal (Annexe)...............32 D5
Hôtel des Augustins....................33 B5
Hôtel des Quatre Dauphins...........34 C5
Hôtel La Caravelle.......................35 D5
Hôtel Le Manoir..........................36 A4

EATING   (pp99-100)
Béchard.....................................37 B5
Brémond....................................38 D5
Charlotte....................................39 A4
Icône...40 C5
Jacquèrres..................................41 B4
La Truffe Cendrée........................42 B4
Le Comptoir des Oliviers...............43 B3
Le Formal...................................44 B4
Le Passage.................................45 B4
Le Zinc d'Hugo...........................46 B4
Leonard Parli..............................47 B6
Monoprix...................................48 B5
Place aux Huiles.........................49 B5
Yôji...50 B5

DRINKING   (p100)
Les Deux Garçons.......................51 C4
L'Orienthé.................................52 B5

ENTERTAINMENT   (p101)
Bar Sextius................................53 A4
Chapelle de Ste-Catherine............54 C3
Ciné Mazarin..............................55 B5
Cinéma Renoir............................56 C5
Église Ste-Marie Madeleine..........57 C4
La Belle Époque..........................58 C4
Le Cézanne................................59 B5
Le Scat Club..............................60 B4
Théâtre du Jeu de Paume.............61 D4

SHOPPING   (pp101-2)
Savon de Marseille......................62 B4

TRANSPORT   (pp102-3)
Aix en Bus Point Accueil.............(see 13)
Bus Station................................63 A6
Cycles Zammit............................64 C3
Trott' Aix..................................65 A4

particuliers and a rash of fountains. Tree-shaded cours Mirabeau is described by many as Provence's most beautiful street.

Orientation
Cours Mirabeau stretches from La Rotonde – a roundabout with a huge fountain on place du Général de Gaulle – east to place Forbin. Vieil Aix (Old Aix) is north of cours Mirabeau. South of cours Mirabeau is the Mazarin quarter, whose regular street grid was laid out in the 17th century. A series of one-way boulevards rings the entire city centre.

Information
BOOKSHOPS
Book in Bar (☎ 04 42 26 60 07; 1bis rue Cabassol; ☾ 9am-7pm Mon-Sat) Excellent English-language bookshop and reading café.
Paradox (☎ 04 42 26 47 99; 15 rue du 4 Septembre; ☾ 10am-12.30pm & 2-6.30pm Mon-Sat) English books and British groceries.

EMERGENCY
Police (☎ 04 42 91 91 11; place B Niollon)

INTERNET ACCESS
Hub Lot Cybercafé (☎ 04 42 21 37 31; 15-27 rue Paul Bert; per min €0.06; ☾ 8am-midnight) WiFi access, helpful service from the English owner and a sometimes lively bar.
Net Games (www.netgames.fr in French; 52 rue de l'Aumône Vieille; 10/30/60 min €1/2/3; ☾ 10am-midnight) Vast place packed with game-addicted teens.

INTERNET RESOURCES
Mairie-aixenprovence (www.mairie-aixenprovence.fr in French) Official city website.

LAUNDRY
There are laundrettes at 3 rue de la Fontaine, 34 cours Sextius, 3 rue de la Fonderie and 60 rue Boulegon; open 7am or 8am to 8pm.

MEDICAL SERVICES
Hospital (Centre Hospitalier Général du Pays d'Aix; ☎ 04 42 33 50 00; av des Tamaris)

MONEY
Find commercial banks on the southern side of cours Mirabeau and along cours Sextius.
L'Agence (☎ 04 42 26 84 77; 15 cours Mirabeau) Amex agent.

POST
Post Office (sq Mattéi)

VISA FOR AIX

Buy a €2 *Visa pour le Pays d'Aix* from any tourist office to get a stack of discounts on admission fees, transport tickets, guided tours and the like in and around Aix.

TOURIST INFORMATION
Maison de la Nature et de l'Environnement (☎ 04 42 93 15 80; 2 place Jeanne d'Arc; ☾ 10am-12.30pm & 2-6pm Mon-Fri) Green source for information on the environment and ways to explore it (nature walks, discovering Mediterranean flora and so on).
Tourist Office (☎ 04 42 16 11 61; www.aixenprovencetourism.com; 2 place du Général de Gaulle; ☾ 8.30am-9pm Jul & Aug, 8.30am-7pm Mon-Sat, 10am-1pm & 2-6pm Sun Sep-Jun)

Sights & Activities
Keen to escape the crowds? Take a leafy stroll to **Parc Jourdan**, a spacious green area dominated by Aix's largest fountain, home to the city's primary **pétanque pitch** and host to various cultural events (see p101). Peaceful moments can also be enjoyed around the **Pavillon de Vendôme** (☎ 04 42 21 05 78; 32 rue Célony; ☾ 10am-12.30pm & 1.30-5.30pm Wed-Mon), an 18th-century house framed by manicured French gardens. Inside are contemporary and digital art exhibitions.

COURS MIRABEAU
Aix's social scene centres on cours Mirabeau, laid out during the latter half of the 1600s and crowned by a rooftop of green plane trees. Renaissance *hôtels particuliers* line its shady southern side, and trendy cafés adorned with young beauties basking in the shade of their sunglasses spill across pavements on the sunny northern side.

Art and photography exhibitions are held in the **Galerie d'Art du Conseil Général des Bouches du Rhône** (☎ 04 42 93 03 67; 21bis cours Mirabeau; admission free; ☾ 10.30am-1pm & 2-7pm). The cast-iron fountain at the western end of cours Mirabeau, **Fontaine de la Rotonde** (1860), personifies justice, agriculture and fine arts. **Fontaine du Roi René** (1819) at the avenue's eastern end on place Forbin is decorated with a 19th-century statue of King René holding a bunch of Muscat grapes, a variety he is credited with introducing to the region. Moss-covered **Fontaine d'Eau Chaude** (cnr cours Mirabeau & rue Clémenceau) spouts 34°C water.

MAZARIN QUARTER & VIEIL AIX

The Mazarin quarter is known for its aristocratic 17th- and 18th-century town houses. Streets and squares to stroll include **rue Mazarine**, south of cours Mirabeau; **place des 4 Dauphins**, two blocks further south; **rue de l'Opéra**, east of cors Mirabeau; and stunning, cobbled **place d'Albertas**, created just west of place St-Honoré for the Marquis d'Albertas in 1745. On Sunday don't miss a jaunt to **place de l'Hôtel de Ville**, where the city's brass band blasts out tunes. From here rue Gaston de Saporta leads to **Cathédrale St-Sauveur**, opposite the **former university** (1741).

CATHÉDRALE ST-SAUVEUR

Aix's **cathedral** (rue Gaston de Saporta) incorporates architectural features representing every major period from the 5th to the 18th centuries. The main Gothic structure, built from 1285 to 1350, includes the Romanesque nave of a 12th-century church as part of its southern aisle. The chapels were added in the 14th and 15th centuries. There is a 5th-century sarcophagus in the apse. Soulful Gregorian chants and organ concerts are sometimes held here.

The 15th-century Triptyque du Buisson Ardent (Triptych of the Burning Bush) in the nave is by Nicolas Froment. It is usually only opened for groups. Nearby is a triptych panel illustrating Christ's passion. The tapestries encircling the choir date from the 18th century, and the fabulous gilt organ is baroque.

FONDATION VASARELY

The **Fondation Vasarely** (☎ 04 42 20 01 09; 1 av Marcel Pagnol; adult/7-18 yrs €7/4; ☒ 10am-1pm & 2-7pm Mon-Fri, 10am-7pm Sat & Sun) is 4km west of town. It is the creation of Hungarian-born artist Victor Vasarely, the 'father of Op Art', who cheered up grey urban areas with huge, colourful works that integrated art with architecture. Vasarely's works are displayed here in 14 hexagonal spaces, recognisable by their contrasting black-and-white geometrical designs. Take bus No 4 from La Rotonde to the Vasarely stop.

TRAILING PAUL CÉZANNE

Cézanne (1839–1906), Aix's most celebrated son (at least after his death), did much of his painting in and around the city. If you're interested in the minute details of his day-to-day life, follow the **Circuit de Cézanne** around

town; ask at the tourist office for the relevant brochure. Cézanne was a close friend of the French novelist Émile Zola (1840–1902), who also spent his youth in Aix; the tourist office has details on following his footsteps, too.

Cézanne's last studio, on a hill 1.5km north of the tourist office, is as it was when he died. Although none of his works are displayed in the **Atelier Paul Cézanne** (☎ 04 42 21 06 53; www.atelier-cezanne.com; 9 av Paul Cézanne; adult/under 16 yrs €5.50/free; ☒ 10am-6pm Jul & Aug, 10am-noon & 2-5 or 6pm Sep-Jun), his tools are. In July and August the tourist office organises gastronomic and literary evenings here.

Take bus No 1 from the St-Christophe stop near the Rotonde to the Cézanne stop.

THERMES SEXTIUS

Enjoy Aix's sexy past at **Thermes Sextius** (☎ 04 42 23 81 82; www.thermes-sextius.com; 55 cours Sextius), a spa built on the site of the thermal springs that soothed weary feet in Roman Aquae Sextiae in the 1st century BC. The excavated remains of the Roman spa are displayed beneath glass in reception.

MUSEUMS

Aix's finest, the **Musée Granet** (☎ 04 42 38 14 70; place St-Jean de Malte), in a 17th-century priory of the knights of Malta, was closed for renovation until 2006 at the time of research.

An unexceptional collection of historical artefacts is displayed in the **Musée du Vieil Aix** (☎ 04 42 21 43 55; 17 rue Gaston de Saporta; adult/14-18 yrs €4/2.50; ☒ 10am-noon & 2-5pm Tue-Sun Nov-Mar, 10am-noon & 2.30-6pm Tue-Sun Apr-Oct).

The **Musée des Tapisseries** (Tapestry Museum; ☎ 04 42 23 09 91; 28 place des Martyrs de la Résistance; adult/under 25 yrs €2/free; ☒ 10-11.45am & 2-5.45pm Wed-Mon) is in a former archbishop's palace. Books, manuscripts and Provençal faïence (earthenware) fill the **Musée Paul Arbaud** (☎ 04 42 38 38 95; musee.arbaud@free.fr; 2a rue du 4 Septembre; adult/under 10 yrs €2.50/free; ☒ 2-5pm Mon-Sat).

Montagne Ste-Victoire geology is unearthed at the **Musée d'Histoire Naturelle** (Natural History Museum; ☎ 04 42 27 91 27; www.museumaix .fr.st in French; 6 rue Espariat; adult/under 25 yrs €2/free; ☒ 10am-noon & 1-5pm Mon-Sat).

Tours

The tourist office runs thematic walking tours (adult/six to 25 years €8/4), many of them in English. From April to mid-October it runs bus excursions too.

Festivals & Events

The most sought-after tickets in Aix's sumptuous cultural calendar are for July's **Festival d'Aix-en-Provence** (Festival International d'Art Lyrique d'Aix-en-Provence; www.festival-aix.com), which brings drama and theatre to the city.

Other festivals include **Danse à Aix** in January and May; the two-day **Festival du Tambourin** (Tambourine Festival) in mid-April; the **Aix Jazz Festival** and **Les Festes d'Orphée**, a baroque music festival, in July; the **Fête Mistralienne**, which marks the birthday of Provençal hero Frédéric Mistral on 13 September; and the solemn **Bénédiction des Calissons**, held the same month in Église St-Jean de Malte.

Aix's **Fête de l'Huile d'Olive Nouvelle et de la Truffe**, held on place Jeanne d'Arc in December, marks the season's new olive oil.

Sleeping

The tourist office's **reservation centre** (☎ 04 42 16 11 84/85; resaix@aixenprovencetourism.com) can tell you what's available where.

BUDGET

Auberge de Jeunesse du Jas de Bouffan (☎ 04 42 20 15 99; fax 04 42 59 36 12; 3 av Marcel Pagnol; dm incl breakfast €15; ◌ mid-Jan–mid-Dec) A hop, skip and jump from Vasarely's striking handiwork, this hostel is handy for early-to-rise art buffs into cheap sleep. Rooms are locked from 9am to 5pm and rates include sheet hire. Ride bus No 4 from La Rotonde to the Vasarely stop.

Camping

Camping Arc en Ciel (☎ 04 42 26 14 28; rte de Nice; 2 adults, tent & car €17.10; ◌ Apr-Sep) Enjoy peaceful wooded hills out back and the rushing of cars on a busy motorway out front at this Aixois camp site, 2km southeast at Pont des Trois Sautets. Take bus No 3 to Les Trois Sautets stop.

MID-RANGE

Hôtel Cardinal (☎ 04 42 38 32 30; fax 04 42 26 39 05; 24 rue Cardinale; s/d from €55/65; ◌ reception 7am-11.30pm) The Cardinal is a charming place in a charming street with 29 very charming rooms, each clad in a mix of modern and period furniture. The annexe (12 rue Cardinale) has small self-catering suites. Breakfast comes with classical music.

Hôtel Le Mozart (☎ 04 42 21 62 86; hotelmozart@ wanadoo.fr; 40 cours Gambetta; s/d from €49/57; ◌ reception 7am-11.30pm; P) Undoubtedly the greatest

asset of this simple but satisfactory two-star hotel, 700m south of the city, is its green breakfast terrace and the on-site parking it sports – be it outside on the steep driveway (free) or in a garage (€7) underground.

Hôtel Le Manoir (☎ 04 42 26 27 20; www.hotel manoir.com; 8 rue d'Entrecasteux; d/tr from €54/72; P) Sleep beneath hefty wooden beams and wake up to breakfast in a 16th-century cloister at this immaculately kept three-star choice, well-placed away from the madding crowds. The hotel has a garden.

Hôtel des Quatre Dauphins (☎ 04 42 38 16 39; fax 04 42 38 60 19; 54 rue Roux Alphéran; s/d/tr €55/70/100) The dozen rooms to be found in the heart of old Aix are decked in traditional Provençal style. Pets stay for €8 a night and reservations require a deposit.

Hôtel La Caravelle (☎ 04 42 21 53 05; www.lacaravelle -hotel.com in French; 20 blvd du Roi René; s with shower €39, d €46-69, q €72; P ◌) You'll find the whole gambit to choose from here: air-conditioned doubles overlooking a garden or smaller, stuffy (no air-con) doubles peeping out through green shutters onto a busy boulevard. Furnishings are unadventurous but serviceable and the cake shop down the road serves a great breakfast.

TOP END

Hôtel des Augustins (☎ 04 42 27 28 59; www.hotel -augustins.com; 3 rue de la Masse; d/ste from €95/185; ◌) There are few hotels that can claim to be in a centuries-old chapel, but this one can. The death bell tolled on this 16th-century convent during the French Revolution, after which it was turned into a hotel. The priciest rooms have Jacuzzis, and you can breakfast on a roof terrace beneath the bell tower in summer.

Grand Hôtel Nègre Coste (☎ 04 42 27 74 22; www .hotelnegrecoste.com; 33 cours Mirabeau; d from €78; P ◌) Louis XIV, so the story goes, played tennis here in 1660. Whatever; fanciful rooms are endowed with 18th-century furnishings from which guests enjoy prime views of slick cours Mirabeau.

Eating

Terraces spill across dozens of backstreet squares, including place des Cardeurs, forum des Cardeurs, place de Verdun, place Richelme and place de l'Hôtel de Ville. Place Ramus, off pedestrianised rue Annonciade, is a restaurant-filled square where buskers often play. Rue de la Verrerie and rue Félibre Gaut have a couple of Vietnamese and Chinese options. *Calissons* (see the boxed text, below) are Aix's sweet-as-sugar-pie speciality.

Le Passage (☎ 04 42 37 09 00; 6bis rue Mazarine & 10 rue Villars; menu €28; ☻ 10am-midnight) Tastebuds flit from Morocco to Italy to Spain to Greece at this chic world-cuisine centre for gourmets, spread across three floors. Dine fine in the contemporary restaurant, eat sweet in the *salon de thé*, munch brunch (11am to 3pm Saturday and Sunday) and stock up at the *épicerie* and *oenothèque* (wine shop).

Charlotte (☎ 04 42 26 77 56; 32 rue des Bernardines; 2-/3-course menu €12.50/14.50; ☻ lunch & dinner Tue-Sat) What a great place this is: fill up on home cooking and smiles galore in its retro interior, which touts few frills but bags of charm. The kitchen is open, dishes are simple (grilled meat, poached egg, apple crumble and so on) and the garden out back is a gem.

Icône (☎ 04 42 27 59 82; 3 rue Frédéric Mistral; 2-/3-course menu €17/20; ☻ lunch & dinner Mon-Sat) Designer cuisine is exquisitely presented on square white platters at this chic, streetsmart restaurant. A DJ spins electric lounge beats and furnishings are a cool pale blue. Rub shoulders with Aix's monied preclubbing set here.

CALISSONS

These sweet almond biscuits, frosted white with icing sugar, have made mouths water since 1473, when privileged guests at the wedding banquet of King René dined on *calissons*. When the Great Plague came into town in 1630 it was *calissons* that supposedly staved off the terrible disease. Today a handful of Aixois *calissonniers* (*calisson* makers) still bake these sweets, which comprise 40% ground almonds and 60% melon and fruit syrup.

Calisson makers include **Béchard** (☎ 04 42 26 06 78; 12 cours Mirabeau); **Brémond** (☎ 04 42 38 01 70; 16 rue d'Italie), dating from 1830; **Roy René** (☎ 04 42 26 67 86; 10 rue Clémenceau), which runs guided tours of its out-of-town factory (10am Tue & Thu; €1); and **Leonard Parli** (☎ 04 42 26 05 71; 33 av Victor Hugo). The tourist office has a complete list.

Eight or nine calissons (100g), plainly rather than ornately wrapped, cost €3.

Le Zinc d'Hugo (☎ 04 42 27 69 69; 22 rue Lieutaud; lunch menus €13-17, dinner menus €20 & €26; ☻ lunch & dinner Tue-Sat) For an informal bistro bite, look no further than Hugo's, where dishes on the menu are poetically split between *à l'ombre du figieurs* (in the shade of fig trees), *lire entre les vignes* (to read between vines) and *l'eau à la bouche* (water in the mouth).

Yôji (☎ 04 42 38 48 76; 7 av Victor Hugo; menus €13.50-32.50; ☻ lunch & dinner Mon-Sat, dinner Sun) Sink your teeth into raw fish flesh at Aix's well-known Japanese and Korean sushi bar, which offers a succulent range of menus. The tinkling water garden adds a soothing Zen touch.

Le Formal (☎ 04 42 27 08 31; 32 rue Espariat; lunch 2-/3-course menu €17/20, plat du jour €11, dinner menus €27 & €40; ☻ lunch & dinner Tue-Fri, dinner Sat; ✗) The Formal more than lives up to its name with the formal dining and service it proffers. Savour *sushi de St-Jacques* and the other divine dishes for which this romantic restaurant is known in a vaulted cellar. One room is reserved for smokers (cigars not welcome).

SELF-CATERING

Aix is among Provence's premier market towns. A mass of fruit and vegetable stands are set up every morning on place Richelme, just as they have been for centuries. Another food market fills place des Prêcheurs on Tuesday, Thursday and Saturday mornings.

Jacquèrres (9 rue Méjanes) A fantastic *épicerie* that sells cheese, cold meats, sausages and 300 types of whisky.

La Truffe Cendrée (9 rue de l'Aumône Vieille) Sells regional food products, including truffles in season.

Le Comptoir des Oliviers (14 rue Gaston de Saporta) and **Place aux Huiles** (59 rue d'Italie) sell olive oil.

If all else fails, try the **Monoprix** (cours Mirabeau; ☻ 8.30am-8pm Mon-Sat) supermarket.

Drinking

See opposite for pubs with live music.

Les Deux Garçons (☎ 04 42 26 00 51; 53 cours Mirabeau; ☻ lunch & dinner) A former intellectual hang-out with a stunning interior from 1792, this Aixois hot spot is just the place to pose and peer over a pastis.

L'Orienthé (5 rue de Félibre Gaut; ☻ 3 or 4pm-1am Mon-Thu, 3 or 4pm-2am Fri & Sat, 3 or 4-9am Sun) For a touch of the Orient, take off your shoes and take it easy at this trendy tea house, brewery for 50-odd different teas.

DANCE IN AIX

Never has Aix been more at the forefront of contemporary dance in France, as a quick look at, through, in and around the future **Centre Chorégraphique National** (CNN, National Choreographic Centre; rue des Allummettes) testifies. At the time of writing, France's first purpose-built choreography centre – a stunning glass-and-steel box with 378-seat auditorium, roof deck and glass-walled rehearsal studios – was scheduled to open in Aix in spring 2005. It will drive contemporary dance in the region, spearheaded by resident dance company Ballet Preljocaj.

Ballet Preljocaj, founded in 1984, presents exciting opportunities to see one of Europe's most cutting-edge, creative – and at times shocking – companies at work. In its city-centre studios at the **Cité du Livre**, a matchstick factory–turned–cultural centre, the **Ballet Preljocaj** (☎ 04 42 93 48 00; www.preljocaj.org; 8-10 rue des Allumettes) opens its rehearsals to the public once a month, runs dance workshops for adults and children, and hosts afternoon *'gouter-danse'* and evening *'aperitif-danse'* events. That is, when the company is not on tour.

Entertainment

The free *Agenda Culturel d'Aix-en-Provence*, published every two months by the tourist office, lists what's on where.

THEATRE, OPERA & CLASSICAL MUSIC

August brings open-air performances (theatre, cinema, cabaret, circus, video projections etc; tickets €1) to Parc Jourdan (p97), **Théâtre de Verdure du Jas de Bouffan** (av St-John Perse), and the Carrières d'Ocre in Rognes (p103) during the month-long Les Instant d'Été.

Théâtre du Jeu de Paume (☎ 04 42 99 12 00; 17-21 rue de l'Opéra) was built in 1756 on the site of a royal tennis court; the curtain rises in the ornate Italianate auditorium most evenings, June to September.

Classical concerts (☎ 04 42 99 37 11) are held in two enchanting little churches, **Église Ste-Marie Madeleine** (place des Prêcheurs) and the 17th-century chapel **Chapelle de Ste-Catherine** (20 rue Mignet).

By 2007 Aix will be graced with a stunning new venue, the €33.66 million **Salle de Spectacles Pays d'Aix**, designed by world-renowned Italian architect Vittorio Gregotti. The theatre will seat 1300.

LIVE MUSIC & DISCOS

Several pubs are sprinkled on and around rue de la Verrerie.

La Belle Époque (☎ 04 42 27 65 66; 29 cours Mirabeau) One of a dozen café-bars on cours Mirabeau, the Beautiful Age is a good bet for its 'happy hour' that lasts a good couple of hours, its big-screen TVs and evening DJs who spin Latino, house and funk.

Bar Sextius (☎ 04 42 26 07 21; 13 cours Sextius; ⏱ 8-2am Mon-Sat) This small intimate watering hole hosts reggae and raga beats on Tuesdays, live bands on Thursdays and DJs spinning house on Saturdays.

Le Scat Club (☎ 04 42 23 00 23; 11 rue de la Verrerie; ⏱ 11pm-6am Tue-Sat) This Aix institution presents rock and jazz bands – and the occasional disco – to a young, casual crowd.

CINEMA

Le Cézanne (☎ 0 892 687 270; www.lecezanne.com in French; 1 rue Marcel Guillaume; ticket adult/student €8.50/6.70) See the latest box-office hits in English at this 12-screen theatre.

Two cinemas screen only foreign films (invariably in English) with French subtitles: **Ciné Mazarin** (cinemazarin@wanadoo.fr; 6 rue Laroque) and **Cinéma Renoir** (24 cours Mirabeau); for programme details call ☎ 0 892 687 270. Tickets for both cinemas are adult/student €7.50/6.50.

Shopping

A flower market sets place des Prêcheurs ablaze with colour on Monday, Wednesday, Friday and Sunday mornings. On Tuesday, Thursday and Saturday the flower market moves to place de Hôtel de Ville and a flea market fills place de Verdun. Place de Hôtel de Ville hosts a book market on the first Sunday of the month.

The chic shops for designer fashion strut their stuff along pedestrianised rue Marius Reynaud (which winds its way behind the Palais de Justice on place de Verdun) and its continuation, rue Espariat. Marseille soap and a bounty of upmarket skincare products are sold at **Savon de Marseille** (63 rue des Cordeliers).

Santons (see Little Saints, p102) are sold at several workshops, including **Santons Fouque** (☎ 04 42 26 33 38; www.santonsfouque.fr;

LITTLE SAINTS

The custom of creating a crèche with figurines of Mary, Joseph, shepherds, kings, oxen, a donkey and so on dates from the Avignon papacy of John XII (1319–34). But it was only after the 1789 Revolution and consequent Reign of Terror that these figures were cut down in size as the people of Provence handcrafted them in the secrecy of their homes: hence, the birth of the *santon* and the Provençal crèche.

Santons (from *santoùn* in Provençal, meaning 'little saint') stand between 2.5cm and 15cm high. The first colourfully painted terracotta figures were created by Marseillais artisan Jean-Louis Lagnel (1764–1822), who came up with the idea of crafting clay miniatures in a plaster mould and allowing them to dry before firing the figures at 950°C. *Santonniers* (*santon* makers) still stick to Lagnel's method today.

In a traditional Provençal crib – set up in churches and peoples' homes in early November and dismantled after the three kings have delivered their gifts during Epiphany – there are 55 *santons* ranging from the tambourine man, chestnut seller, fishwife and woman with aïoli, to the tinsmith, scissor grinder, a trumpet-blowing angel and the patron saint of *santon* makers – St Francis of Assisi. Since 1803 *santonniers* have flocked to Marseille each December to take part in the **Foire aux Santonniers**, which sees the length of La Canebière transformed into one great big *santon* fair. In nearby Aubagne, during the two-day **Biennale de l'Art Santonnier** held the same month, *santonniers* flood the town with little saints, run *santon*-making workshops and so on.

Santons dating from the 18th and 19th centuries are displayed in Marseille's magical **Musée du Santon** (Map pp80-1; ☎ 04 91 13 61 36; 49 rue Neuve Ste-Catherine, *1e*; metro Vieux Port; admission free; ⊗ 10.30am-12.30pm & 2-6.30pm Tue-Sat). The museum houses the private collection of *santonnier* Marcel Carbonnel and has a shop selling *santons* crafted in his adjoining **workshop** (admission free; ⊗ guided visits 2.30pm Tue & Thu).

65 cours Gambetta), where the Thumbelina-sized figures have been crafted since 1934.

Getting There & Away

BUS

From the **bus station** (☎ 04 42 91 26 80; av de l'Europe) there are buses to/from Marseille (€4.20, 35 minutes via the A51/one hour via the N8, every five to 10 minutes), Marseille-Provence airport (€8.20, 35 minutes, two an hour between 4.45am and 10.30pm), Arles (€9.80, 1¾ hours, two to six daily) and Avignon (€11.80/14 via national roads/the A7 *autoroute*, one to 1½ hours, two to five daily).

Sumian buses serve Apt, Castellane and the Gorges du Verdon (see p189 for details).

CAR & MOTORCYCLE

The following car rental agencies also have offices at the Gare d'Aix TGV train station:
Avis (☎ 04 42 21 64 16; 11 blvd Gambetta)
Europcar (☎ 04 42 27 83 00; 55 blvd de la République)
Hertz (☎ 04 42 27 91 32; 43 av Victor Hugo)
National Citer (☎ 04 42 93 07 85; 42 av Victor Hugo)

TRAIN

Non-TGV trains chug between Aix's central station and Marseille (€6.10, 30 minutes, 16 to 24 daily), while TGV services use Gare d'Aix TGV, 8km west. Within the region the only destinations served by TGV are Marseille (€7.10, 15 minutes), Avignon (€26.60, 20 minutes) and Nice (€30.60, 3¼ hours).

Getting Around

BICYCLE & SCOOTER

Trott' Aix (☎ 04 42 93 14 35, 06 23 95 16 67; 9 rue Fermée; ⊗ 10am-7pm Mon-Sat) rents electric bicycles (€25 per day) and electric *trottinettes* (scooters; €20) as well as bog-standard road bikes (€15 per day). Cycle shop **Cycles Zammitt** (☎ 04 42 23 19 53; 27 rue Mignet; ⊗ 9am-12.30pm & 3-7.30pm Tue-Sat) has mountain bikes.

Those with a used public transport ticket for that day can rent a set of wheels for €6 a day from **Relais Aix en Vélo** (☎ 04 42 26 78 92; La Rotonde, 2 av des Belges; ⊗ 9.30am-noon & 12.30-6pm Mon-Sat), run by Aix en Bus.

BUS

Aix en Bus (www.aixenbus.com), with a **Point Accueil** (Information/ticket desk; ☎ 04 42 26 37 28; place du Général de Gaulle; ⊗ 8.30am-7pm Mon-Sat) in the tourist office, runs buses and minibuses in town. A single ticket/carnet of 10 costs 1.10/7.70 and a one-day pass is €3.50.

Minibus No 1 links the train and bus stations with La Rotonde and cours Mirabeau. The **Navette Aix-TGV-Aéroport** (☎ 04 42 93 59 13) links the bus station with the TGV train station (€3.80, 15 minutes) and Marseille-Provence airport (€7.70, 30 minutes).

AROUND AIX
Mountains painted by Cézanne, a truffle kingdom and a WWII concentration camp lie within easy reach of Aix.

Montagne Ste-Victoire
Among Cézanne's favourite haunts was Montagne Ste-Victoire, a mountain ridge immortalised on canvas numerous times by artists over the centuries. Garrigue covers its dry slopes and its foot is carpeted with 32 sq km of vineyards, from which Coteaux d'Aix-en-Provence wine originates.

Heading east on the D17 from Aix, you pass local artists at their easels in the roadside pine forests trying to reproduce works painted by Cézanne – including *La Montagne Ste-Victoire au Grand Pin* (1887) – along this stretch. His cubist works *Les Baigneurs* and *Les Baigneuses* (The Bathers) were painted in the **Vallée de l'Arc** around the small mining town of **Gardanne** (population 19,679), 10km south off the D6. Before leaving Aix, pick up a copy of the tourist office's *In Cezanne's Footsteps* to discover other places in the Montagne Ste-Victoire area that Cézanne painted. Between 1902 and 1906 the artist produced 11 oil and 17 watercolour paintings here.

Mountain flora and fauna can be found at **Écomusée de la Forêt Méditerranéenne** (☎ 04 42 51 41 00; www.institut-foret.com in French; chemin de Roman; adult/under 15 yrs €5.30/3; ☺ 10am-6pm Jul & Aug, 9am-7pm Sep-Jun) in Gardanne, and along the *sentier de découverte* (discovery path) at the **Maison de Ste-Victoire** (☎ 04 42 66 84 40; ☺ 10am-6pm Mon-Fri, 10am-7pm Sat & Sun) in St-Antonin-sur-Bayon. The latter, in converted stables, shelters fauna and flora exhibits and has mountains of information on **walking** and **mountain-biking** around Montagne Ste-Victoire. Note that the entire mountain, save the roads that cross it, is closed between 1 July and 1 September due to the threat of forest fire.

Returning to Aix via the westbound D10, you pass Vauvenargues, with the 14th-century **Château de Vauvenargues**, in the grounds of which Picasso is buried. The red-brick castle, purchased by the artist in 1958, still belongs to the Picasso family and cannot be visited.

Rognes
pop 4191 / elevation 311m
Little-known Rognes languishes in medieval splendour 17km north of Aix. Originally built on the slopes of Foussa, part of the Chaîne de la Trévaresse, the village tumbled down to the bottom of the hill in 1909 after an earthquake struck it.

Almost 75% of Provence's black truffles are snouted out here. The village's **Grand Marché Truffes et Gastronomie** (Truffle and Gastronomy Market), held the Sunday before Christmas, opens with a Bénédiction des Truffes (truffle blessing) in the church.

The **tourist office** (☎ 04 42 50 13 36; office.tourisme.rogne@wanadoo.fr; 5 cours St-Étienne) knows what's on at the **Carrières d'Ocre** (rte de St-Cannat), a theatre in a former ochre mine.

At **Les Olivarelles** (☎ 04 42 50 24 27; chemin Font de Vabre; menus €21-50; ☺ lunch & dinner Fri & Sat, lunch Sun) truffle ice cream, lamb roasted in truffle juice and *foie gras de canard* are among the exquisite creations of highly regarded chef Pau Dietrich. His gorgeous countryside manor, 6km northwest of Rognes along the D66, sits amid scented garrigue.

A HORRIBLE DETOUR

Drive 6km west of Aix along the D9 to reach **Tuileries des Milles**, a red-brick tile factory in Les Milles that manufactured 30,000 tonnes of bricks and tiles a year from 1882 until 31 August 1939, when it was turned into a WWII concentration camp. By June 1940 some 3500 artists and intellectuals – predominantly Germans living in the Marseille region, among them surrealist painters Max Ernst (1891–1976) and Hans Bellmer (1902–75) – were interned at **Camp des Milles**. Emotive paintings and prose drawn on the walls by the prisoners in the refectory remain, as does one of the wagons used to transport prisoners by rail from Les Milles to Auschwitz.

Unnervingly, the camp remains almost intact. In 1946 it briefly reopened as a factory; the refectory became a carpenter's workshop. Since 1993 it has been preserved as a **memorial** (☎ 04 42 24 34 68; admission free; ☺ 9am-noon & 12.45-5pm Mon-Fri); the wagon can be visited by appointment only.

The Camargue

CONTENTS

THE CAMARGUE

THE CAMARGUE

Black bulls, white horses, pink flamingos, paddy fields and cowboys: famed for its desolate beauty and bird life beyond belief, this haunting and sparsely populated 780-sq-km delta is the wild child of Provence. Formed by sediment deposited by the River Rhône as it flows into the Mediterranean, the Camargue promises adventure by the 4WD-load: galloping on horseback, cycling around saltpans, canoeing, or brushing through bull rushes in search of the 400-plus species of birds that live here are but some of the oodles of incredible things to see and do.

Shaped like a crab, the wet 'n soggy park-protected Camargue sits plump within a neat triangle formed by the River Grand Rhône (east) and the Petit Rhône (west). The Roman town of Arles – the place where van Gogh lopped off his left ear – rides on the crab's north-facing back, while the seaside town of Stes-Maries de la Mer clings to its little right toe and the walled city of Aigues-Mortes hovers nearby. The Étang de Vaccarès and Étang du Fangassier are two large lakes in the centre of the Camargue where 25,000 couples of *flamants roses* (pink flamingos) nest, hatch and raise their offspring in spring.

Salt and rice are mainstays in this 'Wild West'. Vast evaporation salt pools glint in the Provençal sun around Aigues-Mortes and Salin de Giraud, while the delta's drier northern sections produce almost 70% of France's annual rice yield. Then, of course, there is the creamy grey *cheval de Camargue* (Camargue horse), and the bull – a feisty beast which, among other things, could end up on your plate.

HIGHLIGHTS

- Do Arles: see scenes **Vincent van Gogh** (p111) painted, sketches Picasso drew in the **Musée Réattu** (p111) and the Roman's idea of fun at the **Roman amphitheatre** (p109)
- Let your hair down at a **rice** or **bull festival** (p112) in Arles or at a **Roma pilgrimage** (p115) in Stes-Maries de la Mer
- Feast on *tellines* (Lilliputian Mediterranean clams) fresh from the Golfe de Beauduc at **Chez Marc et Mireille** (p121)
- **Gallop** (p107) along endless sand, **cycle** (p107) or discover the wetland and its brilliant **bird life** (p107) on foot
- Be a **gardian** (Camargue cowboy; p116) for a week
- Huff and puff your way past paddy fields aboard *Le Train des Alpilles* **steam train** (p114)

★ Arles

★ Stes-Maries
de la Mer

Chez Marc ★
et Mireille

GET SET GO!

Get set to go with that perfect safari picnic, built with local produce fresh from the morning market:
Monday Stes-Maries de la Mer
Wednesday Aigues-Mortes, Arles
Friday Stes-Maries de la Mer
Saturday Arles
Sunday Aigues-Mortes

National & Regional Parks

Storks, bee-eaters and 160 other migratory species are among the many species protected by the **Parc Naturel Régional de Camargue** (PNRC), an 863-sq-km park set up in 1970 to preserve the wetland's fragile ecosystems by maintaining an equilibrium between ecological considerations and economic mainstays: agriculture, salt production, hunting, grazing and tourism.

At the heart of the PNRC is the **Étang de Vaccarès**, a 600-sq-km lake afforded additional protection by the **Réserve Nationale de Camargue**. The 135-sq-km reserve, established

in 1927, protects the lagoon, its nearby peninsulas and islands.

Another 20 sq km between Arles and Salin de Giraud is managed by the Conservatoire du Littoral (see the boxed text, p36).

INFORMATION CENTRES
Maison du Parc Naturel Régional de Camargue
(☎ 04 90 97 86 32; www.parc-camargue.fr in French; Pont du Gau; ☺ 10am-6pm Apr-Sep, 9.30am-5pm Mon-Thu, Sat & Sun Oct-Mar) Four kilometres northwest of Stes-Maries de la Mer off the D570.
Réserve Nationale de Camargue information centre (☎ 04 90 97 00 97; snpn.reserve .de.camargue@wanadoo.fr; La Capelière; ☺ 9am-1pm & 2-5pm Wed-Mon) On the D36B in La Capelière.

Dangers & Annoyances

Savage mosquitoes flourish in the Camargue in summer, feeding on the blood of hapless passers-by just as they have for countless aeons. In June and July, worse still, there are millions of also seemingly invisible, scalp-eating *aoûtats* (harvest mites or midges) to contend with. Pack *plenty* of insect repellent – then pack more.

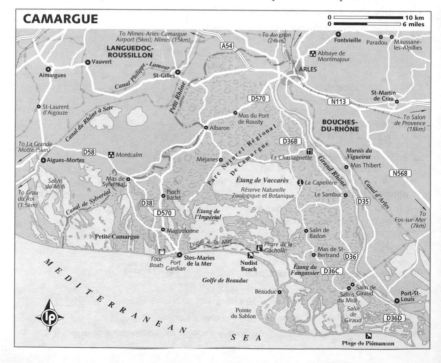

Activities
BIRD-WATCHING & WALKING
From the glassed-in foyer at the **Maison du Parc Naturel Régional de Camargue** (opposite) you can watch birds in the nearby marshes through powerful binoculars, and several nature discovery trails can be picked up in its grounds.

Next door, in the **Parc Ornithologique du Pont de Gau** (☎ 04 90 97 82 62; parc.pont-de-gau@provnet.fr; Pont du Gau; adult/4-10 yrs €6.50/3.50; ☺ 9am-sunset Apr-Sep, 10am-sunset Oct-Mar), several kilometres of paths wend their way through reed beds and marshes. Pink flamingos fly overhead or wade through the watery landscape, making it the best place in the Camargue to view the birds. Guided walks around the park are available. Salin de Badon in southeastern Camargue is another prime bird-watching spot.

There are numerous other walking trails along the sea embankments and the coast in the PNRC. One of the most dramatic paths, the Digue à la Mer (p119), is atop the dike between Stes-Maries and Salin de Giraud. Shorter nature trails start from the Musée de la Camargue (p111) southwest of Arles; and La Capelière (p119), Salin de Badon (p119) and Domaine de la Palissade (p120) in the southeastern Camargue.

Park offices sell detailed maps of the area, including the 1:25,000 IGN Série Bleue maps, Nos 2944E and 2944O.

CANOEING
Kayak Vert (☎ 04 66 73 57 17; www.kayak.camargue.fr; Mas de Sylvéréal), 14km north of Stes-Maries off the picturesque D38C, rents canoes to explore Camargue waterways by paddle power for €9.50 per hour. The canoeing centre also runs half-/one-/two-/three-day guided expeditions for €17/24/47/70 and offers a combined canoe (10km) and bicycle trip (16km) departing from Stes-Maries (€27).

CYCLING
As long as you can put up with the insects and stiff sea breezes, travelling by bicycle is the finest way to explore the very flat Camargue. East of Stes-Maries, areas along the seafront and further inland are reserved for walkers and cyclists. Cycling is forbidden on beaches, but you can bike along the Digue à la Mer.

SEA CHANGE
At some places along the coast, the delta continues to grow, sweeping one-time seaside towns kilometres from the Mediterranean. Elsewhere, sea currents and storms have, in recent centuries, washed away land that had been around long enough for people to build things on it. The course of the Rhône has changed repeatedly over the millennia, but the Grand Rhône (which carries 90% of the river's flow) and the Petit Rhône have followed their present channels for about 500 years.

Le Vélo Saintois and Le Vélociste in Stes-Maries de la Mer (see p118), both open Easter to early October, distribute cycling itineraries (20km to 70km long) with route descriptions in English and deliver bicycles to your door.

HORSE RIDING
Plenty of roadside farms along the D570 into Stes-Maries de la Mer offer *promenades à cheval* (horse riding) for €14/26 per one/two hours.

South of Pioch Badet on the D85a to Stes-Maries, the **Mas de Frigoules** (☎ /fax 04 90 97 51 41, 06 12 48 10 03) organises overnight rides (€70) and day-long rides on the beach (€55). For longer treks (two to seven days) contact **Promenades des Rieges** (☎ 04 90 97 91 38; www.promenadedesrieges.com; rte de Cacharel), just north of Stes-Maries de la Mer.

The **Domaine Paul Ricard de Méjanes** (☎ 04 90 97 10 62; mejanes@ricard.fr; ☺ Apr–mid-Oct), a leisure complex on the northeastern bank of the Étang de Vaccarès in Méjanes, 20km southwest of Arles, also has horses.

The spot for scenic rides in the wilder southeastern Camargue is Domaine de la Palissade (p120).

Tours
Boat excursions sail from Aigues-Mortes (p118) and Stes-Maries (p115).

La Maison du Guide en Camargue (☎ /fax 04 66 73 52 30, 06 12 44 73 52; www.maisonduguide.camargue.fr) in Montcalm, 10km northwest of Stes-Maries on the D58, organises guided tours by foot, boat and bicycle.

In Arles, **Camargue Organisation** (☎ 04 90 96 94 44; 14bis rue de la Calade; ☺ 9am-6pm Mar-Oct) runs English-language 4WD tours from March

THE CAMARGUE

PRETTY IN PINK

The pink or greater flamingo *(Phoenicopterus ruber)* in flight is a breathtaking sight. Equally majestic is the catwalk stance – neck high, breast out – adopted by this elegant, long-legged creature when strutting through shallow waters.

Flamingo courtship starts in January, with mating taking place from March to May. The single egg laid by the female in April or May is incubated in a mud-caked nest for one month by both parents. The young chicks shakily take to the skies when they are about three months old. By the time they reach adulthood (around five years old), their soft grey down has become a fine feather coat of brilliant white or pretty rose-pink.

This well-dressed bird lives to the grand old age of 34 (longer if kept in captivity). It stands between 1.5m and 2m tall and has an average wing span of 1.9m. When the flamingo feels threatened, its loud hiss is similar to the warning sound made by a goose. It feeds on plankton, sucking in water and draining it off with its disproportionately heavy, curved bill.

Some flamingos remain in the Rhône delta year-round. Come September, several thousand take flight to Spain, Tunisia and Senegal where they winter in warmer climes before returning to the Camargue in February in time for early spring.

---

to October. Morning/afternoon 'safari-photo' Jeep tours last 2½ and 3½ hours respectively and cost €25/30 (€12.50/15 for under 12 years). **Camargue Découverte** (☎ /fax 04 90 96 69 20; 1 rue Émile Fassin) is another Arles-based Jeep-safari company. **Camargue Safaris 4x4 Gallon** (☎ 04 90 97 86 93; camargue-safari .gallon@wanadoo.fr; 22 av Van Gogh) and **Safari Photo du Delta** (☎ 04 90 97 89 33; 17 av de la République) are Stes-Maries de la Mer equivalents.

ARLES
pop 50,513

Vincent van Gogh's famous canary-yellow house, known the world over by art-lovers, was in Arles. Long since demolished, it was one of dozens of Arlésian sights, streets and surrounding rural areas that Arles' most famous resident immortalised on canvas.

The city where van Gogh lived and worked in 1888 is at the northern tip of the Camargue alluvial plain and sits on the River Grand Rhône, slightly south of where the Petit Rhône splits off from it. Arles began its ascent to prosperity and political importance in 49 BC, when Julius Caesar – backed by the Arlésians – captured and plundered Marseille. Soon after, Arles replaced Marseille as the region's major port and within a century and a half begged a magnificent 20,000-seat amphitheatre and a 12,000-seat theatre to entertain its citizens. Both still entertain today.

Avignon and Nîmes are 30km from Arles. Pulling into town aboard *Le Train des Alpilles* steam train (p114) is unforgettable.

Orientation

Central Arles is ensnared by the Grand Rhône to the northwest, blvd Émile Combes to the east and, to the south, by blvd des Lices and blvd Georges Clémenceau. It is shaped like a foot, with the train station, place de la Libération and place Lamartine (where van Gogh once lived) at the ankle, Les Arènes at the anklebone and the tourist office squashed under the arch.

Information

Find commercial banks on place de la République.

Cyber Sal@delle (☎ 04 90 93 13 56; 17 rue de la République; 5/30/60 min €1/2/3.50; ☽ 9am-7pm Mon-Sat, to 8pm Jul & Aug) Eat, drink and surf here.

Forum Harmonia Wilson (☎ 04 90 93 65 39; 3 rue du Président Wilson; ☽ 9am-7pm Mon-Sat) Excellent selection of Provence-related books (in French) and maps.

Laundrette (6 rue de la Cavalerie; ☽ 7am-9pm)

Main Post Office (5 blvd des Lices)

Main Tourist Office (☎ 04 90 18 41 20; www.tourisme .ville-arles.fr; blvd des Lices; ☽ 9am-6.45pm mid-Mar–Sep, 9am-5.45pm Mon-Sat, 10.30am-2.30pm Sun Oct–mid-Nov, 9am-4.45pm Mon-Sat, 10.30am-2.30pm Sun mid-Nov–mid-Mar)

Point Web (☎ 04 90 18 91 54; 10 rue du 4 Septembre; 10/60 min €1/6; ☽ 9am-12.30pm & 1.30-7.30pm Mon-Sat)

Police (Comissariat de Police; ☎ 04 90 18 45 00; 1 blvd des Lices)

Tourist Office Annexe (av Paulin Talabot; ☽ 9am-1pm Mon-Sat)

Ville-Arles (www.ville-arles.fr) Official city website.

Roman Arles

Familiarising yourself with the fabulous
story of Roman Arles at the state-of-the-art
Musée de l'Arles et de la Provence Antique (☎ 04 90
18 88 88; www.arles-antique.org in French; av de la Première
Division Française Libre; adult/12-18 yrs €5.50/4; ☙ 9am-
7pm Mar-Oct, 10am-5pm Nov-Feb), 1.5km southwest
of the tourist office on the Presqu'île du
Cirque Romain, is an excellent way to kick
off sightseeing in the city. The museum's
rich collection of Pagan and Christian art –
including Roman statues, artefacts, marble
sarcophagi and a renowned assortment of
early Christian sarcophagi from the 4th century – is impressive and illuminating.

LES ARÈNES

Sporting contests, chariot races and the
bloody spectacles so beloved by the Roman
public were staged at the **amphitheatre** (☎ 04 90
96 03 70; entrance rond-point des Arènes; adult/12-18 yrs €4/3;
☙ 9am-7pm May-Sep, 9am-6pm Mar, Apr & Oct, 10am-5pm
Nov-Feb), built in the late 1st or early 2nd century AD. An audience of 20,000 would watch
wild animals pitted against other animals or
gladiators (usually slaves or criminals), fighting each other until one of them was killed
or surrendered (in the latter case their throat
was usually then slit). Executions were carried out by the executioner or by pushing the
victim into the arena with a wild animal.

In the early medieval period, during
the Arab invasions, the theatre, measuring
136m by 107m (making it marginally larger
than its counterpart in Nîmes), was transformed into a fortress; three of the four
defensive towers can still be seen around
the structure. These days the amphitheatre
holds 12,000 and draws a full house during
the bullfighting season.

Opening hours at Les Arènes vary depending on what is on. Tickets for bullfights, the Wednesday-evening *courses
Camarguaises* (see p116) in June, July and
August (adult/child €6/3), and other events
are sold at the **Bureau de Location** (☎ 04 90
96 03 70; arenes.arles@wanadoo.fr; rond-point des Arènes;
☙ 9am-noon & 2.30-6pm Mon-Fri, 10am-1pm Sat).

THÉÂTRE ANTIQUE

For centuries Arles' **Roman theatre** (rue de la
Calade; adult/12-18 yrs €3/2.20; ☙ 9am-7pm May-Sep,
9am-noon & 2-6pm Mar & Apr, 9am-noon Oct, 10am-noon
& 2-5pm Nov-Feb), dating from the 1st century BC, was quite a convenient source of

construction materials. Nowadays little of
the original structure remains, except for
two imposing columns. Open-air performances are occasionally hosted here.

LES ALYSCAMPS

This large **necropolis** (adult/12-18 yrs €3.50/2.60;
☙ 9am-7pm May-Sep, 9am-noon & 2-6pm Mar & Apr, 9am-
noon Oct, 10am-noon & 2-5pm Nov-Feb), 1km southeast
of Les Arènes, was founded by the Romans
and taken over by Christians in the 4th century. It became a popular last resting place
because of the presence of Christian martyrs
among the dead, said to work miracles.

The necropolis was badly maintained
during and after the Renaissance, making
it a shadow of its former self. Van Gogh and
Gauguin painted it with great vividness.

THERMES DE CONSTANTIN & CRYPTOPORTICUS DU FORUM

Arles' **Roman baths** (rue du Grand Prieuré; adult/12-18
yrs €3/2.20; ☙ 9am-7pm May-Sep, 9am-noon & 2-6pm Mar
& Apr, 9am-noon Oct, 10am-noon & 2-5pm Nov-Feb) were
built in the 4th century and are only partly
preserved. The **Cryptoporticus du Forum** (rue
Balze; adult/12-18 yrs €3.50/2.60; ☙ 9am-7pm May-Sep,
9am-noon & 2-6pm Mar & Apr, 9am-noon Oct, 10am-noon
& 2-5pm Nov-Feb), an underground storeroom
carved out in the 1st century BC, is accessed
via a 17th-century Jesuit chapel.

Other Sights

Romanesque **Église St-Trophime** (rue Jean Jaurès), once a cathedral, stands on the site
of several earlier churches. It was built in
the late 11th and 12th centuries – perhaps
using stone cut from the Théâtre Antique –
and was named after a late-2nd- or early-
3rd-century bishop of Arles.

Unlike the interior, almost unadorned save
for a few tapestries, the western portal facing
place de la République is richly decorated
in 12th-century stone carvings. Two lateral

ARLES MUSEUM PASSES

The **Pass Monuments** (Monuments Pass;
adult/12 to 18 yrs €13.50/12) is valid for three
months. It covers as many guided tours
(p111) as your feet can take, as well as admission to all Arles' museums, monuments
and Roman relics. Tourist offices and museums sell it.

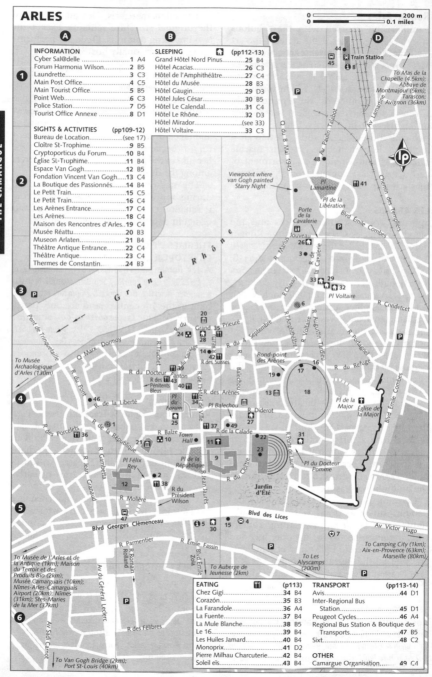

ARLES

| 0 | 200 m |
| 0 | 0.1 miles |

INFORMATION
Cyber Sal@delle 1 A4
Forum Harmonia Wilson............2 B5
Laundrette.................................3 C3
Main Post Office.......................4 B4
Main Tourist Office...................5 B5
Point Web.................................6 C3
Police Station............................7 D5
Tourist Office Annexe 8 D1

SIGHTS & ACTIVITIES (pp109-12)
Bureau de Location...............(see 17)
Cloître St-Trophime...................9 B5
Cryptoporticus du Forum........10 B4
Église St-Trophime..................11 B4
Espace Van Gogh....................12 B5
Fondation Vincent Van Gogh...13 C4
La Boutique des Passionnés.......14 B4
Le Petit Train...........................15 C4
Le Petit Train...........................16 C4
Les Arènes Entrance................17 C4
Les Arènes...............................18 C4
Maison des Rencontres d'Arles..19 C4
Musée Réattu..........................20 B3
Museon Arlaten.......................21 B4
Théâtre Antique Entrance........22 C4
Théâtre Antique.......................23 C4
Thermes de Constantin............24 B3

SLEEPING (pp112-13)
Grand Hôtel Nord Pinus............25 B4
Hôtel Acacias..........................26 C3
Hôtel de l'Amphithéâtre...........27 C4
Hôtel du Musée.......................28 B3
Hôtel Gaugin..........................29 D3
Hôtel Jules César.....................30 B5
Hôtel Le Calendal....................31 C4
Hôtel Le Rhône.......................32 D3
Hôtel Mirador......................(see 33)
Hôtel Voltaire..........................33 C3

Viewpoint where
van Gogh painted
Starry Night

To Mas de la
Chapelle (4.5km);
Abbaye de
Montmajour (5km);
Tarascon;
Avignon (36km)

To Musée
Archaéologique
d'Arles (130m)

To Camping City (1km);
Aix-en-Provence (63km);
Marseille (80km)

To Musée de l'Arles et de
la Antique (1km); Maison
du Terroir et des
Produits Bio (2km);
Musée Camarguais (10km);
Nîmes-Arles-Camarguais
Airport (20km); Nîmes
(31km); Stes-Maries
de la Mer (37km)

To Auberge de
Jeunesse (2km)

To Les
Alyscamps
(200m)

To Van Gogh Bridge (2km);
Port St-Louis (40km)

EATING (p113)
Chez Gigi..................................34 B4
Corazón...................................35 B3
La Farandole............................36 A4
La Fuente.................................37 B4
La Mule Blanche.....................38 B5
Le 16.......................................39 B4
Les Huiles Jamard....................40 B4
Monoprix.................................41 D2
Pierre Milhau Charcuterie........42 B4
Soleil eïs..................................43 B4

TRANSPORT (pp113-14)
Avis...44 D1
Inter-Regional Bus
Station..................................45 D1
Peugeot Cycles........................46 A4
Regional Bus Station & Boutique des
Transports.............................47 B5
Sixt..48 C2

OTHER
Camargue Organisation............49 C4

chapels were added in the 14th century. The choir and the ambulatory are from the 15th century, when the structure was significantly enlarged. Across the courtyard is the serene **Cloître St-Trophime** (rue Jean Jaurès; adult/12-18 yrs €3.50/2.60; 9am-6.30pm May-Sep, 9am-6pm Mar, Apr & Oct, 10am-5pm Nov-Feb), a cloister surrounded by superbly sculptured columns.

Montmajour Abbey (04 90 54 64 17; rte de Fontvieille; adult/under 18 yrs €6.10/free; 9am-7pm May-Sep, 10am-5pm Wed-Mon Oct-Mar, 9am-7pm Wed-Mon Apr), 5km northeast of Arles on the D17, is a medieval ensemble featuring an 11th-century main building and crypt, a Romanesque cloister built by Benedictine monks in the 12th century and a hermitage dedicated to St Peter.

MUSEUMS

The **Museon Arlaten** (04 90 96 08 23; 29 rue de la République; adult/12-18 yrs €4/3, 1st Sun & last Wed of the month free; 9.30am-1pm & 2-6.30pm Jul & Aug, 9.30am-1pm & 2-6.30pm Tue-Sun Jun, 9.30am-12.30pm & 2-5 or 6pm Tue-Sun Sep-May) was founded by Provençal poet Frédéric Mistral in 1896 to preserve and display everyday objects related to traditional Provençal life: furniture, crafts, costumes, ceramics etc. Find the museum in a 16th-century town house built around Roman ruins.

The **Musée Réattu** (04 90 96 37 68; 10 rue du Grand Prieuré; adult/12-18 yrs €4/3; 10am-12.30pm & 2-7pm May-Sep, 10am-12.30pm & 2-5.30pm Mar, Apr & Oct, 1-5.30pm Nov-Feb), inside a 15th-century priory, exhibits photography, modern and contemporary works of art, and paintings by 18th- and 19th-century Provençal artists.

Contemporary art exhibitions also take place at the **Maison des Rencontres d'Arles** (04 90 96 63 69; www.rencontres-arles.com; 10 rond-point des Arènes; various admission prices; 9am-noon & 2-6pm Mon-Fri), known for its international photography festival (see p112).

Inside a sheep shed built in 1812, the **Musée de la Camargue** (04 90 97 10 82; Mas du Pont de Rousty; adult/10-16 yrs €5/2.50; 9am-7pm Jul & Aug, 9am-6pm Apr, Jun & Sep, 10am-5pm Wed-Mon Oct-Mar), 10km southwest of Arles on the D570 to Stes-Maries, introduces the history, ecosystems, flora and fauna of the delta. Much attention is given to traditional life in the Camargue, including raising sheep and cattle, salt production and local arts. A 3.5km nature trail (1½ hours) leads from the museum to an observation tower.

STREET BEATS

Roma bands such as Los Reyes, Arles' very own Gypsy Kings (discovered while busking in St-Tropez), Chico & the Gypsies (founded by former Gypsy King Chico Bouchikki) and Manitas de Plata have all sung on the streets of Arles and Stes-Maries de la Mer at some point in their vibrant careers. For an outstanding collection of tracks by these and other artists, shop at **La Boutique des Passionnés** (04 90 96 59 93; www.passionnes .com in French; 14 rue Réattu; 2-7pm Mon, 9am-7pm Tue-Sat), a top-quality music shop in Arles.

The best time to watch Roma bands perform on the streets is during the **Festival Mosaïque Gitane** in Arles in mid-July and the Stes-Maries de la Mer pilgrimages (see Pélerinage des Gitans, p115) in May and October. The musicians (exclusively male) are usually encircled by Roma women dancing Camargue flamenco (reminiscent of Spanish flamenco).

TRAILING VAN GOGH

None of van Gogh's original works remain in Arles but fans can follow him around town with (see below) or without a guide (ask at the tourist office for its van Gogh itinerary). His canary-yellow house – the subject of *La Maison Jaune* (1888) and the place where, more famously, he sliced off his left ear – was on Place Lamartine.

Art exhibitions take place at the **Espace Van Gogh** (04 90 49 37 40; place Félix Rey), the hospital where van Gogh spent time as a depressed patient in 1889 and painted several works including his portrait of the hospital's courtyard garden, *Le Jardin de la Maison de Santé* (1989). The hospital is a cultural centre today.

Works by artists inspired by van Gogh are showcased at the **Fondation Vincent Van Gogh** (04 90 49 94 04; www.fondationvangogh-arles .org; 24bis rond-point des Arènes; adult/8-18 yrs €7/5; 10.30am-8pm Apr Oct, 11am-5pm Tue-Sun Nov-Mar).

Tours

Between July and September the tourist office runs guided city tours (adult/12-18 years €4/1.60 plus admission fees), including once-weekly city tours in English, morning trips to a *manade* (bull farm; see the boxed text, p116) and a van Gogh tour departing at 5pm on Tuesday.

Le Petit Train d'Arles (☎ 04 93 41 31 09; adult/under 10 yrs €6/3; ☼ 10am-5pm Apr-Oct) is an easy way of glimpsing the main sights without any wear and tear on your feet. Tours with English commentary take 35 minutes and depart from in front of Les Arènes and blvd des Lices.

Festivals & Events

Bullfights fill Les Arènes and bulls run riot in the streets during Eastertime's **Férla de Pâques**. The two-week **Fêtes d'Arles** at the end of June brings dance, theatre and music to Les Arènes.

In early July **Les Rencontres Internationales de la Photographie** (International Photography Festival; www.rip-arles.org) attracts photographers from around the world, although photography exhibitions remain until mid-September.

The **Festo Vierginenco** in mid-July, celebrated since 1904, honours young girls who don the traditional Arlésienne costume (consisting of a long full skirt, lacy shawl and cap) for the first time. During **Un Été au Ciné** in July and August, films (free admission) are shown on giant screens rigged up in various outdoor venues around town.

September's week-long **Fête des Prémices du Riz** marks the start of the rice harvest.

Sleeping

BUDGET

Auberge de Jeunesse (☎ 04 90 96 18 25; arles@fuaj .org; 20 av Maréchal Foch; dm incl breakfast, dinner & sheets €24.10; ☼ Feb-late Dec) Precisely 100 beds await HI card–holding travellers at Arles' friendly hostel, 2km south of the centre, which also organises bike rental (€10.70 a day) and horse riding (€11/53.50 per hour/day). To reach it, take bus No 3 from blvd Georges Clémenceau or No 8 from place Lamartine to the Fournier stop.

On quaint place Voltaire there's a line-up of respectable one- or two-star hotels:

Hôtel Le Rhône (☎ 04 90 96 43 70; 11 place Voltaire; d with washbasin €26, with shower €31-33, d/tr with shower & toilet €39/43) Spick, span and run with pride by bright and cheery people; three rooms have a square-facing balcony.

Hôtel Gaugin (☎ 04 90 96 14 35; hotel-gaugin .arles@wanadoo.fr; 5 place Voltaire; d with shower €30, d/tr with shower & toilet €35/44) Spot the blue-and-yellow façade.

Hôtel Mirador (☎ 04 90 96 28 05; www.hotel-mirador .com; 3 place Voltaire; d with shower €30, with shower & toilet €35-38; P ⬚) Garage parking €7.

Hôtel Voltaire (☎ 04 90 96 49 18; 1 place Voltaire; d with washbasin/shower €25/28, with shower & toilet €36) A dozen bare-bone rooms, some of which sport a table-clad balcony overlooking the pretty square.

Camping

Camping City (☎ 04 90 93 08 86; www.camping-city .com; 67 rte de Crau; 2 people, tent & car €16; ☼ Apr-Sep; P) To get to this green and tree-shaded site, 1km southeast of the centre on the Marseille road, take bus No 2 from blvd Georges Clémenceau to the Hermite stop.

MID-RANGE

Hôtel de l'Amphithéâtre (☎ 04 90 96 10 30; www .hotelamphitheatre.fr; 5-7 rue Diderot; s/d from €41/45, terrace ste low/high season €109/145; P ⁑) Stunning inside, this beautiful hotel is decked out in a contemporary fashion to contrast with its heavily beamed, 17th-century exterior. Classical music soothes guests as they enter, breakfast (€6) is a feast and the hotel is wheelchair-friendly.

Hôtel Le Calendal (☎ 04 90 96 11 89; www.lecal endal.com; 5 rue Porte de Laure; d from €45, buffet lunch €14; P) Known as much for its tea room and restaurant, tucked beneath the shade of palm trees in a peaceful bird-twittering walled garden, as for its graceful rooms, this 17th-century house-turned-hotel is a sure bet. The help-yourself lunch buffet (noon to 4pm) is the best late-lunch option in town.

Hôtel du Musée (☎ 04 90 93 88 88; www.hotel dumusee.com.fr; 11 rue du Grand Prieuré; s/d/tr/q from €42/48/65/85; P ⁑) Twenty-eight lovely rooms are tucked away in this appealing, spacious and historic hotel. A shaded terrace garden out back makes breakfast extra special. Covered parking costs €7.

Hôtel Acacias (☎ 04 90 96 37 88; www.hotel-acac ias.com; 1 rue Marius Jouveau; d low/mid-/high season €48/51/55; ⁑ ⬚) Painted a fresh and rosy pink, Arles' most modern, mid-range choice touts 33 comfortable air-conditioned rooms and a lift to boot.

TOP END

Grand Hôtel Nord Pinus (☎ 04 90 93 44 44; www.nord -pinus.com; place du Forum; s/d/ste/apt €125/137/275/412; P ⁑) Bullfighting's feisty spirit pervades this age-old hotel where everyone from Cocteau to Picasso – not to mention matadors and *razeteurs* (bullfighters) galore – have stayed since it first opened its hefty wooden doors in 1865. Garage parking is €15.

Hôtel Jules César (☎ 04 90 52 52 52; www.hotel -julescesar.fr; 9 blvd des Lices; d €132-158, ste €300-385; P ☒ ☎) Arles' other four-star choice resides in a 17th-century convent with Roman-style portico, chapel, walled garden, cloister and sumptuous Provençal-style rooms. Garage parking/breakfast clocks in at €12/16 and pet dogs can stay for €12. Its restaurant **Lou Marques** (lunch menus €20-27, dinner menus €37-75; ☺ lunch & dinner Mon-Sat) is a gastronomic treat.

Eating
RESTAURANTS
Traffic-ridden blvd Georges Clémenceau and blvd des Lices are lined with plane trees and brasserie pavement terraces. In the historic heart, place du Forum is an intimate square shaded by eight large plane trees and filled with restaurant terraces.

Corazón (☎ 04 90 96 32 53; corazon.arles@wanadoo .fr; 1bis rue Réattu; starters/mains/desserts €9/11/9.50; ☺ lunch & dinner Tue-Sat) Warm goat cheese dripping in lavender honey and *coquilles St-Jacques au saffron* are the imaginative dishes cooked up at this contemporary choice. Changing painting, sculpture, furniture and lamp exhibitions – all of an ultramodern nature – add the ultimate funky touch.

Le 16 (☎ 04 90 93 77 36; 16 rue du Docteur Fanton; lunch menu €12; ☺ lunch & dinner Mon-Fri, lunch Sat) Combine boldly striped tablecloths, a rainbow of lamps inside and a flowery pavement terrace outside with excellent market-inspired cuisine and you get this fabulous little number – named after the number of the street on which its stands.

Chez Gigi (☎ 04 90 96 68 59; gigietcie@wanadoo.fr; 49 rue des Arènes; ☺ lunch & dinner Wed-Sat) French-Canadians Marcel and Gigi are the creative force behind this refreshingly different and fun 'soul food' restaurant guaranteed to please *végetariens, cannibales et amoureux de la mer* (vegetarians, carnivores and seafood lovers) alike. Dig the *steak á lettres* (beef-chop letter box).

La Mule Blanche (☎ 04 90 93 98 54; 9 rue du Président Wilson; mains from €15; ☺ lunch & dinner Mon-Sat) The White Mule has Arles' loveliest pavement terrace – beneath a very, very, very large plane tree – and gets packed out by 12.30pm. It's brasserie-style cuisine.

LUNCH ON THE MOVE

For a simple and satisfying lunch on the move, stop off at **Les Huiles Jamard** (☎ 04 90 49 70 73; pjamard@aol.com; 46 rue des Arènes; sandwiches €3.50-4.50), a rustic olive-oil shop (signposted Les Huiles d'Olive) where sandwiches are constructed from a juicy range of fillings: the mozzarella, avocado, tomato, basil and olive oil is this author's choice.

For dessert, look no further than **Soleil eïs** (☎ 04 90 93 30 76; cnr rue des Thermes & rue du Docteur Fanton; 1/2/3 scoops €1/1.80/2.60; ☺ 2-6.30pm), a great little ice-cream shop run by an American (despite its German-inspired name – *eïs* means ice cream in German). Nowhere will you wrap your tongue around a better ice than here: home-made ice creams and sorbets are stuffed with fresh fruit and strictly *sans additives* (free of additives).

La Fuente (☎ 04 90 93 40 78; 20 rue de la Calade; menus €16.50 & €24; ☺ lunch & dinner Tue-Sun) King prawns (*gambas*) flambéed in cognac, lobster tails grilled in basil butter and fish paella are the house specialities at La Fuente, a classic dining choice with a vaulted interior and classically square interior courtyard.

SELF-CATERING
Maison du Terroir et des Produits Bio (☎ 04 90 96 13 93; www.villanatura.com; chemin de Séverin; ☺ 9.30am-12.30pm & 2.30-7.30pm Mon-Sat, from 10am Sun) Out of town, locally grown regional (olive oil, honey, rice, sausage) and *bio* (organic fruit, veg etc) products fill this vast building, impossible to miss on the A54/D570/N113/D36 roundabout.

Shops that sell *saucissons d'Arles* (local bull-meat sausages):
La Farandole (11 rue des Porcelets)
Pierre Milhau Charcuterie (11 rue Réattu)

Les Huiles Jamard (see the boxed text, above) sells olive oil for €18 per litre. **Monoprix** (place de la Libération; ☺ 8.30am-7.30pm Mon-Thu, 8.30am-8pm Fri & Sat) is a central supermarket.

Getting There & Away
AIR
Nîmes-Arles-Camargue airport (Aéroport de Nîmes-Arles-Camargue or Aéroport Nîmes-Garons; ☎ 04 66 70 49 49) is 20km northwest of Arles on the A54.

THE CAMARGUE

STEAMING AROUND

Huffing and puffing past paddy fields and sunflower meadows aboard **Le Train des Alpilles** (☎ 04 90 18 81 31; www.rdt13.fr; diesel return adult/4-12 yrs €8/5, steam return €10/7; ☻ Wed, Thu, Sat & Sun) places this unique wetland landscape in a different perspective, as van Gogh – who painted the steam train in 1888 – would have undoubtedly agreed.

The train, which runs mid-April to mid-September, links Arles with Fontvieille (best known for its windmill immortalised by Alphonse Daudet; see p155), 7km northeast by rail. The scenic 40-minute trip is made by a 030T steam locomotive on weekends (departing 10am, 1.30pm & 3.10pm Saturday and Sunday from Arles; 10.50am, 2.20pm & 4pm Sat & Sun from Fontvieille), and by a 1950s diesel train the rest of the week (10am and 2pm Wednesday and Thursday from Arles; 11am and 5pm Wednesday and Thursday from Fontvieille). Maximum speed is 20km/h and for passengers taking the last train of the day from Fontvieille, it's a one-way ride. Fares include admission to the small railway museum at the **RDT13 train station** (17bis av de Hongrie, Arles), from where trains arrive/depart.

BUS

The inter-regional bus station is on av Paulin Talabot, opposite the train station, but most buses use the bus stops on blvd George Clémenceau. The **Boutique des Transports** (☎ 0 810 000 816; 34 blvd George Clémenceau; ☻ 7.45am-12.45pm & 1.15-6pm Mon-Fri) sells bus tickets.

From Arles there are buses to/from Stes-Maries de la Mer (€4.80, one hour, four to five daily), Salin de Giraud (€4.80, 40 minutes, two to four daily) and many places en route such as Mas du Pont de Rousty, Pioch Badet and Pont de Gau.

From Arles you can travel by bus to/from Nîmes (€5.50, 50 minutes, four daily Monday to Saturday) and Avignon (€7.10, 45 minutes, 11 daily). For information on services to/from Aix-en-Provence (€9.80, 1¾ hours, two to six daily), Fontvieille (€2.40, 20 minutes, eight daily Monday to Saturday, two daily Sunday) and Salon de Provence (€4.90, 1¼ hours, eight daily Monday to Saturday, two daily Sunday) call ☎ 04 42 97 52 12.

CAR & MOTORCYCLE

Car-rental agencies:

Avis (☎ 04 90 96 82 42; av Paulin Talabot) In the train station.

Sixt (☎ 04 90 93 02 17; 4 av Paulin Talabot)

TRAIN

Arles train station (av Paulin Talabot) serves major rail destinations including Nîmes (€6.70, 30 minutes), Marseille (€11.90, 50 minutes), Avignon centre (€5.80, 55 minutes) and Avignon TGV (€7.10, 45 minutes).

Getting Around

BICYCLE

Hire a bike from **Peugeot Cycles** (☎ 04 90 96 03 77; 15 rue du Pont) for €15 per day.

STES-MARIES DE LA MER

pop 2200

No more than a seaside village marooned at what seems like the end of the world between the Étang de l'Impérial and the sea, Stes-Maries de la Mer *is* the Camarguaise outback. At its heart towers a magnificent fortified Romanesque church which, as it has done for centuries, serves as a pilgrimage site for Europe's colourful Roma population.

Away from the madding crowds in the small pedestrian village, a stunning coastline laced with 30km of uninterrupted sandy beach basks in the sun. Nudists bare it all near the Phare de la Gacholle (p120), a lighthouse 11km east of the village.

Orientation & Information

Most things you need are lined up between av Van Gogh and the sea. From the bus stop on av d'Arles (the southern end of the D570), head south along av Frédéric Mistral then east across place des Remparts and place Portalet to get to central place de l'Église.

Laundrette (24 av d'Arles) Near the tourist office.

Tourist Office (☎ 04 90 97 82 55; www.saintesmaries .com in French; 5 av Van Gogh; ☻ 9am-8pm Jul & Aug, 9am-7pm May, Jun & Sep, 9am-6pm Apr & Oct, 9am-5pm Nov-Mar) Has an ATM outside.

Sights

Donjon-style **Église des Stes-Maries** (place de l'Église) was built between the 12th and 15th centuries. Its sober, dim interior shelters a beautiful elevated choir and a crypt where the statue of St Sarah – the highly revered patron saint of the Roma – is kept. A sea of smoky candles burns at the foot of the overdressed black statue which, at pilgrimage time, is showered with at least 40 or 50 brightly coloured dresses (see Pélerinage des Gitans, below). St Sarah's relics – found in the crypt by King René in 1448 – are enshrined in a gaudy wooden chest, stashed in a hole cut in the stone wall above the choir. From the rooftop **Terrasse de l'Église** (church terrace; adult/12-18 yrs €2/1.30; ☺ 10am-8pm Jul & Aug, 10am-12.30pm & 2-6.30pm Mon-Fri, 10am-7pm Sat & Sun Mar-Jun, Sep & Oct, 10am-noon & 2-5pm Wed, Sat & Sun Nov-Feb) a fabulous panorama unfolds.

Les Arènes, the amphitheatre next to Port Gardian, can only be visited during bull-fights; the tourist office has details. Bull-fights can also seen on Sunday, Easter to mid-July, at the **Arènes de Méjanes** (☎ 04 90 97 10 60; Domaine de Méjanes), on the Paul Ricard complex 30km north in Méjanes.

About 10km north of Stes-Maries is **Château d'Avignon** (☎ 04 90 97 58 58; rte d'Arles; guided tour adult/under 16 yrs €3/free; ☺ 10am-5pm Jul, Aug, Oct & Mar, 10am-5pm Wed-Mon Apr, Jun & Sep), an 18th-century chateau furnished almost exactly as it was by wealthy Marseille merchant Louis Noilly

Prat, who used the place as a hunting lodge in the 1890s. He kitted out the castle with hot and cold running water, central heating and other gadgets revolutionary at the time. Next door is the fascinating Maison du Cheval Camargue (see A Bullish Affair, p116).

Tours

For walking, cycling and horse-riding tours see p107. For a 12km-long, 45-minute tour by white electric train from Stes-Maries, hop aboard **Le Petit Train Camarguais** (☎ 06 09 96 02 65; adult/child €5/4; ☺ Apr-Oct), with hourly departures from in front of the tourist office.

From March to November, several companies run boat trips from Port Gardian in Stes-Maries, including **Le Camargue** (☎ 04 90 97 84 72; bateau.camargue@wanadoo.fr; 5 rue des Launes) and **Les Quatre Maries** (☎ 04 90 97 70 10; www.lesquatre maries.com in French; 36 av Théodore Aubanel). Both charge around €10/5 per adult/under 16 years for a 1½-hour trip. The **Tiki III** (☎ 04 90 97 81 68; tiki3@wanadoo.fr) is docked at the mouth of the Petit Rhône, 1.5km west of Stes-Maries.

Festivals & Events

The village bursts with life during the **Pélerinage des Gitans** (Roma pilgrimages; see the boxed text, below) on 24–25 May and 17–18 October. Bullfights animate Les Arènes

---

PÉLERINAGE DES GITANS

Europe's Roma population is said to have its roots in Camargue's shifting waters, where Roma people from all over Europe flock each May and October to honour their patron saint, Sarah. According to Provençal legend, Sarah was the servant of Mary Jacob and Mary Salome, who (along with other New Testament figures) fled the Holy Land by boat and drifted in the open sea until landing near the River Rhône in AD 40.

Pilgrimages set the streets of Stes-Maries de la Mer ablaze with song, music and dance. The May festivities last for three days, the first two of which celebrate the feast day of Mary Jacob (25 May) and see Roma party with great gusto. Many hit the road for the long journey home on the third day, which honours the Marquis de Baroncelli Jaron (1869–1943), a local herdsman responsible for rekindling many a Camarguaise tradition in the 19th century. Fewer travel to the autumn pilgrimage, which falls on the Sunday closest to Mary Salome's feast day (22 October).

In anticipation of a pilgrimage, a wooden chest above the choir in Église des Stes-Maries is lowered to the altar so the pilgrims can touch it and pray by its side. The chest is believed to contain the skeletons of Sarah, Mary Jacob and Mary Salome, discovered in the church in 1448. Following a solemn mass, a black statue of Sarah is carried from the church crypt through the streets and down to the sea, to symbolise the arrival of the Roma patron saint. The procession is led by *gardians* (see A Bullish Affair, p116) on horseback, who escort the statue to the seashore, where it is placed in a wooden fishing boat in the sea and blessed. The pilgrims pour into the sea fully clothed. The same ritual is showered upon statues of Mary Jacob and Mary Salome on 25 May when, following the benediction of the sea, the sacred relics in the church are winched back up to their safe hidey-hole.

during Easter; most Sundays in May and June; in mid-June for the village's five-day **Fête Votive** when it celebrates traditional Camargue traditions; and in mid-August during the **Feria du Taureau** (bull festival).

Sleeping

BUDGET

Hostel

Auberge de Jeunesse (☎ 04 90 97 51 72; fax 04 90 97 54 88; half-board €24.40; ☼ reception 8.30-11am & 5-10pm) Head 8km north of Stes-Maries along the Arles-bound D570 to reach this charming hostel, in the old village school in Pioch Badet. Tables and chairs lounge beneath trees, there

are bicycles to rent and horse-riding expeditions can be organised. A HI card (or nightly stamp) is obligatory. Les Cars de Camargue buses from Arles to Stes-Maries drop you at the door in Pioch Badet (see p114).

Cabanes

Aspiring cowboys can rent a self-catering *cabane de gardian* (see A Bullish Affair, below); the tourist office has details. Most sleep up to five people and can be rented on a weekly basis from April to September. There is a cluster for hire on av Riquette Aubanel, a narrow lane (the D38) leading from Stes-Maries past the port to Aigues-Mortes.

A BULLISH AFFAIR

Unlike the *mise à mort* bullfighting *(corrida)* popular in Spain, Latin America and parts of southern France, bullfighting in the Camargue does not end with a dead bull.

In *courses Camarguaises* (Camargue-style bullfights), *razeteurs* (bullfighters) dressed in white try to remove ribbons or *attributs* (rosettes) tied to the bull's horns with hooks held between their fingers. It originates from the 15th century when dogs, lions and bears were let loose in a ring to chase a bull. Finally slammed as cruel in the 19th century, the other animals were then banished from the ring, leaving man to pit his wits alone against the feisty *taureau* (bull).

Bulls are bred (mainly for bull fighting) on a *manade* (bull farm) by *manadiers*, who are helped in their daily chores by *gardians* (Camargue cowboys who herd cattle on horseback). These mounted herdsmen are honoured by the **Fête des Gardians** in Arles in May, during which they parade through town on horseback clad in leather hats, chequered shirts and boots. *Gardians* traditionally live in *cabanes de gardians* (whitewashed, thatched-roof cottages sealed with a strip of mortar).

Many *manades* also breed the cowboys' best friend: the *cheval de Camargue* (Camargue horse), recognised as a breed in its own right since 1978. Creamy grey in colour, it has a square-shaped head, is 13.1 hands in size and is exceptionally robust and agile. **Maison du Cheval Camargue** (House of the Camargue Horse; ☎ 04 90 97 76 37; Mas de la Cure, chemin de la Bardouine, Stes-Maries de la Mer), managed by the Conservatoire du Littoral (see the boxed text, p36), promotes and develops the breed. The research centre was closed to the public at the time of writing, but check with the Stes-Maries de la Mer tourist office (p114) as guided visits might well be a thing of the future.

Several bull farms open their doors to visitors, including the **Manade Jacques Bon** (☎ 04 90 97 28 50; www.manade-jacques-bon.com; Le Sambuc), a farm in Le Sambuc with 400 head of cattle and 40 horses, and the **Mas de la Bélugue** (☎ 04 42 86 82 44; www.h-yonnet-labelugue.com in French) in Salin de Giraud. A typical *journée Camarguaise* (around €35, including a bull-chop 'n rice lunch and a farm tour on horseback or by 4WD), including equestrian and bull-raising traditions unique to the Camargue – the branding of young bulls with the farm emblem, the *course Camarguaise* and so on – can be seen first-hand at either farm.

Unforgettable are the one-week *stages de monte gardiane* (Camargue cowboy courses) run by the **Manade Salierène** (☎ 04 66 86 45 57; www.manadesalierene.com in French; Mas de Capellane), 11km west of Arles in Saliers. An initiation/perfection course (€500 including accommodation and meals with the *manadier's* family) comprises up to six/seven hours a day on horseback learning how to ride the Camargue's rough terrain, herd bulls and so on.

Courses Camarguaises fill amphitheatres in Arles (see p109) and Stes-Maries de la Mer (see p115). *Recortadores* (a type of bull-baiting with lots of bull-jumping and vaulting) can also be caught during the bullfighting season (Easter to September). A calendar of *courses Camarguaises* is posted online by the **Fédération Française de la Course Camarguaise** (French Federation of Camargue Bullfights; ☎ 04 66 26 05 35; www.ffcc.info in French; 485 rue Aimé Orand, 3000 Nîmes).

Camping

Camping Le Clos du Rhône (☎ 04 90 97 85 99; leclos@ laposte.net; rte d'Aigues-Mortes; 2 adults, tent & car low/ mid-/high season €15.20/20.50/21.40; ❤ Mar–mid-Dec; P ⛆) Be it a fridge (€4) or four-person bungalow (low/mid/high season €245/376/ 556) you want, this well-organised, seaside site will keep hot-and-bothered cowboys cool and looking good.

Camping La Brise (☎ 04 90 97 84 67; labrise@laposte .net; rue Marcel Carrière; 2 adults, tent & car low/mid/high season €11.40/18/18.90; ❤ Dec-Oct; P ⛆) More than 1000 campers can pitch up at this large site, northeast of the centre by the seashore, where a mind-boggling array of activities and entertainment is organised. It also has bungalows to rent.

MID-RANGE
Farmhouse

Mas de la Grenouillère (☎ 04 90 97 90 22, 06 80 25 68 58; chemin Bas des Launes; d/tr/q €60/80/100; P ⛆) La Grenouillère (literally 'Frog Farm'), 500m further along the same dirt track as L'Étrier Camarguais, has small but comfortable rooms with a small veranda overlooking open fields, a choir of frogs to croak guests to sleep at night, and horses.

Hotels

Heaps of hotels – mostly three- or four-star and costing at least €60 per night – line the D570, the main Arles–Stes-Maries road.

Les Vagues (☎ /fax 04 90 97 84 40; 12 av Théodore Aubanel; d with washbasin €31-38.50, with shower & toilet €45.75; P) The Wave, very appropriately, overlooks the water from its handsome perch alongside the road running along the port, west of the tourist office. Look for the blue-and-white building that looks like a boat. Its restaurant, equally appropriately, cooks up shellfish in every shape and size.

Hôtel Méditerranée (☎ 04 90 97 82 09; 4 av Frédéric Mistral; d with shower €40, d/tr with shower & toilet €61/65) Flower boxes add a pretty and welcoming touch to this small and well-kept hotel right in the heart of the village. Breakfast on the garden terrace ensures a great start to the day.

TOP END
Farmhouses

Numerous *mas* (Provençal farmhouses) surrounding Stes-Maries provide some of the Camargue's most pleasing accommodation.

L'Étrier Camarguais (The Camargue Stirrup; ☎ 04 90 97 81 14; www.letrier.com; chemin Bas des Launes; d incl breakfast €115; ❤ Apr-Sep; P ⛆ ⛆) This farmhouse-hotel made from 'a dream, flowers and the sun' is an absolutely idyllic joint, 1km along a dirt track signposted off the D570 1km north of Stes-Maries. Dining is poolside and rooms with garden terrace are rustic, traditional and very equestrian in feel.

Mas du Tadorne (☎ 04 90 97 93 11; www.masdu tadorne.camargue.fr; chemin Bas des Launes; d/tr/q low season €135/140/200, high season €160/167/225; P ⛆ ⛆) The Camargue is at its wildest at this cowboy-inspired hotel-restaurant, saddled with four stars, where saddles straddle the walls and horses are saddled waiting to go outside. The poolside grill is a very tasty evening choice.

Chambres d'Hôtes

The tourist office has a complete list of *chambres d'hôtes* (B&Bs).

Mas de Bardouine (☎ 04 90 97 16 55, 06 21 05 05 09; mas-bardouine@avignon-et-provence.com; d €76-100; P ⛆) Interior furnishings are nothing short of exquisite at this fabulous five-room *chambre d'hôte*, housed in what was a hunting lodge in the 18th century. Guests can use the library and Internet access is available. An extra bed can be put in any of the five rooms for an extra €20 a night. Hosts Jean Pierre and Jeanne do not accept payment by credit card.

Eating

Stes-Marie is loaded with unspectacular, snack-style places. In summer the seafront is practically one large terrace; the early morning fish market that operates here is a fabulous spot to buy some locally caught *tellines* (Lilliputian Mediterranean clams).

Brasserie de la Plage (☎ 04 90 97 84 77; 1 av République; mains around €15, sandwiches/salads €4.50/8; ❤ lunch & dinner) Take your pick of the whole dining spectrum here, be it a simple sandwich with sea view, a rack of bulls ribs (€22) or an absolutely splendid *plateau royal* (seafood platter for two people; €95) straight from the sea.

Hostellerie du Pont de Gau (☎ 04 90 97 81 53; rte d'Arles; menus €18.50-50) This Logis de France hotel with just nine rooms (d €50) is actually best known for its excellent restaurant, a handy spot for lunch after visiting the neighbouring Parc Ornithologique (p107).

THE CAMARGUE

Getting There & Away

Stes-Maries has no bus station; buses use the shelter at the northern entrance to town on av d'Arles (the continuation of rte d'Arles and the D570).

For bus details to/from Arles (via Pont du Gau and Mas du Pont de Rousty), see p114. In summer there are two buses daily from Stes-Maries to Nîmes (1¼ hours) via Aigues-Mortes.

Getting Around

Le Vélo Saintois (☎ 04 90 97 74 56; www.levelosaintois .com; 19 rue de la République) charges €15/34 for one/three days' bike rental. It also rents children's bicycles (€13.50 per day) and tandems (€30 per day). Ask for a copy of its free English-language tour brochure (also posted on its website) before pedalling off.

Le Vélociste (☎ 04 90 97 83 26; place Mireille) charges similar rates and likewise distributes a brochure with cycling routes. It also organises cycling, canoeing and horseriding trips.

Both deliver bikes to your hotel for free.

AIGUES-MORTES

pop 5000

The curiously named walled town of Aigues-Mortes (literally 'Dead Waters') sits on the Camargue's western edge, 28km northwest of Stes-Maries in the Gard *département* (department). A sleepy place, it was built on marshy flat land in the mid-13th century by Louis IX so the French crown would have a Mediterranean port under its direct control. At the time the area's other ports were governed by rival powers, including the counts of Provence. In 1248 Louis IX's ships – all 1500 of them – gathered here before setting sail to the Holy Land for the Seventh Crusade.

Information

The **tourist office** (☎ 04 66 53 73 00; www.ot-aigues mortes.fr; ⊗ 9am-8pm Jul & Aug, 9am-noon & 2-6pm Mon-Fri, 10am-noon & 2-6pm Sat & Sun Sep-Jun) is inside the walled city at Porte de la Gardette.

Sights

The sturdy, rectangular ramparts of Aigues-Mortes – the tops of which afford great views over the marshlands – can be easily circumambulated from the **Tour de Constance** (☎ 04

66 53 61 55; adult/under 18 yrs €6.10/free; ⊗ 10am-6pm May-Aug, to 4.30pm Nov-Apr), named by Louis VII after his sister. Count on 30 minutes for the 1.6km wall-top walk. Inside the impregnable fortress, with its 6m-thick walls, you can visit the 32m-tall tower that served as a Huguenot women's prison after the revocation of the Edict of Nantes in 1685. The word *register* ('to resist' in old French) on the millstone in the centre of the prison was carved by heroine inmate Marie Durand, jailed here for 38 years.

SALINS DU MIDI

From the top of Aigues-Mortes' southern ramparts there are magnificent views of the pink-hued saltpans that stretch south. By road the lone D979 follows the narrow land bar that cuts across the still pools. Alternatively, hop aboard the **salt train** (☎ 04 66 51 17 10; www.salins.fr) that salt producer La Baleine operates daily between March and October. Tickets for the informative, one-hour train ride (with English commentary and a visit to La Baleine's museum and shop), cost €6.80/5 per adult/four to 13 years. Heading towards the Salins du Midi, La Baleine train stop is clearly flagged on the left just before the bridge.

Between May and August tours of the salt works and marshes are possible. The tourist office has details.

Boat Trips

Between March and November, boats line up at Aigues-Mortes port to take tourists on safaris around the Camargue's wild waters; the tourist office has a list of operators. Tickets cost €7/4.50 per adult/three to 12 years for a 1½-hour safari and €10/6 for a 2½-hour trip.

Sleeping & Eating

Hostel-Restaurant St-Louis (☎ 04 66 53 72 68; www .lesaintlouis.fr; 10 rue Amiral Courbet; s/d from €62/79; P ⊠) A medieval welcome at the foot of the Tour de Constance awaits guests staying at the St-Louis. Its patio is a delight to dine on and comfortable rooms ensure a good night's rest. Look for the building with the ornate wrought-iron balconies.

The walled city is loaded with eating places. Pretty place St-Louis, at the southern foot of Grande Rue, has heaps of open-air cafés and terrace restaurants, most sporting *menus* averaging €18 and starring *gardianne de taureau* (a traditional bull-meat stew from the Camargue) for €10 or so. Bakeries and food, grocery and butcher shops bespeckle Grande Rue.

L'Oustau Camarguais (☎ 04 66 53 79 69; 2-4 rue Alsace-Lorraine; menu €20; ☼ lunch & dinner high season, lunch & dinner Fri-Wed low season) Those fantastic little *tellines* hand-plucked from the sandy shores are among the fish dishes featured on the menu here. Dine beneath age-old beams, enjoy changing art exhibitions on the walls and tap your toe to the occasional musical event while you munch. Meat eaters, don't miss the *civet de taureau aux saveurs de garrigue* (bull stew flavoured with Provence scrubland herbs).

La Salicorne (☎ 04 66 53 62 67; 9 rue Alsace-Lorraine; lunch formule €26, menu €32; ☼ lunch & dinner) Simple but elegant, the Salicorne (a type of edible seaweed) stands out. Jean-Claude cooks up quintessential Provençal dishes with an imaginative twist in an old-world setting. Reservations are recommended.

Getting There & Away

From Aigues-Mortes' tiny train station on rte de Nîmes, there are a handful of trains and SNCF buses to/from Nîmes (€6.30, 45 minutes).

SOUTHEASTERN CAMARGUE

The wetland is at its most savage around the eastern shores of the Étang de Vaccarès. Much of this area is protected and off limits to tourists. A memorable day trip is to head south along the D570 from Arles, turn left (southeast) onto the D36, then bear right along the narrow D36B to La Capelièr and Salin de Badon, and along its continuation, the D36C, to Salin de Giraud. Return to Arles via the northbound D36, a larger road which shadows the Grand Rhône.

Arles to Digue à la Mer

Midway along this 48km stretch – where the D36B kisses Vaccarès' eastern shores – is **La Capelière**, a minuscule hamlet where the Réserve Nationale de Camargue runs its excellent **Centre d'Information Nature** (Nature Information Centre; ☎ 04 90 97 00 97; www.reserve-camargue .org in French; adult/under 12 yrs €3/1.50; ☼ 9am-1pm & 2-6pm Apr-Sep, 9am-1pm & 2-5pm Wed-Mon Oct-Mar). As well as exhibitions, a 1.5km-long **Sentier des Rainettes** (Tree-frog Trail), studded with

---

AUTHOR'S CHOICE

Mas de St-Bertrand (☎ 04 42 48 80 69; rte du Vaccarès; d/tr/q/five-person room €35/45/55/60; mains around €10; ☼ restaurant 8am-8pm Wed-Mon Feb–mid-Nov) Luxurious it is not, but this fabulously authentic *gîte rural* – a former sheepfold – makes for a great rough-it (ish) place to stay, eat and have fun. Low-ceilinged chalets come with a small grassy terrace; Madame creates sculptures out of old rusty farm tools (displayed both in the grounds and in her workshop); horses to ride (€15/58 per hour/day) are stabled out front; there are bikes to rent (two hours/two to five hours/five+ hours €5/10/15); the bar sells mozzie spray (€6); and the very informal restaurant does the most fabulous home cooking: *côte de taureau grillé à la fleur de sel* (€13), *gardianne de taureau maison* (€11) and *tellines de Golfe de Beauduc* (€7) are perennial favourites. Find the Mas de St-Bertrand 80m past the Digue à la Mer turn-off on the D36C to Salin de Giraud.

---

four wildlife observatories (two of which are wheelchair accessible), enables you to discover flora and fauna native to freshwater marshes.

The centre runs three observatories and 4.5km of nature trails at **Salin de Badon**, former royal saltpans about 7km further south along the D36B. Unlike at La Capelière, the bird-watching towers fall within the Réserve Nationale de Camargue. Photography is therefore forbidden and visitors need a permit (adult/under 12 years €3/1.50; issued at the Centre d'Information Nature in La Capelière) to enter. The site is accessible to permit holders from sunrise to sunset daily. A ticket covering access to the latter and the nature information centre in La Capelière costs €4.50/2.

A beautiful stroll along what seems to be the edge of the world can be enjoyed on the **Digue à la Mer** (admission free; ☼ 9am-1pm & 2-6pm Apr-Sep, 9am-1pm & 2-5pm Oct-Mar), a sea dike built in the 19th century to cut the delta off from the sea. A 20km-long walking and cycling track runs along the length of the dike; there's also a shorter 10km circuit and a 2.3km footpath that cuts down to a lovely sandy beach. Walking on the fragile sand dunes is forbidden. Bird-watching is

---

AUTHOR'S CHOICE

La Chassagnette (☎ 04 90 97 26 96; restaurantchassa@aol.com; rte du Sambuc; lunch/ dinner menu €52; ☺ lunch & dinner Thu-Tue, dinner Wed mid-Dec–Oct) More fashionable than fashionable (making advance reservations a must), this Michelin-starred gem of a *bio* eating place – a restored 19th-century sheepfold surrounded by vast farmlands – is well worth the 13km trip from Arles along the southbound D36. Cuisine is strictly organic and creative, with every last fruit and vegetable coming straight from the stunning gardens – scarecrow-guarded, no less – that unfold from in front of the restaurant terrace or from the market. Meat is likewise 100% free-range and roasted 'openrotisserie' style in a central fireplace.

---

bliss in this neck of the woods: grey herons, little egrets, shelduck, avocet, the Kentish plover, oystercatcher and the yellow-legged gull are among the dozens of species to strut past.

To access the dike, follow the D36B for 17km southwest from La Capelière to Parking de la Gacholle where motorists must park; the final 3km is a rollercoaster second-gear drive along an unsealed, potholed road. From the car park, a 1km-long footpath (a particularly popular cycle ride for families) leads to the **Phare de la Gacholle** (☺ 11am-7pm Sat, Sun & school holidays), a lighthouse from which bird's-eye ocean views can be relished and exhibitions on the coast enjoyed.

Salin de Giraud & Beyond

The chequered evaporation saltpans (*marais salants*) of **Salin de Giraud** cover 140 sq km and produce about one million tonnes

---

FREEBIE

The sea wind might be wicked when it really blows and even basic sanitary facilities are nonexistent, but Plage de Piémanson (right) is one of France's last remaining free camp sites where seemingly every last Tom, Dick and Harry pitch up come the sunny months. Tents and caravans alike are a dime a dozen.

---

of salt per year, making them one of Europe's largest. *Sel* (salt), which takes three years to produce, is harvested in September and then stored in giant mountains. Pass the entrance to Salin de Giraud on the D36 and continue south along the D36D for a stunning panorama of the marsh village, the saltpans and the salt mountains. A couple of kilometres south is a **point de vue** (viewing point) where you can pull up and breathe in the salty sea air. Come here to watch the salt being harvested between August and mid-October.

Alternatively, view the pans from the back of the electric tourist train which departs two to five times daily between March and October from in front of **Les Salins de Giraud** (☎ 04 42 86 71 80; www.salins.fr; adult/4-13 yrs €6.80/5; ☺ 10.15am-12.15pm & 2.30-6pm Mar-Jun, Sep & Oct, 9.30am-12.30pm & 2-7pm Jul & Aug), in Salin de Giraud village. A small ecomuseum inside the village salt works displays old photographs and tools.

The final 12km leg of this southbound journey is unforgettable. Drive slowly to enjoy the views and stop to see pink flamingos wading through the water. About 8km south of Salin de Giraud is **Domaine de la Palissade** (☎ 04 42 86 81 28, 06 87 84 33 72; palissade@free.fr; rte de la Mer; admission €2.30; ☺ 9am-5pm Apr-Oct), a nature centre run by the Conservatoire de l'Espace Littoral et des Rivages Lacustres, which organises forays in the marshes on foot and horseback. There are a couple of observation towers here for nature-spotting on the estate, a 1km-long **sentier de découverte** (discovery trail), and various audiovisual displays in the main house to help visitors learn about local flora and fauna.

The road reaches the Mediterranean about 4km further south. Caravans and camper vans can park overnight in the camp site on the sand here, overlooking **Plage de Piémanson**. Bear east (left) from the car park and walk 1400m to get to the nudist section of the very windy beach.

Salin de Giraud is 15km east of the Digue à la Mer via the winding D36C. The **tourist office** (☎ 04 42 86 80 87; place des Gardians; ☺ 9am-12.30pm & 3-6pm Thu-Mon mid-Jun–mid-Sep), in a traditional cowboy's *cabane* on the central square in Salin de Giraud, has information on the few other accommodation options in this isolated part of the world.

Vallon des Auffes (p76), along Marseille's main coast road

Fish for sale at Marseille's Vieux Port (p71)

Cafés line Aix-en-Provence's cours Mirabeau (p97)

Le Panier quarter (p83), Marseille

PASCALE BER

Restaurants in Arles (p108)

JEAN-BERNARD CARILLET

Pink flamingoes in the
Camargue (p108)

Gardians in the Camargue (p116)

JEAN-BERNARD CA

Pélerinage des Gitans (p115), Stes-Maries de la Mer

STEVE DAVEY

A FISHY DETOUR

There is no tastier (or fishier, come to that) detour than the bone-shaking 15km ride along unsealed tracks to **Pointe de Beauduc**: from Salin de Giraud, head north along the D36C for 4km, then turn right along a narrow country lane signposted 'Chez Marc et Mireille' (look for a shabby white sign). Follow this road for 2km and at the T-junction turn right onto a gravel potholed road. From here it is a slow, bumpy, windy and breathtakingly picturesque drive for 9km to what feels like the end of the world.

An alternative is to cycle from Stes-Maries de la Mer: a 22km mountain-bike ride via the Digue à la Mer (p119) and Phare de la Gacholle (p120); both bike-rental companies in Stes-Maries (p118) have route details. Bikes can also be picked up in Salin de Giraud from the **Station Elf** (☎ 04 42 86 81 31; rond-Point Charles de Gaulle; half-/full day €10/15; ☼ 7.30am-7pm Mon-Sat) petrol station.

The 'end of the world' – alias beach endowed **Beauduc** overlooking the **Golfe de Beauduc** – is in fact a shantytown of bric-a-brac shacks, caravans and ramshackle homes where an alternative bunch of seafaring people live alongside one of the hottest addresses in the Camargue: **Chez Marc et Mireille** (☎ 04 42 48 80 08; Plage de Beauduc; fish per 100g €2-5; ☼ lunch & dinner Thu-Sun Apr-Sep, lunch Sat & Sun Oct-Mar). This old fishermen's hut–turned–beach restaurant is dimly lit, smoky and swelteringly hot. The toilet is outside. Dead flies stick to the nets covering the small windows and the chipped crockery does not match. Yet people totter in on their high heels from far and wide to feast on the fantastic grilled fish – *muge* (mullet), *saupe* (salema), *dorade* (sea bream), *bar* (bass), turbot and so on – served here. *Poutargue de Beauduc* (mullet roe from the Gulf of Beauduc) and *tellines à l'aoïli* (nail-sized Lilliputian Mediterranean clams with a garlic sauce) are dishes typical to these remote parts. Fish aside, a salad, cheese and a choice of two desserts (fruit or flan) are the only items on the menu.

Chez JuJu (☎ 04 42 86 83 86; Plage de Beauduc; ☼ lunch summer, lunch Sat & Sun Oct-Mar), the throbbing ramshackle hut opposite with part-straw roof, serves snails (€15) as well as fish.

Back to Arles

Some 8km north of Salin de Giraud on the D36 is the very informal **Musée du Riz du Petit Manusclat** (☎ 04 90 97 29 44; adult/under 12 yrs €3.50/free; ☼ 10am-5.30pm Mon-Sat, Sun & in winter by appointment) in Petit Manusclat. The history of the Camargue rice industry, which dates from the 13th century, is explained. Rice production has dropped sharply since the 1960s but it remains a key part of the Camarguais economy: almost 70% of France's annual rice yield – equivalent to 8 million quintals (400,000 tonnes) – is produced here.

In **Le Sambuc**, 1km further north along the same road, there are a couple of places where you can ride horses, and the fabulous Manade Jacques Bon (see A Bullish Affair, p116), where you can experience life on a bull farm. A night spent at the absolutely charming and authentic farm hotel **Le Mas de Peint** (☎ 04 90 97 20 62; www.masdepeint.com; d €197-254, ste €321-378; lunch/dinner menu €34/43; ☼ closed mid-Jan–mid-Mar & mid-Nov–mid-Dec) is a particularly memorable experience.

The **Station Biologique de la Tour du Valat** (☎ 04 90 97 20 13), just west of here, is a biology research station. It covers 25 sq km and opens

to the public one day per year (in January). In 1970 the station instigated the construction of the artificial **Étang du Fangassier**. The 4000-sq-metre island serves as a flamingo breeding colony, as a few years previously flamingos had started to breed less in the region.

On the eastern bank of the Grand Rhône is the **Mas Thibert** (☎ 04 90 98 70 91; www.mas-du-vigueirat.com; ☼ 10am-5pm Tue-Sun Feb-Nov), from where the **Marais du Vigueirat** – 10 sq km of extensive marshland protected by the Conservatoire du Littoral – can be discovered. The family-friendly **Sentiers de l'Étourneau** nature trails (free) can be followed alone, but the rest of the reserve can only be explored with a guide. Two-hour guided nature walks (€7) depart at 8am and 6pm Tuesday to Sunday, June to August; and five-hour equivalents (€10) depart at 7pm on Wednesday and weekends in February, March and September to November. The eight heron species that frequent these dense swamps are among the many bird species to be seen. For the less agile, the nature here can be observed from a horse-drawn carriage (€13, departures 10am and 1pm Tuesday to Sunday April to September).

Avignon Area

Hilltop villages, purple lavender fields, fruit orchards, Roman relics and a feast of markets and farmhouse *chambres d'hôtes* (B&Bs): this vast area is quintessential Provence at its best. Yet there is more to this well-trodden patch of land than meets the eye.

Papal Avignon, the city of theatre and nursery rhymes around which the Vaucluse *département* (department) revolves, acquired its ramparts and reputation as a city of art, culture and finesse during the 14th century when Pope Clement V and his court fled Rome's political turmoil for Provençal peace. Between 1309 and 1377 seven French-born popes ploughed magnificent sums of money into the Rhône-side city, building, among other things, Europe's largest Gothic palace and planting what would become extraordinary vineyards in a sleepy mining hamlet a few kilometres north. Avignon's future as a European city of culture, festival host and TGV hub was made.

Looking north, the fan-shaped Vaucluse opens up into a multitude of contrasting landscapes, climaxing with stark stone-capped Mont Ventoux (1912m), the region's highest mountain, where the legendary mistral blows at hair-raising speeds of 300km/h. Walking and cycling opportunities abound here, there is spelunking on the sinkhole-ridden Plateau d'Albion and mountains of other outdoor activities to entertain.

Gourmets visiting this neck of olive groves won't want to leave: amid the fierce, silver-ridged southern cut of the Alpilles, oil mills invite you to taste and buy while hilltop villages slumber in the sun. Hop west across the Rhône and life is one big *féria*.

AVIGNON AREA

HIGHLIGHTS

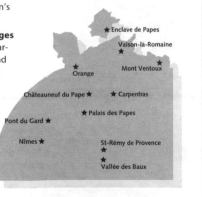

- Find out how the Popes entertained at Avignon's **Palais des Papes** (p126)

- See some of the world's greatest **Roman vestiges** in Orange (p136), Vaison-la-Romaine (p138), Carpentras (p146), St-Rémy de Provence (p151) and Nîmes (p159), and of course the **Pont du Gard** (p162)

- Smell sweet. Think purple. Follow the **lavender road** (p144)

- View **Mont Ventoux** from every angle – on a scenic drive (p141), or by bike, by quad, on foot, from the air or on a pair of skis (p145)

- Take a gourmet tour: **wine** in Châteauneuf du Pape (p135); **truffles and sweets** in Carpentras (p148); **olive oil** in the Vallée des Baux (p154); and **truffles** in a papal enclave (p140)

★ Enclave de Papes
Vaison-la-Romaine ★
★ Orange
★ Mont Ventoux
Châteauneuf du Pape ★   ★ Carpentras
★ Palais des Papes
Pont du Gard ★
Nîmes ★
St-Rémy de Provence ★
★ Vallée des Baux

AVIGNON & AROUND

AVIGNON
pop 85,935

With its world-famous performing arts festival, Europe's largest Gothic palace, outstanding Côtes du Rhône wine, a nursery rhyme bridge and a historic walled city – a pocket of which falls under Unesco World Heritage protection – it is understandable why wealthy Avignon comes across as smugger than smug. This city has it all: historic treasures, a clutch of interesting museums, great dining and a cutting-edge bar and café scene kept on its toes by a substantial student population.

Should Avignon's frenzy of things to see and do leave you gasping for breath, pop a *papaline d'Avignon,* a pink chocolate ball laced with a potent liqueur concocted from Mont Ventoux herbs. Still whacked? Pop across the River Rhône for a shot of lunch away from the tourist crowd in the quiet sister towns of Villeneuve-lès-Avignon or Les Angles.

Orientation

Avignon's main avenue, cours Jean Jaurès, runs north from the train station, outside the walled city, past the tourist office to café-clad place de l'Horloge. Place du Palais, the square abutting the Palais des Papes, is 200m north of here.

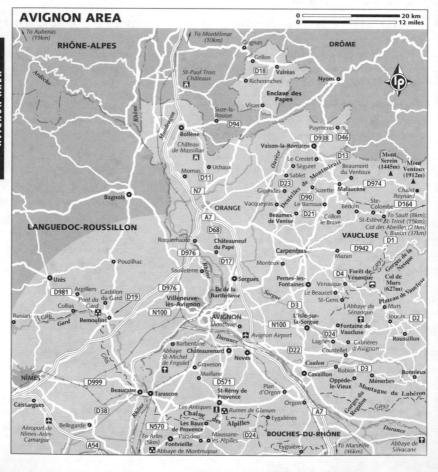

The Quartier des Teinturiers (dyers' quarter), around rue des Teinturiers and southeast of place Pie, is Avignon's bohemian patch of town.

Villeneuve-lès-Avignon and Les Angles are adjacent suburbs on the west bank of the River Rhône, and are reached by crossing the two branches of the river as well as Île de la Barthelasse, the island that divides them.

Information

BOOKSHOPS

Shakespeare (☎ 04 90 27 38 50; 155 rue de la Carreterie; ☺ 9.30am-12.30pm & 2-6.30pm Tue-Sat) English-language bookshop and tearoom.

EMERGENCY

Police Station (☎ 04 90 16 81 00; blvd St-Roch)

INTERNET ACCESS

Ad'Art Informative (☎ 04 90 86 68 70; www.adart .fr.st in French; 32 rue de la Balance; per hr €2; ☺ 10am-12.30pm & 2.30-7pm Tue-Sat)

Chez W@M (☎ 04 90 86 19 03; www.chezwam.fr in French; 41 rue du Vieux Sextier; per 15/60 min €1/3.50; ☺ 8-1am Mon-Fri, noon-1am Sat & Sun)

INTERNET RESOURCES

www.avignon-et-provence.com Sleeping and eating options in Avignon and Provence.

www.avignon.fr/en Official city website.

LAUNDRY

Laundrettes (48 rue de la Carreterie, 26 rue Lanterne & 66 place des Corps Saints; ☺ 7am-8 or 9pm) Pay €2.80 to wash a 6kg load.

LEFT LUGGAGE

Bagages Consigne (Avignon bus station, 58 blvd St-Roch; ☺ 6am-10pm May-Sep, 7am-7pm Oct-Apr) Pay €3.40/5/7.50 per small/medium/big bag per 72 hours.

MEDICAL SERVICES

Hôpital Général Henri Duffaut (☎ 04 32 75 33 33; 305 rue Raoul Follereau) Marked on maps as Hôpital Sud (bus No 1 or 3 to end of line); 2.5km south of the central train station.

MONEY

Banque de Lyonnais (13 rue de la République) Twenty-four-hour banknote exchange machine.

POST

Central Post Office (cours Président Kennedy)

TO MARKET, TO MARKET, TO BUY A ...

... whole pig not, but certainly one of the fat little beasts chopped up and ready to cook. Unless stated otherwise, markets happen from around 8am to noon. Covered food markets in Avignon (p132) and Nîmes (p161) operate daily.

Monday Fontvieille, Nîmes

Tuesday Beaumes-de-Venise, Maussane-les-Alpilles, Tarascon, Vaison-la-Romaine

Wednesday Malaucène, Sault, St-Rémy de Provence, Valréas

Thursday Eryragues, L'Isle-sur-la-Sorgue, Maillane, Nyons, Orange, Vaison-la-Romaine, Villeneuve-lès-Avignon

Friday Carpentras, Châteauneuf du Pape, Fontvieille, Graveson (farmers' market; 4pm to 8pm May to October), Nîmes (organic/bio)

Saturday Orange (June to September), Pernes-les-Fontaines, Richerenches (truffles; November to March), Vaison-la-Romaine

Sunday L'Isle-sur-la-Sorgue, Vaison-la-Romaine (July and August)

TOURIST INFORMATION

Central Tourist Office (☎ 04 32 74 32 74; www.ot -avignon.fr; 41 cours Jean Jaurès; ☺ 9am-6pm Mon-Sat, 10am-5pm Sun Apr-Oct, 9am-6pm Mon-Fri, 9am-5pm Sat, 10am-noon Sun Nov-Mar) Longer hours during July's Avignon Festival.

Gare TGV Tourist Office (☎ 04 32 74 32 74; Courtine; ☺ 10am-5pm Mon-Sat)

Pont d'Avignon Tourist Office (☎ 04 32 74 32 74; Pont St-Bénézet; ☺ 10am-7pm Apr-Sep)

Sights

Avignon's most interesting attractions are within its roughly oval walled city – 1.5 sq km of history surrounded by 4.3km of ramparts built between 1359 and 1370. The most historic pocket of the medieval city around the imposing Palais des Papes has been a Unesco World Heritage site since 1995. To glimpse Avignon's nine popes in their fashionable garbs of the day, peek at their **trompe l'oeil portrait** on the side of the *conseil général* (general council) building, off rue Viala.

Université d'Avignon (Avignon University; www .univ-avignon.fr; 74 rue Louis Pasteur), founded by Pope Boniface VIII in 1303, resides in all its splendour inside **Porte St-Lazare**, the gate linking the eastern part of the walled city with the modern world.

PALAIS DES PAPES

Europe's largest Gothic palace, the **Papal Palace** (☎ 04 90 27 50 00; www.palais-des-papes.com; place du Palais; adult/8-17 yrs mid-Mar–Oct €9.50/7.50, Nov–mid-Mar €7.50/6; ⏰ 9am-9pm Jul, 9am-8pm Aug & Sep, 9am-7pm Apr-Jun & Oct, 9.30am-5.45pm Nov-Mar) was built in the 14th century as a fortified palace for the pontifical court. Papal banquets held here were of tremendous proportions. A feast to celebrate Clement VI's coronation in 1342 comprised 118 oxen, 1033 spit-roasted sheep, 1195 geese, 7428 chickens, 50,000 sweet tarts, 39,980 eggs and 95,000 loaves of bread, among numerous other things. Since 1947 the **Cours d'Honneur** (Courtyard of Honour) has hosted the Avignon theatre festival.

The basic admission fee includes a seven-language audioguide to direct you around 24 of the palace's bare and undecorated stone halls; the palace's **Grande Chapelle** (Great Chapel), where temporary exhibitions are held; and the **Musée de l'Oeuvre**, with its collection of interactive maquettes, archaeological pieces, statues and other works illustrating medieval papal life; and a stroll around **La Bouteillerie**, a wine boutique where you pay to taste wine.

Guided tours in English run once or twice daily in summer. Alternatively, pay €24.50 for a two-hour Visite Palais Secret (secret palace tour; French only) around previously unexplored parts of the palace (the baths, bedrooms where the popes kept caged nightingales, secret towers, rooftop walkways etc), followed by brunch (and stunning panorama) on the **Great Dignitaries' Terrace**. Tours depart Saturday and Sunday, September to June, and must be booked in advance.

AVIGNON PASSION

Whether in town for a few hours or several days, anyone intent on seeing two or more sights needs to frogmarch themselves straight to the tourist office to pick up an *Avignon Passion* museum pass. It is free, valid for 15 days and – from your second museum or monument visit on – gets you and four others a bonanza of 20% to 30% discount on entrance fees, walking tours and boat cruises in Avignon and Villeneuve-lès-Avignon. Discounted pass prices are the same as reduced rates students and those aged eight to 17 years pay.

Combination tickets covering admission to the palace and Pont St-Bénézet (adult/ eight to 17 years March to October €11.50/9, November to mid-March €9.50/7.50) are available.

PLACE DU PALAIS

In the 14th and 15th centuries bishops and archbishops lived in the big **Petit Palace** (Little Palace; place du Palais). Today the **Musée du Petit Palais** (☎ 04 90 86 44 58; musee.petitpalais@wanadoo .fr; place du Palais; adult/under 12 yrs €6/free; ⏰ 10am-1pm & 2-6pm Wed-Mon Jun-Sep, 9.30am-1pm & 2-5.30pm Wed-Mon Oct-May), it houses an outstanding collection of 13th- to 16th-century Italian religious paintings.

From the Romanesque **Cathédrale Notre Dame des Doms** (1671–72), walkways wend uphill to the **Jardins des Doms**, bluff-top gardens affording wonderful views of the Rhône, Pont St-Bénézet, Villeneuve-lès-Avignon and the Alpilles. Steps link the limestone rock top, **Rocher des Doms**, with riverside blvd de la Ligne.

From the same square, the flatter **Promenade des Papes** – signposted along rue de Mons – leads to the **Verger d'Urbain V**, gardens since gravelled over where the popes grew sweet-smelling plants and herbs and kept exotic animals in cages.

PONT ST-BÉNÉZET

Legend claims this bridge, immortalised by the French nursery rhyme *Sur le Pont d'Avignon* (On the Bridge of Avignon), was built by St Bénézet (St Benedict), a pious lad from Savoy who was told in three visions to get the Rhône spanned at any cost.

Tall stories aside, **Pont d'Avignon** (☎ 04 90 27 51 16; rue Ferruce, entrance on cours Châtelet; adult/8-17 yrs mid-Mar–Oct €4/3.30, Nov–mid-Mar €3/2.50; ⏰ 9am-9pm Jul, 9am-8pm Aug & Sep, 9am-7pm Apr-Jun & Oct, 9.30am-5.45pm Nov-Mar) – properly called Pont St-Bénézet – was built between 1177 and 1185 across both channels of the River Rhône and Île de la Barthelasse to link Avignon with what later became Villeneuve-lès-Avignon. The original 900m-long wooden structure was rebuilt in stone around 1350, only for four of its 22 spans to be washed away by floods in 1669. Discover what happened after that in the onsite **Musée du Pont St-Bénézet** (⏰ same hr as bridge).

Combination tickets for the bridge and the Palais des Papes are available; see p126.

MUSEUMS

Most museums languish in 17th- and 18th-century *hôtels particuliers* (private mansions): Hôtel de Villeneuve-Martignan (1741–54) shelters a fine-arts museum, the **Musée Calvet** (☎ 04 90 86 33 84; 65 rue Joseph Vernet; adult/12-18 yrs €6/3; ⊙ 10am-noon & 2-6pm Wed-Mon), with its 16th- to 20th-century painting collection. An archaeological collection slumbers in the **Musée Lapidaire** (Statuary Museum; ☎ 04 90 86 33 84; 27 rue de la République; adult/12-18 yrs €2/1; ⊙ 10am-noon & 2-6pm Wed-Mon), in the 17th-century chapel of a former Jesuit college.

A block east, view masterpieces by van Gogh, Sisley and Cézanne in the **Musée Angladon** (☎ 04 90 82 29 03; www.angladon.com; 5 rue Laboureur; adult/7-14 yrs €6/1.50; ⊙ 1-6pm Wed-Sun Sep-Jun).

The **Musée Louis Vouland** (☎ 04 90 86 03 79; www.vouland.com; 17 rue Victor Hugo; adult/12-18 yrs €6/3; ⊙ 10am-noon & 2-6pm Tue-Sat, 2-6pm Sun May-Oct, 2-6pm Tue-Sun Nov-Apr) displays an interesting collection of 17th- and 18th-century decorative arts and a collection of Provence-inspired paintings.

Minimalist art, photography and video are represented in the **Musée d'Art Contemporain** (☎ 04 90 16 56 20; www.collectionlambert.com; 5 rue Violette; adult/under 18 yrs €5.50/4; ⊙ 11am-6pm or 7pm Tue-Sun).

Natural history is the drive behind the fusty collection of botanist Espirit Requien (1788–1851) in the **Musée Requien** (☎ 04 90 82 43 51; musee.requien@wanadoo.fr; 67 rue Joseph Vernet; admission free; ⊙ 9am-noon & 2-6pm Tue-Sat).

QUARTIER DES TEINTURIERS

Rue des Teinturiers follows the course of the River Sorgue through Avignon's old dyers' district – busy until the 19th century. Some water wheels still turn. Beneath plane trees stands the 16th-century **Chapelle des Pénitents Gris** (rue des Teinturiers) and the chapel and belltower of the former **Couvent des Cordeliers** (rue des Teinturiers), Avignon's largest convent when it was founded in 1226. Inside lies the grave of Laura, the muse of Italian poet Petrarch.

SYNAGOGUE

Avignon's neoclassical **synagogue** (☎ 04 90 85 21 24; 2 place Jérusalem; ⊙ 10am-noon & 3-5pm Mon-Thu, 10am-noon Fri) was first built in 1221. A 13th-century oven used to bake unleavened bread for Passover can still be seen, but the rest of the present round, domed neoclassical structure dates from 1846; a fire destroyed the original edifice in 1845. Visitors must be modestly dressed and men must cover their heads as is custom.

Activities

BOATING

Les Grands Bateaux de Provence (☎ 04 90 85 62 25; www.avignon-et-provence.com/mireio in French; allées de l'Oulle), based at the landing stage opposite **Porte de l'Oulle**, runs dinner cruises down the River Rhône from Avignon to Arles and Châteauneuf du Pape (both four to seven hours, €41 to €54).

In summer you can dine aboard a boat (adult/under 12 years €23.50/12, 1¼ hours) or make a return trip (adult/under 12 years €7/3.50, 1¼ hours, six daily, mid-June to mid-September) aboard its boat-bus to Île de la Barthelasse and Villeneuve-lès-Avignon.

ROLLERBLADING

Avignon en Rollers (☎ 06 74 03 21 80; www.avignon enrollers.asso.fr in French), the local rollerblading club, meets for a weekly blade (7km to 10km, one hour) on Friday at 8.30pm in front of the post office. It arranges longer trips into the surrounding countryside too.

WALKING

The **Club Alpin Français** (☎ 04 90 82 66 17; caf.avignon@free.fr; 3 rue St-Michel; ⊙ 6-8.30pm Thu) helps wannabe walkers get going.

WINE TASTING

Find out everything about Côte du Rhône wines at the **Maison des Vins** (☎ 04 90 27 24 00; www.vins-rhone.com; 6 rue des Trois Faucons). Its series of free booklets, detailing nine different colour-coded *routes touristiques* (tourist trails) in the Côtes du Rhone wine region, lists dozens of estates where you can taste, buy, eat, drink, be merry and sleep.

Avignon for Children

The white trains, **Les Trains Touristiques d'Avignon** (☎ 06 11 35 06 66; place du Palais; admission €6; ⊙ every 15 min 10am-7pm mid-Mar–Jun & Sep–mid-Oct, 10am-8pm Jul & Aug), that trundle around town are a winner with kids. Adults too enjoy the 45-minute sightseeing tour.

Otherwise, there is a playground in the **Jardins des Doms** (p126); and **Medieval Avignon city tours** (July and August; French only) run by the tourist office for older children.

AVIGNON

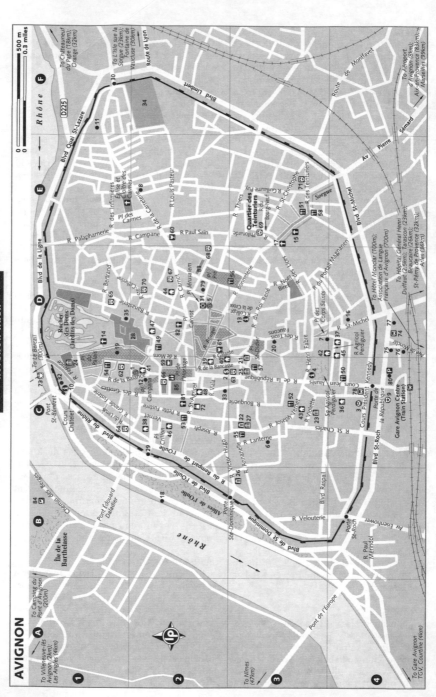

AVIGNON AREA

In Les Angles, planets loom large at the **Parc d'Astronomie, du Soleil et du Cosmos** (☎ 04 90 25 62 82; www.parcducosmos.com in French; av Charles de Gaulle), an astronomy park where young masterminds can follow a 1¼ hour trail through garrigue to unravel the mysteries of the universe. Call ahead to check what workshops/guided visits it has that day.

Tours
The tourist office runs many city tours, including English-language ones on foot (adult/under eight years €10/7, two hours, three times weekly) from April to October.

Festivals & Events
The world famous **Festival d'Avignon** (www .festival-avignon.com), founded in 1947, is held each year in July. It attracts hundreds of actors, dancers, musicians and other artists who perform some 300 shows a day in every imaginable venue. Alongside this expensive, prestigious and government-subsidised official festival runs the fringe **Festival Off** (www.avignon-off.org in French).

Tickets for official festival performances cost €5 to €33. Programme and ticket information is available online and at the **Bureau du Festival** (☎ 04 90 14 14 14; Cloître St-Louis, 20 rue de la Portail Boquier; ☽ 11am-6pm Mon-Fri mid-Jun–early Jul, 11am-8pm daily during festival). Tickets can be reserved by telephone, via the website or at branches of FNAC (€1.60 booking fee) from early June onwards. Unsold tickets are available up to three hours before the performance starts from the Bureau du Festival and from the actual venue 45 minutes before the performance begins.

Tickets for Festival Off performances are likewise available from FNAC and the **Bureau du Off** (☎ 04 90 84 01 47; www.avignon-off .org in French; Conservatoire de la Musique, place du Palais; ☽ 11am-9pm Jul). The annual Carte Public Adhérent-Avignon Off (€13) pays for itself in the 30% discount it yields on all Festival Off performances and in 600-odd theatres countrywide the rest of the year.

Sleeping
During the July festivals it is impossible to bag a room unless you snagged it months in advance.

BUDGET
Hôtel Innova (☎ 04 90 82 54 10; fax 04 90 82 52 39; 100 rue Joseph Vernet; d with shower €32, d/tr/q with shower & toilet €45/49/57; ☽ 1st-fl reception 7am-8pm) A short stroll from the train station, this bright and

friendly hotel has 11 small but wholesome rooms and a comfortable lounge-cum-breakfast room where guests can sit and chat. The latter should have an Internet point (for guests) by 2005. Minimum payment by credit card is €40.

Hôtel Monclar (☎ 04 90 86 20 14; www.hotel-monclar.com; 13 av Monclar; s/d with washbasin from €20/30, with shower €26/36, with shower & toilet €45/45; P) The Monclar occupies a peppermint-shuttered 18th-century building by the train station (next to the tracks in fact, meaning noise can be a problem) and has considerable charm. Better still, it has a back garden.

A trio of hotels with acceptable rooms sits just off the main commercial shopping street:

Hôtel Colbert (☎ 04 90 86 20 20; www.lecolbert-hotel.com; 7 rue Agricol Perdiguier; s/d/tr with shower & toilet €45/49/68)

Hôtel du Parc (☎ 04 90 82 71 55; www.hotelduparc.fr.fm; 18 rue Agricol Perdiguier; s/d with washbasin €20/35, with shower €35/42, with shower & toilet €38/47)

Hôtel Le Splendid (☎ 04 90 86 14 46; www.avignon-splendid-hotel.com; 17 rue Agricol Perdiguier; s with washbasin/shower/shower & toilet €30/37/40, d/tr with shower & toilet €49/70)

Île de la Barthelasse sports five camp sites to pitch up, including **Camping du Pont d'Avignon** (☎ 04 90 82 63 50; www.camping-avignon.com; chemin de la Barthelasse; 2 adults, tent & car very low/very high season €9.60/20.65; ☉ mid-Mar–Oct; P ☎), a pretty green site that touts five sets of prices, ranging from very low (March) to very high (August) season. It rents bungalows and chalets too.

MID-RANGE
The tourist office has a list of many lovely pool-clad *chambres d'hôtes* around Avignon, costing €70 to €150 per night for a double with breakfast.

Villa Agapé (☎ 04 90 85 21 92; www.villa-agape.com; 13 rue St-Agricol; d €90-140; P ☒ ☒) This elegant townhouse wrapped around a swimming pool in central Avignon has three rooms, two named after the host's grown-up daughters, Caroline and Olivia, whose rooms they once were. Its entrance is the inconspicuous wooden door next to the pharmacy.

Hôtel Le Médiéval (☎ 04 90 86 11 06; hotel.medieval@wanadoo.fr; 15 rue Petite Saunerie; s/d/tr €40/53/74, 2-/3-person studio from €392/413) In a restored 17th-century mansion, the Medieval has a splendid interior courtyard, studios to

rent on a three-day or longer-term basis and a clutch of rooms with papal-palace views.

Hôtel de Garlande (☎ 04 90 80 08 85; hotel-garlande@avignon-et-provence.com; 20 rue Galante; s/d €105/118/128; ☒ ☒) In the same mould as Médiéval, this is a lovely two-star 12-room place well housed in a historic *hôtel particulier* overlooking a quiet narrow street. Larger rooms have a fridge and air-con, and little dogs can stay for €6.10 a night.

Hôtel de Blauvac (☎ 04 90 86 34 11; www.hotel-blauvac.com; 11 rue de la Bancasse; small s/d €56/59, larger s/d/tr/q €66.50/70.50/84/90) The third in Avignon's trio of old and graceful twin-starred hotels bang in the centre of things, historic Hôtel de Blauvac was the town residence of the Marquis de Blauvac in the 17th century. Rates rise by €3.50 in July.

Hôtel du Palais des Papes (☎ 04 90 86 04 13; www.hotel-avignon.com in French; 3 place du Palais; s/d from €75/85, ste 110-160; ☒) Charming, old and old-worldly, there's no prizes for guessing what guests staying in the pricier rooms gaze out on at the Papal Palace Hotel. Only three of its 27 rooms are air-conditioned.

Le Petit Manoir (☎ 04 90 25 03 36; www.hotel-lepetitmanoir.com in French; 15 av Jules Ferry; d from €47; P ☒) Across the river in Les Angles, this Logis de France hotel has a shady pool, a good restaurant and is an excellent mid-range choice if you have kids in tow. Rooms are spread between several buildings and some have a balcony; others, a table-clad terrace by the pool.

Hôtel Mignon (☎ 04 90 82 17 30; www.hotel-mignon.com; 12 rue Joseph Vernet; d/tr from €39/44; ☐) Tucked amid designer clothes shops, this cute hotel (*mignon* means 'cute' in French) has 15 spotless, well-kept and soundproofed rooms. Prices include breakfast and there is an Internet point for guests at reception (open until 11pm).

TOP END
La Mirande (☎ 04 90 85 93 93; www.la-mirande.fr in French; 4 place de la Mirande; d low/high season from €240/340, ste low/high season from €560/640, menus €38-92; P ☒ ☒ ☐ ☒) French newspaper *Le Figaro* once described the city's most exclusive hotel – in a 14th-century cardinal's palace behind Palais des Papes – as a 'place of pilgrimage for men and women of taste'. Its restaurant is praiseworthy and innovative. Parking costs an impressive €18 per night.

Cloître St-Louis (☎ 04 90 27 55 55; www.cloitre -saint-louis.com; 20 rue du Portail Boquier; d low/high season from €100/155; P ⊠ ⊠ ⬚ ⬚) Exquisite four-starred rooms languish in a Jesuit school dating from 1589 at Cloister St-Louis. The ultra-modern wing with rooftop pool to splash around in is the creation of French architect Jean Nouvel.

Hôtel d'Europe (☎ 04 90 14 76 76; www.hotel -d-europe.fr; 12 place Crillon; d/ste €129/616; P ⊠ ⊠ ⬚ ⬚) An inner courtyard to breakfast in and a Pope-sized €33 Sunday brunch are stand-outs at Hôtel d'Europe, inside a *hôtel particulier* built for the Marquis de Graveson in 1580 and host (from 1799 onwards) to everyone from Napoleon to Salvador Dali and Picasso. Its restaurant has a Michelin star.

Eating
RESTAURANTS
Maison Nani (☎ 04 90 82 60 90; 29 rue Théodore Aubanel; salads €9, mains around €10; ✆ lunch Mon-Sat, dinner Fri & Sat) This busy place markets itself as 'the restaurant of the Avignonnais' and serves hearty salads, meats and other sunny bistro-style dishes in a flamboyant interior splashed with ochre. Nani is a simple place and does not take credit cards.

Le Grand Café (☎ 04 90 86 86 77; 4 rue des Escaliers Ste-Anne; lunch/dinner menu €18/30; ✆ lunch & dinner Tue-Sat) Inside the La Manutention cultural centre, this cutting-edge contemporary café-restaurant cooks up memorable Mediterranean cuisine in a fabulous old-and-new warehouse setting.

La Compagnie des Comptoirs (☎ 04 90 85 99 04; www.lacompagniedescomptoirs.com; 83 rue Joseph Vernet; starters/mains from €15/20; ✆ lunch & dinner Tue-Sat, lunch Sun) Reception flashes orange neon, the lounge bar (p132) is a green square and Christophe Fluck cooks world cuisine at this striking minimalist place, built around an 18th-century cloister. The imaginative menu – crab and avocado sushi and the like – has, unusually, some strong vegetarian choices.

Le Vernet (☎ 04 90 86 64 53; 58 rue Joseph Vernet; menu du jour €22; ✆ lunch & dinner) Light summery cuisine – roast quail in a raspberry vinegar sauce, white tuna or *soupe de pêches* – is the mainstay of this down-to-earth but elegant courtyard restaurant, hidden behind a wall opposite the Calvet and Requien museums.

Le Marmiton (☎ 04 90 85 93 93; 4 place de la Mirande; menus €49 & €90, table d'hôte €85; ✆ dinner Tue-Sat) Foodies as keen to know how to prepare Provençal food as eat it should not miss the four-course table d'hôte feasts cooked before your very eyes around a scrubbed wooden table in La Mirande's famous kitchen.

Le Bercail (☎ 04 90 82 20 22; 162 chemin Canotiers, Île de la Barthelasse; mains around €20; ✆ lunch & dinner) The Fold (as in a sheep fold or to return to the fold) is a romantic spot by the river to munch on pizza cooked in a wood-fired oven. Listen to the Rhône lap by and gaze at awe-inspiring views of Pont d'Avignon and the walled city across the water while you dine. Better still, you can sail here (p133); the boat jetty fronts the busy terrace restaurant.

Le Moutardier (☎ 04 90 85 34 76; moutardier@ wanadoo.fr; 15 place du Palais; menus €27-39; ✆ lunch & dinner) In the medieval days of the Avignon popes, the *souffleur* blew the fire to get it going, the *rôtisseur* roasted the meat on it and the *moutardier* made the mustard – hence the name of Avignon's most scenic terrace restaurant, which can be found lazing in the shade of the Palais des Papes. It is one of the few places to tout a fully-fledged vegetarian menu.

Woolloomooloo (☎ 04 90 85 28 44; www.woolloo .com; 16bis rue des Teinturiers; lunch menus €11 & €15, dinner menus 17 & €24; ✆ lunch & dinner Tue-Sun) Next to an old paper mill, Woolloomooloo is an Avignon institution with its striking feast of eclectic antique and contemporary furnishings. Vegetarian and Antillean dishes dominate.

L'Empreinte (☎ 04 32 76 31 84; 33 rue des Teinturiers; couscous €10-18; ✆ lunch & dinner Mon-Sat) Bedazzle your eyes with brightly coloured rugs, wall art and tile-topped tables while your tummy is bedazzled with Mediterranean cuisine. Cultural happenings fill this trendy spot Thursday evenings.

Christian Étienne (☎ 04 90 86 16 50; www.christian-etienne.fr; 10 rue de Mons; lunch menu €30, dinner menus €50-95; ✆ lunch & dinner Tue-Sat) Avignon's best-known chef conjures up culinary creations from his eponymous rooftop restaurant overlooking Palais des Papes. Étienne's *menu homard* (€70) involves a whole lobster cooked three different ways while his *menu confiance* (€95) – trust the chef – is one big and very delicious surprise.

C'est La Lune (It's the Moon; ☎ 04 90 25 40 55; montée Valadas, Les Angles; mains around €15; ✆ lunch & dinner Jul-Sep, dinner Oct-Jun) The panoramic view of Avignon and flower-bedecked swimming pool (open to lunch guests until 7pm) are as alluring as the jumbo salads and meats, laid-back beach feel and bohemian-styled interior at Avignon's best-kept secret. Come dusk, techno beats until well into the early hours. It's across the river in Les Angles.

SELF-CATERING

Les Halles d'Avignon (☎ 04 90 27 15 15; www.halles -avignon.com in French; place Pie; ❨ 6am-1.30pm Tue-Sun) Shop for fresh fruit, veg, fish, cheese and so on at this covered market.

Erio Convert (45 cours Jean Jaurès) One of the region's best bakeries with a superb range of breads, pastries and filled baguettes.

La Tropézienne (22 rue St-Agricol) *Papalines d'Avignon* and other naughty-but-nice sweets.

Drinking

Avignon's celebration of the region's first Côtes du Rhône wines of the year, the **Fête des Côtes du Rhône Primeurs** in mid-November, is a great excuse to drink. Otherwise, place de l'Horloge hums with café-life day and night. Across the river **C'est La Lune** (p131) is also a fabulous place to soak up the local scene.

L'Opéra Café (☎ 04 90 86 17 43; 24 place de l'Horloge; lunch formule/plat du jour €13/9, menu €32; ❨ lunch & dinner) Theatrically inspired and contemporary, this one stands out from the place de l'Horloge's café crowd.

Le Lounge (☎ 04 90 85 99 04; www.lacompagnie descomptoirs.com; 83 rue Joseph Vernet; ❨ Tue-Sat) The Lounge, albeit a very green one, is chic and trendy. DJs, concerts and happenings happen Thursday and Sunday.

Pick-Up Café (☎ 04 90 85 49 77; http://pickup cafeavignon.free.fr in French; 18 rue du Portail Matheron; petit menu/plat du jour €4.50/8; ❨ Mon-Sat) A year-round fringe festival spirit pervades this pocket-sized bistro bar, choc-a-block with bric-a-brac.

Tapalocas (☎ 04 90 82 56 84; www.tapalocas.com in French; 15 rue Galante; tapas €2.20) Drink, be merry and feast on a tapas menu as long as a giant's arm.

Entertainment

Tickets are sold at the tourist office and **FNAC** (☎ 04 90 14 35 35; 19 rue de la République; ❨ 10am-7pm Mon-Sat). For event listings, pick up the free weekly magazine, *César* or fortnightly *Rendez-vous d'Avignon* at the tourist office.

> **DID YOU KNOW?**
>
> Pernod was concocted in 1870 by absinthe inventor Jules Pernod in his house at 75–77 rue Guillaume Puy in the Quartier des Teinturiers.

NIGHTCLUBS

Red Zone (☎ 04 90 27 02 44; 25 rue Carnot; www.red zonebar.com in French; admission varied; ❨ 9pm-3am) DJs mix Thursday to Sunday at this popular club where salsa, soul and dance steal the dance floor. Monday is Afro night and live bands play Wednesday.

The Red Lion (☎ 04 90 86 40 25; www.leredlion .com; 21-23 rue St Jean le Vieux) Part ye olde English pub, part nightclub, this lively spot sports a different dance genre each evening.

L'Esclave (☎ 04 90 85 14 91; 12 rue du Limas; ❨ from 11pm) Avignon's gay hide-out is tucked in an inconspicuous building save for a signature rainbow flag.

CLASSICAL MUSIC, OPERA, BALLET & THEATRE

The season at the **Opéra Théâtre d'Avignon** (☎ 04 90 82 81 40; place de l'Horloge), built in 1847, runs October to June.

There are dozens of theatres, among them the mainstream **Théâtre du Bourg Neuf** (☎ 04 90 85 17 90; bourgneuf@wandoo.fr; 5bis rue du Bourg-Neuf) and **Théâtre du Chêne Noir** (☎ 04 90 86 58 11; www.theatreduchenenoir.asso.fr in French; 8bis rue Ste-Catherine). The **Théâtre du Chien qui Fume** (The Dog who Smokes; ☎ 04 90 85 89 49; www.chienquifume .com in French; 76 rue des Teinturiers) is an alternative venue in the dyers' district.

JAZZ

AJMI (Association pour Le Jazz & La Musique Improvisée; ☎ 04 90 86 08 61; www.jazzalajmi.com in French; 4 rue des Escaliers Ste-Anne) is a popular jazz club inside the arts centre, **La Manutention**. Concert tickets cost €15.

CINEMA

Watch nondubbed films, old and new, at **Cinéma Utopia** (☎ 04 90 82 65 36; www.cinemas -utopia.org in French; 4 rue des Escaliers Ste-Anne; tickets day/evening €3/5), inside La Manutention.

Shopping

Place des Carmes buzzes with a flower market on Saturday and a flea market on Sunday.

Avignon's smartest shopping streets are rue St-Agricol and rue Joseph Vernet, southwest of place de l'Horloge. Find art and antique galleries on rue du Limas and inside the **covered mall** (23 rue St-Agricol) beneath Hôtel du Petit Louvre.

Getting There & Away

AIR
Aéroport d'Avignon (☎ 04 90 81 51 51; www.avignon .aeroport.fr in French; chemin Felons, Montfavet) is 8km southeast.

BUS
From the **bus station** (☎ 04 90 82 07 35; 58 blvd St-Roch/5 av Monclar), there are two to five services daily to/from Aix-en-Provence (€11.80/14 via national roads/the A7 *autoroute*, one to 1½ hours), Apt (€7.20, 1¼ hours), Arles (€8.50, 1½), Cavaillon (€3.30, one hour), Vaison-la-Romaine (€7, 1¼ hours), Nîmes (€8, 1¼ hours) and Pont du Gard (€6.60, 45 minutes). Orange (€5.50, 45 minutes) and Carpentras (€3.80, 45 minutes) are served by 20-odd buses daily. Tickets are sold aboard.

International bus companies **Linebùs** (☎ 04 90 85 30 48, 04 90 86 88 67) and **Eurolines** (☎ 04 90 85 27 60) are at the bus station; see p353 for details.

CAR & MOTORCYCLE
Car rental agencies:
Avis (☎ 08 20 61 16 50; Avignon Centre train station, 42 blvd St-Roch)
Europcar (☎ 04 90 85 01 40; Avignon Centre train station, 42 blvd St-Roch)
National Citer (☎ 04 90 85 96 47; 2a av Monclar)

TRAIN
Avignon has two train stations: Gare Avignon TGV in the southwest suburb of Courtine, and central **Gare Avignon Centre** (42 blvd St-Roch), where local trains to/from Orange (€4.80, 20 minutes) and Arles (€5.80, 20 minutes) arrive/depart. Some TGVs to/ from Paris stop at Gare Avignon Centre, but TGV services to/from Nîmes (€13.30, 45 minutes), Marseille (€21.90, one hour), Nice (€45.50, 2½ hours) and so on only use Gare Avignon TGV.

Getting Around

BICYCLE & CAR
Motorists can park their cars in **Vinci Park Gare Centre** (☎ 04 90 80 74 40; blvd St-Roch & blvd

St-Ruf; ⏰ 24hr) beneath the train station and borrow a bike for free to get around.

Provence Bike (☎ 04 90 27 92 61; www.provence -bike.com in French; 52 blvd St-Roch; ⏰ 9am-12.30pm & 3-6.30pm Apr-Jun, Sep & Oct, 9am-6.30pm Jul & Aug) rents road/mountain bikes for €12/15 a day and €60/75 a week including helmet, repair kit and road book with map and route description (in English). The shop also rents tandems, scooters and motorbikes. Out of season, arrange rental by telephone (same number).

BOAT
In July and August cross the Rhône aboard the **Bac du Rocher des Doms** (admission free; ⏰ 2-5.30pm Wed, 10am-noon & 2-6.30pm Sat & Sun mid-Feb, Mar & Oct-Dec, 2-5.30pm Wed, 10am-noon & 2-6.30pm Sat & Sun Apr, Jun & Sep, 11am-9pm Jul & Aug), a shuttle boat that sails between the jetty on blvd de la Ligne and Île de la Barthelasse every 15 minutes.

BUS
A single-/double-journey ticket costs €1.05/ 1.80 direct from the bus driver and a 10-journey carnet costs €8 at the **TCRA office** (☎ 04 32 74 18 32; www.tcra.fr in French; av de Lattre de Tassigny); children under five years ride for free.

Navettes (shuttle buses) link Gare Avignon TGV with the centre (€1.05, 10 to 13 minutes, twice hourly between 6.15am and 11.30pm); buses use the bus stop in front of the post office on cours Président Kennedy Monday to Saturday, and the Cité Administrative bus stop around the corner on cours Jean Jaurès on Sunday.

Bus No 11 links Avignon with Villeneuve-lès-Avignon and bus No 10 serves Les Angles.

VILLENEUVE-LÈS-AVIGNON
pop 12,078

This so-called 'City of Cardinals', across the Rhône from Avignon, was founded in the late 13th century but only found its feet in the 14th century when cardinals, prelates and so on from the Papal court built sumptuous *livrées* (residences), churches and convents here. At the same time the French crown established a garrison in Villeneuve-lès-Avignon to keep an eye on events in the Papal-controlled city on the other side of the river.

Information

Tourist Office (☎ 04 90 25 61 33; www.villeneuveles avignon.fr; 1 place Charles David; ☼ 9am-12.30pm & 2-6pm Mon-Sat Sep-Jun, 10am-7pm Mon-Fri, 10am-1pm & 2-7pm Sat & Sun Jul, 9am-12.30pm & 2-6pm Aug) Runs two-hour guided city tours in English in July and August.

Sights

The Avignon Passion museum pass (p126) is valid here.

A breezy 15-minute stroll from Avignon across Pont Édouard Daladier brings you to Villeneuve-lès-Avignon, originally linked to its big-sister city by the **Pont d'Avignon** (p126). The defensive, 32m-tall tower that looms on your left – and affords a magnificent panorama from the top of its interior 172-step

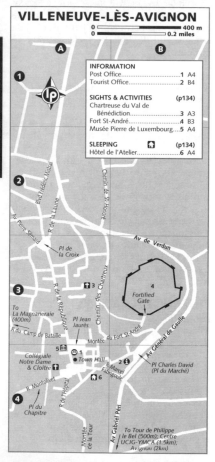

VILLENEUVE-LÈS-AVIGNON

INFORMATION
Post Office..........................1 A4
Tourist Office......................2 B4

SIGHTS & ACTIVITIES   (p134)
Chartreuse du Val de
Bénédiction........................3 A3
Fort St-André.......................4 B3
Musée Pierre de Luxembourg...5 A4

SLEEPING   (p134)
Hôtel de l'Atelier.................6 A4

spiral staircase – is the **Tour de Philippe le Bel** (adult/12-18 yrs €2/1; ☼ 10am-12.30pm & 2-6.30pm Apr-Sep, 10am-noon & 2-5.30pm Tue-Sun Oct-Jan & Mar), built in the 14th century at the western end of Pont d'Avignon. Several **walking and cycling nature trails** start from the foot of the tower; the tourist office has details.

Keen to spy on Papal Avignon, King Philippe le Bel (1285–1314) built **Fort St-André** (☎ 04 90 25 45 35; adult/under 18 yrs €4.60/free; ☼ 10am-noon & 2-6pm Apr-Sep, 10am-noon & 2-5pm Oct-Mar) – a fine example of medieval military architecture – on Mont Andaon.

Pope Innocent VI lived in a palatial *livrée* in Villeneuve-lès-Avignon which, once he became pontiff in 1352, became the **Chartruese du Val de Bénédiction** (☎ 04 90 15 24 24; www.chartreuse.org in French; 60 rue de la République; adult/under 18 yrs €6.10/free; ☼ 9am-6.30pm Apr-Sep, 9.30am-5.30pm Oct-Mar), a cloistered Carthusian monastery with 40 cells. Guided tours in English (1¼ hours) take in the delicately carved Gothic mausoleum of the pope.

During the French Revolution the monastery was shut down and its treasures stolen. View 15th- to 17th-century paintings and precious pieces of plundered religious art in the **Musée Pierre de Luxembourg** (☎ 04 90 27 49 66; 3 rue de la République; adult/under 18 yrs €3/free; ☼ 10am-12.30pm & 2-6.30pm Apr-Sep, 10am-noon & 2-5.30pm Tue-Sun Oct-Jan & Mar).

Sleeping & Eating

La Magnaneraie (☎ 04 90 25 11 11; www.hostellerie -la-magnaneraie.com; 37 rue du Camp de Bataille; d/ste from €100/230, menus €29-53; ℗ ☒ ⬛ ⬛) Sleep, eat and imagine you're in heaven at this quintessentially Provençal pad – think stone farmhouse, lavish and rambling gardens and a restaurant that guarantees to titillate with its gastronomic creations.

Hôtel de l'Atelier (☎ 04 90 25 01 84; hotel -latelier@libertysurf.fr; 5 rue de la Foire; d low/high season from €46/56; ℗) Charming rooms with old beamed ceilings and period furnishings fill this good-value two-star abode.

Centre UCJG-YMCA (☎ 04 90 25 46 20; www .ymca-avignon.com; 7bis chemin de la Justice; s/d/tr/q with shared bathroom €22/28/33/44, with private bathroom €33/44/51/51, breakfast/dinner €5/12; ℗ ⬛) This hostel organises activities, including guided tours of Avignon and its surrounds. Take bus No 10 to the Pont d'Avignon stop.

Villeneuve also has several stunning *chambres d'hôtes* guaranteed to charm.

NORTH OF AVIGNON

Vaucluse fans out northeast from the lucrative vineyards of Châteauneuf du Pape and the Roman treasures of Orange, through to the rocky Dentelles de Montmirail, the slopes of Mont Ventoux and the harsh and uninhabitable Plateau d'Albion in the Vaucluse's easternmost corner.

If you don't have a car, you can labour from town to town by bus, but the frequency and pace of services are in keeping with the tempo of Provençal life – slow.

CHÂTEAUNEUF DU PAPE
pop 2098

Wealthy Châteauneuf du Pape, 18km north of Avignon, was a mining hamlet called Calcernier after its limestone quarries until 1317, when Pope John XXII (r 1316–34) built a pontifical residence here. Moreover, he planted vineyards – the source of the extraordinarily rich and full-bodied red wines for which the village is famed today.

Châteauneuf du Pape vineyards, covered with large smooth stones (*galets*), cover 32 sq km between Avignon and Orange on the Rhône's left bank. The vines are tended by 350 *vignerons*, many of whose annual production is sold years in advance, making it impossible for tourists to so much as whiff the region's top wines commanding €300-odd a bottle. A bottle of run-of-the-mill red from 2002/2000 sells for €11/17.

The best wines of the last *millésime* (vintage) are cracked with gusto around 25 April during the **Fête de la St-Marc**.

Château des Papes

This ruined **papal castle**, built between 1317 and 1333, stands on a hillock (118m) at the village's northern end. It was plundered and burnt during the Wars of Religion, and further destroyed by German troops on 20 August 1944. From its foot there are sweeping views of Avignon, the Plateau de Vaucluse, the Lubéron, the Rhône and beyond. Steps lead to the village from the car park next to the castle.

Wine Tasting

Most producers allow cellar visits and offer *dégustation gratuite* (free wine-tasting) *sur rendez-vous* (by appointment) only; the

---

PLATEAU D'ALBION

There's more to the Plateau d'Albion than meets the eye.

France's land-based nuclear missiles were stationed on this harsh and uninhabitable moonscape from 1965 until 1996, when President Chirac ordered the missiles to be deactivated and the military site to be manned by the French Foreign Legion instead. The last nuclear missile and concrete silo was dismantled in February 1998.

What was once France's biggest secret is riddled with natural pot-holes and caverns. The plain can be uncovered – above or below ground – with the **Association Spéléologique du Plateau d'Albion** (☎ 04 90 76 08 33; www.aspanet.net in French; 2 rue de l'Église), a spelunking club in the plain's only real village, **St-Christol d'Albion** (population 555, elevation 850m), 11km south of Sault. Spelunking starts at €50 per day; the association also arranges mountain-biking expeditions. Basic accommodation (€10/5/25 for dorm bed/breakfast/half-board) is available in the club's *refuge* (hut).

---

tourist office (☎ 04 90 83 71 08; tourisme-chato9-pape@wanadoo.fr; place du Portail; 🕑 9.30am-1pm & 2-7pm Mon-Sat, 10am-1pm & 2-6pm Sun) has details. In the village itself there are several *caves* (wine cellars) where you can simply stroll in, taste and buy.

Essentially a ploy to sell wine from the Caves Brotte-Père Anselme, the **Musée du Vin** (☎ 04 90 83 70 07; www.brotte.com; av Louis Pasteur; admission free; 🕑 9 or 9.30am-noon & 2-6 or 7pm) displays old tools and is an opportunity nonetheless to soak up the pungent smell of wine and ask beginner-level questions without feeling silly.

Sleeping & Eating

La Mère Germaine (☎ 04 90 83 54 37; www.lameregermaine.com; place de la Fontaine; d €54-69; lunch menu €16, evening menus €22-85; P) Eight charming rooms slumber up top at this village restaurant with a splendid terrace to feast on. The *menu pontifical* includes seven surprise courses accompanied by seven different glasses of papal wine.

La Marmite (☎ 04 90 83 78 45; 22 rue Joseph Ducos; menus €14-19; 🕑 lunch & dinner Wed-Mon) Up the hill from the village square, the Cooking

A SCENIC DETOUR

The best way to appreciate the Châteauneuf vineyards (bar drinking their wine) is to get lost in them. Follow av St-Joseph (the west-bound D17) out of the village, then turn right (north) at the *'circuit touristique'* sign along chemin de l'Arnasque and chemin de Pradel. Then sit back, relax and motor on down through stone-crusted vineyard after vineyard. Stop at **Château Mont Redon** (☎ 04 90 83 72 75; www.chateaumontredon.fr; ☉ 8am-7pm Thu-Tue, 8am-noon & 2-6pm Wed) for a quick tipple before rounding the corner for a fantastic full frontal of Mont Ventoux.

Pot is so refreshingly simple for such an upmarket village that it risks being labelled retro. It cooks regional cuisine.

Hostellerie du Château des Fines Roches (☎ 04 90 83 70 23; www.chateaufinesroches.com; d €150-200, menus from €30; P ☒) Princesses will feel right at home at this dreamlike, turreted castle amid sprawling vineyards. It's 2km south along the Avignon-bound D17.

La Sommellerie (☎ 04 90 83 50 00; www.hotel-la-sommellerie.com; d/ste from €85/115, menus €29-80; P ☒ ☒) It was a sheepfold in the 17th century. Now it is a haven of peace and tranquillity, 3km out of the village along the westbound D17. Cooking courses are one of chef Pierre Paumel's specialities.

Getting There & Away

Rapides du Sud-Est (☎ 04 90 34 15 59) operates buses to/from Orange (€2.60, 15 minutes, one or two daily). In Châteauneuf buses use the stop on av du Général de Gaulle.

ORANGE

pop 28,889

A magnificent history, magnificent Roman relics and a less-than-magnificent National Front mayor are the distinguishing features of this small town that is otherwise really rather dull.

Named after the princely dynasty (the House of Orange) that ruled the city from the 12th century, Orange – through a 16th-century marriage with the German House of Nassau – became an active player in the history of the Netherlands and, later, (through William III, alias William of Orange) Britain

and Ireland. A stronghold of the Reformation, the city was ceded to France in 1713. To this day many members of the royal house of the Netherlands are known as the princes and princesses of Orange-Nassau.

Information

MONEY

There are a couple of commercial banks on place de la République.

POST

Post Office (blvd Édouard Daladier)

TOURIST INFORMATION

Tourist Office (☎ 04 90 34 70 88; 5 cours Aristide Briand; ☉ 9.30am-7pm Mon-Sat Apr-Jun & Sep, 9.30am-7pm Mon-Sat, 10am-4pm Sun Jul & Aug, 10am-1pm & 2-5pm Mon-Sat Oct-Mar)

Tourist Office Annexe (place des Frères Mounet; ☉ 10am-1pm & 2.15-6pm or 7pm Mon-Sat, 10am-12.30pm & 2.30-6pm Sun Apr-Sep) Opposite the Théâtre Antique.

Sights

The Roman **Théâtre Antique** (☎ 04 90 51 17 60; rue Madeleine Roch; adult/7-17 yrs €7.50/5.50, family ticket €23; ☉ 9am-6pm Mar & Oct; 9am-7pm Apr, May & Sep; 9am-8pm Jun-Aug; 9am-5pm Nov-Feb), designed to seat 9000 or so, was built during the time of Augustus Caesar (r 27 BC–AD 14). Its stage wall – the only such Roman structure still standing in its entirety (minus a few mosaics and the roof) – is 103m wide and 37m high. Admission includes a seven-language audioguide and covers entrance to the **Musée d'Orange** (☎ 04 90 51 18 24; rue Madeleine Roch; ☉ 9.30am-7pm Apr-Sep, 9am-noon & 1.30-5.30pm Oct-Mar) opposite, known for its Roman land survey registers.

The other big sight – literally – is Orange's **Arc de Triomphe** (av de l'Arc de Triomphe), a 19m tall and wide triumphal arch, 450m from the centre, that was built around 20 BC. Exceptional friezes on the 8m-thick walls commemorate Julius Caesar's victories during the Gallic Wars.

Festivals & Events

Concerts and films fill the Théâtre Antique during **Les Nuits du Théâtre Antique**, June to August. The last fortnight in July brings **Chorégies d'Orange** (☎ 04 90 34 24 24; www.choregies.asso.fr), a series of weekend operas, classical concerts and choral performances.

Sleeping

Hôtel St-Florent (☎ 04 90 34 18 53; stflorent@yahoo
.fr; 4 rue du Mazeau; d with shower/shower & toilet
€35/48; **P**) Flamboyant wall murals and
belle époque wooden beds adorned with
crushed and studded velvet make this small
family-run joint stand out. Parking costs
€6 a night.

Hôtel Le Glacier (☎ 04 90 34 06 26; www.le-glacier
.com in French; 46 cours Aristide Briand; d €52-70, f €61-70;
P ⊠) Three generations of family effort
ensures a warm welcome, 28 well-equipped
rooms and willing hosts who rent bikes
and recommend itineraries of surrounding villages.

Château de Massillan (☎ 04 90 40 64 51; www
.chateau-de-massillan.com; d from €170; **P** ⊠ 🖳 🖵)
With its glass chandeliers, turrets, bathtubs
with legs and enormous park, this chateau –
owned by Henri II's lover Diane de Poitiers
in the 16th century – is everything a fairy-
tale castle should be. It is 9km north of Orange in Uchaux (signposted off the D11).

Camping Le Jonquier (☎ 04 90 34 49 48; 1321
rue Alexis Carrel; 2 people, tent & car low/high season
€17.50/22.20; ⊙ Apr-Sep; **P**) Near the Arc de
Triomphe, this site is across from a football
pitch. Take bus No 1 from the République
stop (on av Frédéric Mistral, 600m from the
train station) to the arch, then walk 100m
back, turn right onto rue des Phocéens and
right again onto rue des Étudiants.

Eating

La Roselière (☎ 04 90 34 50 42; 4 rue du Renoyer; mains
from €10; ⊙ lunch & dinner Tue-Sat) With its bric-
a-brac décor and air of rebellion blowing
through the place, this bistro makes a refreshing change from the norm. Look for
the sax sign and wine bottle outside.

La Table Vigneronne de Provence (☎ 04 90 51
76 50; i-t-v@wanadoo.fr; Palais du Vin, on the N7 opposite
Orange-Sud motorway exit; menus €14.90-32.50; ⊙ lunch
Mon-Fri, lunch & dinner Sat) A soulless location it
might have next door to the **Palais du Vin**
(☎ 04 90 11 50 00; N7; ⊙ 10am-7pm) – home to
600 wines to buy – but the food and wine
served at this winegrowers' restaurant will
impress. The seven-course *'symphonie'*
menu includes seven glasses of different
regional wines, each perfectly matched to
the course it accompanies.

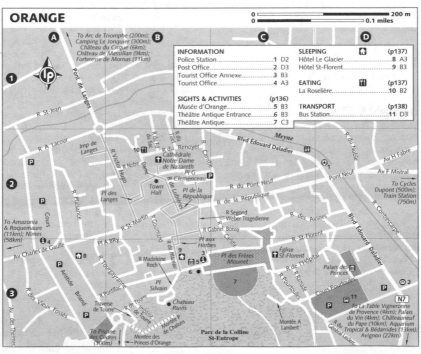

TOP FIVE ORANGE THINGS FOR KIDS

- **Piscine des Cèdres** (☎ 04 90 34 09 68; Colline St-Eutope; ⏰ 10am-7pm Jul & Aug) Open-air swimming pool, scenically placed atop St-Eutope hill in the centre of Orange.

- **Amazonia** (☎ 04 66 82 53 92; rte d'Orange, Roquemaure; adult & over 4 yrs/under 4 yrs €12/free, 2nd/3rd child over 4 yrs €11/8; ⏰ 11am-6pm school holidays, 11am-6pm Sat &/or Sun rest of yr) Adventure park for kids aged four to 12 years, 10km south.

- **Château du Cirque** (☎ 04 90 29 49 49; www.alexis-gruss.com; Piolenc; adult/child with show Mon-Fri €14/12, Sat & Sun €22/16; ⏰ 10am-5pm Tue-Fri, 10am-7.30pm Sat & Sun May-Sep) Trapeze and clowning workshops, horses and elephants to see, clown make-up sessions (€3), calash rides (€3), a circus museum – and a circus – in a wood 6km north of town.

- **Forteresse de Mornas** (☎ 04 90 37 01 26; Mornas; adult/5-12 yrs €7/5; ⏰ 10am-12.30pm & 2-6.30pm Apr-Sep) Fortress with animations galore 11km north in Mornas.

- **Aquarium Tropical** (☎ 04 90 33 06 87; 30 petite rte de Sorgues, Bédarrides; adult/3-12 yrs €6/4; ⏰ 10am-noon & 2-7pm Tue-Sun) Aquarium with 300 species, 13km south; handy for a rainy day.

Getting There & Around

From the **bus station** (☎ 04 90 34 15 59; cours Pourtoules), **Rapides du Sud-Est** (☎ 04 90 34 13 39) runs buses to/from Avignon (€5.10, 45 minutes, about 20 daily), Carpentras (€4.20, 40 minutes) and Vaison-la-Romaine (€5.10, 45 minutes).

From the **train station** (☎ 04 90 11 88 64; av Frédéric Mistral), 1km east of place de la République along rue de la République, trains run to Avignon Centre (€4.80, 20 minutes, 17 daily), Marseille (€18.90, 1½ hours, 10 daily) and beyond.

Cycles Dupont (☎ 04 90 34 15 60; 23 av Frédéric Mistral) rents bikes for €15 a day.

VAISON-LA-ROMAINE

pop 5986 / elevation 193m

Extensive Roman ruins, a medieval city and tourists by the coach-load grace Vaison-la-Romaine, a Roman city split by the ever-flooding River Ouvèze: the Romans and their modern counterparts built on the northern bank and Vaison's medieval townsfolk settled on the southern bank.

Like Malaucène and Carpentras, 10km and 27km to the south, Vaison is handy for embarking on adventures in the Dentelles de Montmirail and up Mont Ventoux. Want to escape the crowds? Take a walk on the wildly odd side around the curious Jardin des Neuf Damoiselles.

Information

Tourist Office (☎ 04 90 36 02 11; www.vaison-la -romaine.com; place du Chanoine Sautel; ⏰ 9am-noon

& 2-5.45pm Mon-Sat, 9am-noon Sun) Guided city tours in English April to October.

Sights

GALLO-ROMAN VAISON

The ruined remains of Vasio Vocontiorum, the Roman city that flourished here from the 6th to 2nd centuries BC, are unearthed at two sites. At **Puymin** (av du Général de Gaulle; adult/12-18 yrs €7/3; ⏰ 10am-noon & 2-5pm Oct-Mar, 9.30am-12.30pm & 2-6pm Apr & May, 9.30am-6pm Jun & Sep, 9.30am-6.45pm Jul & Aug) you can see **houses**, **mosaics**, the still-functioning **Théâtre Antique** (built around AD 20 for an audience of 6000) and an **archaeological museum** with a hefty collection of statues – including the silver bust of a 3rd-century patrician and likenesses of Hadrian and his wife Sabina.

La Villasse (⏰ 10am-noon & 2-5pm Oct-Mar, 9.30am-12.30pm & 2-6pm Apr-Jun & Sep, 9.30am-12.30pm & 2-6.45pm Jul & Aug), to the west of the same road, is enchanting at night. The tourist office runs evening tours (€6/4.50 with/without a guide), June to mid-September.

Admission to Puymin includes a visit to the latter and to the 12th-century Romanesque **cloister** (€1.50; ⏰ 10am-noon & 2-5pm Oct-Mar, 9.30am-12.30pm & 2-6pm Apr-Jun & Sep, 9.30am-12.30pm & 2-6.45pm Jul & Aug) of the **Cathédrale Notre-Dame de Nazareth**, a five-minute walk from the car park opposite the tourist office.

HAUTE VILLE MÉDIÉVALE

In the 6th century the Great Migrations forced the population to move to the hill across the river. In the 12th century the counts of Toulouse built a **château** atop the hill, modernised in the 15th century only for it to be later abandoned. From it narrow, cobblestone alleys lead downhill past restored medieval houses to the river and **Pont Romain** (Roman Bridge). The resettlement of the original site began in the 17th century.

Festivals & Events

In July dance takes centre stage at Puymin's Théâtre Antique during the two-week **Festival de Vaison-la-Romaine** (www.vaison-festival .com in French) and polyphonic performances can be seen at the Cathédrale Notre-Dame de Nazareth during the **Festival des Choeurs Lauréats**.

Choralies, a two-week choral festival held every three years in August, is the largest of its kind in Europe. The next takes place in 2007.

Sleeping

Centre à Coeur Joie (☎ 04 90 36 00 78; http://acj.mus icanet.org in French; av César Geoffray; d/tr per person with half-board €35/33; ☺ mid-Feb–mid-Dec) Half-board is the only option at this well-run choral centre, 500m southeast of town along the river with great Mont Ventoux views. Rates in July and August/winter are 10% more/less.

Camping du Théâtre Romain (☎ 04 90 28 78 66; www.camping-theatre.com; chemin du Brusquet; adult/tent low season €4.70/4.90, high season €5.50/7.50; ☺ Mar–mid-Nov; P ☺) Opposite the Roman theatre at Puymin, this well-equipped site rents bicycles.

Hôtel Burrhus (☎ 04 90 36 00 11; www.burrhus.com; 1 place Montfort; d €44-50, ste €98; ☺ mid-Dec–mid-Nov, closed Sun Jan & Feb; P ☺) A twin set of stars

seems a paltry accolade for the mid-range pick of Vaison, set bang slap on the town's buzzing café-clad square. Rooms are smart, spacious and furnished with contemporary style and flair.

Eating

The streets around the tourist office and Roman ruins buzz with restaurants and bistros. Wine, honey, truffles and so on are sold at the **Maison des Vins et des Produits du Terroir** (place du Chanoine Sautel; ☺ 9am-noon & 2-5.45pm Mon-Sat), in the tourist office basement.

Chez Jérémy: Le Petit Café (☎ 04 90 36 20 32; 47 Grande Rue; salads €10; ☺ lunch & dinner Tue-Sun) A notable stand-out on the pedestrian street linking Roman Vaison with the river, Jeremy's place is laid-back, friendly, a little bit bohemian and tummy-tickling: giant-sized salads built from the unexpected are dished up in wooden bowls.

Moulin à Huile (☎ 04 90 36 20 67; www.moulin -huile.com; quai Maréchal Foch; lunch/dinner menus €42/100; ☺ lunch & dinner Tue-Sat, lunch Sun) Savour the full monty gastronomic experience (the lobster menu stuns) courtesy of renowned chef Robert Bardot at the Oil Mill – an old apricot-coloured riverside mill on the southern bank. This illustrious choice has three stunning rooms too.

Getting There & Away

From the **bus station** (av des Choralies), where **Lieutard buses** (☎ 04 90 36 05 22) is based, there are limited services to/from Carpentras (€3.90, 45 minutes) via Crestet, Malaucène and Le Barroux; Orange (€4.60, 45 minutes) and Avignon (€7, 1¼ hours).

AN ODDITY DETOUR

From the hectic touristy centre of Vaison-la-Romaine, head west out of town along the D975 towards Orange. Within minutes an enormous and almighty strange stone garden comes into view. Flick your left-hand indicator on and pull up into the gravel car park next to it.

The creation of sculptor Serge Boÿer, the **Jardin des Neuf Damoiselles** (Garden of Nine Damsels) inspires lofty contemplation. A central square of nine granite blocks (the 'nine damsels') pierces the heart of the garden, each block representing one of Europe's nine cities of culture in 2000 and engraved with a short poem of love and peace, written by a native poet of that city. Around this, 72 hefty boulders – each representing a different town in the world with respective inscriptions – spiral in concentric circles to form a monumental sundial. A path ensnares the entire ensemble.

Intended as a memorial to those who died during Vaison's 1992 floods, the serene stone garden on the bank of the River Ouvèze is a place of poetry, philosophy and alchemy today. Read into it what you will.

ENCLAVE DES PAPES

French king Charles VII (r 1422–61) refused point-blank to sell any of his kingdom to the papacy, the result being the Enclave des Papes – a papal enclave in France which, from 1318 until the French Revolution in 1789, belonged to the Pope. Part of the Vaucluse since 1791, this bizarre ball of land measuring no more than 20km in diameter remains an enclave today – wholly surrounded by the Drôme department.

Medieval **Valréas** (population 9500, elevation 250m), 29km north of Vaison-la-Romaine, is the primary town here. During the 19th century the town was known for its cardboard production, the history of which unfolds in the world's only **Musée du Cartonnage et de l'Imprimerie** (Cardboard & Printing Museum; ☎ 04 90 35 58 75; musee-cartonnage -imp@cg84.fr; 3 av Maréchal Foch; adult/under 12 yrs €3.50/free; ⏰ 10am-noon & 3-6pm Tue-Sat, 3-6pm Sun). During the **Nuit du Petit St-Jean** on 23 June,

---

BLACK DIAMONDS

Provence's cloak-and-dagger truffle trade is far from glamorous. In fact, the way these diamond dealers operate – out of a car boot, payment exclusively by cold, hard cash – is a real black business.

Little known Richerenches, a deceptively wealthy village shielded within the thick walls of a 12th- to 13th-century Templar fortress, is the congruous setting for Provence's leading wholesale truffle market where the far-from appetising-looking (in fact, very ugly) fungus sells for €130 or so per 100g. Once a year villagers celebrate a truffle Mass in the village church, during which parishioners offer up truffles instead of cash to the Lord. The Mass falls on the closest Sunday to 17 January, the feast day of Antoine, the patron saint of truffle-harvesters. Call Richerenches' **Point Tourisme** (☎ 04 90 28 05 34; www.richerenches.fr in French; rue du Campanile; ⏰ 2-6pm Mon, 9am-12.30pm & 2-6.30pm Tue-Fri, 9.30am-12.30pm Sat) for details.

Crisp, cold Saturday mornings during the truffle season (November to March) see av de la Rebasse – Richerenches' main street – resound with the furtive whisperings of local *rabassaïres* (truffle hunters) selling their weekly harvest to a big-time dealer from Paris, Germany, Italy or beyond. No more than four or five cash-laden dealers attend the weekly market. Each sets up shop – the boot (trunk) of their car – on the street, from where they carefully inspect, weigh and invariably buy kilos of the precious black fungi. Their *courtiers* (brokers) mingle with the truffle hunters to scout out the best truffles and keep tabs on deals being cut by rival dealers.

Truffle hunters, harvesters and dealers alike store the ugly, mud-caked truffles in grubby white plastic bags. Individuals seeking black diamonds generally have their own dealer whom they telephone to place an order: **Dominique and Eric Jaumard** (☎ 04 90 66 82 21; www.truffes-ventoux .com; La Quinsonne), 7km southwest of Carpentras in Monteux, have hunted, harvested and sold truffles from their land for a couple of decades and are more open than most. Between November and March you can go truffle-hunting with them and their dogs, or discover the taste of fresh truffles during a truffle-tasting workshop. Year round they sell (less tasty) frozen or canned truffles as well as truffle juice, truffle vinegar, acacia and truffle honey, truffle olive oil and so on.

Many a truffle traded at Richerenches market ends up in a can at the world's largest truffle cannery, **Plantin** (☎ 04 90 46 41 44; www.plantin.com; rte de Nyons; ⏰ 8am-noon & 1.30-5.30pm Mon-Fri), 7km northeast of Vaison-la-Romaine in Puymeras, where the fungus has been conserved in jars for year-round consumption since 1930. The cannery, which handles between 20 and 30 tonnes of truffles a year, is just west of Puymeras village on the D46/D938 junction.

In season, fresh truffles can also be picked up at general food markets in Vaison-la-Romaine (Tuesday), Valréas (Wednesday), Nyons (Thursday) and Carpentras (Friday); and at the truffle-specialist shop in St-Rémy de Provence (p154), inspired by France's top truffle chef Clément Bruno (p297). Restaurants in the Vaucluse particularly known for their truffle cuisine include Christian Étienne in Avignon (p131) and Chez Serge in Carpentras (p148).

The history of truffles is unearthed in the **Musée de la Truffe et du Tricastin** (Truffle Museum; ☎ 04 75 96 61 29; ⏰ 2-6pm Mon, 9am-noon & 2 or 3-6 or 7pm), 14km west of Richerenches in St-Paul Troix Châteaux. The village celebrates a **Fête de la Truffe** the second Sunday in February. A comprehensive online information source is www.truffle-and-truffe.com.

Valréassiens in traditional dress and bearing torches parade through the old-town streets, climaxing with the crowning of a three- to five-year-old boy as the new Petit St-Jean (Little St John).

Lavender fields and treasure troves of truffles buried underground (see opposite) surround Valréas and the fortified villages of **Grillon**, **Visan** and **Richerenches**. From here age-old olive groves stretch across the border south to Vaison-la-Romaine and east to **Nyons** (population 6948, elevation 271m), a foodie town, 14km from Valréas, famed for its olives and olive oil. The **Institut du Monde de l'Olivier** (☎ 04 75 26 90 90; monde-olivir@wanadoo.fr; 40 place de la Libération) runs olive workshops and there are several mills where you can buy the Nyons' fruity AOC olive oil. Don't leave without biting into a big fat *saucisson aux olives de Nyons* (Nyon olive sausage) from the **Boucherie Guy Dineile** (2 rue de la Résistance) or, should you be travelling *en famille*, cooling down and splashing around at **Nyonsoleïado** (☎ 04 75 26 06 92; promenade de la Digue; adult/6-16 yrs €4/3; ☼ 10.30am-7.30pm Jul & Aug, 11am-7pm Jun & Sep), an aqua park with water slides, paddling pools and beach area. Men note: in true French fashion, trunks are not allowed (so dig out those skin-tight Speedos big boys!).

Hop 3km across the enclave's western border to **Suze-la-Rousse** (population 1591) to learn about wine at France's **Université du Vin** (University of Wine; ☎ 04 75 97 21 34; www.universite-du-vin.com in French), inside the 12th- to 14th-century Château de la Suze.

Information

Nyons Tourist Office (☎ 04 75 26 10 35; www.nyons tourisme.com; place de la Libération; ☼ 9.30am-noon & 2.30-6pm Mon-Sat, 10am-1pm Sun)
Valréas Tourist Office (☎ 04 90 35 04 71; www.ot -valreas.info; place Aristide Briand; ☼ 9.15am-12.15pm & 2-5, 6 or 7pm Mon-Sat)

DENTELLES DE MONTMIRAIL & AROUND

Immediately south of Vaison loom the pinnacles of the Dentelles de Montmirail, a series of lacy limestone rocks that thrust into the sky like needles. Vineyards cling to the lower parts of the rocky slopes, and climbers dangle perilously from the south-facing rocks around Gigondas. This area, stretching as far east as Mont Ventoux, makes great walking terrain; Régis at the Gîte d'Étape

---

A DETOUR WITH VIEWS

For a startling twin-set view of Mont Ventoux (east) and the Dentelles de Montmirail, motor on up – or pedal – for 9km along the wiggly D90 from Malaucène to Suzette. The panoramas that unfold from the Col de la Chaine (472m), 4km west, and the Col de Suzette (392m), a further 3km, will leave you gagging for more.

---

des Dentelles de Gigondas (p142) arranges **guided walks**, **rock climbs** and **bike rides**.

Looping the lacy outcrop of the Dentelles by car or bicycle is a good day trip: from Vaison-la-Romaine start by taking the southbound D938 towards Carpentras, which snakes around the eastern side of the Dentelles to Le Barroux. Just south of Le Barroux, follow the westbound D21 to Beaumes de Venise, from where you can continue north to Gigondas, Sablet, Séguret and back to Vaison-la-Romaine.

Malaucène (population 2581, elevation 350m), 10km south of Vaison-la-Romaine, is the starting point for forays into the Dentelles and up Mont Ventoux. Its **tourist office** (☎ /fax 04 90 65 22 59; ot-malaucene@axit.fr; place de la Mairie; ☼ 10am-noon & 2.30-4.30pm Mon-Sat) covers the entire Mont Ventoux area.

Le Barroux
pop 574 / elevation 325m
Yellow-stone Le Barroux tumbles down the hillside around medieval **Château du Barroux** (☎ 04 90 62 35 21; http://chateau.barroux.free.fr; adult/child €3.50/free; ☼ 10am-7pm Sat & Sun Apr & May, 2.30-7pm Jun, 10am-7pm Jul-Sep, 2-6pm Oct). Classical music concerts and art exhibitions are occasionally held here.

Gregorian chants are sung at 9.30am (10am Sunday and holidays) by the industrious Benedictine monks at **Abbaye Ste-Madeleine** (☎ 04 90 62 56 31; rte de Suzette), a lavender-surrounded monastery built in Romanesque style in the 1980s. Monk-made bread, cakes and the like are sold in the monastery shop. Hats, mini skirts, bare shoulders and mobile phones are forbidden in the church.

Thirty llamas live in relative freedom at the **Ferme Expérimentale d'Élevage de Lamas** (☎ 04 90 65 25 46; rte du Lac du Paty; admission free; ☼ guided visits with advance reservation), a llama farm 1km along the D19 to Bédoin.

Beaumes de Venise & Gigondas

At the foot of the loop around the Dentelles de Montmirail sits **Beaumes de Venise** (population 2070, elevation 126m), 10km southwest of Le Barroux at the crossroads of the D21 and the D90, which leads north into the massif. The village is known for its **Or Blanc** – fruity and sweet golden Muscat wines – best drunk young, chilled to 6°C or 8°C and served as a digestif. Juicy melons from Cavaillon form the perfect partner to Beaumes de Venise's wines. The **Maison des Dentelles** (☎ 04 90 62 94 39; otbeaumes@wanadoo.fr; place du Marché; ☽ 9am-noon & 2-7pm Mon-Sat) has a list of estates where you can taste and buy the nectar.

Beaumes' other tasty treat is olive oil: try it and buy it at the **Moulin à Huile de la Balméenne** (☎ 04 90 62 93 77; av Jules Ferry; ☽ 8am-noon & 2-6.30pm Mon-Sat, 2-6.30pm Sun Apr-Aug; 8am-noon & 2 6.30pm Mon-Sat Sep-Mar), in business since 1856.

Yellow-stone **Gigondas** (population 648, elevation 282m), 5km northwest, offers ample wine-tasting opportunities. Wine cellars stud the central square, place du Portail, from where rue du Corps de Garde climbs to Gigondas' ruined chateau, campanile-clad church and cemetery. Contemporary sculptures en route form **Le Cheminement de Sculptures**; ask for a map of the sculpture trail at the **tourist office** (☎ 04 90 65 85 46; ot-gigondas@axit.fr; place du Portail; ☽ 10am-noon & 2-6 or 7pm Mon-Sat Sep-Jun, 9.30am-12.30pm & 2.30-6.30pm Jul & Aug). The latter also has information on walking and cycling routes in the Dentelles.

Sleeping & Eating

Most mid-range choices listed offer delicious dining too.

BUDGET

Gîte d'Étape des Dentelles de Gigondas (☎ 04 90 65 80 85; www.provence-trekking.com; dm €12, d or tr per person with shared bathroom €14, sheets €3; ☽ Mar-Dec) Next to Gigondas' fire station, this comfortable *gîte* has two 13-bed dorms and a clutch of two- and three-bedded rooms. Experienced mountain guide and rock climber Régis, who runs the place, organises hikes, mountain-bike rides and climbing expeditions.

There are several camp sites just north of Bédoin along the D974 east of Le Barroux.

MID-RANGE

Many *mas* (farmhouses) open their doors to *chambre d'hôte* guests; several are on the northbound D23 to Séguret. Tourist offices have complete lists of *chambres d'hôtes*.

Ferme Le Degoutaud (☎ 04 90 62 99 29; www .degoutaud.fr.st; rte de Malaucène, 5km north of Malaucène along the D90 to Suzette; s/d/tr/q with breakfast €45/57/62/71, self-catering cottage for 4/7 €450/560, dinner €20; P ☝) A family favourite, this authentic working farm dating to the 16th century is hard to beat. It has three rooms, self-catering cottages and poolside views that leave you breathless. **La Treille** (☎ 04 90 65 03 77; rte de Malaucène, Suzette), along the same scenic road, is also worth considering.

La Respelido (☎ /fax 04 90 36 03 10; http://lares pelido.crestet.free.fr; Le Crestet; d with kitchenette/tr with Mont Ventoux view €60/75; ☽ Mar-Oct; ✗) In the hilltop village of Le Crestet, 14km south of

---

A VILLAGE CHRISTMAS

Nowhere is a traditional Provençal Christmas celebrated more than in **Séguret** (population 892, elevation 250m), a yellow-tinged village that clings to a rocky outcrop 9km south of Vaison-la-Romaine.

Festivities open at dusk on Christmas Eve with *Cacho Fio*. During this Provençal ceremony a log – usually cut from a pear, olive or cherry tree – is placed in the hearth, doused with fortified wine, blessed thrice by the youngest and oldest family members, then set alight. In keeping with tradition, the fire has to burn until the three kings arrive on 6 January.

Although many still celebrate *Cacho Fio* at home, it is only in Séguret that the village people gather to bless and burn a log together. This takes place in the Salle Delage, adjoining Chapelle Ste-Thecle on rue du Four. Later, villagers wend their way up to Église St-Denis where, during *Li Bergié*, the Christmas nativity scene is brought to life with real-life shepherds, lambs and a baby in a manger. This *crèche vivant* (living crèche) is followed by midnight Mass, celebrated in Provençal.

After Mass, families rush home for *Caleno vo Careno* (see p59).

Vaison la Romaine, speak sweetly to host Monsieur Veit at this guesthouse (a former oil mill) and he'll tell you all there is to know about the area.

Mas de Magali (☎ 04 90 36 39 91; fax 04 90 28 73 40; quartier Chante Coucou, Le Crestet; high season half-board per person €62.50-73.40, low season d €89; P ☒ ☙) The chances are you won't want to budge an inch once you find this wonderful hotel-restaurant, beautifully hidden amid flowers, mountains, twittering birds and panoramic views. Follow the signs from the bottom of the D76 leading up to Le Crestet village.

La Ferme des Bélugues (☎ 04 90 65 15 16; chemin de Choudeirolles, rte ru Paty; s/d/tr €65/76/90; P ☙) 'Bliss' best describes this little-publicised farmhouse *chambre d'hôte*, submerged in nature just outside Le Barroux village (follow the D928 north, then bear east along the D19 towards Bédoin). It is particularly suited to those happy to picnic some evenings, given there is a small kitchen for guests. The pool is nothing short of magnificent.

Mas de la Lause (☎ 04 90 62 33 33; www.provence -gites.com in French; chemin de Geysset, rte de Suzette, Le Barroux; s/d with breakfast €48/55, ste with kitchen for 2/3/4 €69/83/110, dinner menu adult/child €16/7; ☙ mid-Mar–mid-Oct; P ☙) This friendly farmhouse *chambre d'hôte* is a wise move for the kid-laden: there are a couple of swings and a small pool in the garden, the *suite mistral* sleeps four, and Christophe – who runs the place with wife Corine – cooks up child-as well as adult-sized evening *menus*. The farmhouse is signposted after the village of Le Barroux, along the road to Suzette.

Malaucène has a couple of unstartling hotels. Otherwise try:

Les Géraniums (☎ 04 90 62 41 08; les.geraniums@ wanadoo.fr; Le Barroux; d €45, half-board per person €43, menus €18-46; ☙ Apr–mid-Nov; P) In summer half-board is obligatory at this charming, yellow-stone hotel with luxurious doubles furnished in traditional Provençal style. Reserve in advance to feast on food and views on its restaurant terrace.

Hôtel Montmirail (☎ 04 90 65 84 01; www.hotel montmirail.com; s/d from €52/72; ☙ mid-Mar–Oct; P) A three-star 19th-century mansion in a remote spot midway between Gigondas and neighbouring Vacqueyras is the alluring shape Hôtel Montmirail takes. The 'his-and-her' dressing gowns in the bathroom add a luxurious touch.

AUTHOR'S CHOICE

Les Abeilles (The Bees; ☎ 04 90 12 38 98; www .abeilles-sablet.com; 4 rue de Vaison, Sablet; s/d with breakfast low season €60/90, high season €80/120, menus €45, €55 & €65; ☙ lunch & dinner Tue-Sun) Until very recently the talk about town in Gigondas, where they invested several years in building up L'Oustalet's legendary reputation, Johannes and Marlies Sailer are now busy working their culinary magic on this happening little place, which was called Coco Café in the 1920s. With a terrace shaded by plane trees, a menu crammed with edible temptations such as duck breast roasted in honey and lavender followed by warm cherry soup, and a couple of rooms up top, contentment is pretty much guaranteed. Advance reservations are strongly recommended.

Domaine de Cabasse (☎ 04 90 46 91 12; www .domaine-de-cabasse.fr; rte de Sablet, Séguret; d low/high season from €85/103; ☙ mid-Mar–Oct; P ☙) This wine-producing estate on the plains, 800m south from Séguret village, sports 12 rooms, a pool, tennis courts and wines galore to taste.

L'Oustalet (☎ 04 90 65 85 30; place Gabrielle Andéol, Gigondas; menus from €35; ☙ lunch & dinner Feb-Dec, closed Mon Oct-Apr) Gigondas' upmarket choice has a fine wine cellar stuffed full of Gigondas wine to accompany its stuffed pork trotters, roasted pigeon and other meaty specialities.

MONT VENTOUX

This *désert de pierre* (stone desert) – a 25km narrow ridge east of the Dentelles de Montmirail – is Provence's most prominent geographical feature thanks to its height and supreme isolation. From afar, Mont Ventoux's stone-capped top (1912m) appears snow-capped – which it is December to April. Accessible by road in summer, the radar- and antenna-studded peak affords spectacular views of Provence, the southern Alps and beyond. Since 1990 the mountain and its surrounds have been protected by Unesco's **Réserve de Biosphère du Mont Ventoux**.

Mont Ventoux is the boundary between the fauna and flora of northern France and that of southern France. Some species, like the snake eagle, numerous spiders and a variety of butterflies, are found only here. The mountain's forests were felled 400 years ago to build ships, but since 1860 some areas have been reforested with a variety of species, including the majestic cedar of Lebanon. The mix of deciduous trees makes the mountain especially colourful in autumn. The broken white stones that cover the top are known as *lauzes*.

Since the summit is considerably cooler than the surrounding plains – there can be a difference of up to 20°C – and receives twice as much precipitation, bring warm clothes and rain gear. With winds of up to 300km/h recorded you could say Mont Ventoux is breezy (the mistral blows here 130 days a year on average).

Near the southwestern end of the Mont Ventoux massif is the agricultural village of **Bédoin** (population 2657, elevation 295m) and, 4km further east along rte du Mont Ventoux (D974), neighbouring **Ste-Colombe**. Road signs here tell you if the *col* (mountain

pass) over the summit is closed. At the eastern end of the Mont Ventoux massif is **Sault** (population 1190, elevation 800m), which is surrounded by a patchwork of purple lavender in July and August. In winter **Mont Serein** (1445m), 16km east of Malaucène and 5km west of Mont Ventoux's summit on the D974, is transformed into a bustling ski station.

Information

INTERNET RESOURCES

www.lemontventoux.net (in French) Ventoux-bound walkers and cyclists should make this their first stop.

www.mab-france.org Follow the links to the Mont Ventoux Biosphere Reserve.

TOURIST INFORMATION

Bédoin Tourist Office (☎ 04 90 65 63 95; ot-bedoin@axit.fr; place du Marché; ⏰ 8.30am-12.30pm & 2-6pm Mon, 9am-12.30pm & 2-6pm Tue-Fri, 9.30am-12.30pm & 2-6pm Sat, 9.30am-12.30pm Sun)

Sault Tourist Office (☎ 04 90 64 01 21; www .saultenprovence.com; av de la Promenade; ⏰ 9am-1pm

---

THE PERFUME OF PROVENCE

If there's one aroma associated with Provence, it's *lavande* (lavender). Lavender fields once seen, never forgotten include those surrounding Abbaye de Sénanque near Gordes and the Musée de la Lavande in Coustellet, and those carpeting the arid Sault region, east of Mont Ventoux on the Vaucluse plateau. In the neighbouring Lubéron the vast lavender farms sweeping the Plateau de Valensole and those in Lagarde d'Apt are particularly memorable.

The sweet purple flower is harvested when it is in full bloom, between 15 July and 15 August. It is mechanically harvested on a hot dry day, following which the lorry-loads of cut lavender, known as *paille* (straw), are packed tight in a steam still and distilled to extract the sweet essential oils.

Authentic lavender farms, all the rage in Provence in the 1920s, are a dying breed today. Since the 1950s lavandin – a hybrid of fine lavender and aspic, cloned at the turn of the 20th century – has been mass produced for industrial purposes. Both blaze the same vibrant purple when in flower, but lavandin yields five times more oil than fine lavender (which produces 1kg of oil from 130kg of cut straw). Since 1997 *huile essentielle de lavande de Haute Provence* – essential lavender oil from Haute-Provence – has been protected by its own *appellation d'origine contrôlée* (AOC).

Approximately 80% of Provence's 400 lavender farms produce lavandin today. The few remaining traditional lavender farms – like Château du Bois, which can be visited (see p177) – usually colour higher areas. Wild lavender needs an altitude of 900m to 1300m to blossom, unlike its common sister, which sprouts anywhere above 800m. Some 80% of essential oils produced in the region's 150 distilleries is exported.

A list of lavender farms, distilleries and gardens open to visitors feature in the free brochure *Les Routes de la Lavande: La Provence par les Sens* (The Lavender Roads: Experiencing Provence through the Five Senses), also available in English from tourist offices or the association **Les Routes de la Lavande** (☎ 04 75 26 65 91; www.routes.lavande.com; 2 av de Venterol, BP 36, F-26111 Nyons).

Several restaurants in the region, notably the Hostellerie du Val de Sault (p145) in Sault, dish up lavender. Lavender honey is another tasty treat. Lavender festivals *(fêtes de la lavande)* are celebrated in Valensole (3rd Sunday in July), Sault (15 August), and Digne-les-Bains and Valréas (both first weekend in August).

& 2-7pm Mon-Sat, 9am-1pm Sun Jul & Aug, 9am-1pm &
2-6pm Mon-Sat, 9.30am-12.30pm Sun May & Jun, 9am-
1pm & 2-4 or 5pm Mon-Sat Sep-Apr)

Activities

CYCLING

In summer cyclists labour up the sun-baked
slopes of Mont Ventoux. The tourist offices distribute *Massif du Mont Ventoux:
9 Itinéraires VTT*, a free booklet detailing
nine mountain-bike itineraries ranging
from an easy 3.9km (one hour) to a gruel-
ling 56.7km (seven to eight hours) tour of
Mont Ventoux.

In Malaucène **ACScycles** (☎ 04 90 65 15 42;
acscycles84@tiscali.fr; av de Verdun; ⌚ closed Sun & Mon
Oct-Apr) rents road and mountain bikes for
€9/12 per half-/full day. **Albion Cycles** (☎ 04
90 64 09 32; rte de St-Trinit) in Sault and **Bedoin
Location** (☎ 04 90 65 94 53; info@bedoin.location.com;
chemin de la Ferraille) in Bédoin charge similar
rates. ACScycles repairs bikes and all three
can suggest cycling routes.

FLYING

View the region's most legendary mountain from up high with **Air Ventoux** (☎ 04
90 66 35 81; airventoux@hotmail.com). Forty-minute
flights (€67 per person for three passengers)
take off from airstrips in Montfavet (near
Avignon) and Pernes les Fonatines (near
Carpentras).

QUADING

Keep your feet firmly on the ground with
Ventoux Quad (☎ 06 19 06 05 92; www.ventoux
-quad.com in French; rte de la Madeleine; 1hr/half-day/day
€50/90/150), a quad-hire place in Crillon le
Brave that organises one-day and weekend
quading adventures around Ventoux.

SKIING

December to March, locals ski Ventoux's
slopes. **Chalet Reynard** (☎ 04 90 61 84 55), at
the intersection of the D974 and the eastbound D164 to Sault, is a small ski station (1440m) on the southern slopes. Two
drag lifts (*téléskis*) serve two blue runs. A
half-/full-day pass costs around €10/15 and
you can hire skis, boots and poles for the
same price again per half-/full day. Cross-
country skiing is also popular and there is
a luge nonskiers can bomb down.

Station de Mont Serein (1400m), 5km west
of the summit on the colder northern side,

is the main ski station with 12km of downhill pistes served by eight drag lifts. Skis,
ski schools, piste maps and ski passes are
available from the **Chalet d'Accueil** (☎ 04 90
63 42 02; adpmv@infonie.fr), in the resort centre.
Chalet Liotard is a mid-station, 100m further
uphill.

WALKING

The GR4 crosses the Dentelles de Montmirail before climbing up the northern face of
Mont Ventoux. It then joins the GR9, both
trails following the bare, white ridge before
parting ways. See p43 for more details.

Bédoin, Sault and Malaucéne tourist offices have information on exploring Mont
Ventoux on foot, including guided evening
strolls (adult/child €7.50/5.35) and 12-hour
night climbs (€10) up Ventoux in July and
August. Online, www.lemontventoux.net
(in French) details three walks and 20 cycling routes around Ventoux.

Find out about flora and fauna at Sault's
Centre de Découverte de la Nature (Nature Discovery
Centre; ☎ 04 90 64 13 96; av de l'Oratoire; adult/under
8 yrs €3/free; ⌚ 10am-noon & 2-6pm Mon-Fri Sep-Jun,
10am-noon & 3-7pm Tue-Sun Jul & Aug).

Sleeping & Eating

Places listed in the Dentelles de Montmirail
section are also handy for exploring Mont
Ventoux.

Chalet Liotard (☎ /fax 04 90 60 68 38; d €50, half-
board per person €45, lunch menu €16; ⌚ lunch & dinner
Dec-Sep; P) Also known as Chez Coco et
Mimi, this mid-station inn is practically alpine in its cosiness with its warming cuisine
and roaring winter fire. Its seven rooms
sleep two to four people and dinner is à la
carte only (no *menu*).

La Maison (☎ 04 90 65 15 50; Beaumont du Ventoux; d €56-66, menu €28; ⌚ hotel Apr-Oct, restaurant
lunch & dinner Wed-Sun Apr-Jun, Sep & Oct, daily Jul & Aug;
P) First and foremost a charming terrace
restaurant beneath linden trees, Michèle
Laurelot has since added three simple but
tastefully furnished rooms to her winning
repertoire. Laurelot's *petits farcis* (stuffed
vegetables), *tian* (vegetable and rice gratin)
and hot peach sauce are legendary.

Hostellerie du Val de Sault (☎ 04 90 64 01 41;
www.valdesault.com; rte de St-Trinit; menus from €32, half-
board per person from €98; ⌚ Mar-early Nov; ⟰ P)
One of those serene *relais du silence* abodes
where noise in any form is frowned upon,

SWEET TIP
Don't leave Sault without savouring a slab of sweet lavender-honey and almond-flavoured nougat or bitter-sweet macaroons made by **André Boyer** (☎ 04 90 64 00 23; place de l'Europe), a nougat maker featured in the *Guinness World Records* book for cooking up the largest bar of nougat (12.45m long and 180kg in weight). Pop into his village square shop in Sault to stock up and/or arrange a factory visit.

this 11-room haven of peace slumbers 2km north of Sault along the D950 to Banon. Its restaurant by the pool is renowned and its Jacuzzi – with picture-postcard views of Mont Ventoux from the bubbling tub – is pure lux.

Getting There & Away
The Mont Ventoux summit can be reached from Sault via the tortuous D164 or from Malaucène or St-Estève via the switchback D974. This 1930s mountain road can be snow-blocked until as late as April.

CARPENTRAS
pop 27,249 / elevation 102m
It might well have been a key trading centre in Greek times and the capital of the papal-driven Comtat Venaissin during the 14th century, but the reason most people visit this drowsy agricultural town, 25km from Avignon and Orange, today is to shop at its sumptuous morning market (p148): ogle at the rainbow of herbs, spices, sweet *berlingots* (hard-boiled sweets), breads of all shapes, sausages of all sizes; nip into the medieval synagogue – the oldest such structure still in use in France – for a quick peek; then sit down to a black diamond (p148) lunch.

Orientation
In the 19th century the city's 16th-century fortifications and walls were replaced by a ring of boulevards: av Jean Jaurès, blvd Alfred Rogier, blvd du Nord, blvd Maréchal Leclerc, blvd Gambetta and blvd Albin Durand. Inside is the partly pedestrian old town.

Information
LAUNDRY
Laundrette (⊙ 7am-8pm; blvd du Nord)

MONEY
Commercial banks line place Aristide Briand and blvd Albin Durand.

POST
Post Office (65 rue d'Inguimbert)

TOURIST INFORMATION
Tourist Office (☎ 04 90 63 00 78; tourist. carpentras@axit.fr; Hôtel Dieu, place Aristide Briand; ⊙ 9.30am-12.30pm & 2-6pm Mon-Sat Oct-May, 9am-7pm Jun-Sep)

Sights & Activities
SYNAGOGUE
In the 14th century Jews expelled from territory controlled by the French crown sought refuge in the Comtat Venaissin, where they lived under papal protection – the result being Carpentras' marvellous but inconspicuous **synagogue** (☎ 04 90 63 39 97; place Juiverie; admission free; ⊙ 10am-noon & 3-5pm Mon-Thu, 10am-noon & 3-4pm Fri). Founded in 1367, it was rebuilt between 1741 and 1743, and restored in 1929 and 1954. The 1st-floor sanctuary is decorated with wood panelling and liturgical objects from the 18th century. Below, there's an oven used until 1904 to bake matzo, Passover's unleavened bread.

CATHÉDRALE ST-SIFFREIN
Carpentras' one-time **cathedral** (☎ 04 90 63 08 33; place du Général de Gaulle; ⊙ 10am-noon & 2-4pm Wed-Mon) was built in the Méridional Gothic style between 1405 and 1519. The classical doorway was added in the 17th century. Inside the **Trésor d'Art Sacré** (Treasury of Religious Art) displays liturgical objects and reliquaries from the 14th to 19th centuries, including St-Mors, the Holy Bridle-bit supposedly made by St-Helen for her son Constant.

ARC DE TRIOMPHE
Hidden in a corner off rue d'Inguimbert – next to the cathedral and behind the **Palais de Justice** in an episcopal palace built in 1801 – what's left of this **triumphal arch** is the town's only Roman relic, built under Augustus in the 1st century AD. On the opposite side of the square are the paltry remains of a 7th-century **Cathédrale Romane**, predominantly destroyed in 1399.

Carpentras' northern outskirts are crossed by the remains of a 10km-long **aqueduct** that supplied water to the city between 1745 and 1893. For a heady glimpse of all 48 arches, follow the signs to Orange from the centre.

MUSEUMS

The unrivetting **Musée Comtadin** (234 blvd Albin Durand; admission €1; ⏱ 10am-noon & 2-6pm Wed-Mon Apr-Oct, 10am-noon & 2-4pm Nov-Mar), home to local history and folklore artefacts, and the art-driven **Musée Duplessis** (☎ 04 90 63 04 92; 234 blvd Albin Durand; admission €1; ⏱ 10am-noon & 2-6pm Wed-Mon Apr-Oct, 10am-noon & 2-4pm Nov-Mar) share the same building.

Furniture, faïence and *objets d'art* in the Louis XV and Louis XVI styles form the backbone of the **Musée Sobirats Arts Décoratifs**

(112 rue du Collège; admission €1; ⏱ 10am-noon & 2-6pm Wed-Mon, 4pm Nov-Mar).

SWIMMING

Art Deco fans can dive into the lovely **piscine couverte** (covered swimming pool; ☎ 04 90 60 92 03; rue du Mont de Piété; adult/3-15 yrs €2/1.50; ⏱ various hr Fri-Wed). It was built by the Caisse d'Épargne in 1930 and has since been restored to its geometric glory. The water temperature is 20°C.

Tours

The tourist office organises fabulous tours, including city tours (adult/10 to 18 years €4/2.50, 1½ hours), nature treks (adult/10 to 18 years €6/3, three hours), *berlingot* factory

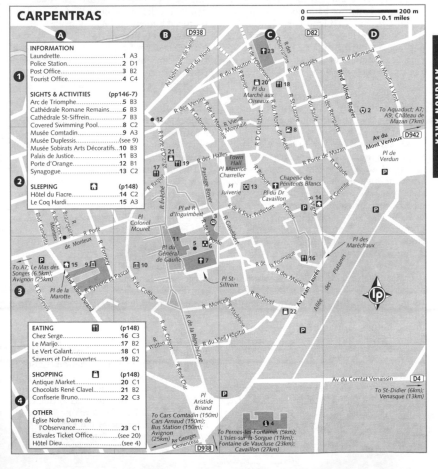

tours (free, 45 minutes), wine-tasting workshops (adult/under 16 years €3/free, one hour), truffle hunts (adult/under 12 years €9/6, two hours) and farm trips (adult/four to 12 years €10/5, two hours). Book at least 24 hours in advance.

Festivals & Events

Carpentras hosts the two-week music, dance and theatre festival **Estivales** (ticket office ☎ 04 90 60 46 00; estivales@ville-carpentras.fr; 4 place aux Marché aux Oiseaux) in open-air venues around town in July.

Sleeping

Hôtel du Fiacre (☎ 04 90 63 03 15; www.hotel-du-fiacre.com; 153 rue Vigne; s/d/tr/ste from €46/50/75/105; P ⊠ ⊒) This solid mid-range choice conjures up a bunch of bathroom-clad rooms above a restaurant–piano bar. Lighting up is only no go in six of the 18 rooms and parking is an extra €6 per 24 hours.

Le Coq Hardi (☎ 04 90 63 00 35; www.hotelcoqhardi.com; 36 place de la Marotte; s/d/tr/q €43/50/60/71; P ⊒) The green table-clad garden out back makes this restored post house stand out from the town-centre crowd. It has a restaurant too, should you not to want to wander far.

Mas des Songes (☎ 04 90 65 49 20; www.masdessonges.com in French; 1631 impasse du Perrusier; d €140-180; P ⊠ ⊒ ⊜) The stuff of dreams, this stunning five-room *maison d'hôte* oozes style, panache and flair out of every corner. Décor is strictly contemporary – lots of light and air – and the view from the pool will leave you breathless. Prices include breakfast and afternoon tea. Find it 6.5km west of Carpentras in the truffle land of Monteux.

Château de Mazan (☎ 04 90 69 62 61; www.chateaudemazan.fr; place Napoléon; d from €120; P ⊠ ⊒ ⊜) In the 18th century this charming castle, 7km east of Carpentras in Mazan, belonged to the notorious Marquis de Sade (p175). Today it is Carpentras' regal out-of-town choice.

Eating

Chez Serge (☎ 04 90 63 21 24; www.chez-serge.com; 90 rue Cottier; lunch formule €13.10, plat du jour €9, menu €26; ⊕ lunch & dinner Mon-Sat) Serge – the Marseillais chef born to Armenian parents – cooks up a mean pizza alongside a wealth of traditional bistro fare and truffle dishes to die for at

his lovely linden tree–shaded restaurant. By 12.30pm the terrace is heaving.

Le Vert Galant (☎ 04 90 67 15 50; www.restaurant-vert-galant.com in French; 12 rue de Clapiès; menus €28, €36 & €46; ⊕ closed Sun evening & Mon lunch Oct-Apr, Sun & Mon lunch May-Sep) An old boy on the block he might be, but Michael Castelain continues to pull in the punters with his truffles, *carpaccio de coquilles St-Jacques à l'orange* (clam carpaccio with orange), oyster sorbet and non-seasonal culinary wonders.

Le Marijo (☎ 04 90 60 42 65; 73 rue Raspail; lunch formule €12, menus €20 & €25; ⊕ lunch & dinner) Superb three- and four-course menus laden with regional fare – including truffle omelettes, aïoli Provençal (see p56) and *pieds et paquets* (tripe-wrapped sheep feet) – are served at this overwhelmingly Provençal restaurant. A note on the menu outside reads 'we have traduced a menu in English inside'.

Saveurs et Découvertes (7 rue des Halles; ⊕ 8.30am-6.30pm Tue-Sat) Indulge in aromatised green leaves, an apple and apricot infusion or one of 80 other tea types at this sweet little tea and chocolate shop.

Shopping

Antique Market (place du Marché aux Oiseaux; ⊕ 8am-noon Fri Apr-Oct) Browse the junk and clunk to uncover some great treasures at Carpentras' weekly antique market

Chocolats René Clavel (☎ 04 90 63 07 59; 30 rue Porte d'Orange) Fantastical sculptures carved from *berlingot*, a hard caramel candy first cooked up in Carpentras in 1844.

Confiserie Bruno (☎ 04 90 63 04 99; www.confiseriebono.fr; 280 allée Jean Jaurès) *Berlingots* since 1925.

Food Market (allée des Platanes & place Aristide Briand; ⊕ 8am-noon Fri) Shop at the Vaucluse's biggest and best market for everything from truffles (November to March) to wicker baskets, cooking pots, fruit, veg and fresh produce galore.

Getting There & Away

From the **bus station** (place Terradou) there are hourly services to/from Avignon (€3.80, 45 minutes) and less frequent services to/from Cavaillon (€4.60, 45 minutes), L'Isle-sur-la-Sorgue (€3.40, 20 minutes), Sault (€5.50, 1¼ hours) and Vaison-la-Romaine (€3.90, 45 minutes). **Cars Comtadins** (☎ 04 90 67 20 25; 192 av Georges Clémenceau) or **Cars Arnaud** (☎ 04 90 63 01 82; 8 av Victor Hugo) have schedules.

AVIGNON AREA

AROUND CARPENTRAS

From Carpentras a circular day trip takes travellers through a water world of fountains and water wheels, gushing springs and breathtaking gorges.

Pernes-les-Fontaines

pop 10,309

A former capital of the Comtat Venaissin, Pernes-les-Fontaines, 5km south of Carpentras, is named after the 40 fountains that spring from its stone walls and squares. Upon discovering the Font de Bouvery source in the 18th century, the town mayor graced the town with monumental mushrooms of fountains like the grandiose, moss-covered **Fontaine du Cormoran**, **Fontaine Reboul** and **Fontaine du Gigot**. Pick up a fountain map at the **tourist office** (☎ 04 90 61 31 04; www.ville-pernes-les-fontaines.fr in French; place Gabriel Moutte; ☺ 9am-12.30pm & 2.30-7pm Mon-Fri, 9am-12.30pm & 2.30-6pm Sat).

L'Isle-sur-la-Sorgue

pop 17,443

A further 11km south sits this chic spot known for its antique shops and graceful waterways. L'Isle dates from the 12th century when villagers built huts on stilts above what was then a swampy marshland. By the 18th century it was a thriving silk-weaving centre surrounded by canals ploughed by water wheels powering its paper mills and silk factories.

On Sunday morning its quays are swamped with book and antique sellers, and a gaggle of market stalls selling other wares. **Le Quai de la Gare** (☎ 04 90 20 73 42; 4 av Julien Guigue), near the train station, houses 35 antique dealers, and another 100 deal in **Le Village des Antiquaires** (☎ 04 90 38 04 57; www.villagegare.com; 2bis av de l'Égalité), an antique shopping mall fronted by an 18th-century mill. Don't expect any bargains.

The **tourist office** (☎ 04 90 38 04 78; www.ot -islesurlasorgue.fr; place de la Liberté; ☺ 9am-12.30 or 1pm & 2 or 2.30-6 or 6.30pm Mon-Sat, 9.30am-12.30 or 1pm Sun) has plenty of information regarding accommodation.

Fontaine de Vaucluse

pop 661

The mighty spring that gives Fontaine de Vaucluse its name is the spot where the River Sorgue ends its subterranean course and gushes to the surface. At the end of winter and in early spring, up to 200 cu metres of water per second spill forth from the base of the cliff, forming one of the world's most powerful springs. During drier periods the reduced flow seeps through the rocks at various points downstream from the cliff and the spring becomes little more than a still, very deep pond. Following numerous unsuccessful human and robotic attempts to reach the bottom, a remote-controlled submarine touched the 315m-deep base in 1985.

INFORMATION

Tourist Office (☎ 04 90 20 32 22; officetourisme .vaucluse@wanadoo.fr; chemin de la Fontaine; ☺ 9am-1pm & 2-8pm Mon-Sat)

SIGHTS

Fontaine has several museums: the Resistance movement is covered at the **Musée de la Résistance 1939–45** (☎ 04 90 20 24 00; chemin de la Fontaine; adult/12-16 yrs €3.50/1.50; ☺ 10am-noon & 2-5 or 6pm Wed-Mon Oct-May, 10am-6pm Wed-Mon Jun-Sep); earthly stalactites and speleology are the subjects of the **Écomusée du Gouffre** (☎ 04 90 20 34 13; chemin de la Fontaine; adult/12-18 yrs €5/3.25; ☺ 9.30am-noon & 2-6pm Feb-May, Oct & Nov; 9.30am-7pm Jun-Sep); and you'll find traditional Provençal figurines at the **Musée du Santon** (☎ 04 90 20 20 83; adult/12-16 yrs €2/1; ☺ 10am-12.30pm & 2-6.30pm).

Vallis Clausa (☎ 04 90 20 34 14; chemin de la Fontaine; admission free; ☺ 9 or 10am-12.20pm & 2-6.50pm) is a reconstructed paper mill, built where Fontaine's original mill was located from 1522 until 1968. Flower-encrusted paper,

---

CANOEING

Ploughing through the 8km of water between Fontaine de Vaucluse and L'Isle-sur-la-Sorgue is an incredibly relaxing way to discover this busy part of Provence in peace. Once on the waterways, nature prevails. Late April to early November, **Canoë Évasion** (☎ 04 90 38 26 22; rte de Fontaine de Vaucluse), next to Camping de la Coutelière on the D24 from Fontaine de Vaucluse towards Lagnes; and **Kayak Vert** (☎ 04 90 20 35 44; www.canoefrance.com) in Fontaine de Vaucluse, both rent canoes and organise river expeditions. A canoe or kayak with guide costs €18 per person.

made by hand as it was in the 16th century, is sold in its boutique.

Italian Renaissance poet Pétrarque (Petrarch in English) lived in Fontaine from 1337 to 1353, where he immortalised Laura, his true love, in verse. The **Musée Pétrarque** (☎ 04 90 20 37 20; musee-biblio-petrarque@cg84.fr; adult/12-16 yrs €3.50/1.50; ⏱ 10am-noon & 2-6pm Wed-Mon Jun-Sep, 10am-noon & 2-6pm Sat & Sun Mar, Apr, May & Oct-Dec) looks at his work, sojourn and broken heart. A combined ticket covering the latter and the Resistance museum costs €4.60/2.80 for adults/12 to 16 years.

Pays de Venasque

The hilltop villages around **Venasque** (population 980, elevation 320m), 13km southeast of Carpentras, form 'Venasque Country'. Seldom explored yet beautiful, it is well worth the drive.

Venasque's village **baptistry** (☎ 04 90 66 62 01; adult/under 12 yrs €3/free; ⏱ 9.15am-noon & 1-5 or 6pm Jan–mid-Dec) was built in the 5th century on the site of a Roman temple and is one of France's oldest structures.

The fortress village of **Le Beaucet** (population 354, elevation 300m), tumbles down the hillside 6km south via the winding D314. Two kilometres south along chemin des Oratoires (the D39A) in the hamlet of **St-Gens** is a small Romanesque basilica, rebuilt in 1884. The hermit Gens, who lived with wolves and performed rainmaking miracles, died here in 1127.

The **Forêt de Vénasque**, crossed by the GR91 walking trail, lies to the east of Venasque. Heading across the Col de Murs (627m) mountain pass to the pretty village of **Murs** (population 420), 5km east, you can see remains of the **Le Mur de la Peste** (see p177). Continuing north, the GR91 makes a beeline for the magnificent **Gorges de la Nesque**, from where Sault and the eastern realms of the Ventoux can be accessed. On the **Col des Abeilles**, north of the gorges on the D1, you can hire a donkey to accompany you along the gorges or up Mont Ventoux at **Les Ânes des Abeilles** (☎ 04 90 64 01 52; anesdesabeilles@wanadoo.fr; Col des Abeilles). Donkeys carry up to 30kg and walk 3km to 4km an hour; a day/weekend costs €38/61.

Venasque **tourist office** (☎ 04 90 66 11 66; www.venasque.fr; Grande Rue; ⏱ 10am-noon & 2-6pm Mon-Sat Jun-Sep, shorter hr Oct-Apr) has information on the entire area.

Sleeping & Eating

Hôtel du Poète (☎ 04 90 20 34 05; www.hoteldupoete.com; Fontaine de Vaucluse; d €90-240, ste €260-290; ⏱ Feb-Dec; P ⏼ ⏾) Given the continuous gushing of water guests hear at this three-star mill-hotel, it is inevitable that room names don musical overtones – *concerto*, *symphonie* and so on. Part of its lovely garden sits on decking above the river.

La Figuière (☎ 04 90 20 37 41; http://la.figuiere.free.fr in French; chemin de la Grangette, Fontaine de Vaucluse; B&B for 2 people €75-85, menus €20 & €28, ⏱ Tue-Sun) The definite appeal of this village bistro with three charming rooms up top is the peace, quiet and calming relief its tree-shaded terrace provides. Find it just off Fontaine's busy main street.

Mas La Bonoty (☎ 04 90 61 61 09; www.bonoty.com; chemin de la Bonoty, Pernes-les-Fontaines; d with breakfast €75-85; P ⏾ ⏼) This elegant farmhouse-hotel languishes amid apricot and cheery trees, an olive grove and lavender fields. Unusually, rooms, named after flowers, have tea- and coffee-making facilities.

Auberge La Fontaine (☎ 04 90 66 02 96; www.auberge-lafontaine.com; place de la Fontaine; d €125, bistro/restaurant menu €18/38; P) Venasque's up-market inn, sitting plump in the heart of the charming village, runs cookery courses and hosts a rash of elegant and atmospheric dinner-concerts. The cheaper, more informal bistro has an à la carte menu as well as fixed-price *menus*, unlike the restaurant, which touts fixed *menus* only.

Le Mas des Abricotiers (☎ 04 90 66 19 16; www.bleu-provence.com; 193 chemin des Terres Mortes, St-Didier; B&B for 2 people €60-94; P ⏾ ⏼ ⏼) It might be on Dead Lands Lane but this age-old farmhouse, 5km east of Pernes-les-Fontaines, creates the prettiest of Provençal scenes with its warm apricot-coloured walls, cooling wooden shutters and riot of roses, apricot trees and vines outside. The entire place is nonsmoking.

Auberge de Jeunesse (☎ 04 90 20 31 65; fax 04 90 20 26 20; chemin de la Vignasse, Fontaine de Vaucluse; dm 8.90, camping €5.30, breakfast/dinner/sheets €3.50/8.60/2.80; ⏱ reception 8-10am & 5.30-11pm) Fontaine's rural, out-of-town hostel takes the guise of a stone farmhouse, 1.2km from the centre along the *'route touristique'* to Gordes (signposted off the D24).

There are camp sites in Pernes-les-Fontaines and Fontaine de Vaucluse, and a hiker-friendly *gîte d'étape* in Murs.

Getting There & Away

Fontaine de Vaucluse is 21km southeast of Carpentras and about 7km east of L'Isle-sur-la-Sorgue. From Avignon **Voyages Arnaud** (☎ 04 90 38 15 58) runs buses to/from L'Isle-sur-la-Sorgue (€3.50, 40 minutes, three to four daily), Fontaine de Vaucluse (€4.40, one hour, three to four daily); and between Carpentras and L'Isle-sur-la-Sorgue (20 minutes).

L'Isle-sur-la-Sorgue train station is not served by passenger trains.

Getting Around

Scoot around Pernes-les-Fontaines from **Vélo & Oxygène** (☎ 04 90 61 37 37; 284 rue Émile Zola) for around €15 a day.

In L'Isle-sur-la-Sorgue, try **Christophe Tendil** (☎ 04 90 38 19 12; 10 av Julien Guigue).

LES ALPILLES

South of Avignon is the oh-so-wild Chaîne des Alpilles, a barren chain of savage limestone rocks that titillates the senses with its thick carpet of herbal garrigue and olive groves. To the north and south sits St-Rémy de Provence and Maussane-les-Alpilles respectively, a town and a village linked by the Vallée des Baux where AOC olive oil (p55) is made.

Les Alpilles stretch east to the River Durance, west to the River Rhône and are traversed by the GR6 walking path.

ST-RÉMY DE PROVENCE

pop 10,007

St-Rémy – the main kick-off point for Alpilles mountain forays – is a colourful place with a colourful past. The Greeks and then the Romans settled Glanum on the city's southern fringe. The philosopher Nostradamus (1503–66) was born in a house on rue Hoche in St-Rémy, only later moving to Salon de Provence to compile his influential prophecies. Three centuries on, a tormented Vincent van Gogh (1853–90) sought refuge in St-Rémy, painting some of his best-known works here between 1889 and 1890.

Sheep, sheep and more *moutons* (sheep) fill the streets on Pentecost Monday during the **Fête de la Transhumance**, which marks the movement of the flocks to pastures new. On 15 August 50 horses lug a cart laden with local produce through town to celebrate **La**

Carreto Ramado, and September closes with a 10-day festival in honour of the town's patron saint.

St-Rémy is a gastronomic mecca with a couple of notable chefs and one of France's best chocolate-makers in its fold. The famed, smooth, rich oils from the Vallée des Baux can also be tried and tasted here.

Information

INTERNET RESOURCES

www.alpilles.fr Excellent tourist information site for St-Rémy and its Alpilles surrounds.
www.alpilles.com An equally informative alternative.

TOURIST INFORMATION

Tourist Office (☎ 04 90 92 05 22; www.saintremy-de-provence.com; place Jean Jaurès; ☉ 9am-noon & 2-7pm Mon-Sat, 9am-noon Sun mid-Jun–mid-Sep; 9am-noon & 2-6pm Mon-Sat mid-Sep–mid-Jun)

Glanum

Accessible only with a guided tour following flood damage in 2003, this vast **archaeological site** (☎ 04 90 92 23 79; rte des Baux; adult/under 18 yrs €4.10/free; ☉ 9.30am-6.30pm, last tour 5.30pm) features excavated remains from the Gallo-Greek (3rd to 1st centuries BC) to the Gallo-Roman (1st century BC to 3rd century AD) eras. Among the archaeological finds uncovered are parts of Glanum's temple, public baths dating from 50 BC and the forum – enjoy great views of these for free from the Taberna Romana (p153). Smaller fragments of treasure dug up will eventually be displayed in the **Musée du Site de Glanum** (☎ 04 90 92 64 04; 1 rue du Parage; ☉ currently closed for renovation), inside the Renaissance Hôtel de Sade in the centre of St-Rémy.

Glanum, 2km south of the centre on the southbound D5, is easy to find: look for **Les Antiques**, a spectacular pair of Roman monuments comprising a **triumphal arch** (AD 20) and **mausoleum** (30–20 BC), on the opposite side of the road.

Van Gogh Sights

The Dutch-born artist retreated to **Monastère St-Paul de Mausole** (☎ 04 90 92 77 00; maison.sante.st.paul@wanadoo.fr; adult/under 12 yrs €3.40/free; ☉ 9.30am-7pm Apr-Oct, 10.15am-4.45pm Nov-Mar). Van Gogh voluntarily admitted himself to the asylum on 3 May 1889 and stayed until 16 May 1890, accomplishing 100 drawings and about 150 paintings, including his

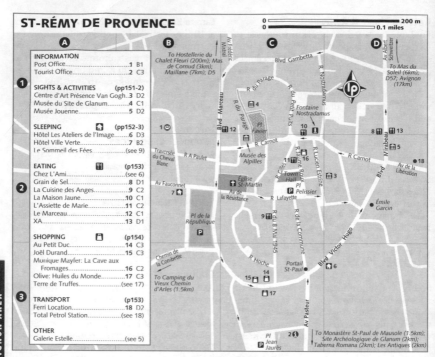

ST-RÉMY DE PROVENCE

0 — 200 m
0 — 0.1 miles

INFORMATION
Post Office...........................1 B1
Tourist Office.......................2 C3

SIGHTS & ACTIVITIES (pp151-2)
Centre d'Art Présence Van Gogh..3 D2
Musée du Site de Glanum........4 C1
Musée Jouenne....................5 D2

SLEEPING (pp152-3)
Hôtel Les Ateliers de l'Image......6 D3
Hôtel Ville Verte..................7 B2
Le Sommeil des Fées............(see 9)

EATING (p153)
Chez L'Ami........................(see 6)
Grain de Sel.......................8 D1
La Cuisine des Anges.............9 C2
La Maison Jaune..................10 C1
L'Assiette de Marie...............11 C2
Le Marceau........................12 C1
XA.................................13 D1

SHOPPING (p154)
Au Petit Duc.......................14 C3
Joël Durand.......................15 C3
Monique Mayfer: La Cave aux
    Fromages.......................16 C2
Olive: Huiles du Monde..........17 C3
Terre de Truffes.................(see 17)

TRANSPORT (p153)
Ferri Location......................18 D2
Total Petrol Station.............(see 18)

OTHER
Galerie Estelle....................(see 5)

To Hostellerie du Chalet Fleuri (200m); Mas de Cornud (3km); Maillane (7km); D5

To Mas du Soleil (6km); D57; Avignon (17km)

Blvd Gambetta

R Nostradamus

Av Albert Schweitzer

R du Parage

R du Petit Puits

Fontaine Nostradamus

Av Frédéric Mistral

Blvd Marceau

Blvd du Parage

R Carnot

Pl Favier

R Lucien Estrine

R Carnot

N Mirabeau

Av de la Libération

Émile Garcin

Traverse du Cheval Blanc

R A Paulet

Musée des Alpilles

Town Hall

Pl Pelissier

Av Fauconnet

Église St-Martin

Av de la Résistance

R Lafayette

R de la Commune

Pl de la République

R du 8 Mai 1945

Chemin de la Combette

R Hoche

Portail St-Paul

Blvd Victor Hugo

To Camping du Vieux Chemin d'Arles (1.5km)

Av Pasteur

Pl Jean Jaurès

To Monastère St-Paul de Mausole (1.5km); Site Archéologique de Glanum (2km); Taberna Romana (2km); Les Antiques (2km)

famous *Les Iris* (Still Life with Iris, 1890) and *Le Champ de Blé au Cyprès* (Yellow Cornfield, 1889) during his stay. A prison camp during WWI, the building is now a clinic with a **Romanesque cloister** and **reconstruction of van Gogh's room** that can be visited.

From the monastery entrance, information boards mark the **promenade sur les lieux peints par van Gogh** walking trail that leads to the places where van Gogh painted. In town, his life and works are unravelled at the **Centre d'Art Présence Van Gogh** (☎ 04 90 92 34 72; 8 rue Lucien Estrine; adult/student €3.20/2.30; ☯ 10.30am-12.30pm & 2.30-6.30pm Tue-Sun late Mar-Dec).

Provençal and other natural scapes painted from a contemporary perspective hang in the **Musée Jouenne** (☎ 04 32 60 00 51; 20 blvd Mirabeau; adult/under 12 yrs €4/free; ☯ 10am-12.30pm & 3-7pm Tue-Sun), a hybrid museum, art gallery and cultural centre showcasing works by French 1950s hotshot Michel Jouenne (b 1933).

Tours

The tourist office runs various one-hour guided tours (€6.50), including a van Gogh one and nature forays in the Alpilles.

Sleeping

Le Sommeil des Fées (☎ 04 90 92 17 66, 06 14 41 41 31; www.alpilles-delices.com; 4 rue du 8 Mai 1945; B&B for 2 people €55-75) The Sleepiness of Fairies, a five-room *chambre d'hôte* in town, is magical. Rooms are beautifully furnished, named after fairies and overlook a pretty old-town patio and garden.

Hôtel Ville Verte (☎ 04 90 92 06 14; www.hotel-villeverte.com; 18 place de la République; d €47-70; ☯ Feb-Dec; P ✖ ✿) This charming place with 37 double rooms and a bunch of self-catering studios first opened its doors in the 19th century. In 2004 it was given a major facelift.

Hostellerie du Chalet Fleuri (☎ 04 90 92 03 62; fax 04 90 92 60 28; 15 av Frédéric Mistral; d €67; P) Part of the Logis de France chain, this flowery chalet with pretty rooms and a leafy terrace specialising in Provençal cuisine lives up to its name.

Mas du Soleil (☎ 04 90 94 10 23; www.gite-masdu soleil.com; rte d'Avignon; 6-/8-person gîte per week from €460/560; P) Those with kids will be hard-pushed to find a better place to stay than this 19th-century farmhouse split into two

Théâtre Antique (p136), Orange

Bridge over River Sorgue, L'Isle-sur-la-Sorgue (p149)

Cheese seller at market,
St-Rémy de Provence (p125)

The legendary Pont d'Avignon (p126)

DAVID TOM

Sunrise over Roussillon (p171)

STEVE FALLON

Silver bories (p171) near Apt

Farmhouse in a field of poppies in the Lubéron (p165)

BARBARA VAN

STELLA HELLANDER

Cakes for sale at Lourmarin's Friday morning market (p181)

self-catering *gîtes*. Its lawn is the size of a football pitch, the laundry room was a pigsty once upon a time and melons grow in greenhouses out back.

Camping du Vieux Chemin d'Arles (☎ 04 90 92 27 22; campingstremy@free.fr; Vieux Chemin d'Arles; 2 adults, caravan/tent & car €10; ☺ Dec–mid-Nov) Pitching up at this small family-run farm is a pleasure. Sporting a couple of swings and a seesaw for little kids, the farm is 1.5km down a country lane from St-Rémy's place de la République.

Eating

La Cuisine des Anges (☎ 04 90 92 17 66; 4 rue du 8 Mai 1945; menu €25; ☺ lunch & dinner Tue, Wed & Fri-Sun, lunch Thu) Tucked down a charming backstreet above Le Sommeil des Fées, the Cuisine of Angels is a cute find cooking up light summery Provençal fare – marinated peppers, grilled fish, beef with a garlic *confit* and so on – with a feminine flourish.

L'Assiette de Marie (☎ 04 90 92 32 14; 1 rue Jaume Roux; menu €29; ☺ lunch & dinner Fri-Wed) Knick-knacks from another era clutter this old-world bistro, known for its delicious mix of traditional dishes like Provençal lamb casserole and contemporary pasta creations. Imaginative salads are served al fresco at lunch time.

Grain de Sel (☎ 04 90 92 00 89; 25 blvd Mirabeau; starters/mains/desserts €12/18/6.50; ☺ lunch & dinner high season, dinner mid-season, lunch & dinner Fri-Mon low season) A discrete note on the menu at this temple to modernity and minimalism subtly tells diners seeking a quick and speedy nosh to go elsewhere. Exquisite dishes at the Salt Grain demand time – to prepare, cook, appreciate and savour.

Le Marceau (☎ 04 90 92 37 11; 13 blvd Marceau; menus €23 & €36; ☺ lunch & dinner Mon, Tue & Sun, dinner Thu & Sat) Dine beneath age-old beams at this simple yet refined restaurant. *Anchoïade* (anchovy paste) and aïoli are among the many regional treats that drive chef Alain Assaud's menu.

Also recommended:

XA (☎ 04 90 92 41 23; 24 blvd Mirabeau; menu €24; ☺ lunch & dinner Thu-Tue Mar-Oct) XA stands for Xavier – the chef's husband who mans this female ode to contemporary cuisine.

La Maison Jaune (☎ 04 90 92 56 14; lamaisonjaune@wanadoo.fr; 15 rue Carnot; menus €30-55; ☺ dinner Tue, lunch & dinner Wed-Sun summer, lunch Tue-Sun winter) Traditional cuisine with a twist served in a stark, modern interior or terrace with old-town views.

AUTHOR'S CHOICE

Hôtel Les Ateliers de l'Image (☎ 04 90 92 51 50; www.hotelphoto.com; 36 blvd Victor Hugo; d €150-380, ste €300-600; ☐ P ☒ ☒ ☒) Photography workshops (p338) are a snippet of what this innovative and stylish 'photography hotel' offers. Its architecture and interior design is stunning. The gardens feature a vegetable patch, water gardens and labyrinth, and one suite has its own tree house accessed via a drawbridge. Jazz concerts set the cocktail bar jiving and chef Masao Ikeda cooks up Franco-Japanese culinary creations in **Chez L'Ami** (☎ 04 90 92 78 40; lunch menus €15-22), a sushi bar-cum-restaurant designed with 'a friend's home' in mind.

Taberna Romana (☎ 04 90 92 65 97; www.taberna -romana.com; rte des Baux; menus €11-19; ☺ 9am-7pm Apr-Sep) Roman cuisine; munch a hard-boiled egg with fennel sauce and savour the free Glanum panorama.

Getting There & Around

Buses to Tarascon and Nîmes operated by **Cévennes Cars** (☎ 04 66 29 27 29) depart from place de la République. Avignon-bound buses run by **Sociétés Rapides du Sud-Est** (☎ 04 90 14 59 00) leave from blvd Victor Hugo.

Ferri Location (☎ 04 90 92 10 88; 35 av de la Libération; ☺ 7.30am-noon & 1.30-7.30pm Mon-Fri, 8am-noon & 2-6pm Sat), inside the Total petrol station, rents mountain bikes for €18 a day. Helmets/child seats cost €1.50/2.30.

AROUND ST-RÉMY DE PROVENCE

Several tip-top sights lie within easy reach of St-Rémy, an area composed of vineyards, olive groves and garrigue, whose powerful herbal fragrance clears the stuffiest of noses in spring and summer.

Les Baux de Provence

pop 443 / elevation 185m

From St-Rémy de Provence, snail-slow sightseeing coaches caterpillar 10km southwest to one of France's most visited tourist attractions, fortified Les Baux de Provence. Some 2.5 million people a year visit this hilltop village that gave its name to bauxite, the chief ore of aluminium first mined here in 1822. In Provençal 'baou' appropriately means 'rocky spur'.

Château des Baux (☎ 04 90 54 55 56; www
.chateau-baux-provence.com; adult/student/7-17 yrs
€7/5.50/3.50, family ticket €19; ☽ 9am-6.30pm Mar-Jun
& Sep-Nov; 9am-8.30pm Jul & Aug; 9am-5pm Dec-Feb), a
once-magnificent fortress destroyed during
the reign of Louis XIII in 1633 and ruined
ever since, crowns this tourist-packed village. Unbeatable views of the surrounding
Chaîne des Alpilles can be enjoyed from its
rocky 70,000 sq metres.

The cinematically minded can catch a
sound-and-light show screened across 4000
sq metres of rock at the **Cathédrale d'Images**
(☎ 04 90 54 38 65; www.cathedrale-images.com; rte de
Maillane; adult/8-16 yrs €7/4.10; ☽ 10am-7pm Feb-Sep,
10am-6pm Oct-early Jan), a cold redundant limestone quarry (bring a warm jumper) on the
village outskirts.

Amid the overkill of crass souvenir shops
and boutiques selling bad art, **Olive: Huiles du
Monde** (Grande Rue; ☽ 9.30am-7pm Mar–mid-Nov), a
cave à huile d'olive (olive oil cellar) is worth
sniffing out – the oil can be floral, peppery,

bitter, herbaceous and so on. The stuff made
at **Moulin Castelas** (☎ 04 90 54 50 86; info@castelas
.com; Mas de l'Olivier; ☽ 9am-6.30pm), at the foot of
the village, is said to have a nose of greenery
and a scent of freshly cut grass.

The **tourist office** (☎ 04 90 54 34 39; www.lesbaux
deprovence.com; Maison du Roy, rue Porte Mage), immediately on your left as you enter the walled
village, has accommodation information.

A noteworthy *chambre d'hôte* in the vil-
lage is **Le Prince Noir** (The Black Prince; ☎ 04 90 54
39 57; www.leprincenoir.com; rue de Lorme; d €79, d/tr
with kitchen & terrace €160/185, ste for 2/3/4 with terrace €132/157/182), with art-strung walls and
rooms built into the rock face.

Two glittering Michelin stars lure gourmets from far and wide to the ultra-tasty
restaurant at **L'Ousta de Baumaniere** (☎ 04 90
54 33 07; www.oustaudebaumaniere.com; d €210-450, half-
board for 2 people per night €698-738, lunch/dinner menu
€70/145; Ⓟ ⊠ 🖥 🐾), an exceptional 16th-
century place to sleep and eat that has at-
tained legendary status in the 60-odd years
it has been open.

Maussane-les-Alpilles & Around
pop 2000

Maussane-les-Alpilles, 3km south of Les
Baux on the Alpilles' southern fringe, shelters some of Provence's best-known *moulins
d'huile* (oil mills), where five different types
of freshly harvested olives are pummelled
and pressed into smooth, golden olive oil.

A tour of the **Moulin Jean-Marie Cornille**
(☎ 04 90 54 32 37; www.moulin-cornille.com; rue Charloun
Rieu; ☽ free guided tours 10.30am Tue & Fri, shop 9am-
6pm Mon-Sat, 11am-6pm Sun), a 17th-century mill
run as a cooperative since 1924, ends with
dégustation (tasting) and buying (from €17
per litre). Depending on the year's harvest
(which produces anything from 140,000L
to 300,00L), oil can sell out by mid-August.
New stock comes in mid-December.

From Maussane stunning views of the
fierce, silver-ridged Alpilles can be enjoyed
along the eastbound D78. A 6km drive
southeast along the D17 brings you to **Mouriès**
(population 2525), where some of the valley's
best olive oil is milled at the **Moulin Coopératif**
(☎ 04 90 47 53 86; www.moulincoop.com; Quartier Mas
Neuf; ☽ 9am-noon & 2-6pm Mon-Sat, 2-6pm Sun, to 7pm
Jun-Sep). The village celebrates a **Fête des Olives
Vertes** (green olive festival) in mid-September
and the arrival of the year's new oil with a
Grand Marché des Huiles Nouvelles in December.

TOP FIVE TASTY BUYS

■ **Chocolates to die for** at **Joël Durand's
boutique** (☎ 04 90 92 38 25; 3 blvd Victor
Hugo). Durand's astonishing use of
Provençal herbs and plants – lavender,
rose petals, violet, thyme, mint etc –
makes him one of France's top 10
chocolate-makers. Chocolates cost
€60 per kilogram.

■ **Historical biscuits** baked by food his-
torian Anne Daguin using old Roman,
Renaissance, Alpine and Arlésien recipes
at her shop **Au Petit Duc** (☎ 04 90 92 08
31; 7 blvd Victor Hugo).

■ **Olive oil** from Provence at **Olive: Huiles du Monde** (☎ 04 90 92 53 93; 16 blvd
Victor Hugo). Taste 30 different oils at its
bar à huiles (oil bar).

■ **Truffles** at **Terre de Truffes** (16 blvd
Victor Hugo), a classy boutique inspired
by chef Bruno (p297) and selling truffles
in all forms.

■ **Yummy and unusual cheeses** at **Monique Mayfer: La Cave aux Fromages**
(☎ 04 90 92 32 45; 1 place Joseph Hilaire), a
fabulous cheese shop with a 12th-
century ripening *cave* (cellar) to visit.

AUTHOR'S CHOICE: TIP-TOP

Make a day of it by lunching at one of these tasty eating spots around St-Rémy.

■ **Le Bistrot du Paradou – Chez Jean Louis** (☎ 04 90 54 32 70; 3km west from Maussane-les-Alpilles on the D17 to Le Paradou; lunch/dinner menus €38/43; ⚇ lunch & dinner Mon-Sat Apr-Sep, lunch Mon-Sat Oct-Mar; (P)) Courageous diners, determined to savour every last mouthful of Jean-Louis' one fixed menu, snap up every table by 12.30pm at this authentic bistro. The cheeseboard is ponging and spoils for choice.

■ **Le Margaux** (☎ 04 90 54 35 04; 1 rue Paul Revoil, Maussane-les-Alpilles; menus €27.50 & €35.50; ⚇ lunch & dinner Wed-Mon, every 2nd week lunch & dinner Thu-Mon) Sardines marinated in aniseed, *fricassée de lapin aux senteurs des Alpilles* (rabbit cooked with Alpilles scents) and other delicious dishes are served with a quiet flourish in this elegant garden restaurant wrapped around an olive tree and green lawn in the village centre. Crisp white linen tablecloths, napkins and silver ice buckets tell you where you are.

■ **Le Romarin** (☎ 04 90 95 58 43; 11 av Bertherigues, Barbentane; menus €11.50, €15.50 & €21.50; ⚇ lunch & dinner Thu-Mon) Cosy Rosemary (as in the herb) is your quintessential village restaurant – chequered tablecloths, flower boxes and super nosh makes you feel right at home. The aubergine, tomato, parmesan and goat cheese crumble is not to be missed.

■ **Le Saint-Georges** (☎ 04 90 92 44 62; www.valmouriane.com; Domaine de Valmouraine, petit rte des Baux; menus €27-65, d low/high season from €120/165; (P) ⚇ ⚇ ⚇ ⚇) St-George is the plump choice for those seeking a fine-dining experience – Pascal Volle's *menu dégustation à l'huile d'olive* (olive oil-tasting menu) is a real treat. Should you find you can't move afterwards, the farmhouse on this idyllic country estate has rooms.

Eyguières (population 5392), 15km further east, is dominated by the Alpilles' highest point (493m). Nearby in **Eygalières** (population 1850, elevation 134m), a 16th-century Renaissance mansion (today a four-star hotel) safeguards the **Jardin de l'Alchimiste** (☎ 04 90 90 67 77; www.jardin-alchimiste.com; Mas de la Brune; adult/student €5/4, guided visit with drink €8; ⚇ 9am-7pm Tue-Sat May, 9am-7pm Sat, Sun & holidays Jun-early Oct), an alchemist's garden where herbs and plants blossom. **Orgon** (population 2268), 9km further north, is guarded by **Notre Dame de Beauregard** (1878), a church perched up high on a needle of rock with eagle-eye views of the Alpilles, TGV railway line and motorway.

Maussane-les-Alpilles (☎ 04 90 54 52 04; www .maussane.com; place Laugier de Monblan), **Mouriés** (☎ 04 91 13 84 13; www.mouries.com; 2 rue du Temple) and **Orgon** (☎ 04 90 73 09 54; av Georges Coste) have small tourist offices.

Fontvieille
pop 3566

Sleepy Fontvieille, 10km west of Maussane along the D17, is famed for its windmill immortalised by Alphonse Daudet in his short stories *Lettres de mon Moulin* (Letters from my Windmill; 1869). Despite the

French author being born in Nîmes and spending most of his life in Paris, he shared a strong spiritual affinity with Provence and is regarded as a Provençal writer.

Contrary to popular belief, **Le Moulin de Daudet** (Daudet's windmill), which dates back to 1814 and houses the **Musée de Daudet** (adult/6-12 yrs €2.50/1.50, parking €2; ⚇ 9am-7pm Jun-Sep, 10am-noon & 2-5pm Nov, Dec & Feb-May), is not the windmill where the writer spent hours sunk in literary thought. From the windmill-museum, a 1½-hour trail leads past the ruined **Moulin Ramet** to **Moulin Tissot-Avon** – Daudet's true haunt, defunct since 1905.

The trail continues to **Château de Montauban** (closed for renovation), home to Daudet's cousins with whom he stayed when in town. Check at the **tourist office** (☎ 04 90 54 67 49; www.fontvieille-provence.com; 5 rue Marcel Honorat; ⚇ 9am-7pm Mon-Sat, reduced hr in winter) for an update on chateau visits.

Le Laetitia (☎ 04 90 54 72 14; rue du Lion; d with sink/shower €26/33, d/tr/q with shower & toilet €38/48/57; (P)) It might only have one star but this small family-run hotel is a rock-solid bet for families and couples motoring around the region. A riot of flowers graces its inviting table-clad garden out front.

The most exciting way to get to Fontvieille is by steam train from Arles (see p114).

Maillane to the Rhône

Mistral (p52) was a native of **Maillane** (population 1880), 7km northwest of St-Rémy. The poet was born in a farmhouse on its outskirts but moved into the centre of the village with his mother following the death of his father. Upon marrying, 46-year-old Mistral left home, only to move with his 19-year-old wife into the **house** (☎ 04 90 95 74 06; 11 av Lamartine; adult/student €3.50/1; ☺ 9.30-11.30am & 2.30-6.30pm Tue-Sun Apr-Sep, 10-11.30am & 2-4.30pm Tue-Sun Oct-Mar) – today a museum – opposite his mother's. Mistral is buried in the village cemetery.

Continuing 3km north towards the River Rhône, you hit **Graveson** (population 3190) with its sweet-smelling, garden-clad **Musée des Arômes et du Parfum** (Museum of Aromas & Perfumes; ☎ 04 90 95 81 55; www.viearome.com in French; petite rte du Grès; adult/under 12 yrs €4/free; ☺ 10am-noon & 2-6pm), unique **Les Figuières du Mas de Luquet** (☎ 04 90 95 72 03; www.lesfiguieres .com; chemin du Mas de la Musique), a fig farm where 150 variations of the fruit tree grow; and **Musée Auguste Chabaud** (☎ 04 90 90 53 02; www .museechabaud.com in French; cours National; adult/student €4/2; ☺ 10am-noon & 1.30-6.30pm Jun-Sep, 1.30-

6.30pm Oct-May), dedicated to the Nîmes-born fauvist painter who spent most of his life in Graveson. In July during the **Fête de St-Éloi** a flower-decorated cart is pulled through the village by 20 horses.

From Graveson the scenic D81 meanders through the gently rolling hills of the **Massif de la Montagnette**. Hidden in its leafy green south is **Abbaye St-Michel de Frigolet**, a neo-gothic abbey (1863–66) with vast grounds and a tower-topped **hotel-restaurant** (☎ 04 90 90 52 70; www.frigolet.com; s/d/q €63/81/134.50, lunch/ dinner menu €12.50/21; P).

Barbentane (population 3780), a medieval village dominated by the 28m-tall **Tour Anglica** (1385) and classical 17th-century **Château de Barbentane** (☎ 04 90 95 51 07; adult/6-15 yrs €6/4.50; ☺ 10am-noon & 2-6pm Easter-Oct), sits in the north of the massif. The village has a **tourist office** (☎ 04 90 90 85 86; www.barbentane.fr in French; Les Cours; ☺ 2-6pm Mon, 9.30am-noon & 2-6pm Tue-Fri, 9.30am-noon Sat) and a particularly lovely *chambre d'hôte* in the guise of **Le Mazet de la Dame** (☎ 04 90 90 91 73; www.la-dame.com; d/ste €83/100; P ♨).

TARASCON & BEAUCAIRE

The mighty chateaux of **Tarascon** (population 12,991) and **Beaucaire** (population 13,940) glare at each other across the Rhône. Each year during June's **Fête de la Tarasque**, a Chinese-style dragon parades through Tarascon to celebrate St Martha's slaying of Tarasque, a dragon that lurked in the Rhône according to Provençal legend.

Louis II had **Château de Tarascon** (☎ 04 90 91 01 93; adult/18-25 yrs/under 18 yrs €6.10/3/free; ☺ 9am-7pm Apr–mid-Sep, 9am-noon & 2-5pm Tue-Sun mid-Sep-Mar) built in the 15th century to defend Provence's political frontier. The interior was richly decorated under King René (1434–80), but was later stripped and used as a mint and then as a prison until 1926.

Shabby and dusty Beaucaire was plagued by a dragon, Drac de Beaucaire, who slept in the Rhône but prowled the streets of Beaucaire by day disguised as a man. Or so legend says. One day Drac snatched a washerwoman and took her back to his filthy hovel where she tended his baby son, Le Draconnet, for seven years. Years after her release she spotted Drac in Beaucaire. Upon greeting him, Drac was so horrified to have his disguise blown that he poked out the woman's eyes. A sculpture of him can be seen on place de la République.

RAZZING AROUND THE ALPILLES

Razzing around by quad is the windy way to tour this rocky neck of the woods. Rent one of these feisty little numbers (regular driving or motorbike licence required) from **Provence Quad Location** (☎ 04 90 15 40 47; www.provence-quad-location.com; 4 av Riboun; half-/full day €85/130, half-/full day guided quad treks €100/160; ☺ 8am-noon & 2-7.30pm May-Oct) in Graveson. Count on covering 60km a day. The same company also rents road (€8/10 per half-/full day), mountain (€10/15 per half-/full day) and children's (€6/10 per half-/full day) bikes.

Failing motor power, there's always horse power to razz around. In Mouriès **La Meynaude** (☎ 04 90 47 69 26; rte de Servannes; 2hr/ half-day trek €31/38, dm for rider/walker €31/38; ☺ year-round with advance reservation) is a *gîte d'étape* that runs treks around the Alpilles on horseback and offers basic overnight accommodation.

Beaucaire's ruined 11th-century castle, **Château de Beaucaire** (☎ 04 66 59 26 72; www.aigles -de-beaucaire.com; place du Château; adult/5-11 yrs €8/5.50; ☺ three afternoon shows daily mid-Mar–mid-Nov), can only be entered during falconry displays. The town's other animal spectacle is the running of 100 bulls through the streets, accompanied by Camargue cowboys on horseback, to open the week-long **Foire de Beaucaire** in mid-July.

Southwest of Beaucaire on the D38 towards Bellegarde is the **Mas des Tourelles** (☎ 04 66 59 19 72; www.tourelles.com; adult/5-16 yrs €4.60/1.50; ☺ 10am-noon & 2-7pm Mon-Sat, 2-7pm Sun Jul & Aug; 2-6pm Apr-Jun, Sep & Oct; 2-6pm Sat Nov-Mar), a farm where you can learn how the Romans made wine. In the cellar, taste farm-made Roman *mucsum* (honeyed wine) and *defrutum* (grape juice).

Tourist offices in **Beaucaire** (☎ 04 66 59 26 57; www.ot-beaucaire.fr; 24 cours Gambetta; ☺ 8.45am-12.15pm & 2-6pm Mon-Fri, 9.30am-12.15pm & 3-6pm Sat) and **Tarascon** (☎ 04 90 91 03 52; www.tarascon.org; 59 rue des Halles; ☺ 9am-7pm Mon-Sat, 9.30am-12.30pm Sun Jul & Aug; 9am-noon & 2-6pm Mon-Fri, 9am-noon & 2-5pm Sat, 9.30am-12.30pm Sun Sep & Jun; 9am-noon & 2-6pm Mon-Fri, 9am-noon & 2-5pm Sat Oct-May) have more details.

ACROSS THE RIVER RHÔNE

The Romans left a couple of great legacies on the Rhône's western bank: Nîmes and an enormous aqueduct. Neither is strictly part of the Provence-Alpes-Côte d'Azur *région* (they are in Languedoc-Roussillon) but both make an easy and spectacular day trip.

Infamous for its unpredictable weather, torrential rains and floods (as was the case of 2002) rapidly raise water levels in the region by 2m to 5m, while during long, dry spells the River Gard can all but disappear.

NÎMES

pop 137,740

Lazy, laid-back Nîmes, a little bit Provençal but with a soul as Languedocien as cassoulet, is graced by some of Europe's best-preserved Roman public buildings. Founded by Augustus, the Roman Colonia Nemausensis reached its zenith in the 2nd

---

DENIM

During the 18th century Nîmes' sizeable Protestant middle class, barred from government posts and various forms of employment, turned its energies to trade and manufacturing. Among the products made in the Protestant-owned factories was a twilled fabric known as *serge*. The soft but durable material became very popular among workers and, stained blue, was the 'uniform' of the fishermen of Genoa.

When Levi Strauss (1829–1902), a Bavarian-Jewish immigrant to the USA, began producing trousers in California during and after the gold rush of 1849, he soon realised that miners needed garments that would last. After trying tent canvas, he began importing the *serge de Nîmes*, now better known as denim (a short form of *de Nîmes* meaning 'from Nîmes').

---

century, receiving its water supply from a Roman aqueduct system that included the Pont du Gard, an awesome bridge 23km to the northeast. The sacking of the city by the Vandals in the early 5th century began a downward spiral in fortunes, from which Nîmes never recovered.

Contemporary architectural creations, notably Norman Foster's Carrée d'Art, are the city's other distinctive trademark. French designer Philippe Starck has left his stamp in the form of the city coat of arms (featuring a palm tree and a crocodile) that he redesigned in 1987, and a bus stop called **Abribus** on av Carnot. Fountain-decorated **place d'Assas** (1989) is the work of new realist Niçois painter Martial Raysse.

Nîmes, only 44km southwest of Avignon, becomes more Spanish than French during its frenetic *férias*, bullfighting festivals that – unlike in neighbouring Camargue – end with a dead bull.

Orientation

Everything, including traffic, revolves around Les Arènes. Just north of the amphitheatre, the fan-shaped, largely pedestrianised old city is bounded by blvd Victor Hugo, blvd Amiral Courbet and blvd Gambetta. North of place aux Herbes, one of the main squares, lies the carefully preserved Îlot Littré – the old dyers' quarter.

AVIGNON AREA

NÎMES

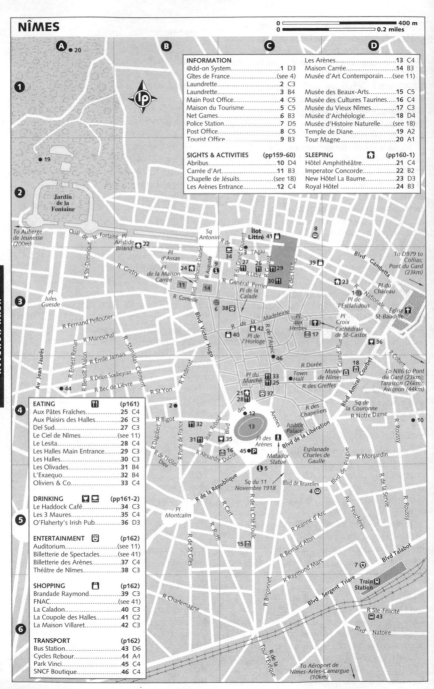

0   400 m
0   0.2 miles

AVIGNON AREA

INFORMATION		Les Arènes.....................................13 C4
@dd-on System.........................**1** D3		Maison Carrée...............................**14** B3
Gîtes de France......................(see 4)		Musée d'Art Contemporain.....(see 11)
Laundrette................................**2** C3		
Laundrette................................**3** B4		Musée des Beaux-Arts.................**15** C5
Main Post Office.......................**4** C5		Musée des Cultures Taurines......**16** C4
Maison du Tourisme..................**5** C5		Musée du Vieux Nîmes...............**17** C3
Net Games................................**6** B3		Musée d'Archéologie..................**18** D4
Police Station...........................**7** D5		Musée d'Histoire Naturelle......(see 18)
Post Office................................**8** C5		Temple de Diane.........................**19** A2
Tourist Office...........................**9** B3		Tour Magne.................................**20** A1

SIGHTS & ACTIVITIES	(pp159–60)	SLEEPING	(pp160–1)
Abribus...............................**10** D4		Hôtel Amphithéâtre..................**21** C4
Carrée d'Art........................**11** B3		Imperator Concorde.................**22** B2
Chapelle de Jésuits............(see 18)		New Hôtel La Baume...............**23** D3
Les Arènes Entrance............**12** C4		Royal Hôtel............................**24** B3

EATING		(p161)
Aux Pâtes Fraîches............................**25** C4
Aux Plaisirs des Halles.......................**26** C3
Del Sud...**27** C3
Le Ciel de Nîmes...........................(see 11)
Le Lesita...**28** C4
Les Halles Main Entrance....................**29** C3
Les Halles...**30** C3
Les Olivades.....................................**31** B4
L'Exaequo..**32** B4
Oliviers & Co....................................**33** C4

DRINKING		(pp161–2)
Le Haddock Café...............................**34** C3
Les 3 Maures....................................**35** C4
O'Flaherty's Irish Pub........................**36** D3

ENTERTAINMENT		(p162)
Auditorium.....................................(see 11)
Billetterie de Spectacles....................(see 41)
Billetterie des Arènes.........................**37** C4
Théâtre de Nîmes..............................**38** C3

SHOPPING		(p162)
Brandade Raymond...........................**39** C3
FNAC...(see 41)
La Caladon.......................................**40** C3
La Coupole des Halles........................**41** C2
La Maison Villaret..............................**42** C3

TRANSPORT		(p162)
Bus Station.......................................**43** D6
Cycles Rebour...................................**44** A4
Park Vinci...**45** C4
SNCF Boutique.................................**46** C4

Southeast of Les Arènes is esplanade Charles de Gaulle, a large open square, from where av Feuchères leads southeast to the train and bus stations.

Information

INTERNET ACCESS
@dd-on System (☎ 04 66 76 13 93; 11 rue Nationale; per 1/5hr €3/11; ☼ 11am-midnight Mon-Fri, 11-2am Sat)
Net Games (25 rue de l'Horloge; per 30/60 min €2/3; ☼ 10am-midnight) Has 40 computers.

INTERNET RESOURCES
www.nimes.fr Official city website.
www.sortiranimes.com Indispensable city-entertainment guide.

LAUNDRY
Laundrette (14 rue Nationale; ☼ 7am-9pm)
Laundrette (24 rue Porte de France; ☼ 8am-8pm)

MEDICAL SERVICES
A list of pharmacies open at night is posted in the window of the tourist office.
SOS Médecins (☎ 04 66 23 69 23; ☼ 24hr) Call-out doctor service.

MONEY
Commercial banks line blvd Amiral Courbet and the western side of Blvd Victor Hugo.

POST
Main Post Office (1 blvd de Bruxelles)

TOURIST INFORMATION
Maison du Tourisme (☎ 04 66 36 96 30; www.cdt -gard.fr; 3 place des Arènes; ☼ 8am-8pm Mon-Fri, 9.30am-noon Sat Jul & Aug, 8.45am-6pm Mon-Fri, 9.30am-noon Sat Sep-Jun) Information on the Gard *département*.
Tourist Office (☎ 04 66 58 38 00; www.ot-nimes.fr; 6 rue Auguste; ☼ 8am-8pm Mon-Wed & Fri, 8am-9pm Thu, 9am-7pm Sat, 10am-5pm Sun Jul & Aug; 8.30am-7pm Mon-Fri, 9am-7pm Sat, 9am-5pm Sun Sep-Jun) City info.

Sights

LES ARÈNES
This superb Roman **amphitheatre** (places des Arènes; adult/10-16 yrs €4.65/3.40; ☼ 9am-7pm mid-Mar–mid-Oct, 10am-5pm mid-Oct–mid-Mar), reminiscent of the Colosseum in Rome, was built around AD 100 to seat 24,000 spectators. It is better preserved than any other such structure in France, even retaining its upper storey – unlike its Arles counterpart. The interior has four tiers of seats and a system

---

SIGHTSEEING CENT SAVERS

The truly dedicated can buy a three-day pass (adult/10-16 years €10/5), covering admission to all museums, from the tourist office or the first place you visit. Otherwise, curtail museum visits to the first Sunday of the month when admission is free.

---

of exits and passages (called, engagingly, *vomitories*) designed so that patricians attending the animal and gladiator combats never had to rub shoulders with the plebs up top. In July and August free guided tours in English depart four times daily. A ticket covering admission to Les Arènes and the Tour Magne is also available; see p160.

Year round Les Arènes (covered by a high-tech removable roof October to April) stages plays, music concerts and bullfights; see p162 for ticket details.

MAISON CARRÉE & CARRÉ D'ART
The rectangular, Greek-style temple known as the **Maison Carrée** (Square House; place de la Maison Carrée; admission free; ☼ 9am-7pm mid-Mar–mid-Oct, 10am-5pm mid-Oct–mid-Mar) is one of the world's best preserved Roman temples. Built around AD 5 to honour Augustus' two nephews, Gaius and Lucius, it survived the centuries as a meeting hall (during the Middle Ages), a private residence, a stable (in the 17th century), a church and, after the Revolution, an archive. Host to occasional historical exhibitions, it is entered through six symmetrical Corinthian columns.

The striking glass-and-steel building directly opposite is the **Carrée d'Art** (Square of Art; ☎ 04 66 76 35 77; 15 place de la Maison Carrée), home to the municipal library, mediatheque, Musée d'Art Contemporain (see p160) and a tip-top lunch spot (see p161). The creation of British architect Sir Norman Foster (1935–1993), it perfectly reflects the Maison Carrée and is everything modern architecture should be: innovative, complementary and beautiful.

JARDIN DE LA FONTAINE
The **Fountain Garden** was laid out around the Source de la Fontaine (the site of a spring, temple and baths in Roman times). It retains an elegant air, with statue-adorned paths running around deep, slimy-green

AVIGNON AREA

waterways. Don't miss the **Temple de Diane** to the left of the main entrance.

A 10-minute walk uphill through the terraced garden takes you to the crumbly white shell of **Tour Magne** (adult/child €2.50/2; 9am-7pm mid-Mar–mid-Oct, 10am-5pm mid-Oct–mid-Mar), the largest of the many towers that ran along the city's 7km-long Roman ramparts. A spiral staircase of 140 steps leads to the top. A combination ticket covering Tour Magne and Les Arènes costs €5.70/4.65 per adult/child.

MUSEUMS
A wonderful Roman mosaic uncovered here in 1883 and an unsurprising collection of Flemish, Italian and French works are in the **Musée des Beaux-Arts** (Fine Arts Museum; ☎ 04 66 67 38 21; musee.beauxarts@ville-nimes.fr; 20-22 rue de la Cité Foulc; adult/10-16 yrs €4.45/3.20; 11am-6pm Tue-Sun).

Enjoy the modern face of art at the airy **Musée d'Art Contemporain** (Contemporary Art Museum; ☎ 04 66 76 35 80; carreart@mnet.fr: place de la Maison Carrée; adult/10-16 yrs €4.65/3.40; 11am-6pm Tue-Sun), on the 2nd floor of the Carrée d'Art. The permanent collection features works from the 1960s to 1990s.

The city's former 17th-century Jesuit college shelters the **Musée d'Archéologie** (Archaeological Museum; ☎ 04 66 76 74 80; 18bis blvd Amiral Courbet; adult/10-16 yrs €4.45/3.20; 10 or 11am-6pm Tue-Sun), which brings together columns, mosaics and sculptures from the Roman and pre-Roman periods; the **Musée d'Histoire Naturelle** (Natural History Museum; ☎ 04 66 76 73 45; 13bis blvd Amiral Courbet; adult/10-16 yrs €4.45/3.20; 10 or 11am-6pm Tue-Sun); and the **Chapelle des Jésuits** (13bis blvd Amiral Courbet), sacred host to cultural happenings.

Those here for a bullfight can gem up on bullish history and culture at the **Musée des Cultures Taurines** (Museum of Bullfighting Culture; ☎ 04 66 36 83 77; musee.taureau@ville-nimes.fr; 6 rue Alexandre Ducros; adult/10-16 yrs €5.50/3.30; 10am-6pm Tue-Sun, to 10pm Thu Jul & Aug).

The same ticket gets you into the markedly less interesting **Musée du Vieux Nîmes** (place aux Herbes; musee.vieux-nimes@ville-nimes.fr; admission free; 11am-6pm Tue-Sun), an eccentric history museum in a 17th-century episcopal palace. One room showcases denim (with smiling pin-ups of Elvis, James Dean and Marilyn Monroe to boot), and two others are entirely devoted to a collection of domestic graters and mincers.

Tours
The tourist office arranges 1½- and two-hour **thematic city tours** (French only; adult/child €5.50/4.50) at 10am on Tuesday, Thursday and Saturday in summer, and at 2.30pm on Saturday the rest of the year.

Festivals & Events
The three big *férias* – the three-day **Féria Prima-vera** (Spring Festival) on the last weekend in February, the five-day **Féria de Pentecôte** (Pentecost Festival) in June, and the three-day **Féria des Vendanges** to mark the start of the grape harvest on the third weekend in September – revolve around *corridas* (a bull bred to be aggressive is killed in a bloody ceremony involving picadors, toreadors, matadors and horses) and *novilladas* (fights with bulls less than four years old). Tickets cost €17 to €93 and reservations must be made months ahead via the Billetterie des Arènes or FNAC (see p162).

Courses Camarguaises (see p116) are held on the weekend before a *féria* and at other times during the bullfighting season. The best bulls are rewarded with a couple of bars from Bizet's opera *Carmen* as they leave the arena.

In July and August during **Les Jeudis de Nîmes** festival, concerts set the streets rocking on Thursday evenings.

Sleeping
For *chambre d'hôte* and self-catering accommodation contact **Gîtes de France** (☎ 04 66 27 94 94; www.gites-de-france-gard.asso.fr; 3 place des Arènes), in the Maison du Tourisme. Most hotels tout three sets of seasonally adjusted prices, plus another rate for *férias*.

BUDGET
Auberge de Jeunesse (☎ 04 66 68 03 20; nimes@fuaj .org; 257 chemin de l'Auberge de Jeunesse; dm with breakfast €13.25; P) About 2.5km northwest of the train station, this botanical park-surrounded hostel has 80 beds split across two- to six-bedded dorms. Internet access, laundry facilities and bicycle rental are available. From the train station take bus No 2 (Alès or Villeverte direction) to the Stade stop, from where it is a 500m walk uphill.

MID-RANGE
Royal Hôtel (☎ 04 66 58 28 27; fax 04 66 58 28 28; 3 blvd Alphonse Daudet; s/d with shower €46/62, s with bathroom

€51-66, d with bathroom €67-87) With canvases just about everywhere, a huge dove cage beside reception and local intelligentsia discoursing over coffee in **La Bodeguita** (🕐 6pm-late Mon-Sat), the in-house Spanish café, it's evident that *la patronne* is herself an artist. Some rooms overlook place d'Assas (p157), itself a work of modern art.

Hôtel Amphithéâtre (☎ 04 66 67 28 51; hotel-amphitheatre@wanadoo.fr; 4 rue des Arènes; s €37-40, d €47-59; 🕐 Feb-Dec; ✗ 🐾) The Amphithéâtre, just up the road from its namesake, was once a pair of 18th-century mansions. Recently adopted by a young and dynamic family, its rooms are named after writers or painters inspired by Provence: Montesquieu and Arrabal – both large with a balcony overlooking pedestrian place du Marché – are particularly welcoming. Paul Valéry, Diderot and Beaumarchais on the third floor have air-con.

TOP END

New Hôtel La Baume (☎ 04 66 76 28 42; www.new-hotel.com; 21 rue Nationale; s/d €95/120; ✗ 🐾 🖥) Far from new, this 34-room hotel with period-furnished rooms (some with frescoed ceilings) occupies an attractive 17th-century town mansion. A glorious interior courtyard and every comfort – bar human warmth – are distinguishing features.

Imperator Concorde (☎ 04 66 21 90 30; www.hotel-imperator.com in French; quai de la Fontaine; d €99-148, ste €183-319; 🅿 🐾 🖥) The city's most exquisite garden-restaurant, L'Enclos de la Fontaine, and the literary-inspired Hemingway Bar are but some of the charms of this dreamy four-star, honeymooners' type of pad.

Eating
RESTAURANTS & CAFÉS

Place aux Herbes, place du Marché with its crocodile and very large palm tree, and the western side of place de la Maison Carrée buzz with café life. Several cosy dining spots are on place de l'Esclafidous, a tiny square, hard to find but a gem once found.

L'Exaequo (☎ 04 66 21 71 96; 11 rue Bigot; menus €25-70; 🕐 lunch & dinner Mon-Fri, dinner Sat) Chef Valentin Lerch cooks up memorable market-driven cuisine at Nîmes' most contemporary eating spot. Interior design is minimalist, a palm tree sprouts on the terrace and the *filet de taureau grillé* is capable of converting the most devout of bull lovers.

Aux Plaisirs des Halles (☎ 04 66 36 01 02; 4 rue Littré; menus €19-45; 🕐 lunch & dinner Tue-Sat) With its long-running reputation as one of the city's best, the Pleasures of the Market Hall lives up to its name. Feast on its *menu de la ballade des halles* – a €35 gastronomic stroll through the market hall – on a quiet terrace save a tinkling fountain and clinking wine glasses. For the cheese course, pick the local AOC *pélardon*.

Le Ciel de Nîmes (☎ 04 66 36 71 70; place de la Maison Carrée; lunch/evening mains €14/20; 🕐 lunch & dinner Tue-Sat, until 2am Thu-Sat) The stunning view of Nîmes' Roman temple is a definite distraction at the Sky of Nîmes, a chic 3rd-floor hang-out in the Carré d'Art – not that the chef needs to distract. Dishes are simple, exemplary and much-loved by fashionable Nîmois.

Del Sud (☎ 04 66 67 22 50; 10 rue Littré; plat du jour €8.50, lunch platter €11, dinner menu €18; 🕐 lunch & dinner Tue-Sat) Also called L'Épicerie, Del Sud cooks up Mediterranean cuisine in a 15th-to 18th-century courtyard proffering good views of otherwise-hidden *hôtels particuliers*. The lunch-time platters are particularly popular.

Also recommended:

Le Lesita (☎ 04 66 67 29 15; 2 blvd des Arènes; lunch menu €26, dinner menus €45 & €65; 🕐 lunch & dinner Tue-Sat, lunch Sun) The newest kid on the block, near the amphitheatre.

Les Olivades (☎ 04 66 21 71 78; 18 rue Jean Reboul; lunch formule €11, menu €18.50; 🕐 lunch & dinner Tue-Fri, dinner Sat) Wine specialist, bistro-style restaurant.

SELF-CATERING

Fresh pasta has been the mainstay of **Aux Pâtes Fraîches** (rue des Broquiers) since 1948; and regional olive oil fills **Oliviers & Co** (10 rue de l'Hôtel de Ville).

The only respectable place to food shop is the city's 'gourmet soul', alias **Les Halles** (rue Guizot, rue Général Perrir & rue des Halles; 🕐 6.30am-1pm), the city's vast covered food market dating to 1885.

Drinking

Le Haddock Café (☎ 04 66 67 86 57; 13 rue de l'Agau; lunch menu €9, dinner menus €11.40, €14.50 & €18.30; 🕐 11am-3pm & 7pm-1am Mon-Sat) A highlight of Nîmois nightlife, this alternative café-bar hosts changing art exhibitions, concerts, theme nights and chalks up some excellent-value lunch-time deals on its board outside.

O'Flaherty's Irish Pub (☎ 04 66 67 22 63; 21 blvd Amiral Courbet; ✆ 11-2 or 3am, Mon-Fri, 5pm-2 or 3am Sat & Sun) Down pints, meet Anglophone travellers and foreign students, get into the local band scene and jive to jazz (Wednesday) at this busy Irish drinking hole.

During *férias* it's the brash, brasserie-style **Les 3 Maures** (☎ 04 66 36 23 23; 10 blvd des Arènes), with its heavily bullish theme, that fills up.

Entertainment

What's-on listings fill *Nîmescope* and *Nîmescoop,* two fortnightly entertainment magazines, both freely distributed at the tourist office.

Tickets for bullfights and cultural events are sold at the **Billetterie de Spectacles** (☎ 04 66 36 33 33; 22 blvd Gambetta), at FNAC, inside La Coupole des Halles indoor shopping centre; at the **Billetterie des Arènes** (☎ 04 66 02 80 90; www.arenesdenimes.com in French; 4 rue de la Violette; ✆ 9.30am-noon & 1.30-6pm Tue-Fri, 10am-1pm Sat); and on the latter's website.

Plays, ballet, modern dance and music recitals fill the **Théâtre de Nîmes** (☎ 04 66 36 65 00; 1 place de la Calade). Documentaries and films (French only) are screened in the **auditorium** (☎ 04 66 76 35 36) inside the Carré d'Art.

Shopping

Caladons – honey and almond-studded biscuits, typical to Nîmes – are sold at most *pâtisseries,* including **La Caladon** (27 rue de la Madeleine), where 200g will set you back €7.80. Rival *croquants Villaret* – rock-hard finger-shaped almond biscuits – have been baked by the Villaret family at **La Maison Villaret** (cnr rue de la Madeleine & place de l'Horloge) since 1775.

Brandade de Nîmes is the trademark of **Brandade Raymond** (☎ 04 66 67 20 47; 34 rue Nationale), a veteran delicatessen and caterer who has made the traditional salted cod paste since 1879. A 125g tin costs €1.86.

Getting There & Away

AIR

Also called Aéroport Nîmes-Garons, **Aéroport de Nîmes-Arles-Camargue** (☎ 04 66 70 49 49; www.nimes.cci.fr in French) is 10km southeast on the A54 to Arles.

BUS

From the **bus station** (☎ 04 66 29 52 00; rue Ste-Félicité) there are buses to/from Pont du Gard (€5.40, 45 minutes, five to six daily), Avignon (€7.30, 30 minutes, 10 or more daily) and Arles (€5.75, 30 to 45 minutes, four to eight daily).

International bus operators **Eurolines** (☎ 04 66 29 49 02) and **Linebùs** (☎ 04 66 29 50 62) have neighbouring offices at the far end of the terminal.

TRAIN

The city's **train station** (blvd Talabot) is at the southeastern end of av Feuchères. In town, tickets are sold at the **SNCF Boutique** (11 rue de l'Aspic; ✆ 8.30am-6.50pm Tue-Sat). Destinations include Avignon Centre (€7.50, 45 minutes, 10 or more daily) and Arles (€6.70, 30 minutes, nine daily). A number of SNCF buses and trains head to Aigues-Mortes (€6.30, 40 minutes/one hour by train/bus) in the Camargue.

Getting Around

TO/FROM THE AIRPORT

From the bus station, **STD Gard** (☎ 04 66 29 27 29; www.stdgard.com in French) runs shuttle buses to/from the airport (€5.10, 30 minutes) to coincide with flight times. Bus drivers sell tickets.

BICYCLE

Motorists parked in **Park Vinci** (place des Arènes; ✆ 24hr) can pick up a bike for free.

Otherwise, rent wheels for €15 a day from **Cycles Rebour** (☎ 04 66 76 24 92; 38 rue de l'Hôtel Dieu).

PONT DU GARD

The Pont du Gard, a Unesco World Heritage site, is an exceptionally well-preserved, three-tiered Roman aqueduct that was once part of a 50km-long system of canals built around 19 BC by Agrippa, Augustus' powerful deputy and son-in-law, to bring water from the Eure Springs in Uzès, 25km northwest, to Nîmes. The scale is huge: the 35 arches of the 275m-long upper tier, running 50m above the River Gard, contain a 1.2m by 1.75m watercourse that, for a century and a half, carried 35,000 cubic metres of water a day. The Romans took 15 years to build the aqueduct, which remained in use until the 3rd century.

From giant car parks either side of the River Gard, you can walk along the road bridge, built in 1743 and running parallel with the aqueduct's lower tier. The best

AVIGNON AREA

view of the Pont du Gard is from upstream, beside the river, where you can swim on hot days. The aqueduct is illuminated from 40 minutes or so after dusk until midnight nightly in July and August, and on Fridays and Saturdays in June and September.

The Pont du Gard receives well over a million visitors a year, averaging a mind-boggling 15,000 or so daily in July and August. Admission to the site is free, but parking costs €5, plus you have to pay another €5 to join a guided tour (in English). Tours depart from **Le Portal** (☺ 9.30 or 10am-5.30 or 7pm, closed Mon morning), a vast complex designed by French architect Jean-Paul Viguier on the left bank. It houses **La Grande Expo du Pont du Gard** (admission €6), a museum that explores the history of the Pont du Gard and Nîmes' Roman aqueduct; a cinema where you can watch a 30-minute **film** (admission €3); and the **Ludo** (admission €4.50) educational centre where kids learn the fun way about the Romans' watery way of life. To retreat from the ever-increasing commercialism, follow the 1.4km-long **Mémoires de Garrigue** (☺ 9.30am-6pm Apr–mid-Oct) walking trail through typical Mediterranean bush, scrubland and olive groves, though to get the most out of it you'll need to buy the explanatory booklet in English (€4).

Those intending to spend the day at the Pont du Gard can buy a combined ticket (adult/child €10/8) covering the latter sights plus parking. The €20 family ticket covers the same for two adults and two children aged up to 17 years.

Information

Accueil du Pont du Gard (☎ 0 820 903 330; www .pontdugard.fr; Le Portal, rte du Pont du Gard; ☺ 9.30 or 10am-5.30 or 7pm, closed Mon morning) Tickets, information, parking tickets, guided visits, workshops and so on.

Canoeing & Cycling

The beautiful wild River Gard descends from the Cévennes mountains and flows through the hills in a long gorge, passing under the Pont du Gard. Between March and October you can hire canoes to paddle around beneath the aqueduct from **Kayak Vert** (☎ 04 66 22 80 76; kayak.vert@wanadoo.dr) or **Canoë Le Tourbillon** (☎ 04 66 22 85 54; location@canoe-le-tourbillon. com), both based in Collias, 4km upstream, under the village's single bridge. Both companies organise half-day 6km-long group

---

---

paddles from Collias to the Pont du Gard and full-day trips from **Russan**, 22km upstream, to Collias.

Kayak Vert and Canoë Le Tourbillon also rent mountain bikes. From the Pont du Gard, a 30km signposted circuit heads northwest towards Uzès in Languedoc; ask at the Accueil du Pont du Gard for a brochure outlining the route.

Sleeping & Eating

Camping La Sousta (☎ 04 66 37 12 80; www.lasousta .com in French; av du Pont du Gard; 2 people, tent & car low/mid/high season €11/14/18; ☺ reception 8am-7.30pm Mar-end Oct; P ♨) This well-equipped site beneath trees touts three stars and is a handy five-minute walk from the aqueduct on the southern side (right bank); follow the D981. It also has mobile homes to rent on a weekly basis (from €390/530 for two/six people) and less comfy wooden chalets (from €312/436).

Le Mas du Mon Père (My Father's Farmhouse; ☎ 04 66 37 16 25; La Bégude; s/d/tr/q with breakfast €39/50/60/70, adult/child evening meal €16/8; P) Escape the tourist mayhem of the Pont du Gard at this idyllic farmhouse *chambre d'hôte* where birds twitter, sheep graze, donkeys eeh-ore and kids have a field day. Find it on the D19 at the Pont du Gard end of La Bégude. Bookings can be made via the Gîtes de France website (www.gites -de-france.fr).

Le Mas de Castille (☎ 04 66 22 97 72; mas-cas tille@avignon-et-provence.com; Quartier du Château, Argilliers; d with breakfast €65, 4-course evening meal with aperitif €25; P 🏊) Guests have the run of the garden and small swimming pool at this charming *chambre d'hôte*, 4km west of the Pont du Gard in the tiny hamlet of Argilliers (signposted off the D981 along the D3bis).

Getting There & Away

The Pont du Gard is 23km northeast of Nîmes and 26km west of Avignon. Buses from Avignon and Nîmes stop 1km north of the bridge. To get to Collias (€5.10, one hour, two daily) take bus No 168 from Nîmes' bus station – or hitch.

The Lubéron

The gently rolling Lubéron hills stretch from Cavaillon (west) to Manosque (east), and from Apt south to the River Durance and a stunning Romanesque abbey. Oaks grow on the steep northern face of the main range – a compact massif with the gentle summit of Mourre Nègre (1125m) – and more Mediterranean flora carpets its drier southern face. Down on the lower slopes, fruit orchards and vineyards grow like there's no tomorrow.

Walking paths, cycling routes and scenic drives galore crisscross the region, the majestic Combe de Lourmarin (Lourmarin Coomb) dramatically dividing the so-called Petit Lubéron (west) from the wilder Grand Lubéron (east).

The Lubéron – much of which is protected by the Parc Naturel Régional du Lubéron – is greener, less densely populated and extremely affluent compared to the rest of the Vaucluse *département* (department), of which it is a part. Most of its lower-lying land is farmed, forming a rich, manicured patchwork of vineyards, olive groves and fruit farms as toylike as the perfectly restored, golden-stone *mas* (Provençal farmhouses). *Bories* (beehive-shaped huts built in the Bronze Age) dot the northern part of the region, while ochre sands, sculpted by the wind and rain over the centuries into fantastic formations, colour it a fantastic fire red and orange.

HIGHLIGHTS

- OD on cherries in **Apt** (opposite): market-fresh, candied, as ice cream or in the **Musée de l'Aventure Industrielle du Pays d'Apt** (opposite)

- Revel in the regional paint palette: red (ochre) in **Rustrel** (p172) purple (lavender) in **Lagarde d'Apt** (p177) and silver (stone *bories;* beehive-shaped huts) in **Viens** (p173)

- Take a breather from the Grand Lubéron's relentless gorges and fortresses with lunch on a farm at **Ferme Auberge Le Castelas** (p181)

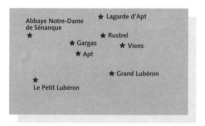

- Follow the ochre trail by pedal power, stopping in Gargas to tour Europe's remaining **ochre quarry** (p172)

- Reel in the sacred splendour of the Romanesque **Abbaye Notre-Dame de Sénanque** (p172)

APT

pop 11,500 / elevation 250m

This small but sweet town founded by the Romans is considered Lubéron's capital. The engine room of the Pays d'Apt in the 18th century thanks to its thriving earthenware and candied-fruits industries, contemporary Apt holds appeal for its Provençal markets and peaceful, park-protected surrounds. Cherries, grapes and other fruits still grow in sweet abundance and are candied by a handful of veteran *fruits-confits* makers.

Apt is a handy pit stop for cyclists and walkers: the Lubéron en Vélo cycling itinerary (see the boxed text, p38) passes through, as does the GR9 (a long-distance walking path).

Information

Commercial banks stud place de la Bouquerie.

Infotelec (☎ 04 90 04 46 40; www.luberon.org in French; 44 quai de la Liberté; per hr €5; ☺ 9am-noon & 3-7pm Mon-Sat) Internet access.

Laundrette (4 av Victor Hugo; ☺ 7am-8pm)

Le Queen Victoria (☎ 04 90 74 60 02; 94 quai de la Liberté; per hr €5; ☺ 10-1.30am) Surf in the pub; slow connection.

Luberon-news (www.luberon-news.com) Info on the entire region.

Post Office (105 av Victor Hugo)

Tourist Office (☎ 04 90 74 03 18; www.ot-apt.fr in French; 20 av Philippe de Girard; ☺ 9am-7pm Mon-Sat, 9.30am-12.30pm Sun Jul & Aug, 9am-noon & 2-6pm Mon-Sat, 9.30am-12.30pm Sun May, Jun & Sep, 9am-noon & 2-6pm Mon-Sat Oct-Apr)

Sights & Activities

The tourist office has info on walks around Apt, some passing the 11th-century **Ancienne Cathédrale Ste-Anne** (rue Ste-Anne; ☺ 8.30am-6pm Mon-Sat), where the relics of St Anne and illuminated 11th- and 12th-century manuscripts rest.

Three museums paint historical Apt in chronological order. The **Musée de Paléontologie** (Palaeontology Museum; ☎ 04 90 04 42 00; 60 place Jean Jaurès; adult/under 18 yrs €1.50/free; ☺ 8.30am-noon & 1.30-7pm Mon-Sat Jul-Sep, 8.30am-noon & 1.30-6pm Mon-Fri Oct-Mar) has prehistoric beauty (flora) and beast (fauna) displays in the Maison du Parc (see the boxed text, p169).

The **Musée d'Histoire et d'Archéologie d'Apt** (History & Archaeology Museum; ☎ 04 90 04 76 65; 27 rue de l'Amphithéâtre), built on the site where gladiators were once pitted against beasts in

---

MORNING MARKET MADNESS

Monday Cadenet, Cavaillon and Lauris

Tuesday Apt (farmers market April to December), Cucuron, Gordes, Lacoste, La Tour d'Aigues, St-Saturnin-lès-Apt

Wednesday Bonnieux (mid-May to September), Coustellet (evening farmers market from 5.30pm June to September), Mérindol, Pertuis (farmers market)

Thursday Ansouis, Céreste, La Tour d'Aigues (farmers market mid-May to September)

Friday Bonnieux, Cavaillon, Lourmarin, Pertuis, Roussillon

Saturday Apt, Cadenet (farmers market May to October), Cavaillon (farmers market April to December), Lauris (farmers market 2pm to 5pm winter, 5pm to 8pm summer), Manosque, Oppède-le-Vieux, Pertuis (farmers market), Vaugines

Sunday Coustellet (farmers market April to November), Vaugines, Villars (June to September)

---

the Roman amphitheatre, is a saunter down memory lane in Roman Apta Juliaare. At the time of writing it was closed for work, and expected to reopen in mid-2005.

The **Musée de l'Aventure Industrielle du Pays d'Apt** (Industrial History Museum; ☎ 04 90 74 95 30; musee@apt.fr; 14 place du Postel; adult/under 12 yrs €4/free; ☺ 10am-noon & 3-6.30pm Mon-Sat, 3-7pm Sun) is in an old candied-fruit factory. The museum focuses on industrial history – candied-fruit trade, ochre mining, earthenware and so on – from the 18th century.

Tasting and buying traditional *fruits confits* is a sweet pastime. Thirty tonnes of cherries a day are candied at the **Confiserie Kerry Aptunion** (☎ 04 90 76 31 43; www.kerryaptunion.com; rte Nationale 100, quartier Salignan; ☺ shop 9am-noon & 2-6pm Mon-Sat, guided factory tours 10.30am & 2pm Mon-Fri Aug), the world's largest crystallised-fruits factory, 2.5km west of town. Guided factory tours (free) must be booked, but the shop can be visited any time.

Festivals & Events

Apt marks Ascension in May with a **jazz festival** and enjoys a **Fête de la Cerise** (Cherry Festival) in June. Tasting and buying cherries in all shapes, forms and sizes – bite-sized, gobstoppers, fresh, candied and turned into jam – is the main thrill of this fun-filled, street-packed celebration. The **Cavalcade d'Apt**, Apt's Pentecost celebration in June since 1883, climaxes with an evening ball.

THE LUBÉRON

THE LUBÉRON

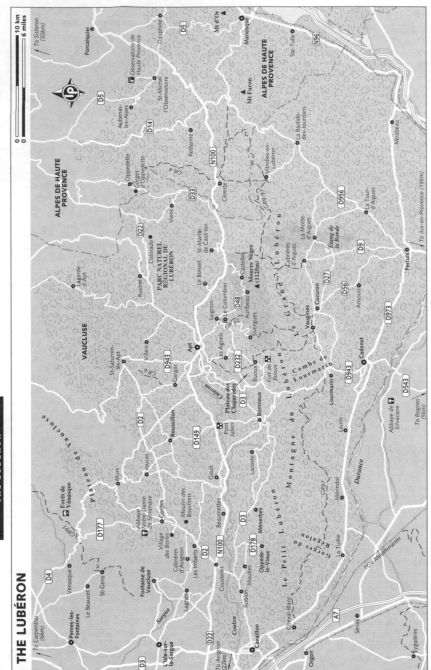

Sleeping

Le Couvent (☎ 04 90 04 55 36, 06 08 90 15 88; www
.loucouvent.com in French; 36 rue Louis Rousset; d/ste
incl breakfast low season €75/90, high season €90/120;
P 🖳 🖭) This stylish *maison d'hôte* (upmarket B&B) with sage-green shutters
boasts five stunning rooms – each named
after the colour scheme it flaunts – in a
restored 17th-century convent. If you're a
group of three, plump for chocolate (extra
bed €18); quads choose blue.

Auberge du Lubéron (☎ 04 90 74 12 50; www.auberge
-luberon-peuzin.com; 8 place Faubourg du Ballet; d €52-73, tr
€93; menus €29-59; P 🔀) Part of Logis de France,
this cosy hotel on the opposite side of the
river has rooms split across two old buildings
and a renowned restaurant: *lapin aux figues
confites et thym* (rabbit with candied fruit and
thyme) is among the unusual dishes using
candied fruit for which chef Serge Peuzin is
known. Garage parking is €7.

Hôtel L'Aptois (☎ 04 90 74 02 02; www.aptois
.fr.st; place Lauze de Perret; d with washbasin €32 or €34,
with shower, €46, with shower & toilet €48; P) This
26-room cyclist-friendly hotel with 1980s
mirrored reception rents bikes and tandems
to hotel guests, prepares picnic hampers for
pedal-powered guests and provides a two-
wheeler breakdown service.

Eating

La Cuisine de Marianne (☎ 04 90 04 87 45; 87 rue de la
République; menu €10; 🕑 lunch Mon-Sat) Discerning
Aptois adore this *table familiale*, a simple
lunchtime spot where diners fill up on the
one fixed *menu* which – incredibly for the

price and quality of home-baked food –
includes wine and coffee. Get here dot on
noon to snag a seat.

Thym, te voilà (☎ 04 90 74 28 25; 59 rue St-Martin;
mains €9; 🕑 11.30am-6pm Tue-Sat) Delicious soups
(hot and cold), savoury tarts and sweet flans
are among the home-made delights on the
short but sweet menu of this lovely little tea
room, complete with inviting open kitchen
where a smiling Carine cooks, chats and
dishes up charm by the plateful. The mint
leaf floating in the water is a nice touch.

Le Goût des Choses (☎ 04 90 74 27 97; 3 place
du Septier; 🕑 lunch Tue-Sat) Vegetarians will
feel particularly at home at this rustic
and unpretentious tea room and *saladerie*
(salad house), sitting plump in a courtyard
wrapped around a small fountain.

Bistro de France (☎ 04 90 74 22 01; 67 place de la
Bouquerie; meals around €15; 🕑 lunch & dinner Mon-Wed,
Fri & Sat) Never was there a more quintessential bistro than this: a prime spot for
coffee, lunch, apéritif or quick pick-me-up
after the market.

La Régal Bio (☎ 04 90 74 52 48; 266 av de Roumanille,
rte de Gargas; menus from €18; 🕑 lunch & dinner Mon-
Sat, dinner Sat with reservation) Its location in the
Les Bourguignons industrial quarter is not
pretty, but providing you look at what's on
your plate – an organic feast – you won't
complain. Find Les Bourguignons signposted off the D443 to St-Saturnin-lès-Apt.

Markets aside (see the boxed text, p167),
try **L'o à la Bouche** (98 rue St-Pierre) or **Via Domitia**
(19 quai Léon Sagy), two *épiceries fines* (upmarket grocery shops).

PARC NATUREL RÉGIONAL DU LUBÉRON

The 1650-sq-km Lubéron Regional Park, created in 1977 and recognised as a Biosphere Reserve by
Unesco in 1997, encompasses 67 villages (population 155,000), desolate forests and unexpected
gorges. The GR6, GR9, GR92 and GR97 walking trails all cross it, as does a 230km-long **cycling
route** (see the boxed text, p38). For amblers, there is a **botanical trail** through the park's oldest cedar forest (Bonnieux; p174); a trail around **ochre cliffs** (Roussillon; p171); and a **bories
discovery path** (Viens; p173).

Information, maps and guides are available at the **Maison du Parc** (☎ 04 90 04 42 00; www
.parcduluberon.fr; 60 place Jean Jaurès, Apt; 🕑 8.30am-noon & 1.30-7pm Mon-Sat Jul-Sep, 8.30am-noon & 1.30-6pm
Mon-Fri Oct-Mar). Between March and August, those not keen to go it alone can join a thematic
nature workshop-walk (French only; adult/under 18 years €5/free). The Egyptian vulture, eagle
owl, wild boar, Bonelli's eagle and the Etruscan honeysuckle are some of species you might
learn about and see.

Guides sold at the Maison du Parc include *topoguide Le Naturel Régional Parc du Lubéron à pied*
(PN07; €11.95), detailing 24 walks including the GR trails (available in English); and the *topoguide
Walks in Provence* (PN04; €11.95), which outlines 24 shorter walks (3km to 20km).

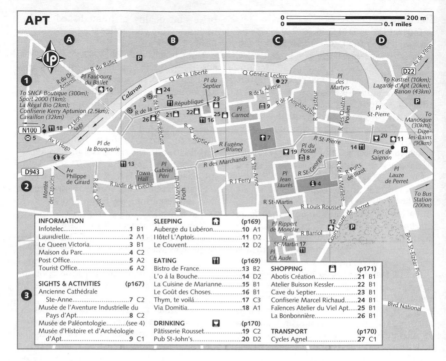

APT

Drinking

Place de la Bouquerie abounds with cafés. Rue St-Pierre is another hot spot, as is the pavement terrace at **Pub St-John's** (☎ 04 90 74 58 59; place St-Pierre).

Pâtisserie Rousset (☎ 04 90 74 14 34; 196 rue des Marchands) is a smart *salon de thé* (tea house) where you can sit down for a soothing cuppa and bowl of cherry-and-lavender ice cream.

Getting There & Away

Tickets for trains departing from other destinations are sold at the **SNCF boutique** (☎ 04 90 74 00 85; 26 blvd Victor Hugo; 🕑 8.30am-5.50pm Mon-Fri, 8.30am-4.50pm Sat), in Apt's former station building.

Buses leave from the **bus station** (☎ 04 90 74 20 21; 250 av de la Libération) to/from Avignon (€7.20, 1¼ hours, three or four daily) via Cavaillon (€4.70, 50 minutes), Digne-les-Bains (€7.30, two hours, one or two daily); and Manosque (€6.40, one hour, twice daily). Twice-daily buses between Apt and Marseille (€8.45, 2½ hours) stop in Bonnieux, Lourmarin, Cadenet, Pertuis and Aix-en-Provence.

Getting Around

Equip yourself with pedal power at **Sport 2000** (☎ 04 90 04 30 00; 669 av Victor Hugo; 🕑 2-7pm Mon, 10am-12.30pm & 2-7pm Tue-Fri, 9.30am-7pm Sat), a vast sports shop with a bike-rental outlet 1km from the tourist office. Rental starts at €19/113 a day/week, including helmet and puncture-repair kit.

Similar rates are charged at **Cycles Agnel** (☎ 04 90 74 17 16; 86 quai Général Leclerc; 🕑 8.30am-noon & 2.15-7pm Tue-Fri, 8.30am-12.15pm & 2.15-5.30pm Sat).

AROUND APT

From Apt a good day trip is to head northwest to Roussillon, Gordes and the Abbaye de Sénanque – three of Provence's hottest tourist spots – and return via the pretty villages of **Joucas** (population 321), St-Saturnin-lès-Apt (population 2393) and hilltop **Villars** (population 700).

Heading in the opposite direction, Provence's very own Colorado (p172) makes for a colourful day trip. Alternatively, walk with a donkey with **Vivre au Pas des Ânes** (☎ 04 90 75 12 49; www.vivre-au-pas-des-anes.com; Le Petit Jas), a farm where you can hire donkeys to ride or bear the load for €10/25/38 per hour/half-day/day. Bear 10km east from Apt along the N100 and after the first left turn for St-Martin de Castillon, turn left to Le Petit Jas.

Roussillon
pop 1190 / elevation 360m

Some two millennia ago, the Romans used the distinctive ochre earth around Roussillon, set in the valley between the Plateau de Vaucluse and the Lubéron range, for producing pottery glazes. These days the whole village – even gravestones in the cemetery – is built of the reddish stone.

In the village a 1km-long **Sentier des Ocres** (Ochre Trail; adult/under 10 yrs €2/free; ☺ 9am-7.30pm Jul & Aug, 10am-5.30pm Sep–mid-Nov & Mar-Jun, 9am-noon & 1-5pm Tue-Sun mid-Nov–Feb) wends through fairytale groves of chestnuts, maritime pines and scrub to the bizarre ochre formations created by erosion and winds over the centuries. Don't wear white.

Workshops (some in English), exploring the colouring properties of ochre, and factory tours are held at the **Conservatoire des Ocres et Pigments Appliqués** (Applied Pigment & Ochre Conservatory; ☎ 04 90 05 66 69; info@okhra.com; rte d'Apt; guided tours 6 times daily adult/student €5/3; ☺ 9am-1pm & 2-6pm Tue-Sun), on the D104 east towards Apt.

Roussillon, 9km east of Gordes, is inaccessible by public transport. Motorists must park in car parks (€2) outside the village, a 300m walk away. Camping des Sources (p173), 5km south, rents bikes. The **tourist office** (☎ 04 90 05 60 25; www.roussillon-provence.com in French; place de la Poste; ☺ 9am-noon & 1.30-6.30pm Tue-Fri, 10am-noon & 2-5.30pm Mon & Sat) has information on walks in and around the village.

Gordes
pop 2127 / elevation 372m

On the white, rocky southern face of the Vaucluse plateau, the tiered village of Gordes – one of Provence's most photographed – forms an amphitheatre over the Rivers Sorgue and Calavon.

The village, 20km west of Apt, is crowned by an 11th-century chateau where art exhibitions and the **Musée Pol Mara** (☎ 04 90 72 02 75; place du Château; adult/10-17 yrs €4/3; ☺ 10am-noon & 2-6pm) are housed. Don't miss the original 7.2m-long Renaissance fireplace inside the art museum. The **tourist office** (☎ 04 90 72 02 75; www.gordes-village.com; place du Château; ☺ 9am-noon & 2-6pm Mon-Sat, 10am-noon & 2-6pm Sun) is in the guards' hall of the chateau.

Heading 3.5km south along rte de St-Pantaléon (D148) you hit the **Moulin des Bouillons** (☎ 04 90 72 22 11; rte de St-Pantaléon; adult/10-17 yrs €4.50/3; ☺ 10am-noon & 2-6pm Apr-Oct, 10am-noon & 2-6pm Wed-Mon Nov-Mar), an oil mill with a 10m-long press weighing seven tonnes.

Buses, operated by Cavaillon-based **Les Express de la Durance** (☎ 04 90 71 03 00), link Gordes with Cavaillon two to four times daily. Motorists must park in the car park (€3) opposite the bright-blue piece of monumental art by Hungarian sculptor Victor de Vasarely (an honorary citizen of Gordes since 1983) at the bottom of the village.

Village des Bories
The **Village des Bories** (☎ 04 90 72 03 48; adult/10-17 yrs €5.50/3; ☺ 9am-sunset) is 4km southwest of Gordes off the D2 towards Cavaillon. *Bories* are one- or two-storey beehive-shaped huts constructed without mortar using thin

---

TOP FIVE SOUVENIRS WITH STYLE

For something different to take home, shop at:

- **Abotis Création** (☎ 04 90 04 56 86; www.abotis.com; 120 rue de la République) Unusual handcrafted furniture stained with natural pigments.

- **Atelier Buisson Kessler** (☎ 04 90 04 89 61; 20 place Septier) Small *poterie* (pottery) workshop specialising in contemporary, big 'n bold bowls, plates and tiles.

- **Cave du Septier** (☎ 04 90 04 77 38; www.vcommevin.com in French; place Septier) For many, the region's best-stocked wine cellars; rare and highly sought-after vintages.

- **Confiserie Marcel Richaud** (48 quai de la Liberté) and **La Bonbonnière** (57 rue de la Sous-Préfecture) Candied figs, cherries and other fruits.

- **Faïences Atelier du Viel Apt** (☎ 04 90 04 03 96; 61 place Carnot) Earthenware featuring the gold 'n mud-coloured marbled finish that was all the rage in 18th-century Apt.

THE LUBÉRON

wedges of limestone. They were first built in the area in the Bronze Age and were continuously lived in, renovated and even built anew until as late as the 18th century. It is not known what purpose they first served but over the centuries they have been used as shelters, workshops, wine cellars and storage sheds. The 'village' contains about 20 such structures, restored to the way they were about 150 years ago.

Abbaye Notre-Dame de Sénanque

Some 4km northwest of Gordes off the D177 is this picture-postcard Cistercian **abbey** (☎ 04 90 72 05 72; www.senanque.fr; adult/6-18 yrs €6/2.50; 🕑 10am-noon & 2-6pm Mon-Sat, 2-6pm Sun Feb–mid-Nov, 2-5 or 6pm mid-Nov–Jan), framed by fields of lilac lavender in July. The abbey was founded in 1148 and is inhabited by a few young monks today. Mass is celebrated at noon on weekdays and 9am Sunday. Visiting hours may be reduced in the future.

St-Saturnin-lès-Apt

Rooftop views of St-Saturnin-lès-Apt, 9km north of Apt, and the surrounding Vaucluse hilltops can be enjoyed from the **17th-century windmill**, 1km north of the village off the D943 to Sault. Follow signs for Le Château Les Moulins.

In the village, learn how olives are turned into oil at the **Moulin à Huile Jullien** (☎ 04 90 75 45 80; 1 rue Albert Trouchet). Its boutique can be visited any time but the mill can only be visited during the December olive harvest.

Rustrel & Around

The main reason for visiting Rustrel (population 621), 10km northeast of Apt, is to explore the **Colorado Provençal** (p172). For

---

OCHRE

Although ochre has been used in the Lubéron since Roman times, it was not until 1785 that large deposits of the hydrated oxidised iron-and-clay sands were mined industrially. In 1929 – the peak of the ochre industry – some 40,000 tonnes of ochre were mined around Apt, 90% of which was exported to other parts of Europe and America.

Traditionally used as a pigment to colour pots and buildings, ochre comes in some 25 shades, ranging from delicate yellow to vivid orange and fire red. Discover these vibrant hues first-hand along short walking trails in Rustrel's **Colorado Provençal** (☎ 04 32 52 09 75; 🕑 9am-dusk), a savage landscape of red-ochre sand where rock formations like the phallic **Cheminée de Fée** (literally 'Fairy Chimney') – a fiery pillar that men are known to stare wistfully at – protrude in all their erect magnificence. The extraordinary collection of rock formations was, in fact, part of a quarry where ochre was mined from the 1880s until 1956.

Colour-coded trails for two of the most dramatic trails – the 'blue' **Sentier de Cheminée de Fée** (1km) and the 'red' **Sentier du Sahara** (1.5km) – can be picked up in the Parking des Mille Couleurs car park, signposted south of Rustrel village off the D22 to Banon. Parking costs €2.50 (free November to March) or €3.50 including a trail map which, despite its poor quality, is essential to get around.

An equally dramatic discovery course is **Colerado Aventures** (☎ 06 78 26 68 91; colorado aventure@wanadoo.fr; adult/child €18/16; 🕑 10am-5pm Jun-Aug, 10.30am-4.30pm Wed, Sat & Sun Apr, May & Sep, 10.30am-4pm Sun Feb, Mar & Oct), a Tarzan-style obstacle course rigged between red rocks in a forest. The site, signposted off the D22, is a good 15-minute walk – and rough to boot, so bring sturdy boots – from the car park.

It is not just in Rustrel you can see red: in Gargas (population 3000, elevation 280m), 4km west of Apt, Europe's **last remaining ochre quarry**, run by **Sociétés Ocres en France** (www .ocres-de-france.com in French), can be visited by guided tour on Friday mornings. The quarry produces around 1000 tonnes of ochre a year, 45% of which is exported. Tours must be booked in advance through the **mairie** (town hall; ☎ 04 90 74 12 70; info@ville-gargas.fr; adult/under 16 yrs €6/ free) and include a visit to the village's **ochre exhibition** (place des Jardins; adult/under 16 yrs €1.50/1; 🕑 9am-noon & 4-6pm Mon, Tue & Thu).

In rust-coloured Roussillon there is an ochre walking trail and a conservatory dedicated to exploring ochre's colouring qualities; if that's not enough, there's the **Ocres en Vélo** cycling trail (see the boxed text, p38).

THE LUBÉRON

aerial views of the rock formations, take off with paragliding school **Rustr'aile Colorado** (☎ 04 40 04 96 53; Le Stade), signposted on the D112. Baptism flights cost €70.

The eastbound D22 and D33 link Rustrel with **Viens** (population 500), a starting point for forays into the **Gorges d'Oppedette**, a limestone canyon. From Viens the 3km-long **Circuit des Bories** takes afternoon strollers past several *bories*; yellow markers flag the footpath. In Roman times the Via Domitia passed through **Céreste** (population 1045, elevation 380m), 8km south. Just outside Céreste on the D31, **Le Frigoulet** (☎ 04 92 79 05 87; humannfrigoulet@aol.com) is a family-run lavender farm that can be visited.

From Céreste the N100 pushes east to Haute-Provence. Lavender fiends can access this neighbouring region via the northbound D14, a scenic road strung with purple in season. **Reillanne**, 8km east off the D14, has a couple of particularly lovely places to sleep and eat.

Céreste **tourist office** (☎ 04 92 79 09 84; www .cereste.fr in French; place de la République; 9.30am-12.30pm & 2-6pm Mon, Tue, Thu & Fri, 9.30am-12.30pm Wed, 10am-noon Sat & Sun) has information on all these villages and rents mountain bikes (€8/15/80 per half-day/day/week).

Walking, cycling and motoring are the only ways to get around.

Sleeping

La Mas de la Beaume (☎ 04 92 72 02 96; www.la beaume.com; Gordes; d incl breakfast low/high season from €104/115; P ☀) Languishing behind a stone wall at the top of the road leading to Gordes, this five-room *maison d'hôte* delights. Olive trees stud the garden, hostess Nadine adores old furniture and flowers, and breakfast is built from home-grown and market produce.

Auberge de Reillanne (☎ /fax 04 92 76 45 95; Reillanne; d €68-72, half-board per person €65; Apr–mid-Oct; P) Tucked down a gravel track off the D14 south of Reillanne, this stone manor house will charm the socks off the fussiest of guests with its six rustic rooms surrounded by green fields.

Hostellerie L'Aiguebelle (☎ 04 92 79 00 91; place de la République, Céreste; s/d with shower €31/34, with shower & toilet €46/48; menus €15-30; mid-Feb–mid-Nov; P) The grilled duck coated in lavender honey, not to mention the ultrawarm welcome guaranteed at this authentic village inn, make a

---

---

stop here more than worthwhile. It belongs to the Logis de France association.

La Bastide de Gordes (☎ 04 90 72 12 12; www .bastide-de-gordes.com; Gordes; d with village/valley views low season from €140/210, high season from €167/230; P ✗ ✗ ☐ ☀) Among the region's heavenly four-star pads, Gordes' upmarket choice is an orgy of marble furnishings, magnificent views and arcaded stone terraces. Its wine cellar stocks 400 *etiquettes* (wine labels) and there is a spa (those two-hour wellbeing cures sound just the job).

Camping des Sources (☎ 04 90 72 12 48; rte des Murs, Gordes; 2 adults, tent & car from €15; Mar-Sep; P ☀) This large pool-clad site touts four- to six-person mobile homes and chalets, and hires out wheels (summer only) for the energetic keen to explore the area by pedal power.

Eating

David (☎ 04 90 05 60 13; restaurant.david@wanadoo.fr; place de la Poste, Roussillon; menus €29.50-50; lunch & dinner Thu-Sat, lunch Sun Feb–mid-Nov) Perched high on a cliff, David dishes up views of ochre and vineyards accompanied by sophisticated cuisine. The most expensive *menu*, *autour du homard*, is a lobster feast.

Mas de Tourteron (☎ 04 90 72 00 16; Elisabeth .bourgeois@wanadoo.fr; chemin de St-Blaise, Les Imberts; menus €31 & €49; ☺ lunch & dinner Wed-Sun Apr-Oct, lunch & dinner Wed-Sat, lunch Sun Mar) Chef Elisabeth Bourgeois is the secret behind this dining legend, frequented by gourmets for almost a decade. A top address without pretension, dining at this farmhouse with opulent gardens and vegetable patch is like visiting someone at home. Find it 3.5km from Gordes village.

Auberge Perry (☎ 04 92 76 51 95; cnr N100 & D214 to Reillanne; menus €13-27; ☺ lunch & dinner Wed-Mon) Plopped in the quiet countryside east of Céreste, the Auberge Perry is an atmospheric farmhouse with rustic-inspired menus to match (including one for kids at €8). The house *terrine de lapin aux pignons de pin* (rabbit terrine with pine kernels) will appease the most sophisticated palate.

LE PETIT LUBÉRON

The rocky landscape of the 'little Lubéron' embraces the western part of the massif and is studded with the region's best-known *villages perchés*. These busy hilltop villages are perched aloft stony spurs and offer good views of the region's lower-lying treasures, including its thick cedar forests. See p12 for a hilltop villages itinerary.

Côtes du Lubéron vineyards line southbound rte de Bonnieux (D3) from Apt to Bonnieux; Bonnieux tourist office has lists of estates where you can taste and buy. The Lubéron's other nectar is honey (p173).

Bonnieux Tourist Office (☎ 04 90 75 91 90; ot-bon nieux@axit.fr; 7 place Carnot; ☺ 2-6pm Mon, 9.30am-12.30pm & 2-6pm Tue-Sat) has information on most villages in the area.

Bonnieux

pop 1436 / elevation 425m

Bonnieux, 11km southwest of Apt and 26km east of Cavaillon, is Le Petit Lubéron's best-known village – straggled as it is along the D36. From place de la Liberté, 86 steps lead to its 12th-century **Église Vieille du Haut**, while the history of breadmaking is unravelled in the **Musée de la Boulangerie** (☎ 04 90 75 88 34; 12 rue de la République; adult/12-18 yrs €3/1.50; ☺ 10am-noon & 2.30-6 or 6.30pm Wed-Mon Apr-Oct), a former bakery.

South of Bonnieux is **Forêt des Cèdres** (1861), a protected cedar forest through which a

> **ESCAPE THE CROWDS**
>
> At the end of the day, leave the busy hilltop villages of Le Petit Lubéron behind and head a few kilometres east to the less-visited villages on the Plateau de Claparèdes (p180) to eat and sleep.

sentier botanique (botanical trail) leads. Heading north, there is local wine to be tasted and bought in the village cooperative, **Caves des Vignerons de Bonnieux** (☎ 04 90 75 80 03; www.cave -bonnieux.com; La Gare de Bonnieux; ☺ 9am-12.30pm & 2.30-6.30pm Mon-Sat), and a three-arched Roman bridge, **Pont Julien** (27 BC–AD 14), to see 6km north on the D149.

SLEEPING

There are a few camp sites around the village and dozens of *chambres d'hôtes* (B&Bs).

Au Pied du Lubéron (☎ 04 90 75 94 08; www .au-pied-du-luberon.com; quartier St-Jean; d incl breakfast €80; ☺ B&B Oct-Mar; **P** **⊠**) In the same family since 1861, this old stone property has been beautifully renovated by hosts who are clearly very green-fingered. In their past lives, Petit Fontaure was a lavender distillery and Petit St-Jean was a *magnanerie* where silkworms were bred. Between April and September both properties are rented as *gîtes* (self-catering accommodation) from €700 a week. Find them 3.3km from Bonnieux along the D194; the last 1.5km is a single-lane track.

La Vieille Bastide (☎ 04 90 75 60 11; www.lavieille bastide.com; chemin du Four; d incl breakfast low season €102-123, high season €120-145; **P** **⊠** **⊠**) A beast of a *bastide* (country manor), four of the six fresh and airy rooms at this vast *chambre d'hôte*, signposted off the D194, have their own terrace-cum-garden. In summer guests barbecue evening meals in the poolside *cuisine d'été* (summer kitchen). Credit cards are not accepted.

Hôtel Le César (☎ 04 90 75 96 35; www.hotel-cesar .com; place de la Liberté; d with shower/shower & balcony €38/46, with shower, toilet & terrace €70-92; menu €23) Bonnieux's quintessential village hotel – named after the Pagnol film – has brushed up its rooms to bring them up to scratch with the stunning valley views they sport. A couple are across the street in an annexe. The restaurant has panoramic views and pint-sized appetites are welcomed with a €11.50 *menu*.

EATING

Le Fournil (☎ 04 90 75 83 62; 5 place Carnot; lunch/dinner menu €25/36; ⓨ lunch & dinner Wed, Thu, Fri & Sun, dinner Tue & Sat) The Bakehouse is a cut above the average village restaurant – literally. Its glass-and-steel interior is cut into a rock face, with a fountain in front around which Provençal creations like courgette cake with tiny prawns, thyme-dressed shoulder of lamb or *soupe de cerise au vin rouge* (cherry and red-wine soup) are served. Bagging a table without a reservation is practically impossible.

Auberge de l'Aiguebrun (☎ 04 90 04 47 00; www .aubergedelaiguebrun.com; d low season €134-164, high season €164-234; lunch/dinner menu €25/55; **P** ⚇ ⚐) Sleep in a *cabanon* (wooden chalet) by the river or in the main house, dine at stone tables on a cobbled terrace with green views, and stroll through gardens charmed with peacocks, a greenhouse and dovecote. Find this *bastide* hidden in the dramatic heart of the Combe de Lourmarin, 6km southeast of Bonnieux off the D943 to Apt.

GETTING THERE & AROUND

Buses to/from Apt and Marseille stop in Bonnieux (see p170). **Mountain Bike Lubéron** (☎ 04 90 75 89 96, 06 83 25 48 07; www.mountainbike luberon.com; rue Marceau; ⓨ 8.30am-noon & 1.30-6.30pm Mon-Fri) rents bikes for €14/25/74 per day/weekend/week. It also has children's seats (€3 per day) and trailers (€5 per day) for hire, and delivers bikes within a 15km radius (free).

Lacoste

pop 417 / elevation 320m

It was to 9th-century Château de Lacoste, 6.5km west of Bonnieux, that the notorious Marquis de Sade (see Sadism, below) retreated in 1771 when his writings became too scandalous for Paris. His 45-room palace, once maintained by 20 servants, remained nothing more than an eerie ruin until 2002 when designer Pierre Cardin stepped in.

So captivated was the French couturier with the stone pile that he bought it and transformed it into a 1000-seat theatre and opera stage, host to July's month-long **Festival de Lacoste**. **Espace La Costa** (☎ 04 90 75 93 12), in the village, sells festival tickets (€25 to €140) and has information on guided tours of the chateau site (including the incredible 1600-sq-metre subterranean conference space in the old Roman quarry beneath the chateau) planned for the future.

SLEEPING & EATING

Café de Sade (☎ 04 90 75 82 29; rue Basse; dm €14, d with shower €44, with shower & toilet €48-53; ⓨ restaurant mid-Mar–mid-Dec, gîte d'étape closed Mon Sep-Jun) The village Café de Sade serves cheap fodder beneath a leafy trellis, sells newspapers and runs a *gîte d'étape* (hikers accommodation) with 30 dorm beds split across two dorms. Breakfast/sheet hire costs €6.50/4 and half-board with dorm accommodation is €31.50 per person.

Hôtel de France (☎ 04 90 75 82 25; d with washbasin €30, with shower €37, with shower & toilet €45) Six

---

SADISM

The Marquis de Sade (1740–1814) gave rise to the term 'sadism'. A complex character whose research into pleasure led to an eroticisation of pain, his sexually explicit novels – *120 Journées de Sodome* (120 Days of Sodom; 1785), *Justine* (1791) and *Juliette* (1798) – caused an outrage and were banned when published in the late 18th century. Equally shocking were the sex scandals surrounding Sade's own life, 27 years of which were spent in prison.

De Sade spent chunks of his childhood in Provence where his family had owned Château de Lacoste since 1627. His ancestors included Hugues de Sade and his wife Laura, a lifelong muse for Italian poet Petrarch. At the age of 22 de Sade wed Parisian bourgeoisie Renée Pélagie de Montreuil, although marriage never tampered with his love for orgies. In 1771, following his ostracism by Parisian society for accosting and flagellating a woman who took him to court for rape, de Sade moved to Château de Lacoste with his wife and three children. He was later tried on charges of sodomy and attempted poisoning after indulging in a whipping session with four prostitutes and his manservant in Marseille.

Château de Lacoste was looted by revolutionaries in 1789, and subsequently sold by de Sade, who spent the last 11 years of his life in a mental asylum where he died, far from mad, aged 74. His works weren't freely published until after WWII.

simple but charming double rooms offer splendid value at this village hotel which doubles as the village bar. The village visible from the terrace is Bonnieux.

Ferme de l'Avellan (☎ 04 90 75 85 10; chemin de St-Jean; d incl breakfast from €50; ⊗ Easter–Nov) There is nothing fancy or manicured about Danielle Ravoire's working farm, set amid vines and cherry orchards. Meals are strictly *bio* (organic). Find it 1km from Lacoste village, at the end of an unpaved track signposted off the D106. To eat here, you must book in advance.

Ménerbes

pop 1007 / elevation 230m

Continue 6km west of Lacoste on the D109 to Ménerbes, a pretty hilltop village marked firmly on the tourist trail by British novelist Peter Mayle, who lived in a *mas* just outside the village from 1986 until 1993. (His former home, 2km southeast of the village on the D3 to Bonnieux, is the second house on the right after the football pitch.)

Meandering up to the village crown – a stiff climb – rewards with great views, the 12th-century village **church** and the **Maison de la Truffe et du Vin** (House of Truffle & Wine; ☎ 04 90 72 52 10; place de l'Horloge; ⊗ 10am-noon & 3-7pm Tue-Sun), housed in the former hospice (called Hôtel d'Astier de Montfaucon) on the cobbled square here. In July and August it organises two-hour wine-tasting sessions (€35 including lunch). To get here (the village is a maze), follow the signs for '*église-mairie*'.

AUTHOR'S CHOICE

La Magnanerie (☎ 04 90 72 42 88; www.magnanerie.com; rte de Bonnieux, Lieu-dit le Roucas; d incl breakfast low/high season €80/90, extra bed €20; ⊗ mid-Mar–mid-Nov; P ⚐) Six stylish rooms are descriptively named – *la grande* is big, *la rose* is pink and so on – at this friendly *maison d'hôte* where hosts Nathalie and Vincent really haven't missed a thing. Guests fed up with dining out can barbeque (and mingle with other guests) in the summer kitchen; there's a fridge to stash drinks in; and the peach room with mezzanine up top and terrace below is ideal for families with kids. Credit cards are not accepted. Find La Magnanerie 200m down a single-track unpaved lane, signposted off the D103.

Sample Côtes du Lubéron wine and discover 1000 different corkscrews (we like the one with the balls) at the **Musée du Tire-Bouchon** (Corkscrew Museum; ☎ 04 90 72 41 58; www.musee-tirebouchon.com; adult/under 15 yrs €4/free; ⊗ 10am-noon & 2-7pm Apr-Oct, 10am-noon & 2-5pm Mon-Sat Nov-Mar), on the Domaine de la Citadelle, a wine-producing estate on the D3 to Cavaillon. The museum is the brainchild of Yves Rousset-Rouard, village mayor and former French MP who resides in the restored chateau atop Ménerbes. In the 1970s he produced films, notably the soft porn *Emmanuelle* (1974).

If snails are more your cup of tea, try the **Parc aux Escargots** (☎ 04 90 72 22 26, 06 61 14 48 84; www.leparcauxescargots.com in French; Les Grès; 1hr guided visit adult/5-16 yrs €4/3; ⊗ 9am-7pm May-Oct), signposted off the D24. Some 30,000-odd gastropods live on the family-run park, which just happens to specialise in snail cuisine. Dishes can be sampled.

SLEEPING & EATING

La Bastide de Marie (☎ 04 90 72 30 20; www.labastidedemarie.com; rte de Bonnieux, quartier de la Verrerie; d with half-board low/high season from €390/435; ⊗ Mar-Nov; P ⚒ ⚐ 🖥 ⚐) Featured in *Tatler, Cosmopolitan, Town & Country* and so on as that country retreat of 1000 dreams, this heavenly 18th-century house amid vineyards stuns – and soothes. Soft golds, creams, coffees and slates fill the interior – all very design, very fresh, very unlike a hotel. Prices include everything (breakfast, afternoon tea, dusk-time apéritif, dinner with wine) except lunch, and the swimming pool is definitely Provence's most chic. From Ménerbes, follow the eastbound D103 for 4km.

Café du Progrès (☎ 04 90 72 22 09; place Albert Roure; plat du jour around €10) Less heady budgets will enjoy the wholesome lunches and snacks dished up on the flowery terrace of this village tobacconist-cum-bar.

Oppède-le-Vieux

pop 1246 / elevation 300m

Large car parks designated for tourist traffic sit at the foot of Oppède-le-Vieux, 6km southwest of Ménerbes. This medieval village (located on a rocky outcrop) was abandoned in 1910 by villagers who moved down the valley to the cultivated plains to earn their livings. A steep rocky path leads to the hillside **ruins**. The 16th- to 18th-century **church**, under constant

A LAVENDER DETOUR

From **Buoux** an invigorating cycling or driving route takes you north on the D113 to a set of crossroads straddled by lavender fields – blazing blue in July. From here you can bear west along the D232 to Bonnieux; east along the D48 to Auribeau (4.3km; see A Curious Detour, p182) and Castellet (7km); or northeast to Saignon (see A Curious Detour, p182) and Le Boisset (from where you can link up with the N100). Otherwise you can continue on a northbound lavender trail to Apt.

After passing more lavender fields, the D113 climbs to **Les Agnels**, where lavender, cypress leaves and rosemary are distilled at the **Distillerie Agnel** (☎ 04 90 74 22 72, rte de Buoux). It dates from 1895 and can be visited by guided tour (three times daily July and August, three times daily Tuesday to Sunday May, June and September).

Lavender-lovers should not miss the Musée de la Lavande (below), 22km west of Apt, and its 800,000-sq-metre lavender farm, **Château du Bois** (☎ 04 90 76 91 23), 25km north of Apt in **Lagarde d'Apt**. Here a 2km-long lavender trail passes field after field of purple lavender, abuzz with bees and aflutter with butterflies from late June until mid-July when the sweet-smelling flower is harvested.

restoration, hosts concerts during August and celebrates mass in honour of Oppède's patron saint (St Laurent) on 10 August.

From the car parks, signs lead you to the **Sentier Vigneron d'Oppède**, a 1½-hour wine-growers' trail through olive groves, cherry orchards and vineyards. Panels tell you what grape varieties you are looking at, how to train a vine 'lyre' style etc.

Oppède-les-Poulivets, the new village, is 1km north of Oppède-le-Vieux.

Coustellet

Coustellet, on the noisy N100, is uninspiring beyond its **Musée de la Lavande** (☎ 04 90 76 91 23; www.museedelalavande.com; adult/under 15 yrs €5/free; ☒ 10am-noon & 2-6 or 7pm Feb-Dec). The museum has stills used to extract the sweet-smelling scent and a shop selling lavender-scented products. Most informative is the short video (in English), which explains how the

WHAT A PEST

The plague, brought to the region in 1720 aboard a ship from Asia, was such a terrible scourge that the king of France ordered a 1.5m-high dry-stone wall to be built in 1721 to prevent the killer disease spreading further into Papal-controlled Comtat Venaissin.

Roughly 6km of the **Mur de la Peste** (literally 'Wall of the Plague') remains standing today – in Cabrières d'Avignon, around Lagnes and in the Pays de Venasque.

purple flower is harvested and distilled (see The Perfume of Provence, p144).

Thirsty travellers can fill up with table wine for €1.10 per litre or *appellation d'origine contrôlée* (AOC) Côtes du Lubéron wine for €1.75 per litre at the **Cave du Lubéron** (☎ 04 90 76 90 01), at the southern end of Coustellet on the D2. The Sunday-morning **farmers market** takes place at the intersection of the N100 and the D2.

Cabrières d'Avignon
pop 1431 / elevation 167m

Cabrières d'Avignon, 5km north of Coustellet, was one of the most unfortunate Waldensian villages (see Martyr Villages, p179). Its **12th-century chateau** (closed to visitors) has since been restored and is in private hands, while the old *moulin à huile* (oil mill) is a **wine tasting school**.

Pine and cedar forests, crisscrossed with paths and picnic tables, shroud the northern village fringe. Herbs and flowers are used to flavour honey made at the village *miellerie* (see Honey Houses, p173) and dishes cooked up at **Le Vieux Bistrot – Le Bistrot à Michel** (☎ 04 90 76 82 08; Grande Rue; lunch formule €13; ☒ lunch & dinner Tue-Sun), the only place (and very lovely too) to eat in the village.

Lagnes
pop 1509 / elevation 110m

Yellow-brick Lagnes, 5km west, offers little to do beyond strolling its cobbled streets and visiting an occasional art exhibition in its *vieux lavoir* (old wash house), off place

THE LUBÉRON

du Fontaine. For the quintessential Provençal sleeping and eating experience check into **Le Mas des Grès** (☎ 04 90 20 32 85; www.masdesgres.com; rte d'Apt; d with half-board low/mid-/high season from €139/159/169; P ☂), a farmhouse with 14 rooms decked in warm hues of rust, ochre and gold.

CAVAILLON
pop 25,058

Western gateway to the Lubéron, Cavaillon sits 28km southeast of Avignon. Bizarrely, it is its sweet cantaloupe melons – mountains of which fill the early-morning Monday market May to September – for which it is best known.

Melons particularly abound during the **Fête du Melon** in July. The four-day festival is, in short, one mean excuse to overindulge in mountains – quite literally – of the town's sweeter-than-sweet cantaloupe melons. Prévôt is Cavaillon's melon-mad chef and the **tourist office** (☎ 04 90 71 32 01; www.cavaillon-luberon.com in French; place François Tourel; 3hr tour adult/under 12 yrs €6/free; ☉ 9am-12.30pm & 2-6.30pm Mon-Sat mid-Mar–mid-Oct plus 10am-noon Sun Jul & Aug, 9am-noon & 2-6pm Mon-Fri, 10am-noon Sat mid-Oct–mid-Mar) arranges melon-tasting tours.

Sights

An **arch** (place François Tourel) built by the Romans in the 1st century BC adorns the square in front of the tourist office, at the western end of cours Bournissac, Cavaillon's main shopping street. Three blocks north the 12th-century **Cathédrale Notre Dame et St-Véran** (☉ 8.30am-noon & 2-6pm Mon-Fri Apr-Sep, 9am-noon & 2-5pm Mon-Fri Oct-Mar) boasts a fine Roman cloister.

Cavaillon's beautiful **synagogue** (1772–74) houses the **Musée Juif Comtadin** (Jewish Museum; ☎ 04 90 76 00 34; rue Hébraïque; adult/under 12 yrs €3/

QUENCH YOUR THIRST …

…with a taste of Provence, be it some *sirop au mimosa* (a nonalcoholic fizzy mimosa drink), a swift shot of *crème au melon* (a melon liqueur) or a slow glass of *délice de Cavaillon* (a melon-flavoured apéritif) or *apéritif à la truffe* (a truffle-flavoured apéritif). Buy all four at the *épicerie fine* **Le Clos Gourmand** (☎ 04 90 78 05 22; 8 place du Clos, Cavaillon).

---

free; ☉ 9.30am-12.30pm & 2.30-5.30pm Wed-Mon Apr-Oct, 9am-noon & 2-5pm Mon & Wed-Fri Nov-Mar), inside the former bakery of the Jewish community, which is also worth visiting.

Tours

The tourist office takes bookings for a bounty of guided tours, including half-day nature walks around Cavaillon with a National Forestry Office guide (€6); three-hour cycle rides (€6); two-hour tours of one of the many nearby hilltop villages (€3); and wine-tasting sessions with farmhouse brunch (€35).

Sleeping & Eating

There are camp sites in Robion, 6km east of Cavaillon, and Maubec, 9km east, and a couple of dead-central hotels on place du Clos and cours Bournissac.

Mas des Amandiers (☎ 04 90 06 29 60; www.mas-des-amandiers.com in French; 48 chemin des Puits Neufs; s/d incl breakfast from €70/75, dinner Tue, Thu & Sat €25; P ☂) The artistically inclined will enjoy staying at this farmhouse with a name inspired by almond trees. Monet, Michelangelo and Cézanne overlook pool-clad gardens, dinner is served thrice-weekly and there's a painting school.

Le Mas du Tilleul (☎ 04 90 71 29 92; www.toutnet.com/lemasdutilleul in French; 12 quartier Grand Grès, rte d'Avignon; d incl breakfast low/high season €40/50, dinner Mon-Sat with advance reservation €25; ☉ Tue-Sun Apr-Oct with reservation; P ✗) Part of the Bienvenue à la Ferme association, this farm has no-frills rooms with shared bathroom and a fabulous table d'hôte where organic, farm-grown/reared produce can be tucked into with relish. Vegetarians are well catered for.

Jean-Jacques Prévôt (☎ 04 90 71 32 43; 353 av de Verdun; lunch menu €25, dinner menus €43-95; ☉ lunch & dinner Tue-Sat) Melon memorabilia adorns the inside of Cavaillon's best address. May to September Prévôt conjures up his melon-inspired *menu* (€70). Truffles (January and February), game and chocolate (November and December), asparagus (March and April) and artichokes and aubergines (May to November) are other seasonal products he honours.

Roger Auzet et Fils (☎ 04 90 78 06 54; 61 cours Bournissac; ☉ Mon-Sat) This popular bakery is great for unusual bread types (walnut, rye, Roquefort, thyme and onion) as well as well-stuffed sandwiches and cakes to eat in its café or on the trot.

Getting There & Away

From the bus stop beside the train station there are daily bus services to/from L'Isle-sur-la-Sorgue (€2.10, 15 minutes, three or four daily), Aix-en-Provence (€7.90, 1½ hours, three daily), Marseille (€10.20, one hour, three daily) and Avignon (€3.20, one hour, five to 20 daily).

From the **train station** (place de la Gare) there are trains to/from Marseille (€11.90, 1½ hours, eight or so daily) and Avignon Centre (€5.50, 30 minutes, seven daily).

Getting Around

Cyclix Cavaillon (☎ 04 90 78 07 06; 166 cours Gambetta; 🕑 9am-12.15pm & 3-7pm Tue-Sat) rents tandems for €28/140 per day/week, mountain bikes for €19/92 and road bikes for €16/78, all including helmet, repair kit and mapped itinerary. Bikes can be delivered for €0.61 per kilometre return.

CAVAILLON TO CADENET

Southeast of Cavaillon the busy D973 skims the Lubéron's southern boundary, delineated by the River Durance and the valley it carves. Some 243 species of birds typical of the riverbanks can be seen from the **Observatoire Ornithologique**, a bird centre run by the Parc Naturel Régional du Lubéron near the Mérindol-Mallemort dam

(signposted 1.5km from the roundabout at the entrance to Mérindol on the D973). Spot herons and great cormorants in abundance along the 3km-long **bird sanctuary trail** (1½ hours) marked with yellow blazes.

Mérindol (population 1800, elevation 200m) itself, crossed by the GR6 about 15km east of Cavaillon, was another Waldensian martyr village (see the boxed text, below).

Lauris (population 1800, elevation 200m), 10km further east, is a handsome hilltop village crowned with an 18th-century **chateau** surrounded by terraced gardens. Tinctorial plants, many rare, grow in the **Jardin Conservatoire de Plantes Tinctoriales** (☎ 04 90 08 40 40 48; couleur.garance@online.fr; adult/under 10 yrs €7/free; 🕑 2-5pm Wed-Mon late May & Oct, 3.30-7pm Jun-Sep, by appointment Nov-Mar). Workshops explore dyes traditionally made from these plants.

The **tourist office** (☎ 04 90 08 39 30; ot-lauris@axit .fr; 12 place de l'Église; 🕑 9.30am-12.30pm & 2.30-6pm Mon-Sat) has details on open-air concerts, theatrical performances and July's **Hot Jazz festival** held around the chateau.

Wickerwork is the mainstay industry of **Cadenet** (population 3937), 7km upstream (east). Learn about the cultivation of *osier* (wicker) on the riverbanks and its exploitation in the **Musée de la Vannerie** (☎ 04 90 68 24 44; av Philippe de Giraud; adult/under 12 yrs €3/free; 🕑 10am-noon & 2.30-6.30pm Wed-Sat, 2.30-6.30pm Sun Apr-Oct).

MARTYR VILLAGES

Cabrières d'Avignon, Buoux and Lourmarin were among 11 Lubéron villages brutally massacred on 9 and 10 April 1545 under the terms of the Arrêt de Mérindol, a bill passed by the Aix parliament condemning Waldensian heretics to death. In Cabrières alone more than 700 men were killed in cold blood and the women of the village were locked in a barn of straw and burnt alive.

The Waldenses (Vaudois) were a minority Protestant group who sought refuge in the remote Lubéron hills (and other backwater parts of France and Italy) following the excommunication of their leader Pierre Valdès from the Catholic Church in 1184. The wealthy merchant from Lyon, who rid himself of material possessions in 1176, incurred the wrath of Pope Lucius III for his fervent preachings of a religion based on the gospels and poverty – itself an enigma in the splendidly rich Catholic Church in medieval times.

In 1532 the Waldenses joined the Reformation, leading to their eventual downfall. What remains of the original castrum in Mérindol guards a memorial to the estimated 3000 murdered and 600 sent to the galleys in the Lubéron in two bloody days in April 1545.

By 1560 there were few Waldenses left in France. In the 1680s large communities reappeared in remote mountain valleys in Piedmont (northern Italy), where they were granted the right to free worship in 1848. The Waldensian church, a Calvinist form of Protestantism, remains particularly strong there today.

La Muse (☎ 04 90 72 91 64; www.routevaudoisluberon.com in French; 3 rue du Four; 🕑 2.30-5.30pm Sat, 9.30am-noon Wed), in Mérindol, is a Waldensian library and research centre that can be visited; call in advance to check someone is there.

The little drummer boy, alias André Estienne (1777–1837), is Cadenet's other known product. A drummer in the Lubéron regiment from the age of 14, Estienne's ferocious drumbeat assured victory for Napoleon I at Arcole (Italy) in 1796 over the Austrians, who thought it was gunfire. A statue of **Le Tambour d'Arcole** (the drummer of Arcole) stands on place du Tambour and there are others in Paris. In 1804 Estienne was decorated with the Légion d'Honneur.

Cycling itineraries can be picked up at Cadenet's **tourist office** (☎ 04 90 68 38 21; ot-cade net@axit.fr; 11 place du Tambour).

Abbaye de Silvacane

The lovely **Silvacane Abbey** (☎ 04 42 50 41 69; adults/under 18 yrs €6.10/free; ☻ 9am-6pm Apr-Sep, 10am-1pm & 2-5pm Wed Mon Oct-Mar) is the third in the trio of medieval Provençal abbeys built in an austere Romanesque style in the 12th century. It sits south of the Durance, 7km southeast of Cadenet. The Cistercian monks, responsible for the magnificent architectural creations, built Abbaye de Silvacane between 1175 and 1230. Today it hosts classical concerts and three colonies of bats (several hundred in total) in its cloister.

LE GRAND LUBÉRON

The deep **Combe de Lourmarin** cuts through the massif in a near-perfect perpendicular from Bonnieux to Lourmarin, thus marking the great divide between Le Petit and Le Grand Lubéron. Dramatic gorges, grand fortresses and one of the region's best *fermes auberges* (farmhouse inns) are trademarks.

Buoux

pop 117

Several kilometres northeast of Bonnieux and 8km south of Apt is Buoux, dominated by the splendid hilltop **ruins of Fort de Buoux**. As a traditional Protestant stronghold, Buoux was destroyed in 1545 (see Martyr Villages, p179) and again in 1660. The fort and old village ruins, perilous in places due to loose rocks and so on, can be explored on foot. Painted white arrows mark an optional return route via a magnificent 'hidden' spiralling staircase cut in the rock.

Local climbing club **Améthyste** (☎ 04 90 74 05 92; http://amethyste1901.free.fr in French; La Baume) organises rock climbing and walks.

AUTHOR'S CHOICE

Chambre de Séjour avec Vue (☎ 04 90 04 85 01; www.chambreavecvue.com in French; Saignon; d incl breakfast €75, studio incl breakfast €100, dinner with wine €25) Polish Kamila Jaccaud, together with French artist husband Pierre, is the creative force behind this unique *demeure d'art et d'hôte*: a 16th-century village house transformed into *chambre d'hôte*-cum-art studio where resident artists display their works. Guests can meander as they please, crossing a little wooden bridge to the garden where bronze sculptures, terracotta urns and contemporary designer chairs lounge beneath trees. Leaves adorn crisp linen pillows, each room has its own bathroom and some a kitchen too.

SLEEPING & EATING

Auberge des Seguins (☎ 04 90 74 16 37; dm with half-board €30, d with shower/shower & toilet with half-board per person €42/47; menus from €25; ☻ Mar–mid-Nov; **P** ☒ ☒) Dramatically placed 2.5km from Buoux village beneath cliffs in the Vallée de l'Aiguebrun, this rambling *gîte d'étape* is classy. Dine on the shaded veranda or loll in the pool and gaze out at giant tiger-striped rocks in what feels like the middle of nowhere. The *magret de canard* (duck breast) with fresh cherries or peaches is sublime.

La Sparagoule (☎ /fax 04 90 74 47 82; dm/s/d/tr €11/30/40/50; **P**) Just up the hill from Auberge de la Loube, this cosy upmarket *gîte d'étape* languishes in an old stone house with burgundy shutters and two white cats. Breakfast costs €4.50 and you can get a picnic/evening meal for €6/12.

Auberge de la Loube (☎ 04 90 74 19 58; lunch/dinner menu €21/27.50, with cheese €29.50; ☻ lunch & dinner Tue-Sat, lunch Sun) One of the lucky few to be mentioned by Peter Mayle in *A Year in Provence*, this inn continues to lure punters with its flowery surrounds and house speciality – *hors d'oeuvres Provençaux de la Loube* (€13), a humungous wicker tray of Provençal treats such as tapenade, *anchoïade* (anchovy sauce), quail eggs, melon slices, cherry tomatoes and fresh figs. Payment is in cash only.

Plateau de Claparèdes

Lavender fields carpet this plateau to form a purple oval between Buoux (west), Sivergues (south), picture-postcard **Saignon** (north) with its curious vegetable garden (see A Curious Detour, p182) and **Auribeau** (east).

Beyond cycling, walking and scenic motoring, the star attraction of this pretty pocket is its accommodation.

A five-room renovated mill plump in the middle of nowhere, **Le Moulin des Fondons** (☎ 04 90 75 10 63; www.moulindesfondons.com in French; Auribeau; s/d/tr/q incl breakfast from €42/58/77/92, dinner adult/child €12/18.50, half-board in gîte d'étape €35; P 🐴) is a great getaway. There is a climbing frame and swing for kids, horse riding and walks galore. The mill is signposted off the D48, 2.5km west of Auribeau. The final 500m is a partly unpaved, single-track lane.

In the 11th and 12th centuries it was three presbyteries; now **Auberge de Presbytère** (☎ 04 90 74 11 50; www.auberge-presbytere.com; place de la Fontaine, Saignon; d €68-115, menu adult/child €32/19.50; ☿ mid-Feb–mid-Nov; P ✗) is a village inn with rooms and terrace restaurant overlooking the village fountain and wash house. Half-board (€133 to €196 for two people) for single-night Saturday stays is obligatory.

To get to all these places without a car or bicycle, use your feet or thumb.

Lourmarin
pop 1127 / elevation 230m

Lourmarin lures with its lovely Renaissance **chateau** (☎ 04 90 68 15 23; chateaudelourmarin@wanadoo.fr; adult/student/10-18 yrs €5/3/2.50; ☿ 10-11.30am & 3-6pm Jul & Aug, shorter hr Sep-Dec & Feb-Jun), host to classical-music concerts.

Nobel Prize–winning writer Albert Camus (1913–60) and his wife are buried in the village cemetery; his tombstone is

planted with rosemary, hers with lavender. Discover these and other herbs and plants at the **Ferme de Gerbaud** (☎ 04 90 68 11 83; adult/child €4.75/free; ☿ 90-min guided visits 5pm Tue, Thu & Sat Apr-Oct, 3.30pm Sat Nov-Mar, boutique 2-7pm), a farm devoted to aromatic plants.

The **tourist office** (☎ 04 90 68 10 77; www.lourmarin.com; av Philippe de Giraud; ☿ 9.30am-1pm & 3-7pm Mon-Sat, 9.30am-noon Sun) has leaflets detailing walks and bike rides around the village, not to mention oodles of information on the village's fabulous Friday morning **market**, where local produce of the edible variety tends to reign.

Guests of **Le Moulin de Lourmarin** (☎ 04 90 68 06 69; www.moulindelourmarin.com; d €190-310, lunch formule €26; P ✗ 🐴 🖳 🐴), a restored 18th-century oil mill, have free reign of the pool and botanical garden of France's youngest Michelin-starred chef, Édouard Loubet.

Vaugines & Cucuron

From Lourmarin the D56 follows the GR97 footpath 5km east to **Vaugines** (population 469), the village where Claude Berri's Pagnol films *Manon des Sources* and *Jean de Florette* (1986) were partly shot. Take one look at the horse-chestnut tree and moss-covered fountain on central place de la Fontaine and you'll understand why.

Cucuron (population 1792, elevation 350m), 2km further east, is the starting point for walks up **Mourre Nègre** (1125m). Its **tourist office** (☎ 04 90 77 28 37; ot.cucuron@axit.fr; rue Léonce Brieugne; ☿ 9am-noon & 2-6.30pm Mon-Sat) sells walking/cycling maps and guides.

Curious palettes keen to consume a meal to remember should call in at the highly

---

AUTHOR'S CHOICE

Ferme Auberge Le Castelas (Chez Gianni; ☎ 04 70 74 60 89; le_castelas@yahoo.fr; Sivergues; dm €19, dm with half-board €39, s/d with half-board €89/118, extra bed €19; lunch formule €19, dinner menu incl wine €30; ☿ lunch & dinner Mar-Dec by reservation only) Nowhere beats this off-the-beaten-track farm for dining. Built solely from farm produce (stroke the goats when you arrive), *La Pause de Berger* (the Shepherd's Pause) – allas lunch – comprises bite-sized pieces of toast topped with *tomme* (a mild cows' milk cheese) followed by wooden platters of ham and goats' milk cheese. Wine costs an additional €20 a bottle and dining is on benches around shared wooden tables; on windier days the tree-sheltered table in the field is a good bet. The dinner *menu* (two starters followed by ham or sausage, a roast, cheese and dessert) is only available evenings and on Sunday lunch *sur réservation* (with advance reservation).

To get to the farm (look for the black piglets in the field), follow the only road through the village of Sivergues (ignore the *'fin de la route'* – 'end of the road' – sign at the village entrance) and continue for 1.5km along the potholed gravel track.

A CURIOUS DETOUR

Heading west to Apt from Céreste there is a curious little detour to be had which, stunning scenery aside, gets you off the busy N100 and onto quiet country lanes.

At the bottom of St-Martin de Castillon, turn left off the main road and follow the road up to Castellet. Continue for 2km, driving around a sharp hairpin bend and further uphill to bring you to quaint stone Auribeau (elevation 586m). In the village, park on rte Jean Moulin, from where a 5.4km walking trail up Mourre Nègre can be picked up. Nip to the top of the street for a panorama of lavender fields and charred cherry-tree stumps (destroyed in summer fires), then stroll along rue du Château, splashing your face with water from the fountain on place de la Fontaine before hopping back in the car.

Continue out of the village along the same D48, passing a place where you can buy *miel* (honey) and *extrait traditionnel de lavandin* (lavender extract) on your left and that field of burnt tree stumps. From here the road snakes uphill for 700m, climaxing with a succession of swift glimpses of stone-capped Mont Ventoux as you round several sweeping bends. Wait until you reach the third bend (where there is a picnic area) before stopping.

Four kilometres further, the russet-red village of Saignon planted atop a crag – this time with Mont Ventoux as the backdrop – makes you gasp again. Drive downhill around the huge hairpin to the village and turn right at the post office, following the signs for **Le Potager d'un Curieux** (☎ 04 90 74 44 68; chemin de la Molière; admission free; 🕑 sunrise-sunset Mon-Fri), 2.6km away. The 'vegetable garden of an inquiring mind' is the creation of Jean-Luc Danneyrolles and his passion for rare and ancient fruits and vegetables.

respected **La Petite Maison** (☎ 04 90 77 18 60; www.la-petite-maison.com; place de l'Étang; menus €24.50-75.50; 🕑 dinner Sat, lunch & dinner Sun & Tue-Fri), from which a Michelin star shines out brightly. Game, black and white truffles, asparagus and blueberries are seasonal temptations to star on its table.

Pays d'Aigues

Many consider rugged Pays d'Aigues the last remaining stronghold in Lubéron yet to be colonised by *résidence secondaire* (second-home) owners. The **Étang de la Bonde**, a lake with beach 3km south of Cabrières d'Aigues on the D9, is one of the few public spots to swim.

In **Ansouis** (population 1057) eccentrics adore the **Musée Extraordinaire** (☎ 04 90 09 82 64; adult/under 16 yrs €3.50/1.50; 🕑 2-6 or 7pm), set up by Marseille-born painter and diver Georges Mazoyer, whose passion for the sea is reflected in the museum's fossilised exhibits. **Château d'Ansouis** (☎ 04 90 09 82 70; adult/6-18 yrs €6/3; 🕑 2.30-6pm Sun Nov-Easter, 2.30-6pm Wed-Mon Easter-Jun & Oct, 2.30-6pm Jul-Sep) is still inhabited but can be visited by guided tour. Classical-music concerts fill its gardens in August.

Château Val Joanis (☎ 04 90 79 20 77; www.val -joanis.com; rte de Cavaillon; admission free; 🕑 10am-7pm Apr-Oct, 2-6pm Tue-Sat Mar & Nov), 8km southeast

in Pertuis, is known for its vineyards and traditional 19th-century terraced garden. In summer it hosts luncheons beneath the plane trees, wine tastings, concerts and other cultural and gastronomic events. Only the gardens can be visited.

La Tour d'Aigues (population 4010, elevation 270m), 5km northeast, is dominated by the 12th- to 15th-century **Château de Tour d'Aigues** (☎ 04 90 07 50 33; www.chateau-latourdaigues .com in French; adult/8-18 yrs €4.50/2; 🕑 2-5pm Sun & Mon, 10am-noon Tue, 10am-noon & 2-5pm Wed-Sat Jan-Mar, Nov & Dec, 2.30-6pm Sun & Mon, 10am-1pm Tue, 2.30-6pm Wed-Sat Apr-Jun, Sep & Oct, 10am-1pm & 2.30-6.30pm Jul & Aug). It hosts temporary exhibitions, a **Musée des Faïences** full of 18th-century earthenware, and courtyard concerts.

Provence Lubéron (☎ 04 90 07 30 00; www .provence-luberon.net in French), in the chateau, provides tourist information on the Pays d'Aigues.

MANOSQUE

pop 20,309 / elevation 387m

Manosque is a perfect stepping stone between toy-town Lubéron and its wilder eastern neighbour Haute-Provence (p184). Provençal writer Jean Giono (1895–1970) was born and bred here, and has an arts centre dedicated to him. Immediately north, **Mont d'Or** (meaning 'mount of gold') offers good views of the town's red rooftops and Lubéron hills beyond. **Mont Foron** (600m), 10km west, likewise proffers fantastic panoramic views.

Cycling routes are mapped on a board in front of the **tourist office** (☎ 04 92 72 16 00; www.manosque-tourisme.com in French; place du Docteur Joubert; ◔ 9am-12.15pm & 1.30-6.30pm Mon-Sat, 10am-noon Sun).

Manosque has an **Auberge de Jeunesse** (☎ 04 92 87 57 44; av de l'Argile, Parc de la Rochette; dm adult/child €8/4; ◔ reception 8-10am & 5-10pm Feb-Nov), 1km west from the centre, and several hotels. Four-star **Hostellerie de la Fuste** (☎ 04 92 72 05 95; www.lafuste.com; rte d'Oraison;

d €145-185; **P** ✗ ❄ ☐ ⚤), a 17th-century manor 6km east on the D4, is the most prestigious.

The **bus station** (☎ 04 92 87 55 99; blvd Charles de Gaulle) is 500m from the centre. Exit the station, turn left on blvd Charles de Gaulle, then right to av Jean Giono. Buses are run by the **Société des Cars Alpes Littoral** (☎ 04 92 51 06 05) and Digne-based **Société des Autocars Dignois** (☎ 04 92 31 50 00). About 10 daily buses serve Marseille (€9.10, 1½ hours).

From the **train station** (place Frédéric Mistral), 2km south of the centre, there are six daily trains to/from Marseille (€14.10, 1¼ hours) and Sisteron (€8.10, one hour).

Haute-Provence

CONTENTS

If you're searching for peace, tranquillity and unbeatable scenery, look no further. Haute-Provence is the region at its rawest, with mass tourism yet to grasp the mountains in its tainted claw.

The splendid snowcapped peaks of the southern Alps dominate the north, while the southeastern valleys are sprinkled with hilltop villages where the tempo of life has barely shifted gear since medieval times. Southwest you'll find Europe's largest canyon, tearing through a land of limestone gorges and shimmering green lakes. Purple lavender mantles the lower-lying Plateau de Valensole, on the left bank of the River Durance, which skirts the region's western side.

Provence's largest national park, the Parc National du Mercantour, sprawls protectively across a large part of the Alpes-de-Haute-Provence *département,* in an arc along the French–Italian border. A stupendous collection of 36,000 Bronze Age petroglyphs can be viewed in the Vallée des Merveilles, wildlife and mountain flowers abound, and there's a wealth of outdoor activities on offer. In summer choose between walking, cycling, whitewater rafting, or tackling the impressive *via ferrata* (literally 'iron way') climbing trails. In winter go snow-trekking or skiing.

An enchanting narrow-gauge railway crosses part of the region, stopping at numerous picturesque villages. Exploring is tough without your own wheels and a sturdy set of walking boots.

HIGHLIGHTS

- Throw yourself into a raft and whitewater down the glorious **Gorges du Verdon** (p186)
- Ride the wild side of Provence on the mountain railway from **Digne-les-Bains** (p192) – stunning views guaranteed!
- Climb dizzying peaks and dangle in thin air on the *via ferrata* (see the boxed text p204), in the **Vallée de la Vésubie** (p201), **Puget-Théniers** (p194) and the **Vallée de la Tinée** (p200)
- Track down prehistoric rock drawings in the **Vallée des Merveilles** (p202), aka the 'Valley of Wonders'
- Sniff Provence's perfumes in the Prieuré de Salagon's sensual gardens in **Mane** (p196)
- Snack on goats' cheese wrapped in chestnut leaves in **Banon** (p196)
- Soar with the region's vultures on a paragliding course at **St-André-les-Alpes** (p191)

Vallée de la Tinée ★
Vallée des Merveilles ★
Digne-les-Bains ★
Vallée de la Vésubie ★
★ Banon
St-André-les-Alpes ★
★ Mane
★ Puget-Théniers
★ Gorges du Verdon

GORGES DU VERDON

Europe's largest canyon, 700m deep in places, was carved by the emerald-green River Verdon, which slices its way through a huge limestone plateau on the southern fringe of Haute-Provence. A favourite area for whitewater activities and paragliding, the 25km-long gorge is also a place to bird-watch, and has its own colony of reintroduced griffon vultures. The canyon has been protected by the **Parc Naturel Régional du Verdon** since 1997.

ORIENTATION

The gorges actually begin at Rougon – near the confluence of the Rivers Verdon and Jabron – and continue until the Verdon River flows into Lac de Ste-Croix. Castellane (northeast) and Moustiers Ste-Marie (northwest) are the main gateways into the region's most fabulous sight.

Maps

You can walk most of the canyon along the often-difficult GR4, a route covered by Didier-Richard's 1:50,000 map No 19, *Haute-Provence-Verdon*.

INFORMATION

Castellane Tourist Office (☎ 04 92 83 61 14; www .castellane.org; rue Nationale; ✆ 9am-12.30pm & 2-6.45pm Mon-Sat, 10am-12.30pm Sun)
Moustiers Ste-Marie Tourist Office (☎ 04 92 74 67 84; www.ville-moustiers-sainte-marie.fr; place de l'Église; ✆ 10am-12.30pm & 2-7.30pm)
Both offices organise gorge excursions and stock information on outdoor activities.

DANGERS & ANNOYANCES

The river in the upper part of the canyon can rise very suddenly if the hydroelectric dams upstream are opened, making it difficult, if not impossible, to cross. Check water levels and weather forecasts with the tourist office before you set out.

THE CANYON

Spectacular views abound from two cliff-side roads that link Moustiers Ste-Marie and Castellane. The river, which gets that amazing colour from its unusually high fluorine content, can be visited by foot, mountain bike or raft.

The **rte des Crêtes** (the D952 and D23) follows the northern rim and passes the **Point Sublime viewing point** at the canyon's entrance, from where the GR4 walking trail leads to the bottom of the canyon. At its eastern end, the steep and narrow D317 climbs 3km to the quaint village of **Rougon** (population 85, elevation 963m).

The **Corniche Sublime** (D19 to D71) skims the southern rim and takes you to landmarks like **Balcons de la Mescla** (Mescla Terraces) and **Pont de l'Artuby**, Europe's highest bridge (182m). See the boxed text opposite for details on bungee jumping from the bridge.

A complete circuit of the Gorges du Verdon involves about 140km of relentless driving along winding roads. The only real village en route is **La Palud-sur-Verdon** (population 300, elevation 930m), 2km northeast of the northern bank of the canyon. There, the **Maison des Gorges du Verdon** (☎ 04 92 77 32 02; www.lapaludsurverdon.com; ✆ 10am-1pm & 4-7pm mid-Jun–mid-Sep, 10am-noon & 4-6pm mid-Mar–mid-Jun & mid-Sep–mid-Nov), inside a 17th-century cha-

---

MOUNTAIN MARKETS

A sprawling splash of life and colour, the Provençal market is a particular treat in Haute-Provence, when it prods sleepy little mountain towns into frantic action. Delicacies include wild-boar sausages, fragrant herbs, AOC olive oil, locally made cheeses (including leaf-wrapped Banon; see p196), lavender honey and all the olives your poor stomach can stand. The food markets listed below start early in the morning and go until noon or 1pm.

Monday Forcalquier
Tuesday Breil-sur-Roya, Colmars-les-Alpes, Seyne-les-Alpes
Wednesday Barcelonnette, Castellane, Digne-les-Bains, La Foux d'Allos, La Palud-sur-Verdon, Sisteron, St-André-les-Alpes, Tende
Thursday Allemagne-en-Provence, Allos, Les Salles-sur-Verdon, Montagnac, Sospel
Friday Colmars-les-Alpes, Entrevaux, Moustiers Ste-Marie, Quinson, Seyne-les-Alpes
Saturday Barcelonnette, Castellane, Digne-les-Bains, Sisteron, St-André-les-Alpes
Sunday Bauduen (summer only), La-Palud-sur-Verdon (summer only)
Daily St-Martin-Vésubie

HAUTE-PROVENCE

teau, hosts exhibitions on gorge flora, fauna and geology and organises guided walks.

The bottom of the canyon, first explored in its entirety in 1905, presents walkers and whitewater rafters with a stiff series of cliffs and narrows. The GR4 runs along the gorge, taking two days to complete; short descents into the canyon are possible from a number of points. Bring a torch (flashlight) and drinking water. Camping on gravel beaches along the way is illegal.

CASTELLANE

pop 1539 / elevation 723m

Small-town Castellane is the favoured starting point for expeditions into the gorges and teems with tourist facilities. Central place Marcel Sauvaire and adjoining place de l'Église shelter hotels and countless whitewater-sports shops.

The most dramatic sight in Castellane is **Chapelle Notre Dame du Roc** (1703), built on an impossibly high and precarious needle-shaped rock. A 45-minute walking trail leads from place de l'Église to the chapel. Each year on 15 August (Assumption Day), a procession of pilgrims goes by torchlight up to the rock to celebrate Mass.

Mermaid mythology and fossil facts are the subject of the **Musée Sirènes et Fossiles** (☎ 04 92 83 19 23; sirenes@club-Internet.fr; place Marcel Sauvaire; adult/7-15 yrs €3.85/2.75; ☼ 10am-noon & 2-5pm Wed-Sun May-Sep, 9am-noon & 2-5pm Wed-Sun Apr & Oct). The fascinating **Musée de la Résistance** (☎ 04 92 83 78 25; rte de Digne; adult/12-18 yrs €3/1.50; ☼ 9am-7.30pm Apr-Sep, by appointment only Oct-Mar), about 1.5km along the road to Digne, is a private collection dedicated to war-time heroes of the Resistance.

MOUSTIERS STE-MARIE

pop 635 / elevation 634m

Quaint little Moustiers Ste-Marie nestles on a rocky shelf beneath two towering limestone cliffs. A 227m-long gold chain bearing a shining star hangs between the rocks – suspended, so legend claims, by a knight grateful to have returned safely from the Crusades.

Underneath the star, perched on a cliff ledge, is the 12th-century **Chapelle Notre Dame de Beauvoir** and its waterfall. A steep trail leads up from rue de la Bourgade, passing 14 stations of the cross en route; count on a good 30-minute climb.

In the 17th and 18th centuries, the village's decorative faïence (earthenware) graced Europe's palaces. Antique masterpieces can be admired in the **Musée de la Faïence** (☎ 04 92 74 61 64; museedemoustiers@wanadoo.fr; rue de la Bourgade; adult/16-18 yrs €2/1; ☼ 9am-noon & 2-6pm Wed-Mon Apr-Jun, Sep & Oct, 9am-noon & 2-7pm Wed-Mon Jul & Aug). The industry was resurrected last century, but Moustiers' 19 modern-day potteries mainly produce tat.

ACTIVITIES

Castellane is the main base for water-sport centres, all offering similarly priced guided trips from April to September, with advance booking required. High-adrenalin activities include rafting (€55/75 per half-/full day) and canyoning (€45/65) expeditions; hot-dogging – bombing down the river in an inflatable canoe (€30); hydrospeed trips – with a bodyboard (€45); and water-rambling with mountain bikes (€10/20 per half/full day).

Aboard Rafting (☎ 04 92 83 76 11; www.aboard -rafting.com; 8 place de l'Église)

Action Aventure (☎ 04 92 83 79 39; www.action -aventure.com in French; 12 rue Nationale)

Acti-Raft (☎ 04 92 83 76 64; http://actiraft.com; rte des Gorges du Verdon).

Aqua Verdon (☎ 04 92 83 72 75; www.aquaverdon .com in French; 9 rue Nationale)

Aqua Viva Est (☎ 04 92 83 75 74; www.aquavivaest .com; 12 blvd de la République)

Buena Vista Rafting (☎ /fax 04 92 83 77 98; www .buenavistarafting.com; 31 rue Nationale)

Easy Rafting (☎ 04 92 83 74 02; easyrafting@hotmail .com; 2 rue du Mitan)

Montagne & Rivière (☎ 04 92 83 67 24; www.rafting -castellane.com; 20 rue Nationale)

...a list of *chambres*
...canyon.

...**uberge** (☎ 04 92 83 62 06; mapetite
...bertysurf.fr; 8 blvd de la République; d/tr/q from
...0/67; **P**) This is the most stylish joint in
...own and teeters on the edge of being upmarket. Noteworthy for its spanking-new
bathrooms, peaceful garden with a 100-
year-old lime tree and quality restaurant.

Grand Hôtel du Levant (☎ 04 92 83 60 05; www
.touring-levant.com; place Marcel Sauvaire; d/tr/q €43/80/85;
P) An impressive pile with cool, dim, newly
decorated rooms, many of which have a
grandstand view of the dramatic chapel. The
doubles are particularly good value.

Hôtel Restaurant de la Forge (☎ 04 92 83
62 61; fax 04 92 83 65 81; place de l'Église; d from €42)
Yet another decent mid-range hotel-with-
restaurant, this little place sits at the foot
of the Rock. Rooms have dinky wooden
shutters and comfy beds.

For a cuisine so Provençal that even Frédéric Mistral (see p52) would be proud, head

for the **Restaurant du Commerce** (☎ 04 92 83 6100;
place de l'Église; menus €22 & €29; ☺ closed Oct-Feb).

Around Castellane

Along the approach to Castellane, the river
is lined with 11 crowded camp sites, open
from April or May to September. Count on
paying from €13 to €21 for two adults with
a tent and car in high season.

Gîte de Chasteuil (☎ 04 92 83 72 45; www.gite
dechasteuil.com; Hameau de Chasteuil; B&B s/d/tr from
€50/55/71) The old schoolhouse in the 16th-
century hamlet of Chasteuil has been converted into a sweet, sunny *chambre d'hôte*
with super mountain views. Situated 8km
southwest of Castellane.

Auberge du Point Sublime (☎ 04 92 83 60 35;
point-sublime@wanadoo.fr; La Palud-sur-Verdon; d from
€50; ☺ Apr–mid-Oct; **P**) This 14-room roadside inn, at the foot of the D317 route to
Rougon, is a delightful place to sleep and
eat.

Le Mur d'Abeilles (☎ 04 92 83 76 33; murabeilles@
wanadoo.fr; Rougon; pancakes €4.40-8.70) It's well
worth the steep climb out of the canyon
to visit this fab creperie, in Rougon at the

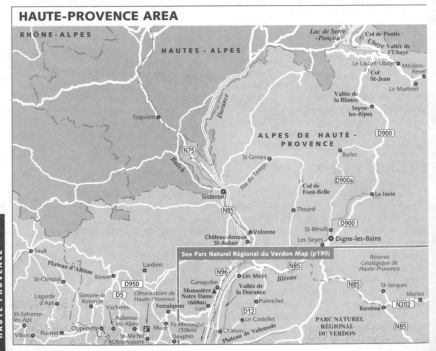

HAUTE-PROVENCE AREA

gorge's eastern end. Sweet and savoury pancakes are served on a terrace with killer views. Taste and buy honey, fresh from hives embedded in the wall.

Moustiers Ste-Marie

The central hotels are so-so, but there are some lovely options along the chemin de Quinson, off the northbound rte de Riez (the D952).

Auberge de la Ferme Rose (☎ 04 92 74 69 47; www.lafermerose.fr.fm in French; chemin de Quinson; d €70-140; ℗ ✗) 'Rustic beauty in buckets' sums up this old farm. More expensive rooms have air-con and private terraces.

Hôtel Le Clos des Iris (☎ 04 92 74 63 46; www.closdesiris.fr; chemin de Quinson; high-season d €65; ℗) Down the same country lane, this charming blue-shuttered house has an untamed flowery garden dotted with tiled tables. Rooms all have shady private terraces looking onto the lawns. Advance booking essential.

Les Santons de Moustiers (☎ 04 92 74 66 48; www.les-santons.com in French; place de l'Église; menus €24 & €33; ✗ closed Tue) Firmly planted on the tourist trail, but this restaurant has tasty

food nonetheless. Try for a table above the moss-covered waterfall.

La Ferme Ste-Cécile (☎ 04 92 74 64 18; www.ferme-ste-cecile.com in French; quartier St-Michel; menus €22, €31 & €42.50; ✗ closed Mon & mid-Nov–Dec) Fresh fish with garlic ice cream is among the delicious culinary surprises to be enjoyed at this authentic *ferme auberge* (farmhouse restaurant), 1km out of the centre along the D952.

GETTING THERE & AWAY

Public transport is limited. **Autocars Sumian** (☎ 04 42 67 60 34) runs buses from Marseille to Castellane (€19.90, 3½ hours) via Aix-en-Provence, La Palud-sur-Verdon and Moustiers Ste-Marie. They leave on Monday, Wednesday and Saturday from July to mid-September (Saturday only during the rest of the year).

VFD (☎ 04 93 85 24 56) operates a daily bus from Grenoble to Nice via Digne-les-Bains and Grasse, stopping en route in Castellane (from Nice €17.22, 2¼ hours). Tourist offices in Castellane and Moustiers Ste-Marie have schedules.

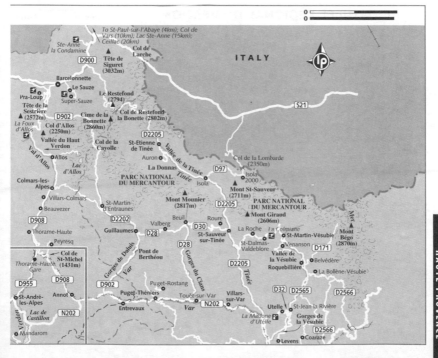

LACS DU VERDON

The Verdon lakes are a spectacular sparkling green and look so natural in their lus-
cious surroundings that it's hard to believe
they were created by the national electricity
company. Swim, participate in all kinds of
water sports, or just sunbathe on the pebbly
shores. Be sure to stick to designated bathing areas, as other sections of the lakes are
dangerous for swimmers.

LAC DE STE-CROIX

Formed in 1974, this is the largest of
the lakes, stretching 10km southwest of
Moustiers Ste-Marie. Pretty **Bauduen** (population 276) sits on its southeastern banks.
Camp sites dot the lakeside D71 and D249,
leading to the village. Bauduen has a small
tourist office (☎ /fax 04 94 84 39 02; http://bauduen
-sur-verdon.com in French; rue de Juterie), as does **Les
Salles-sur-Verdon** (☎ 04 94 70 21 84; www.sallessur
verdon.com; place Fontfreye).

On the western banks, **Ste-Croix de Verdon**
(population 103, elevation 525m) is the only

village. At the lake shore, the **École Française
de Voile** (☎ 04 92 77 76 51) rents out sailboards
(beginners per hour €13). Five minutes'
walk along the beach, **Le Petit Port** (☎ 06 73 65
60 09) hires out electric boats (per half-hour
€16) and catamarans (per 20 minutes €10),
or lets you bounce on a floating trampoline
(per 15 minutes €3).

LAC DE QUINSON

Lac de Quinson sits at the southernmost
foot of the lower Gorges du Verdon.

In **Quinson** (population 354), the high-
tech **Musée de la Préhistoire des Gorges du
Verdon** (☎ 04 92 74 09 59; www.museeprehistoire
.com; rte de Montmeyan; adult/6-18 yrs €7/5, family ticket
€19; ☺ 10am-6pm Wed-Mon Feb, Mar & Oct–mid-Dec,
10am-7pm Wed-Mon Apr-Jun & Sep, 10am-8pm daily Jul
& Aug, closed mid-Dec–end Jan), designed by British architect Norman Foster, explores the
gorges' prehistoric past and archaeological treasures. In July and August it runs
expeditions to the **Grotte de la Baume Bonne**,
a prehistoric cave discovered by archaeologists in the 1960s. Twice-weekly **guided
tours** (adult/6-18 yrs €3.80/3.10) entail a two-hour

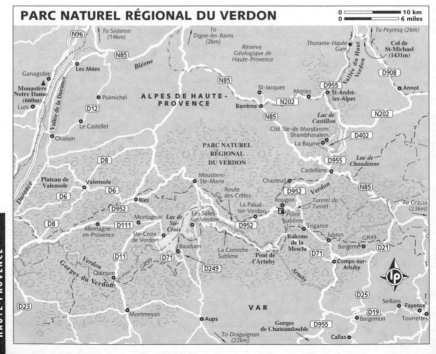

PARC NATUREL RÉGIONAL DU VERDON

walk through difficult rocky terrain and up metal staircases. Walking shoes, a hat and water are essential. Reserve in advance at the museum. Quinson's **tourist office** (☎ 04 92 74 01 12; www.quinson.fr in French; place de la Mairie; 🕑 10am-12.30pm & 2.30-6pm, closed Tue & Sun outside high season) also has details.

Endearing **Montagnac** (population 326), 11km north of Quinson off the D11, is known for its fresh truffles, available from November to March. Eight kilometres west is **Allemagne-en-Provence** (population 384), which adopted its German-influenced name during the Wars of Religion (1562–98) when the Baron of Germany besieged the place. Its centrepiece is the storybook 12th- to 16th-century **Château d'Allemagne** (☎ 04 92 77 46 78, 04 92 77 73 84; adult/6-12 yrs €5/2.50; 🕑 for guided tours only 4pm & 5pm Tue-Sun Jul–mid-Sep, 4pm & 5pm Sat & Sun Apr-Jun & mid-Sep–Oct), a privately inhabited donjon-style building that has a few *chambres d'hôtes* (see right).

LACS DE CHAUDANNE & CASTILLON

Two cool, turquoise lakes decorate the eastern end of the Gorges du Verdon. Lac de Chaudanne's banks are steep-sided, but Lac de Castillon has gently sloping beaches where you can swim and hire paddle boats (per hour €13), including the beach just south of St-André-les-Alpes and right on the lake's southwestern tip.

From the latter, the single-track D402 cuts into the mountains to the walled Cité Ste-de Mandarom Shambhasalem (see the boxed text p193).

St-André-les-Alpes (population 832, elevation 914m) is France's leading paragliding centre: spread your wings at **Aérogliss** (☎ 04 92 89 11 30; www.aerogliss.com; chemin des Iscles), where a five-day beginner's course costs €460. In the village, the **tourist office** (☎ 04 92 89 02 39; www.ot-st-andre-les-alpes.fr; place Marcel Pastorelli; 🕑 9am-noon & 2-7pm Mon-Sat, plus 10am-1pm Sun high season) has more information on activities.

Also in St-André-les-Alpes, 30 types of sausage are sold at the **Maison du Saucisson** (House of Sausages; ☎ 04 92 89 03 16; fax 04 92 89 09 56; place de Verdun; 🕑 closed Mon winter), including donkey, ostrich and wild boar (from €24 per kg).

St-André is linked with eastern Provence and the coastal resort of Nice by a narrow-gauge railway (see the boxed text p194).

AUTHOR'S CHOICE

Hôtel Restaurant La Bastide de Moustiers (☎ 04 92 70 47 47; www.bastide-moustiers.com; chemin de Quinson; d €145-250; 🅿 🗶 🔀 🖫) This stunning four-star hotel, located in a 17th-century country house, is unbearably perfect, with gorgeous rose archways, Starck-designed fittings, a Michelin-starred restaurant and even *baby deer* for your kids to pet! One room is adapted for people with disabilities.

SLEEPING

There are numerous camp sites in and around Ste-Croix de Verdon; ask at the Castellane tourist office.

Les Cougnas (☎ 04 92 89 18 78; lescougnas@club-Internet.fr; rte de Nice, St-André-les-Alpes; bed in 4- to 6-bed r €13, bed in d €17, breakfast/dinner €4/13) This pleasant *gîte d'étape* (hiker's accommodation) overlooks Lac de Castillon. A highlight is watching paragliders drop from the sky while you have breakfast.

Camping Les Iscles (☎ 04 92 89 02 29; fax 04 92 89 02 56; rte de Nice, St-André-les-Alpes; car & tent/adult €1.75/3.65; 🕑 May-Sep) A well-kept municipal site next to St-André's paragliding school.

Hôtel Lac et Forêt (☎ 04 92 89 07 38; lacforet@club-Internet.fr; rte de Nice; d from €29, menu €15) Next door to Les Cougnas, rooms in this friendly family-run hotel are spacious and bright, with good views of the lake. There's a tasty restaurant downstairs.

Château d'Allemagne (see left; B&B d/ste €80/140; 🅿 🖫) Satisfy your inner prince or princess by staying in one of three regal rooms in this fairy-tale castle. Guests are allowed to stroll in the private park.

EATING

Domaine d'Aiguines (☎ 04 92 34 25 72; fax 04 92 34 29 09; St-Jacques; menus €17, €22 & €25) Strictly for those who love ducks – on a plate. Home to hundreds of the birds, this duck farm cooks up out-of-the-ordinary farm-made foie gras, pan-fried duck salad and other ducky dishes. A peacock, chickens and dogs amuse guests in the yard out front. Follow the N202 for 13km west from St André-les-Alpes and turn left (north) just before Barrême, along the narrow D118 to the hamlet of St-Jacques. Opening hours are variable, so don't just turn up on the off chance: book ahead.

RÉSERVE GÉOLOGIQUE DE HAUTE-PROVENCE

The 1900-sq-km Réserve Géologique de Haute-Provence contains spectacular fossil deposits, including the footprints of prehistoric birds. Its main town is Digne-les-Bains.

You'll need a detailed regional map or *topoguide* (sold at the Digne-les-Bains tourist office; right) to the Digne and Sisteron areas and your own transport to get to the 18 sites. Most of them are around **Barles** (population 114, 24km north of Digne) and **Barrême** (population 442, 28km southeast). There's an impressive limestone slab with some 500 ammonites 3km north of Digne on the road to Barles. The reserve runs museums in Sisteron (p195) and Castellane (p187).

The **Centre de Géologie** (☎ 04 92 36 70 70; www .resgeol04.org; Parc St-Bénoît; adult/7-14 yrs €4.60/2.75; 🕙 museum 9am-noon & 2-5.30pm Sat-Thu, to 4.30pm Fri Apr-Oct, 9am-noon & 2-5.30pm Mon-Fri Nov-Mar, park 8am-7pm Apr-Oct, 8am-7pm Mon-Fri Nov-Mar), 2km north of Digne off the road to Barles in St-Bénoît, is the reserve's HQ. Take TUD bus No 2 from Digne to the Champourcin stop (across the bridge; €1), then follow the road to the left that's signposted 'Musée-Promenade', a dramatic 15-minute walk along a rocky overhang above the river (cars aren't allowed up).

DIGNE-LES-BAINS

pop 17,680 / elevation 608m

The land of snow and melted cheese collides with the land of sun and olives around Digne-les-Bains. The town is in the centre of the Réserve Géologique de Haute-Provence and is named after its thermal springs, which are visited annually by around 11,000 people seeking cures for rheumatism and other ailments.

The area's shale is rich in fossils and protected by the Réserve Géologique de Haute-Provence. Rte Napoléon (the N85), which Bonaparte followed in 1815 after escaping from Elba, passes though Digne-les-Bains.

Orientation

Digne-les-Bains is on the eastern bank of the Bléone. The major roads into town converge at rond-point du 11 Novembre 1918, 400m northeast of the train station. Blvd Gassendi heads northeast from the roundabout to place du Général de Gaulle, the main square.

Information

Tourist Office (☎ 04 92 36 62 62; www.ot-digne lesbains.fr in French; place du Tampinet; 🕙 8.45am-12.30pm & 1.30-6.30pm Mon-Sat & 10am-noon & 3-6pm Sun Jul & Aug, 8.45am-noon & 2-6pm Mon-Sat Sep-Jun) Overlooking rond-point du 11 Novembre 1918.

Sights

It's worth darting into the **Cathédrale Notre-Dame du Bourg** (av du Camping), at the eastern end of town. Built between the 12th and 13th centuries, it has a simple, clean-cut Romanesque interior and contains some unusual painted murals. Once archaeological works have finished, the crypt will also be opened to visitors.

VULTURE CULTURE

The griffon vulture *(Gyps fulvus)*, with its spectacular 3m wingspan, was once common in Provence. It was a useful carrion eater, which helped prevent water pollution. However, the shotgun and loss of food sources like the bear and wolf caused its disappearance almost a century ago.

In 1999, 12 young birds were reintroduced into the wild at Rougon. It took them two weeks to learn to fly again, but they eventually settled happily in the Gorges du Verdon. By 2004 a total of 90 vultures had been released and they have now formed a breeding colony.

Watching the vulture's expansive, soaring flights over the canyon is awe-inspiring. Between June and September the **Association Vautours en Haute-Provence** (☎ 04 92 83 69 55; www .verdon.vautours.org in French), together with the Office National des Forêts (National Forests Office) and Ligue pour la Protection des Oiseaux, organises guided vulture-watching walks around Rougon. Half-day walks depart from Castellane's tourist office at 9am on Wednesday (9.30am from Rougon) from June to September (plus Tuesday and Thursday in July and August). It costs €6/3 for adults/students (children under 10 free); wear a sturdy pair of boots.

AUM SWEET AUM

Angels with machine guns guard the gates of the **Cité Ste-de Mandarom Shambhasalem** (Holy City of Mandarom Shambhasalem; ☎ 04 92 83 63 83; www.aumisme.org; adult/student/10-18 yrs €5/3/2; ☽ 3-5pm Sat & Sun, 3-5pm daily during Easter & summer school holidays), glittering like an outpost of Disneyland on Lac de Castillon's western shores. Europe's largest Buddha (22m) gazes into the eyes of a huge concrete-and-iron Christ, and the pair is surrounded by sparkling temples representing the world's major religions.

Aumism, a religion founded in 1969, is a strange kettle of fish. The 15 monks who live permanently in the 'city' dress in multicoloured robes and mirrored headbands and pray for world peace while chanting the holy word 'Aum'. All is love, light and dinging bells; but scratch the surface and out spews controversy.

Buddha and Christ used to stand with a third figure, at 33m the tallest of the trio. Built in 1990, this crowned, white-robed effigy was none other than the religion's founder Gilbert Bourdin (1923–98), aka the Holy Lord Hamsah Manarah, who had just declared himself the new Messiah.

It was a statue too far, and drew the hostile attention of local ecologists, planning officials, anti-cult group ADFI and the French police, who became increasingly jumpy about Mandarom after the Solar Temple mass suicides of the mid-1990s. Legal battles led to the statue's eventual demolition in 2001, much to the sect's dismay.

Sinister cult or persecuted religious order? The truth, no doubt, is out there... Decide for yourself on an intriguing guided tour.

MUSÉE ALEXANDRA DAVID-NÉEL

Digne was home to explorer, writer, anarchist and philosopher Alexandra David-Néel (1868–1969), who travelled incognito to Tibet in the early 20th century. Her extraordinary life and all-consuming passion for the country are celebrated at the **Musée Alexandra David-Néel** (☎ 04 92 31 32 38; www .alexandra-david-neel.org; 27 av Maréchal Juin; admission free; ☽ guided tours 10am, 2pm & 4pm Oct-Jun, 10am, 2pm, 3.30pm & 4.30pm Jul-Sep), based in the home where she spent her last years. Visits are by guided tour only; tours last 1½ hours (some are in English). The museum is just over 1km from town on the Nice-bound N85. By bus, take TUD bus No 3 to the Stade Rolland stop (€1).

Activities

Between mid-February and early December you can enjoy a thermal bath (29° to 49°C) at **Les Thermes de Digne-les-Bains** (☎ 04 92 32 32 92; www.eurothermes.com in French).

Rando Lavande (☎ 04 92 32 27 44; www.chez.com/ randolavande in French; 7 rue de Provence) organises tailor-made mountain walks and snowshoeing expeditions (from €20 per person per day), run by mountain guide Jean Louis Béatrix.

Ramble with a donkey from **Lambert Âne** (☎ 04 92 31 60 37; www.lambertane.com in French; Le Château-Lambert) or **Poivre d'Âne** (☎ 04 92 34 87 12; http://poivre.ane.free.fr; La Bastide des Férauds),

northwest of Digne in Thoard. Donkey hire costs €31/46 per half-/full day.

Festivals & Events

Digne is known for its lavender, harvested in July or August and honoured with the five-day **Corso de la Lavande** on the last weekend of August. Musicians flock to town, colourful floats made from the fragrant blue herb parade through the streets and torch-lit celebrations continue into the night.

The **Journées Tibetaines** (Tibetan Days), an annual celebration of Tibetan culture, is held at the Musée Alexandra David-Néel over three days in August.

Sleeping & Eating

Hôtel Central (☎ 04 92 31 31 91; www.lhotel-central .com in French; 26 blvd Gassendi; s/d from €29/42) Most of the shuttered rooms in this central two-star place overlook a quiet pedestrian street. Reception is on the 1st floor; guests need a code to enter after dark. There's a discount if you're visiting Digne's spa.

Hôtel Villa Gaïa (☎ 04 92 31 21 60; www.hotel villagaia.fr; 24 rte de Nice; d €81-95; ☽ Apr-Oct; **P**) Set in Italianate gardens, complete with tinkling fountain, this beautifully restored villa really feels like a home, not a hotel. The bright, breezy rooms contain antique furniture and there's a tennis court for the sporty. It's 2km west of town.

La Chauvinière (☎ 04 92 31 40 03; 56 rue de l'Hubac; menus €19 & €24; ☺ lunch & dinner Tue-Sun) In the pedestrianised old town, this restaurant has a sunny terrace and serves a regional menu.

A food market fills place du Général de Gaulle Wednesday and Saturday mornings.

Getting There & Around

BUS

From the **bus station** (☎ 04 92 31 50 00; place du Tampinet), there are buses to and from Nice (€14.60, 2¼ hours, one or two daily); Marseille (€14.10, 2¼ hours, two to four daily); Castellane (€11.50, one hour, two daily); La Foux d'Allos (€9.90, two hours, two or three weekly during the ski season and July and August) via Colmars and Allos; Barcelonnette (€8.30, 1½ hours, one bus daily); Manosque (€5.40, 1¼ hours, two to four daily); and Apt (€10.20, two hours, two daily).

During the ski season **Société des Cars Alpes Littoral** (SCAL; ☎ 04 92 51 06 05) runs a daily bus

---

ALONG THE MOUNTAIN RAILWAY

The Digne–Nice narrow-gauge railway chugs from the mountains to the sea, rising to 1000m altitude, and offers breathtaking views of landscapes scarcely navigable by road. The 151km track was built between 1890 and 1911, and passes 50 tunnels, 16 viaducts and 15 metal bridges on its precipitous journey.

The train stops at numerous little villages en route. You can buy direct tickets to the place you want to visit; or, if you're travelling the whole route, it's possible to hop out, explore, and join a later train. Travelling east from Digne, highlights (with prices and journey times) include:

- **St-André-les-Alpes** (€6.60, 50 minutes; see p191).

- **Thorame-Haute** (€8.20, one hour; population 174, elevation 1012m) Despite its pinprick size, this village is a vital bus link between southern Provence and the Allos ski resorts. After Thorame-Haute, the **Col de St-Michel** (1431m) and the ancient shepherds' village of **Peyresq** flash past. The 3.5km-long tunnel here took 400 workers some two years to construct.

- **Annot** (€9, one hour 25 minutes; population 1020, elevation 700m) This sweet old town has a couple of interesting 17th-century chapels, both a short walk from the village. The **tourist office** (☎ 04 92 83 23 03; www.annot.fr in French; blvd St-Pierre) has details.

- **Entrevaux** (€11.15, one hour 50 minutes; population 752) The 17th-century fortified village tumbles dramatically down the hillside from a Vauban-built citadel. Across the drawbridge is an oil and flour mill that can be visited. The **tourist office** (☎ 04 93 05 46 73; tourisme@entrevaux .info) is inside the old city gate.

- **Puget-Théniers** (€12.15, one hour 55 minutes; population 1624, elevation 405m) The 1909 steam locomotive *Train des Pignes* is stationed here: from May to October it shunts between Puget and Annot (€6.80 return, 50 minutes). Passengers seeking hearty Haute-Provence fodder in Puget – including *secca de boeuf* (mountain-dried beef) – should head for **Auberge des Acacias** (☎ 04 93 05 05 25; fax 04 93 05 06 82; lunch/dinner menu €12.20/17.55; ☺ closed Wed), 1km east of Puget on the N202 (get off at 'Le Planet' train stop). In Puget itself, **Edelweiss** (☎ 04 90 05 01 00; 1 place Adolphe Cornil; lunch menu €12, dinner menus €16.50 & €25; ☺ closed Mon) cooks up succulent mountain lamb in lavender pastry. There's also a *via ferrata* here (see the boxed text, p204).

- **Touët-sur-Var** (€13.20, two hours 10 minutes; population 445) Another pleasant gastronomic stop, the perched village's **Auberge des Chasseurs** (☎ 04 93 05 71 11; menus €17 & €32) is renowned for its seasonal game dishes – don't miss the wild boar.

The entire trip from Digne-les-Bains to Nice takes 3¼ hours. There are four to five trains daily and a single fare is €17.65. A single Annot–Nice fare is €10.10 (€24.40 with the steam train between Puget and Annot). Bicycles cannot be taken onto the train, but are sent as baggage (€8) – contact the railway for information.

Updated fares and schedules are on Chemins de Fer de Provence's website at www.train provence.com.

in either direction between Marseille and Pra-Loup (€25.10, 4½ hours) via Digne-les-Bains (€14.10, 2¼ hours) and Barcelonnette (€22.50, four hours). Transporting a pair of skis costs €2.70.

If you plan to use local buses a lot, invest in a 10-ticket carnet (€5.70), sold in the tourist office.

TRAIN

From the train station, a 10-minute walk west of the tourist office on av Pierre Sémard, there are four daily trains to and from Marseille (€19.90, 2½ hours).

Digne-les-Bains is also served by the scenic narrow-gauge railway, operated by **Chemins de Fer de Provence** (☎ /fax 04 92 31 01 58; www.train provence.com; av Pierre Sémard), which links Digne to Nice (see the boxed text, opposite).

VALLÉE DE LA DURANCE

The impetuous waters of the 324km-long River Durance, an affluent of the Rhône, follow the Via Domitia, the Roman main road from Italy that allowed them to infiltrate the whole of France. It's a bit off the tourist trail today, but this has advantages: you can explore monasteries and museums in peace, star-gaze at St-Michel's Centre d'Astronomie away from light pollution and snack on the region's comestibles without having to share!

ORIENTATION

The Durance Valley ploughs from Sisteron in the north down to the eastern side of Parc Naturel Régional du Verdon. The three main towns along this 100km stretch are Manosque, on the eastern edge of the Lubéron (see p182); industrial **Château-Arnoux** (population 5000) with its 16th-century castle on the confluence of the Rivers Durance and Bléone; and Sisteron.

SISTERON

pop 7232 / elevation 485m

The town's main lure is its **Musée Terre et Temps** (Museum of Earth & Time; ☎ 04 92 61 61 30; musee_terre_et_temps@libertysurf.fr; 6 place Général de Gaulle; ⏰ 10am-1pm & 3-7pm Jul & Aug, 9.30am-12.30pm & 2-6pm Thu-Mon Apr-Jun, Sep & Oct), inside a former 17th-century chapel. It's one of a trio of museums (see also Musée Sirènes

et Fossiles, p187, and Centre de Géologie, p192) run by the Réserve Géologique de Haute-Provence, and it focuses on time itself, with a Foucalt's Pendulum, sundials and a miraculous water clock.

From the museum, motorists can follow the rte du Temps (Time Rd), a marked itinerary that follows the eastbound D3 to remote **St-Geniez**, from where it climbs over the Col de Font-Belle (1708m) before plummeting south to the medieval fortified village of **Thoard** and Digne-les-Bains. Information panels en route highlight geological sights.

The annual **Festival des Nuits de la Citadelle** (Citadel Nights Festival; www.francefestivals.com//sisteron/ indexuk.htm; tickets €25-50), established in 1928, is held from mid-July to mid-August. Its open-air classical-music concerts take place in the wonderful surroundings of Vauban's **Château de Sisteron** (☎ 04 92 61 27 57; fax 04 92 61 29 54; adult/5-12 yrs €4.70/2.35; ⏰ 9am-6pm Apr-Nov, 9am-7pm Jul & Aug), a 13th- to 16th-century fortress perched on a rock above the *cluse* (transverse valley); contact the **tourist office** (☎ 04 92 61 12 03; www.sisteron.com; Hôtel de Ville; ⏰ 9am-7pm Mon-Sat & 10am-1pm Sun mid-Jun–mid-Sep, 9am-noon & 2-6pm Mon-Sat mid-Sep–mid-Jun) for information.

AROUND SISTERON

In **Les Mées** (population 2973), 20km south of Sisteron, is the **Rocher des Mées**, a row of rocky pinnacles that stand 100m tall. They were once a gaggle of monks who were turned to stone for lusting after Saracen women, so legend claims.

Ten kilometres south in **Ganagobie**, the 10th-century Benedictine **Prieuré de Ganobie** (☎ 04 92 68 00 04; www.ndganagobie.com in French; ⏰ 3-5pm) showcases an exquisite 12th-century floor mosaic – the largest of its kind in France – in its chapel (the only section of the monastery open to visitors).

FORCALQUIER

pop 4375 / elevation 550m

Forcalquier sits atop a rocky perch 19km southwest of Ganagobie. Steep steps lead to the citadel and octagonal-shaped chapel at the top of the village, where **carillon concerts** are held: the **tourist office** (☎ 04 92 75 10 02; www.forcalquier.com; 13 place du Bourguet; ⏰ 9am-7pm Mon, 9am-12.30pm & 2-7pm Tue-Sat, 10am-1pm & 3-6pm Sun mid-Jun–mid-Sep, 9am-noon & 2-6pm Mon-Sat mid-Sep–mid-Jun) has details.

STAR-SPANGLED SCREENINGS

In July and August action-packed, crowd-rousing movies are shown every night on massive screens beneath the stars. These atmospheric events are hosted by a clutch of villages, including Annot, Allemagne-en-Provence, Banon, Castellane, Forcalquier, Moustiers Ste-Marie and Ste-Croix de Verdon. The most breathtaking venue is the Centre d'Astronomie (below right), near St-Michel l'Observatoire, where films have a science-fiction theme.

Screenings start at 9.30pm and cost €4. **Le Cinéma de Pays** (☎ 04 92 78 13 25; http://cinepays.free.fr in French) runs the **Nuits du Cinéma en Plein Air** programme; film choices and venues are available online.

France's only heritage-listed **cemetery** (place du Souvenir Français; ⏲ 9am-5pm) lies 1km north of the centre, distinguished by its age-old yew trees cut to form high, decorative alleys.

Fiery liqueurs like Bigarade (bitter orange), La Farigoule (thyme), *amandine* (almond), and of course pastis (see the boxed text, p58), have been distilled at the **Distilleries et Domaines des Provences** since 1898. Taste and buy at its **Espace Dégustation** (☎ 04 92 75 15 41; www.distilleries-provence.com in French; 9 av St-Promasse; ⏲ 9am-7pm Mon-Sat & 9am-noon Sun Jul & Aug, 9am-noon & 2-6pm Mon & Wed-Sat Sep-Jun).

You can also sample local aperitifs at **Le Lapin Tant Pis** (☎ 04 92 75 38 88; info@lecomptoirdespoivres.com; 10 av St-Promasse; menu €58; ⏲ dinner Mon-Sat Jul & Aug, rest of year by appointment only), a boldly unconventional restaurant run by eccentric chef and spice-gatherer Gérard Vives. He feeds a maximum of 15 diners, so book ahead; credit cards are not accepted.

The AOC Haute-Provence olive-oil harvest can be tested at **Oliviers & Co** (☎ 04 92 75 00 75; 5 rue des Cordeliers; menus around €18), a shop that dishes up light Mediterranean cuisine in the adjoining bistro.

AROUND FORCALQUIER

The delightful **Prieuré de Salagon** (☎ 04 92 75 70 50; www.musee-de-salagon.com in French; adult/12-18 yrs €5/2.60; ⏲ 10am-noon & 2-7pm May-Sep, 2-6pm Oct-Dec & Feb-Apr), 4km south in **Mane**, is a 13th-century priory with the most fascinating gardens. Aromatic herbs grow in a medieval garden, perfumes typical of the region (lavender, mint, mugwort and sage) fill its **Jardin de Senteurs** and there's a formal section showcasing plants from around the world.

From Forcalquier, if you have your own transport, a delicious detour can be made to **Banon** (population 940, elevation 760m), renowned for its *chèvre de Banon* cheese, made from goats' milk and wrapped in chestnut leaves. The **Fromagerie de Banon** (☎ 04 92 73 25 03; fax 04 92 73 31 94; rte de Carniol) sells its cheeses at the Tuesday-morning market on place de la République and at the wonderful cheese-and-sausage shop **Chez Melchio** (☎ 04 92 73 23 05; place de la République; ⏲ 7.30am-12.30pm & 2.30-7pm Wed-Sun). The **tourist office** (☎/fax 04 92 73 36 37; place de la République; ⏲ 9am-12.30pm & 3-6pm Tue-Sat plus 10am-noon Sun summer) has a list of farms in the surrounding countryside where you can sample fresh cheese. In May Banon celebrates its annual **Fête du Fromage** (Cheese Fair).

A bunch of villages peek at Forcalquier from the hilltops west of town: **Vachères** (population 260, elevation 830m), 30km west; **Oppedette** (population 40, elevation 525m) with its lovely gorges crossed by the GR4; **Lurs** (population 347, elevation 600m); and **Simiane-la-Rotonde** (population 532), host to the international music festival **Les Riches Heures Musicales** in August. Tickets costing €26 are sold at Forcalquier tourist office (p195).

OBSERVATORY

The **Observatoire de Haute-Provence** (☎ 04 92 70 64 00; www.obs-hp.fr) is a national research centre situated 10km southwest of Forcalquier at the end of the D305 from the village of **St-Michel l'Observatoire**. It can be visited by a 30-minute **guided tour** (☎ 04 92 76 69 09; adult/6-12 yrs €2.50/1.50; ⏲ 2-4pm Wed Jul & Aug, 3pm Wed Oct-Mar); buy tickets from the *billetterie* (ticket office) in the village square. Shuttle buses run every 30 minutes from St-Michel l'Observatoire (2km).

From St-Michel l'Observatoire, the eastbound D5 flashes past **Centre d'Astronomie** (☎ 04 92 76 69 69; www.centre-astro.fr in French; Plateau du Moulin à Vent), an astronomy centre that organises star-filled multimedia events and educational workshops. Learn how to **watch stars** (adult/6-16 yrs €8.75/7; ⏲ 9pm Fri & Sat) with the naked eye and telescopes.

Accommodation and food are available in St-Michel l'Observatoire at the friendly **Hôtel-Restaurant l'Observatoire** (☎/fax 04 92 76

63 62; place de la Fontaine; s/d €41/49, lunch/dinner menu €14/26). Rooms, decorated in warm Provençal colours, are welcoming, the food is great and there's a little bar where you can eavesdrop on the latest village gossip.

GETTING THERE & AROUND
There are buses that leave from the **Sisteron bus station** (☎ 04 92 61 22 18) to and from Aix-en-Provence (€10.40, 2½ hours, four daily), Marseille (€13.30, two hours, four daily) and Nice (€17.90, 3¾ hours, one daily) via Digne-les-Bains (€3.60, 45 minutes).

In Forcalquier **Voyages Brémond** (☎ 04 92 75 16 32) and **Autocars Sumian** (☎ 04 91 49 44 25) run buses to and from Marseille (€10.30 and €9.30, two hours, up to five daily). Voyages Brémond also runs buses to Manosque (€3.20, 30 minutes, three per day Monday to Saturday, one Sunday). Daily services to and from Avignon (€10, two hours) and Digne-les-Bains (€6.70, one hour) are by **Barlatier** (☎ 04 32 76 00 40). All buses leave from the stop on place Martial Sicard, except on Monday when (because of the market) they depart from in front of the cathedral.

St-Michel l'Observatoire is accessible by one daily bus from Manosque (30 minutes) and Forcalquier (€1.30, 15 minutes).

PARC NATIONAL DU MERCANTOUR

The Mercantour National Park is Provence at its most majestic. Europe's highest mountain pass, **Col de Restefond la Bonette** (2802m), strides through the Vallée de l'Ubaye, the park's most northern and wildest area. Come winter, the Ubaye and its southern sisters, the Vallées du Haut Verdon and de la Tinée, offer fine skiing. The Vallées de la Vésubie, des Merveilles and de la Roya offer a heady mix of gorges, ageless rocks and white waters, all within easy reach of the Côte d'Azur.

The Parc National du Mercantour is home to a dazzling array of birds, including the golden eagle and the bearded vulture. Its higher-altitude plains shelter marmot, mouflon and chamois (a mountain antelope), as well as the *bouquetin* (Alpine ibex), reintroduced into the region in the early 1990s. In lower wooded areas, red

and roe deer are common. Wild boar roam throughout, and wolves (see the boxed text, p198) are making a comeback.

Camping in the park is not allowed.

ORIENTATION
The park's uninhabited heart covers 685 sq km in the northeast of the region and embraces six valleys: (northwest to southeast) Ubaye, Haut Verdon, Tinée, Vésubie, Merveilles and Roya. The park abuts Italy's Parco Naturale delle Alpi Marittime to the east and is surrounded by a 1465-sq-km partially protected and inhabited peripheral zone.

INFORMATION
There are permanent Parc National du Mercantour **Maison du Parc** (www.parc-mercantour.fr) offices in St-Martin-Vésubie (p201), Tende (p203) and Valberg (p201); and summer bureaux in St-Étienne de Tinée and St-Sauveur-sur-Tinée (p201), Lac d'Allos (p199) and Sospel (p203). They provide detailed information on all aspects of the park and sell maps and guidebooks.

For tourist information see the relevant town sections.

VALLÉE DE L'UBAYE
Desolate and wild, the Ubaye Valley is an isolated stretch of land sandwiched between the Parc Régional du Queyras (north) and the Parc National du Mercantour (south). Winter skiing and excellent summer whitewater rafting are its two main activities. The valley is crossed by the D900, which closely shadows the banks of the River Ubaye.

Barcelonnette (population 3316, elevation 1135m), founded by the count of Barcelona in 1231, is the valley's only town. From the 18th century until WWII, some 5000 Barcelonnettais emigrated to Mexico to seek their fortunes in the silk and wool-weaving industries. Their colourful history unfolds in the **Musée de la Vallée** (☎ 04 92 81 27 15; musee .vallee@wanadoo.fr; 10 av de la Libération; adult/child under 18 €3.20/1.60; ☽ 10am-noon & 2.30-7pm Jul & Aug, 3-6pm Tue-Sat Jun & Sep, shorter days & hrs Oct-May).

Information
Barcelonnette's **tourist office** (☎ 04 92 81 04 71; www.barcelonnette.net in French; place Frédéric Mistral; ☽ 9am-noon & 2-7pm Jul & Aug, 9am-noon & 2-6pm Mon-Sat Sep-Jun) has a list of guides who organise walks, and biking and canoeing trips.

HAUTE-PROVENCE

OF WOLVES AND MEN...

Strychnine, clubs, traps, guns...human responses to the wolf are rarely friendly, and sustained hunting over 1000 years led to the creature's eventual disappearance from France in 1930.

But good news! In 1992 two 'funny-looking dogs' were spotted in the Parc National du Mercantour near Utelle. Since then the wolves have been making a natural slow return, loping across the Alps from Italy; there are now around 30 in the park.

The grey wolf *(canis lupus)* is something of a misnomer: its thick, furry coat also comes in shades of black, red, tawny, cinnamon and white. It lives for around 10 years, in packs of two to 12 animals, with complex social rules. Howling is its most dramatic form of communication – the sound can travel for 16km in open spaces and generally scares the pants off people. As early ecologist Aldo Leopold (1887–1948) put it, 'Only the mountain has lived long enough to listen objectively to the howl of a wolf'.

Contrary to popular belief, the wolf doesn't feed on grandmothers, woodcutters or small girls with red hoods. Its diet includes fruit, eggs, fish, insects, mice and mushrooms in the summer months, and sheep and goats in winter. And this is where the conflict begins: the wolf's feeding habits make it a bane to farmers.

In 2004, after loud complaints, Minister of Ecology Serge Lepeltier gave authorisation for one troublesome animal in the park to be shot. However, conservationists argue that wolves are blamed disproportionately for sheep deaths: in France, one in a hundred lost sheep will be taken by a wolf, while the other 99 die from illness, wild dogs or accident.

Chances of bumping into a wolf in the park are almost nil. Unlike the beasts of myth and fairy tale, they're wary animals, and will run in the opposite direction if they sniff you! Summer leaf coverage makes them hard to spot and the wolves usually pad back to Italy when the weather's nice. Just be glad they're out there somewhere.

Alternatively, contact the big pink **Maison de la Vallée de l'Ubaye** (☎ 04 92 81 03 68; www .ubaye.com in French; 4 av des Trois Frères Arnaud). The walking and climbing club **Club Alpin Français** (☎ 04 92 81 28 18; www.cafubaye.com) shares its postal address, but is to be found at the back of the town hall (rue Mairie).

Activities

CYCLING

The Vallée de l'Ubaye is linked to the outside world by seven mountain passes. Cyclists tough enough to conquer them all, including Col de Restefond la Bonette (2802m), are given a medal; the Maison de la Vallée de l'Ubaye in Barcelonnette (see above) has details.

In **Le Martinet** both whitewater-sports bases (see right) rent mountain bikes (€8/26 per hour/day) and arrange guided rides. River has a mini mountain-bike (VTT) course for kids, 20km of forest trails, 1.7km of downhill tracks and a 450m bi-cross (scramble) circuit for adult riders.

SKIING

Pra-Loup (1500m and 1600m) is the main resort in the Vallée de l'Ubaye, 8.5km from Barcelonnette. It's connected by a lift system to the La Foux d'Allos resort in the Vallée du Haut-Verdon (see opposite). Pra-Loup has 170km of runs: its 73 pistes (35 of which are red or black) are suited to intermediate and advanced skiers, while boarders can surf in the snow park. Nearby are **Sauze** (1400m) and **Super-Sauze** (1700m).

A six-day **Ski Pass Vallée** (☎ 04 92 84 11 54; www.skipass-praloup.com in French; adult/6-12 yrs €130/105) covers the above resorts plus **Ste-Anne La Condamine** (1800m). Pra-Loup's **École du Ski Français** (ESF; ☎ 04 92 84 11 05; www .esf-praloup.com; Les Mélèzes bldg) charges €95/115 in low/high season for six group-skiing lessons and €105/122 for the equivalent on a snowboard. Skis, boots and poles can be hired for around €20 per day.

Pra-Loup's **tourist office** (☎ 04 92 84 10 04; www.praloup.com; Maison de Pra-Loup; ☼ 9am-7pm winter) has information on the entire valley.

WHITEWATER SPORTS

Canoe-rental places line the D900 between Le Lauzet-Ubaye and Barcelonnette. In Le Martinet, south off the D900, are **AN Rafting** (☎ 04 92 85 54 90; www.an-rafting.com in French; Pont du Martinet) and **River** (☎ 04 92 85 53 99; www.river.fr in

French). Both arrange whitewater activities, including two- to three-hour rafting (€36), hot-dogging (€37) and canyoning (half-/full day €43/63) expeditions. **Adventure Rio Raft** (☎ 04 92 81 91 15), at the adjoining Camping du Rioclar in Méolans-Revel, 12km west of Barcelonnette, has similar rates.

Sleeping & Eating

Camping du Rioclar (☎ 04 92 81 10 32; www.rioclar .com; av Georges Pompidou; 2 adults, tent & car €19; ☾ mid-Jun–mid-Sep; P ☎) In Méolans-Revel, this large site is ideally close to the hamlet's water-sports centre.

Le Cheval Blanc (☎ 04 92 81 00 19; 12 rue Grenette; d €45; P) In the old post office in Barcelonnette, the White Horse is a friendly, family-run affair. Its Provençal **restaurant** (lunch/dinner menu €15/20) is open to nonguests from May to September.

Barcelonnette's place Manuel overflows with restaurants. The tourist offices have glossy brochures for the ski resorts.

Getting There & Around

The nearest train station is in Gap (outside the scope of this guidebook), 60km to the north.

From Barcelonnette **Autocars SCAL** (☎ 04 92 81 00 20) runs one bus daily to and from Marseille (€22.50, four hours) and Digne-les-Bains (€8.30, 1½ hours). During the ski season there's one daily direct bus between Pra-Loup and Marseille (€25.10, 4½ hours).

Buses in the Vallée de l'Ubaye are run by **Autocars Maurel** (☎ 04 92 81 20 09). There are three Barcelonnette–Le Martinet buses a day (€1.70) and four daily shuttle buses between Barcelonnette and Sauze. Shuttles

between Sauze (3.5km south of Barcelonnette) and Super-Sauze (5km further south) are free.

VALLÉE DU HAUT VERDON

The breathtaking **Col d'Allos** (2250m) links the Vallée de l'Ubaye with its southern neighbour, the Vallée du Haut Verdon. The mighty River Verdon has its source here at La Tête de la Sestrière (2572m).

La Foux d'Allos (elevation 1800m), immediately beyond the mountain pass (snow-blocked in winter), is an unattractive ski resort 23.5km south of Pra-Loup and connected to it by cable car. Its **tourist office** (☎ 04 92 83 02 81; www.valdallos.com) is in the Maison de la Foux on the main square. In the upper village close to the lift stations, there's an **auberge de jeunesse** (☎ 04 92 83 81 08; la-foux-allos@ fuaj.org; dm/sheet hire €8.90/2.80; ☾ reception 8-10am & 7-8pm mid-Jun–mid-Sep, 8am-7pm Dec-Apr). HI cards are obligatory but non-HI members can stay for an extra €2.90 per night in summer. The hostel overlooks Les Chauvets ski slope.

Allos (population 650, elevation 1400m), 8km further south on the D908, bears the same concrete-block stamp as its ugly sister and is just as deserted outside of the ski season, except in July and August when hotels reopen their doors to walkers.

Lac d'Allos is Europe's largest Alpine lake (62 hectares) and the valley's main draw. To get there, you'll need your own transport. Drive 12km to the end of the bumpy D226, then follow the 40-minute walking trail that leads to the lake (2226m) from the car park. Route maps and walking information are available from the **Parc National du Mercantour hut** (☎ 06 32 90 80 24) that operates from the car park in July and August.

AN ICY DETOUR

If paragliding is passé and rafting no longer floats your boat, **Aqua-Logis** (☎ 04 92 45 00 68; www .aqualogis.com; La Gravière, Ceillac; beginner €46; ☾ office 4-6pm) runs beginner's courses in ice diving during winter, when the lake is frozen. The outfit is based in Ceillac, which lies just outside the Haute-Provence region, 39km north of St-Paul-sur-l'Abaye.

Diving (15 minutes) takes place at Lac Ste-Anne (2408m), where a hole is cut through the ice; skiers gain access by the Ste-Anne lift, while non-skiers can take the Girardin chair lift, then walk or snowshoe to the lake (1½ hours).

Coral reefs and rainbow-coloured fish are out (you might see frozen trout if you're lucky); it's the miracle of a frozen underwater world that makes the dive so different.

Ski rental and ski pass (half/full day €14/17) aren't included in the price. As with regular diving, you'll need a medical certificate.

Lower in the valley, two ideal retreats are **Beauvezer** (population 287, elevation 1770m) and **Colmars-les-Alpes** (population 385, elevation 1250m). Colmars is a formidable Vauban-fortified village surrounded by high thick walls. Its Savoy fort can be visited via the little **museum** (place Joseph Girieud; adult/child under 10 €3/free; ☿ 10am-noon & 3.30-6.30pm Jul & Aug). The **tourist office** (☎ 04 92 83 41 92; colmarslesalpes@wanadoo.fr; Ancienne Auberge Fleurie; ☿ 9am-12.15pm & 2-5.45pm Mon-Sat Sep-Jun, 8am-12.30pm & 2-6.30pm Jul & Aug) has accommodation details.

Getting There & Away

In Colmars-les-Alpes, **Haut Verdon Voyages** (☎ 04 92 83 95 81) runs buses between Digne-les-Bains and La Foux d'Allos (€9.80, two hours, one daily), stopping at St-André-les-Alpes, Thorame-Haute, Colmars and Allos.

On Saturday during the ski season (usually mid-December to early April), direct shuttle buses link La Foux d'Allos with Nice and Marseille airports. You'll need to check fares and schedules, as they change every year.

You can take the mountain railway (see the boxed text, p194) from Nice to Thorame-Haute.

VALLÉE DE LA TINÉE

The **Col de Restefond la Bonette** (2802m) links Barcelonnette and the Vallée de l'Ubaye with the tamer, more southern Vallée de la Tinée. In winter, when the snowy pass is closed, the 149km-long Tinée Valley can only be accessed up its southern leg from Nice. The narrow road (D2205) wiggles along the French–Italian border to **Isola** (875m), where it plummets sharply south towards the coast.

The steep D97 makes an eastbound climb to **Isola 2000** (elevation 2000m), a purpose-built ski resort from where the **Col de la Lombarde** (2350m) crosses into Italy.

St-Étienne de Tinée (population 1684) is a lovely Alpine village 15km northwest of Isola village on the D2205. There are endless walking opportunities in summer around the Cime de la Bonette (2860m): contact the summer Maison du Parc National du Mercantour information centre (see opposite) for details. Thrill-seekers can scale new heights at the **Via Ferrata La Tradtionelle** in Auron; see the boxed text p204.

Southbound, the road twists through beautiful gorges to **St-Sauveur-sur-Tinée** (population 459, elevation 490m), gateway to the Parc National du Mercantour.

St-Sauveur to Guillaumes

From St-Sauveur-sur-Tinée, the spectacular D30 takes you 24km west to **Beuil** (population 334, elevation 1450m), from where you can access the dazzling **Gorges du Cians**, carved from burgundy-coloured rock.

Typical flora can be viewed in the **Arboretum Marcel Kroenlein** (☎ 04 93 57 38 02; fax 04 93 35 00 50; admission free) in Roure, a few hair-raising kilometres west of St-Sauveur off the D30. From the 1920s until 1961 villagers here used a 1850m-long cable to transport their milk and cheese down the mountain and their food provisions up – you can still see the cable.

Further west is **Valberg** (elevation 1700m), a ski resort that lures walkers and mountain bikers in summer. At the **Espace Valberg Aventure** (☎ 04 93 23 24 25; ☿ Jul & Aug) you can scale trees, cross rope bridges and monkey around dozens more Tarzan-inspired obstacles; routes are graded yellow (ages four to 10; €10), green (beginner; €14, 1½ hours) and blue and red (advanced; €23, three hours). The forested site can be accessed via the Croix du Sapet chairlift; a single ride with/without mountain bike costs €4.10/3.60. Valberg also has a summer luge (one/three rides €3/8).

Guillaumes (elevation 800m), 20km west again, is the starting point for forays into the **Gorges de Dalius**, which is also chiselled from the wine-coloured rock. Thrill-seekers can bungee jump with **Top Jump** (☎ 04 93 73 50 29; http://topjump.free.fr in French; €60; ☿ Sun Apr-Sep, plus Sat Jul) from Pont de la Mariée, an 80m-high stone footbridge across the gorges.

Pont de Berthéou, another bridge 8km south of Guillaumes on the D2202, is the starting point for the scenic Sentier du Point Sublime (4km, 1½ hours), a beautiful walk that takes you through oak and pine forest and past red rock formations to the 'sublime point', where there's a stunning clifftop view. Panels on the way highlight interesting flora and fauna. Guillaumes' **tourist office** (☎ 04 93 05 52 73; www.pays-de-guillaumes.com in French; place Napoléon III; ☿ 9am-noon & 2-6pm) has more information.

Information

Parc National du Mercantour runs information centres in the valley in **Valberg** (☎ 04 93 02 58 23; rue Jean Mineur), **St-Sauveur-sur-Tinée** (☎ 04 93 02 10 33; 11 av des Blavets; ☿ Jul & Aug) and **St-Étienne de Tinée** (☎ 04 93 02 42 27; fax 04 93 02 41 33; quartier de l'Ardon; ☿ Jul & Aug).

Tourist offices in **Isola 2000** (☎ 04 93 23 15 15; www.isola2000.com; Galerie Marchande) and **Valberg** (☎ 04 93 23 24 25; www.valberg.com; place du Quartier) also stock information on outdoor activities.

Sleeping & Eating

Isola 2000 has a host of unappealing concrete blocks.

Hôtel La Renaissance (☎ 04 93 05 59 89; mlltjn@aol.com; 3 place Napoléon; d from €44, menu €17; ☿ closed mid-Nov–Dec; **P**) In Guillaumes, at the northern mouth of the Gorges de Daluis, this is opposite the sheepfolds where the weekly village sheep fair takes place. It has 11 simple rooms and a restaurant.

Auberge de la Gare (☎ 04 93 02 00 67; av des Blavets, St-Sauveur-sur-Tinée; menu €14) In the village of St-Sauveur-sur-Tinée, this cheap bistro cooks filling food like your mum would make – almost. It's also where locals relax and watch the world hurry past on the D2205, a surprisingly hypnotic pastime.

Getting There & Away

Three daily buses run between Nice and Isola 2000 (€27.10, 2½ hours) from December to April, with one or two daily the rest of the year. Call ☎ 04 93 85 92 60 for information.

AUTHOR'S CHOICE

Le Valbergan (☎ 04 93 02 50 28; valbergan@aol .com; 2 av Valberg, Valberg; menus €22 & 29; ☿ closed Sun dinner & Mon) The mountain cuisine here is guaranteed to warm the cockles of your heart: specialities are *raclettes* (melted cheese over boiled potatoes, served with pickles and ham); cheese fondues; *fondues bourguignonnes* (beef cubes fried in oil); and fish or meat *pierrades* (meat grilled on a stone slab).

Better than the food, though, is the amazing panoramic view: feast your eyes and soul on the mountains as you fill your tum. It's particularly satisfying in winter, when you're curled up in the warmth.

During the ski season, buses serve Nice-Côte d'Azur airport (€27.10, two hours).

Société Broch (☎ 04 93 31 10 52) operates one daily bus year-round between Nice, Nice-Côte d'Azur airport and Valberg (€11.70, two hours).

VALLÉE DE LA VÉSUBIE

The Vésubie, a dead-end valley accessed from the south, is less wild than its northwestern neighbours, Vallées de la Tinée and du Haut Verdon, due to its proximity to Nice and the Côte d'Azur.

The hairpin-laced **Gorges de la Vésubie** weaves its way from the valley's southern foot. For a stunning aerial view of the gorge and its surroundings, head for **La Madone d'Utelle** (1181m), a pilgrimage site settled by Spanish sailors in the 9th century and crowned with a chapel (1806). From the mountain village of **St-Jean la Rivière** (on the D2565), a stone bridge crosses the River Var, from where a steep, winding mountain pass (D32) leads west to **Utelle** (population 489), 6km northeast of La Madone.

About 18km north of St-Jean along the D2565, just past the turning for **La Bollène-Vésubie** (elevation 964m), you arrive at a crossroads. Bear east along the snakelike D171 to get to **Belvédère** (population 495, elevation 820m), a hilltop village where you can learn how milk is made in the **Musée du Lait** (Milk Museum); visits are arranged by the **tourist office** (☎ 04 93 03 51 66; mairie .belvedere@smtm06.fr; 1 place Colonel Baldoni).

The valley's main outdoor-activity base is attractive **St-Martin-Vésubie** (population 1089, elevation 1000m), 13km north of Belvédère; for information on walks, see p202. For a panorama of the village, follow the steep D31 up to **Venanson** (elevation 1164m), a hamlet perched on a rock above St-Martin.

Activities

CYCLING

Colmiane Sports and Ferrata Sport (see p204) both hire mountain bikes (per day €20).

PARAGLIDING

High-fliers can paraglide in St-Dalmas-Valdeblore (elevation 1350m), 5km west of La Colmiane. The **tourist office** (☎ 04 93 23 25 90; www.colmiane.com) in La Roche, a hamlet 4km west of St-Dalmas-Valdeblore, has a list of paragliding schools.

SKIING

The small ski station of La Colmiane, 7km west of St-Martin-Vésubie across Col de St-Martin, has one chair lift. It whisks skiers and walkers up to Pic de la Colmiane (1795m), where 30km of ski slopes and several walking and mountain-bike trails can be accessed. A single-/eight-ride card costs €3.50/20 and a one-day pass is available for €9.50. The chair lift runs from 10am to 6pm daily.

VIA FERRATA

The **Via Ferrata du Baus de la Frema** (☎ 04 93 02 89 54) is 3km from La Colmiane ski station along an unpaved track. **Colmiane Sports** (☎ 04 93 02 87 00) and **Ferrata Sport** (☎ 04 93 02 80 56) both rent *via ferrata* gear (€14 for helmet, harness and karabiners).

The **Bureau des Guides** (☎/fax 04 93 02 88 30) in La Colmiane can help you around the *via ferrata* for €40. It also organises guided climbs (€35 per half-day), canyoning (€60 per day) and whitewater rafting (from €35).

For more information about *via ferrata* see the boxed text p204.

WALKING

In St-Martin-Vésubie, **Escapade Bureau des Guides** (☎ 04 93 03 31 32; place du Marché; 10.30am-12.30pm & 4.30-7.30pm Jul & Aug) leads three walks per week into the Vallée des Merveilles (€26). The **Maison du Parc** (☎ 04 93 03 23 15; mercantour.vesubie@wanadoo.fr; 8 rue Kellermann Sérurier; 9am-noon & 2.30-6.30pm Mon-Sat) runs a wealth of weekly themed walks on mushrooms (adult/10 to 17 years €5/2.50), flowers, insects, birds, mammals or birds of prey (€19/10). It also does five-day all-inclusive donkey treks (€540/489). The **tourist office** (☎ 04 93 03 21 28; www.saintmartinvesubie.fr in French; place Félix Faure) has a list of mountain guides who lead walks and ski tours. Walks are graded from easy to difficult.

A good map for walks in the area is Didier-Richard's No 9 or IGN's Série Bleue map No 3741OT *Vallée de la Vésubie, Parc National du Mercantour* (€9.50), available at bookshops and national park offices.

Sleeping & Eating

Gîte d'Étape RandoSportNature (☎ 04 93 02 82 86; http://lorenzo.garofalo.free.fr in French; St-Dalmas-Valdeblore; dm €15, breakfast €6, half-board €35) Lorenzo,

an experienced mountain guide, runs this place, five shared rooms in a little stone house. He organises mountain walks, fishing, mushrooming and mountain-bike expeditions (from €23 per person) for interested guests.

Gîte du Boréon (☎ 04 93 03 27 27; giteduboreon@free.fr; 248 rte de Salèse, Le Boréon; dm €12.50, half-board €30) This *gîte* has a lake view; you can gaze on its frozen prettiness in winter, too, if you reserve in advance. Located 5km northwest of St-Martin on the D89.

Camping La Merio (☎ 04 93 03 30 38; www.univers-nature.com/la-merio in French; 1344 rte de la Colmiane, St-Martin-Vésubie; 2 people, tent & car €14; Jun-early Sep) Beneath trees next to a river, the camp site is just 1km southwest of the village on the road to Colmiane. There are free 24-hour showers.

La Trappa (☎ 04 93 03 21 50; place du Marché, St-Martin-Vésubie; menus €18 & €22; closed Mon) In this family-run village restaurant, you can eat snails in garlic butter, game terrine, herby lamb and other 'mountain' food. It sits in a quiet square, with the sound of trickling water vaguely audible – very peaceful.

Auberge del Campo (☎ 04 93 03 13 12; menus from €24) A charming farmhouse inn run by a very humorous patron. The stone building dates from 1785 and offers sweeping views of the gorges and village from its hillside terrace. A roaring fire warms the place in winter and the menu oozes fresh local produce. Located 2km west of St-Jean la Rivière on the D32.

Getting There & Away

Two to three weekly buses are run by **Transport Régional des Alpes-Maritimes** (☎ 04 93 85 92 60) between Nice and La Colmiane (€13.50, two hours), plus one a day on weekends only to and from La Colmiane via St-Martin-Vésubie (€10.10, 1¾ hours).

VALLÉE DES MERVEILLES

One of the world's most precious collections of Bronze Age petroglyphs can be found in this 'Valley of Wonders', sandwiched between the Vésubie and Roya Valleys. There are over 36,000 rock engravings of human figures, bulls and other animals, spread over 30 sq km around Mont Bégo (2870m). They date from between 1800 and 1500 BC and are thought to have been made by a Ligurian cult.

The main access routes into the valley are the eastbound D91 from St-Dalmas de Tende in the Vallée de la Roya, or the dead-end D171, which leads north to the valley from **Roquebillière** (population 1513) in the Vallée de la Vésubie. The moonscape valley is snow-covered much of the year and the best time to visit is July to September. Access is restricted: walkers should only visit the valley with an official guide (see opposite and p204).

Maps
IGN's Série Bleue map No 3841OT *Vallée de la Roya, Vallée des Merveilles* (€9.50) covers the area in a scale of 1:25,000.

VALLÉE DE LA ROYA
The Roya Valley once served as a hunting ground for King Victor Emmanuel II of Italy and only became part of France in 1947. In this valley is the pretty **Breil-sur-Roya** (population 2023, elevation 280m), 62km northeast of Nice. There are good views from the Col de Brouis (879m), which links **Sospel** (population 2937), 21km south, with the Roya Valley.

The dramatic **Gorges de Saorge**, 9km north of Breil-sur-Roya, lead to fortified **Saorge** (population 398, elevation 520m), which overlooks the valley and is set in a natural amphitheatre. The vertiginous village is a maze of narrow, cobbled streets and 15th- to 17th-century houses. A baroque church and cloister decorated with 17th-century frescoes form part of the **Monastère de Saorge** (☎ 04 93 04 55 55; fax 04 93 04 52 37; adult/18-25 yrs €4.60/3.10; ☼ 10am-noon & 2-6pm Wed-Mon Apr-Oct, to 5pm Nov-Mar), founded in 1633.

Immediately north, the **Gorges de Bergue** lead to **St-Dalmas de Tende**, which is the main gateway into the Vallée des Merveilles. From St-Dalmas de Tende, the D91 winds 10km west along the Vallon de la Minière to **Lac des Mesches** (1390m), from where trails lead into the valley past the Refuge des Merveilles (2111m). Alternatively, continue 5km to the mountain resort of **Casterino** to pick up more northern trails.

Equally scenic is the eastbound D143 from St-Dalmas de Tende to **La Brigue** (elevation 770m) and 4km further on to **Notre Dame des Fontaines**, a fabulous church hidden at the foot of the mountain. Dubbed the Sistine Chapel of the southern Alps, it

shelters beautifully preserved frescoes by 15th-century Piedmontese painters Jean Canavesio and Jean Baleison. Contact the tourist office in La Brigue (see below) for a **guided visit** (4 per day Fri-Mon May-Sep; with/without commentary €3.20/1.50).

In **Tende** (population 1890, elevation 830m), 4km north of St-Dalmas de Tende, the **Musée des Merveilles** (☎ 04 93 04 32 50; www.museedesmerveilles.com; av du 16 Septembre 1947; adult/14-16 yrs €4.55/2.30, 1st Sun of month free; ☼ 10am-6.30pm Wed-Mon May–mid-Oct, 10am-5pm Wed-Mon mid-Oct–Feb & Apr) explains the natural history of the valley and exhibits numerous archaeological finds.

Also in Tende, the small but sweet **Maison du Miel et de l'Abeille** (House of Honey & Bees; ☎ 04 93 04 76 22; descente aux Moulins; adult/7-16 yrs €1.60/0.80; ☼ 1.30-5.30pm Mon-Fri, 9am-noon & 1.30-5.30pm Sat & Sun mid-Jun–mid-Sep) shows how the region's honey is made. Visit **La Maison du Fromage** (☎ 04 93 04 64 82; 13 av du 16 Septembre 1947, Tende) for fabulous cheese and smoked ham.

In July the valley celebrates **Les Baroquiales**, a baroque art and music festival with period markets, 17th-century restaurant menus and street entertainment. **Concerts** (☎ 04 93 04 24 41; fax 04 93 04 99 91; tickets €10-20) are held indoors and outdoors throughout the valley.

Just 5km north of Tende, the **Tunnel de Tende** – engineered in 1882 – provides a vital link into Italy.

Information
There are several small but efficient tourist offices:

Breil-sur-Roya (☎ 04 93 04 99 76; www.breil-sur-roya .fr in French; place Bianchéri)

La Brigue (☎ 04 93 04 60 04; www.labrigue-tourisme .org in French; place St-Martin)

Sospel (☎ 04 93 04 15 80; www.sospel-tourisme.com in French; Le Pont-Vieux)

Tende (☎ 04 93 04 73 71; www.tendemerveilles.com in French; av du 16 Septembre 1947)

Activities
VIA FERRATA
The Maison de la Montagne et des Sports (see p204) rents equipment for Tende's dizzying **Via Ferrata des Comtes Lascaris** (for details see the boxed text, p204) and can provide you with a guide (€46). Alternatively, contact the **Bureau des Guides** (☎ 04 93 04 77 85; www.berengeraventures.com in French; Cagnorina) in Tende.

HAUTE-PROVENCE

VIA FERRATA

During WWI Italian troops moved swiftly and safely through the Dolomites – the natural frontier between Italy and Austria – using iron-rung ladders and steel cables bolted into the rocky mountainside. Today, similar routes known as *via ferrata* (meaning 'iron way' in Italian) allow adventurous tourists to scale Alpine rock faces without knowing the first thing about rock-climbing.

Haute-Provence sports a clutch of *via ferrata* courses, rigged at dizzying heights and guaranteed to get the blood pumping. Anyone (with guts) can do it: harnessed climbers are attached to the rock by two lines. To move along the rock-face safely, climbers unclip one karabiner then attach it further along the steel cable, before unclipping and then clipping the second.

Courses range in length from 3½ hours to 5½ hours; first-timers can tackle short sections. Giddying elevations of up to 2274m are reached and *ponts Himalayen* (rope bridges with steel cables at waist height), *ponts de singe* (monkey bridges with steel cables above your head) and *tyroliennes* (zip lines, requiring climbers to pull themselves along, legs dangling) are hair-raising features of most.

Climbers need a *casque* (helmet), *mousquetons* (a harness attached to two cables with shock-absorbers and karabiners) and a sturdy pair of walking shoes. Gloves also come in handy. Everything but boots and gloves can be hired on-site for around €14. Course admission costs an additional €5. Tickets and equipment hire are generally handled by the local tourist office.

There are four *via ferrata* in the northeast of the region: **Baus de la Frema** (☎ 04 93 02 89 54; near La Colmiane, Vallée de la Vésubie); **Les Demoiselles du Castagnet** (☎ 04 93 05 05 05; Puget-Théniers); **La Traditionelle** (☎ 04 93 23 02 66; Auron, Vallée de la Tinée); and the **Circuit des Comtes Lascaris**, which is split across three sites – in La Brigue and Tende in the Vallée de la Roya, and in Peille (see p235); contact the tourist information centres in those towns for details. The Peille section is not recommended for beginners.

Those who'd rather not scale new heights alone can hook up with a local mountain guide: see p201, p202 and p203. Online, see www.viaferrata.org.

WALKING & CYCLING

Merveilles, Gravures & Découvertes (☎ 06 83 03 90 13; gravureinfo@yahoo.fr; 10 montée des Fleurs, Tende) runs daily guided archaeological walks to Mont Bégo (adult/12 to 18 years €8/4) and weekly night visits (€4 per person) in July and August.

In July and August the **Parc National du Mercantour office** (☎ 10am-1pm & 2.15-7pm Fri-Wed mid-Jun–mid-Sep), inside Sospel's old city gate, organises guided walks and distributes a map detailing 19 mountain-biking itineraries. Cycling club **Sospel VTT** (☎ 06 70 76 57 05; www.sospelvtt.net in French; Sospel) rents wheels. In Tende the **Maison de la Montagne et des Sports** (☎ /fax 04 93 04 77 73; mmstende@aol.com; 11 av du 16 Septembre 1947) hires bikes and can tell you about 23 bike trails departing from Tende, Col de Tende, La Brigue and Casterino.

WHITEWATER SPORTS

Breil-sur-Roya is *the* water-sports base. **Roya Évasion** (☎ 04 93 04 91 46; www.royaevasion .com in French; 1 rue Pasteur) organises kayaking, canyoning and rafting trips on the River Roya, as well as walks and mountain-bike expeditions. **AET Nature** (☎ 04 93 04 47 64; www .aetcanyoning.com; 392 chemin du Foussa), with a bureau on central place Bianchéri, organises similar trips. A day's canyoning costs between €45 and €65, depending on the level of difficulty.

Jeep Tours

Luc Fioretti (☎ 06 82 19 61 55; lucfioretti@9online.fr; rue Antoine Vassallo, St-Dalmas de Tende) runs one-day 4WD Jeep tours (€63 per person).

Sleeping & Eating

Hôtel Le Roya (☎ 04 93 04 48 10; fax 04 93 04 92 70; place Bianchéri; d from €42, formule gîte per person €16) Le Roya is a simple inn in Breil-sur-Roya that also offers a nifty *formule gîte* (B&B) for breakfast-keen walkers happy to share a room with a stranger. The public car park outside makes way for the market on Monday evening and Tuesday.

Le Miramonti (☎ 04 93 04 61 82; fax 04 93 04 78 71; 5-7 rue Vassalo, Tende; d from €35, menus €13.80 & €19.80) Rooms are high ceilinged and light, and the restaurant, serving Piedmontese specialities, absolutely throngs with people –

book ahead. The Miramonti also organises Jeep tours (from €61) into the Vallée des Merveilles.

Castel du Roy (☎ 04 93 04 43 66; www.castelduroy .com; rte de Tende; high season d/tr/q €70/90/110, menu €23; ☺ Apr-Oct; P ☻) Signposted off the Tende-bound N204 from Breil-sur-Roya, this place is famous for the delicious food in its traditional restaurant, the charming hotel rooms, and the five acres of green and flowery grounds. Many rooms are adapted for visitors with disabilities.

Restaurant Le Roya (☎ 04 93 04 47 38; place de Brancion; menu €23, trout €12, lunch-time formule €13; ☺ closed Sun dinner & Mon) Sitting next to the church in Breil-sur-Roya, this restaurant/ hotel serves food in a picturesque 16th-century mill. Choose your own trout and one of eight toppings to go with it.

Getting There & Away

SNCF trains run several times per day along the Nice–Turin line through the valley. Prices and times from Nice are: Sospel (€6.30, 40 minutes), Breil-sur-Roya (€6.90, one hour), St-Dalmas de Tende (€9.40, 1¼ hours) and Tende (€10.30, 1½ hours).

Buses (☎ 04 93 04 01 24) link Sospel with Menton on the coast (€4.90, 40 minutes, four to five daily).

Nice to Menton

CONTENTS

Three rollercoaster coastal roads, each higher and more hazardous than the last, link Nice and Menton (and the 30km of towns in between). They're justly celebrated for their breathtaking sea views and luxurious villas. In the 1920s motorists raced the coastal *Train Bleu* from Paris along these roads. Speed fiends today should opt for the inland A8 motorway, which continues east to Ventimiglia (Vintimille in French) in Italy.

Nice makes an ideal base for exploring the rest of the Côte d'Azur. The city is a fantastic blend of old-world opulence and modern grit, and has plenty of decently priced places to stay. The millionaires' playground of Monaco, swanky Cannes and other Riviera hot spots are only a short hop away, via excellent train and bus services.

Of course beaches are a huge attraction along this stretch of coastline, but don't let yourself become too hypnotised by the sandy strips and sparkly sea. The Niçois hinterland is a maze of remote *villages perchés* (hilltop villages) and hairpin mountain passes, a spiky contrast to the lazy littoral. Hire a car and take off into the back of beyond.

HIGHLIGHTS

- Admire the colour-saturated masterpieces of Matisse and Chagall at their **museums** (p215) in Nice

- Escape the sun-seeking hordes on a tranquil coastal stroll around Cap Martin, Cap d'Ail and St-Jean-Cap Ferrat, along the **Corniche Inférieure** (p228)

- Tour the eagle's-nest village of **Peillon** (p235), then lunch at the **Beau Séjour** (p241) in Gorbio

- Decide how you'd decorate *your* multimillion-dollar mansion, by visiting two of France's finest houses: **Villa Grecque Kérylos** (p231) and **Villa et Jardins Ephrussi de Rothschild** (p230)

- Party like a champion at Nice's **Carnival** (p219) or Menton's citron-worshipping **Lemon Festival** (p238)

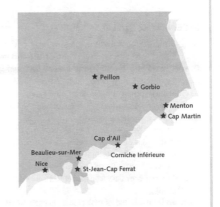
★ Peillon
★ Gorbio
★ Menton
★ Cap Martin
Cap d'Ail ★
Beaulieu-sur-Mer ★
Corniche Inférieure
Nice ★
★ St-Jean-Cap Ferrat

NICE

pop 342,738

Nice, the capital of the Côte d'Azur, is *not* 'nice': what an insult! Nice is a sparky, sexy city, with a gritty underside that keeps it grounded. If Nice were a person, it would wear designer cocktail dresses with old army boots, cause lots of trouble and be mad as hell about that insipid adjective.

Bursting with packed-out pubs, bars and clubs at night, the old town's maze of narrow lanes is just as intriguing by day. There's an old harbour and hilltop gardens to explore, and great markets to nose around in too. The city's fantastical *belle époque* architecture, Matisse, Chagall and modern-art museums and buzzing cultural scene will have artistic types in raptures. The famous Nice Carnival sets the streets ablaze each year at Mardi Gras with a merry-go-round of masked parades, 'big-head' floats and a 'battle of flowers'.

Rich English folk – Queen Victoria for one – were the first to spot Nice's potential as a seaside resort (for more on Nice's past see p22). If the hectic pace of the city gets too much, follow the Victorian example with a slow stroll along the glorious promenades, or wander over the long, pebbly beaches to dip your toes in the sparkling Baie des Anges (Bay of Angels).

Nice also makes a great base from which to explore the rest of the Côte d'Azur:

accommodation is plentiful and cheap for the region, and it's only a short hop to Monaco, Cannes and other Riviera hot spots.

ORIENTATION

Av Jean Médecin runs south from near the main train station to place Masséna, close to both the beach and old town. The modern city centre, the area north and west of place Masséna, includes the pedestrian shopping streets of rue de France and rue Masséna. The local and intercity bus terminals are three blocks east of place Masséna.

From the airport, 6km west, famous promenade des Anglais runs along the curving beachfront (the Baie des Anges), becoming quai des États-Unis near the old town. Vieux Nice (Old Nice) is crunched into a 500-sq-metre area enclosed by blvd Jean Jaurès, quai des États-Unis and the hill known as Colline du Château.

The wealthy residential neighbourhood of Cimiez, home to several outstanding museums, is north of the centre.

INFORMATION
Bookshops

Brouillon de Culture (☎ 04 93 62 28 32; 23 rue de l'Hôtel des Postes; ⏰ 9am-noon & 2.30-7pm Mon-Sat) Second-hand English reference books.

Cat's Whiskers (☎ 04 93 80 02 66; catswhiskersnice@aol .com; 30 rue Lamartine; ⏰ 9.30am-noon & 2-6pm Mon & Thu, to 7pm Tue, Wed & Fri, 10am-12.30pm & 3-7pm Sat) New and second-hand English-language novels and guides, plus Vodka the beautiful Labrador.

NICE: MARKETVILLE!

Nice is a cracking town for markets, and cours Saleya in Vieux Nice is the place to find them. From Tuesday to Sunday, the chaotic **fruit and vegetable market** (⏰ 6am-1pm) and the colourful **flower market** (⏰ 6am-5.30pm Tue-Sat, 6am-1pm Sun) sprawl down its entire length. Some of the flower stalls sell *fruits confits* (glazed or candied fruits), a speciality of the region.

Hoarders should try the large all-day **antique market** (⏰ 8am-5pm Mon), also on cours Saleya; the all-day **book market** (⏰ Sat) outside the Palais de Justice; the **collectors' market** (⏰ 8am-1pm Sun) on place Durandy, overflowing with stamps, coins and telephone cards; and the **permanent flea market** (⏰ 10am-6pm Tue-Sun) down by the port.

For the catch of the day, delve further into the old town for the **fresh fish market** (⏰ 6am-1pm Tue-Sun), on fishy fountained place St-François.

If you can tear yourself away, there are some other interesting markets in the area:

Beaulieu-sur-Mer Daily food market (place du Marche; ⏰ morning); antique market (place de Gaulle; ⏰ 3rd Sun of month)

Menton Les Halles (Indoor fresh produce market; ☎ 04 93 35 75 93; quai de Monléon; ⏰ 5am-1pm Tue-Sun); food market (Vieux Port; ⏰ Sat morning)

Villefranche-sur-Mer Art and antique market (place Amélie Pollonnais; ⏰ all day Sun)

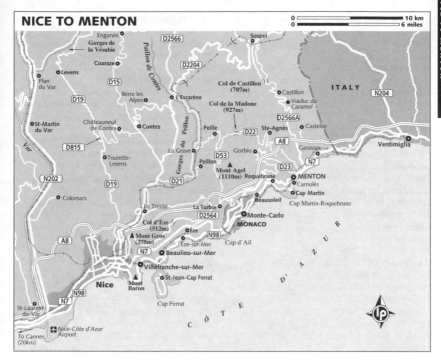

NICE TO MENTON

Magellan Librairie de Voyages (☎ 04 93 8231 81; 3 rue d'Italie; ✆ 2-7pm Mon, 9.30am-1pm & 2-7pm Tue-Sat) Excellent selection of maps and travel guides (including Lonely Planet) in English.

Cultural Centres
Holy Trinity Anglican Church (☎ 04 93 87 19 83; www.anglican-nice.com; 11 rue de la Buffa) Functions as an Anglophone cultural centre. Sunday Mass is celebrated at 11am. The adjoining cemetery contains the grave of tuberculosis-sufferer Henri Francis Lyte (1793–1847), a British vicar from Devonshire who wrote the hymn *Abide with Me*.

Emergency
Foreign Tourist Department (☎ 04 92 17 20 63; 1 av Maréchal Foch; ✆ 8am-noon & 2-6pm) At police HQ; this is where you should report lost or stolen passports.
Police Headquarters (☎ 04 92 17 22 22; 1 av Maréchal Foch; ✆ 24hr)

Internet Access
Rue Pertinax and rue Assalit, near the train station, are packed with late-opening Internet places. Many have English keyboards and all charge around €3 to €4 per hour.

@ Cyber Point (☎ 04 93 92 70 63; cybercom_nice@ yahoo.com; 10 av Félix Faure; per hr €6; ✆ 10am-8pm Mon-Sat) Opposite the bus station. English keyboards.
Panini & Web (☎ 04 93 88 72 75; 25 promenade des Anglais; ✆ 10am-9pm) By the sea. Surfing 'n' sandwich special offers, eg *panino* (Italian-style sandwich) and 30 minutes of Internet access €5.50.

Laundry
Launderette (13 rue du Pont Vieux, Vieux Nice; per 6kg wash €2.50; ✆ 7am-9pm)
Launderette (rue Alberti; per 5kg wash €3; ✆ 8am-8pm)
Taxi Lav' (22 rue Pertinax; per 5kg wash €2.80; ✆ 7am-9pm)

Libraries
Anglo-American library (12 rue de France; ✆ 10-11am & 3-5pm Tue-Thu & Sat, 3-5pm Fri) Up the passageway opposite 17 rue de France. Short-term membership available.
Bibliothèque Louis Nucéra (☎ 04 97 13 48 00; 2 place Yves Klein; ✆ 1-6pm Tue-Sat Jul & Aug, 10am-7pm Tue & Wed, 2-7pm Thu & Fri, 10am-6pm Sat Sep-Jun) Next to the Musée d'Art Moderne et d'Art Contemporain.

Medical Services
Dentist (☎ 04 93 80 77 77) Phone for emergency treatment at night/Sunday.

Hôpital St-Roch (☎ 04 92 03 33 75; 5 rue Pierre Dévoluy) Has a 24-hour emergency service.

Pharmacie Masséna (☎ /fax 04 93 87 78 94; 7 rue Masséna; ♥ 24hr)

Pharmacie Riviera (☎ 04 93 62 54 44; 66 av Jean Médecin; ♥ 24hr)

SOS Médecins (☎ 08 01 85 01 01) Phone for emergency home visits.

Money

There are plenty of banks and ATMs all over the city, including in the train station car park.

Amex (☎ 04 93 21 59 79; Gate A2, Terminal 1, Nice-Côte d'Azur Airport) The nearest Amex office to Nice.

Le Change (☎ 04 93 88 56 80; 17 av Thiers; ♥ 7.30am-8pm) Opposite the train station. Decent exchange rates.

Post

Main Post Office (23 av Thiers; ♥ 8am-7pm Mon-Fri, 8am-noon Sat) Near the train station.

Port Branch Office (8 quai Papacino; ♥ 8.30am-noon & 1.45-5.30pm Mon, Tue, Thu & Fri, 8.30-noon & 2.15-5.30pm Wed, 8.30am-noon Sat)

Vieux Nice Branch Office (2 rue Louis Gassin; ♥ 8.30am-6pm Mon, Tue, Thu & Fri, 9am-6pm Wed, 8.30am-noon Sat)

EASY RIDERS

If walking the promenade des Anglais is unthinkably hard work and skating its length seems a tad passé, hop aboard a Segway personal transporter. **City Segway Tours** (☎ 01 56 58 10 54; www.citysegwaytours .com/nice; 16 rue de la Buffa; tours €45; ♥ 10.30am Mar-Nov, 6.30pm Apr-Oct) runs three-hour jaunts on these electronic, two-wheeled gyroscopic chariots, taking you effortlessly (but very conspicuously) along the seafront and into the old town. Everyone has a 30-minute practice at mastering the controls first (movement is controlled using your balance), and safety helmets are provided. It's a fun, if slightly silly, way to see the city.

Day tours include shopping for a picnic on cours Saleya, which you eat in the lovely Parc du Château above town; or opt for an atmospheric night trip round Vieux Nice.

Groups are limited to seven people (over 12 years only), so book ahead: reservations are by telephone or Internet.

Tourist Information

All three tourist offices hand out free city maps and make free hotel reservations.

Airport Tourist Information Desk (☎ 08 92 70 74 07; ♥ 8am-10pm) In the arrivals hall of Terminal 1.

Beachfront Tourist Office (☎ 04 92 14 48 00; 5 promenade des Anglais; ♥ 8am-8pm Mon-Sat, 9am-7pm Sun mid-Jun–mid-Sep, 9am-6pm Mon-Sat mid-Sep–mid-Jun)

Main Tourist Office (☎ 04 93 87 07 07; www .nicetourisme.com; av Thiers; ♥ 8am-8pm Mon-Sat, 9am-7pm Sun) To the left as you exit the train station.

Parc National du Mercantour Headquarters (☎ 04 93 16 78 88; www.parc-mercantour.fr; 23 rue d'Italie; ♥ 9am-6pm Mon-Fri) Provides comprehensive information about the park, including the free *Les Guides RandOxygène* series, which details hiking, mountain-bike and canyoning routes.

SIGHTS
Vieux Nice

The twisting, mellow-hued rabbit warren that is Nice's old town has scarcely changed since the 1700s. At its northeastern corner lies arcade-lined **place Garibaldi**, built during the late 18th century and named after Giuseppe Garibaldi (1807–82). Born in Nice to a fishing family, Garibaldi went on to become a sailor, merchant captain, guerrilla fighter, leader of the Red Shirts, and popular hero of Italian unification; he's now buried in the Parc du Château cemetery (see p211).

The baroque **Palais Lascaris** (☎ 04 93 62 05 54; 15 rue Droite; admission free; ♥ 10am-6pm Wed-Mon) was owned by the Lascaris-Ventimiglia family in the 17th century. Its elaborately frescoed state apartments contain some fine Flemish tapestries, a collection of faïence and many gloomy religious paintings, and there's an 18th-century pharmacy on the ground floor.

The parallel **rue Bénoît Bunico** served as Nice's Jewish ghetto after a 1430 law restricted where Jews could live. It runs into rue de la Préfecture, the old city's main artery, dominated at its western end by the imposing **Palais de la Préfecture**, the 17th-century home of the princes of Savoy; and the **Palais de Justice**, the imposing law courts built in neoclassical style in 1885. Head south to reach **cours Saleya**, buzzing with bars and restaurants and splashed with colour by the flower market. Nearby, **Matisse's house**, where he lived in the 1920s, is at 1 place Charles-Félix. There's no plaque: look out for the lions.

Sweet-chiming baroque churches in Vieux Nice include **Cathédrale Ste-Réparate** (place Rossetti), honouring the city's patron saint; blue-grey and yellow **Église St-Jacques Le Majeur** (place du Gésu); and **Église St-Giaume** (1 rue de la Poissonnerie), all dating back to the mid-17th century. The slightly later **Chapelle de la Miséricorde** (cours Saleya), built between 1740 and 1780, is also worth a glance.

Parc du Château

Vieux Nice's eastern extremity is flanked by the **Parc du Château** (Castle Park; ☺ 8am-8pm Jun-Aug, to 7pm Apr, May & Sep, to 6pm Oct-Mar), a towering 92m-high rock offering a cinematic panorama of Nice and the sparkling Baie des Anges. The 12th-century castle, after which the hill and park are named, was razed by Louis XIV in 1706; only the 16th-century **Tour Bellanda**, the round tower you can see from quai des États-Unis, remains.

The park is a great place for picnics and for kids to screech about in. Its other simple attractions include **Cascade Donjon**, an 18th-century artificial waterfall crowned with a viewing platform; a couple of amusement-park rides for tots; and open-air concerts in summer. The cemetery containing **Garibaldi's grave** covers the northwestern section of the park.

To get here, ride the **lift** (ascenseur du château; rue des Ponchettes; single/return adult €0.70/1, 4-10 yrs €0.40/0.50; ☺ 9am-7.50pm Jun-Aug, 9am-6.50pm Apr, May & Sep, 10am-5.50pm Oct-Mar) from beneath Tour Bellanda (worth it to burst out onto such a devastatingly beautiful view). Alternatively, plod up the staircases on montée Lesage or the eastern end of rue Rossetti.

Promenade des Anglais

Palm-lined promenade des Anglais, paid for by Nice's English colony in 1822, is a fine stage for a stroll along the beach and the Baie des Anges. It's particularly atmospheric in the evening, with whizzing Rollerbladers and epic sunsets over the sea. Don't miss the magnificent façade of **Hôtel Negresco**, built in 1912 for the Romanian Henri Negresco, or the Art Deco **Palais de la Méditerranée**, the prized property of American millionaire Frank Jay Gould and France's top-earning casino until the 1970s, when his luck changed and the place closed

down. Completely renovated, it reopened in 2004 as a plush four-star hotel and casino.

East towards Vieux Nice, promenade des Anglais becomes **quai des États-Unis**, named after the United States in honour of President Wilson's decision in 1917 to join WWI. Changing contemporary art exhibitions are hosted by two former fish halls on the quay: **Galerie des Ponchettes** (☎ 04 93 62 31 24; 77 quai des États-Unis; admission free; ☺ 10am-6pm Tue-Sun), a 19th-century vaulted building which was also used as a public *lavoir* (wash house) in the 1840s, then as a fish market until Matisse persuaded the council to revamp it in 1950; and **Galerie de la Marine** (☎ 04 93 62 37 11; 59 quai des États-Unis; admission free; ☺ 10am-6pm Tue-Sun). At the quay's eastern end, a huge and sombre **war memorial**, hewn from the rock, commemorates the 4000 Niçois who died in both world wars.

At the southern end of av Jean Médecin, Nice's main commercial street, sits **place Masséna**, with early-19th-century, neoclassical arcaded buildings painted in shades of ochre and red. Its western end is dominated by the 19th-century **Jardin Albert 1er**. The giant arc languishing on the lawn was designed by sculptor Bernard Venet to commemorate the centenary of the appellation 'Côte d'Azur', dreamt up by French poet Stéphane Liégeard (1830–1925). **Espace Masséna**, a public square with sparkling fountains, a Rollerblading dome and ornamental gardens, straddles the eastern side of place Masséna.

NICE

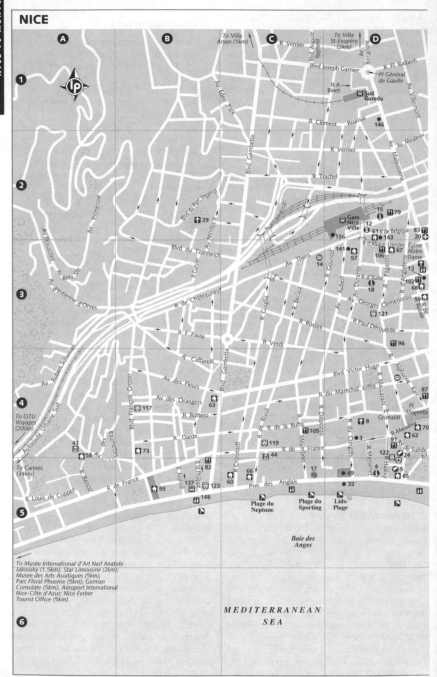

To Musée International d'Art Naïf Anatole
Jakovsky (1.5km); Star Limousine (2km);
Musée des Arts Asiatiques (5km);
Parc Floral Phoenix (5km); German
Consulate (5km); Aéroport International
Nice-Côte d'Azur; Nice Ferber
Tourist Office (5km)

MEDITERRANEAN
SEA

Baie des
Anges

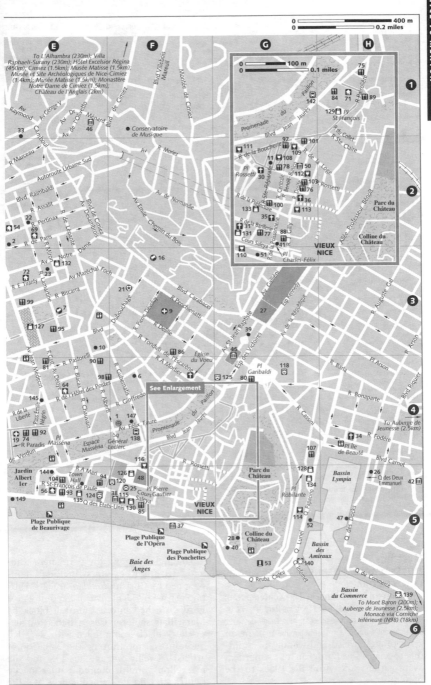

To L'Alhambra (230m); Villa
Raphaeli-Surany (230m); Hôtel Excelsior Régina
(450m); Cimiez (1.5km); Musée Matisse (1.5km);
Musée et Site Archéologiques de Nice-Cimiez
(1.4km), Musée Matisse (1.5km); Monastère
Notre Dame de Cimiez (1.5km);
Château de l'Anglais (2km)

NICE TO MENTON

Museums

MUSÉE D'ART MODERNE ET D'ART CONTEMPORAIN

The **Musée d'Art Moderne et d'Art Contemporain** (Mamac; Museum of Modern and Contemporary Art; ☎ 04 93 62 61 62; www.mamac-nice.org; promenade des Arts; adult/student €4/2.50; ☼ 10am-6pm Tue-Sun), in an appropriately weird-and-wonderful building, specialises in European and American avant-garde works from the 1960s to the present.

Highlights among the permanent 2nd- and 3rd-floor exhibits include items wrapped by Christo; *Entablature* (1971) by pop artist Roy Lichtenstein; a red model-T Ford crunched into a 1.6m-tall block by Marseillais sculptor César; Ben's tongue-in-cheek black 'room' filled with scrawled quotations, questioning the validity of art itself (well, someone has to); and the marvellous, multicoloured papier-mâché figures of Niki de Saint-Phalle – it's the second-largest collection of her work in the world. Nice-born Arman, part of the 1960s New Realism movement, also gets space for his mundane objects (rubbish, letters, children's toys) encased in Perspex containers. Born as Armand Fernandez, Arman was inspired by a printer's mistake in 1958 to drop the 'd' from his name.

At the top of the building, humpbacked wooden bridges (slippery) connect the four marble towers, crowned with a rooftop garden and gallery featuring pieces by another of the city's sons, Yves Klein (1928–62). Temporary exhibitions fill the ground and 1st floors.

Art films and cult movies are screened twice a month in the auditorium. The **Jardin Maréchal Juin**, a modernist red concrete garden, hugs Mamac's eastern side.

MUSÉE MATISSE

The **Musée Matisse** (Matisse Museum; ☎ 04 93 81 08 08; www.musee-matisse-nice.org; 164 av des Arènes de Cimiez; adult/student €4/2.50; ⊙ 10am-6pm Wed-Mon) houses a splendid assortment of works by Henri Matisse. Its permanent collection is displayed in a red-ochre 17th-century Genoese villa overlooking the olive-tree–studded **Parc des Arènes**. Temporary exhibitions are hosted in the futuristic basement building. The reception hall of the museum is dominated by a colourful, 4.1m by 8.7m paper cutout frieze entitled *Flowers and Fruits*, designed by Matisse for the inner courtyard of a Californian villa in 1953.

Well-known pieces in the permanent collection include Matisse's blue paper cutouts of *Blue Nude IV* (1952) and *Woman with Amphora* (1953).

Take bus No 15, 17 or 22 from the bus station to the Arènes/Musée Matisse stop.

MUSÉE NATIONAL MESSAGE BIBLIQUE MARC CHAGALL

The **Musée National Message Biblique Marc Chagall** (Marc Chagall Biblical Message Museum; ☎ 04 93 53 87 20; www.rmn.fr; 4 av Docteur Ménard; adult/18-25 yrs €5.50/4.40, during temporary exhibitions extra €1.20; ⊙ 10am-5.50pm Wed-Mon Jul-Sep, 10am-4.50pm Oct-Jun) houses the largest public collection of works by Belarusian painter Marc Chagall (1887–1985), known for his characteristic flying animals, flowers, violinists and kissing couples.

The exuberant swathes of colour used by Chagall to illustrate Old Testament themes are set off by the severity of this purpose-built museum. The main hall contains 12 huge interpretations (1954–67) of stories from Genesis and Exodus. In an antechamber, an unusual mosaic of Elijah in his fiery chariot, surrounded by signs of the zodiac,

MATISSE – THE ESSENTIAL ELEMENTS

Henri Matisse (1869–1954) was passionate about pure colour. His paintings epitomised the radical use of violent colour, heavy outlines and simplified forms characteristic of Fauvism.

Matisse was a latecomer compared to contemporaries such as Picasso, only becoming interested in painting at the age of 20, when he was bedridden for months with appendicitis. He studied art for many years under the symbolist painter Gustave Moreau. While visiting Brittany he met Australian artist John Russell, who introduced him to the works of van Gogh, Monet and other impressionists, prompting Matisse's change from a sombre palette to brighter colours.

By the early 1900s Matisse was well known in Paris but was still struggling financially. His stint as an impoverished artist ended at the first Fauvist exhibition (1905), called this by a staggered art world who deemed it to be the work of *fauves* (wild animals). The ensuing explosion of controversy, repulsion and adoration fired Matisse to stardom. By 1913 he had paintings on display in London and New York.

In the 1920s Matisse moved to Nice but continued to travel widely. During these years he painted prolifically but was less radical; his work's characteristic sensuality and optimism, however, were always present. The 1930s saw him return to more experimental techniques and a renewed search for simplicity, in which the subject matter was reduced to essential elements. His Tahitian drawings date from this decade.

In 1948 he began working on a set of stained-glass windows for the astonishing Chapelle du Rosaire in Vence (see p265). Matisse died and was buried in Nice, in the cemetery of the Monastère Notre Dame de Cimiez (p217) in 1954.

FREE MUSEUM BUS

You're allowed to travel free on bus No 15 between the Matisse, Chagall and Archaeology Museums. Ask the ticket desks at each museum to supply you with a bus ticket.

is viewed through a plate-glass window and reflected in a small pond. Five paintings (1960s) based on the *Song of Songs* form the most startling series, an explosion of passionate red (in contrast to the sea greens, deep purples and blues of the main room) dedicated to his wife Vava.

Take bus No 15 to the Musée Chagall stop, or walk (signposted from av de l'Olivetto).

MUSÉE ARCHÉOLOGIQUE DE NICE-CIMIEZ

The ruins of the ancient Roman city of Cemenelum lie on the eastern side of the Parc des Arènes. Discover its rocky history in the **Musée Archéologique de Nice-Cimiez** (Archaeology Museum; ☎ 04 93 81 59 57; 160 av des Arènes de Cimiez; adult/student €4/2.50; ☼ 10am-6pm Wed-Mon). Both the public baths and amphitheatre – the venue for outdoor concerts during the Nice Jazz festival (p219) – can be visited.

Bus Nos 15, 17 and 22 go from the bus station to the Arènes stop.

MUSÉE INTERNATIONAL D'ART NAÏF ANATOLE JAKOVSKY

Over 1000 works of naive art from all over the world are gathered at the **Musée International d'Art Naïf Anatole Jakovsky** (Anatole Jakovsky International Naive Art Museum; ☎ 04 93 71 78 33; av de Fabron; admission €4; ☼ 10am-6pm Wed-Mon), housed in the 19th-century Château Ste-Hélène, 2km west of the city centre. The mansion was built by François Blanc, who founded the casino in Monte Carlo, and later served as the country home of a perfume manufacturer.

Romanian art critic Anatole Jakovsky (1909–83), who moved to southern France in 1932, kick-started the museum by donating his vast collection. Pieces date from the 18th century to the present day.

To get to the museum, take bus No 8, 10, 11 or 12 from the local bus station to the Fabron stop, from where it's a 500m walk, or take bus No 34 to the Musée Art Naïf stop.

MUSÉE DES ARTS ASIATIQUES

A striking white-marble building designed by Japanese architect Kenzo Tange houses Nice's **Musée des Arts Asiatiques** (Museum of Asian Arts; ☎ 04 92 29 37 00; www.arts-asiatiques.com in French; 405 promenade des Anglais; adult/student €6/4, 1st Sun of month free; ☼ 10am-6pm Wed-Mon May–mid-Oct, 10am-5pm Wed-Mon mid-Oct–Apr). It showcases ornamental treasures from Cambodia, China, India and Japan. The museum is in Nice's spacious **Parc Floral Phoenix**, near the airport; take bus No 9 or 10 from the bus station, or No 23 from the train station.

MUSÉE DES BEAUX-ARTS

This **fine arts museum** (☎ 04 92 15 28 28; www.musee-beaux-arts-nice.org; 33 av des Baumettes; adult/student €4/2.50; ☼ 10am-6pm Tue-Sun) is housed in a fantastic cream-and-apricot villa built in 1878 for the Ukrainian princess Elisabeth Vassilievna Kotschoubey. Its decorative stucco friezes and six-column rear terrace overlooking luxuriant gardens are typical of houses dating from Nice's *belle époque*.

The collection is a mishmash of absolute gems, like Jan Brueghel's *Allegory of Water* and *Allegory of Earth,* and yawnsome 18th-century portraits. Fauvist appreciators will relish a roomful of Raoul Dufy's works. Also impressive are sculptures by Rodin, and some late impressionist pieces by Bonnard, Monet and Sisley. Local lads Jules Chéret (1836–1932), the 'Father of the Poster', and Alexis Mossa (1844–1926), who painted truly hideous symbolist works, also feature. The latter is more famous for adding wildly decorated floats to the Nice Carnival than for his watercolours.

There are English **guided tours** (adult/child €3/1.50; ☼ 3pm Fri).

From the bus station, take bus No 38 to the Musée Chéret stop outside.

MUSÉE DE PALÉONTOLOGIE HUMAINE DE TERRA AMATA

East of the port, this **museum** (☎ 04 93 55 59 93; 25 blvd Carnot; adult/student €4/2.50; ☼ 10am-6pm Tue-Sun) displays objects from a site inhabited 400,000 years ago by the predecessors of *Homo sapiens.* Bus No 32 links the local bus station and the museum; alight at the Carnot stop.

MUSÉE D'ART ET D'HISTOIRE

Also called **Musée Masséna** (☎ 04 93 88 11 34; 65 rue de France), this museum is closed for renovation until 2007. If you're in the area, cast your eyes at the **Palais Masséna**, the building in which the museum is based – it's a marvellous Italianate neoclassical villa dating from 1898.

Cathédrale Orthodoxe Russe St-Nicolas

The **Cathédrale Orthodoxe Russe St-Nicolas** (Russian Orthodox Cathedral of St Nicolas; ☎ 04 93 96 88 02; av Nicolas II; ☺ 9am-noon & 2.30-6pm, closed Sun morning), consecrated in 1912, is crowned by multicoloured onion domes and is the biggest Russian Orthodox Church outside Russia. Step inside and let the icons and frescoes transport you to 17th-century Moscow. Shorts, miniskirts and sleeveless shirts are forbidden.

Monastère Notre Dame de Cimiez

Matisse is buried in the cemetery of the **Monastère Notre Dame de Cimiez** (☎ 04 93 81 00 04; ☺ 8.30am-12.30pm & 2.30-6.30pm). The artist's grave is signposted 'sépulture Henri Matisse' from the cemetery's main entrance (next to the monastery church on av Bellanda). Raoul Dufy (1877–1953), who spent many years in Nice, is also buried here.

The monastery houses a small **museum** (admission free; ☺ 10am-noon & 3-6pm Mon-Sat) illustrating the everyday lives and activities of its Franciscan monks. The adjoining **Église Notre Dame** (admission free; ☺ 9am-6pm) holds pieces of precious medieval art by Louis Bréa, and a monumental 17th-century baroque altar, carved in wood and decorated with gold leaf. Surrounding the buildings is

---

SMITH'S FOLLY

From Nice ferry port, glance up at Mont Boron, home to celebrities such as Elton John. The pink confection you can see is **Château de l'Anglais**, built in 1859 for an English engineer called Robert Smith, renowned at the time as being the only foreigner to live in Nice year-round. Locals quickly dubbed his castle – now protected as a historical monument – Smith's folly. It has since been split into private apartments.

Jardin du Monastère, filled with cypress trees and an abundance of sweet-smelling roses, and offering a sweeping panorama of the Baie des Anges. The Nuits Musicales de Nice (p219) are held in the cloisters in July and August.

Take bus No 15, 17 or 22 from the bus station to the Arènes stop.

Villa Arson

Sensational temporary photographic and contemporary art exhibitions are displayed at the **Centre National d'Art Contemporain** (☎ 04 92 07 73 73; www.cnap-villa-arson.fr; 20 av Stéphane Liégeard; admission free; ☺ 2-7pm Wed-Mon Jul-Sep & 2-6pm Wed-Mon Oct-Jun), inside the 18th-century **Villa Arson**, about 1km north of the town centre.

Take bus No 36 to the Villa Arson stop, or bus No 4, 7 or 26 to the Fanny stop on blvd de Cessole.

A CIMIEZ DETOUR

Belle époque Nice was ab fab. The wedding-cake mansions, palaces and pastel-painted concrete gateaux that sprang up in abundance were utterly fantastical. For a break from the crowded beaches, museums and old town, take a detour to the Cimiez quarter. Cimiez, 2.5km northeast of the train station, is Nice's wealthy residential district and the place where the cream of these lavish mansions can be found.

From the town centre, follow av Jean Médecin north, passing under the train tracks, then turning right onto av Mirabeau. The Musée National Message Biblique Marc Chagall is signposted at the end of the street; follow the signs just past the museum, to blvd de Cimiez. Just across this road is the Haussmann-style **Conservatoire de Musique** (8 blvd de Cimiez), dating from 1902. At No 46 is **L'Alhambra** (1901), an opulent private mansion set on a small, palm-tree–studded mound and surrounded by a high wall, though not high enough to hide the Moorish minarets that rise from the sparkling white building. **Villa Raphaeli-Surany** (1900), opposite at No 35, is adorned with intricate mosaic reliefs. The boulevard's crowning jewel is **Hôtel Excelsior Régina** (71 av Régina), built in 1896 to welcome Queen Victoria to Nice (a statue of the queen stands in front). Henri Matisse later lived here. This titanic building houses private apartments and a handful of medical practices today.

ACTIVITIES

For outdoor information, contact the Parc National du Mercantour headquarters (p210), or the **Club Alpin Français des Alpes-Maritimes** (☎ 04 93 62 59 99; www.cafnice.org in French; 14 av Mirabeau; ☒ 4-8pm Mon-Fri).

Beaches & Boats

If you don't like the feel of sand between your toes, Nice's beaches – covered with smooth, round pebbles – are for you. Free public sections of beach alternate with 15 private beaches (open April to October) that cost upwards of €11 per day to use. **Lido Plage** (☎ 04 93 87 18 25; lidoplage@wanadoo .fr), opposite the Palais de la Méditerranée, hosts romantic candlelit dinners, discos and salsa evenings on the beach. **Plage Publique des Ponchettes**, opposite Vieux Nice, gets the most packed with oiled bodies laid out to bake.

From June to mid-September all manner of watery thrills are on offer from the public sections of Lido Plage, **Plage du Neptune** (opposite Hôtel Negresco) and **Plage du Sporting** (opposite 25 promenade des Anglais). Take to the air with a parachute strung to the back of a motorboat (one/two people €40/55), be dragged at speed in a *bouée* (rubber ring; €20), water-ski (€25) or have a blast on a jet ski (€35).

Trans Côte d'Azur (☎ 04 92 00 42 30; www .trans-cote-azur.com; quai Lunel) runs one-hour boat trips along the coast, departing from the port at 3pm daily June to September (Tuesday, Wednesday, Friday and Sunday October to May). Tickets cost €11/6 for adults/four to 10 years. It also runs excursions several times a week (mid-June to mid-September) to Île Ste-Marguerite (€23/16), St-Tropez (€43/26), Monaco (€20/15) and San Remo (€35/20) in Italy. Reservations are vital.

Diving & Snorkelling

The **3B Plongée** (☎ 04 93 26 09 03; phplus@wanadoo .fr; 3 quai des Deux Emmanuel) diving shop sells equipment and offers diving advice. Portside dive companies **Le Poseidon** (☎ 06 11 80 81 81; www.poseidon-nice.com; quai Lunel) and **Nice Diving** (☎ 04 93 89 42 44; www.nicediving.com; 14 quai des Docks) organise courses, expeditions and equipment rental (around €40/35 for a baptism/night dive and €290 for a sevendive course) from April to October.

Rollerblading

Skaters speed along the smooth, long promenade des Anglais. Hire blades from **Roller Station** (☎ 04 93 62 99 05; 49 quai des États Unis) for €5 per day, or a skateboard or *trottinette* (microscooter) for €3/6/9 per hour/five hours/day. Nicea Location Rent (p227) also rents *rollers* (Rollerblades) and *trottinettes*. Bring some ID for a deposit.

Local blading association **Nice Roller Attitude** (☎ 06 09 07 57 19; www.nice-roller-attitude .com) runs mass skates around town, departing from outside the Hôtel Beau Rivage (p221) at 9pm, usually on the last Friday of the month (but check first, because it does vary).

NICE FOR CHILDREN

Nice is a fascinating city, but it doesn't have many attractions aimed specifically at kids. Its museums are grown-up affairs; the Musée d'Art Moderne et d'Art Contemporain (p214) is probably the most childfriendly. Kids can let off steam by skittering up and down promenade des Anglais on Rollerblades, scooters or skateboards (see above). Leg-weary littl'uns might appreciate a toot-tooting trip on one of the tourist trains (see below). Older children (over 12) will love the novelty of the Segway (see the boxed text, p210), although the longish tour time might fray tempers. The Parc du Château (p211) is good for a relaxed picnic, with lots of running-about room and a playground. If you're here in February or March, the Nice Carnival (see opposite) is an extravaganza you shouldn't miss.

You might be better off making a bargain: a day of Nice museums for you, then a day trip to Monaco (p319), which is one giant playground!

To locate a babysitter (same word in French), call **Allo Mary Poppins** (☎ 04 93 53 07 37). Minimum babysitting time is three hours.

TOURS

Whip through Vieux Nice on one of the **Trains Touristiques** (☎ 06 16 39 53 51; www.petit trainnice.com; adult/under 9 yrs €6/3; ☒ closed mid-Nov–Jan & when raining). The 40-minute round trip takes in the flower market, old town and parc du Château, leaving every 30 minutes from 10am from promenade des Anglais, opposite Jardin Albert 1er.

For a more leisurely and further-ranging journey, try the open-topped buses of **Le Grand Tour** (☎ 04 92 29 17 00; one-day pass adult/student/senior/child €17/13/13/9), which go round the port, up to Cimiez, and along promenade des Anglais. Hop on and off at any one of 12 stops: the most central is on promenade des Anglais, near the Trains Touristiques. Passes are available from the tourist offices, or on the bus.

Trans Côte d'Azur (see opposite) runs boat trips around the Baie des Anges.

FESTIVALS & EVENTS

The celebrated two-week **Carnaval de Nice** (Nice Carnival; www.nicecarnaval.com) has been held each year around Mardi Gras (Shrove Tuesday) since 1294, and today attracts around 1.2 million spectators! Highlights include the *batailles de fleurs* (battles of flowers), when hundreds upon thousands of fresh blossoms are tossed into the crowds from passing flower-parade floats; and the ceremonial burning of the carnival king on promenade des Anglais, followed by an enormous fireworks display, at the end of the festivities.

The week-long **Nice Jazz Festival** (www.nicejazzfest.com) jives in July, its main venue being the olive grove behind the Musée Matisse (p215) in Cimiez. Equally atmospheric is the two-day **Fête au Château**, an outdoor music festival held in Parc du Château in mid-June. During the **Festival de Musique Sacrée** (Festival of Sacred Music), Russian sacred chants meet Mozart's *Requiem* for two weeks in late June. During the three-week **Les Nuits Musicales de Nice** in mid-July/early August, classical-musical concerts are held in the cloisters of Monastère Notre Dame de Cimiez (p217) and in the gardens around the Musée d'Art Moderne et d'Art Contemporain (p214).

SLEEPING

Nice has a surfeit of reasonably priced places to stay: most one- and two-star places are clustered around the station (on rue d'Angleterre, rue d'Alsace-Lorraine, rue de Suisse, rue de Russie and av Durante) and dotted throughout the modern centre. Only the very best hotels in Nice have sea views. Accommodation can be hard to find in July and August when most places brandish *complet* (full) signs by 10am.

Budget

Le Petit Louvre (☎ 04 93 80 15 54; www.hotelgoodprice.com; 10 rue Emma Tiranty; s €35-38, d €41-46, tr €54; ☼ Feb-Oct) Midway between the sea and the train station is a colourful backpacker favourite run by humorous sax-player M Vila. It's packed with personality and contains an eclectic collection of home-made paintings sure to make you smile. There's cereal and fruit for breakfast as well as the usual baguette, croissant and coffee. All rooms have washbasins, more expensive ones have showers, too.

Hôtel Belle Meunière (☎ 04 93 88 66 15; fax 04 93 82 51 76; 21 av Durante; dm with/without shower €20/15, d with shower & toilet €49.50; ☼ reception 7.30am-midnight Feb–mid-Nov) A bustling, comfortable place a minute's walk from the train station, with a tree-studded garden that's great for meeting people. Get a key code if you're staying out after midnight. Prices include breakfast.

Also recommended:

Backpacker's Chez Patrick (☎ 04 93 80 30 72; www.chezpatrick.com; 1st fl, 32 rue Pertinax; dm/d €21/45) Central, run by the cheery Patrick. Dorms are 3-, 4- or 5-person.

Auberge de Jeunesse (☎ 04 93 89 23 64; fax 04 92 04 03 10; rte Forestière du Mont Alban; dm incl breakfast €14.40; ☼ reception 7am-noon & 5pm-midnight Jan-Oct) About 5km east of the train station, with stunning views of downtown Nice. Rooms locked from 10am to 5pm, midnight curfew. Catch bus No 14 from the bus station to L'Auberge stop; beware – the last one leaves at 8.20pm!

AUTHOR'S CHOICE

Villa St-Exupéry (☎ 04 93 84 42 83; www.villasaintexupery.com; 22 av Gravier; dm €22, s €28-35, d €48; ☼ Jul-Sep; P ▯) Readers have raved about this 60-room summer hostel, and no wonder. Totally renovated, rooms are clean and fresh, almost all have en suite showers, and some have balconies with marvellous views over Nice. It attracts a lively set of backpackers from all over the world, and has a slew of fine facilities: free Internet access, laundry room (€5), fully equipped kitchen...and none of those cursed French curfews. Rates include breakfast.

At 2.5km north of the train station it might seem a tad remote, but the super-friendly staff may be able to pick you up if you warn them in advance, and there's a good bus service (No 21 to town, No 23 to the station, night bus No N3).

Mid-Range

TRAIN STATION

Hôtel Plaisance (☎ 04 93 85 11 90; hotelplaisance@ wanadoo.fr; 20 rue de Paris; s/d €56/71; ✕) A pleasing two-star pile with 34 soundproofed rooms and a relaxed feel.

Hôtel Normandie (☎ 04 93 88 48 83; www.hotel normandie.cote.azur.fr; 18 rue Paganini; s/d/tr/q from €60/72/82/92; P ✕) This welcoming place has been entirely renovated. Cool, clean rooms all have baths or showers, and the TVs receive CNN.

Hôtel du Midi (☎ 04 93 88 36 72; www.atlashotels .fr; 16 rue d'Alsace-Lorraine; s/d/tr/q €80/95/110/125; ✕) On the same street as the Normandie is the more upmarket, three-star Midi, which has also been tarted up recently. Its tasteful tiled rooms are wonderfully cool in summer.

CITY CENTRE & BEACH

Hôtel Notre Dame (☎ 04 93 88 70 44; www.nicenotre dame.com; 22 rue de Russie; s/d/tr/q €39/42/54/67) This glimmering, modern place, named after its location near Église Notre Dame, is under new management. The English owner is a real sweetie, and rooms are spacious with private toilets and showers. It's under 10 minutes' walk from the train station.

Hôtel Regence (☎ 04 93 87 75 08; www.hotelregence .com; 21 rue Masséna; d €65-78; ✕) Cool, civilised and close to the sea, this well-situated hotel is on a pedestrianised street near the promenade des Anglais and Jardin Albert 1er.

Hôtel Félix (☎ 04 93 88 67 73; www.hotel-felix .com; 41 rue Masséna; d €50-75; ✕ 💻) This has considerable appeal, with its breakfast terrace and brightly coloured, soundproofed rooms. Some have balconies overlooking pedestrianised rue Masséna.

Hôtel Cronstadt (☎ 04 93 82 00 30; www.hotelcron stadt.com; 3 rue Cronstadt; s/d/tr from €67.50/85/117.50) The Cronstadt is hidden inside the Palais Adly: enter the building, cross the ravishing Arabian Nights courtyard garden, press the buzzer at the far end, and *don't* be put off by the eccentric and unhelpful owner. Rooms are quiet and graceful, all with garden views, and it's the closest two-star to the sea.

Hôtel Lafayette (☎ 04 93 85 17 84; www.nouvel -hotel.com/lafayette; 32 rue de l'Hôtel des Postes; s/d from €84/90; ✕) It advertises itself as 'small and friendly', and it isn't wrong: staff are so chirpy, you expect them to sprout wings and flap and flap tweeting. Décor is soulless, but

families of four can squeeze into one of their larger doubles (€140), and there's free luggage store.

Résidence Hôtelière Astoria (☎ 04 95 15 25 45; www.residenceastoria.com; 6 blvd François Grosso; mini/ standard/large studio per week €280/420/450; ✕ reception 8.30am-7.30pm; ✕) These nifty two-person studios, near the sea 1.5km from Vieux Nice, contain bathrooms (with shower), fridges and hotplates. Outside July and August it's possible to hire them per month for around half price. The Astoria also has a pretty garden where guests can breakfast. A lift is to be installed in 2005, allowing disabled access. Free cots.

Hôtel Clémenceau (☎ 04 93 88 61 19; fax 04 93 16 88 96; 3 av Georges Clémenceau; s €38-43, d €46-58, tr €65, q €80) This hotel has old-fashioned, chintzy rooms and unsmiling staff, but many of the rooms here have access to little kitchens (€10), which are a boon if you want to self-cater. It's also handily placed in the shopping district, about 10 minutes from the beach.

Hôtel Carlone (☎ /fax 04 93 44 71 61; 2 blvd François Grosso; s/d/tr/q from €50/60/75/90; P) A stone's throw from the sea and the Musée des Beaux-Arts, with light, airy rooms, and private parking for an extra €7 per night.

VIEUX NICE

Hôtel Villa la Tour (☎ 04 93 80 08 15; www.villa-la -tour.com; 4 rue de la Tour; s €49-120, d €52-125; ✕) The only hotel in Vieux Nice was set up by a former manager at the Hôtel Negresco, so good service and charm are a given. The well-equipped rooms (some with balconies) are individually decorated with contemporary flair, there's a cute little roof patio, but best of all, you're just a stumble from the bars and *socca* (pancake) joints of the old town.

Top End

Many of the upmarket hotels have private beaches so you can bask away from the riffraff.

Hôtel Negresco (☎ 04 93 16 64 00; www.hotel -negresco-nice.com; 37 promenade des Anglais; d with courtyard/garden & sea views from €220/310; P ✕) A classified historical monument, with each room decorated in styles ranging from Louis XIII to Art Deco. Owner Jeanne Augier has turned it into a semimuseum, with Van Loo paintings, Aubusson carpets and crystal chandeliers furnishing the lavish *belle époque* interior. Only the doormen, forced to wear feathered caps, don't look impressed.

Hôtel Le Méridien (☎ 04 97 03 44 44; www.le meridien-nice.com; 1 promenade des Anglais; d from €240; P ⊠ ⚃ ⚔) This four-star hotel has a rooftop pool, health club and casino.

Hôtel Beau Rivage (☎ 04 92 47 82 82; www.nice beaurivage.com; 24 rue St-François de Paule; d from €210; P ⚃) Matisse (1916) and Russian playwright Anton Chekhov (1891) both stayed here. Completely overhauled in 2004, this place is full of sleek, sharp lines, hickorywood and chrome furnishings, and has plasma TVs.

Four Points Elysée Palace (☎ 04 93 97 90 90; reservation@elyseepalace.com; 59 promenade des Anglais; d from €230; P ⊠ ⚃ ⚔) The building's concrete rear is adorned with giant statues of Venus baring a breast to passers-by. Pure Art Deco style, capped by a rooftop pool.

Hôtel Hi (☎ 04 97 07 26 26; www.hotel-hi-nice .cote.azur.fr; 3 av des Fleurs; r €175-500; ⊠ ⚃ ▫ ⚔) Step inside this hi-tech Philippe Starck–designed place and you could be forgiven for thinking you've somehow boarded an ultrastylish, candy-coloured, interstellar spaceship. Striking rooms contain bright panels of colour, modern entertainment systems and glam guests like fashion designer Jean Paul Gaultier or rock stars REM. The building is topped by a modish rooftop plunge pool.

EATING
Restaurants
TRAIN STATION
There are lots of cheap eats, particularly at the Vietnamese and Chinese restaurants clustered on rue Paganini, rue d'Italie and rue d'Alsace-Lorraine.

Voyageur Nissart (☎ 04 93 82 19 60; 19 rue d'Alsace-Lorraine; menus €11.50, €15 & €19; ☻ closed Mon) No frills, just good solid portions of traditional food, served speedily and with a smile. The menu's translated into three languages, but the clientele are mostly locals who are onto a good thing.

Restaurant au Soleil (☎ 04 93 88 77 74; 9 rue d'Italie; menu €12, plat du jour €8; ☻ closed Sat Nov & Dec) Run by a friendly husband-and-wife team since 1960, this place serves local cuisine, including an all-day omelette breakfast for €5.50. Its hearty menu includes a 25cL *pichet* (jug) of wine.

CITY CENTRE & BEACH
Pedestrianised rue Masséna and its nearby streets and squares, including rue de France and place Magenta, are crammed with touristy cafés and restaurants. Most don't offer particularly good value, but there are exceptions.

La Cantine de Lulu (☎ 04 93 62 15 33; 26 rue Alberti; starters/mains around €9/14; ☻ closed Mon dinner, Sat & Sun & Aug) Dishes up local specialities and all the great classics such as *escalope de veau à la crème* (veal escalope in a cream sauce) A huge aïoli is served up on the first Friday of the month. Its small seating area gets packed: turn up early.

Grand Café de Turin (☎ 04 93 62 29 52; 5 place Garibaldi; full meal around €25) With an authentic 1900 interior, this is one of Nice's most traditional seafood spots. Shellfish, including sea urchins in season, are prepared beneath the arches on the pavement terrace.

Les Viviers (☎ 04 93 16 00 48; 22 rue Alphonse Karr; lunch/dinner menu from €18/25; ☻ closed Sun & Aug) A temple to seafood, with a magnificent choice of oysters, urchins and other shellfish, all consumed to the sweet tinkle of a piano. Diners seeking a less rarefied atmosphere should try the Viviers bistro next door.

La Maison de Marie (☎ 04 93 82 15 93; 5 rue Masséna; mains around €20) A distinctive feature here is the beautiful flowery pergola arching over the terrace. Settle under the leaves and sample local specialities on the *menu Niçois* (€18).

Texas City (☎ 04 93 16 25 75; 10 rue Dalpozzo; salads €9.50, mains €12-20; ☻ closed mid-Jan) A slice of the purest Americana run by friendly owner Frank. Just the ticket for homesick Texans, or for anyone wanting filling US and Tex-Mex food. Fajitas, enchiladas and chilli mix company with T-bone steaks, burgers and chocolate brownies. Keep your eye on the buffalo: he looks as though he likes guacamole.

Boccaccio (☎ 04 93 87 71 76; 7 rue Masséna; seafood platters €31-92) Flanked by over-the-top golden angels blasting on trumpets, this place wins first prize for 'most dramatic entrance'. The specialities here are seafood platters, fish dishes and Spanish-influenced meals. Six oysters/seafood paella/bouillabaisse swim in at €12/25/50.

Le Speakeasy (☎ 04 93 85 59 50; 7 rue Lamartine; menus €12-14; ☻ noon-2.15pm Mon-Sat, 7-9.15pm Thu & Fri) A teeny slice of veggie heaven, serving unusual organic meals and juices. Takeaways are also available.

Le Comptoir (☎ 04 93 92 08 80; 20 rue St-François de Paule; lunch/dinner menu €18/32; ✆ closed Sat & Sun lunch) This smart place has an Art Deco–style terrace, close to the beach, serving Italian and French cuisine, and an adjoining nightclub.

La Cigale Orientale (☎ 04 93 88 60 20; 7 av de Suède; full meal around €25; ✆ 9.30am-midnight) Refresh your tastebuds with Lebanese, Greek and Asian cuisine, served up in a trendy interior. Dining reservations are essential, particularly on Friday and Saturday evenings when they let out the belly dancers. You can also stock up on stuffed vine leaves, falafel and hummus to munch on the move: vegetarians will welcome the choices.

Indyana (☎ 04 93 80 67 69; 11 rue Gustave Deloye; mains €30-60) The first rule of Indyana: reserve. Dressy customers nibble on minimalist Asian and world-cuisine preparations here.

Terres de Truffes (☎ 04 93 62 07 68; 11 rue St-François de Paule; mains from €29; ✆ closed Sun) This top-notch deli-bistro, set up by acclaimed chef Bruno, serves the region's famous fungi in all its forms – right down to truffle caramel with apple pie!

Chantecler (☎ 04 93 16 64 00; 37 promenade des Anglais; lunch/dinner menus €45/90; ✆ closed Jan) Inside Hôtel Négresco, Chantecler has lost one of its two Michelin stars (down the back of a Regency sofa?), but is still a mind-blowing extravaganza of impeccably served French cuisine. Vegetarians get their own evening *menu* (€85).

VIEUX NICE

Vieux Nice's narrow streets are crammed with restaurants, cafés and pizzerias. In

---

summer, dozens of outdoor eating and drinking places on cours Saleya, place Pierre Gautier and place Rossetti stay buzzing until well past midnight.

Lou Pilha Leva (place Centrale; dishes from €2) This *socca* spot heaves with merrily munching families and couples. Buy your food at the counter before sitting down: waiters only serve drinks.

L'Escalinada (☎ 04 93 62 11 71; 22 rue Pairolière; menu €20; ✆ closed mid-Nov–mid-Dec) With its smiling staff and candlelit terrace, this enchanting little place is usually jammed with diners. Fare is meaty with a capital M: specialities include *secca d'Entrevaux* (dried beef; €13) and *testicules de mouton panés* (sheep testicles in batter; €12.50).

Delhi Belhi (☎ 04 93 92 51 87; 22 rue de la Barillerie; menu €21.50; ✆ dinner Mon-Sat) The world's most grossly named restaurant thankfully provides first-rate Indian food! Atmospheric, and very welcome if you've overdosed on Niçois cuisine. It's a small place, so book ahead.

L'Atelier (☎ 04 93 53 44 94; 5 rue de la Barillerie; mains around €18; ✆ 7-11.30pm Tue-Sun) This select restaurant has a split-level dining room, with mezzanine floor perched above the bar. Dishes flirt with Italian, Tunisian and Moroccan influences: from mild *linguine aux écrivisses* (crayfish pasta) to spicy *lamb à l'harissa*.

Restaurant du Gésu (☎ 04 93 62 26 46; 1 place du Gésu; pizzas from €7.50; ✆ closed Sun) Decorated with football pennants, and with a terrace in front of Église du Gésu St-Jacques le Majeur, this lively place prepares tasty pizzas and pasta.

Nissa Socca (☎ 04 93 80 18 35; 5 rue Ste-Réparate; menus €12.50/14/15; ✆ closed Sun & lunch Mon) Probably Nice's cheapest eating place. Don't expect miracles, just low-priced traditional grub. A (jokey?) sign asks children to scream and cry outside…make of that what you will.

PORT AREA

Zucca Magica (☎ 04 93 56 25 27; 4bis quai Papacino; lunch/dinner menu €15/22; ✆ closed Sun & Mon) Bursting with vegetarian surprises and guaranteed to thrill. Italian chef Marco Folicardi moved from Rome to Nice to open his much-vaunted egg, cheese and vegetable restaurant…lucky, lucky Nice and poor old Rome! Weekend reservations are essential.

NIÇOIS NIBBLES

Local specialities, especially common in Vieux Nice, include:

Beignets d'aubergines/de courgettes Slices of aubergine/zucchini fried in batter.

Farcis Stuffed vegetables (especially zucchini flowers).

Pissaladière Anchovy, onion and black olive pizza.

Socca Griddle-fried pancake made from chickpea flour and olive oil, served with pepper.

Salade Niçoise Ingredients vary slightly: usually green salad with boiled egg, tuna and anchovy.

Cafés & Quick Eats

Terrace cafés and bars just made for beer quaffing and cocktail sipping abound on cours Saleya.

Le Pain Quotidien (☎ 04 93 62 94 32; 1 rue St-François de Paule; breakfast €7.50, brunch €19.50; ☾ 7am-7pm) Startlingly good organic breakfasts and creamy hot chocolate. For a lazy start to the weekend, take a leisurely brunch (Saturday and Sunday only) alongside the fragrant flower market.

Fenocchio (☎ 04 93 80 72 52; 2 place Rossetti; ice cream from €9; ☾ 9am-midnight Jul & Aug, 9am-midnight Tue-Sun mid-Feb–Jun & Sep–mid-Nov) You could dither forever over the 70-plus flavours of ice cream and sorbet made on the spot at this marvellous *glacier*. Eschew dull old familiars and tuck into a new taste sensation: lavender, ginger, liquorice, mandarin, thyme, or even tomato-basil and prune for the truly adventurous! Huge portions justify the steep-looking prices. Take away, or order at the counter and take a seat on the little terrace.

Oliviera (☎ 04 93 13 06 45; 8bis rue du Collet; platters €8-16; ☾ closed dinner Sun & Mon) This highly regarded olive-oil parlour, around since 1922, offers a series of light lunchtime platters. Pastas and crunchy salads are drizzled with some of its 26 varieties of oil.

Maïl's (☎ 04 93 85 28 17; 26 rue de l'Hôtel des Postes; plat du jour €12; ☾ 8am-midnight) With funky interior furnishings, including swings at the bar, this place is popular with beautiful youths. Nibble light Italian lunches, or be a devil and indulge in an early cocktail.

Chez Thérésa (☎ 04 93 85 00 04; 28 rue Droite) This *socca* maker, going since 1925, doles out chickpea pancakes from a hole in the wall. There's also a stall at the cours Saleya food market.

Self-Catering

Rue du Collet and its continuation, rue Pairolière, is lined with cheese shops, bakeries and fruit shops.

J Multari (☎ 04 93 92 01 99; 58bis av Jean Médecin; ☾ 6.30am-8.30pm Mon-Sat) A top-notch bakery producing traditional *michettes* (cheese-, olive-, anchovy- and onion-stuffed breads) and slobberlicious cakes. It has four smaller outlets (22 rue Gioffrédo, 8 blvd Jean Jaurès, 2 rue Alphonse Karr and 13 cours Saleya); the main branch has an ever-popular in-house café.

Central supermarkets include **Intermarché** (5 blvd Gambetta; ☾ 8.30am-8.30pm Mon-Sat, 9am-noon Sun) and **Monoprix** (42 av Jean Médecin; ☾ 8.30am-8.30pm Mon-Sat).

See also Nice: Marketsville! (p208).

DRINKING

Vieux Nice in particular explodes with pubs, each hooking boisterous young crowds with live music and beguiling happy-hour offers. Most open 11am to 2am daily.

Master Home (☎ 04 93 80 33 82; 11 rue de la Préfecture) Thirty types of beer, 110 cocktails and over 20 different whiskies woo the alcohol-lover into this 'Scottish-style' pub next door to the infamous Wayne's. There are also four computers with Internet access (€6 per hour).

De Klomp (☎ 04 93 92 42 85; 6 rue Mascoïnat) Next door to Master Home, this dark-wood Dutch-themed place attracts a more mature crowd (locals and visitors) than other bars in the old town. There are 18 beers on tap and 100 bottled beers from all over the world, plus around 60 whiskies. Nightly live music often has a jazz/funk focus.

Wayne's (☎ 04 93 13 46 99; 15 rue de la Préfecture) The kraazy team at Wayne's put on wild summer beach parties, quizzes, Sunday karaoke and live bands every night from 9.30pm. Cheap happy-hour pints of cocktails fuel the hard-core carousing.

Guinness-serving Irish pubs include **McMahons Pub** (☎ 04 93 13 84 00; 50 blvd Jean Jaurès); **O'Neill's** (☎ 04 93 80 06 75; 40 rue Droite), which has the occasional pub quiz; and **O'Hara's** (☎ 04 93 80 43 22; 22 rue Droite), with pub grub until 1.30am and the BBC on the box. Popular student/backpacker places include **Jonathan's Live Music Pub** (☎ 04 93 62 57 62; 1 rue de la Loge) and **Thor Pub** (☎ 04 93 62 49 90; 34 cours Saleya).

If you want fewer spewing neighbours and more sophistication, stick with late-opening bar-restaurants.

Sensory (☎ 04 93 76 01 04; 24 quai Lunel; Tue-Sun til 1am) At the port, brand-new Sensory is tastefully furnished in mellow purple and dusky red, and specialises in 'sensual food and sounds'. Consume morsels like creamy crab, and avocado and mango salad (€12), while being immersed in swirly electronica. Weekend DJs.

La Casa del Sol (☎ 04 93 62 87 28; 69 quai des États Unis; Tue-Sat) House music reigns at this early-evening port of call, frequented by affluent 30-somethings. The fab view of the Baie des Anges makes a perfect background for a seafood snack or pre-club cocktail session. Live DJs hit the decks from midnight on.

ENTERTAINMENT

Cinema and theatre schedules are online at www.nice.webcity.fr (in French). For general entertainment listings, pick up *Nice Rendezvous* (free) from the tourist offices, or buy *Semaine des Spectacles* (€0.80, weekly) from newsstands. Tickets for most events are sold at **FNAC** (billeterie ☎ 08 92 68 36 22; www.fnac.com in French; 24 av Jean Médecin), inside the Nice Étoile shopping centre.

Nightclubs

Clubs are usually open from midnight to around 5am, with admission costing upwards of €15, but this often includes a free drink.

Ghost (☎ 04 93 92 93 37; 3 rue de la Barillerie) An essential stop on the local clubber's weekend circuit, this place has a relaxed vibe, with snug red sofas and trip-hoppy tunes. Ring to be let in.

Le Saramanga (☎ 04 93 96 68 00; 45-47 promenade des Anglais) Prominently situated near the beach, Saramanga has a relaxed dress code and is where many tourists end up.

Le Grand Escurial (☎ 04 93 82 37 66; 29 rue Alphonse Karr; Thu-Sat Jul & Aug, Fri & Sat rest of yr) This huge industrial-style complex is Nice's largest nightclub, with a restaurant, two bars, light shows and live bands; if you're seeking an intimate atmosphere, look elsewhere. The music, aimed at a potential 1200 punters, is crowd-pleasing stuff. Croissants are served before kicking-out time.

Cinemas

Nice has two cinemas screening original-language films: **Cinéma Nouveau Mercury** (☎ 08 36 68 81 06; 16 place Garibaldi) and **Cinéma Rialto** (☎ 04 93 88 08 41; 4 rue de Rivoli). Tickets cost €7 (concession €4).

Theatre

Théâtre de Nice (☎ 04 93 13 90 90; esplanade des Victoires) This modern theatre, a block west of place Garibaldi, stages classical music, plays and dance performances.

Gay & Lesbian Venues

Le 6 (☎ 04 93 62 66 64; www.le6.fr; 6 rue de la Terrasse; 9.30pm-2.30am Tue-Sun) The hottest bar, with retro-futurist décor and live music from midnight to 1am. The pre-club place to be seen.

Le Klub (☎ 04 93 16 27 56; www.leklub.net; 6 rue Halévy; 11pm-5am Wed-Sun) The hippest gay venue in town, ruled by techno, house and high fashion. The ever-popular Top 50 nights (every second Sunday) draw the wildest crowds. Admission free, except Saturday (€12 to €14).

Blue Boy Entreprise (☎ 04 93 44 68 24; 9 rue Jean-Baptiste Spinetta; from 11pm) Nice's oldest gay club contains a relaxed crowd of regulars. Admission free, except Saturday (€10).

Live Music

Most pubs in Vieux Nice have live pop or rock bands nightly: see p223.

Opéra de Nice (☎ 04 92 17 40 00; www.opera-nice.fr; 4-6 rue St-François de Paule) Operas and orchestral concerts are held October to mid-June at the Garnier-designed Opéra de Nice (1885). Tickets, available at the **box office** (☎ 04 92 17 40 79; opera-billetterie@ville-nice.fr; 9.30am-6pm Mon-Sat) inside the opera house, cost €7 to €70.

SHOPPING

See also Nice: Marketville! (p208) and Shop, Don't Drop (opposite).

Antiques

Quality antique shops cram the streets west of the port. Shop for antiques under one roof at portside **Les Puces de Nice** (place Robilante; 10am-7pm Jun-Sep, 10am-6pm Tue-Sat Oct-May).

Fashion

Rue Paradis, av de Suède, rue Alphonse Karr and rue du Maréchal Joffre are the places to go for beautiful fashion boutiques,

---

SHOP, DON'T DROP

If you're short on shopping time, contact **Riviera Shuttle** (☎ 06 16 29 74 68; www
.rivierashuttle.com). They'll lend you a car and driver, who will whirl you round Nice (from €35 per person per half-day), hurtle you to the chic boutiques of Monaco (from €45 per person) or cruise you along Cannes' Croisette (from €55 per person). No stressful city driving, no parking nightmares, just pure purchasing pleasure!

---

including dedicated designer kids' and maternity clothes shops.

Centre Commercial Nice Étoile (☎ 04 92 17 38 17; 30 av Jean Médecin; ♥ 10am-7.30pm Mon-Sat) An indoor shopping centre containing mainstream fashion shops, FNAC and so on.

Food & Wine

Buy truffle oil (€20 per 25cL), truffle purée (€90 per 80g) or a jar of truffles in acacia honey (€21.50) in the boutique of Terres de Truffes (p222), and attempt to re-create the bistro's dishes back home.

Other specialists:

Confiserie Florian (☎ 04 93 55 43 50; www.confiserie florian.com; 14 quai Papacino; kitchen tours ♥ 9am-noon & 2-6.30pm) For chocolate-coated orange slices, almonds, figs and tangerine slices.

J P Paci (☎ /fax 04 93 92 93 48; confiseriepaci@aol.com; 19 av Notre Dame) A tiny chocolatier, selling chocolates shaped like cheeses, and mushrooms made of marzipan.

Les Grands Caves Caprioglio (☎ 04 93 85 66 57; 16 rue de la Préfecture) The best place for wine (from €1.20 per litre); also sells absinthe, spirits from all over Provence and olive oil (from €5.50 per litre).

Moulin à Huile d'Olive Alziari (☎ 04 93 85 76 92; 14 rue St-François de Paule) Dedicated olive-oil shop (extra virgin €9 per litre).

GETTING THERE & AWAY
Air

Nice's international airport, **Aéroport International Nice-Côte d'Azur** (☎ 08 20 42 33 33, 08 36 69 55 55; www.nice.aeroport.fr) is 6km west of the city centre. Several budget airlines have services to Nice from the UK (see p352) and continental Europe (see p352).

Boat

Ferries to and from Corsica (p355) use Nice's **ferry terminal** (Gare Maritime; ☎ 04 93 13 78 78).

Terminal 1 (quai du Commerce) is used by **SNCM ferries** (ticket counter ♥ 6am-7pm Mon-Fri, 6am-noon & 1-5pm Sat, 6am-10am & 1-5pm Sun).

Terminal 2 (quai Infernet) is used by **Corsica Ferries** (ticket counter ♥ 6-8am & 9am-6pm Mon-Fri, 6-8am & 11am-6pm Sat & Sun).

Bus

The train is the fastest means of transport along the coast, but there's also a slow and frequent bus service. The **intercity bus station** (☎ 04 93 85 61 81; 5 blvd Jean Jaurès; information counter ♥ 8.30am-5.30pm Mon-Fri, 9am-noon & 1-4pm Sat) is used by some two dozen bus companies, including **Intercars** (☎ 04 93 80 08 70), which runs various long-haul services to European destinations (see p353).

For sporadic buses to the mountain villages north of Nice, see p235.

Several bus companies serve towns along the coast and in the Provençal hinterland:

Phocéens Cars (☎ 04 93 85 66 61) Ticket office at 2 place Masséna.

Rapides Côte d'Azur (RCA; ☎ 04 93 85 64 44, 04 97 00 97 00; www.rca.tm.fr)

Société Broch (☎ 04 93 31 10 52)

Société des Cars Alpes-Littoral (☎ 04 92 51 06 05)

Transports Alpes-Maritimes (TAM; ☎ 04 93 89 41 45)

Train

Nice's main train station, **Gare Nice Ville** (Gare Thiers; ☎ 08 36 35 35 35; av Thiers) is 1.2km north of the beach. In town, tickets are sold at the **SNCF Boutique** (cnr rue de la Liberté & passage E Negrin; ♥ 9.30am-6.30pm Mon-Sat).

There are fast, frequent services (up to 40 daily in each direction) from Nice to towns along the coast between St-Raphaël and Ventimiglia (Italy), including Antibes (€3.60, 30 minutes), Cannes (€6.30, 40 minutes), Menton (€4, 35 minutes), Monaco (€3.10, 25 minutes) and St-Raphaël (€9.40, 45 minutes).

The mountain railway operated by **Chemins de Fer de la Provence** (☎ 04 97 03 80 80; www.trainprovence.com) offers a scenic trip to Digne-les-Bains (€17.40, 3¼ hours, four or five times daily) from Nice's **Gare du Sud** (☎ 04 93 82 10 17; 4bis rue Alfred Binet). See the boxed text (p194) for full details.

GETTING AROUND
To/From the Airport

Sunbus No 99 provides a speedy link between Nice's main train station and the airport (€3.50, 15 minutes, every 30 minutes between 8am and 9pm). Bus No 98 runs between the bus station and the airport (€3.50, 15 minutes, every 20 minutes between 6am and 9pm). Otherwise, there's the cheaper – and substantially slower – bus No 23 (€1.30, every 20 minutes between 6am and 8pm) between the train station and airport.

From the airport bus station, next to Terminal 1 at Nice airport, there are daily buses to many of the destinations in the table below (prices slightly more), including Cannes, Grasse, Isola 2000, Menton (departures to coincide with flight times), Valberg and Vence.

A taxi from the airport to Nice centre costs from €25 to €30, depending on the time of day and terminal.

To/From the Port

Free shuttle buses operated by the Chamber of Commerce & Industry shunt ferry passengers between the port, train station and a handful of upmarket hotels. Alternatively, bus Nos 1 and 2 run between the Port stop and av Jean Médecin (€1.30).

Bicycle

Always, Holiday Bikes, JML and Nicea Location Rent (see opposite) rent road and/or mountain bikes for around €5/8/15/70 per hour/half-day/day/week.

Bus

Local city buses are run by Sunbus, which has its main hub, the Station Centrale, on three sides of sq Général Leclerc. Tickets cost €1.30/16 for a single/14 rides. After you time-stamp your ticket, it's valid for one hour and can be used for one transfer or return. The Nice by Bus pass (one/five/seven days €4/12.95/16.75) includes a return trip to the airport. You can buy single trips,

BUSES FROM NICE

Destination	Cost (€)	Duration	Frequency	Bus Company
Aix-en-Provence	23.50	2¼hr	5 per day Mon-Sat, 1 Sun	Phocéens Cars
Antibes	4.20	1hr	15 daily	RCA
Beaulieu-sur-Mer	2.30 return	11min	every 15min daily	RCA
Beausoleil	3.80	40min	7 daily Mon-Sat, 3 Sun	RCA
Cagnes-sur-Mer	3.00	25min	every 40min from 6.55am Mon-Fri, 7.45am Sat, 8.15am Sun until 8.15pm	RCA
Cannes	5.90	2hr	15 daily	RCA
Digne-les-Bains	14.70	2¼hr	1-2 daily	Société des Cars Alpes-Littoral
Èze	2.50	20min	7 daily Mon-Sat, 3 Sun	RCA
Golfe-Juan	5.10 return	1hr	15 daily	RCA
Grasse	6.30	1½hr	8-18 daily	RCA/TAM
Hyères	23.00	2hr	2 daily Mon-Sat	Phocéens Cars
Isola 2000	27.10	2½hr	3 daily Dec-Apr, 1-2 daily rest of yr	☎ 04 93 85 92 60
La Colmiane	13.50	2hr	2-3 per week, plus 1 Sat & Sun	TAM
La Turbie	3.00	35min	4 daily Mon-Sat	RCA
Marineland (Biot)	3.80	40min	at least 15 daily	RCA
Marseille	23.50	2½hr	5 daily Mon-Sat, 1 Sun	Phocéens Cars
Menton	5.10 return	1½hr	every 15min from 6am Mon-Sat, 6.30am Sun until 8pm	RCA
St-Martin-Vésubie	10.10	1¾hr	1 Sat & Sun	TAM
St-Paul de Vence	4.20	45min	every 40min from 6.55am Mon-Fri, 7.45am Sat, 8.15am Sun until 8.15pm	RCA
Sisteron	17.90	3¾hr	1 daily Mon-Sat	Société des Cars Alpes-Littoral
Toulon	23.00	2½hr	2 daily Mon-Sat	Phocéens Cars
Valberg	11.70	2hr	1-2 daily	Société Broch
Vence	4.70	1hr	every 40min from 6.55am Mon-Fri, 7.45am Sat, 8.15am Sun until 8.15pm	RCA
Villefranche-sur-Mer	1.80 return	8min	every 15min btwn 6am & 8pm	RCA

14-trip cards and a day card on the bus. The other passes are sold in *tabacs* (tobacconists) and kiosks as well as at the **Sunboutique information office** (☎ 04 93 13 53 13; www.sunbus.com; 10 av Félix Faure; ⏱ 7.15am-7pm Mon-Fri, 8am-6pm Sat) or its **smaller outlet** (☎ 04 92 17 52 54; 29 av Malausséna; ⏱ 8am-5.45pm Mon-Fri, 8am-12.15pm Sat).

Bus No 12 links the train station with promenade des Anglais (15 minutes). To get from the train station to Vieux Nice, take bus No 30. To get to the local bus station, turn left on leaving the train station and walk to the end of av Thiers: from av Jean Médecin, bus Nos 1, 2, and 17 go to the local bus station (10 minutes).

The night-bus service, Noctambus, runs north, east and west from place Masséna every 30 minutes from 9.10pm to 1.10am (same prices as day buses).

Car & Motorcycle

Very handily, car rental agencies **ADA** (☎ 04 93 82 27 00), **Avis** (☎ 04 93 87 90 11; www.avis.com), **Budget** (☎ 04 93 16 24 16), **Europcar** (☎ 04 93 82 17 34; www.europcar.fr), **Hertz** (☎ 04 97 03 01 20; www .hertz.fr) and **National Citer** (☎ 04 93 16 01 48; www .citer.fr) are all to be found in one small annexe adjoining the train station at 12 av Thiers (also in town and at the airport).

Opposite the station, **Holiday Bikes** (☎ 04 93 16 01 62; www.holiday-bikes.com; 34 av Auber) and neighbouring **JML** (☎ 04 93 16 07 00; fax 04 93 16 07 48; 34 av Auber) rent 50cc scooters/125cc motorcycles for around €35/60 per day. **Nicea Location Rent** (☎ 04 93 82 42 71; www.nicealocationrent.com; 12 rue de Belgique) is a little more expensive.

Always (☎ 04 93 16 10 32; www.alwayscar.net; 25 promenade des Anglais) rents 50/100/125cc scooters for €38/53/60 per day and also has hip buggy-style scoot cars for €60/80 per half-/full day. For limousine hire, contact **Star Limousine** (☎ 04 92 29 44 44; info@starlimousine.fr; 455 promenade des Anglais).

Parking in Nice costs a stiff €2-plus per hour. Many hotels without private parking have deals with nearby car parks: when making your reservation, ask if the hotel can give you a discount parking card.

Taxi

Nice has numerous **taxi ranks** (☎ 04 93 13 78 78; ⏱ 24hr), including outside the train station; near place Masséna on av Félix Faure; on place Garibaldi; on promenade des Anglais; and outside the major museums. Journeys

---

ROUTE TO THE FUTURE

If there seems to be loads of roadworks in Nice, it could be that you're looking at the muddy beginnings of the €32 million tram system, the most ambitious regional transport scheme in France. With the fifth largest population in France and eight million visitors a year, the congested city was choking on its own exhaust fumes. Its new tram system is to be a gulp of fresh air.

Line 1 will link the north and the east of the city: its 8.7km should be operational by 2007. Line 2 will run from the port, along rue Hôtel des Postes/rue de la Buffa, then along promenade des Anglais to beyond the airport, eventually stretching all the way to Cagnes-sur-Mer. During the initial stages (2003 to 2006), buses will begin running along sections of the Line 2 route, to be replaced by trams in 2010.

So if you're stuck in a traffic jam in Nice, don't curse those workmen. Just think of the clean, green transport machine waiting at the end of the line.

---

are metered, and rates should be clearly displayed inside the cab. Night rates apply between 7pm and 7am.

THE THREE CORNICHES

Three parallel coastal roads, offering unparalleled views, link Nice and Menton, passing quaint perched villages, epic monuments and the principality of Monaco on the way. The Corniche Inférieure (aka Basse Corniche, the Lower Corniche and the N98) sticks closely to the nearby train line and villa-lined waterfront. The Moyenne Corniche (the N7) is the middle road, clinging to the hillside and affording great views if you can find somewhere to pull over. The Grande Corniche leaves Nice as the D2564 and has the most breathtaking panoramas of all.

Accommodation is pricey and limited: it's simplest to stay in Nice and make easy day or half-day trips from there. The Corniche Inférieure is well served by bus and train from Nice; the two higher roads, and the entire Niçois hinterland, are practically inaccessible without your own car.

CORNICHE INFÉRIEURE

Heading east from Nice to Menton, the Corniche Inférieure, built in the 1860s, passes through the towns of Villefranche-sur-Mer, St-Jean-Cap Ferrat, Beaulieu-sur-Mer, Èze-sur-Mer, Cap d'Ail and Monaco. Look for the pretty pink Château de l'Anglais (see the boxed text, p217) atop Mont Boron as you leave Nice.

Getting There & Away

The lower coastal road is well served by buses and trains. Bus No 100 operated by Rapides Côte d'Azur is the fastest bus. It runs the length of the Corniche Inférieure between Nice and Menton, stopping at all the villages along the way (daily, every 15 minutes between 6am and 8pm), including Villefranche-sur-Mer (€1.80 return, eight minutes) and Beaulieu-sur-Mer (€2.30 return, 11 minutes). The more roundabout bus No 111 runs seven times a day Monday to Saturday, and serves St-Jean-Cap Ferrat (€2.30, 25 minutes) as well as Villefranche (10 minutes) and Beaulieu (45 minutes).

The first train from Nice along the coast to Ventimiglia (Italy) is at 5.25am. Between 7am and 6pm, there's a service every 10 to 20 minutes (every 30 to 50 minutes from 6pm to 1am). Most stop at:

Destination	Cost (€)	Duration
Villefranche-sur-Mer	1.40	8min
Beaulieu-sur-Mer	1.70	14min
Cap d'Ail	2.60	21min
Monaco	3.10	25min
Cap Martin-Roquebrune	3.50	32min
Carnolès	3.80	36min
Menton	4.00	38min

Between July and September, buy a Carte Isabelle (p361) if you intend making several train trips along the coast in one day. If you're merely making a return day trip to Menton, however, stopping en route in Villefranche-sur-Mer and Beaulieu-sur-Mer, it's cheaper to buy a straightforward Nice–Menton return ticket.

Villefranche-sur-Mer

pop 6877

Heaped above a perfect harbour, this picturesque village overlooks the Cap Ferrat peninsula and is a popular port of call for passing cruise ships. Its well-preserved, 14th-century old town has a rash of evocatively named tiny streets, broken up by twisting staircases and glimpses of the glittering sea. Eerie, arcaded **rue Obscure**, a block in from the water, is a historical monument.

Above the old fishing harbour, **Port de la Santé**, lies place Amélie Pollonnais, filled by an **art and antique market** on Sundays. From here a coastal path runs around the citadel to Port Royal de la Darse, fortified between 1725 and 1737 and sheltering pleasure boats today. En route there are good views of Cap Ferrat and the wooded slopes of the Golfe de Villefranche (Gulf of Villefranche), which served as a Russian naval base in the 19th century during their conflicts with the Turks.

Villefranche was a favourite of Jean Cocteau, who sought solace here in 1924 following the death of his companion Raymond Radiguet.

ORIENTATION & INFORMATION

From Villefranche-sur-Mer train station, follow the signposts to the old town, whose main street (rue du Poilu) is on the same vertical level as the station; or take the steps down to quai Amiral Courbet and the shingle beach. To get to rue Obscure from the harbour, walk up the unpromising-looking staircase at 7–9 quai Amiral Courbert (between La Mère Germaine and L'Oursin Bleu restaurants), then turn immediately right.

The **tourist office** (☎ 04 93 01 73 68; www.villefranche-sur-mer.com; Jardin François Binon; ☼ 9am-noon & 2-6pm Mon-Sat) is right at the top of Villefranche, in the newer town. From place Philbert, outside the citadel, follow av du Marechal Joffre upwards, then bear left onto av du Marechal Foch. The office is 100m further along on your left.

CHAPELLE ST-PIERRE

The 14th-century waterfront **Chapelle St-Pierre** (☎ /fax 04 93 76 90 70; admission €2; ☼ usually 10am-noon & 4-8.30pm Tue-Sun summer, 9.30am-noon & 2-6pm Tue-Sun autumn, to 5pm winter, 9.30am-noon & 3-7pm Tue-Sun spring, closed mid-Nov–mid-Dec) was a neglected spot, used by fishermen to store their nets, until Jean Cocteau (1889–1963) got his hands on it. He'd been plotting the project for 10 years, but it was only in 1957 at the age of 68 that he began work, transforming the building with sweeping, mystical frescoes. Scenes of angels, St Peter's life and the Roma (Gypsies) of Stes-Maries de la Mer (see Pélerinage des Gitans, p115) are interspersed with patterns, stars and the creepy apocalyptic Eye of God design. The engraving above the (oddly, inner) door reads 'Enter this building as if it were made of living stone'.

A mass is celebrated here on 29 June, the feast day of St Peter, patron saint of fishermen.

CITADEL

The imposing **Fort St-Elme** (place Emmanuel Philibert) was built by the duke of Savoy between 1554 and 1559 to defend the gulf. Nowadays the walls shelter a scattering of cultural doodahs, including the town hall, some well-combed public gardens and a clutch of museum collections, the most interesting being the **Fondation Musée Volti** (☎ 04 93 76 33 27; admission free; ☺ 10am-noon & 2.30-7pm Mon & Wed-Sat, 2.30-7pm Sun Jul & Aug, 9am-noon & 2-5.30pm Mon & Wed-Sat, 2-5.30pm Sun Oct & Dec-May, to 6pm Jun & Sep), which displays voluptuous bronzes by Villefranche sculptor Antoniucci Volti (1915–89).

In summer there are some fine outdoor events. The **Petits Matins de la Citadelle** (Citadel Early Mornings; ☎ 04 93 01 73 68; €8) take place at 9am on Fridays from April to September: after a civilised breakfast in the museum garden, you're taken on a comprehensive tour of the fortress and old town. Evening attractions include the 15-minute **changing of the guard**, starting at 7pm in July and August; and the **Théâtre de la Citadelle** (☎ 04 93 01 73 68; tickets €6), screening open-air films daily at 9.30pm from mid-June to mid-September.

ACTIVITIES

Affrétement Maritime Villefranchois (☎ 04 93 76 65 65; amv.sirenes@wanadoo.fr; Port de la Santé; ☺ 9am-noon & 2-6pm Tue-Sun Jun-Sep) runs weekly boat trips to Cap Ferrat (adult/child €8/5, one hour) and Monaco (€14/10, two hours) from June to September. Boats leave from the Gare Maritime at Port de la Santé, at the western end of quai Amiral Courbet. The same company also sells tickets for dolphin- and whale-watching expeditions (see the boxed text, above).

Dark Pelican (☎ /fax 04 93 01 76 54; www.darkpelican .com; Port de la Santé) hires boats of all shapes and sizes, starting at €60/110 per morning/

WHALE-WATCHING

Acti'Loisirs (☎ 04 93 62 00 16; www.actiloisirs .com) runs cetacean-spotting expeditions from Villefranche-sur-Mer. Dolphins (common, striped and bottlenose) and whales (fin, long-finned pilot and sperm) roam around the Mediterranean during the summer months; with a bit of luck, you'll be able to see these startling creatures leaping from the seas. Bring binoculars and keep your fingers crossed.

From June to September, boats depart at 8.30am and 1.30pm on Tuesday, Friday, Saturday and Sunday from Port de la Santé. An English-speaking marine biologist is planted on board to tell you what's what. Expeditions last four hours and tickets cost €40/29 for adults/under 12 years.

day for a five-person, no-licence-required Fun Yak 450 (€500 deposit).

Underwater photography is one of the many activities offered by the diving centre **Aqua Pro Dive International** (☎ 04 93 01 71 04; apdi-pantxoa@wanadoo.fr; 16 rue du Poilu). It rents all the gear.

SLEEPING & EATING

Hôtel Welcome (☎ 04 93 76 27 62; www.welcomehotel .com; 1 quai Amiral Courbet; d/ste from €132/199; ☺ closed mid-Nov–mid-Dec; ᴾ ✷) Cocteau stayed at this restored 17th-century convent, opposite the Chapelle St-Pierre, when he was in town. All of its rooms have wrought-iron balconies overlooking the old port. The helpful reception desk will make reservations for you, and there's an upmarket 'wine pier' where you can toast the sunset with a cocktail or glass of *vin rouge*.

Hôtel Provençal (☎ 04 93 76 53 53; www.hotel provencal.com; av Maréchal Joffre; d with garden/sea views €78/105; ✷) With its warm mustard-coloured façade and family-run atmosphere, the Provençal oozes charm. Over half of its rooms overlook the citadel gardens or harbour, and you can breakfast on a terrace shaded by orange trees. Wheelchair access.

Quai Amiral Courbet is lined with pavement restaurants where you can crack open freshly caught crustaceans.

La Mère Germaine (☎ 04 93 01 71 39; 9 quai Amiral Courbet; menu €45; ☺ closed mid-Nov–Christmas) The great-grandmother of Villefranchois cuisine, cooking up prized bouillabaisse and other fishy delights since 1938.

Le Joïa (☎ 04 93 76 62 40; 18 rue du Poilu; ☽ dinner) For something a little different, try welcoming Joïa's decent-value Asian and European dishes, served on a picturesque terrace in the old town.

St-Jean-Cap Ferrat
pop 2555

St-Jean-Cap Ferrat, once a drowsy fishing village, lies on a spectacular wooded peninsula that now glitters with millionaires' mansions. Most are off limits, but the bogglingly ornate Villa et Jardins Ephrussi de Rothschild is open to visitors and is an absolute must-see.

Famous former residents of Cap Ferrat read like a *Who's Who* of the 19th and 20th centuries: writer Somerset Maugham owned the luxurious Villa Mauresque (his regular guests included Noël Coward, Ian Fleming, TS Eliot and Evelyn Waugh); and Charlie Chaplin, Churchill and Cocteau holidayed here (not together).

Some 14km of eucalyptus-scented walking paths crisscross the cape; ask for a map from the **tourist office** (☎ 04 93 76 08 90; ot.stjeanc apferrat@tiscali.fr; 59 av Denis Séméria; ☽ usually 8.30am-noon & 1-5pm Mon-Sat). A coastal path links the fine-shingle **Plage de Passable** on the western side with the café-lined **port** on the east. Walking right round the cape (8km) only takes a couple of hours.

VILLA ET JARDINS EPHRUSSI DE ROTHSCHILD

An unbelievably over-the-top *belle époque* confection, the **Villa et Jardins Ephrussi de Rothschild** (☎ 04 93 01 33 09; adult/7-17 yrs €8.50/6.50; ☽ 10am-7pm Jul & Aug, to 6pm Feb-Jun & Sep-Oct, 2-6pm Mon-Fri, 10am-6pm Sat & Sun Nov-Feb) were commissioned by the eccentric Baroness Béatrice Ephrussi de Rothschild in 1912, and took 40 architects seven years to build. Pink, pink, pink is everywhere (the Baroness's favourite animals were flamingos because of their colour), and the sugary effect is heightened by Fragonard paintings, frilly Louis XVI furniture and flowery porcelain, all in 18th-century style. It's so extreme, you just have to love it. The first floor costs a further €2 to see (tour only), and includes the Monkey Room, decorated with painted monkey friezes on the panelled walls and filled with Béatrice's collection of cheeky porcelain chimps.

Absolutely out of this world are the villa's seven themed gardens. Stroll through Spanish, Japanese, Florentine, stone, cactus and pink rose areas, before entering the romantic French garden, landscaped to resemble a ship's deck (the Baroness had her 30 gardeners dress as sailors to complete the effect). A stream flows from the Temple of Love to a pool at the heart of the complex, where musical fountains dance every 20 minutes. Magical.

Bus No 111 linking Nice and St-Jean-Cap Ferrat stops at the foot of the driveway leading to the villa, at the northern end of av Denis Séméria (the D25). By train, get off at Beaulieu-sur-Mer, then it's a 20-minute walk.

SLEEPING & EATING

Hôtel Clair Logis (☎ 04 93 76 51 81; www.hotel-clair -logis.fr; 12 av Centrale; d €105-170; ☽ closed Nov–mid-Dec & Feb; **P** ☒) This peaceful 19th-century villa is set in wonderful parkland; Général de Gaulle stayed here in the 1950s. The most handsome rooms are in the main building. One is adapted for people with disabilities.

L'Oursin (☎ 04 93 76 04 65; oursin@wanadoo.fr; 1 av Denis Séméria; s/d €50/85; ☒) A good 'cheapie' by local standards, close to the port. The two best rooms have sea views: book ahead.

La Voile d'Or (☎ 04 93 01 13 13; www.lavoiledor.fr; av Mermoz; d from €400; **P** ☒ ☒) Live the Cap Ferrat good life at this luxury hotel, with sauna, two seawater swimming pools, private beach and sumptuous rooms. Prices halve in low season.

Beaulieu-sur-Mer
pop 3701

Another popular *belle époque* resort for Europe's artists, poets and princes. French architect Gustave Eiffel lived at the waterfront Villa Durandy (now converted into luxury holiday apartments; see opposite) from 1896 until his death in 1923. His next-door neighbour was Théodore Reinach, oddball scholar and originator of the awesome Villa Grecque Kérylos, Beaulieu's main draw.

Remnants of the resort's golden age include the **Grand Casino** (☎ 04 93 76 48 00; www .casinobeaulieu.com; 4 av Fernand Dunan), built in 1928 and still drawing wildcards until 4am or 5am daily; and neighbouring La Rotonde (1899), a curvy, wedding-cake-white structure built as a hotel, used as a hospital during WWII and housing a small local-history museum today. Across from the harbour are the **Jardins de L'Olivaie**, the venue for a two-week Jazz Parade in August.

Beaulieu's shingle **beach** overlooks the Baie des Fourmis (Bay of Ants). From here, promenade Maurice Rouvier leads south-west beneath a hedgerow of *lauriers-roses* (oleanders) to the port of St-Jean-Cap Fer-rat, a pleasant 2.5km stroll. For other scenic seaside walks, ask at the **tourist office** (☎ 04 93 01 02 21; www.ot-beaulieu-sur-mer.fr; place Georges Clemenceau; ☷ 9am-12.30pm & 3-7pm Mon-Sat, 9am-12.30pm Sun), next to the train station.

VILLA GRECQUE KÉRYLOS

'REJOICE!' says the mosaic in the entrance hall of the **Villa Grecque Kérylos** (☎ 04 93 76 44 09; www.villa-kerylos.com; av Gustave Eiffel; adult/child €7/5.50; ☷ 10am-7pm Jul & Aug, 10am-6pm Feb-Jun, Sep & Oct, 2-6pm Mon-Fri & 10am-6pm Sat & Sun Nov-Jan), and it would be churlish not to. Like the Villa Ephrussi (opposite), this is another seven-years-in-the-making mansion that's eccentric and beautiful in equal measure. Scholar-archaeologist Théodore Reinach (1860–1928) and architect Emmanuel Pontremoli (1865–1956) designed the house in 1902, basing the rooms and everything in them on ancient Greek models. The result: a perfect reproduc-tion of a 1st-century Athenian villa.

Excellent audio guides lead you from the *balanéion* (bathroom), with its dolphin-decorated marble tub, to the *triklinos* (dining room), complete with Greek-style reclin-ers, frescoes and gold-leaf ceiling. Several hundred square metres of mosaics cover the floors (look out for the wonderful Min-otaur), and meticulously made walnut, rosewood, coral, marble and lemonwood furniture fills the rooms. It's all so immacu-late, you long to see where Théodore's kids lived (sadly, it's out of bounds).

In the gardens, a botanical trail highlights the ancient uses of plants typical to Greece and the French coast. On Wednesday and Saturday, you and your children can have a go at making Greek pottery in the basement ceramic workshop.

SLEEPING & EATING

Hôtel Résidence Eiffel (☎ 04 93 76 46 46; www.residence-eiffel.com; rue Gustave Eiffel; 4-/6-person studios per week from €959/1358; ℗ ☒ ☲) Gustave Eif-fel's former home, now divided into 75 cosy apartments with kitchenettes (two adapted for wheelchairs), which are good value for families or groups. Facilities include pri-vate beach access, swimming pool (April to October), table tennis and badminton. The lovely terrace restaurant and tea salon, with stonking sea views, are open to all.

La Réserve (☎ 04 93 01 00 01; www.reservebeaulieu .com; 5 blvd du Maréchal Leclerc; d with port/sea views from €475/840, ste from €1380) Beaulieu's decadent hang-out since WWII is famed, four-star and very pink. Big-name guests have in-cluded Churchill, Walt Disney and Picasso. Hide from the paparazzi in the private salt-water pool, fitness centre, spa, billiard room and gourmet restaurant.

Hôtel Riviera (☎ 04 93 01 04 92; contact@hotel -riviera.fr; 6 rue Paul Doumer; d €52-75; ☒ ☲) A breath of air for nonsmokers, this tastefully renovated hotel is completely smoke-free. Rooms are cool and clean as fresh paint.

Cap d'Ail
pop 4565

Strolling and swimming are the main attrac-tions on the unpoetically named Cape of Garlic (actually derived from the Provençal 'Cap d'Abaglio' meaning 'Cape of Bees'). Motion-picture pioneer Auguste Lumière's grand house (1902) still stands among the palm trees and pines at 8 av Charles Blanc, while the spectacular **amphitheatre** that Coc-teau designed is used as a youth theatre by the **Centre Méditerranéen d'Études Françaises** (☎ 04 93 78 21 59; centremed@monte-carlo.mc; chemin des Oliviers).

Smoking and dogs are banned on **Plage Mala**, Cap d'Ail's shingle beach tucked into a cove. From Cap d'Ail train station, walk down the steps to av Raymond Gramaglia, a promenade from where Cap d'Ail's splen-did **Sentier du Littoral** (coastal path) can be accessed. Information panels along the way explain the lush flora and plush villas you pass; during rough seas the seaside path is closed. Bear west (right) for a 20-minute amble around rocks to the beach, or east for a more strenuous stroll to Monaco. The **tourist office** (☎ 04 93 78 02 33; www.cap-dail.com; 87bis av du 3 Septembre; ☷ 9am-noon & 2-6pm Mon-Fri, 9am-noon Sat), in the village centre on the N98, has plenty more information on walks in the area.

July kicks off with the three-day **Fête de l'Abeille** (Bee Festival). In August there are four days' worth of jazz concerts at the seaside

Amphithéâtre de la Mer (☎ 04 93 78 02 33; fax 04 92 10 74 36; place Marquet), overlooking Cap d'Ail's small port. Concerts generally start at 9.30pm and tickets, available from the tourist office, cost €10 to €12 (€35 for all four evenings).

Relais International de la Jeunesse (☎ 04 93 78 18 58; fax 04 93 53 35 88; av Raymond Gramaglia; dm incl breakfast €14; ☻ Apr-Sep), Cap d'Ail's stunning seaside hostel, is based in a villa perched above the sea. Travellers have to vacate their rooms between 9.30am and 5pm, and a curfew is enforced from 11pm.

Restaurant La Pinède (☎ 04 93 78 37 10; www .pinede-riviera.com; 10 blvd de la Mer; menus €27, €37 & €47) is a former fisherman's hut overlooking the Med on the Cap d'Ail coastal path, and a great spot to eat a refined fish lunch and while away the afternoon on the sea-facing terrace. From the train station, walk down the steps and head straight for the sea.

Cap Martin

Cap Martin is the coastal quarter of Cap Martin-Roquebrune (see opposite). The green headland is best known for its sumptuous villas, presumptuous collection of royal honorary citizens and famous past residents, among them Winston Churchill, Coco Chanel, Marlene Dietrich, the architect Le Corbusier, designer Eileen Gray and Irish poet WB Yeats.

Exploring on foot is a pleasurable pastime. Av Le Corbusier follows the coast east, around Baie de Roquebrune to the northern end of the cape where it turns into promenade Le Corbusier. The beach, **Plage du Buse**, is a two-minute stroll from the train station on av de la Gare. The hilltop village of Roquebrune is an hour's walk (2km) – up numerous staircases – from the station, while Monte Carlo is three hours (7km) away by foot.

The **tourist office** (☎ 04 93 35 62 87; www.roque brune-cap-martin.com; 218 av Aristide Briand; ☻ 9am-1pm & 3-7pm Mon-Sat, 10am-1pm & 3-7pm Sun Jul & Aug, 9am-12.30pm & 2-6.30pm Mon-Sat Jun & Sep, to 6pm Oct-May), at the northern end of the cape midway between Carnolès and Cap Martin-Roquebrune train stations, distributes a free map of walking trails around Cap Martin. It also arranges guided tours (10am Tuesday and Friday) of Corbusier's seashore studio (for more on Le Corbusier see the boxed text, p49). Roquebrune, Cap Martin's medieval counterpart (see p234), has a couple of delightful eating options.

MOYENNE CORNICHE

Cut through rock in the 1920s, the Moyenne Corniche takes you from Nice past the Col de Villefranche (149m), Èze and Beausoleil (the French town bordering Monaco's Monte Carlo).

Èze
pop 2742 / elevation 429m

More like toy town than anywhere else on the Riviera! This rocky little village perched on an impossible peak is undeniably picturesque, but you spend a lot of time staying out of other people's photographs and waiting for them to get out of yours. Its coastal counterpart Èze-sur-Mer is accessible by road or train from the Corniche Inférieure.

When German philosopher Friedrich Nietzsche (1844–1900) stayed here, he started writing *Thus Spoke Zarathustra*; the path that links Èze-sur-Mer and Èze is named after him. Walt Disney holidayed in Èze, and in 2002 U2 guitarist The Edge got married on a luxury yacht moored off the coast here.

Ask at the **tourist office** (☎ 04 93 41 26 00; www.eze-riviera.com; place du Général de Gaulle; ☻ 9am-7pm) for details of guided tours that explore the old town and Jardin Exotique (€6, including garden admission).

SIGHTS & ACTIVITIES

Steep streets lead to the medieval hilltop village, which is crammed with dinky art galleries, boutiques and cafés. Its crowning glory is the chateau ruins, brightened by a cactus-laden, oil-scented **Jardin Exotique** (☎ 04 93 41 10 30; adult/11-16 yrs €3/2; ☻ 9am-8pm Jul & Aug, 9am-5pm Jun & Sep), with marvellous views but cheeky admission fee.

Perfumery Fragonard (p269) has a **factory** (☎ 04 93 41 05 05; admission free; ☻ 8.30am-6.30pm Feb-Oct, 8.30am-noon & 2-6.30pm Nov-Jan) on the eastern edge of Èze that you can visit, and a small **outlet** (av du Jardin Exotique; ☻ 10am-7pm Mar-Oct, 10am-12.30pm & 2-7pm Nov-Feb) in the village.

SLEEPING & EATING

Èze's hotels are small and it's frantically popular: book accommodation well ahead.

Hermitage du Col d'Èze (☎ 04 93 41 00 68; fax 04 93 41 24 05; Col d'Èze; d €49-69; ☻ restaurant closed Tue lunch & Wed; P ☒ ☒) This old-style 14-room inn is set spectacularly at the top of a mountain pass, 2.5km from the village centre.

The Gorges du Verdon (p186) in Haute-Provence

Colourful ski gondolas above the Col d'Allos
in the Vallée du Haut Verdon (p199)

Woman in traditional
Provençal dress from
Digne-les-Bains (p192)

Lavender field outside Banon (p196)

DAVID TOMLINSON

Hilltop village of Roquebrune (p233)

GREG ELMS

Pissaladière, a Niçoise speciality (p222)

Fête des Citrons (p238), Menton

DAVID TOMLINSON

Musée Matisse (p215), Nice

DAN HERRICK

Food is strictly local fare and delicious to boot – a guaranteed taste of the region.

Château de la Chèvre d'Or (☎ 04 92 10 66 66; www.chevredor.com; rue du Barri; d €360-650; menus €60, €75 & €130; P 🅿 🔀 🕿) A gastronomic restaurant of the highest calibre, guaranteed to thrill the most jaded palates. Hotel facilities are fantastic too: sauna, *hammam* (Turkish bath), fitness centre, spa, infinity-edge swimming pool…the list is endless!

Le Golf Hôtel (☎ 04 93 41 18 50; fax 04 93 41 26 58; place de la Colette; d €88-140) The Golf's eight rooms are always booked months in advance. The restaurant below serves up decent grub.

Hôtel Arc en Ciel (☎ 04 93 41 02 66; www.arcenciel eze.com; av du Jardin Exotique; d €58; 🕙 closed Jan; 🔀) At the foot of the road leading up to the village. It's a simple place to stay, but the rooms, decked out in Provençal fabrics, are pleasant enough.

Camping Les Romarins (☎ 04 93 01 81 64; www .camping-romarins.com; Col d'Èze; 2 adults, tent & car €22.20; 🕙 Apr-Oct) At the western end of the Col d'Èze, 2km above the village. Sites have dramatic views of Cap Ferrat.

Getting There & Away
Bus No 112 operated by Rapides Côte d'Azur serves the Moyenne Corniche, stopping at Èze village (€2.50, 20 minutes) and Beausoleil (€3.80, 40 minutes) on the way to and from Nice. Buses run seven times a day Monday to Saturday, and three times daily on Sunday and holidays.

By train from Nice, get off at Èze-sur-Mer train station on the Corniche Inférieure, where shuttle buses transport tourists up and down the hill between May and October (single/return €3.80/6.85; eight buses in either direction daily, coinciding with train arrivals and departures). Failing that, it's a 3km uphill trudge on foot to Èze village.

GRANDE CORNICHE
Shot through with spectacular tunnels and blinding hairpin bends, Napoléon's Grande Corniche is quite literally a cliffhanger. Hitchcock was sufficiently impressed to use it as a film backdrop for *To Catch a Thief* (1956), starring Cary Grant and Grace Kelly. Ironically, the Hollywood actress, who met her Monégasque Prince Charming while making the film, died in 1982 after crashing her car on this very same road. Fasten those seatbelts, folks.

Observatoire de Nice & Astrorama
The **Observatoire de Nice** (☎ 04 92 00 30 11; www.obs -nice.fr), a 19th-century monument 5km northeast of Nice centre at the top of Mont Gros (375m), was designed by French architects Gustave Eiffel and Charles Garnier. It sits amid 35 hectares of landscaped parkland and has ravishing views over Nice and the coast. When the observatory opened in 1887, its telescope – 76cm in diameter – was among the largest in Europe. Guided tours (adult/child €4.50/2.50, 1½ hours) of the observatory are held at 3pm on Wednesday and Saturday.

Watch the skies at **Astrorama** (☎ 04 93 41 23 04; www.astrorama.net in French; adult/student & 7-10 yrs €7/5, 'spectacles aux étoiles' €10/7; 🕙 6-10.30pm Fri & Sat Sep-Jun, 6-10.30pm Mon-Sat Jul & Aug), a planetarium and astronomy centre 8km further northeast along the Grande Corniche in **La Trinité**.

There's a combined ticket (€9.50) for the Observatoire de Nice and Astrorama, but you have to visit them both on the same day.

La Turbie
pop 3043 / elevation 480m
La Turbie teeters on a promontory above Monaco and offers a stunning night-time vista of the principality. By day, an unparalleled aerial view can be had from the gardens of the **Trophée des Alps** (Trophy of the Alps; ☎ 04 93 41 20 84; 18 av Albert I; adult/12-25 yrs €4/2.50; 🕙 9.30am-6pm Apr–mid-Jun, 9.30am-7pm mid-Jun–mid-Sep, 10am-5pm Tue-Sun mid-Sep–Mar), a dramatic 2000-year-old triumphal monument built by Emperor Augustus in 6 BC on the highest point of the old Roman road. The 45 Alpine tribes he conquered are listed on the inscription carved on the western side of the monument. Steps lead to the top, and there's a small **history museum** at the base.

La Turbie village is unexciting bar its small but intact old town, neatly packed around the baroque-style **Église St-Michel** (1777). From the village, a mountain road leads to the top of **Mont Agel** (1110m), the slopes of which are graced with the greens of **Monte Carlo Golf Club** (☎ 04 93 41 09 11; fax 04 93 41 09 55; rte du Mont Agel), an elite 18-hole golf club dating to 1911.

Roquebrune
pop 11,966
Cap Martin-Roquebrune, sandwiched between Monaco and Menton, became part of France in 1861; prior to that it was a free town following its revolt against Grimaldi

rule in 1848. The town stretches north from the exclusive suburb of Cap Martin on the coast (see p232) to the hilltop village perched 300m high on a pudding-stone lump.

A fantastic feudal castle dating from the 10th century crowns medieval Roquebrune. The crenellated mock-medieval **Tour de l'Anglais** (Englishman's Tower) near the entrance was built by wealthy British lord William Ingram, who bought the chateau in 1911. His archaeological vandalism caused such outrage that **Château de Roquebrune** (☎ 04 93 35 07 22; place Ingram; adult/7-18 yrs €3.50/1.60; ❂ 10am-12.30pm year-round, plus 3-7.30pm Jul & Aug, 2-6.30pm Apr-Jun & Sep, 2-6pm Feb, Mar & Oct, 2-5pm Nov-Jan) was immediately classified as a historical monument to protect it from further modification. The four floors are atmospheric, and concerts are held here in July and August; the programme is available from Easter from the Cap Martin tourist office (p232).

Of all Roquebrune's steep and tortuous streets, rue Moncollet – with its arcaded passages and stairways carved out of the rock – is the most impressive. The architect Le Corbusier (see the boxed text, p49) is buried in the cemetery at the top of the village.

SLEEPING & EATING

Hôtel-Restaurant Les Deux Frères (☎ 04 93 28 99 00; www.lesdeuxfreres.com; place des Deux Frères; s €65, d €91 or €101; lunch/dinner menu €24/45; ❂ restaurant closed Mon year-round, lunch Tue summer, dinner Sun winter) Boasting 10 really lovely seaview rooms, this hotel also has a stylish restaurant terrace perched above the water. Sample the excellent-value lunchtime *menu* (including half a bottle of wine), overlooked by a miserable-looking statue of *France Triumphant*: perhaps she missed out on the grapefruit sorbet.

Au Grand Inquisiteur (☎ 04 93 35 05 37; 18 rue du Château; menus €24.50 & €36; ❂ closed Mon & Tue) This rock-cave restaurant could be a film set for a movie about mad monks. Meat and fish dishes are the speciality here, carried to your table from the kitchen across the street! *Menus* include cheese or dessert (add another €4 if you want both).

Getting There & Away

Rapides Côte d'Azur's bus No 116 to and from Nice stops at La Turbie (€3, 35 minutes) en route to Peille (€4.70, one hour, four buses per day Monday to Saturday). Other than that, you need your own wheels.

ARRIÈRE-PAYS NIÇOIS

Studded with medieval hilltop villages, the Niçois hinterland stretches inland from Nice to Menton.

CONTES TO COARAZE

Roman **Contes** (population 6600), 16km north of Nice, sits on a ship-shaped rock above the River Paillon de Contes. Before plodding up from the modern town, nip into the **tourist office** (☎ 04 93 79 13 99; fax 04 93 79 26 30; place A Olivier; ❂ 2-6pm Mon-Fri), level with the river/D15.

At **Le Site des Moulins** (☎ 04 93 79 19 17; www .musee-contes.fr in French; admission €2; ❂ 9.30am-12.30pm & 2-5pm Sat, closed Nov), at the northern end of Contes on the D15, olives have been crushed at the still-functioning **Moulin à Huile de la Laouza** since the 13th century. Discover the ins and outs of olive-oil making here and buy locally made olive oil in its shop. The neighbouring **Moulin à Fer**, a 13th- to 14th-century water-powered forge where agricultural tools were made, shelters a recreation of a 1900s Contoise kitchen.

Châteauneuf de Contes, 6km west, is a hamlet at the foot of the overgrown ruins of an older village, abandoned prior to WWI. A path leads from the road to the crumbling ruins, which – territorial goats allowing – can be freely explored on foot. To get to the ruins, follow rte de Châteauneuf (the D815) through Châteauneuf de Contes, and bear left at the wrought-iron roadside cross along rte des Chevaliers de Malte. The ruins are signposted and located 2km from here.

Continuing west along the D815, then south along the D19, you come to **Tourrette-Levens** (population 4000, elevation 465m), a particularly dramatic hilltop village crowned with a **Château Musée** (Castle Museum; ☎ 04 93 91 03 20; place du Château; admission free; ❂ 2-7pm summer, 2-5pm winter), which houses an exotic butterfly collection and natural-history museum. Enchanting concerts are held in its grounds during **Les Nuits Musicales** (Musical Nights) in July and August. Like Gorbio (p240), Tourrette-Levens has an annual **Proucession daï Limassa** on Corpus Christi in June.

The **Maison des Cantons des Alpes d'Azur** (☎ 04 93 08 76 31; fax 04 93 29 23 10), 10km west on the N202 in **Colomars** (population 2885, elevation 334m), has information on all these villages.

Coaraze (population 659, elevation 650m), a tiny place 9km north of Contes on the Col St-Roch (D15), has a dinky old town and celebrates an **olive festival** on 15 August. Its small **tourist office** (☎ /fax 04 93 79 37 47; office .de.tourisme.coaraze@tiscali.fr; 7 place Ste-Catherine) has details. Look out for the Jean Cocteau sundial on the town hall, and the lizard mosaic on place Félix-Giordan, alongside a poem telling how the villagers caught the devil. Poor old Satan had to cut off his tail to escape! ('Coaraze' derives from the Provençal words 'coa raza' meaning 'cut tail'.)

Truly fantastic futurist works fill the **Musée Figas** (☎ 04 93 79 31 87; www.museefigas.asso.fr; Engarvin; adult/7-18 yrs €4/2; ☽ 3-6pm Sat & Sun summer, 2-5pm Sat & Sun winter), designed by painter Marcel Figas (b 1935) and home to his oils. From Coaraze, continue north along the D15 towards Col St-Roch and after 6km turn left to **Engarvin**.

Sleeping & Eating

Auberge du Soleil (☎ 04 93 79 08 11; fax 04 93 79 37 79; half-board from €61 per person; menu €20; ☽ mid-Mar–mid-Nov) Tucked at the top of Coaraze, the inn contains 10 lovely double rooms, a garden and pool. Its terrace overlooks mountains and makes a good spot for a very tasty lunch.

Lou Madonics (☎ 04 93 79 03 52; place des Barbets, Châteauneuf de Contes; full meal around €15) With its pea-green shutters, candy-striped covered terrace, *pétanque (boules)* pitch and simple *cuisine familiale* (family kitchen), this place has all the ingredients for a long and lazy informal lunch.

Getting There & Away

To and from Nice, **Transport Alpes-Maritimes** (TAM; ☎ 04 93 89 41 45; www.cg06.fr) operates hourly buses Monday to Saturday (six on Sunday) to Contes (€3.40, 45 minutes), two or three of which continue Monday to Saturday to Coaraze (€4.70, 20 minutes). For information about daily bus services between Nice and Tourrette-Levens (€2.50, 45 minutes), call ☎ 04 93 85 61 81.

PEILLE & PEILLON

Quaintly restored **Peille** (population 2055, elevation 630m) is quite untouched by tourism tackiness despite the raving reports it gets as being among the hinterland's most intact perched villages. Its eastern entrance is guarded by the 12th-century **Chapelle St-Roch** (place Jean Mioul).

In the teeny **Musée du Terroir** (☽ 2-6pm summer), captions are written in Pelhasc. This is a dialect specific to Peille and distinguishable from the Niçois dialect by its absent 'r's and silent 'l's (for instance, the Peillasques say 'carriea' instead of 'carriera', Niçois for 'street'). Peille celebrates a **Fête du Blé et de la Lavande** (Wheat and Lavender Festival) in early August.

Not for the faint-hearted is the **Via Ferrata de Peille**, part of the Circuit des Comtes Lascaris (see the boxed text, p204), cut into rock above Peille and classed as very difficult. The course is a 10-minute walk from the village and scales the Baous de Caster and Barma de la Sié rock formations, with full complement of ladders, monkey bridges and zip lines. The full monty takes 3½ hours to conquer, but it's possible to tackle just one or two of the four sections (each 45 minutes to an hour long). Tickets and equipment hire are handled by **Bar l'Absinthe** (☎ 04 93 79 95 75; 6 rue Félix Faure; half-/full day €17/25); advance reservations are strongly recommended.

Six kilometres of hairpin bends southwest of Peille on the D53 towards Peillon is **La Grave** (population 500), a blot-on-the-landscape cement works where the hinterland's limestone is turned into cement. The best aerial view of Peille and La Grave is from the **Col de la Madone** (927m), a hair-raising stone-tunnelled mountain pass (the D22) that runs east from Peille to Ste-Agnès.

Peillon (population 1229, elevation 456m), 14km northeast of Nice, is known for its precarious *nid d'aigle* (eagle's nest) location. From the village car park, a footpath leads to the **Chapelle des Pénitents Blancs**, noteworthy for its set of macabre 15th-century frescoes. Longer trails lead to Peille, La Turbie and Chapelle St-Martin. North of Peillon, the **Gorges du Peillon** (D21) cuts through the Peillon Valley to **L'Escarène** (population 2138), an important mule stop in the 17th and 18th centuries for traders working the rte du Sel (Salt Rd) from Nice to Turin in Italy.

Sleeping & Eating

Auberge de la Madone (☎ 04 93 79 91 17; info@ch -demeure.com; 2 place Auguste Arnulf, Peillon; d from €95; menus €45 & €75; ☽ closed mid-Oct–mid-Dec, restaurant closed Wed; P) At the foot of the village of Peillon, this upmarket three-star hotel also creates delicious local Peillonnais cuisine that draws diners from far and wide. Rooms and tables need booking well in advance.

Getting There & Away
See p234 for details of buses to Peille.

MENTON & AROUND

MENTON
pop 29,266

You'd have thought Eve was in enough trouble, but as she was thrown out of Eden, she managed to steal one of the garden's Golden Fruits. On arriving at Menton, she was so reminded of paradise that she planted the fruit's seeds here, and Menton has been famous for its lemons ever since! Frenzied citrus worship takes place at the two-week-long Fête des Citrons in February.

Besides Adam and Eve, Gustave Flaubert, Guy de Maupassant, Katherine Mansfield and Robert Louis Stevenson all found solace in Menton in the past. Jean Cocteau lived here from 1956 to 1958 and made a number of important artistic contributions to the town. Today, Menton mainly draws Italians from across the border, and retains a magnetic charm free from airs and graces. Its lush, subtropical microclimate has helped create some of the Riviera's most beautiful gardens, and its old town is appropriately pretty and precipitous.

Historically, Menton, along with neighbouring Cap Martin-Roquebrune, found itself under Grimaldi rule until 1848, when its people rebelled and declared themselves independent. In 1861 the two towns voted to become part of France, forcing Charles III of Monaco to sell them to Napoleon III for four million francs.

Orientation
The old town and port are wedged between Baie de Garavan, to the east, and Baie du Soleil, which stretches 3km west to Cap Martin-Roquebrune. Promenade du Soleil and its continuations quai Général Leclerc and quai de Monléon skirt the length of Menton's shingle beach. There are more beaches directly northeast of the old port and east of Port de Garavan, Menton's main pleasure-boat harbour. Av Édouard VII links the train station with the beach.

Information
Banks abound on rue Partouneaux. Café des Arts (p239) has Internet access for €6 per hour.

Post Office (☎ 04 93 28 64 84; 2 cours Georges V; ⏲ 8am-6.30pm Mon-Wed & Fri, to 6pm Thu, 8.30am-noon Sat) Cyberposte available.

St John's Anglican Church (☎ 04 93 57 20 25; av Carnot) 5000-plus English books on loan.

Service du Patrimoine (☎ 04 92 10 97 10; fax 04 93 28 46 85; Hôtel de Lantagnac, 24 rue St-Michel) Responsible for garden tours, which can be arranged at the tourist office too. Also acts as ticket office for the town's festivals.

Tourist Office (☎ 04 92 41 76 76; www.villedementon .com; Palais de l'Europe, 8 av Boyer; ⏲ 9am-7pm Mon-Sat, 9.30am-12.30pm Sun May-Sep, 8.30am-12.30pm & 2-6pm Mon-Fri, 9am-noon & 2-6pm Sat Oct-Apr) Arranges guided tours and garden visits (see the boxed text, p239) in conjunction with the Service du Patrimoine.

Sights & Activities
Down by the port, a small 17th-century fort crowns the spur of land between Menton's bays. It was built in 1636 to defend Menton and was later used as a salt cellar, prison and lighthouse. Today this seafront bastion is the **Musée Jean Cocteau** (☎ 04 93 57 72 30; hugues -delatouche@ville.menton.fr; sq Jean Cocteau; adult/under 25 yrs €3/2.25, 1st Sun of month free; ⏲ 10am-noon & 2-6pm Wed-Mon), displaying crayon drawings, tapestries and ceramics by the French artist. Cocteau restored the building himself, decorating the 2m-thick alcoves, outer walls and reception hall with pebble mosaics. His gravestone, looking out to sea, reads *Je reste avec vous* (I remain with you). In 1957 Cocteau decorated Menton's **Salles des Mariages** (Registry Office; place Ardoïno; adult/18-25 yrs €1.50/1.15; ⏲ 8.30am-12.30pm & 2-5pm Mon-Fri), inside the town hall, with scenes of Orpheus' and Eurydice's wedding, galloping horses and starry local lovers.

Near the museum is **Les Halles** (☎ 04 93 35 75 93; quai de Monléon; ⏲ 5am-1pm Tue-Sun), Menton's bustling indoor market. Walk under the arches to the east of the block and cross café-filled place aux Herbes to get to rue St-Michel, the main pedestrianised street in the old town.

From place du Cap a ramp leads up to the Italianate **Basilique St-Michel Archange** (☎ 04 93 35 81 63; ⏲ 10am-noon & 3-5.15pm Mon-Fri), considered the grandest baroque church in southern France. Its creamy façade is flanked by a 35m-tall clock tower and a 53m-high steeple (1701–03). The square outside hosts a music festival in August; see p238. Up the steps on place de la Conception is apricot-coloured **Chapelle des Pénitents Blancs** (☉ 3-5pm Mon), built in 1689, which has an ornate trompe l'oeil cupola inside.

It's a shame the occupiers of prime real estate **Cimetière du Vieux Château** (☉ 7am-8pm May-Sep, 7am-6pm Oct-Apr) can't appreciate the immense views. Walk right up montée du Souvenir to reach the main gates of the ornate 19th-century cemetery (side gates are locked). The inventor of rugby, Reverend William Webb Ellis (1805–72), is buried in the southwestern corner. For more grave-musing and marvellous vistas, continue north along the steep chemin du Trabuquet to the **Cimetière du Trabuquet**.

A little out of the town centre along the coast is 18th-century Palais Carnolès, a former summer residence of Monaco's royal family. It houses Menton's **Musée des Beaux-Arts** (☎ 04 93 35 49 71; 3 av de la Madone; admission free; ☉ 10am-noon & 2-6pm Wed-Mon), surrounded by the **Jardin de Sculptures**, a lemon and orange grove full of weird artworks.

Between 1920 and 1921 novelist Katherine Mansfield (1888–1923) stayed in the **Villa Isola Bella** (av Katherine Mansfield), in the upmarket neighbourhood of Garavan, to attempt to ease her worsening tuberculosis. Her short story *The Doves' Nest*, published the year she died, is about a group of lonely women living in a villa on the French Riviera.

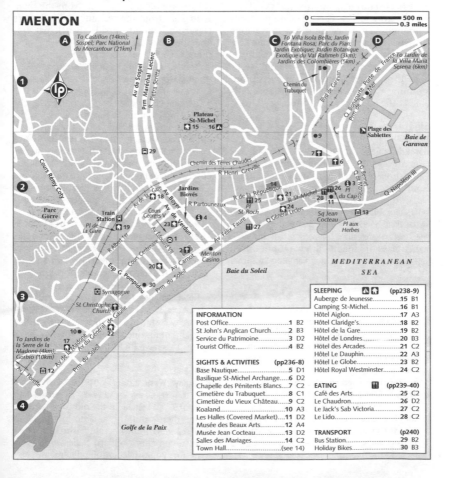

INFORMATION		SLEEPING 🛏️ (pp238-9)	
Post Office..................................1 B2		Auberge de Jeunesse.................15 B1	
St John's Anglican Church........2 B3		Camping St-Michel....................16 B1	
Service du Patrimoine...............3 D2		Hôtel Aiglon..............................17 A3	
Tourist Office.............................4 B2		Hôtel Claridge's.........................18 B2	
		Hôtel de la Gare.........................19 B2	
SIGHTS & ACTIVITIES (pp236-8)		Hôtel de Londres.......................20 B3	
Base Nautique...........................5 D1		Hôtel des Arcades......................21 C2	
Basilique St-Michel Archange....6 D2		Hôtel Le Dauphin.......................22 A3	
Chapelle des Pénitents Blancs....7 C2		Hôtel Le Globe...........................23 B2	
Cimetière du Trabuquet............8 C1		Hôtel Royal Westminster............24 C2	
Cimetière du Vieux Château......9 C2			
Koaland....................................10 A3		EATING 🍽️ (pp239-40)	
Les Halles (Covered Market).....11 D2		Café des Arts.............................25 B2	
Musée des Beaux Arts...............12 A4		Le Chaudron..............................26 D2	
Musée Jean Cocteau.................13 D2		Le Jack's Sab Victoria.................27 C2	
Salles des Mariages...................14 C2		Le Lido......................................28 D2	
Town Hall...............................(see 14)			
		TRANSPORT (p240)	
		Bus Station................................29 B2	
		Holiday Bikes............................30 B3	

Base Nautique (☎ 04 93 35 49 70; promenade de la Mer) rents dinghies/catamarans/kayaks for €19/31/8 per hour.

For tots, Menton holds no greater joy than **Koaland** (☎ /fax 04 92 10 00 40; 5 av de la Madone; ☺ 10am-noon & 3pm-midnight Wed-Mon summer, 10am-noon & 2-7pm Wed-Mon winter), a jungle playground with minigolf, carousel, rides including a dinky rollercoaster, and go-karts. Admission to the park is free, but rides cost €1.10/5/11 for one/six/16 tickets, and karting costs €2.50/10 for one/five goes.

Festivals & Events

Menton's fabulous two-week **Fête des Citrons** (Lemon Festival; www.feteducitron.com), when giant sculptures made from 130 tonnes of lemons are wheeled through the streets, kicks off on Mardi Gras in February. Mid-July brings contemporary dance and jazz to various gardens during the **Rencontres de Danse Contemporaine**. The classical **Festival de Musique**, held in front of Basilique St-Michel Archange throughout August, is an even more stunning affair. Tickets for events are available at the Service du Patrimoine (p236).

Sleeping

BUDGET

Hôtel de la Gare (☎ /fax 04 93 57 69 87; place de la Gare; s/d €32/42; ✗) Has nine rooms above Le Chouchou sandwich bar, near the station. Rooms are strictly nonsmoking.

On top of plateau St-Michel you'll find both the **Auberge de Jeunesse** (☎ 04 93 35 93 14; fax 04 93 35 93 07; dm incl breakfast €14.40, sheet hire €2.80; ☺ reception 7am-noon & 5-10pm; P), which has a midnight curfew (10pm out of season); and the two-star **Camping St-Michel**

FOOD FIGHT

An odd Menton legend is the origin of its **Fête de Bazaïs**, held in August, when everyone gathers round a huge cauldron of bean soup set up on quai Gordon Bennett. In the Middle Ages, so the story goes, plague, famine and incessant raiding by vicious Barbary pirates threatened to wipe out the town. The surviving residents, rather than turning on each other, clubbed together the food they had left and turned it into a body-and-soul-saving soup. Faced with such unnatural cooperation, the evil marauders fled.

(☎ 04 93 35 81 23; fax 04 93 57 12 35; 2 adults, tent & car €15). The plateau is a vertical 1km walk from the train station up the Escher-like escaliers des Orangers, or take a No 6 bus.

MID-RANGE

Hôtel Aiglon (☎ 04 93 57 55 55; aiglon.hotel@wanadoo .fr; 7 av de la Madone; d incl breakfast from €131; P ☒ ☒) In a former merchant's house, this three-star place has an air of *belle époque* quality. The heated pool, with an upmarket restaurant alongside, is open year-round. A good family choice, with playground and table tennis. Parking costs €6 per day.

Hôtel de Londres (☎ 04 93 35 74 62; www.hotel -de-londres.com; 15 av Carnot; d from €59; ☒) A member of the reliable Logis de France chain, this pretty hotel is set back from the main road 25m from the sea, and has a flowery terrace-restaurant outside. Beach parasols and loungers are loaned out for free, and there's table tennis for the kids.

Hôtel Le Dauphin (☎ 04 93 35 76 37; www.hotel -ledauphin.com; 408 promenade du Soleil; s/d with sea views €75/86, s/d with mountain views €56/61; P ☒) If you want sea views at a reasonable price, the three-star Dolphin is for you: bask on the wooden balconies and watch the waves.

Hôtel des Arcades (☎ 04 93 35 70 62; fax 04 93 35 35 97; 41 av Félix Faure; d incl breakfast with washbasin/ shower & toilet €56/60; menus €15 & €21.50) On the edge of the old town. There are no frills, but it's one of Menton's most picturesque options. Its **bar-restaurant** (reservations ☎ 04 93 28 34 09), under the arches, is a local favourite.

Hôtel Le Globe (☎ 04 92 10 59 70; fax 04 92 10 59 71; 21 av de Verdun; s/d from €48.78/53.36; ☺ closed Nov & Dec; P) Another sturdy Logis de France choice, with comfortable rooms and a tasty in-house **restaurant** (reservations ☎ 04 93 57 19 97) serving traditional dishes.

Hôtel Claridge's (☎ 04 93 35 72 53; www.claridges -menton.com; 39 av de Verdun; s/d from €37.40/57.58; P ☒) A two-star place handy for the station. The air-conditioned rooms cost a few euros more. TVs have English-language channels.

TOP END

Hôtel Royal Westminster (☎ 04 93 28 69 69; 1510 promenade du Soleil; s/d with sea views €85/125, s/d with town views €67/97; ☒) Close to the old town and the shore: there's nothing and no-one to block that sea view! Entirely refurbished in sedate style, it contains a billiard table, library and gym for your delectation. There are also

TOP FIVE GARDENS IN MENTON

Menton's maze of beautiful gardens, with pools, winding paths and exotic plantings, is a true Eden. Each one has a different horticultural appeal and historical charm, heightened by summer concert programmes.

■ **Jardin Botanique Exotique du Val Rahmeh** (☎ 04 93 35 86 72; av St-Jacques; adult/child €4/2; ⏰ 10am-12.30pm & 3-6pm Wed-Mon Apr-Sep, 10am-12.30pm & 2-5pm Oct-Mar) Laid out in 1905 for Lord Radcliffe, governor of Malta. Debt forced its botany-mad English owner, Maybud Campbell, to sell her prized one-hectare garden to the state in 1967; it now belongs to the French National History Museum. The terraces are renowned for their exotic fruit-tree collections and subtropical plants, including the only European specimen of the Easter Island tree *Sophora toromiro*, now extinct on the island. The tourist office runs guided visits (€7) here at 3pm on Monday.

■ **Jardin Fontana Rosa** (☎ 04 92 10 33 66; av Blasco Ibañez; ⏰ tour only) Created by Spanish novelist Vicente Blasco Ibañez in the 1920s and dedicated to writers. Its vivid colours are meant to conjure up Spain, but with fanciful benches, pergolas, pools and ceramics the effect is more of a delightful fairyland. The garden was extensively renovated in 2004–05, so should be in top condition. On the same street, **Parc du Pian** (av Blasco Ibañez; admission free) comprises a 1000-year-old grove of 530 olive trees spread across three hectares.

■ **Jardin de la Villa Maria Serena** (☎ 04 92 10 33 66; 21 promenade Reine-Astrid; ⏰ tour only) France's most temperate garden, where the temperature never falls below 5°C! The garden, known for its palm trees, frames the white Villa Maria Serena, designed in a grandiose Second Empire style by Charles Garnier in 1866. Guided visits (€5) depart at 10am on Tuesday; the tourist office has details.

■ **Jardins de la Serre de la Madone** (☎ 04 93 57 73 90; 74 rte du Val de Gorbio; admission €8; ⏰ tour only) It was an American gardener, Lawrence Johnston, who made this historic garden what it is today. After laying out the gardens at Hidcote Manor (Gloucestershire, UK), the botanical buff moved to the French coast where he planted dozens of rare plants, picked up from his travels around the world. The seven-hectare garden, abandoned for decades, is now being slowly restored by a small but enthusiastic army of gardeners. From February to October the tourist office runs guided tours (€8) departing at 9.30am Tuesday to Sunday. The gardeners will also show you round at 3pm on the same days.

■ **Jardins des Colombières** (rte des Colombières Garavan; ⏰ tour only) Olive trees, cypresses, lavender and other non-exotic plants feature in this series of lovely little gardens 5km north of town, each inspired by a different personality in Greek mythology. They were designed by Ferdinand Bac (1859–1952), comic writer and the illegitimate son of Napoleon III. Contact the tourist office for details of visits.

---

dinner dances on Wednesday evenings (per person/couple €35/60). Wheelchair access.

Eating

Menton doesn't have any outstanding restaurants; you'll have to train it to another town if your gourmet tastebuds are shrivelling. As well as the solid hotel restaurants in the Sleeping section, there are places to eat galore along av Félix Faure, its pedestrianised continuation rue St-Michel, and place aux Herbes. Pricier terraces with sea views line promenade du Soleil (watch waiters dice with death to bring you a coffee).

Café des Arts (☎ 04 93 35 78 67; 16 rue de République; pasta/salads/meats €8/8/12) An unstuffy place, with a stylish traditional-with-a-twist interior, laid-back staff and Internet access. Light meals are served at lunchtime only: in the evening, this becomes a loud and lively bar where food is scoffed at and alcohol is king.

Le Jack's Sab Victoria (☎ 04 93 57 91 22; promenade du Soleil; lunch/dinner menu €13.50/18.50) An upbeat spot with beachfront terrace, appetising snacks, and a well-heeled, sunglasses-wearing, 20s-to-50s crowd.

Le Chaudron (☎ 04 93 35 90 25; 28 rue St-Michel; menu €19.50; ⏰ closed Tue dinner & Wed) It's salads and traditional fare here, including stuffed courgette flowers (€10.50).

Le Lido (☎ 04 93 28 48 71; 24 rue St-Michel; menus €16 & €30) A bustling seafood bar, with piles of *langoustine* (small saltwater lobster), oysters, sea urchins and prawns served in seafood platters (€18 per person).

Getting There & Around

BICYCLE

To wheel along that long, long prom, rent a mountain bike/50cc scooter for €13/30 per day (€230/500 deposit) from **Holiday Bikes** (☎ 04 92 10 99 98; www.holiday-bikes.com; esplanade G Pompidou).

BUS

From the **bus station** (☎ 04 93 28 43 27, office ☎ 04 93 35 93 60; 12 promenade Maréchal Leclerc) there are buses to and from Monaco (€2.10, 30 minutes), Nice (€5.10, 1¼ hours), Ste-Agnès (€7.20 return, 45 minutes) and Sospel (€4.70 one way, 45 minutes). **Bus RCA** (☎ 04 93 85 64 44) runs a service to Nice-Côte d'Azur airport (€16.10, 1½ hours, departures to co-incide with flight times) via Monaco.

TRAIN

Trains to Ventimiglia (Italy) cost €2.10 and take 10 minutes. For information on Côte d'Azur train services see p225.

AROUND MENTON

A string of mountain villages peer down on Menton from the **Col de Castillon** (707m), a hair-raising pass that wends its way up the Vallée du Carei from the coast to Sospel (21km), the gateway to the Parc National du Mercantour (see p203). The road cuts through **Forêt de Menton**, a thick forest traversed with walking trails, then passes the **Viaduc du Caramel**. In former times the viaduct was used by the old Menton–Sospel tram, which used to trundle along the valley.

One of France's youngest villages, **Castillon** (population 280), just south of the top of the pass, is a model of modern rural planning. The original village was destroyed by an earthquake in 1887, then bombed in 1944. It was built anew in 1951, perched on the mountain slopes in true Provençal fashion. Castillon has a small **tourist office** (☎ 04 93 04 32 03; www.castillon06.com; rue de la République). The Sospel–Menton bus stops in the village.

About 5km northeast of Menton along the D24 is **Castellar**. En route you pass by the former home of designer Eileen Gray (see Trailing Le Corbusier, p49). Climb the steep and narrow streets, scale stairs and cut through tiny covered passages to reach place Clémenceau, at the summit of the village, from where there is a magnificent panorama across the valley. Both the GR51 and GR52 walking paths pass through Castellar.

Gorbio & Ste-Agnès

The flowery hilltop village of **Gorbio** (population 1162, elevation 360m), 10km northwest of Menton, is best known for its annual **Fête Dieu** (Corpus Christi) feast day in June. During the traditional **Procession aux Limaces**, villagers light up Gorbio's medieval cobbled streets with snail shells set in pots of sand and filled with burning olive oil. Other than that, exploring its maze of cobbled streets and lunching away several lazy hours at Beau Séjour (see opposite) are its chief attractions.

A walking trail (2km) leads from Gorbio to **Ste-Agnès** (population 1200, elevation 780m), supposedly Europe's highest 'seaside village' and a fantastic mountain escape. From montée du Souvenir, 187 rocky steps lead to the rubbly 12th-century **chateau ruins** (2-5pm Tue-Sun; admission by donation) with its intriguing flower beds, based on allegorical gardens found in medieval French poetry. Some friendly goats graze between the rocks, and views of the coastline are breathtaking.

The drawbridged entrance to the huge underground **Fort Ste-Agnès** (☎ 04 93 35 84 58; adult/7-14 yrs €3.05/1.52; 3-6pm Tue-Sun Jul-Sep, 2.30-5.30pm Sat & Sun Oct-Jun) lies at the top of the village. The 2500-sq-metre defence was built between 1932 and 1938 as part of the 240km-long Maginot line, a series of fortifications intended to give France time to mobilise its army if attacked. The fort is in good nick; it was maintained throughout the Cold War for use as a nuclear fallout shelter!

The tourist office at Menton (see p236) holds information on the two villages. In Ste-Agnès, the **Espace Culture et Tradition** (☎ 04 93 35 87 35; association.les.peintres.du.soleil@wanadoo.fr; rue du Seigneur Baroum; admission free; 9.30am-5pm Tue-Sat, 2-5pm Sun), a small exhibition space, has a few leaflets about the village.

SLEEPING & EATING

Camping Fleur de Mai (☎ /fax 04 93 57 22 36; rte du Val de Gorbio; adult/tent/car €12/4/13; ☼ mid-Sep–mid-Apr) Probably the busiest camp site along this stretch of coast, located midway between Menton and Gorbio.

Hôtel St-Yves (☎ 04 93 35 91 45; rue des Sarassins, Ste-Agnès; d €32, half-/full board per person €42/52; menu €12) Near the fort entrance, with simple but pleasant rooms in ice-cream colours and staff who make you feel really welcome. The restaurant's open wood fire is great on nippy winter evenings.

Beau Séjour (☎ 04 93 41 46 15; Gorbio; menus €21, €24 & €30; ☼ closed Wed & Oct-Apr) The stuff of Provençal dreams: the auberge's beautiful jasmine-covered terrace overlooks the fountain and 300-year-old elm tree in the quiet village square. Inside, a pianist plays while diners enjoy regional fare cooked with a twist. Credit cards not accepted.

Getting There & Away

From Menton there are buses to and from Ste-Agnès (€7.20 return, 45 minutes, two or three daily), Gorbio (€6.30 return, 30 minutes) and Castellar (€5.90 return, 25 minutes). A pass covering return transport from Menton to all three villages costs €16.

Cannes Area

CANNES AREA

Glittering, showbizzy Cannes sets camera flashes popping at its renowned 10-day International Film Festival in May, and year-round outside the ultrahip bars of its 'Magic Square'.

With its glamorous buildings, long beaches and fascinating inhabitants, the town is undoubtedly a celebrity in its own right…but don't let its dazzling white smile distract you from exploring further afield. For a day trip, skip across the Baie de Cannes to the Îles de Lérins, two perfectly formed islands packed with historical interest.

Northeast along the coast is beautiful little Antibes, nuzzling next to Vallauris and Golfe-Juan (Picasso territory). Then there's a cluster of arty, inland villages crowned with Matisse's Vence, Chagall's St-Paul de Vence and Renoir's Cagnes-sur-Mer. Perfumeries fill the air with scent in Grasse.

The most stunning natural feature of the entire Côte d'Azur – apart from the sky-blue sea, of course – is the lump of red porphyritic rock known as the Massif de l'Estérel. At its foot is St-Raphaël, a beachside resort town a couple of kilometres southeast of Roman Fréjus.

CANNES AREA

HIGHLIGHTS

- Find yourself a tiny, beribboned dog and join the crowds on **La Croisette** (p246), the Riviera's classiest promenade

- Sail to the **Îles de Lérins** (p253) to see where the mysterious Man in the Iron Mask was imprisoned

- Create your own bespoke perfume in fragrant **Grasse** (p269)

- Bathe yourself in the intense coloured light of Matisse's **Chapelle du Rosaire** (p265) in Vence; or view Picassos in **Antibes** (p258) and **Vallauris** (p255), and Renoirs in **Cagnes-sur-Mer** (p263)

- Admire the cartoon-like monsters, monks and mermaids in Fréjus' medieval **cloister** (p277)

- Visit **Château de la Napoule** (p272), the closest thing to Gormenghast you'll ever see

- Go wild for water sports – water-skiing, parascending, riding a rubber tyre or diving – up and down the coast

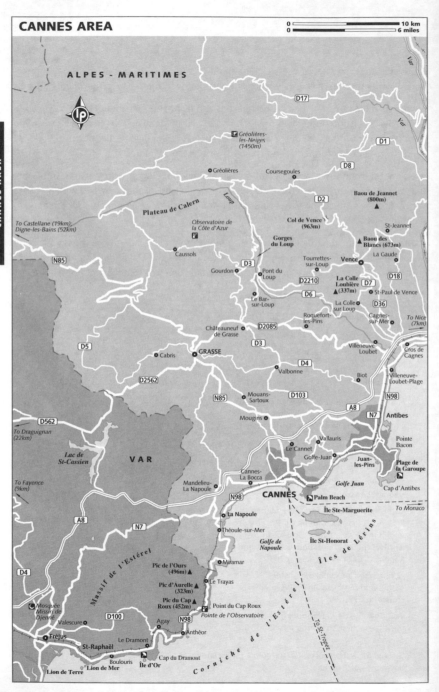

CANNES AREA

0 |———————————————| 10 km
0 |———————————————| 6 miles

ALPES - MARITIMES

Gréolières-les-Neiges (1450m)

Gréolières

Courségoules

D17

Var

D1

D8

D2

Baou de Jeannet (800m)

Plateau de Calern

Loup

Observatoire de la Côte d'Azur

To Castellane (19km); Digne-les-Bains (52km)

Caussols

N85

Col de Vence (963m)

St-Jeannet

Baou des Blancs (673m)

La Gaude

Gorges du Loup

Tourrettes-sur-Loup

Vence

Gourdon

D3

Pont du Loup

D2210

La Colle Loubière (337m)

D7

D18

Le Bar-sur-Loup

D6

St-Paul de Vence

La Colle sur Loup

D36

Châteauneuf de Grasse

D2085

Roquefort-les-Pins

Cagnes-sur-Mer

To Nice (7km)

D5

Cabris

GRASSE

D3

Villeneuve-Loubet

Cros de Cagnes

D2562

Valbonne

D4

Biot

Villeneuve-Loubet-Plage

To Draguignan (22km)

D562

N85

Mouans-Sartoux

D103

A8

N98

N7

Antibes

Mougins

Lac de St-Cassien

VAR

Vallauris

Le Cannet

Golfe-Juan

Juan-les-Pins

Pointe Bacon

To Fayence (9km)

Mandelieu-La Napoule

Cannes-La Bocca

Golfe Juan

Plage de la Garoupe

Cap d'Antibes

A8

N7

CANNES

Palm Beach

Île Ste-Marguerite

To Monaco

D4

Mosquée Missiri de Djenné

Valescure

D100

La Napoule

Théoule-sur-Mer

Golfe de Napoule

Île St-Honorat

Îles de Lérins

Massif de l'Estérel

Miramar

Pic de l'Ours (496m)

Pic d'Aurelle (323m)

Le Trayas

Pic du Cap Roux (452m)

Point du Cap Roux

Pointe de l'Observatoire

Fréjus

Agay

N98

Anthéor

St-Raphaël

Le Dramont

Boulouris

Lion de Terre

Lion de Mer

Île d'Or

Cap du Dramont

Corniche de l'Estérel

To St-Tropez

CANNES TO NICE

The 32km-stretch of coast that lies between Cannes and Nice is heavily developed, but packed with intriguing finds. It's particularly rich in artistic connections: in the late 1940s Picasso had a studio in the upmarket port of Antibes, lived in the neighbouring potters' village of Vallauris and quite often lunched with Matisse, Chagall and Fernand Léger in the hilltop village of St-Paul de Vence.

CANNES

pop 68,214

It's the banknotes of the affluent, spent with absolute nonchalance, that keep Cannes' exorbitant hotels, restaurants, boutiques, nightclubs and liner-sized yachts in business. All the wealth is truly hypnotic: revel in the luxury, even if it is second-hand, and play spot-the-celeb, -bodyguard or -shady millionaire.

For those who aren't seduced by Cannes' hedonistic air, there's enough natural beauty here to make a trip worthwhile: the harbour, bay, old quarter of Le Suquet, and the beaches and their bathers all spring into life on a sunny day.

Cannes, of course, is famous the world over for its International Film Festival, which sees the city's population treble overnight (see the boxed text 'Starring at Cannes' on p247).

Orientation

Don't expect glitz 'n' glamour the minute you step into Cannes: seedy sex shops surround the train station and bus stop on rue Jean Jaurès. Things glam up along rue d'Antibes, the main shop-till-you-drop street a couple of blocks south. Several blocks south again is Palais des Festivals, east of the Vieux Port.

Cannes' famous promenade, the magnificent blvd de la Croisette, begins at Palais des Festivals and continues eastwards along Baie de Cannes to Pointe de la Croisette.

Place Bernard Cornut Gentille, where the main bus station is located, fills the north-western corner of the Vieux Port. Perched on a hill just to the west is the quaint, pedestrian quarter of Le Suquet.

Information

BOOKSHOPS

Cannes English Bookshop (☎ 04 93 99 40 08; walstorer@wanadoo.fr; 11 rue Bivouac Napoléon; ⌚ 10am-6.30 or 7pm Mon-Sat) New books.

INTERNET ACCESS

Dre@m Cyber-Café (☎ 04 93 38 26 79; 6 rue du Commandant Vidal; ⌚ 10am-11pm; per hr €4.50) Laptop connection. English keyboards.

Web Center (☎ /fax 04 93 68 72 37; 24-26 rue Hoche; ⌚ 10am-11pm Mon-Sat, noon-8pm Sun; per 30/60min €3/4) English keyboards.

MEDICAL SERVICES

Pharmacies in Cannes rotate late shifts: check the *Nice-Matin* newspaper for timetables.

CANNES AREA MARKETS

This area hums and heaves with markets. Cannes itself sells flowers and food every day of the week; and there's an atmospheric **marché nocturnal** (night market; ⌚ most evenings June to September) for night owls, on the sands of Fréjus Plage.

Monday Cannes, Mouans-Sartoux, St-Raphaël

Tuesday Antibes (September to May), Biot, Cagnes-sur-Mer, Cannes, Fréjus Ville (June to September), Grasse, Mouans-Sartoux, St-Raphaël, Théoule-sur-Mer, Vallauris, Vence

Wednesday Antibes (September to May), Cagnes-sur-Mer, Cannes, Fréjus Ville, Grasse, Mouans-Sartoux, St-Raphaël, Vallauris, Vence (antiques)

Thursday Antibes (September to May), Cagnes-sur-Mer, Cannes, Fréjus Ville (June to September), Grasse, Mouans-Sartoux, St-Raphaël, Vallauris

Friday Antibes (September to May), Cagnes-sur-Mer, Cannes, Fréjus Ville (June to September), Grasse, Mouans-Sartoux, St-Raphaël, Vallauris, Vence

Saturday Antibes (September to May), Cagnes-sur-Mer, Cannes, Fréjus Ville, Grasse, Mouans-Sartoux, St-Raphaël, Vallauris, Vence

Sunday Antibes (September to May), Cagnes-sur-Mer, Cannes, Fréjus Ville (June to September), Grasse, St-Raphaël, Théoule-sur-Mer, Vallauris, Vence

SOS Médecins (☎ 04 93 38 39 38) Twenty-four-hour emergency doctor service.

MONEY
There are several banks along rue d'Antibes and rue Buttura, and ATMs everywhere.
Amex Bureau de Change (☎ 04 93 99 05 45; 8 rue des Belges; ☺ 9am-7pm May-Sep, 9.30am-noon & 1.30-5.30pm Mon-Fri Oct-Apr)
Thomas Cook (☎ 04 93 39 41 45; 8 rue d'Antibes; ☺ 9am-8pm Mon-Fri, 9am-6pm Sat & Sun) Cashes travellers cheques: 6.5% commission charge.

POST
Post Office (☎ 04 93 06 26 50; 22 rue Bivouac Napoléon; ☺ 9am-7pm Mon-Fri, 9am-noon Sat) Foreign currency exchange, ATM and Cyberposte.

TOURIST INFORMATION
Main Tourist Office (☎ 04 92 99 84 22; www.cannes .com; blvd de la Croisette; ☺ 9am-8pm Jul & Aug, 9am-7pm Mon-Sat Sep-Jun) On the ground floor of Palais des Festivals.
Tourist Office Annexe (☎ 04 93 99 19 77; rue Jean Jaurès; ☺ 9am-7pm Mon-Sat) Next to the train station.

Sights & Activities
The obvious place to start a people-watching stroll is on the Riviera's poshest, palm-shaded prom, the **blvd de la Croisette** (La Croisette). To get you in the mood, begin at the eastern end with tea on the terrace of the town's most famous hotel, the Carlton InterContinental (p250); like the rest of Cannes, it's just undergone a facelift. Its twin cupolas, erected in 1912, were modelled on the breasts of the courtesan La Belle Otéro, infamous for her string of lovers (including Britain's King Edward VII and Tsar Nicholas II).

Continue west and choose yourself a dream mansion in the sparkling windows of 140-year-old estate agency **John Taylor & Son** (☎ 04 97 06 65 65; www.john-taylor.fr; 55 blvd de la Croisette; ☺ 9am-12.30pm & 2-5pm Mon-Fri). Several million euros lighter, walk a further two blocks to **La Malmaison** (☎ 04 97 06 44 90, 04 93 99 04 04; 47 blvd de la Croisette; adult/18-25 yrs/under 18 yrs €4/2/free; ☺ 10am-1pm & 3-7pm Tue-Sun Jun-Aug, 10am-1pm & 2.30-6.30pm Tue-Sun Apr, May & Sep, 10am-12.30pm & 2.30-6pm Tue-Sun Oct-Mar), a seaside house (1863) sandwiched between the Grand Hôtel and flashy Noga Hilton, which holds temporary art exhibitions.

Next on the stroll, 400m along La Croisette, is the legendary **Palais des Festivals**

(Festival Palace; ☎ 04 93 39 01 01), a ferociously ugly concrete beast where beauties gather and films are screened during the Cannes festival. Pose for a photograph on those 22 steps leading up to the entrance (you'll have to provide your own glittery dresses and red carpet), then wander along the **allée des Étoiles du Cinéma**, a path of celebrity hand imprints embedded in the pavement.

Watch boats bobbing in the nearby **Vieux Port**, or cross the busy street and cheer on the *pétanque* players on **sq Lord Brougham**. Half the town hangs out here: kids ride the merry-go-round, teens drink shakes outside McDonald's and aspiring models wait to be spotted on the terrace of Palm Square (p251). A **flower market** blooms across the northern side of the square every morning.

Walk diagonally across sq Lord Brougham and join rue Félix Faure. Pass the back of the **Hôtel de Ville** (town hall) and bus station, until you reach the foot of rue St-Antoine. This ancient, restaurant-crammed street snakes north into hilly **Le Suquet**, the oldest town quarter. British chancellor Lord Brougham – the first foreigner to live in Cannes – built the **Villa Eleanor** (1862) here; locals thought he was crackers when he insisted on laying a green lawn around his abode.

The hill is topped by the majestic 12th-century **Église Notre Dame d'Esperance** (☺ 9am-noon & 2.15-6pm Mon autumn & spring, to 4pm Mon winter, 9am-noon & 3-7pm summer) and the **Musée de la Castre** (☎ 04 93 38 55 26; adult €3, 1st Sun of month free; ☺ 10am-1pm & 3-7pm Tue-Sun Jun-Aug, 10am-1pm & 2-6pm Tue-Sun Apr, May & Sep, to 5pm Tue-Sun Oct-Mar), which contains a diverse collection of art, antiquities and ethnographical oddities. It's worth a visit for the chillingly lit masks and funeral effigies, the views from the summit of its 12th-century tower and the fine collection of musical instruments in adjoining **Chapelle de Ste-Anne**.

BEACHES
Unlike Nice, Cannes is blessed with glorious sandy beaches. Most of the stretches along blvd de la Croisette are sectioned off for guests of fancy hotels. Sunbathers pay from €18.50 per day for mattress and parasol on **Plage du Festival** to an astonishing €32 on **Carlton Beach** to lap up the beachside equivalent of room service (lunch delivered to your deck chair, strips of carpet leading to the water's edge etc).

CANNES AREA

STARRING AT CANNES

For 12 days in May, Cannes becomes the centre of the cinematic universe. Over 30,000 producers, distributors, directors, publicists, stars and hangers-on descend to buy, sell or promote more than 2000 films. As the premier film event of the year, it attracts some 4000 journalists from around the world, guaranteeing a global spotlight to anyone with enough looks or prestige to grab it.

At the centre of the whirlwind is the 60,000-sq-metre Palais des Festivals (dubbed 'the bunker' by locals), on the legendary Croisette, where the official selections are screened. Its stark concrete base is adorned with the hand prints and autographs of celebrities: Timothy Dalton, Brooke Shields, Brigitte Bardot, David Lynch, Johnny Halliday and the like.

The palace was built to accommodate the first Cannes Film Festival, scheduled for 1 September 1939 as a response to Mussolini's Fascist propaganda film festival in Venice. Hitler's invasion of Poland brought an abrupt end to the festival but it restarted in 1946. The rest is history.

Over the years the festival split into 'in competition' and 'out of competition' sections. The goal of 'in competition' films is the prestigious Palme d'Or, awarded by the jury and its president to the film that best 'serves the evolution of cinematic art'. Notable winners include Francis Ford Coppola's *Apocalypse Now* (1979), Mike Leigh's *Secrets and Lies* (1996) and the 2004 winner *Farenheight 9/11*, in which American activist Michael Moore challenged the legitimacy and actions of the American administration.

The vast majority of films are 'out of competition'. Behind the scenes there's the *marché* (marketplace), where an estimated €150 million worth of business is negotiated for obscure movies that won't be coming to a theatre near you.

The combination of hard-core commerce and Tinseltown glitz gives the film festival its special magic. For a concentrated dose, put on your best clothes, straighten your shoulders and march confidently into the bar of the Majestic Hotel in the early evening.

Getting film tickets to the Cannes Film Festival is governed by a complex system of passes. Unless you are somehow connected to the film industry and apply well in advance, you will not get one. What you can get are free tickets to selected individual films, usually after their first screening. Look for the booth of the **Cannes Cinephiles** (☎ 04 93 99 04 04), outside the Palais des Festivals, which distributes film tickets daily from 9am to 5.30pm. For the film festival programme, consult the official website www.festival-cannes.org.

This arrangement leaves only a small strip of sand near the Palais des Festivals for the bathing hoi polloi. However, free public beaches **Plage du Midi** and **Plage de la Bocca** stretch for several kilometres west from the Vieux Port along blvd Jean Hibert and blvd du Midi.

If starfish rather than stars float your boat, contact **Plongée Club de Cannes** (☎ 04 93 38 67 57; www.sylpa.com in French; 46 rue Georges Clémenceau), whose vessel the Sylpa is moored on quai St-Pierre. An introductory dive costs €40 including equipment.

BOAT EXCURSIONS
The Îles de Lérins are a 20-minute skip across the bay from Cannes, and make a fine day out year-round; see p254 for how to get there.

Tours
If you haven't time for a stroll through Cannes, hop on **Le Petit Train** (☎ 06 14 09 49 39; www.cannes-petit-train.com; 10.30am-11pm Jul & Aug, shorter operating hrs winter), which sets off from opposite Hôtel Majestic Barrière. Travel along La Croisette and rue d'Antibes (adult/three to 10 years €5/2.50) or go up to Le Suquet (€6/3), or both (€8/5).

Festivals & Events
The Cannes **Festival International du Film** (International Film Festival) is held over 10 days in May; see Starring at Cannes above. In mid-July classical orchestras and solo performers from around the world gather for the 10-day **Nuits Musicales du Suquet** (Suquet Musical Nights). Concerts are held in the square in front of Église Notre Dame d'Esperance.

Sleeping
Hotel prices in Cannes fluctuate wildly. Prices given here are for the high season (June to September here); rooms can be

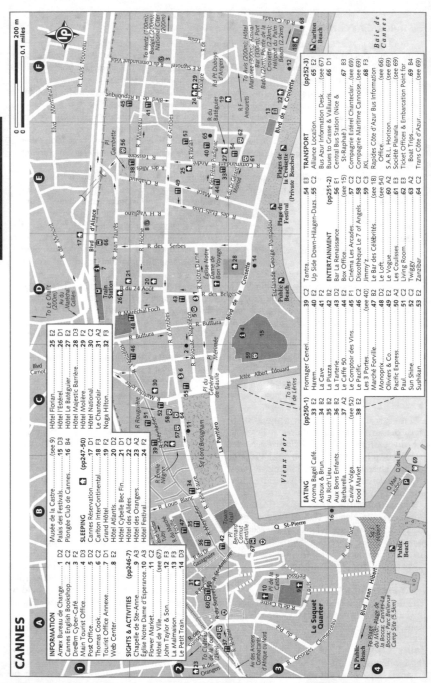

50% cheaper in low season. Staying in Cannes during the May film festival or congress periods is near impossible unless you've booked months in advance. Prices are astronomical, and many places only accept 12-day bookings. If you still want to try, get in touch with **Cannes Réservation** (☎ 08 26 00 06 06; www.cannes-reservation.com; 8 blvd d'Alsace; ⏱ 7am-7pm Mon-Sat).

BUDGET

Le Chalit (☎ 04 93 99 22 11; www.le-chalit.com; 27 av du Maréchal Galliéni; dm Apr-Sep €20, Oct-Mar €18, film festival €25-30, sheets €3; ⏱ reception 8.30am-1pm & 5-8.30pm) Around 300m northwest of the station, this is a very pleasant private hostel. There's one kitchen with a food and drinks machine, and no curfew (but a lockout operates between 10.30am and 5pm in summer). From July to September you have to book for three or more nights.

Hôtel Cybelle Bec Fin (☎ 04 93 38 31 33; fax 04 93 38 43 47; 14 rue du 24 Août; s/d with washbasin €20/26.50, with shower & toilet €40/43; ⏱ closed mid-Nov–mid-Dec) Since rooms this cheap in central Cannes are rarer than panda eggs, it would be churlish to point out the teeny room dimensions. It's an atmospheric old building, and the owners are sweethearts.

Le Chanteclair (☎ /fax 04 93 39 68 88; 12 rue Forville; r with shower/shower & toilet €40/42; ⏱ closed Nov & Dec) A well-run hotel in Le Suquet, with a pretty courtyard and small, functional whitewashed rooms. Rooms are the same price in high or low season.

Hôtel National (☎ 04 93 39 91 92; hotelnational cannes@wanadoo.fr; 8 rue Maréchal Joffre; s/d €45/60; ✕) Friendly, with newly furnished rooms. Reserve, and try to get a room overlooking the courtyard.

Parc Bellevue (☎ 04 93 47 28 97; www.parcbelle vue.com; 67 av Maurice Chevalier, Cannes-La Bocca; 2 adults, tent & car €20; ⏱ Apr-Sep; ✕) A facility-filled, three-star camp site about 5.5km west of the centre. Bus No 9 from Cannes bus station stops 400m away.

MID-RANGE

Hôtel Molière (☎ 04 93 38 16 16; www.hotel-moliere .com; 5-7 rue Molière; s €79, d €97-108; ✕) This is an immaculate place with a pastel-pink, wedding-cake exterior and a picture-postcard garden with shady cypress trees and seating. Most of the comfortable rooms have balconies overlooking the greenery.

AUTHOR'S CHOICE

Château de la Tour (☎ 04 93 90 52 52; www .hotelduchateaudelatour.com; 10 av Font-de-Veyre; d with garden views €120-140, with sea views €130-200, tr or q €240; P ✕ ✔) Set in a grand garden full of fountains and flowers, this is a charming hotel, although try to check your room first: the décor veers wildly from extremely tasteful to pure chintz. A Jacuzzi, spa and swimming pool add to the air of luxury, and families are made to feel very welcome. The château lies about 2km west of the centre; catch bus No 209 from the cental bus station.

Hôtel des Orangers (☎ 04 93 39 99 92; www.charm hotel.com; 1 rue des Orangers; d €130; P ✕) Right in Le Suquet, this large place has shady gardens and a sparkling swimming pool. Rooms, slightly '80s in feel, are decent sized, and some have sea views costing a little extra.

Hotel l'Estérel (☎ 04 93 38 82 82; www.hotel lesterel.com; 15 rue du 24 Août; s/d from €59/69; ✕) This huge block of a building couldn't be handier for the station. Its brand-new rooms are spare, simple and unlikely to offend anyone's sensibilities. The Estérel's best feature is its 6th-floor breakfast room, with rare rooftop views of Cannes.

Hôtel Le Batéguier (☎ 04 93 68 90 00; www.hotel -bateguier.com; 10 rue du Batéguier; s/d with shower €40/50, with shower & toilet €60/80; ✕) A little eight-roomed place with an enviable location – a mere stagger away from Cannes' hippest bars. Rooms are soundproofed and contain TVs.

Hôtel des Allées (☎ 04 93 39 53 90; www.hotel-des -allees.com; 6 rue Émile Négrin; s/d €59/79) This Swiss-run hotel offers clean, comfortable mid-range accommodation on a pedestrian street in the heart of central Cannes. All rooms have TVs, phones and safety boxes, and there are glimpses of the sea from some.

Hôtel Festival (☎ 04 97 06 64 40; www.hotel-festival .com; 3 rue Molière; s/d €105/125; ✕) The Festival features pastel-painted personality-free rooms, teamed rather strangely with dark-grey marble bathrooms. It's centrally placed, and has a Jacuzzi and sauna on site. Its two-bedroom apartment (per night €122 to €168) and three studio flats (per night €76 to €122) have little kitchenettes, more kick to the décor, and are good value for self-caterers; better rates can be negotiated for longer stays.

Hôtel Atlantis (☎ 04 93 39 18 72; www.cannes -hotel-atlantis.com; 4 rue du 24 Août; s/d €58/80; 🐾) Run by a funny, friendly family, the Atlantis has cheerful, basic rooms with hairdryers, telephones and TVs. Unusually for a two-star hotel, there's a sauna and a weights room for guests, tucked into the garret. Try to snag accommodation at the back, overlooking a peaceful pedestrian street.

Hôtel Florian (☎ 04 93 39 24 82; www.hotel-leflorian .com; 8 rue Commandant André; s/d €62/72; 🐾) Central, neat and modern. All rooms have private bathrooms, TVs, telephones and hairdryers.

TOP END
Grand Hôtel (☎ 04 93 38 15 45; www.grand-hotel -cannes.com in French; 45 blvd de la Croisette; s/d with city views €168/198, with sea views €229/269; **P** 🐾) The Grand has an appealing if somewhat 1960s ambience and, compared to its neighbours on La Croisette, offers affordable luxury. It has its own private gardens and slab of beach, which costs €11 to laze on with sunlounger and parasol.

Hôtel Martinez (☎ 04 92 98 73 00; www.hotel-mart inez.com; 73 blvd de la Croisette; d from €380; 🐾 🍴) Arguably the loveliest luxury place in town, this is an ultrasmart Art Deco–style place with huge, fabulous rooms, a posh Givenchy Spa (treatments €40 to €160) and private beach (€24 to €42 for mattress and parasol).

Other luxury places in town:

Carlton InterContinental (☎ 04 93 06 40 06; www .cannes.interconti.com; 58 blvd de la Croisette; d from €620; 🐾 🖥) Among the world's most photographed hotels (see p246 for one reason why). Utterly elegant rooms with contemporary accents and all the mod cons. Private beach (€30 per day).

Noga Hilton (☎ 04 92 99 70 00; www.cannes .hilton.com; 50 blvd de la Croisette; d from €429; **P** 🐾 🖥 🍴) Big, bold and blue, with four panoramic restaurants, a theatre, car park and shopping mall. Modern cream-and-terracotta rooms, some with balconies. Private beach (€30 per day).

Hôtel Majestic Barrière (☎ 04 92 98 77 00; www .majestic-barriere.com; 10 blvd de la Croisette; d from €450; 🐾 🍴) Art Deco palace. Private beach (€35 per day).

Eating
RESTAURANTS
Rue du Marché Forville is the area for less-expensive restaurants. There are lots of little restaurants along pedestrianised rue St-Antoine and rue du Suquet.

Astoux & Brun (☎ 04 93 39 21 87; 21 rue Félix Faure; menu €28, meal around €35; 🕐 noon-3pm & 7-11.30pm) *The* place for seafood. Every type and size of oyster is available, along with elaborate fish platters, lobster, crab, sea urchins, scallops and stuffed mussels. In summer chefs draw the crowds by preparing the shellfish out front. Available to eat in or take away.

Le Comptoir des Vins (The Wine Counter; ☎ 04 93 68 13 26; 13 blvd de la République; menu €25; 🕐 noon-2pm Mon-Wed, noon-2pm & 7.30-10pm Thu-Sat) Not to be confused with La Cave nearby, this well-stocked wine cellar, with 350+ wines, spirits and champagnes, hides a delicious little bistro out the back where you can eat and drink wine in discreet surroundings.

Barbarella (☎ 04 92 99 17 33; 14-16 rue St-Dizier; mains €23-26, menus €28-39; 🕐 7-11.30pm Tue-Sun, open Mon during congress; 🐾) An eye-catching, gay-friendly establishment with sleek Philippe Starck style. Its innovative menu, full of sweet/savoury clashes, contains treats like lemon and vanilla turbot, and asparagus and tiger-prawn ravioli.

Sushikan (☎ 04 93 39 86 13; 5 rue Florian; dishes €2.80-6; 🕐 noon-3.30pm & 6.30-11.30pm Mon-Sat) Raw-fish delicacies are sliced, diced and conveyor-belted at this smart sushi restaurant and takeaway. Looking for love? Get fed *and* find romance at one of their speed-dating-and-sushi evenings!

La Cave (The Wine Cellar; ☎ 04 93 99 79 87; www .restaurant-lacave.com; 9 blvd de la République; lunch menu €28; 🕐 closed Sun & Aug) This tasty little number produces hearty Provençal dishes in a setting reminiscent of an old Parisian bistro.

Pacific Express (☎ 04 93 39 43 43; 6-8 rue du Suquet; menus €27 & €44; 🕐 from 7pm Mon-Sat, closed mid-Nov–Dec; 🐾) With a rash of recommendations, this place on tiny rue du Suquet serves traditional Provençal and Mediterranean dishes until 9pm.

La Piazza (☎ 04 92 98 60 80; 9 place Bernard Cornut Gentille; mains €9-16, lunch/dinner menu €11/19; 🕐 noon-2.30pm & 7-11.45pm) This sprawling, friendly establishment offers the best home-made pasta, risotto and pizza in town.

Aux Bons Enfants (80 rue Meynadier; menu €17; 🕐 closed Sat evening & Sun Oct-Jun) A people's-choice place, offering regional dishes like *aïoli garni* (aïoli with vegetables) and *mesclun* (green salad with dandelion leaves) in a convivial atmosphere. It's easy to miss the narrow doorway, which leads up to the 1st-floor dining area. Credit cards not accepted.

Le Pacific (☎ 04 93 39 46 71; 14 rue Vénizélos; menu €10.50, mains €8-12; ☒ 11.30am-2.30pm Sun-Fri) Not far from the train station, this is a rough-and-ready favourite with locals for its eat-on-the-cheap, three-course *menu*. If you like it, buy a 10-*menu* carnet for €95.

Au Rich'Lieu (☎ 04 93 39 98 75; 66 rue Meynadier; menus €14.90 & €23; ☒ noon-2.30pm & 5-11pm, closed Sun lunch) If you love mussels, try the whopping portions here (€9.60 with fries). Fish dishes and wood-fired pizzas are also available.

Among the rash of tasty places to eat and be seen around Cannes' *carré magique* (see p252) are loungy bar-cum-restaurant **Harem** (☎ 04 93 39 62 70, reservations ☎ 06 18 09 70 28; 15 rue des Frères Pradignac); **Les 3 Portes** (☎ 04 93 38 91 70; 16 rue des Frères Pradignac); and equally trendy **Tantra** (☎ 04 93 39 40 39; 13 rue du Dr Gérard Monod).

CAFÉS
Up Side Down–Häagen-Dazs (☎ 04 93 99 27 70; 5 place du Général de Gaulle; menu €20; ☒ 7am-2am) Night and day, this contemporary caff lures in a buoyant crowd of sightseers, families and teen couples. Waiters sashay round the shaded terrace – they look damn hot, but service can be erratic! For those who can't wait for their ice-cream fix, the back door at 45 rue d'Antibes leads directly into the Häagen-Dazs takeaway.

La Tarterie (☎ 04 93 39 67 43; 33 rue Bivouac Napoléon; eat-in/takeaway menu €6.90/8.40; ☒ 8.30am-4.30pm Mon-Fri; ☒) There's a good range of well-priced salads (€6 to €8), but it's the house specialities – sweet/savoury tarts and *clafoutis* for €3 to €5 per slice – that bring in the crowds.

Le Caffe 50 (☎ 04 93 39 00 01; 10 rue des Frères Pradignac; mains €15-25; ☒ 11am-11pm) Within high-heeled strolling distance from the magic square, this bold, striking place serves light lunches of *panini*, bruschetta and salads, and full-on Italian meals at night.

Aroma Bagel Café (22 rue Commandant André; bagels €7.50-12) Giant-sized bagels are dished up here, crammed with delectable goodies (such as cheese, cream and basil…or hamburgers for you less-traditional types). To eat in or take away.

SELF-CATERING
Cannes' main markets are the morning **food market** (place Gambetta; ☒ closed Mon winter) and the **Marché Forville** (rue du Marché Forville; ☒ Tue-Sun), a covered fruit and vegetable market two blocks north of the bus station. The super-

market Monoprix has entrances on rue Jean Jaurès, rue Maréchal Foch and rue Buttura.

Gather admirable picnic ingredients or foodie presents from the following specialist shops:

Caviar Volga (☎ 04 92 98 17 12; 5 rue Maréchal Joffre; ☒ 9am-7pm Tue-Sat) Caviar emporium.

Fromager Ceneri (☎ 04 93 39 63 68; fax 04 93 68 99 98; 22 rue Meynadier; ☒ 9am-6pm Tue-Sat) One of France's top cheese shops.

Oliviers & Co (☎ 04 93 39 00 38; 4 rue Macé; ☒ 10am-1pm & 3-7.30pm Mon-Sat) Olive-oil shop, with tastings.

Paul (☎ 04 93 38 15 59; 8 rue Meynadier; ☒ 8am-7pm) Freshly baked breads (including honey and olive) and delicious sandwiches.

Sun Shine (☎ 04 93 39 44 56; 5 rue Maréchal Joffre; ☒ 9.30am-7.30pm Mon-Sat) Serious wine cellar.

Entertainment
Tickets for many events are sold at the **box office** (☎ 04 92 98 62 77; ☒ 10am-7pm Mon-Sat), inside the Palais des Festivals tourist office.

The free monthly *Le Mois à Cannes* lists what's on and where. Pick up a copy from the tourist office.

NIGHTCLUBS & BARS
Some cafés double as drinking holes come evening.

Palm Square (☎ 04 93 06 78 27; www.palm-square .com in French; 1 allées de la Liberté) This lavish bar-cum-restaurant is decked out in tasteful colonial style, with tribal knick-knacks, leather seats and tropical tunes. Nibble light lunches with the wannabes, or slink back at dusk to sip cocktails with the stars.

Bar La Renaissance (☎ 04 93 38 38 20; 38 rue Jean Jaurès; ☒ 6-10pm) This small and cosy bar overlooking the bustling market on place Gambetta is down-to-earth and draws a relaxed crowd. Black-and-white photos of yesterday's stars and glamour queens line the walls.

During the film festival, autograph hunters can track down their favourite stars in Cannes' classiest clubs and bars:

Le Bar des Célébrités (☎ 04 93 06 40 06; 58 blvd de la Croisette; ☒ 11-2.30am) At the Carlton InterContinental.

Amiral Bar (☎ 04 92 98 73 00; www.hotel-martinez .com; 73 blvd de la Croisette; ☒ to 2.30am) An ever-popular piano bar at Hôtel Martinez, serving champagne and cocktails to the glitterati.

Jimmy'z (☎ 04 92 98 78 00; pportier@lucienbarriere .com; Palais des Festivals, blvd de la Croisette; ☒ midnight-5am Thu-Sat) The Cannes branch of the legendary Monaco club (see p330).

CANNES AREA

Le Loft (☎ 04 93 39 40 39; 13 rue du Dr Gérard Monod; 10.30pm-2.30am) A more low-key lounge bar where celebrities sometimes play truant from official functions.

Cannes' *carré magique* (magic square) is jam-packed with ultrahip haunts, including **Living Room** (☎ 04 93 99 34 82; 17 rue du Dr Gérard Monod; restaurant from 6pm), whose nonchalant restaurant-bar shields an ultraposey crowd; and **Les Coulisses** (☎ 04 92 99 17 17; www.lescoulisses.com; 29 rue Commandant André), a tiny but glam hot spot near the seafront, where crowds of beautiful Cannois perch on squashy purple seats. Rue Commandant André, rue des Frères Pradignac, rue du Batéguier and rue du Dr Gérard Monod form the magic square's edges.

In Le Suquet, the hip record shop and bar **Twiggy** (☎ 04 93 99 13 32; 3 rue des Suisses; 3pm-12.30am Tue-Sun) is a gay-friendly temple to 1970s pop.

GAY & LESBIAN VENUES
Zanzibar (☎ 04 93 39 30 75; 85 rue Félix Faure; 6pm-6am) The oldest and most venerable gay bar on the coast (opened in 1885), where people come to talk, dance to house music and admire erotic frescoes of well-built sailors.

Discothèque Le 7 of Angels (☎ 04 93 39 10 36; www.discotheque-le7.com; 7 rue Rouguière; admission free-€16; 11.30pm-dawn) Known simply as '7', Cannes' premier gay disco is a high-camp place (drag cabarets etc), which is attracting an increasingly mixed crowd these days.

Le Vogue (☎ 04 93 39 99 18; 20 rue du Suquet; closed Mon) An ambient bar which draws a young, trendy, predominantly gay crowd up to Le Suquet.

CINEMAS
Considering Cannes' international reputation, nondubbed films are hard to find. **Cinéma les Arcades** (☎ 08 92 68 00 39; www.cinefil .com in French; 77 rue Félix Faure; tickets €7.50) The only cinema that regularly screens films in their original languages.

Getting There & Away
AIR
Nice Hélicoptères (☎ 04 93 43 42 42; www.nice helicopteres.com; blvd de la Croisette; one way/return €85.30/145.35; 8am-8pm summer, 8am-5pm winter) flies from Nice to Héliport du Palm Beach, and provides a free shuttle service to Palais des Festivals.

BOAT
Compagnie Maritime Cannoise (CMC; ☎ 04 93 38 66 33; www.ilesdelerins.com in French) runs trips from Cannes to Monaco (9.15am Monday June to September) and St-Tropez (9.15am Tuesday, Thursday and Saturday May, June and September, 9.15am Tuesday to Sunday July and August). A return fare to either costs €30/15 per adult/five to 10 years.

Trans Côte d'Azur (☎ 04 92 98 71 30; www.trans -cote-azur.com) runs boat excursions (reservations essential) to Corniche de l'Estérel (adult/four to 10 years €15/8.50, 2.30pm Monday, Wednesday and Friday June to September); Monaco (adult/four to 10 years €32/16, 8.30am Saturday, 10am Thursday July to mid-September); Porquerolles (adult/four to 10 years €47/21, 8.30am Sunday July to mid-September); St-Tropez (adult/four to 10 years €31/16, 10.15am Tuesday, Thursday, Saturday and Sunday June, 10.15am daily July to mid-September); and San Remo, Italy (adult/four to 10 years €42/19.50, 8.30am Saturday July to mid-September).

There are also seasonal boats from Golfe-Juan (see p256) and the seaside resorts of Mandelieu-La Napoule (see p272) and Théoule-sur-Mer (see p272).

BUS
The train is quicker and cheaper for coastal journeys. Buses to Nice (€5.90, 1½ hours, every 20 minutes) and Nice-Côte d'Azur airport (€12.70 via A8, 40 minutes; €2.20 via regular road, 1½ hours; hourly from 8am to 7pm) leave from the **central bus station** (marked 'Hôtel de Ville' on bus timetables; place Bernard Cornut Gentille). For westbound buses along the Corniche de l'Estérel coast road to St-Raphaël, see p274.

Buses to Grasse (€3.80, 45 minutes) via Mougins (€1.90, 20 minutes), Mouans-Sartoux (€2.30, 25 minutes) and Vallauris (€2.40, 30 minutes) depart every 20 minutes between 6am and 9pm Monday to Saturday and hourly between 8.30am and 8.30pm Sunday from Cannes' second bus station, next to the train station on rue Jean Jaurès. Most services are operated by **Rapides Côte d'Azur** (RCA; information office ☎ 04 93 39 11 39; www.rca.tm.fr in French; 7.30am-noon & 1.30-5pm Mon, Tue, Thu & Fri), which has an information desk at the bus station on rue Jean Jaurès.

TRAIN

Cannes train station is located on rue Jean Jaurès. Destinations within easy reach include St-Raphaël (€5.60, 30 minutes, two per hour), from where you can get buses to St-Tropez and Toulon; and Marseille (€22.80, two hours). Most trains to and from Nice (€5.30, 40 minutes) stop in Antibes (€3.60, 15 minutes).

Getting Around

BICYCLE

Alliance Location (☎ 04 93 38 62 62; www.alliance location.fr; 19 rue des Frères Pradignac; ☯ 9am-6.30pm) rents mountain bikes for €15 per day.

BUS

Cannes and destinations up to 7km away are served by **Bus Azur** (☎ 04 93 45 20 08; place Bernard Cornut Gentille; ☯ 7am-7pm Mon-Fri, 8.30am-noon & 2-6.30pm Sat), with an information desk at the central bus station. A ticket/10-ticket carnet costs €1.30/8.80. A weekly Carte Palm'Hebdo/monthly Carte Croisette costs €9.80/33.25.

Bus No 8 runs along the coast from place Bernard Cornut Gentille to the port and Palm Beach Casino on Pointe de la Croisette. Bus Nos 2 and 9 run from the train station, via the bus station, to/from the beaches in Cannes La Bocca. Line 620 follows the same route but continues further southwest along the coast to Théoule-sur-Mer.

CAR & MOTORCYCLE

All the major car-rental companies have offices in Cannes, including **Avis** (☎ 04 93 94 15 86; 69 blvd de la Croisette); **Budget** (☎ 04 93 99 44 04; 160 rue d'Antibes); **Hertz** (☎ 04 93 99 04 20; 145 rue d'Antibes); and **National Citer** (☎ 04 93 43 58 82; 160 rue d'Antibes).

Car-rental agency **JKL** (☎ 04 97 06 37 77; www .jkl-forrent.com; 21 rue du Canada) offers cars fit for a star (if you absolutely, positively have to get noticed, how about a yellow Humvee for €1,000 a day?).

Alliance Location (☎ 04 93 38 62 62; www.alliance location.fr; 19 rue des Frères Pradignac; ☯ 9am-6.30pm) rents 50cc scooters/125cc motorcycles starting at €40/60 per day.

TAXI

Call ☎ 04 93 38 91 91 or ☎ 04 93 49 59 20 to order a taxi.

ÎLES DE LÉRINS

The two islands making up Lérins – Île Ste-Marguerite and Île St-Honorat – lie within a 20-minute boat ride of Cannes. Known as Lero and Lerina in ancient times, these tiny, traffic-free oases of peace and tranquillity remain a world away from the glitz, glamour and hanky-panky of cocky Cannes.

Wild camping, cycling and smoking are forbidden on both islands. There are no hotels or camp sites on either island and St-Honorat, the smaller of the two, has nowhere to eat either. Take a picnic and a good supply of drinking water with you.

Neither island has a wildly fantastic beach. Pretty coves can be found on the southern side of Ste-Marguerite (a 45-minute walk from the harbour). On the northern side, sunworshippers lie on rocks and mounds of dried seaweed.

Île Ste-Marguerite

The enigmatic Man in the Iron Mask was imprisoned here in the late 17th century (see the boxed text on p254). Covered in sweet-smelling eucalyptus and pine, the island (home to a mere 20 families) is only 1km from the mainland and makes an excellent day trip.

Ste-Marguerite is dominated by the 17th-century **Fort Royal**, built by Richelieu to defend the islands from the Spanish (who occupied the fort anyway from 1635 to 1637), with later additions by Vauban. Today it houses the **Musée de la Mer** (☎ 04 93 43 18 17; adult/18-25 yrs €3/2, 1st Sun of month free; ☯ 10.30am-1.15pm & 2.15-5.45pm Tue-Sun Apr-Sep, to 4.45pm Oct-Mar), with exhibits on the fort's Greco-Roman history and on ships wrecked off the island's coast.

A door to the left in the museum's reception hall leads to the **state prison**, built by Louis XIV. Steamboat inventor Claude François Dorothée was imprisoned here between 1773 and 1774; he came up with his idea while watching slaves row the royal galley to the island. Other inmates included six Huguenots, put into solitary confinement for life in 1689 for refusing to renounce their Protestant faith – look at the triple-grilled windows and you'll understand why they went insane.

Ste-Marguerite is encircled and criss-crossed by walking trails. There's also an underwater snorkel trail off the west coast of the island.

GETTING THERE & AWAY

Compagnie Estérel Chanteclair (☎ 04 93 39 11 82; www.ilesdelerins.com in French), **Compagnie Maritime Cannoise** (CMC; ☎ 04 93 38 66 33; www.ilesdelerins .com in French), **SARL Horizon** (☎ /fax 04 92 98 71 36) and **Trans Côte d'Azur** (☎ 04 92 98 71 30; www.trans -cote-azur.com) all run year-round daily ferries (from around 7.30am, at least hourly) from Cannes to Ste-Marguerite. All charge €10/5 return per adult/five to 10 years, and the journey time is about 20 minutes. Ticket offices and boats are on quai des Îles (on the far side of the quai Max Laubeuf car park at the Vieux Port).

Île St-Honorat

Forested St-Honorat was once the site of a powerful monastery founded in the 5th century. Today it is home to 30-odd Cistercian monks who own the island but welcome people to visit their monastery and four of the seven small chapels dotted around the island, which have drawn pilgrims since the Middle Ages. At 1.5km by 400m, it's the smallest (and most southerly) of the two Lérins islands.

The **Monastere Fortifié** (☎ 04 92 99 54 00; www .abbayedelerins.com in French; admission €2 Jul-Sep, rest of yr free; ⏱ 10.30am-4pm mid-Jun–mid-Sep, 10.30am-12.30pm & 2.30-4pm mid-Sep–mid-Jun) guarding the island's southern shores is all that remains of the original monastery. Visits from July to September are by guided tour only from 10.30am to 12.30pm, and 2.30pm to 4.45pm Monday to Saturday, and from 2.30pm to 4.45pm Sunday. Built in 1073 to protect the monks from pirate attacks, its entrance stood 4m above ground level and was accessible only by ladder (later replaced by the stone staircase evident today). The elegant arches of the vaulted **cloître de la prière** (cloister of prayer) on the 1st floor date from the 15th century, and there's a magnificent panorama of the coast from the donjon terrace.

THE MAN IN THE IRON MASK

'More than 60 names have been suggested for this prisoner whose name no one knows, whose face no one has seen: a living mystery, shadow, enigma, problem.'

Victor Hugo.

The Man in the Iron Mask was imprisoned by Louis XIV (1661–1715) in the fortress on Île Ste-Marguerite from around 1687 until 1698, when he was transferred to the Bastille in Paris. Only the king knew the identity of the man behind the mask, prompting a rich pageant of myth and legend to be woven around the ill-fated inmate.

Political and social satirist Voltaire (1694–1778) claimed the prisoner was the king's brother – a twin or an illegitimate older brother. In 1751 he published *Le Siècle de Louis XIV*, which attested that Louis XIV's usurped brother, face shrouded in iron, arrived on the island in 1661, was personally escorted to the Bastille by its new governor in 1690, and died in 1703 aged around 60. His featureless mask was lined with silk and fitted with a spring mechanism at the chin to allow him to eat. Prison guards had orders to kill anyone who dared remove his iron mask.

Over 60 suggested identities have been showered on the masked prisoner, among them the Duke of Monmouth (actually beheaded under James II), the Comte de Vermandois (son of Louis XIV, said to have died from smallpox in 1683), the Duc de Beaufort (killed by the Turks in 1669) and Molière. Some theorists claimed the man in the iron mask was actually a woman.

The storming of the Bastille in 1789 fuelled yet more stories. Revolutionaries claimed to have discovered a skeleton, the skull of which was locked in an iron mask, when plundering the prison, while others focused on a supposed entry found in the prison register which read *détenu 64389000: l'homme au masque de fer* (prisoner 64389000: the man in the iron mask). Others provoked a storm with their allegations that there was *no* iron mask entry in the prison register – just a missing page. In 1855 an iron mask was found in a scrap heap in Langres, north of Dijon, and subsequently displayed in the town museum.

With the 1850 publication of Alexandre Dumas' novel *Le Vicomte de Bragelonne*, the royal crime became written in stone: in 1638 Anne of Austria, wife of Louis XIII (1617–43) and mother of Louis XIV, gives birth to twins; one is taken away from her, leaving her to bear the secret alone until the terrible truth is discovered. Dozens of iron mask films were made in the last century, including the 1976 version starring Richard Chamberlain, and the 1998 film starring Leonardo DiCaprio.

In front of the donjon is the walled, 19th-century **Abbaye Notre Dame de Lérins**, built around a medieval cloister. In the souvenir shop you can buy the 50% alcohol Lérina, a ruby-red, lemon-yellow or pea-green liqueur concocted by the monks from 44 different herbs.

The Byzantine-inspired **Chapelle de la Trinité** (☼ visits by guided tour only 10.30am-12.30pm & 2.30-4.45pm Mon-Sat, 2.30-4.45pm Sun Jul-Sep) was built between the 9th and 10th centuries on the island's eastern tip.

GETTING THERE & AWAY
Boats to St-Honorat also leave from quai des Îles. They are run by the abbey boat service **Société Planaria** (☎ /fax 04 92 98 71 38; www.abbayedelerins.com), with a return fare costing €10/5 per adult/five to 10 years. Boats run almost hourly from 8am to 4.30pm from May to September, and every one to two hours from 8am to 3pm October to May.

VALLAURIS & GOLFE-JUAN
pop 25,931

The traditional potters' town of Vallauris is rather charmless, but definitely worth visiting for its three memorable museums. One is dedicated to Picasso, who lived in Vallauris with Françoise Gilot from 1948 until 1955.

Clay pots have been created in Vallauris since Roman times. A declining trade in the 16th century was boosted by a group of Genoese potters who moved their studios to Vallauris in order to exploit its clay-rich soil. An artistic revival in the 1940s, spearheaded by Picasso, ensured the trade's survival.

The statue of **L'Homme au Mouton** – a dour bronze figure clutching a sheep – on place Paul Isnard (adjoining place de la Libération) was a gift from Picasso to Vallauris.

Vallauris' satellite resort of Golfe-Juan, 2km south on the coast, is where Napoleon landed following his return from exile in 1815. Today the main reason for visiting is to catch a boat (summer only) to the Îles de Lérins.

Orientation & Information
Vallauris bus station adjoins place de la Libération, the central square in the northern part of town. From here av George Clémenceau, the main pottery-stuffed street, stretches 1.5km south to the **tourist office**

(☎ 04 93 63 82 58; www.vallauris-golfe-juan.fr in French; square du 8 Mai; ☼ 9am-noon & 2-6pm Mon-Sat), in a car park off the D135.

The closest train station is in Golfe-Juan. From Vallauris tourist office head south along the D135 to Golfe-Juan's central square Nabonnand, then continue south along av de la Gare to Golfe-Juan train station. Golfe-Juan **tourist office** (☎ 04 93 63 73 12; www.vallauris-golfe-juan.fr in French; av des Frères Roustan; ☼ 9am-noon & 2-6pm Mon-Fri) is past the train station at the seafront.

Sights & Activities
CHÂTEAU MUSÉE DE VALLAURIS
The **Château Musée De Vallauris** (Vallauris Castle Museum; ☎ 04 93 64 16 05; contact.musee@ville-vallauris.fr; place de la Libération; adult/concession €3.20/1.65; ☼ 10am-12.15pm & 2-6pm Wed-Mon mid-Jun–mid-Sep, 10am-12.15pm & 2-5pm mid-Sep–mid-Jun) hosts three museums: the **Musée National Picasso**, which is based around Picasso-decorated Chapelle La Guerre et La Paix (War and Peace Chapel); the **Musée Magnelli**, devoted to the works of Italian artist Albert Magnelli (1899–1971); and the **Musée de la Céramique** (Ceramic Museum), in which the history of Vallauris' age-old craft is unravelled.

Picasso (1881–1973) was 71 when he started work on his *temple de la paix* (temple of peace) in a disused 12th-century chapel. Dramatic murals painted onto plywood panels are tacked to the church's stone walls. In *War*, on the left, a hideous figure clutches a bloody sword, a sack of skulls and a basket of bacteria (representing germ warfare); books are trampled under the hooves of a black horse. The themes are reversed in *Peace*, on the right: figures gather in harmony, a man writes in a book and a child ploughs the sea with a winged white horse.

The museum is next to Vallauris bus station; steps lead from the station to place de la Libération.

GALERIE MADOURA
A handful of licensed copies of ceramics cast by Picasso are on sale at **Galerie Madoura** (☎ 04 93 64 66 39; www.madoura.com; av Suzanne Ramié; admission free; ☼ 10am-12.30pm & 3-6pm Mon-Fri), the workshop where, in 1946, Picasso first dabbled with clay under the guidance of local potters Georges and Suzanne Ramié. He consequently granted the Ramiés exclusive rights to reproduce his work, resulting in

a limited edition – between 25 and 500 in number – of 633 different Picasso pieces cast between 1947 and 1971.

From the bus station, walk south along av George Clémenceau, then west (right) along av Suzanne Ramié.

MAISON DE LA PÉTANQUE

Everything from the invention of *pétanque* to its contemporary champions can be discovered in the quaint **Maison de la Pétanque** (Provençal Boules House; ☎ 04 93 64 11 36; www.maison delapetanque.com; 1193 chemin de St-Bernard; adult/under 18 yrs €3/free; ☼ 9am-noon & 2-6.30pm Mon-Sat Apr-Sep, Mon-Fri Oct-Mar), a museum dedicated to the region's most popular sport. Amateurs can have a spin on the *pétanque* pitch, and enthusiasts can get their own set of made-to-measure *boules*.

The museum is 2km north of Vallauris bus station. From the station, head north along av de Grasse and at the roundabout bear east (right) along chemin St-Bernard.

BOAT EXCURSIONS

In summer **Maritime Cap d'Antibes** (☎ 04 93 63 91 30; www.ilesdelerins.com in French) sails daily from quai St-Pierre at the Vieux Port in Golfe-Juan to Îles Ste-Marguerite. See right for details.

Sleeping & Eating

Bar Hôtel du Stade (☎ 04 93 64 91 27; 48 av Georges Clémenceau; d with washbasin €25) This cheap 'n' cheerful nine-room place is above a local bar in Vallauris centre; one side of the building overlooks a pedestrianised street. Shared showers and toilets are in the corridor.

Auberge Siou Aou Miou (☎ 04 93 64 39 89; fax 04 93 64 45 60; 105 chemin des Fumades; d €61) This Logis de France property, with the decent standards that implies, is about 1km southwest of Vallauris bus station. Rooms have airy balconies, and there's a blossom-filled terrace and good Provençal restaurant, too.

Maison Lascasse (☎ 04 93 63 14 14; 62 av Georges Clémenceau; ☼ 7am-8pm) A staggering 55 different breads are baked before your eyes at this master bakery.

Getting There & Around

Golfe-Juan train station, from where trains go in both directions along the coast, is 3km south of Vallauris town, making bus the most convenient way of getting to/from Vallauris.

From Vallauris **bus station** (☎ 04 93 64 18 37; cnr av de la Grasse & av Aimé Berger), bus No 6V goes to Cannes train station (€2.70, every 30 minutes). Bus No 5V serves Antibes bus station (€2.70, 10 per day). Buses are less frequent on Sundays.

Envibus No 4V runs between Vallauris bus station and Golfe-Juan train station (€1, every 20 minutes Monday to Saturday, every 35 minutes Sunday). Journey time is 11 minutes.

Maritime Cap d'Antibes (☎ 04 93 63 91 30; www.ilesdelerins.com in French) sails from quai St-Pierre at the Vieux Port in Golfe-Juan to Îles Ste-Marguerite. May to October there are four crossings daily (11.30am, 3pm, 5pm, 6.15pm; 50 minutes). A return ticket to Ste-Marguerite costs €10/5 per adult/five to 10 years. In July and August there are a couple of weekly boat trips to St-Tropez (€28) and also to Monaco (€42). To get to the port from the Golfe-Juan train station, turn right (east) along av de Belgique, then turn right again (south) onto av de la Gare, which cuts underneath the train track towards the sea. At the end of the street, bear south again onto blvd des Frères Roustan, the promenade fronting the Vieux Port.

ANTIBES

pop 72,412

Directly across the Baie des Anges from Nice are Antibes, Cap d'Antibes and neighbouring Juan-les-Pins, which have a surprising range of attractions packed into a relatively small space.

Antibes is the quintessential Mediterranean town, with narrow cobblestone streets festooned with plants and flowers. It boasts a fine Picasso museum, a pleasure-boat harbour (Port Vauban), sandy beaches and 16th-century ramparts. Picasso, Max Ernst and Nicolas de Staël all found Antibes charming. Even the restless Graham Greene (1904–91) settled here with his lover Yvonne Cloetta, from 1966 until the year before his death.

Greater Antibes embraces Cap d'Antibes, an exclusive green cape studded with luxurious walled mansions, and the modern beach resort of Juan-les-Pins. The latter is known for its beautiful 2km-long sandy beach and sizzling nightlife (including a thriving gay scene), a legacy of the 1920s when Americans swung into town with their jazz music and oh-so-brief swimsuits. Party madness peaks at Jazz à Juan, a week-long jazz festival in late July, which attracts musicians and music lovers from all over the world.

Orientation

Antibes is made up of three parts: the commercial centre around place du Général de Gaulle; Vieil Antibes (old Antibes) south of Port Vauban and the Vieux Port; and Cap d'Antibes, to the southwest, including the contiguous community of Juan-les-Pins.

Av Robert Soleau links Antibes train station with place du Général de Gaulle, where the tourist office is located. From here, Juan-les-Pins is a straight 1.5km walk along blvd du Président Wilson, which runs southwest off Antibes' central square.

Information

BOOKSHOPS

Antibes Books–Heidi's English Bookshop (☎ 04 93 34 74 11; 24 rue Aubernon; ⏰ 10am-7pm) The best selection of new and used English-language books on the coast.

INTERNET ACCESS

Xtreme Cybercafé (☎ 04 93 34 14 37; Galérie du Port, 8 blvd d'Aguillon; per hour €5; ⏰ 9.30am-9pm Mon-Sat, 10am-6pm Sun)

LAUNDRY

Laverie (Av du 24 Août; ⏰ Mon-Sat 7.30am-8pm) Charges €4.20 per 6kg.

MONEY

There are several commercial banks on av Robert Soleau in Antibes centre.

Eurochange (☎ 04 93 34 48 30; 4 rue Georges Clémenceau; ⏰ 9am-7pm Mon-Fri, 10am-1pm Sat)

Delta Change (☎ 04 93 34 12 76; 17 blvd Albert 1er; ⏰ 9am-7pm Mon-Sat)

POST

Antibes Post Office (☎ 04 92 90 61 00; place des Martyrs de la Résistance; ⏰ 8am-7pm Mon-Fri, 8am-noon Sat)

Juan-les-Pins Post Office (sq Pablo Picasso; ⏰ 8am-noon & 2.30-6pm Mon-Fri, 8am-noon Sat) Cyberposte.

TOURIST INFORMATION

Antibes Tourist Office (☎ 04 92 90 53 00; www .antibes-juanlespins.com; 11 place du Général de Gaulle; ⏰ 9am-7pm Jul & Aug, 9am-12.30pm & 1.30-6pm Mon-Fri, 9am-noon & 2-6pm Sat Sep-Jun)

Juan-les-Pins Tourist Office (☎ 04 92 90 53 05; www.antibes-juanlespins.com; 55 blvd Charles Guillaumont) Similar opening hours to Antibes office.

> **ANTIBES MUSEUMS FOR LESS**
>
> If you plan to see all of Antibes' museums, buy a **combined ticket** (€10), valid for seven days, available from the tourist office or the six places covered: the Peynet, de la Tour, Archaeology, Picasso and Napoleonic museums, and Fort Carré.

Sights & Activities

VIEIL ANTIBES

Because of Antibes' position on the border of France and Savoy, it was fortified in the 17th and 18th centuries, but these fortifications were ripped down in 1896 to give the city room to expand. From the tourist office on place du Général de Gaulle, bear east along rue de la République to **Porte de France**, one of the few remaining parts of the original city walls.

The **Musée Peynet et du Dessin Humoristique** (☎ 04 92 90 54 30; musee.peynet@ville-antibes.fr; place Nationale; adult/concession €3/1.50; ⏰ 10am-6pm Tue-Sun mid-Jun–mid-Sep, to 8pm Wed & Fri Jul & Aug, 10am-noon & 2-6pm Tue-Sun mid-Sep–mid-Jun) displays over 300 pictures, cartoons, sculptures and costumes by Antibes-born cartoonist Peynet, best known for his Lovers series: even if you don't think you know him, you will when you see his work. The museum also has good temporary exhibitions by other illustrators and cartoonists.

A hectic **marché Provençal** (Provençal market; ⏰ am Tue-Sun Sep-May) sprawls the length of cours Masséna.

At the southern end of cours Masséna, 19th-century Tour Gilli houses **Musée de la Tour** (☎ 04 93 34 13 58; 2 rue de l'Orme; admission free; ⏰ 4-7pm Wed, Thu & Sat Jun-Sep, 3-5pm Wed, Thu & Sat Oct-May), a small arts and traditions museum.

East of cours Masséna is **Cathédrale d'Antibes** (rue St-Esprit; ⏰ 8am-noon & 3-6.30pm Mon-Fri, to 7pm Sat & Sun mid-Sep–mid-Jun, 8am-noon & 3-6.30pm Mon-Fri, to 8pm Sat & Sun mid-Jun–mid-Sep), built on the site of an ancient Greek temple with an ochre neoclassical façade. Its tall, square Romanesque bell tower dates from the 12th century.

Southwest is the **Musée d'Archéologie** (☎ 04 92 90 54 35; Bastion St André; adult/concession €3/1.50; ⏰ 10am-6pm Tue-Sun mid-Jun–mid-Sep, to 8pm Wed & Fri Jul & Aug, 10am-noon & 2-6pm Tue-Sun mid-Sep–mid-Jun), inside the Vauban-built Bastion St-André. Its displays are devoted to Antibes' Greek history.

ANTIBES

INFORMATION	
Antibes Books–Heidi's English	
Bookshop......................................**1** D2	
Delta Change..**2** B4	
Eurochange..**3** C3	
Laverie...**4** B3	
Post Office..**5** B2	
Tourist Office.......................................**6** A2	
Xtreme Cybercafé................................**7** B2	
SIGHTS & ACTIVITIES (pp257-9)	
Access to Beach....................................**8** D2	
Antibes Bateaux Services.....................**9** D2	
Cathédrale d'Antibes..........................**10** D3	
Château Grimaldi................................**11** D3	
InterSport...**12** A3	
Marché Provençal................................**13** C3	
Musée de la Tour.................................**14** C3	

Musée d'Archéologie.........................**15** B4	
Musée Peynet et du Dessin	
Humoristique....................................**16** C3	
Musée Picasso..............................(see 11)	
Tour Gilli.......................................(see 14)	
SLEEPING (p260)	
Le Caméo...**17** C3	
Le Relais du Postillon.........................**18** B2	
Modern Hôtel......................................**19** B3	
Nouvel Hôtel......................................**20** B3	

EATING (pp260-1)	
Cave la Treille d'Or............................**21** B2	
Chez Juliette.......................................**22** C3	
Fromagerie L'Etable............................**23** C3	
Geoffrey's of London..........................**24** B2	
Key West...(see 27)	
Le Brûlot..**25** C3	
Le Pressoir de Bacchus.......................**26** B2	
L'Elephant Bleu..................................**27** C2	
Les Trois Princes Rice Bar....................**28** C3	
Les Vieux Murs...................................**29** C3	

ENTERTAINMENT (p261)	
Absinthe Bar.......................................**30** C3	
Cinéma Casino....................................**31** A3	
Le Latino...**32** C2	

TRANSPORT (p261)	
Bus Station..**33** B3	
Buses to Biot, Vallauris &	
Juan-les-Pins...................................**34** A3	
Envibus Information Office.............(see 33)	

MUSÉE PICASSO

Set on a spectacular site overlooking the sea is **Château Grimaldi**, a 14th-century castle which served as Picasso's studio from July to December 1946. It houses Antibes' star museum, and the first one in the world dedicated to the artist, the **Musée Picasso** (☎ 04 92 90 54 20; fax 04 92 90 54 21; place Mariejol; adult/student mid-Jun–mid-Sep €6/3, mid-Sep–mid-Jun €5/2.50; ☼ 10am-6pm Tue-Sun mid-Jun–mid-Sep, to 8pm Wed & Fri Jul & Aug, 10am-noon & 2-6pm Tue-Sun mid-Sep–mid-Jun). An excellent collection of Picasso's paintings, lithographs, drawings and ceramics is on display, as well as a photographic record of the artist at work.

Particularly poignant is Picasso's *La Joie de Vivre* (The Joy of Life), one in a series of 25 paintings from The Antipolis Suite. The young flower girl, surrounded by flute-playing fauns and mountain goats, symbolises Françoise Gilot, the 23-year-old love of Picasso (1881–1973), with whom he lived in neighbouring Golfe-Juan. Also fascinating is his play on Velázquez' *Las Meninas*, with figures repeated obsessively as he tries to get to the bottom of the mysterious original.

Contemporary works by other artists grace the sculpture-lined terrace and lower exhibition rooms.

FORT CARRÉ & PORT VAUBAN

The impregnable 16th-century **Fort Carré**, enlarged by Vauban in the 17th century, dominates the approach to Antibes from Nice.

Port Vauban, one of the first pleasure ports to be established on the Mediterranean, is between the fort and Antibes' old town.

Inside the fortress, which can be visited by guided tour (Tuesday to Sunday year-round), a pedestrian walkway takes visitors around the stadium hidden within the star-shaped walls. Contact the tourist office for tour details.

CAP D'ANTIBES

You feel like a shrunken Alice in Wonderland on this select peninsula: larger-than-life villas and pine trees loom above you at every turn, and the frenzied sound of cicadas provides an unearthly soundtrack (see Love Song, p33).

The southwestern tip of the cape is crowned by the legendary Hôtel du Cap Eden Roc (see p260), the Côte d'Azur's most exclusive hotel and the owner of the first open-air swimming pool (built in 1914 for WWI servicemen). Dating from 1870, it really hit the big time just after WWI, when a literary salon held here one summer (previous guests came for the winter season only) was attended by Hemingway, Picasso et al. The hotel was immortalised in F Scott Fitzgerald's novel *Tender is the Night* (1934), disguised as the fictional Hôtel des Étrangers.

Other notable names on Cap d'Antibes' guest book include Cole Porter, who rented **Château de la Garoupe** in 1922, and novelist Jules Verne (1828–1905), who lived at **Les Chênes Verts** (152 blvd John F Kennedy).

Immediately northwest of Eden Roc is the **Musée Napoléonien** (☎ 04 93 61 45 32; blvd Kennedy; adult/student €3/1.50; 9.15-11.45am & 2-5.45pm Mon-Fri, 9.15-11.45am Sat, closed Oct), a naval museum inside Tour Sella, which documents Napoleon's return from exile in 1815.

The centre of the cape is dominated by the beautiful **Jardin Botanique de la Villa Thuret** (☎ 04 93 67 88 66; 62 blvd du Cap; admission €1.50; 8am-6pm Mon-Fri Jun-Sep, 8.30am-5.30pm Mon-Fri Oct-May), 3.5 hectares of botanical gardens embracing 2500 species and dating from 1856.

Another lovely garden to visit is the 11-hectare landscaped park around **Villa Eilenroc** (☎ 04 93 67 74 33; av de Beaumont; admission & tours free; park 9am-5pm Wed Sep-Jun, guided tours of villa 9.30am-noon & 1.30-5pm Wed Sep-Jun), on the southern tip of Cap d'Antibes. Eilenroc was designed by Garnier for a Dutchman who

scrambled the name of his wife Cornélie to come up with the villa's name.

Sweeping views of the coastline from St-Tropez to Italy can be enjoyed from **Chapelle de la Garoupe** (☎ 04 93 61 57 63; rte du Phare), filled with poignant offerings from fishing families. The neighbouring lighthouse can't be visited. From here steps lead downhill to av Aimé Bourreau; bear right, then turn left along av Guide to get to sandy **Plage de la Garoupe**, first raked clear of seaweed in 1922 by Cole Porter and American artist Gerald Murphy. A coastal path snakes from here to **Cap Gros**, the cape's southeasternmost tip.

BEACHES & BOATS

Antibes has a small sandy beach, **Plage de la Gravette**, accessible from quai Henri Rambaud. However, for long golden beaches that buzz with business from sunrise to sunset, Juan-les-Pins is the place to go. From the Ponton Courbet, opposite the tourist office on blvd Charles Guillaumont, glass-bottomed boats (adult/two to 12 years €12/6, 1¼ hours) sail around Cap d'Antibes, May to September.

In Antibes, rent a 6cv boat (without licence) to go to sea at **Antibes Bateaux Services** (☎ 06 15 75 44 36; www.antibes-bateaux.com; quai Henri Rambaud) for €100/140 per half-/full day (with €763 deposit). With **Siesta Water Sports** (☎ 06 87 81 55 70; opposite Parking de la Siesta), 2km north of Antibes' old town, you can jet ski, water-ski, wakeboard, strap on a parachute or sit in a rubber ring and be dragged along by a boat.

ROLLERBLADING

Bladers can hire skates for €12 per day at **InterSport** (☎ 04 93 34 20 14; www.intersport.fr in French; 10 av Guillabert; 9am-12.15pm & 2.30-7.15pm Mon-Sat).

Festivals & Events

Cap d'Antibes' premier occasion is **Jazz à Juan** (Festival de Jazz d'Antibes Juan-les-Pins), a week-long festival in late July. There's always a first-rate line-up, and the venues, Juan-les-Pins' **Eden Casino** (☎ 04 92 93 71 71; blvd Édouard Baudoin) and the gardens fronting the beach on square Gould, are superb. Festival programmes and tickets are available from the tourist offices in Antibes and Juan-les-Pins, or you can often buy tickets at the door if you turn up an hour early.

Sleeping

Antibes and Juan-les-Pins have higher accommodation prices than other places on the coast, and it's wise to book ahead.

BUDGET

Relais International de la Jeunesse (☎ 04 93 61 34 40; fax 04 90 83 65 33; 60 blvd de la Garoupe; dm incl breakfast €14, sheets €3; ☒ Mar-Oct, reception 8-11am & 5.30-11pm) The cheapest option, this hostel is beautifully located on the Baie de la Garoupe (3km south of Antibes centre), in Cap d'Antibes. It's possible to pitch a tent on site for €8, not including breakfast. Take bus No 2A from Antibes' bus station to L'Antiquité stop.

MID-RANGE

In Antibes:

Modern Hôtel (☎ 04 92 90 59 05; fax 04 92 90 59 06; 1 rue Fourmilière; s/d €68/82; ☒) The Modern is a favourite: small, sweet and full of character. It's hidden down a narrow pedestrian street in the old town. Rooms have TVs and air-con.

Le Relais du Postillon (☎ 04 93 34 20 77; www .relaisdupostillon.com; 8 rue Championnet; d €44-79; mains €11-27; ☐) A friendly establishment in a sprawling 17th-century coach house. Each of its 16 cosy, characterful rooms overlooks either a quiet courtyard or park. The hotel also runs a smart restaurant-bar-lounge with an accent on good-quality fish dishes, cocktails and song.

Le Caméo (☎ 04 93 34 24 17; fax 04 93 34 35 80; 62 rue de la République; d with shower/shower & toilet €48/59) This is a large place overlooking Vieil Antibes' central square. Staff also manage the bar-restaurant and massive terrace below, so if they're slightly frazzled, don't take it personally.

Nouvel Hôtel (☎ 04 93 34 44 07; 1 av du 24 Août; s/d with washbasin €32.50/48, d with shower & toilet €58) A quintessential French bar with rooms up top. Ask for one on the other side to the Cinéma Casino: flashing neon sign + thin curtains = no sleep. Rooms have a cheerful, scruffy '70s air, TVs and safes.

TOP END

In Cap d'Antibes:

Hôtel La Jabotte (☎ 04 93 61 45 89; www.jabotte .com; 13 av Max Maurey; d €72-130; ☐) Beach bunnies will be well pleased with this hotel, a minute's walk from free, fine-sand Plage de la Salis, 1km south of Antibes' old town. Eat your breakfast in the little courtyard, shaded by a handsome orange tree. There are a few first-come-first-served parking spaces outside.

Two heavenly historical hotels:

Hôtel Belles Rives (☎ 04 93 61 02 79; www.belles rives.com; 33 blvd Édouard Baudoin; r with cape views €220-340, with sea views €485-685; ☒) F Scott and Zelda Fitzgerald stayed at Hôtel Belles Rives – then an untouched spot of paradise called Villa St-Louis – in 1926. A four-star oasis of luxury with original 1930s furniture, its own private jetty and a beach (sunlounger and parasol €30).

Hôtel du Cap Eden Roc (☎ 04 93 61 39 01; www .edenroc-hotel.fr; blvd Kennedy; s/d €420/550; ☒ ☒) Expensive, exquisite and on a par with paradise. Ride the teak-seated cable car down from the hotel to the private beach (free for guests, €40 for nonguests) below and pretend you're in a James Bond movie.

Eating

Terrace restaurants and cafés lace Antibes' old-town streets.

Chez Juliette (☎ 04 93 34 67 37; 18 rue Sade; menus €13, €20 & €26; ☒ 7-11pm Tue-Sun, plus noon-2pm Sun) Popular for its wide choice of guaranteed-to-fill Provençal dishes, including tripe, rabbit stew with polenta or stuffed sardine fillets in tomato sauce.

Les Vieux Murs (☎ 04 93 34 06 73; promenade Amiral de Grasse; lunch/dinner menus €25/40; ☒ closed Tue mid-Sep–May; ☒ ☒) This finely located restaurant is tucked into the old ramparts, next to the crashing waves. Its kitchen staff are no slouches, serving up well-prepared French/Provençal food. Wheelchair access.

L'Elephant Bleu (☎ 04 93 34 28 80; 28 blvd d'Aguillon; dishes €10-23, menus €19-40; ☒ noon-2.30pm & 6.30-11.30pm) The lantern-lit Blue Elephant cooks up tasty Chinese, Vietnamese and Thai cuisine on one of Antibes' trendiest streets. There's a good veggie selection.

Also recommended:

Key West (☎ 04 93 34 58 20; 30 blvd d'Aguillon; ☒ 10am-2pm) Stop by for brunch, or a jumbo English breakfast (€9.80).

Le Brûlot (☎ 04 93 34 17 76; 3 rue Frédérick Isnard; mains €10-18; ☒ 12.30-11.30pm Mon-Sat) Cavernlike setting, carnival theme, with mainly Italian food: pizzas, seafood, pasta.

Les Trois Princes Rice Bar (☎ 04 93 34 12 84; 1 rue des Bains; mains €8-17; ☒ 12.30-2.30pm & 7-11.30pm Tue-Sun) Rice-based dishes from around the world (nasi goreng, biryani etc) with some veggie choices.

For self-caterers, **Le Pressoir de Bacchus** (☎ / fax 04 93 74 93 25; 9 rue Fontvieille) and **Cave la Treille d'Or** (☎ 04 93 34 33 87; 12 rue Lacan) both sell wine; **Fromagerie L'Etable** (cnr rue Sade & rue Guillaumont) sells cheese; and **Geoffrey's of London** (☎ 04 93 34 55 70; Galerie du Port; 9am-7.30pm Mon-Sat) is the place for British and American foodstuffs, from Heinz beans to Hersheys.

Entertainment

Pedestrian blvd d'Aguillon, immediately south of the old city wall by the port in Antibes, is lined with busy 'English' and 'Irish' pubs, heaving with merrily piddled Brits and Aussies.

Absinthe Bar (☎ 04 93 34 93 00; 1 rue Sade) Flirt with the green fairy at this dedicated absinthe bar, decorated in 1860s style and with a brain-pickling 25 varieties of the drink on offer (from €4).

Le Latino (☎ 04 93 34 44 22; www.lelatino.com in French; 24 blvd d'Aguillon; tapas €7.50-17; ☺ food 7pm-midnight, bar 7pm-2am) A busy tapas bar, popular for that essential early-evening apéritif.

Cinéma Casino (☎ 04 93 34 04 37; 6-8 av du 24 Août) Screens films in their original language (usually English) on Tuesday at 8.30pm (tickets €7.50).

Juan-les-Pins has nightlife galore, including one of the largest gay scenes on this stretch of the coast. Try old favourite **Le Voom-Voom** (☎ 04 93 61 18 71; 1 blvd de la Pinède; admission €16; ☺ to 5am), whose techno nights attract DJs from all over Europe.

Getting There & Away
BUS

Antibes **bus station** (☎ 04 93 34 37 60), just off rue de la République, has buses leaving/ arriving every 20 minutes or so between 6am and 8pm to/from Nice (€4.30, 50 minutes), Cagnes-sur-Mer (€2.30, 20 minutes), Golfe-Juan (€1.90, 15 minutes) and Cannes (€2.10, 30 minutes).

Buses to/from Biot (line 10A, €1, 25 minutes, seven to 10 buses daily) and Vallauris (line 5V, €2.40, 30 minutes, seven to 10 buses daily) use the bus stops on place du Général de Gaulle.

TRAIN

From Antibes **train station** (place Pierre Semard), at the end of av Robert Soleau, there are frequent trains to/from Nice (€3.60, 30 minutes) and Cannes (€2.30, 15 minutes).

Unlike Antibes, where many TGVs stop, the smaller **train station** (av de l'Estérel) in Juan-les-Pins is only served by local trains.

Getting Around
BICYCLE

JML Location (☎ 04 92 93 05 06; 93 blvd du Président Wilson; ☺ 9am-6.30pm Mon-Sat, 9.30am-noon & 4-6.30pm Sun) rents bikes/scooters/125cc motorcycles for €12/23/48 per day. The tourist offices have lists of other rental outlets.

BUS

In summer a free minibus (every 10 minutes between 7.30am and 7.30pm Monday to Saturday) shuttles travellers between Antibes centre and Vieil Antibes. The Centre Ville line (shaded blue on the route maps displayed at bus stops) links the train station with place du Général de Gaulle and the bus station. The Vieil Antibes line (shaded red) links the train station with Fort Carré.

Other city buses are run by **Envibus** (☎ 04 93 00 28 41; www.envibus.fr in French). Tickets cost €1/8 for a single ticket/10-ticket carnet. A one-day individual/family pass costs €3/5.

Envibus Nos 1A, 3A and 8A link Antibes bus station and place du Général de Gaulle with sq du Lys in Juan-les-Pins (15 minutes, every 10 to 20 minutes). Bus No 2A from Antibes goes to Eden Roc on Cap d'Antibes (every 30 minutes). Between 15 June and 15 September this bus circles the cape, continuing along the coast from Eden Roc to Juan-les-Pins before returning to Antibes.

BIOT
pop 7849

This charming 15th-century hilltop village was an important pottery-manufacturing centre specialising in large earthenware oil and wine containers. Metal containers brought an end to this, but Biot is still active in handicraft production, especially glass-making and ceramics. The village was also the one-time HQ (1209–1387) of the Knights Templars, then the Knights of Malta: fragments of their presence remain in the quaint streets. Get there early to beat the hordes.

A complete list of glass-blowing workshops (*verreries*) is available at the **tourist office** (☎ 04 93 65 78 00; www.biot-coteazur.com; 46 rue St-Sébastien; ☺ 10am-7pm Mon-Fri, 2.30-7pm Sat & Sun Jul & Aug, 9am-noon & 2-6pm Mon-Fri, 2-6pm Sat & Sun Sep-Jun).

CANNES AREA

Sights & Activities

One of the largest *verreries* is the **Verrerie de Biot** (☎ 04 93 65 03 00; www.verreriebiot.com; chemin des Combes; admission free; ⏱ 9.30am-8pm Mon-Sat, 10am-1pm & 2.30-7.30pm Sun Jul & Aug, 9.30am-6pm Mon-Sat, 10.30am-1pm & 2.30-6.30pm Sun Sep-Jun), at the foot of the village (1km), where you can watch glass-blowers at work, buy the end results, admire on-site art galleries or have lunch at their terrace restaurant.

In town, the **Musée d'Histoire et de Céramique Biotoises** (☎ 04 93 65 54 54; 9 rue St-Sébastien; adult/student €2/1, 1st Sun of month free; ⏱ 10am-6pm Wed-Sun Jul-Sep, 2-6pm Wed-Sun Oct-Jun) has interesting local history displays. A little further along the street is picturesque **place des Arcades**, dating from the 13th century.

MUSÉE NATIONAL FERNAND LÉGER

The **Musée National Fernand Léger** (☎ 04 92 91 50 30; www.musee-fernandleger.fr in French; chemin du Val de Pôme; adult/18-26 yrs €4/2.60; ⏱ 10.30am-6pm Wed-Mon Jul-Sep, 10am-12.30pm & 2-5.30pm Wed-Mon Oct-Jun) is dedicated to the artist Fernand Léger (1881–1955) and contains 360 of his works: paintings, mosaics, ceramics and stained-glass windows. It was built by Léger's wife following his death, and its foundation stone was laid by Braques, Chagall and Picasso. It is due to reopen in March 2005 after renovation works: check first to see if it has. To get there, walk the 2km from Biot centre, or it's on the No 10A (Antibes–Biot) bus route.

MUSÉE BONSAÏ ARBORETUM

This Japanese **bonsai garden** (☎ 04 93 65 63 99; www.museedubonsai.fr.st; 209 chemin du Val de Pôme; adult/student/under 6 yrs €4/2/free; ⏱ 10am-noon & 2-6pm Wed-Mon), created from the private collection of the Okonek family, contains Europe's largest bonsai forest – 6m long! It's next door to the Musée National Fernand Léger.

PARC DE LA MER

Well distanced from the hilltop village is the Disneyland-style **Parc de la Mer** (Sea Park; ☎ 04 93 33 49 49; www.marineland.fr; RN7; ⏱ 10am-midnight Jul & Aug, 10am-8pm Sep-Dec & Feb-Jun), a giant amusement park divided into themed areas. To get to Parc de la Mer take bus No 10A from Antibes bus station to the Marineland stop. By train, turn right out of Biot train station, walk 50m along rte de Nice (N7), then turn right along the D4 signposted 'Marineland & Biot'.

Getting There & Away

Biot village is 4km from Biot train station. From Antibes take bus No 10A from the bus station or place du Général de Gaulle to Biot (€1, 25 minutes, seven to 10 buses daily).

CAGNES-SUR-MER

pop 44,207

Renoir spent his last 12 years in Cagnes-sur-Mer; his old house and studio now house a museum dedicated to the artist. The town is actually more like three places welded together: there's **Haut de Cagnes**, the old hilltop town dominated by the 14th-century Château Grimaldi; **Cagnes Ville**, a fast-growing modern quarter; and **Cros de Cagnes**, a former fishing village by the beach.

The **tourist office** (☎ 04 93 20 61 64; www.cagnes-tourisme.com in French; 6 blvd Maréchal Juin; ⏱ 9am-7pm Mon-Sat, 9am-noon & 3-7pm Sun Jul & Aug, 9am-noon & 2-7pm Mon-Sat Jun & Sep, 9am-noon & 2-6pm rest of yr), just off the A8 in Cagnes Ville, runs annexes in **Haut de Cagnes** (☎ 04 92 02 85 05; place du Château; ⏱ 10am-1.30pm & 4-7pm Jul & Aug, 2-6pm Wed-Sun Apr-Jun & Sep, 2-5pm Wed-Sun Oct–mid-Nov & Jan-Mar) and **Cros de Cagnes** (☎ 04 93 07 67 08; 20 av des Oliviers; ⏱ 9am-noon & 2.30-6.30pm Jul & Aug, 9am-noon Mon-Fri Sep-Jun).

Château-Musée Grimaldi

Built around 1300 by Rainier Grimaldi, **Château-Musée Grimaldi** (☎ 04 92 02 47 30; place Grimaldi; adult/student €3/1.50, combined same-day ticket with Musée Renoir €4.50; ⏱ 10am-noon & 2-6pm Wed-Mon), at the top of the old town, now houses a **Musée de l'Olivier** (Olive-Tree Museum) featuring paintings of olive groves and oily paraphernalia; and a **Musée d'Art Méditerranéen Moderne** (Museum of Modern Mediterranean Art). Between July and September temporary exhibits festoon the walls during the Festival International de la Peinture (International Painting Festival).

Sold during the French Revolution to a wealthy citizen, the castle was bought in 1873 by a doctor who restored it to its 1620s glory. Baroque influences are evident in the grandiose banquet hall and arched galleries. The old Grimaldi boudoir is filled with a bizarre collection of portraits of Suzy Solidor (1900–85), a Parisian cabaret singer and favourite artists' model who spent the last 25 years of her life living in Cagnes-sur-Mer. Among the 40 portraits are pieces by Brayer, Cocteau, Dufy, Kisling and van Dongen.

Musée Renoir

La Domaine des Collettes, today the **Musée Renoir** (☎ 04 93 20 61 07; chemin des Collettes; adult/ student €3/1.50, combined same-day ticket with Château-Musée Grimaldi €4.50; ◷ 10am-noon & 2-6pm Wed-Mon), served as home and studio to an arthritis-crippled Renoir (1841–1919), who lived here with his wife and three sons from 1907 until his death. The artist painted, with a brush bandaged to his fingers, in the north-facing, 2nd-floor studios. The chicken wire covering the window protected Renoir from his children's mis-hit tennis balls.

Works of his on display include *Les Grandes Baigneuses* (The Women Bathers; 1892), a reworking of the 1887 original, and rooms are dotted with photographs and personal possessions. The magnificent olive and citrus groves around the Provençal *mas* (farmhouse; today the boutique) and bourgeois house are as much an attraction as the museum itself.

From Cagnes bus station on place du Général de Gaulle, walk east along av Renoir and its continuation, av des Tuilières, then turn left (north) onto chemin des Collettes. From here the museum is 500m uphill.

Sleeping & Eating

Cagnes Ville has plenty of seaside resort-style restaurants and cafés. There are only two hotels, but several high-class restaurants, in the heights of Haut de Cagnes.

Le Cagnard (☎ 04 93 20 73 21; www.le-cagnard.com; rue Sous-Barri, Haut de Cagnes; d from €190; lunch menu €55, dinner menus €70-90; restaurant ◷ noon-2pm & 7.30-11pm, closed lunch Mon, Tue & Thu & mid-Nov–mid-Dec; Ⓟ ⬚) A fabulous 14th-century nobleman's residence inside the castle walls, where D'Artagnan buckled his swash and Antoine de St-Exupéry slept. Beamed rooms are four-star and *très* romantic. The restaurant is a real gourmet treat, with black-truffle lasagne among its house specialities. The painted ceiling slides back in summer to let in sunshine.

Josy-Jo (☎ 04 93 20 68 76; place Notre Dame de la Protection, Haut de Cagnes; lunch menu €40; ◷ 12.30-2.30pm & 5.30-9.30pm, closed Sat lunch & Sun) The simple-yet-stately Josy-Jo lacks pretension and oozes charm. It specialises in wood-fire grilled meats with a variety of sauces.

Getting There & Around

Cagnes-sur-Mer is served by two train stations, Cagnes-sur-Mer and Le Cros de Cagnes. Most Cannes–Ventimiglia trains stop at both (they're two to three minutes apart).

Buses from Cannes to Nice (every 20 minutes) stop outside Cagnes-sur-Mer (52 minutes) and Le Cros de Cagnes (one hour) train stations, and at Cagnes' central bus station on place du Général de Gaulle. The Grasse–Nice bus (No 500) only stops outside Cagnes-sur-Mer train station (35 minutes, about 10 daily). From Vence, bus No 400 departs every 30 minutes for Cagnes-sur-Mer (20 minutes) via St-Paul de Vence.

A frequent shuttle bus (free, 6.30am to 12.30am June to September, 7am to 10.30pm May and October to December) runs from Cagnes Ville bus station to Haut de Cagnes.

ST-PAUL DE VENCE

pop 2900 / elevation 125m

Once upon a time, St-Paul de Vence was a modest village on a hill overlooking the coast, about 10km north of Cagnes-sur-Mer. Fortified in the 16th century, it remained beautifully intact and attracted artists such as the Belarusian painter Marc Chagall, who moved to the village in 1966. African-American novelist James Baldwin (1924–85) also spent the last years of his life in the village.

It's certainly a magical place, filled with flowers and minute cobbled lanes, but in the height of summer it explodes with tourists and can feel like one giant fortified art gallery. If the village gets too wearing, escape down the road to the extraordinary Fondation Maeght to view some nuggets of truly fine modern art.

Orientation & Information

Rue Grande is the village's backbone, leading right from the main gate to the cemetery.

The **tourist office** (☎ 04 93 32 86 95; www.saint -pauldevence.com; 2 rue Grande; ◷ 10am-7pm Mon-Fri, 10am-1pm & 2 7pm Sat & Sun Jun-Sep, 10am-6pm Mon-Fri, 10am-1pm & 2-6pm Sat & Sun Oct-May) is on the right as you enter the walled village. The **post office** (rte de la Colle), which has an ATM, is outside the walled village opposite the bus stop.

The Village

Strolling the narrow streets is how most visitors pass the time in St-Paul. No less than 36 of its 64 **art galleries** are on rue Grande;

the tourist office has a list. Steps from rue Grande lead east to place de l'Église, where you'll find the **Église Collégiale** (containing a hotchpotch of religious icons) and adjoining **Chapelle des Pénitents**, where free organ recitals are held in July and August. On the same square is the **Musée d'Histoire Locale** (place de l'Église; adult/6-16 yrs €3/2; 🕙 10am-12.30pm & 1.30-5.30pm, closed end Nov), with tableaux bringing St-Paul's history to waxy life.

Marc Chagall and his wife, Vava, are buried in the **cemetery** at the village's southern end. From the entrance, turn right, then left; the Chagalls' simple graves are third on the left, with beach pebbles scattered over them.

The mosaic mural by Fernand Léger, *Les Femmes au Perroquet* (Women with a Parrot), is among the modern artworks at La Colombe d'Or (see right) on place des Ormeaux. This upmarket restaurant is where once-impoverished artists Braque, Chagall, Dufy and Picasso paid for meals with their creations – which today form one of France's largest private art collections. Viewing is strictly for diners.

In front of the restaurant is the gravel **pétanque** pitch where singer/actor Yves Montand once played. The tourist office hires balls (€3.50 per set) and arranges games with local *pétanque* champs (€65 per hour) so you too can rise to the challenge.

Fondation Maeght

The finest art museum in the region is **Fondation Maeght** (☎ 04 93 32 81 63; adult/student/under 10 yrs €11/9/free; 🕙 10am-7pm Jul-Sep, 10am-12.30pm & 2.30-6pm Oct-Jun), inaugurated in 1964 in a purpose-built futuristic building. It hosts an exceptional permanent collection of 20th-century works by Braque, Bonnard, Chagall, Giacometti, Matisse, Miró and Léger, exhibited on a rotating basis, as well as temporary exhibitions.

Behind the galleries is the **Miró Labyrinth**, created by Spanish surrealist Joan Miró (1893–1983). Follow the zigzag path through the terraced garden, studded with gigantic sculptures, comical faces, mosaics and pools of water.

The centre, signposted from rond-point St-Claire, is 800m from the bus stop. A steep driveway leads up to the Foundation. Approaching St-Paul by car, turn left off the D7 from La-Colle-sur-Loup.

Galerie Guy Pieters

This **modern-art gallery** (☎ 04 93 32 06 46; www .guypietersgallery.com; chemin des Trious; 🕙 10am-7pm Mon-Sat Jun-Oct, 10am-12.30pm & 2-6pm Mon-Sat Nov-May), near the bottom of the Fondation Maeght driveway, contains monumental pieces of contemporary work which you can stagger away with if your wallet's big enough. Some of the star pieces (not for sale) include Andy Warhol's *La Grande Passion* (1984), Tom Wesselmann's *Smoker* (1998) and Arman's 2.8m-tall *Music Power* (1985).

Sleeping & Eating

Three- and four-star hotels are the norm, and restaurants are classy (or have classy prices, at least).

Le St-Paul (☎ 04 93 32 65 25; www.lesaintpaul .com; 86 rue Grande; d from €230; lunch menu €45, dinner menus €65-85; 🕙 12.30-2.30pm & 6-11pm; 🍴) One of the Riviera's most exclusive hotels, this place is absolutely exquisite, with romantic rooms, a fireside salon, and a one-star Michelin restaurant to complete the experience.

La Colombe d'Or (The Golden Dove; ☎ 04 93 32 80 02; www.la-colombe-dor.com in French; place de Gaulle; d from €265; mains €25-35; 🕙 12.30-2.30pm & 7.30-10.30pm; 🅿 🍴 🖳) Tables must be reserved long in advance at this legendary restaurant. Peeking at the art collection is out of the question unless you eat there or stay in one of the 26 rooms.

Hostellerie Les Remparts (☎ /fax 04 93 32 09 88; www.stpaulweb.com/remparts; 72 rue Grande; d €40-80; menu €30) The cheapest accommodation in St-Paul, this medieval two-star is as cosy as anything. Its restaurant, specialising in regional cuisine, has a terrace with a jaw-dropping panorama.

Un Coeur en Provence (A Heart in Provence; ☎ /fax 04 93 32 87 81; montée de l'Église; mains €6-23, menus €12-16; 🕙 closed evenings Wed & Sun) This laid-back *salon de thé* (tea room) features soft music and an array of fresh soups, salads, pancakes and tarts (with several vegetarian options) as well as occasional poetry readings.

Getting There & Away

St-Paul de Vence (St-Paul on bus timetables and road signs) is served by bus No 400 running between Nice (€4.30, one hour) and Vence (€1.30, 15 minutes).

VERONICA GARBUTT

The Carlton InterContinental (p250), Cannes

JULIET COOMBE

Relaxing on Cannes' blvd de la Croisette (p246)

Fondation Maeght (p264), St-Paul de Vence

DAN HERRICK

DAN HERRICK

Art galleries line rue Grande (p263), St-Paul de Vence

Boats in Vieux Port (p287), St-Tropez

Casino de Monte Carlo (p326)

Café in St-Tropez (p290)

VENCE

pop 17,184 / elevation 325m

Vence is a pleasant inland town, 4km north of St-Paul de Vence. The area is typically built up with holiday homes and villas, but the medieval centre is perfect for strolling. Vence's most noteworthy feature, though, has got to be Matisse's otherworldly Chapelle du Rosaire, floodlit by the most extraordinary stained-glass windows.

Music fills the streets during the three-week **Nuits du Sud** (Nights of the South) festival, which occupies place du Grand Jardin in late July/early August. A **fruit and vegetable market** fills the central square on Tuesday, Friday, Saturday and Sunday mornings, with an antique market on Wednesdays.

Orientation & Information

Place du Grand Jardin is Vence's central square, overlooked by the **tourist office** (☎ 04 93 58 06 38; www.ville-vence.fr in French; 8 place du Grand Jardin; 🕑 9am-1pm & 2-7pm Mon-Sat Jul & Aug, 9am-12.30pm & 2-6pm Mon-Sat Sep-Jun).

Rue Marcellin Maurel, which touches the northeastern corner of place du Grand Jardin, skirts the medieval city's southern wall. Port du Peyra, the main gate, is at the western end of rue Marcellin Maurel. Place Clémenceau lies at the old town's heart.

Medieval Vence

Porte du Peyra, the main gate of the 13th-century wall encircling the old city, leads to place du Peyra and its **fountain** (1578). Gate and square are named after the old execution block. Imposing **Château de Villeneuve** and its adjoining 12th-century **watchtower** dominate the western edge of the square. Round the back of the castle is the **Fondation Émile Hughes** (☎ 04 93 24 24 23; 2 place du Frêne; adult/12-18 yrs €5/2.50; 🕑 10am-6pm Tue-Sun Jul-Sep, 10am-12.30pm & 2-6pm Tue-Sun Oct-Jun), a cultural centre with 20th-century art exhibitions.

Leading east from place du Peyra is narrow rue du Marché, once the stables for the town, now dotted with delectable food shops. Cut along rue Alsace-Lorraine to reach place Clémenceau, where there's a **market** on Tuesday and Friday mornings. The **Romanesque cathedral** on the eastern side of the square was built in the 11th century on the site of an old Roman temple. It contains Chagall's **mosaic** of Moses (1979), appropriately watching over the baptismal font.

Matisse's Chapelle du Rosaire

Matisse's unmissable **Chapelle du Rosaire** (☎ 04 93 58 03 26; 468 av Henri Matisse; adult/6-16 yrs €2.50/1; 🕑 2-5.30pm Mon, Wed & Sat, 10-11.30am & 2-5.30pm Tue & Thu, guided tour at around 10.45am Sun after Mass finishes, closed mid-Nov–mid-Dec) took four years to create; the artist was 81 when the chapel was completed in 1951.

In 1943 an ailing Matisse moved to Vence and fell under the care of his former nurse and model Monique Bourgeois, who had since become a Dominican nun. She persuaded him to design a chapel for her community; it is still used by the Dominican nuns of the Rosary today.

From the road all that's visible are the blue-and-white ceramic roof tiles and a wrought-iron cross and bell tower. Inside, light floods through the glorious stained-glass windows, painting stark white walls with glowing blues, greens and yellows. To achieve this effect, Matisse set up camp 200m down the road at **Le Rêve** (The Dream; private house, opposite 320 av Henri Matisse), so he could visit the chapel site throughout the day and observe the sun's position before signing off on the architectural plans.

A line image of the Virgin Mary and child is painted on white ceramic tiles on the northern interior wall. The western wall is dominated by the bolder *Chemin de Croix* (Stations of the Cross), numbered in Matisse's frenzied handwriting. St Dominic overlooks the altar. Matisse also designed the chapel's stone altar, candlesticks, cross and the way-out priests' vestments (displayed in an adjoining hall).

The chapel is about 800m north of Vence on rte de St-Jeannet (the D2210). From place du Grand Jardin, head east along av de la Résistance then turn right (north) along av Tuby. At the crossroads, turn right onto av Henri Matisse, from where the chapel is signposted.

Sleeping & Eating

Auberge des Seigneurs (☎ 04 93 58 04 24; fax 04 93 24 08 01; place du Frêne; d €85; 🕑 closed Nov–mid-Mar) This enchanting little hotel-restaurant, in a 15th-century building, is the only accommodation within the medieval walls. Some rooms have spectacular mountain views.

Hôtel La Victoire (☎ 04 93 58 61 30; fax 04 93 58 74 68; place du Grand Jardin; s/d €35/40) The one-star Victoire is a homely place above a busy bar.

Rooms have a charmingly purple, 1970s air, cooling fans and clean bathrooms.

Maison Lacordaire (☎ 04 93 58 03 26; fax 04 93 58 21 10; 466 av Henri Matisse; half-/full board per person €27.50/36.50) Adjoining the Chapelle du Rosaire, this house belongs to the Dominican nuns, who offer beds for the night. Rooms, all with toilet and shower, must be reserved three to eight days in advance.

The old town is rammed with restaurants.

Le P'tit Provençal (☎ 04 93 58 50 64; 4 place Clémenceau; mains €17-20, menus €23-29; ⊙ closed lunch Wed & Thu) Tucked beside the town hall in the heart of the medieval city, this restaurant serves local cuisine on a pavement terrace that couldn't be more picturesque. A notable highlight is roasted rabbit pie with onions and basil.

Le Peyra (☎ 04 93 58 67 63; 11-13 place du Peyra; menus €18 & €23; ⊙ closed Wed lunch & mid-Feb–mid-Mar) Another perfectly situated place, with the Peyra fountain tinkling in the background and an air of high civility. Italian and French dishes weight the menu, with some interesting twists: try their gingerbread *millefeuille* (literally 'thousand leaves') with liquorice ice cream.

Getting There & Away

Bus No 400 to/from Nice (€4.70, 50 minutes) uses the stop on place du Grand Jardin, a few doors down from the tourist office. Buses run every 20 to 30 minutes between 7am and 7pm Monday to Friday, every 50 minutes to one hour between 8am and 7.20pm Saturday, every 50 to 75 minutes between 8.15am and 7.20pm Sunday.

AROUND VENCE

The northbound D2 from Vence leads to the **Col de Vence** (963m), a mountain pass 10km north offering good views of the *baous* (rocky promontories) typical of this region. At the foot of the pass is the **Baou des Blancs** (673m), crowned by the stony remains of the **Bastide St-Laurent**, inhabited by the Templars in the 13th century. Marked walking trails around the pass follow part of the GR51.

Coursegoules (population 323, elevation 1020m), 6km further north along the D2, is a typical Provençal hilltop village with 11th-century castle ruins and fortifications. From here head west along the D2 to **Gréolières**

A STARRY DETOUR

From the village of Gourdon (see below), stargazers can detour 15km west to the **Observatoire de la Côte d'Azur** (1270m; ☎ 04 93 40 54 54; adult/child €4.50/2.50 ⊙ 3.30-5.30pm Sun May-Sep), which is the region's highest observatory, atop the Plateau de Calern near Caussols.

(population 455), yet another fabulous hilltop village. Walkers can then follow the GR4 north to **Gréolières-les-Neiges** (elevation 1450m), a small ski station equipped with 14 lifts (and eight snow canons!), on the northern face of Montagne Cheiron; the GR4 scales Cheiron's 1778m-high peak.

Hook up with the dramatic **Gorges du Loup** 7km south of Gréolières along the D603. The road along the western side of the gorges (the D3) crescendos with the village of **Gourdon** (population 384, elevation 758m). Art Deco works, including pieces from designer Eileen Gray's Paris apartment and seaside villa on Cap Martin (see Trailing Le Corbusier on p49), can be viewed in the **Musée des Arts Décoratifs et de la Modernité** (☎ 04 93 09 68 02; place du Château; admission €10; ⊙ by appointment only) inside Château de Gourdon. Aspiring 'noses' can see what happens to freshly picked lavender, genista, thyme and orange-tree leaves at **La Source Parfumée** (☎ 04 93 09 68 23; lasourceparfumee@wanadoo.fr; rue Principale; admission free; ⊙ 10am-5.30pm), a distillery run by the Galimard perfumery (see p269).

The D6 leads to **Pont du Loup**, mostly visited for the **Confiserie Florian Factory** (☎ 04 93 59 32 91; www.confiserieflorian.com; ⊙ 9am-7pm), in a lovely old 19th-century flour mill. A free 10-minute tour demonstrates how the traditional sweet house makes its jams, crystallised fruits and flowers, and other sweet treats. Citrus trees grow in the pleasant Jardin d'Agrumes and there is – of course – a shop where you can buy Florian products.

From Pont du Loup the eastbound D2210 snakes to Tourrettes-sur-Loup. Some 5km before the village is **Ferme des Courmettes** (☎ 04 93 59 31 93), a 600-hectare goat farm where cheese is made. Guided tours and tasting sessions are available: Vence tourist office has details. **Tourrettes-sur-Loup** (population 3921, elevation 400m), dubbed the 'city of violets', is a picturesque, 15th-century hilltop village crammed with art galleries and craft shops. Violet flowers are crystallised and their leaves, harvested here in May and August, are sold to perfumeries in Grasse for the extraction of essential oils. Tourrettes' annual **Fête des Violettes** (Violet Festival) on the first or second Sunday in March closes with a flower battle. The **tourist office** (☎ 04 93 24 18 93; www.tourrettessur loup.com; 2 place de La Libération; ⏰ 9.30am-12.30pm & 2.30-6.30pm May-Aug, 9.30am-12.30pm & 2.30-6.30pm Mon-Sat Sep-Apr) has more information.

Six kilometres northeast of Vence, at the foot of **Baou de Jeannet** (800m), is the village of **St-Jeannet** (population 3647, elevation 400m), the setting for Peter Mayle's fictional *Chasing Cézanne*. A marked 45-minute trail leads from central place Ste-Barbe to the summit of the promontory. Top off the trip with a visit to **La Gaude** (population 6217), a less-touristy hilltop village 1.5km south of St-Jeannet.

INLAND TO GRASSE

From Cannes, an inland journey takes you along the same road Napoleon Bonaparte trod on his return from exile in 1814. From the island of Elba, he landed at Golfe-Juan, from where he and a clutch of faithful followers marched for six days north to Lyons. Now called **La rte Napoléon** (the N85 today), at that time it was a remote road passing through a couple of medieval villages, including Grasse with its skilled perfumers, then into the mountains of Haute-Provence.

MOUGINS
pop 16,287 / elevation 260m

Mougins is elegant and elite, and prides itself on its arty connections and luxury hotels and restaurants. Picasso discovered the village in 1935 with lover Dora Marr, and lived here with his final love, Jacqueline Roque, from 1961 until his death. His former house (across the valley from the tourist office) is a private residence and cannot be visited, but there are fascinating photos of the artist in Mougins' photography museum.

Mougins absolutely crawls with artists' workshops: the **tourist office** (☎ 04 93 75 87 67; www.mougins-coteazur.org; parking du Moulin de la Croix; ⏰ 10am-8pm Jun-Sep, 2.30-5.30pm Mon, 10am-5.30pm

Tue-Sat Oct-May), in the car park at the foot of the village, has a list of 30 galleries that can be visited.

Musée de la Photographie
Celebrated Riviera photographer Jacques Henri Lartigue (1894–1986) is among the wealth of famous snappers represented in the small but fabulous **Musée de la Photographie** (☎ 04 93 75 85 67; 67 rue de l'Église; adult/child €2/1; ⏰ 10am-8pm Jul-Sep, 10am-noon & 2-6pm Wed-Sat, 2-6pm Sun Oct & Dec-Jun). The museum was set up in 1989 by André Villers, best known for photographing Picasso, and the 2nd floor is filled with his fantastic black-and-white shots of the artist at work and play. Picasso's vitality and passion just leap out of the frames. A collection of antique cameras and early-20th-century photos of Mougins are displayed on the 1st floor, with temporary exhibitions on the ground floor.

The museum is located inside Mougin's medieval Porte Sarrazine, behind the church bell tower.

Other Sights
From May to October art exhibitions are held in the 19th-century **lavoir** (☎ 04 92 92 50 42; 15 av Jean-Charles Mallet; admission free; ⏰ 10am-7pm Mar-Oct); according to the tourist office, some 'determined' laundresses still use the building as a wash house!

Bugatti, Rolls-Royce and Ferrari race into gear 5km south in the **Musée de l'Automobiliste** (☎ 04 93 69 27 80; www.musauto.fr.st in French; 772 chemin de Font de Currault; adult/12-18 yrs €7/4; ⏰ 10am-7pm Apr-Sep, 10am-6pm Oct-Mar), an automobile museum just off the A8.

Sleeping & Eating
In Mougins, all hotel accommodation is four-star. For a list of *chambres d'hôtes*, contact the tourist office.

Le Moulin de Mougins (☎ 04 93 75 78 24; www.moulin-mougins.com; av Notre Dame de Vie; d €140-190, apt €320; lunch menus €48-58, dinner menus €98-115; P ⏰) Alain Lorca's illustrious place is in a 16th-century oil mill, dotted with original sculptures by César and Arman. Feast on Provençal delights like courgette flowers with black truffles in the chandeliered, rich-plum restaurant, or throw off all your cares in the radiant rooms. The mill is 2.5km southeast off the D3 (signposted from the foot of the village).

CANNES AREA

Le Mas Candille (☎ 04 92 28 43 43; www.lemascand ille.com; blvd Clément Rebuffel; r €129-229, ste €195-399; P 🛇 🖭) This luxury hotel, just north of the village, was converted from an 18th-century farmhouse. Its impeccable interior is enhanced by two pools, a Jacuzzi and a 'Zen-style shiseido spa', with massage, aromatherapy and beauty treatments ranging from a 30-minute manicure (€20) to the full monty ultimate pampering day (€335).

La Ferme de Mougins (☎ 04 93 09 03 74; www .lafermedemougins.fr; 10 av St-Basile; menus €30-65; 🛇 closed Sun dinner & Mon low season) A truly romantic eating spot, this farm restaurant lies a couple of kilometres outside Mougins, off the road to Valbonne. It's an upmarket haven of tranquillity, with unforgettable Provençal cuisine served in the elegant gardens (indoors in winter).

L'Amandier (The Almond Tree; ☎ 04 93 90 00 91; place du Commandant Lamy; lunch menu €25, dinner menus €33-50; 🛇 10.30am-10pm) In a rustic 14th-century oil mill, L'Amandier is one of Mougin's less-expensive options. The menu is traditional Provençal and decent enough, but really it's the amazing mountain views from the restaurant's warm stone terraces that you're here to feast on.

L'Eau Vive (☎ 04 93 75 36 35; 713 chemin des Cabrières; 2 people, tent & car €14.50) This camp site is the one low-cost option available, 1.5km south of Mougins off the N85.

Getting There & Away

Mougins is on the Cannes–Grasse bus route. Buses depart every half-hour (hourly on Sunday) from the bus station next to Cannes train station for Mougins (€1.90, 20 minutes). Grasse is a 20-minute bus ride from Mougins (€3).

MOUANS-SARTOUX

pop 9031 / elevation 120m

The **tourist office** (☎ 04 93 75 75 16; www.mouans -sartoux.com; 258 av de Cannes; 🛇 9am-12.30pm & 2-6pm Mon-Fri, 9am-12.30pm Sat) is on the main road through town.

The main draw of Mouans-Sartoux, 4km north of Mougins, is the **Espace de l'Art Concret** (Centre of Concrete Art; ☎ 04 93 75 71 50; gaelle .eac@wanadoo.fr; place Suzanne de Villeneuve; adult/ student/under 12 yrs €2.30/1.15/free; 🛇 11am-7pm Jul & Aug, 11am-6pm Tue Sun Sep-Jun). This contemporary art centre is housed in the 16th-century **Château de Mouans** and in the purpose-built **Donation Albers-Honegger** extension, a controversial (lime-green) concrete block ferociously juxtaposed with its surroundings. All the old familiars (Eduardo Chillida, Yves Klein, Andy Warhol, César, Philippe Starck) are here, along with lesser-known practitioners and temporary exhibitions.

The only central hotel, **Hôtel de la Paix** (☎ 04 92 92 42 80; fax 04 92 92 42 99; 45 rue de Cannes; d with toilet/bath & toilet €38/55) is a cheap choice on the main road. Rooms are dingy but clean, and there's a sunny breakfast terrace.

It's worth coming to **Restaurant du Château** (☎ 04 93 75 54 50; 1 place Suzanne de Villeneuve; plat/menu du jour €8.50/12; 🛇 noon-10.15pm Tue-Sun) just for the shaded terrace, which overlooks unusual Château de Mouans. *Menus* (eg monkfish filet with lemon and cream, followed by peach tart) are good too.

Mouans-Sartoux is on the same Cannes–Grasse bus route as Mougins (see left). A single Mouans-Sartoux–Grasse fare costs €1.30.

GRASSE

pop 44,790 / elevation 250m

For centuries Grasse, with its distinct red and orange roofs rising up pre-Alpine slopes, has been one of France's most important centres of perfume production. Lavender, jasmine, centifolia roses, mimosa, orange blossom and violets are grown in huge quantities in the area to feed the industry. Inhale the essence of cut flowers at the Provençal **market**, which splashes cours Honoré Cresp with colour on the first and third Saturday of the month, or at the morning **market** (🛇 Tue-Sun) on place aux Aires.

Orientation & Information

While the town of Grasse and its suburbs sprawl over a wide area, the old city is a small, mainly pedestrianised area, densely packed into the hillside. The N85, which leads north to Digne-les-Bains and south to Cannes, runs right through Grasse, where it becomes the town's main (often congested) thoroughfare, blvd du Jeu de Ballon.

There are two tourist offices: **Grasse Espace Accueil** (☎ 04 93 36 21 68; place de la Foux; 🛇 9am-7pm Mon-Sat, 9am-1pm & 2-6pm Sun Jul-Sep, 9am-12.30pm & 2-6pm Mon-Sat Oct-Jun), near the bus station; and the central **tourist office** (☎ 04 93 36 66 66; www .grasse-riviera.com; Palais de Congrès; 🛇 9am-7pm Mon-

Sat, 9am-1pm & 2-6pm Sun Jul-Sep, 9am-12.30pm & 2-6pm Mon-Sat Oct-Jun), near the casino.

The **post office** (9-11 blvd Fragonard; 9.30am-12.30pm & 2-6pm Mon-Wed & Thu, 8.30am-noon Sat) is opposite the main entrance to the Fragonard perfumery.

Perfumeries

Don't expect to sniff out Chanel, Giorgio Beverley Hills or Guerlain here: Grasse's 40 or so *parfumeries* (perfumeries) sell their essence to factories or by mail order and are practically unknown. Three of the biggest (Fragonard, Galimard and Molinard) allow visitors into their showrooms, where you're taken through every stage of perfume production, from extraction and distillation

to the work of the perfumer or 'nose'. At the end you'll be squirted with scents, invited to purchase any number, and leave under a fragrant cloud. The perfumes are less expensive than store-bought smellies, where 60% of what you pay is for the fancy bottle.

Fragonard (04 93 36 44 65; www.fragonard .com; 20 blvd Fragonard; admission free; 9am-6.30pm Jun-Sep, 9am-12.30pm & 2-6pm Oct-May) is the most convenient perfume house if you're on foot. It dates back to 1926, and is named after one of the town's original perfume-making families. After meandering round the upstairs perfume museum, join a Fragonard 'factory' tour, which leads you through a former 16th-century tannery; the real perfume production takes place at the modern **Fabrique**

CANNES AREA

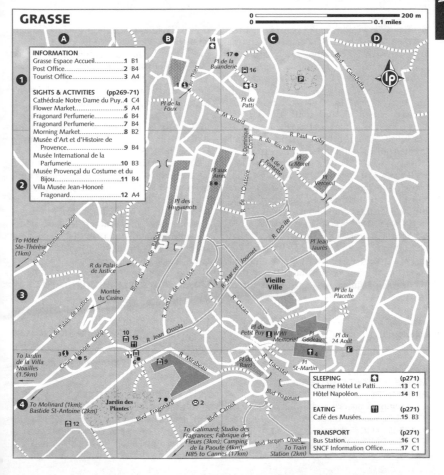

GRASSE

0 ─────── 200 m
0 ─────── 0.1 miles

GRASSE'S PERFUMED HISTORY

Founded by the Romans, Grasse had become a small republic by the early Middle Ages, exporting tanned hides and oil. It may even have earned its name from the trade: *gras* or *matière grasse* means 'fat' in French.

With the advent of perfumed gloves in the 1500s (the doing of France's queen, Catherine de Medicis, who detested the smell of raw leather on her hands), Grasse discovered a new wealth. Glove-makers quickly split from the tanners and set up a separate industry, leading to the eventual creation of perfumeries.

Perfume became all the rage in the 18th century, and business boomed. The production process was a lengthy one: early perfumers left fresh flower petals resting in animal fat for three months, then mixed the fatty substance with alcohol to extract the essences. Unlike today (synthetic products are used in the main), they created perfumes exclusively from flowers: 600kg of fresh flower petals for every 1L of essence!

Grasse's perfume industry employs 3000 people and averages an annual gross revenue of €5.2 million; 60% of its products (perfumes and alimentary aromas) are exported, mainly to Germany, the USA, the UK and Switzerland.

---

des Fleurs (Flower Factory; rte de Cannes; admission free; ☼ 9am-6.30pm Jun-Sep, 9am-12.30pm & 2-6pm Oct-May), out of town on the southbound N85; and at the Fragonard plant in Èze (see p232).

Galimard (☎ 04 93 09 20 00; www.galimard.com; 73 rte de Cannes; admission free; ☼ 9am-6.30pm Jun-Sep, 9am-12.30pm & 2-6pm Oct-May) is 3km from Grasse centre on the southbound N85. Close by is Galimard's **Studio des Fragrances** (☎ 04 93 09 20 00; 5 rte de Pégomas), where you can create your own unique fragrance from 127 different scents. Two-hour **seminars** (incl 30ml bottle of scent €34) are guided by a professional 'nose' (see the boxed text on p271). You must reserve in advance. Galimard also has a flower distillery in Gourdon (p266).

Molinard (☎ 04 93 36 01 62; www.molinard.com; 60 blvd Victor Hugo; admission free; ☼ 9am-6.30pm Mon-Sat Jul-Sep, 9am-12.30pm & 2-6pm Mon-Sat Oct-Jun), 1km out of the centre, is a ritzier affair, founded in 1849. Old copper stills are displayed in the former distillery, designed by architect Gustave Eiffel himself. Molinard also runs 1¼-hour 'create your own perfume' **seminars** (incl 50ml bottle of eau de parfum €40), and you can combine them with a (literal) field trip to see rose and jasmine crops.

Museums
MUSÉE D'ART ET D'HISTOIRE DE PROVENCE
This regional history and art **museum** (☎ 04 97 05 58 00; www.museesdegrasse.com; 2 rue Mirabeau; adult/10-16 yrs €3/1.50, during exhibitions €4/2; ☼ 10am-6.30pm Jun-Sep, 10am-12.30pm & 2-5.30pm Wed-Mon Oct & Dec-May) is inside the stately Hôtel de Clapiers

Cabris. Former owner Jean-Paul de Clapiers loathed his mother, who lived opposite, so much that he had a Gorgon's head carved over his door to leer through her windows. The four-floored museum contains scatterings of everything: faïence pottery, children's toys, furniture, costumes and paintings.

VILLA-MUSÉE JEAN-HONORÉ FRAGONARD
Artist Jean-Honoré Fragonard, born in Grasse in 1732, has been honoured with a **house-museum** (☎ 04 97 05 58 00; www.musees degrasse.com; 23 blvd Fragonard; adult/10-16 yrs €3/1.50, during exhibitions €4/2; ☼ 10am-6.30pm Jun-Sep, 10am-12.30pm & 2-5.30pm Wed-Mon Oct & Dec-May) in the villa where he lived for a year in 1790. His paintings shocked and titillated 18th-century France with their licentious love scenes. Works by other members of his artistic family are also displayed.

MUSÉE PROVENÇAL DU COSTUME ET DU BIJOU
Lace-capped dummies model 18th- and 19th-century clothes and jewellery in this Fragonard-run **museum** (☎ 04 93 36 44 65; www.fragonard.com; 2 rue Jean Ossola; admission free; ☼ 10am-1pm & 2-6pm Feb-Oct, 10am-1pm & 2-6pm Mon-Sat Nov-Jan).

MUSÉE INTERNATIONAL DE LA PARFUMERIE
This **museum of perfume** (☎ 04 93 36 80 20; www .museesdegrasse.com; 8 place du Cours Honoré Cresp) is being revamped and enlarged, and is expected to be closed until 2007.

Other Sights

In springtime the green-fingered should take a stroll around **Jardin de la Villa Noailles** (☎ 04 93 36 07 77; 59 av Guy de Maupassant; admission €10; ⊗ 2-4pm Fri Apr-Jun), English- and Italian-inspired gardens created in 1947 by Charles de Noailles, since restored and protected as a historic monument.

Although rather uninteresting in itself, the 12th century **Cathédrale Notre Dame du Puy** (place Godeau; ⊗ 8.30-11.30am & 3-6pm Mon, Tue, Thu & Fri, 9.30-11.30am & 3-6pm Wed, 9.30-11.30am & 3-7pm Sat, 8-11.15am Sun except when services are on) contains a painting by Fragonard and several early paintings by Rubens, including *The Crown of Thorns* and *Christ Crucified*. Summer concerts are occasionally held here.

Festivals & Events

Grasse's two main events – related to flowers and scents *naturellement* – are **Exporose** in May, and **La Jasminade**, a jasmine festival held the first weekend in August.

Sleeping & Eating

While Grasse might appeal for its perfumeries, the sweetest-smelling sleeping and eating options lie a short drive away in Mougins (p267).

Hôtel Ste-Thérèse (☎ 04 93 36 10 29; www .hotelsaintetherese.com; 39 av Yves Emmanuel Baudoin; r €60-68) Fork out a mere eight euros extra and you can enjoy smashing panoramic views of the valley and orange-roofed town from your own balcony. The hotel's located just over a kilometre up the hill from the casino.

Charme Hôtel Le Patti (☎ 04 93 36 01 00; www .hotelpatti.com; place du Patti; d/tr from €89/99; ⊠) Cheerful two-star Le Patti teeters on the brink of the old town. Rooms are decorated in romantic style, and contain satellite TVs and DVD players. There's also a restaurant with a sunny terrace if you don't want to stray too far for food.

Bastide St-Antoine (☎ 04 93 70 94 94; www .jacques-chibois.com; 48 av Henri Dunant; d €235-400; lunch/ dinner menus €53/130, mains around €45; ⊠ ⊠ P) Overlooking a vast olive grove, this lavish four-star Relais & Chateaux pad is Grasse's most upmarket sleeping and dining choice. Sensual menus are created by well-known French chef Jacques Chibois – oysters with rose petals, anybody?

Hôtel Napoléon (☎ 04 93 36 05 87; fax 04 93 36 41 09; 6 av Thiers; s/d €29/38.50) Bonaparte was probably used to finer lodgings! The Napoléon is nothing to rave about, but it is the cheapest hotel in town. All rooms have a TV (with an English-language channel) and shower, and doubles contain toilets.

Camping La Paoute (☎ 04 93 09 11 42; www .campingpaoute.com; 160 rte de Cannes; 2 people, tent & car €18; ⊗ Jun-Sep; ⊠) This camp site is on the N85 south of Grasse, and has good family facilities.

Grasse's only central restaurants are lacklustre pizza/pasta joints at the northern end of place des Huguenots.

Café des Musées (☎ 04 92 60 99 00; 1 rue Jean Ossola; mains €11; ⊗ 8am-6pm) For a quick and tasty lunch, this café is definitely the best option. Sit on a yellow Jacobsen chair in its modern interior and pick a light Mediterranean-inspired platter.

Getting There & Away

BUS

From the **bus station** (☎ 04 93 36 08 43; place de la Buanderie), there are eight to 10 buses daily to/from Nice (€6.30, 1¼ hours) and Cannes (€3.80, 45 minutes) via Mouans-Sartoux (see p268) and Mougins (see p268).

TRAIN

A section of track between Grasse and Cannes is expected to open in April 2005, with 18 trains per day in either direction. The train station is about 2km south of the centre. The **SNCF information office** (☎ 04 93 36 06 13; ⊗ 8.30am-5.30pm Mon-Sat), near the bus station, has details.

SO YOU WANT TO BE A NOSE?

Professional perfumers are known as 'noses'. There are 250 noses in the world (of which 30 are women), and five famous master noses. Noses combine a natural gift with 10 years of study, including five years at a special nose school in Versailles, Chicago or Zürich.

Noses live a puritanical lifestyle. Tasty, fun things like alcohol, smoking, coffee, garlic and spicy food are strictly forbidden, as they damage the highly sensitive nose's ability to identify – from no more than a whiff – 6000 or so scents.

MASSIF DE L'ESTÉREL

This range of red porphyritic rock is one of the coast's most stunning natural features. Devastating fires in 1985 and 1986 destroyed many of the pine, oak and eucalyptus trees that covered it, but thankfully these are now returning to life. The massif lies immediately southwest of Cannes, with Mandelieu-La Napoule to the north and St-Raphaël to the south. The latter, together with its Roman neighbour, Fréjus, serves as the main gateway to the Massif des Maures (p298) and St-Tropez (p283).

There are all sorts of walks to enjoy in the Massif de l'Estérel, but for the more difficult trails you'll need a good map, such as IGN's Série Bleue (1:25,000) No 3544ET *Fréjus, Saint-Raphaël & Corniche de l'Estérel*, available from bookshops and newsagents. Those not keen to go alone can link up with an organised walk: tourist offices in Mandelieu-La Napoule, Agay, St-Raphaël and Fréjus have details.

CORNICHE DE L'ESTÉREL

A walk or drive along the winding Corniche de l'Estérel (also known as the Corniche d'Or, which translates as the 'Golden Coast', and the N98) is not to be missed – the views are spectacular. Small summer resorts and inlets (good for swimming) are dotted along the 30km coastal stretch, all of which are accessible by bus or train (see p274).

The Corniche de l'Estérel can get very busy in summer: to escape the crowds, choose the inland N7, which runs through the hills and feels like a whole different world.

Mandelieu-La Napoule

This small seaside village contains the coast's most eccentric building, the wonderful, turreted, 14th-century **Château de la Napoule** (☎ 04 93 49 95 05; av Henry Clews; adult/under 10 yrs château & gardens €6/free, gardens only €3/free; ☼ 10am-6pm). American nutcases Henry and Marie Clews arrived on the coast in 1918 and spent 17 years rebuilding the sea-facing Saracen tower and decorating it in twisted-fairy-tale style: the effect is Gormenghast-by-the-Sea. Henry Clews' (1876–1937) grave in a tower in the grounds reads 'Poet, Sculptor, Actor, Grand Knight of La Mancha, Supreme Master Humormystic, Castelan of Once upon a Time, Chevalier de Marie'. In a macabre twist, his tomb and Marie's (opposite) hang open, as though the two corpses have sought each other out after death.

The beautiful gardens, designed by Marie, are in classic French formal style, and are packed with more of Henry's creations, and challenging works by contemporary sculptors. A particularly creepy statue, entitled *The God of Humormystics*, stands in the courtyard: Henry's wedding present to his wife!

The interior of the privately owned chateau can only be seen with a guided tour. From February to October these leave at 11.30am, 2.30pm, 3.30pm and 4.30pm. From November to January it's 2.30pm and 3.30pm (and 11.30am at weekends). The gardens, with tea room and kids' treasure hunt, can be viewed any time from 10am to 6pm.

The chateau's sturdy garden wall is laced by **Plage du Château**, a sandy beach where coastal paths to the neighbouring beaches of **Plage de la Raguette** (10 minutes) and **Plage de la Rague** (30 minutes) start. Pick up more information about coastal walks in the area at the **tourist office** (☎ 04 93 49 95 31; www.ot -mandelieu.fr; 272 av Henry Clews; ☼ 10am-12.30pm & 2-6pm Mon-Fri), downhill on the other side of the street to the castle.

From adjacent pleasure-boat harbour Port de la Napoule, **Compagnie Maritime Napouloise** (☎ 04 93 49 15 88) runs boats to/from Île Ste-Marguerite. From April to September boats sail one to three times daily (adult/four to six years €11/6 return).

Théoule-sur-Mer

Neighbouring Théoule-sur-Mer, 2.5km south along the coast, is dominated by **Château de la Théoule** (☼ closed to visitors), another privately owned folly (and ex-18th-century soap factory) built in the same architectural style as Château de la Napoule. An even bigger eccentricity, the bubble-like **Palais Bulles** (think Teletubby house crossed with old diving helmets), lies well hidden amid trees 5km west of the small seaside resort. It was designed in the 1960s by Hungarian architect Antti Lovag, who now lives in Tourrettes-sur-Loup, and was bought by couturier Pierre Cardin in 1989. Unfortunately, the only chance to get a glimpse of his fanciful palace (other than online at www.palaisbulles.com in French) is during the few cultural events it hosts in June and

July; the **tourist office** (☎ 04 93 49 28 28; www
.theoule-sur-mer.org in French; 1 corniche d'Or; ☺ 9am-
7pm Mon-Sat, 10am-1pm Sun) has details.

Boats to Île Ste-Marguerite sail from the
small port, with three or four departures
Monday and Wednesday to Sunday April
to June, and five or six daily in July and August (adult/five to eight years €11/6 return).
Between April and September shorter boat
excursions with guided commentary also
sail along the Corniche d'Or (adult/five to
eight years €11/6, 1¾ hours).

Le Trayas

Needles of red rock tumble into the sea at Le
Trayas, a pretty seaside resort and the highest
point of the corniche, located 7km south of
Théoule-sur-Mer. The road gets more dramatic as it twists and turns along the coastline past the **Forêt Domaine de l'Estérel**. There
are several parking areas along this stretch
of the corniche where you can stop to picnic,
and there are good views of the spectacular **Rocher de St-Barthélemy** (St-Bartholomew's
Rock) and **Cap Roux** from the **Pointe de
l'Observatoire**, 2km south of Le Trayas.

There's a largish beach at **Anse de la Figue-
irette**, at the northern end of Le Trayas, with
various water sports on offer.

Agay

Agay, 10km or so south of Le Trayas, is
another pleasant resort, celebrated for
its fine views of the **Rade d'Agay**, a perfect
horseshoe-shaped bay embraced by sandy
beaches and abundant pine trees. Numerous water sports and boat excursions are
offered at busy central Plage d'Agay. The
tourist office (☎ 04 94 82 01 85; www.esd-fr.com/agay;
place Giannetti; ☺ 9am-noon & 2-6pm Mon-Sat), opposite the beach, has details.

It's also a good departure point for treks
into the Massif de l'Estérel: follow rte de
Valescure inland, from where various walking trails are signposted, including to **Pic de
l'Ours** (496m), **Pic du Cap Roux** (452m) and **Pic
d'Aurelle** (323m). All three peaks offer stunning panoramas. Forest rangers lead guided
nature walks (€9, 3hr) into the massif: pick up
an itinerary from the tourist office.

Le Dramont

Cap du Dramont, aka Cap Estérel, is crowned
by a military semaphore and sits at the southern end of the Rade d'Agay. From the sema-

phore there are unbeatable views of the Golfe
de Fréjus, flanked by the **Lion de Terre** and the
Lion de Mer, two red porphyritic rocks jutting
out of the sea. Trails lead to the semaphore
from **Plage du Débarquement** in Le Dramont on
the western side of the cape. In Agay, a path
starts from the car park near **Plage du Camp
Long**, at the eastern foot of the cape. Both
beaches are accessible from the N98.

From Plage du Débarquement you can
sail (15 minutes) to **Île d'Or** (Golden Island),
a pinprick island uninhabited bar a mock
'Medieval' tower. Tintin fans may recognise
it: the Île d'Or inspired Hergé's design for
The Black Island.

Hire catamarans (about €35/115 per one/
five hours) and sailboards (from €10 per
hour) from the Accueil Base Nautique, a
wooden hut on the beach.

Overlooking Plage du Débarquement,
1km west of Boulouris on the Corniche de
l'Estérel (N98), is a large **memorial park** (blvd
de la 36ème DI du Texas), which commemorates
the landing of the 36th US Infantry Division on the beach here on 15 August 1944.
A monumental landing craft faces out to
sea. Steps lead down to the beach.

Sleeping

Le Relais des Calanques (☎ 04 94 44 14 06; fax 04 94
44 10 93; rte des Escalles; r €70-110; mains €15; ℗ 🐊)
At the southern end of Le Trayas on the
N98, this hotel offers striking views of the
red-rocked sea. It has its own pool, private
beach and restaurant.

Le Trayas Hostel (☎ 04 93 75 40 23; www.fuaj.org;
9 av de la Véronèse; camping/dm incl breakfast €9/14.50,
sheet hire €3.70; ☺ Mar-Oct, closed 10am-5.30pm) This
HI youth hostel is in the idyllically situated
1930s Villa Solange, with views over the
coast. It's a steep 1.5km up the hill from
the Auberge Blanche bus stop in Le Trayas.
Non-HI cardholders pay €2.90 more per
night. Telephone reservations not accepted.

Campéole Le Draumont (☎ 04 94 82 07 68;
www.campeoles.fr; 2 people, tent & car €31.90; ☺ mid-
Mar–mid-Oct) This pretty site next to Plage
du Débarquement on the western side of
Cap du Dramont has numerous facilities,
including tennis courts and an on-site diving school.

Royal Camping (☎ 04 94 82 00 20; fax 04 94 82
00 20; 2 people, tent & car €23.50; ☺ Feb-Oct) Only a
snack kiosk stands between you and sandy
Plage du Camp Long, at Agay.

Getting There & Away

BUS

RafaelBus (☎ 04 94 83 87 63) runs a service along the Corniche de l'Estérel (labelled 'Ligne de la Corniche d'Or' on timetables) from St-Raphaël to Le Trayas (€2.90, 15 buses daily Monday to Saturday, 10 Sunday).

From Cannes, buses (eight daily Monday to Saturday, five Sunday) stop at Boulouris (€1.10), Cap du Dramont/Le Dramont (€1.70), Agay (€2.20) and Le Trayas (€2.90).

TRAIN

There are train stations at Mandelieu-La-Napoule (4km north of La Napoule), Théoule-sur-Mer, Le Trayas, Agay and Le Dramont. These are served by the Nice–Cannes–St-Raphaël–Fréjus–Les Arcs-Draguignan train route. There are frequent trains (nine to 11 Monday to Saturday; less frequently on Sunday and in winter) from Nice to St-Raphaël, stopping at all the smaller resort stations. From Les-Arcs-Draguignan to Nice, only two trains per day stop at the resorts: change in St-Raphaël.

There are many more trains from Cannes to St-Raphaël (see p253), from where there are regular buses to the smaller places.

ST-RAPHAËL

pop 31,196

Once a tiny fishing hamlet, the resort of St-Raphaël was more or less created by its mayor Félix Martin (1842–99), who took advantage of the new railway to draw in visitors. It became a fabulous place to be seen: in the 1920s F Scott Fitzgerald wrote *Tender is the Night* here, while wife Zelda spent her time drink-diving. During WWII it was one of the main landing bases of US and French troops.

St-Raphaël has lost some teeth and gained a potbelly since its glamour days. Its old town was bombed during the war, and the seafront suburbs have run out of control: they're now entangled with those of Fréjus, 2km away. It's still a great spot for beaches and water sports, though, and is one of France's leading diving centres.

By bicycle, you can cycle all the way to Toulon – a good 100km – on a silky smooth, two-lane coastal cycling track.

Orientation

The remnants of the old town are off rue de la Liberté (which is due north of rue Waldeck Rousseau). The new centre is neatly packed between rue Waldeck Rousseau and promenade de Lattre de Tassigny, which leads west to the Vieux Port. St-Raphaël's beach activities sprawl as far east as Port Santa Lucia (a modern pleasure port 1.5km along the coast) and another 2km west to Fréjus.

Information

Centrale de Reservation: Terres et Mer (☎ 04 94 19 10 60; reservation@saint-raphael.com; rue Waldeck Rousseau; ☼ 9am-7pm Jul & Aug, 9am-12.30pm & 2-6.30pm Mon-Sat Sep-Jun) This office deals with all accommodation reservations (free service).

Crédit Agricole (☎ 08 21 08 04 00; 28 promenade Commandant-Guilbaud; ☼ 8.30am-noon & 1.45-5pm Mon-Fri) Has a currency exchange desk.

Cyber Bureau (☎ 04 94 95 29 36; cyber.bureau@wanadoo.fr; 123 rue Waldeck Rousseau; per hr €7; ☼ 9am-noon & 2-7pm Mon-Fri, 9am-1pm Sat) Inside the train-station shopping centre.

Post Office (☎ 04 94 19 52 00; av Victor Hugo; ☼ 8am-6.30pm Mon-Fri, 8am-noon Sat) Cyberposte.

Tourist Office (☎ 04 94 19 52 52; www.saint-raphael.com; rue Waldeck Rousseau; ☼ 9am-7pm Jul & Aug, 9am-12.30pm & 2-6.30pm Mon-Sat Sep-Jun) Opposite the train station.

Sights & Activities

MUSEUMS

The **Musée Archéologique** (☎ 04 94 19 25 75; place de la Vieille Église; adult/10-18 yrs €1.50/0.70; ☼ 9am-noon & 2-5pm Wed, Thu & Sat, 11am-5pm Wed-Sun school holidays) has an exhibition on underwater archaeology, as well as artefacts from the Neolithic to the Bronze Age.

DIVING

St-Raphaël is a leading diving centre, thanks to the many **WWII shipwrecks** off its coast. These include a 42m-long US minesweeper, and a landing craft destroyed by a rocket in 1944 during the Allied landings. **Aventure sous Marine** (☎ 04 94 19 33 70; www.plongee83.com in French; 56 rue de la Garonne; ☼ 8.45am-3pm) can take you to see them: baptism dives cost €46.

BEACHES & WATER SPORTS

Choose between sand or shingle underfoot: **Plage du Veillat**, the main beach, has shining golden sand; to the east, **Plage Beaurivage** is covered in small pebbles. From June to September, you can waterski, parascend or ride the waves in a rubber tyre from most beaches along this stretch of coastline.

Port Santa Lucia, further east again, is a water-sports hub. **Club Nautique** (☎ 04 94 95 11 66; blvd Raymond Poincaré; ⏰ 8.30am-6pm) rents windsurfing boards/catamarans in July and August for around €46/115 per five hours.

BOAT EXCURSIONS

TMR Les Bateaux de St-Raphaël (Transports Maritimes Raphaelois; ☎ 04 94 95 17 46; bateauxsaintraphael@wanadoo.fr; quai Amiral Nomy, Vieux Port) organises boat excursions to St-Tropez and Port Grimaud (see p291). They also run trips from St-Raphaël to Calanques de l'Estérel (adult/two to nine years €12/7, 1¼ hours, daily July and August, Wednesday and Sunday September and October); Corniche de l'Estérel (adult/two to nine years €14/8, two hours 40 minutes, daily July and August, Wednesday and Sunday September); Île Ste-Marguerite (day excursion adult/two to nine years €23/12, daily July and August, Wednesday and Sunday September).

Festivals & Events

St-Raphaël's fishing community honours its patron saint, St Peter, every August with a two-day **Fête de la St-Pierre des Pêcheurs**. Local fishermen, dressed in traditional costume, joust Provençal-style from flat-bottomed boats moored in the harbour.

Every year St-Raphaël hosts a number of Provençal **jousting competitions**; watch out for members of the Société des Joutes Raphaëloises (Raphaëloises Jousting Society) practising in boats around the Vieux Port.

Sleeping

See p279 for camp sites.

Auberge de Jeunesse Fréjus-St-Raphaël (☎ 04 94 53 18 75; frejus-st-raphael@fuaj.org; chemin du Counillier; dm incl breakfast €14) Near Fréjus Ville, in a 7-hectare park. If you arrive by train, get off at St-Raphaël (6km away), take bus No 7 and walk up the hill. In July and August bus No 6 goes directly to the hostel. From Fréjus train station (6km away) or from place Paul Vernet, bus No 3 is the best option.

Le Jardin des Arènes (☎ 04 94 95 06 34; 31 av du Général Leclerc; s/d with shower €42/50; ⏰ reception 7.30am-12.30pm & 1.30-11pm) This is the cheapest joint in town, but it's clean, central and pleasantly quirky. Stained-glass windows,

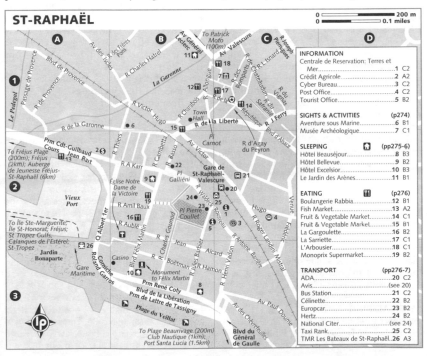

ST-RAPHAËL

| 0 | 200 m |
| 0 | 0.1 miles |

INFORMATION
Centrale de Reservation: Terres et
  Mer..1 C2
Crédit Agricole......................................2 A2
Cyber Bureau..3 C2
Post Office...4 C2
Tourist Office...5 B2

SIGHTS & ACTIVITIES (p274)
Aventure sous Marine...........................6 B1
Musée Archéologique............................7 C1

SLEEPING 🏠 (pp275-6)
Hôtel Beauséjour...................................8 B3
Hôtel Bellevue.......................................9 B2
Hôtel Excelsior....................................10 B3
Le Jardin des Arènes............................11 B1

EATING 🍴 (p276)
Boulangerie Rabbia.............................12 B1
Fish Market..13 A2
Fruit & Vegetable Market.....................14 C1
Fruit & Vegetable Market.....................15 B1
La Gargoulette......................................16 B2
La Sarriette..17 C1
L'Arbousier..18 C1
Monoprix Supermarket.........................19 B2

TRANSPORT (pp276-7)
ADA..20 C2
Avis...(see 20)
Bus Station..21 C2
Célinette..22 B2
Europcar..23 B2
Hertz..24 B2
National Citer.............................(see 24)
Taxi Rank...25 C2
TMR Les Bateaux de St-Raphaël..........26 A3

CANNES AREA

strange curvy doors and a leafy garden all add to the charm.

Hôtel Bellevue (☎ 04 94 19 90 10; fax 04 94 19 90 11; 24 blvd Félix Martin; s/d/tr incl breakfast €46/65/75; 🕑 closed mid-Nov–mid-Dec; 🔀) This two-star hotel has good-value rooms, particularly if you're a crowd of four or five (four- and five-person rooms cost the same as a triple). They're quite spacious, and contain TVs and handy fridges.

Hôtel Beauséjour (☎ 04 94 95 03 75; www.hotel beausejour.fr; promenade René Coty; r with town views €80, with sea views €104-145; 🕑 Apr-Oct; 🔀) Slightly chintzy, but as the only central two-star hotel with ocean views, this is the place if you like waking up to the sounds of the sea and the chink of pennies in the piggy bank.

Hôtel Excelsior (☎ 04 94 95 02 42; www.excelsior -hotel.com; promenade René Coty; d with town views €135, with sea views €156-170; 🔀) Further along the prom is the Excelsior, an elegant old pile near the casino. It's graced with a beautiful tea terrace overlooking the azure sea, and contains two restaurants and an English-style pub. They often do two-night deals outside high season.

Eating

L'Arbousier (☎ 04 94 95 25 00; 4 av Valescure; lunch menu €26, dinner menus €34-55; 🕑 closed lunch Tue, dinner Sun, Mon & mid-Jan–Dec) With its fabulous flowery garden to dine in, and great reputation, this is the town's gastronomic choice. Chef Phillippe Troncy serves up traditional fare using only the freshest seasonal ingredients: check out the lunchtime *repas du marché* (market meal) *menu* (€26).

La Gargoulette (☎ 04 94 95 48 18; 29 rue Aublé; lunch menu €22, dinner menus €29-54; 🕑 lunch & dinner Tue-Fri, dinner Sat) Chef André Quaglia defected from L'Arbousier to set up his own restaurant, so you know the food is quality nosebag. Emphasis is on country cooking and Mediterranean dishes, with parmesan, balsamic vinegar and fresh grilled vegetables everywhere.

La Sarriette (☎ 04 94 19 28 13; 45 rue de la République; menus €15.50 & €23; 🕑 5.30-10pm) This is a pretty place tucked in the shade of a plane tree in the heart of the old town. Dishes are well doused with Provençal herbs and spices.

SELF-CATERING

Boulangerie Rabbia (☎ 04 94 95 07 82; 29 rue Allongue; 🕑 7am-8pm Tue-Sun) This splendid family bakery dates back to 1885, and sells *tarte*

Tropézienne (creamy, sponge-cake sandwich topped with sugar and almonds), *farinette Niçois* (Niçois bread) and bread stuffed with olives, bacon bits, anchovy or goat cheese.

A daily fruit and vegetable market fills place de la République and place Victor Hugo. Fishmongers sell the catch of the day each morning at the Vieux Port **fish market** (cours Jean Bart). There's also a **Monoprix supermarket** (58 blvd Félix Martin; 🕑 8.30am-7.30pm Mon-Sat).

Getting There & Away

BUS

St-Raphaël **bus station** (☎ 04 94 95 16 71; av Victor Hugo) is just behind the train station (accessible via the escalators on the station platforms). It also doubles as Fréjus' main bus station. For information on buses to/from Fréjus see p280.

Estérel Cars (St-Raphaël ☎ 04 94 95 16 71, Fréjus ☎ 04 94 53 78 46) operates buses from St-Raphaël to/from Draguignan (€5.40, 1¼ hours, hourly Monday to Saturday, six per day Sunday) via Fréjus (€5.10).

RafaelBus (☎ 04 94 83 87 63) runs buses along the Corniche de l'Estérel (see p274) from St-Raphaël to Le Trayas. **Sodetrav** (☎ 04 94 97 88 51) runs buses to St-Tropez (€8.90, 1¼ hours, eight to 10 daily) via Saint-Pons (for Port Grimaud; €7.30, 50 minutes) or Grimaud (€7.90, 55 minutes) and Ste-Maxime (€5.70, 35 minutes). Services are less frequent in winter.

TRAIN

The Nice–Marseille train line runs through Fréjus and St Raphaël's **Gare de St-Raphaël-Valescure** (information office ☎ 08 92 35 35 35; rue Waldeck Rousseau; 🕑 9.15am-1pm & 2.30-6pm). Some trains to/from Nice (€9.40, 1½ hours, every 30 minutes) stop at the villages along the Corniche de l'Estérel (p272). There's also a direct service to Les Arcs-Draguignan (see p297; €4.50) in the Var region.

Getting Around

Major car-rental agencies are clustered around the train station: **ADA** (☎ 04 94 95 01 83) and **Avis** (☎ 04 94 95 60 42; www.avis.fr in French) have an office inside; opposite are **Hertz** (☎ 04 94 95 48 68) at No 36, **Europcar** (☎ 04 94 95 56 87; www.europcar.fr in French) at No 56 and **National Citer** (☎ 04 94 40 27 89) at No 20.

Patrick Moto (☎ 04 94 53 65 99; 199 av Général Leclerc) rents mountain bikes (summer only) for €15 per day.

For something out of the ordinary, visit **Célinette** (☎ 06 24 32 89 82; place Galliéni), which rents three-/six-person pedal carts for €15/18 per hour (€50/60 per half-day).

There's a taxi rank outside the station, or call ☎ 04 94 83 24 24 or ☎ 04 94 95 04 25.

FRÉJUS

pop 48,000 / elevation 250m

Fréjus, first settled by Massiliots (the Greek colonists from Marseille) then colonised by Julius Caesar around 49 BC as Forum Julii, is known for its Roman ruins. Once an important port, much of its commercial activity ceased after the harbour silted up in the 16th century.

Fréjus Ville is an appealing old town, with rows of pastel buildings, shady plazas and winding alleys. Its most amazing sight is the episcopal complex, sheltering unique medieval paintings of mermaids and monsters. Outside, place Paul Albert Février hosts **morning markets**: a flower/Provençal market on Wednesday and Saturday; and fruit and veg Tuesday to Sunday, June to September.

Fréjus' golden-sand Fréjus Plage is lined with buildings from the 1950s. Its chic port – full of seafood restaurants with grossly inflated prices – was built in the 1980s. You'll find a **marché nocturnal** (night market) spilling across the sand at Fréjus Plage most evenings, June to September.

Orientation

Fréjus is made up of hillside Fréjus Ville, 3km from the seafront, and Fréjus Plage, on the Gulf of Fréjus. Fréjus' modern port is at the western end of blvd de la Libération and its continuation, blvd d'Alger. The Roman remains are mostly in Fréjus Ville.

Information

There's a phonecard-operated Internet terminal inside the main tourist office.

Banque National de Paris (BNP; ☎ 08 20 82 00 01; 232 rue Jean Jaurès; 🕑 8.30-noon & 1.45-5pm Mon-Fri) Near the main tourist office; with an ATM.

Branch Post Office (blvd de la Libération) Opposite the tourist office kiosk.

Espace Bureautique (☎ 04 94 17 15 70; epace bureautique.as@wanadoo.fr; 58 rue de Grisolle; per hr €4) Internet access.

Gendarmerie Nationale (Police Station; ☎ 04 94 51 40 54; 215 rue de Triberg, Port Fréjus)

Post Office (264 av Aristide Briand; 🕑 8.30am-7pm Mon-Fri, 8.30am-noon Sat)

Tourist Office (☎ 04 94 51 83 83; www.frejus.fr in French; 325 rue Jean Jaurès; 🕑 10am-noon & 2.30-6.30pm Mon-Sat, 10am-noon & 3-6pm Sun Jul & Aug, 10am-noon & 2-6pm Mon-Sat Sep-Jun)

Tourist Office Kiosk (☎ 04 94 51 48 42; 🕑 10am-noon & 3-7pm Jun–mid-Sep) By the beach opposite 11 blvd de la Libération in Fréjus.

Sights

LE GROUPE ÉPISCOPAL

Fréjus' most fascinating sight is **Le Groupe Épiscopal** (Cathedral Close; ☎ 04 94 51 26 30; 58 rue de Fleury; adult/under 18 yrs €4.60/free; 🕑 9am-6.30pm Jun-Sep, 9am-noon & 2-5pm Tue-Sun Oct-May), slap in the centre of town on the foundations of a Roman temple. At the heart of the complex is an 11th- and 12th-century **cathedral**, one of the first Gothic buildings in the region (although it retains certain Roman features).

The beautiful carved wooden doors at the main entrance were added during the Renaissance. The octagonal 5th-century **baptistry** (which incorporates eight Roman columns into its structure) is one of the oldest Christian buildings in France, and is exceptionally well preserved.

Stairs from the narthex lead up to the **cloister**, which looks onto a fine courtyard with a well-tended garden and well. Here you'll find the complex's most stunning feature, its utterly unique 14th- and 15th-century painted **wooden ceiling panels**: 500 of the original 1200 survive. Angels, devils, hunters, acrobats, monsters and a cheery-looking man riding a pig gallivant round the vivid comic-book frames: bring binoculars for a better view.

ROMAN RUINS

West of the old town, past the ancient **Porte des Gaules**, is the mostly rebuilt 1st- and 2nd-century **Les Arènes** (amphitheatre; ☎ 04 94 51 34 31; rue Henri Vadon; admission free; 🕑 10am-1pm & 2.30-6.30pm Mon & Wed-Sat Apr-Oct, 10am-noon & 1.30-5.30pm Mon & Wed-Sat Nov-Mar). It was one of the largest amphitheatres in Gaul, seating an audience of 10,000, and is still used for rock concerts and bullfights today.

At the southeastern edge of the old city is the 3rd-century **Porte d'Orée** (rue des Moulins), the only remaining arcade of monumental

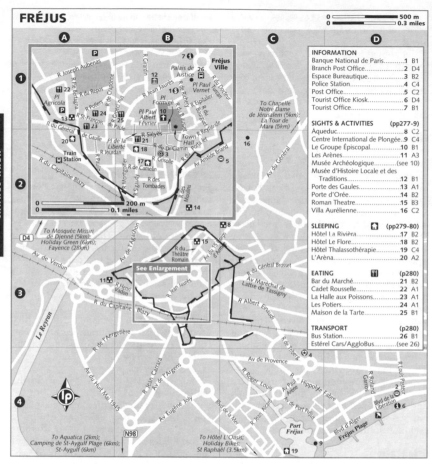

FRÉJUS

INFORMATION
Banque National de Paris..........1	B1
Branch Post Office...................2	D4
Espace Bureautique.................3	B2
Police Station.........................4	C4
Post Office..............................5	C2
Tourist Office Kiosk.................6	D4
Tourist Office.........................7	B1

SIGHTS & ACTIVITIES   (pp277-9)
Aqueduc.................................8	C2
Centre International de Plongée..9	C4
Le Groupe Épiscopal..............10	B1
Les Arènes............................11	A3
Musée Archéologique...........(see 10)	
Musée d'Histoire Locale et des	
Traditions..........................12	B1
Porte des Gaules....................13	A1
Porte d'Orée.........................14	B2
Roman Theatre......................15	B3
Villa Aurélienne....................16	C2

SLEEPING   (pp279-80)
Hôtel La Rivièra.....................17	B2
Hôtel Le Flore.......................18	B2
Hôtel Thalassothérapie..........19	C4
L'Arèna................................20	A2

EATING   (p280)
Bar du Marché......................21	B2
Cadet Rousselle....................22	A1
La Halle aux Poissons............23	A1
Les Potiers...........................24	A1
Maison de la Tarte................25	B1

TRANSPORT   (p280)
Bus Station...........................26	B1
Estérel Cars/AggloBus........(see 26)	

Roman thermal baths. North of the old town are the ruins of a **Roman theatre** (☎ 04 94 53 58 75; rue du Théâtre Romain; admission free; ◷ 10am-1pm & 2.30-6.30pm Mon & Wed-Sat Apr-Oct, 10am-noon & 1.30-5.30pm Mon & Wed-Sat Nov-Mar). Part of the stage and the outer walls are all that can be seen today.

Northeast, towards La Tour de Mare, you pass a section of a 40km-long **aqueduc** (aqueduct; av du 15 Corps d'Armée), which once carried water to Roman Fréjus. Continuing 500m further north, you reach **Villa Aurélienne** (1880; signposted), which hosts temporary photography exhibitions. In its 22-hectare park there's another section of the aqueduct, complete with five moss-covered arches.

CHAPELLE NOTRE DAME DE JÉRUSALEM

Also known as the **Chapelle Cocteau** (☎ 04 94 53 27 06; av Nicolaï, La Tour de Mare; admission free; ◷ 1.30-5.30pm Mon & Wed-Fri, 9.30am-12.30pm & 1.30-5.30pm Sat Nov-Mar, 2.30-6.30pm Mon & Wed-Fri, 10am-1pm & 2.30-6.30pm Sat Apr-Oct), this was one of the last pieces of work embarked upon by Jean Cocteau (1889–1963), best known for the fishermen's chapel he decorated in Villefranche-sur-Mer (see p228). Cocteau began work on Chapelle Notre Dame in Fréjus in 1961, but it remained incomplete until the artist's legal heir, Édouard Dermit, finished his former companion's work in 1988. The altar is made from a millstone.

The chapel is about 5km northeast of the old city in the quarter of La Tour de Mare (served by bus No 13; see p280), on the N7 towards Cannes.

MUSEUMS

Adjoining Fréjus' episcopal complex is the **Musée Archéologique** (☎ 04 94 52 15 78; place Calvini; admission free; ⊙ 10am-1pm & 2.30-6.30pm Mon & Wed-Sat Apr-Oct, 10am-noon & 1.30-5.30pm Mon & Wed-Sat Nov-Mar), housing permanent pieces including a two-headed statue of Hermes and a magnificent 3rd-century leopard mosaic. It also puts on temporary exhibitions of finds from archaeological digs.

The town's history is illustrated in the **Musée d'Histoire Locale et des Traditions** (Local History & Traditions Museum; ☎ 04 94 51 64 01; 153 rue Jean Jaurès; admission free; ⊙ 10am-1pm & 2.30-6.30pm Mon & Wed-Sat Jul & Aug, 10am-1pm Mon & Wed-Fri, 10am-1pm & 2.30-6.30pm Sat Apr-Jun, 10am-1pm & 2.30-6.30pm Sat Sep & Oct, 1.30-5.30pm Mon-Fri, 9.30am-12.30pm & 1.30-5.30pm Sat Nov-Mar).

MOSQUÉE MISSIRI DE DJENNÉ

A collection of surprising war memorials and troop-related buildings lie scattered round Fréjus, including this **mosque** (rue des Combattants d'Afrique du Nord), a replica of one in Djenné, Mali. It was built in 1930 for Sudanese troops stationed at a marine base in Fréjus, and lies 5km north of town on the rte de Bagnols-en-Forêt (the D4 towards Fayence).

Activities

AQUATICA

Bomb down giant water slides, ride rubber rings and go wave-crazy on dozens of different attractions at **Aquatica** (☎ 04 94 51 82 51; www.parc-aquatica.com; adult/under 12 yrs €22/18; ⊙ 10am-7pm Jul & Aug, 10am-6pm Jun & Sep), the Riviera's biggest water park, out of town on the southbound N98. Children under 1m tall get in free.

BEACHES & DIVING

Fréjus Plage, lined with buildings from the 1950s, is an excellent sandy beach.

At the new port, **Centre International de Plongée** (CIP; ☎ 04 94 52 34 99; www.cip-frejus.com; lot 15 & 16 Port Fréjus) does diving courses, fun dives and night dives. Baptisms cost €40/34 for adults/eight to 13 years, including all equipment.

Sleeping

Note to hostellers: it is equally feasible to stay in the hostel in St-Raphaël (see p275).

BUDGET

Hôtel La Riviéra (☎ 04 94 51 31 46; fax 04 94 17 18 34; 90 rue Grisolle; d with shower €35, with toilet and shower or bath €40) A backpackers hotel in the best sense. The rambling old building and dark but neat rooms are kept in good shape by a friendly young couple who clearly enjoy the company of their clientele. The hotel has a restaurant (main course and 0.25L wine €9).

Fréjus has a dozen or so camp sites:

Holiday Green (☎ 04 94 19 88 30; www.holiday-green.com; rte des Combattants d'Afrique du Nord; 2 adults, tent & car €30; ⊙ Apr-Sep; P ☎) The fancy four-star Holiday Green (on the D4 towards Fayence) is one of the best. It's 7km from the beach, but has its own large pool.

Camping de St-Aygulf Plage (☎ 04 94 17 62 49; www.camping-cote-azur.com; 270 av Salvarelli; 2 adults, tent & car from €21; ⊙ Apr-Oct) If you want a seaside site, head south to this huge place in St-Aygulf (6km south of Fréjus): its 1100 places are practically on the beach.

MID-RANGE

In Fréjus Ville:

Hôtel Le Flore (☎ 04 94 51 38 35; fax 04 94 55 59 89; 35 rue Grisolle; s/d €55/60) The Flore is a two-star hotel on a main street, with twisting staircases (watch out for unexpected steps) and decent-sized rooms with TVs; a couple have balconies. Lady the dog and several jumpy Siamese cats patrol downstairs.

Near the sea:

Hôtel L'Oasis (☎ 04 94 51 50 44; fax 04 94 53 01 04; impasse Jean-Baptiste Charcot, Fréjus Plage; r €64; ⊙ mid-Feb–Oct; P ☎ ☎) A 27-room place set amid pine trees, with comfortable rooms that have TV.

TOP END

L'Arèna (☎ 04 94 17 09 40; www.arena-hotel.com; 145 rue du Général de Gaulle; s €80, d €120-145; menus €35, €45 & €55; P ☎ ☎ ☎) A delightful three-star hotel with a flower-lined garden terrace, where you can eat wonderful breakfasts or lounge by the pool. Rooms are summery, if a little on the small side, and there's a decent restaurant serving refined and imaginative food. Recommended.

Hôtel Thalassothérapie (☎ 04 94 52 55 00; www.hotelthalasso-portfrejus.fr; Port-Fréjus West; s €87-107, d €103-126; P ☎ ☎) Stress-heads can enhance their holiday with a range of treatments at the hotel's spa/clinic. A seven-night, six-day massage package costs from €1317 with half-board. Or you could just splash in the pool, relax in the veranda rooms, or stroll straight onto the beach via the hotel gardens.

Eating

Port Fréjus has a few cafés and restaurants with views of bobbing boats. In Fréjus Ville there's a cluster of average-priced, unfussy pizza restaurants (lunch *menus* around €14) on place Paul Albert Février. Also try:

Les Potiers (☎ 04 94 51 33 74; 135 rue Potiers; menus €22.50 & €32; 🕒 noon-2pm & 7.30-9.30pm Thu-Mon, 7.30-9.30pm Wed; 🔀) The cream of the town's restaurants, this quaint and civilised spot is tucked down a peaceful backstreet. Its desserts are particularly memorable: try one of its rainbow of *crèmes brûlées*, flavoured with orange, pistachio, chicory or liquorice.

Bar du Marché (☎ 04 94 51 29 09; 5 place de la Liberté; mains €7.50) At the other end of the scale, this rough and-ready bar serves salads, giant pizzas and bowlfuls of *moules frites* (mussels and fries) on its bustling, bubbly terrace.

Cadet Rousselle (☎ 04 94 53 36 92; 25 place Agricola; menu €12; 🕒 11am-3pm & 6pm-midnight) Dozens of different sweet/savoury crepes (from €2.60/3.25) make for a cheap lunch.

Maison de la Tarte (☎ 04 94 51 17 34; 33 rue Jean Jaurès; 🕒 6am-9pm Mon-Sat) This top-quality *boulangerie*-cum-*tarterie* sells well-filled baguettes and a peachy array of sweet tarts (peach, pear and chocolate, pine kernel, almond), sold by the slice (€1.80 to €2.20) to take away. Be prepared to queue.

Buy fresh fish at **La Halle aux Poissons** (☎ 04 94 51 36 44; 114 rue du Général de Gaulle; 🕒 7.30am-1pm & 4.20-7pm Tue-Fri, to 2pm Sat, 8.50am-noon Sun).

Getting There & Away

BUS

Fréjus bus station (a humble series of stands around a roundabout) is served by local bus company **Estérel Cars/AggloBus** (☎ 04 94 53 78 46; place Paul Vernet).

From Fréjus bus station, Bus Nos 6, 7, 10, 13 and 27 run to St-Raphaël (€1.10, 20 to 35 minutes, every 15 or 20 minutes). From Fréjus train station, Bus No 27 runs to St-Raphaël (€1.10, approximately hourly, less frequently Sunday). From the bus station, there's also a service to/from Draguignan (€5.50, one hour, hourly), and the Nice–Marseille service run by Nice-based Phocéens Cars (p225) stops here twice per day.

TRAIN

The town's **train station** (rue du Capitaine Blazy) is on the Nice–Marseille train route, although few trains stop here beyond services to/from St-Raphaël (€1.20, two minutes, hourly): see p276.

Getting Around

Bus No 6 (hourly) links the beaches of Fréjus Plage with place Paul Vernet in Fréjus Ville. Bus No 13 runs between Fréjus' train station and bus station and Cocteau's Chapelle Notre Dame de Jérusalem. Tickets can be purchased from bus drivers (€1.10/8.40 per ticket/carnet of 10).

Close to the beach, **Holiday Bikes** (☎ 04 94 52 30 65; www.holiday-bikes.com; 41 blvd Severin Decuers; 🕒 9am-noon & 2-6.30pm Mon-Sat), overlooking rond-point des Moulins, rents road bikes/mountain bikes/50cc scooters/125cc scooters for €15/25/40/50 per day.

St-Tropez to Toulon

CONTENTS

ST-TROPEZ TO TOULON

Pouting sexpot Brigitte Bardot came to St-Tropez in the '50s to star in *Et Dieu Créa la Femme* (And God Created Woman; 1956). The film's stunning success changed St-Tropez overnight, from peaceful fishing village into ultra-chic jet-set favourite. The Tropeziens have thrived on their glitzy image ever since: millionaires' yachts jostle for the €90,000-per-week moorings, and an infinite number of tourists jostle to admire them.

Toulon, 20km west of St-Tropez, is France's most important military port. It's a battleship-grey blast of reality on the shining yellow coast, but has some interesting corners. Continuing west, the islands off Toulon's shores, dubbed the Îles du Fun (Islands of Fun), have been transformed into concrete playgrounds by pastis millionaire Paul Ricard.

Between the two towns, fine-sand beaches of buttercream yellow abound: at St-Tropez's 9km-long Plage de Pampelonne; the quiet white coves of Cavalaire-sur-Mer, Le Rayol, Cavalière and Aiguebelle; the resort of Le Lavandou; and La Capte, near pretty palm-tree-lined Hyères, a launch pad for day trips to the golden Îles d'Hyères.

Inland, the surprisingly wild, remote and heavily forested Massif des Maures (from the Provençal word *maouro* meaning dark pine wood) sprawls west from St-Tropez, a hushed, whispering retreat from the Côte d'Azur madness. Walking and cycling routes radiate around Collobrières, famous for its sweet chestnuts. Further north around Draguignan is Pays Dracénois, a region of unspoiled hilltop villages, with fortified gateways leading to tiny winding streets and sleepy squares.

HIGHLIGHTS

- Window-shop, star-spot and ogle yachts in sexy **St-Tropez** (opposite)
- Enjoy endless sun, sea and sand on the shining islands of the **Îles d'Hyères** (p303)
- Cuddle an octopus, then roam the plant-filled paradise of the **Domaine du Rayol** (p301)
- Lose yourself inside the labyrinth of medieval streets in **Ramatuelle** (p292)
- Gorge on the region's delicacies: candied chestnuts in **Collobrières** (p298), black truffles in **Aups** (p296), *tarte Tropézienne* in **St-Tropez** (opposite) and Côtes de Provence wines in **Les Arcs-sur-Argens** (p297)
- Atone for your gluttony in the superbly stark surroundings of the **Abbaye de Thoronet** (p297)
- Slow down and savour simple pleasures in the hilltop villages scattered round **Draguignan** (p295)

Aups ★

Draguignan ★

★ Les Arcs-sur-Argens

Abbaye de ★
Thoronet

★ St-Tropez

Collobrières ★

Ramatuelle ★

Domaine du Rayol ★

★
Îles d'Hyères

PRESQU'ÎLE DE ST-TROPEZ

Jutting out into the sea, between the Golfe de St-Tropez and the Baie de Cavalaire, is the select Presqu'île de St-Tropez (St-Tropez Peninsula). From swanky St-Tropez on the northern coast, fine sandy beaches ring the peninsula. Inland lie the hilltop villages of Gassin and Ramatuelle, both lovely enough to keep their many thousands of visitors charmed.

ST-TROPEZ

pop 5542

Guy de Maupassant (1850–93), arriving in St-Tropez in 1887, was charmed by its quaint beauty and the 'sardine scales glistening like pearls on the cobblestones'. These days, sleek yachts have chased away the simple fishing boats and those same cobblestones are trampled by 100,000 daily visitors in summer. Don't fight the crowds: go with the flow, window-shop for designer clothes, and enjoy the spectacle of rich diners aboard their floating palaces, twirling silver knives and forks.

For a glimpse of an older, gentler village, grab a seat at a café on place des Lices, and watch *pétanque (boules)* being played under the age-old plane trees. If you're there on a Tuesday or Saturday morning, the square's food, flower, clothing and antique market is an unforgettable extravaganza. The former fishing quarter, La Ponche, with its tiny cobbled streets and glimpses of an azure sea, has held on to its intimate, enchanting air.

The most seductive view of St-Tropez, though, is from the water. Arriving by boat, the sprawling citadel, glowing terracotta roofs and church tower, with its distinctive Provençal campanile, are postcard-pretty. You don't need your own yacht, either – see p287 for details on watery ways into town.

Orientation

The old city is packed between quai Jean Jaurès, the main quay of the Vieux Port (old port); place des Lices, a vast shady rectangular square a few blocks inland; and the brooding 17th-century citadel in the northeast. Yachts like spaceships moor in the old port alongside quai Suffren.

From the bus station and Parking du Port at the Nouveau Port (new port), keep following av du Général Leclerc left as it turns into rue Allard; when you reach the end, turning left will take you to the scenic Vieux Port, and turning right, to the place des Lices.

The tourist office produces a very clear (and free) map of the town, as well as a free map of the peninsula.

Information

EMERGENCY

Gendarmerie Nationale (Police Station; ☎ 04 94 12 70 00; rue François Sibilli)

MARKET MANIA

Warm nutty loaves, juicy red tomatoes, herby olives, locally grown fruit, little cakes and lashings of lavender honey…purchase the perfect beach picnic from your nearest market.

Monday Bormes-les-Mimosas (evening craft market mid-June to mid-September), Cavalière (June to September), Ste-Maxime

Tuesday Bandol, Callas, Fayence, Hyères, Lorgues, St-Tropez, Toulon

Wednesday Bormes-les-Mimosas, Cavalaire-sur-Mer, Cogolin, Draguignan, La Garde Frelnet, Salernes, Sanary-sur-Mer, Toulon

Thursday Aups (November to March truffle market), Bargemon, Callas, Collobrières (July and August), Fayence, Grimaud, Hyères, Le Lavandou, Les Arcs-sur-Argens, Ollioules, Port Grimaud, Ramatuelle, Toulon

Friday Cotignac (June to September), Le Castellet, Le Pradet, Le Rayol (April to October), Ste-Maxime, Toulon

Saturday Cogolin, Draguignan, Fayence, Hyères, St-Tropez, Toulon

Sunday Cavalière (all-day flea market), Collobrières, La Garde Freinet, La Londe, Le Croix Valmer, Port Grimaud, Ramatuelle, Salernes, Toulon

ST-TROPEZ TO TOULON

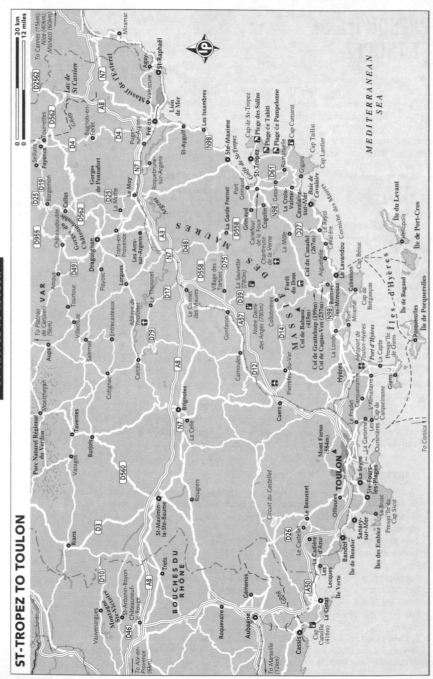

INTERNET ACCESS
Kreatik Cafe (☎ 04 94 97 40 61; infos@kreatik.com; 19 av du Général Leclerc; per 15min €2; 🕑 10–1am)
Le Girafe (☎ 04 94 97 13 09; 36 rue du Portail Neuf) Costs €2.50 for the first 15 minutes, then €0.12 per minute.

LAUNDRY
Laverie du Port (13 quai de l'Épi; per 5.5/16.5kg wash €5.50/13; 🕑 9am–7pm high season)

MEDICAL SERVICES
Hospital: Pôle de Sante (☎ 04 98 12 50 00) In Gassin, 11km from St-Tropez.
Pharmacie du Port (☎ 04 94 97 00 06; 9 quai Suffren; 🕑 8.30am–midnight high season)

MONEY
Change Cambio (☎ 04 94 97 80 70; 18 rue Allard; 🕑 9.15am–10pm high season)

POST
Central Post Office (place Celli)

TOURIST INFORMATION
Tourist Office (☎ 04 94 97 45 21; www.ot-saint -tropez.com; quai Jean Jaurès; 🕑 9.30am–8pm Jul & Aug, 9.30am–12.30pm & 2–7pm Apr–Jun, Sep & Oct, to 6pm Jan–Mar, Nov & Dec)

Sights & Activities

CITADEL
A 17th-century **citadel** dominates the hillside overlooking St-Tropez to the east. The views (and peacocks!) are great, and its dungeons now house a **Musée Naval** (☎ 04 94 97 59 43; adult/8- 18 yrs €4/2.50; 🕑 10am–12.30pm & 1.30-5.30pm Nov-Mar, to 6.30pm Apr-Jul, 10am–12.30pm & 1.30-10.30pm Aug-Oct), dedicated to the town's maritime history and the Allied landings in August 1944.

MUSÉE DE L'ANNONCIADE
The **Musée de l'Annonciade** (☎ 04 94 97 04 01; place Georges Grammont; adult/student/under 12 yrs €5.50/3.50/ free; 🕑 10am–1pm & 3-11pm mid-Jul & Aug, 10am–12pm & 3-7pm Wed-Mon Jun & Sep, 10am–noon & 2-6pm Wed- Mon Oct & Dec-May), in a gracefully converted 16th-century chapel at the Vieux Port, con- tains an impressive collection of modern art infused with the famous Côte d'Azur light. It's a great escape from the crowds and you'll leave with a fresh feeling for the St-Tropez that captivated these painters.

Go dotty over the pointillist collection on the 2nd floor, which includes Signac's *St-Tropez, L'Orage* (1895), *St-Tropez, Le*

A HEADLESS HERO
A grisly legend provided St-Tropez with its name in AD 68. After beheading a Roman officer named Torpes for becoming a Chris- tian, the emperor Nero packed the decapi- tated body into a small boat, along with a dog and a rooster who were to devour his remains. Miraculously, the body came ashore in St-Tropez unnibbled, and the village adopted the headless Torpes as its saint.

Quai (1899) and *St-Tropez, Le Sentier Côtier* (1901). Artists such as Vuillard, Bonnard, Maurice Denis and Valloton (the self-named Nabis group) have a room to themselves, and there are some wild works by the Fau- vists: Matisse spent the summer of 1904 in St-Tropez, starting preliminary studies for *Luxe, Calme et Volupté*. Cubists George Braque and Picasso are also represented.

In summer there are extra art exhibitions in the 19th-century **Lavoir Vasserot** (rue Joseph Quaranta; admission free; 🕑 variable), the former communal washhouse.

LA MAISON DES PAPILLONS
Around 4500 creatures are pinned to the walls in **La Maison des Papillons** (House of Butter- flies; ☎ 04 94 97 63 45; 9 rue Étienne Berny; adult/under 8 yrs €3/free; 🕑 2.30-6pm Mon-Sat Apr-Oct). Dany Lar- tigue, son of Riviera photographer Jacques Henri Lartigue (1894–1986), collected the European species. He can also guide you round the cottage-museum (once the Lar- tigue home) on request.

BEACHES
About 4km southeast of town is the start of the magnificent sandy **Plage de Tahiti**, and its continuation, **Plage de Pampelonne**. The beach runs for about 9km between Cap du Pinet and Cap Camarat, a rocky cape domi- nated by France's second-tallest **lighthouse** (☎ 04 94 79 80 65; admission free; 🕑 2-5pm or 6pm); fabulous views can be enjoyed from the platform at the top of 84 steps.

Pampelonne's two most legendary bars are on the beach – **Le Club 55** (☎ 04 94 55 55 55; www.leclub55.com; 43 blvd Patch; 🕑 lunch only Mar–mid-Nov; advance reservations essential) and **La Voile Rouge** (The Red Sail; ☎ 04 94 79 84 34; rte des Tamaris; 🕑 Apr-Sep), where parts of *And God*

Created Woman were filmed and where the first sightings of topless bathers and later the g-string bikini occurred. To get to the beach on foot, head out of town along av de la Résistance (south of place des Lices) to rte de la Belle Isnarde and then rte de Tahiti. Otherwise, the bus to Ramatuelle runs about 1km inland from the beach.

Closer to St-Tropez, **Plage des Salins** is a long, wide sandy beach 4.5km east of town at the southern foot of Cap des Salins. To get here, follow rte des Salins to its end. On the way you'll pass **La Treille Muscate** (The Wine Trellis), a rambling villa framed with redochre columns wrapped in honeysuckle. Here in 1927 Colette wrote *La Naissance du Jour* (Break of Day), which evokes a 1920s unspoilt St-Tropez. She left town in 1938.

At the northern end of Plage des Salins, on a rock jutting out to sea, is the **tomb of Émile Olivier** (1825–1913), who served as first minister to Napoleon III until his exile in 1870. Olivier's 17-volume *L'Empire Libéral* is preserved in the library of **Château La Moutte**, his former home on Cap des Salins, where musical concerts are held in summer. Its unmarked entrance is on chemin de la Moutte.

Olivier's sea-facing tomb looks out towards **La Tête de Chien** (The Dog's Head), named after the legendary dog who declined to eat St Torpes' remains. Further

south, **Pointe du Capon** is a beautiful cape crisscrossed with walking trails.

Bathers can swim in the buff on aptly named **Plage de la Liberté**, a nudist beach on Pampelonne's northern end; **Plage de la Moutte** on Cap des Salins; or the more secluded **Plage de l'Escalet**, on the southern side of Cap Camarat.

COASTAL WALKS

A picturesque coastal path leads 35km south from St-Tropez to the beach at Cavalaire-sur-Mer, and around the St-Tropez peninsula as far west as Le Lavandou (60km), passing rocky outcrops and hidden bays en route.

In St-Tropez the path, flagged with a yellow marker, starts at **La Ponche**, immediately east of Tour du Portalet at the northern end of quai Frédéric Mistral. From here, trails lead to Baie des Cannebiers (2.7km), La Moutte (7.4km), Plage des Salins (8.5km) and Plage de Tahiti (12km). Alternatively, drive to the end of rte des Salins, from where it is a shorter walk along the coastal path to Plage de Tahiti (2.7km) and nudist Plage de la Moutte (1.7km) on Cap des Salins.

Cap Lardier, the peninsula's southernmost cape, is protected by the Parc National de Port-Cros (see p306). **Cap Taillat**, 1km northeast, is similarly guarded. This tiny spit of sandy land supports a range of important habitats, from seashore to wooded cliffs,

---

BB

Controversial model-turned-actress Brigitte Bardot was the epitome of smouldering sex appeal in the 1950s and 1960s. An icon of sexual liberation, Paris-born Bardot sprang nakedly to stardom in Roger Vadim's *Et Dieu Créa la Femme* (And God Created Woman; 1956) and moved to St-Tropez in 1958.

A year later she met French singer Serge Gainsbourg, with whom she went on to record several breathlessly erotic tracks, including the raunchy 'Harley Davidson', which saw the starlet clad in leather coquetting a motorbike. Gainsbourg's subsequent hit 'Initials BB' (1968), a melodious tribute to the Bardot myth, was a legend of its time.

Animals became Bardot's passion after she retired from the screen. She founded the **Fondation Brigitte Bardot** (☎ 01 45 05 14 60; www.fondationbrigittebardot.fr; 45 rue Vineuse, F-75116 Paris) in 1986, subsequently donating her celebrated 1960s St-Tropez home – Villa La Madrague, overlooking Baie des Cannebiers – to the animal-activist campaign group.

Now married to fourth husband Bernard d'Ormale, a National Front politician, Bardot's own right-wing views have led to four convictions for inciting racial hatred. Her book *Un Cri dans le Silence* (A Cry in the Silence; 2003) spared nothing and nobody: the unemployed, teachers, gays, the disabled, Islam, women in politics and what she termed 'the mixing of genes' all came under attack, rousing the fury of social and religious leaders.

The volatile BB, now 69, has courted controversy for the last 50 years, and shows no sign of stopping!

and hides some of France's rarest plant species as well as a population of Hermann tortoises (see p301).

DIVING & SNORKELLING

Discover St-Tropez's underworld with **Octopussy** (☎ 04 94 56 53 10, 06 10 25 61 26; www.octopussy.fr; ☼ 8.30-9.30am, 11.30am-3pm, 5-7pm Apr-Nov), with a kiosk at the portside car park. Dives cost from €30, plus equipment charge. The **European Diving School** (☎ 04 94 79 90 37; www.EuropeanDiving.com), based at Camping Kon Tiki, also organises similarly priced dives, with reductions for Kon Tiki campers.

BOAT EXCURSIONS

Boat trips around the glamorous Baie des Cannebiers – dubbed the 'Bay of Stars' after the many celebrity villas dotting the coast – are advertised on boards along quai Suffren. A typical company is **MMG** (☎ 04 94 96 51 00; transports.maritimes.mmg@wanadoo.fr), whose **Baie des Cannebiers boat trips** (adult/4-12 yrs €8/4; ☼ 4-5 daily departures Mar-Oct) last one hour.

From April to September **Les Bateaux Verts** (☎ 04 94 49 29 39; bateaux.verts@wanadoo.fr; 14 quai Léon Condroyer) runs various trips departing from the Nouveau Port (opposite Parking du Port), including **glass-bottomed boat trips** (adult/4-10 yrs €9/4.50; 45min) daily around the Bay of St-Tropez. Other destinations include Port-Cros (€26.50/16.80, 8.30am Monday, Thursday, Friday and Sunday, extra sailing Saturday July and August); Porquerolles (€30.60/19.40, 8.30am Monday, Thursday, Friday and Sunday, extra sailing Saturday July and August); and Cannes and Ste-Marguerite (both €26.50/16.80, 9am Wednesday and Sunday).

On Tuesday and Saturday in July and August, **Vedettes Îles d'Or et Le Corsaire** (☎ 04 94 71 01 02; www.vedettesilesdor.fr; 15 quai Gabriel Péri) runs boat trips from the Nouveau Port to Cavalaire-sur-Mer (adult/four to 12 years return €32/25.60, 1¼ hours) and Le Lavandou (return €41.40/33.20, two hours).

Otherwise, shuttleboats between St-Tropez, St-Raphaël, Ste-Maxime and Port Grimaud (see p291) make for a jolly day out.

Walking Tour

Vieux Port – the heart of Tropezien life – is as good a place as any to kick off a stroll. On quai Suffren, a **statue of the Bailli de Suffren** cast

from a 19th-century cannon peers out to sea. The bailiff (1729–88) was a sailor who fought with a Tropezien crew against Britain and Prussia during the Seven Years' War.

In a backstreet a block southwest, stop in at **La Maison des Papillons** (p285).

The charming old fishing quarter of **La Ponche**, where you can shrug off the hectic hustle of the centre, is northeast of the Vieux Port. To get to the harbour from quai Suffren, walk to the northern end of its continuations – quai Jean Jaurès and quai Frédéric Mistral. At the 15th-century **Tour du Portalet**, turn right (east) to the sandy fishing cove. From here, a coastal path (see opposite) snakes its way around the St-Tropez peninsula.

From the southern end of quai Frédéric Mistral, place Garrezio sprawls east from the 10th-century **Tour Suffren** to place de l'Hôtel de Ville. From here, rue Guichard leads southeast to the 18th-century sweet-chiming **Église de St-Tropez**, built in 1785 in an Italian baroque style on place de l'Ormeau. Inside is the bust of St Torpes, honoured during Les Bravades (see below).

Nearby, steps lead up to the **citadel** (p285) from the end of rue de la Citadelle, up montée de la Citadelle.

Back on rue de la Citadelle, and a few blocks south, is **Chapelle de la Miséricorde** (rue de la Miséricorde), built in 1645, with a pretty bell tower and colourful tiled dome. One block further south is **place des Lices**, with a 200m length lined with plane trees and *pétanque* players. The 1757 **Chapelle du Couvent** (av Augustin Grangeon) and **Chapelle Ste-Anne** (av Augustin Grangeon), built in 1618, lie south of here. Inside Chapelle Ste-Anne, there's an impressive collection of ex-votive paintings and centuries-old miniature boats given by Tropezien fishermen. They can be viewed once a year on St Anne's feast day (26 July).

Tours

City walks (adult/under 12 yrs €5/free; ☼ 10.30am Thu Apr-Sep) runs walking tours that depart from outside the tourist office. Tours of Gassin and Ramatuelle are also available, by prior arrangement only.

Festivals & Events

Guns blaze and flags flutter on 15 June during **Les Bravades des Espagnols**, a festival held to mark St-Tropez's victory over 21 Spanish galleons that attacked the port on

ST-TROPEZ

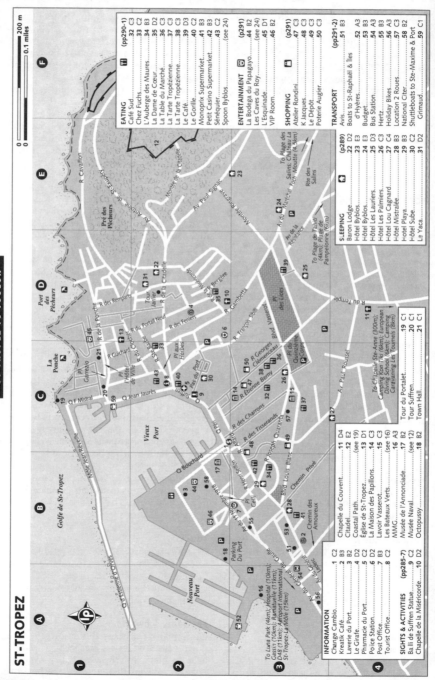

15 June 1637. The colourful street processions are led by the *capitaine de ville* (town captain).

The most important *bravades* (Provençal for 'bravery'), however, fall on 16, 17 (St Torpes' day) and 18 May, and have been celebrated since 1558. Tropeziens dress in traditional costume, and the *capitaine de ville*, along with an ear-splitting army of 140 musket-firing *bravadeurs*, process through the street bearing a bust of the town's saint.

Sleeping
BUDGET

Daahling, don't be crass: of *course* there are no cheap hotels in St-Trop! The tourist office has information on self-catering accommodation. Camping on the beach is illegal but there are around 15 camp sites on the peninsula, including **Camping Kon Tiki** (☎ 04 94 55 96 96; kontiki@wanadoo.fr; rte des Plages; 2 adults, 2 children, tent & car low/mid-/high season €25/35/50; ☿ reception 8am-8pm Apr-Oct; ☐), right on the beach at the northern end of Plage de Pampelonne, with its own diving school and beach huts.

MID-RANGE

Hôtel Sube (☎ 04 94 97 30 04; www.hotel-sube.com; quai Suffren; r with garden view low/high season from €65/90, with sea view €150/250; ✸) Tucked upstairs in an arcade behind the Bailli de Suffren statue at the Vieux Port, this place has a definite maritime air. Beautiful wooden sailing boats and nautical knick-knacks decorate the public spaces, and the terrace of the bar-restaurant gives you a super view of the port. Rooms are spacious and cool; pricier ones have boat-harbour views.

Hôtel Lou Cagnard (☎ 04 94 97 04 24; www.hotel-lou-cagnard.com; 18 av Paul Roussel; d low/high season from €44/53; ☿ Jan-Oct; P ✸) That thing of miracles, a decently priced St-Tropez hotel. In an old Provençal house, rooms aren't fancy but they're clean and light, and there's a jasmine-scented old courtyard garden.

Baron Lodge (☎ 04 94 97 06 57; www.hotel-le-baron.com; 23 rue de l'Aïoli; d low/mid-/high season from €46/53/69; P ✸) At the foot of the citadel, the Baron is unpretentious and has 10 comfortable double rooms, with either sea views or glimpses of the citadel. Staff are helpful and there's a good-value Provençal restaurant.

Hôtel Playa (☎ 04 98 12 94 44; www.playahotel sttropez.com; 57 rue Allard; d low/high season from €90/121; ✸) A young upstart among the town's list of venerable old hotels, Le Playa still has the unsullied shininess of a brand-new car. Its central rooms are simple but smart, but its best feature is its glass-roofed, palm-filled patio, which doubles as art exhibition space.

Hôtel Les Palmiers (☎ 04 94 97 01 61; www.hotel-les-palmiers.com; 24-26 blvd Vasserot; d low/high season from €75/89; P ✸) Crisp, no-nonsense décor and a pleasant courtyard, complete with orange trees and sun-lounges, make this hotel a good spot to stay. It's also very central, with prime views of place des Lices' *pétanque* players from rooms overlooking the square.

Hôtel Les Lauriers (☎ 04 94 97 04 88; fax 04 94 97 21 87; rue du Temple; d from €70; ☿ Christmas & Easter-15 Nov; ✸) Quite nondescript, but none the worse for that: this is a cool, green, anonymous two-star place, set on a quiet street behind the place des Lices.

TOP END

Le Yaca (☎ 04 94 55 81 00; www.hotel-le-yaca.fr; 1 blvd d'Aumale; s/d/apt low season from €250/300/550, high season from €300/380/650; ☿ Mar-early Jan; ✸ ☐ ☎) Sleep where Orson Welles, Errol Flynn and Greta Garbo laid their heads. Utterly without blemish, Le Yaca is hushed and understatedly elegant, with a gorgeous courtyard garden and staff so discreet it's like being waited on by charmingly mannered poltergeists. More expensive rooms have balconies with expansive views over the rooftops to the sea.

Hôtel Mistralée (☎ 04 98 12 91 12; www.hotel-mistralee.com; 1 av du Général Leclerc; d low/mid-/high season from €190/320/450; P ✸ ☎) In a beautifully restored 1850s mansion, this 'boutique hotel' has airy, high-ceilinged rooms, landscaped gardens, a good-sized pool and a soothing sauna.

Hôtel Byblos (☎ 04 94 56 68 00; www.byblos.com; av Paul Signac; s/d from €280/360; ☿ mid-Apr-mid-Oct; ✸ ☎) The Paris jet set, movie moguls and numerous celebs make Byblos their home-from-home. It's the *crème de la crème* of Riviera accommodation, with bouncers to fend off those irritating paparazzi, the scent of fresh banknotes wafting through the air, and an undeniably aphrodisiac atmosphere of pure luxury. Its gourmet restaurant serves impeccable food (see p290), and its nightclub is one of St-Trop's hottest spots.

Eating

You've probably guessed; there aren't many greasy spoons in St-Tropez. Café and restaurant prices are around a third higher than elsewhere on the coast: you're paying for the glamour dust that's been sprinkled over your fish and chips! Count on as much as €5 for a five-sip coffee at some of the trendy cafés.

Don't leave town without sampling a sweet and creamy *tarte Tropézienne*, a sponge cake sandwich filled with custard cream and topped with sugar and almonds.

RESTAURANTS

Quai Jean Jaurès is lined with restaurants; most have €25 *menus* and a strategic view of the silverware and champagne of the yacht brigade. At the northern end of rue des Remparts in the old town, there's a lesser-known cluster of places overlooking Port des Pêcheurs at La Ponche.

L'Auberge des Maures (☎ 04 94 97 01 50; fax 04 94 97 67 24;4 rue du Docteur Boutin; menu €42; ☼ mid-Feb–Nov) The oldest restaurant in town, this is a firm favourite, with quaintly Provençal décor (including a leaf-canopied courtyard), wonderful waiters and delicious food. Opt for a traditional *menu* or go for the *carte barbecue* – a choice of grilled meats including lobster (€46 per 600g) and monkfish (€79 per kg).

Chez Fuchs (☎ 04 94 97 01 25; fax 04 94 97 81 82; 7 rue des Commerçants; menu €35; ☼ Feb-Dec) This casual, unpretentious bar-restaurant is a truly authentic family-run affair where noisy, happy Tropeziens hang out. It's notable for the massive range of cigars it sells, and for its carefully prepared traditional dishes: stuffed courgettes, artichokes *á la barigoule* and seafood. It positively heaves – book ahead.

La Dame de Coeur (☎ 04 94 97 23 16; 2 rue de la Miséricorde; mains €25) With a daily changing menu featuring plenty of fresh-fish dishes, the Queen of Hearts caters to a low-key crowd. No name is signposted outside; look for the playing card.

La Table du Marché (☎ 04 94 97 85 20; www.christophe-leroy.com; 38 rue Georges Clémenceau; menus €18 & €26) An informal bistro where traditional Provençal dishes are concocted from market produce. It also does a fantastic line in cakes, including the *gendarme de St-Tropez*, a huge, chocolaty policeman's hat!

Café Sud (☎ 04 94 97 42 52; 12 rue Étienne Berny; menus €26 & €35; ☼ May-Oct) A tasteful restaurant set in a star-topped courtyard. Specialities include *petits farcis Provençaux* (Provençal filled vegetables) and all things fishy, like the yum clam carpaccio with citrus-fruit dressing. Café Sud's other outlet, **La Plage des Jumeaux** (☎ 04 94 79 84 21; rte de l'Épi; ☼ lunch Thu-Mon, lunch & dinner Jul & Aug) is right on Plage Pampelonne and has the same time-honoured dishes on the menu.

Spoon Byblos (☎ 04 94 56 68 20; www.byblos.com; av du Maréchal Foch; á la carte starter, main & dessert around €70, menu €55) This minimalist Ducasse creation is inside the Hôtel Byblos. The restaurant's concept whiffs of pretension – a 'Grand Tour' through a world menu, following the numbered columns horizontally for the chef's choice or zigzagging to create the culinary unthinkable – but the food itself is beyond reproach.

CAFÉS

Le Café (☎ 04 94 97 44 69; www.lecafé.fr; place des Lices) Artists and intellectuals have been meeting in St-Tropez's most famous café (formerly the Café des Arts) for years. Aspiring *pétanque* players can borrow *boules* from the bar and join the square's illustrious ball-chuckers. Don't confuse this legendary place with the newer, red-canopied Café des Arts on the corner.

Sénéquier (☎ 04 94 97 00 90; quai Jean Jaurès) Sartre wrote parts of *Les Chemins de la Liberté* (Roads to Freedom) here. It's a buzzing, people-watching terrace, with shouty-red tables and chairs, relaxed service, and famous nougat produced on the premises. Breakfast served from 7.30am.

Le Gorille (☎ 04 94 97 03 93; www.legorille.com; 1 quai Suffren; ☼ 7am-4am) Another eminent bistro, named after its previous owner, Henri Guérin, a short, muscular and hairy man! It's worth stopping here for a lunch-time pastis or post-clubbing snack.

SELF-CATERING

A morning fresh fish market fills place aux Herbes (daily in summer, Tuesday to Sunday in winter), under the archway behind the tourist office. Place aux Herbes is also home to an excellent *fromagerie*. On Tuesday and Saturday mornings a massive market, selling everything from fruit and veg to antique mirrors and slippers, fills place des Lices.

La Tarte Tropézienne (☎ /fax 04 94 97 19 77; 9 blvd Louis Blanc & 36 rue Georges Clémenceau), a bakery with two outlets in town, sells the traditional cream-filled sandwich cake created by *boulanger* Micka in Cogolin in 1955. Its fresh sandwiches are a good way to beat St-Tropez's exorbitant restaurant prices.

In-town supermarkets include **Monoprix** (9 av du Général Leclerc) and **Petit Casino** (39 rue Allard).

Entertainment

Clubs are open every night during high season and at weekends only from September to April. Strict door codes apply; if you're beautiful enough to get past the bouncers, prepare to spend around €18 per drink. The 'in' spots to boogie with the stars have always been **Les Caves du Roy** (☎ 04 94 97 16 02; www.byblos.com; av du Maréchal Foch), inside the Hôtel Byblos, and **VIP Room** (☎ 04 94 97 14 70; www.viproom.fr; av du 11 Novembre 1918). Don't just dress to impress; dress to create awe, envy and tomorrow's fashion-mag photos.

La Bodega du Papagayo (☎ 04 94 79 29 50; www .papagayobodega.com; résidence du Nouveau Port, quai Bouchard; menus €25 & €50) Overlooking the old port, this is a voguish restaurant, nightclub and terrace rolled into one. The leopard-skin toilet seats in the ladies' add a touch of *raaaargh*! You can dine here until 1am.

L'Esquinade (☎ 04 94 97 87 44; 2 rue du Four) Tucked near the water in the old fishing quarter of La Ponche; this club is hot, heaving stuff.

Shopping

St-Tropez is loaded with voguish boutiques, gourmet food shops and galleries overflowing with bad art. The Grand Passage, linking rue Allard with rue Georges Clémenceau, is crammed with designer fashion shops. Second-hand designer labels can be picked up at **Le Dépôt** (☎ 04 94 97 80 10; 24 blvd Louis Blanc).

Traditional Tropézienne sandals, supposedly inspired by a simple leather pair brought by Colette from Greece to show her cobbler, are all part of the St-Tropez myth. Buy a pair from €80 at **Atelier Rondini** (☎ 04 94 97 19 55; 16 rue Georges Clémenceau), where the strappy footwear has been crafted since 1927; or at **K Jacques** (☎ 04 94 54 83 63; www.kjacques.com; 25 rue Allard), where the family has cobbled since 1933.

Poterie Augier (☎ 04 94 97 12 55; poterie.augier@ wanadoo.fr; 19 rue Georges Clémenceau) sells massive garden urns, as well as more suitcase-friendly examples of clay craftsmanship.

LE GENDARME DE ST-TROPEZ

Jean Girault's hugely popular 1964 film *Le Gendarme de St-Tropez* sums up the town's sunny hedonism. An ambitious but incompetent police officer, played by Louis de Funès, is transferred to the resort, and makes it his mission to crack down on the local nudists. Meanwhile, his daughter Nicole lies her way into high society and the company of art thieves by pretending her dad is a high-rolling yacht owner.

Fast-paced, farcical and utterly French, the film is infused with catchy tunes and a very Gallic mocking of authority. If you have cause to eat your hat on the Côte d'Azur, make it the chocolate dessert named after the film, baked at La Table du Marché (see opposite) in St-Tropez.

Getting There & Away
AIR

The closest airport is **Aéroport International St-Tropez–La Môle** (St-Tropez–La Môle airport; ☎ 04 94 54 76 40; www.st-tropez-airport.com), 15km west of St-Tropez on the westbound N98.

BOAT

Transports Maritimes Raphaelois (☎ 04 94 95 17 46) runs two to six boats daily from St-Tropez to St-Raphaël (adult/two to nine years same-day return €11/7, 50 minutes) April to August, and boats twice a week in September and October. Boats depart from the Nouveau Port, from the jetty off av du 8 Mai 1945, opposite the bus station.

Between March and October, MMG (see p287) runs *navettes* (shuttleboats) to and from Ste-Maxime (adult/four to 12 years €5.50/2.90 one way, 30 minutes, at least hourly) and Port Grimaud (€4.80/2.50, 20 minutes, nine to 11 daily). Shuttles to and from Les Issambres (€6/3.20, 20 minutes, eight or nine daily) only sail mid-June to October. Boats depart from the pier off quai Jean Jaurès at the Vieux Port. Tickets are sold five minutes before departure from the portside kiosk.

Navettes between St-Tropez and Ste-Maxime operated by Les Bateaux Verts (see p287) sail year round; fares are the same as MMG's.

See p287 for boats to/from the Îles d'Hyères (Porquerolles and Port-Cros).

ST-TROPEZ TO TOULON

BUS

From St-Tropez **bus station** (☎ 04 94 97 88 51; av du Général de Gaulle), buses to and from Ramatuelle (€3, 25 minutes, four daily summer) and Gassin (€3, 25 minutes, four daily summer) run parallel to the coast about 1km inland.

There are also buses to and from St-Raphaël (€8.90, 1¼ hours, six to eight daily) via Grimaud and Port Grimaud (€3.20, 15 minutes), Ste-Maxime (€4.40, 40 minutes) and Fréjus (€8.20, one hour).

Buses to Toulon (€16.60, 2¼ hours, seven daily) go inland before joining the coast at Cavalaire-sur-Mer (€4.10, 30 minutes); they also stop at Le Lavandou (€9.70, one hour) and Hyères (€14, 1½ hours). Services are less frequent in winter.

CAR & MOTORCYCLE

People who do wrong in life are made to drive to St-Tropez when they die: the roads are chock-a-block and parking costs at least €4 per hour at the Nouveau Port. For your sanity's sake, try to get here by other means.

To get out of town, try car-hire places **National Citer** (☎ 04 94 54 85 19; fr-sttropez@citer .fr; rue du 11 Novembre 1918), **Budget** (☎ 04 94 54 86 54; 2 av du Général Leclerc), **Hertz** (☎ 04 94 55 83 00; stt60@hertz.com; rue de la Poste) and **Avis** (☎ 04 94 97 03 10; av du 8 Mai 1945).

Getting Around

TO/FROM THE AIRPORT

Shuttle buses between St-Tropez–La Môle airport and St-Tropez bus station (€18.20, one hour) coincide with flight arrivals/departures.

ALL THE FUN OF THE FAIR

If your kids are sick of sightseeing, pacify them with an evening trip to **Luna Park** (☎ 04 94 56 48 39; www.azurpark.com/sttropez .htm; ☼ 8pm-2am Apr-Sep). There are gentle rides for little 'uns, and beefier ones for braver souls: a big wheel, rollercoaster and crazy crane that hurtles you to 100km/hr in three seconds. Rides are priced individually, but buy a **carte pass** (adult/child €20/10) for savings.

The theme park is between Gassin and St-Tropez, next to the roundabout at Carrefour de la Foux off the N98.

BICYCLE & MOTORCYCLE

In town, family firm **Location 2 Roues** (☎ 04 94 97 00 60; 3-5 rue Joseph Quaranta; ☼ 9am-7pm Mar-Oct) hires road/mountain bikes/50cc scooters/100cc scooters for €10/12/34/44 per day and €42/69/205/264 per week.

Holiday Bikes (☎ 04 94 97 09 39; www.holiday -bikes.com; 14 av du Général Leclerc; ☼ 9am-12.30pm & 3-7pm, closed Jan & Feb) hires 50cc scooters/600cc motorcycles for €40/120 per day. You can also hire bicycles here.

PUBLIC TRANSPORT

Mid-March to October, shuttle buses run every 20 minutes in July and August from the car park (Parking du Port) opposite the bus station to and from av du Général Leclerc, av Gambetta (place des Lices) and quai Suffren (Vieux Port). A single ticket/carnet of 10 costs €1.30/8.60.

The Ramatuelle bus (see left) stops at Plage de Pampelonne (€1.30) – there are bus stops on rte des Plages (the D93) and blvd Patch.

TAXI

St-Tropez is small enough to walk round comfortably, but if necessary, there's a **taxi rank** (☎ 04 94 97 05 27) in front of the Musée de l'Annonciade at the Vieux Port.

GASSIN & RAMATUELLE

The sparsely populated interior of the Presqu'île de St-Tropez is crossed by sprawling vineyards and winding roads that link Gassin and Ramatuelle to the coast.

In medieval **Gassin** (population 2752, elevation 200m), 11km southwest of St-Tropez atop a rocky promontory, narrow streets wend up to the village **church** (1558). The village's most wowing feature is its 360° panoramic view of the peninsula, St-Tropez bay and the Maures forests – don't miss it!

From Gassin, rte des Moulins de Paillas snakes 3km southeast to **Ramatuelle** (population 2174, elevation 136m), an immeasurably picturesque labyrinthine walled village. Its unique name is thought to come from 'Rahmatu'llah', meaning Divine Gift, a legacy of the 10th-century Saracen occupation. Each year in mid-August, jazz and theatre liven up the tourist-packed streets during the two-week **Festival de Ramatuelle**.

The fruits of the peninsula's vineyards – Côtes de Provence wines – can be tested at various chateaux along the D61; **Ramatuelle tourist office** (☎ 04 98 12 64 00; www.ramatuelle-tour isme.com in French; place de l'Ormeau; ☽ 9am-1pm & 3-7.30pm Jul & Aug, 9am-1pm & 3-7pm Mon-Sat Apr, Jun & Sep, 9am-12.30pm & 2-6pm Mon-Fri Oct-Mar) has a list of estates where you can taste and buy.

Sleeping & Eating

Le Giulià (☎ 04 94 79 20 46; 31 av Georges Clémenceau; d €50, menus €15.50 & €23) Ramatuelle's cheapest hotel – and a friendly place at that – has six rooms above a simple bar-cum-restaurant.

Le Vesuvio (☎ 04 94 79 21 60; 19 av Georges Clémenceau; menus €17.50, €19, €20.50 & €25; ☽ lunch & dinner) This 25-year-old restaurant is an old favourite, guaranteed to please with Italianate pizzas and pasta dishes as well as seafood treats such as king prawn and clam kebabs.

GOLFE DE ST-TROPEZ

The brash, flash, beach resort of Ste-Maxime dominates the northern end of the bay, while Port Grimaud, the 'Venice of Provence', draws in crowds to the southwest. Further inland, Grimaud is a charming retreat from the beaches, with its winding medieval streets and ruined fortress.

Accommodation can be booked through the helpful **Maison du Tourisme** (☎ 04 94 55 22 00; www.golfe-infos.com; ☽ 9am-7.30pm Mon-Fri, 9.30am-6.30pm Sat, 10am-6pm Sun mid-Jun–mid-Sep, earlier closing & closed Sun mid-Sep–mid-Jun), overlooking the roundabout in Carrefour de la Foux, 2km south of Port Grimaud on the N98.

Ste-Maxime

pop 11,978

Sandy Ste-Maxime, 14km northwest of St-Tropez, screams BEACH RESORT in capital letters. It's modern, concrete and crawling with sun-catchers: you'd never guess it was founded by monks in AD 1000! Countless water-sports clubs line the beachfront.

The pedestrianised old town, centred around rue Gambetta, is crammed with touristy cafés, craft stalls and souvenir shops. Giant pans of paella, fruit stalls and pastry shops line rue Courbet, a cobbled street leading to the town's main market square, place du Marché. Flowers, fish, olives, oil, wine and *tartes Tropéziennes* are sold in the **covered market** (4 rue Fernard Bessy).

The **tourist office** (☎ 04 94 55 75 55; www.sainte-maxime.com; 1 promenade Simon Lorière; ☽ 9am-8pm Mon-Sat, 10am-noon & 4-7pm Sun Jul & Aug, shorter hr

& closed Sun Sep-Jun) has information on water sports and other seafaring activities.

BOAT EXCURSIONS

From April to September **Les Bateaux Verts** (☎ 04 94 49 29 39; bateaux.verts@wanadoo.fr; 14 quai Léon Condroyer) runs boat excursions from its portside base to Baie des Cannebiers (adult/four to 12 years €11.80/6, at least one daily); Gulf of St-Tropez (€13/7.80, Wednesday, Friday and Saturday), with some stopping in St-Tropez and/or Port-Grimaud; Calanques de l'Estérel (€15.60/9.40, Monday and Wednesday); Capes of Camarat, Taillat and Lardier (€15.60/9.40, Tuesday and Thursday); Cannes (return €26.50/16.80, Wednesday and Sunday); Îles de Lérins (€26.50/16.80, Wednesday and Sunday); Port-Cros (€26.50/16.80) and Porquerolles (€30.60/19.40, four times per week).

GETTING THERE & AWAY

There are regular buses and shuttleboats between St-Tropez and Ste-Maxime (see p291). In Ste-Maxime boats depart from 14 quai Léon Condroyer at the port.

Port Grimaud

Pretty little Port Grimaud, inspired by pictures of prehistoric lagoon towns, was built in the 1960s on top of a 1-sq-km mosquito-filled swamp. Within the high wall that barricades the 'Venice of Provence', colourful cottages stand gracefully alongside yacht-laden waterways. On Thursday and Sunday mornings a **market** fills place du Marché, from where a wooden bridge leads to Port Grimaud's modernist **church**. Inside, sunbeams shine through a stained-glass window designed by Vasarely, which tends to polarise viewers into lovers and haters. A panorama of red rooftops fans out from the **bell tower** (admission €1).

François Spoerry (1912–99), the Alsatian architect who dreamt up this massive waterworld, fought from 1962 to 1966 to get the authorities to agree to his proposal. Now 400,000 visitors a year come to gape at his work, with its mighty 12km of quays, 7km of canals and mooring space for 3000 luxury yachts. Spoerry, who went on to design Port Liberty in New York, is buried in Port Grimaud's church.

Cars are forbidden (the car park outside charges €2.20 per hour); the bronzed residents cruise around in speedboats. *Tenue correcte* (correct dress) is insisted upon, except on the wide sandy beach that can be accessed on foot from Grand Rue.

In summer a small **tourist office** (☎ 04 94 56 02 01; chemin Communal; ⏱ 9am-12.30pm & 3-7pm Mon-Sat, 10am-1pm Sun Jun-Sep) operates on the roadside (N98) in St-Pons Les Mûres, opposite the Porte de Poterne, the main pedestrian entrance into Port Grimaud.

SLEEPING & EATING

Camping des Mûres (☎ 04 94 56 16 17; www.camping -des-mures.com; 2 people, tent & car low/high season €17/22; ⏱ Apr-Sep) Just outside Port Grimaud, this three-star site has plenty of facilities and safe underground access to the beach.

Le Suffren (☎ 04 94 55 15 05; www.hotellerie dusoleil.com; 16 place du Marché; d high season from €140; ❄) Port Grimaud's newest and most affordable hotel is decorated in a smart mix of Art Deco and modern reds and whites. Each of its 19 rooms has a delightful little balcony, overlooking either the market square or the port.

Hôtel Giraglia (☎ 04 94 56 31 33; www.hotelgiraglia .com; place du 14 Juin; d low/high season from €200/250; ❄ ⛱) Upping the ante is this four-star place with rooms oozing romance. Delicious culinary creations are served with a flourish by waiters in dinner jackets at its poolside restaurant.

GETTING THERE & AWAY

There are buses between Port Grimaud and Grimaud (€1.30, 10 minutes, five daily summer) and St-Tropez (€3.20, 15 minutes, six to eight daily summer).

An **electric tourist train** (☎ 04 94 54 09 09; www.nova.fr/petit-train-grimaud) shunts visitors between Port Grimaud and Grimaud (50 minutes, including tour of Grimaud) April to mid-October. From Port Grimaud there are five daily trains between 10.15am and 6.25pm. One-way/return costs €3/5.50 (four to 12 years €2/2.80). In Port Grimaud the stop is opposite Porte de Poterne, the pedestrian entrance to the marine village; in Grimaud it's on central place Neuve.

March to October there are shuttleboats to and from St-Tropez (see p291). A combined ticket covering a return ride on the Port-Grimaud–Grimaud train and St-Tropez shuttleboat costs €13.55/7.20 for adults/four to 12 years.

GETTING AROUND

Bicycle

L'Amiral (☎ 04 94 43 47 32; www.amiral-immobilier .com; 47 Grand Rue) hires bikes for €5/15 per hour/day.

Boat

From mid-June to mid-September **Les Coches d'Eau** (☎ 04 94 56 21 13, fax 04 94 43 42 83; 12 place du Marché) runs 20-minute boat tours of Port Grimaud, departing from place du Marché every 10 minutes between 9am and 10pm daily (shorter hours outside July and August). Tickets are €3.50/2 for adults/three to 12 years.

Across the bridge on place de l'Église, you can hire a *barque électrique* (electric boat), costing €18 per 30 minutes for up to four people, between Easter and mid-November.

Inside Porte de Poterne, **Nautic Location** (☎ 04 94 56 00 13; www.nautic-location.com; 1 place des Artisans) hires speedboats (for licence-holders; deposit required) and less powerful six-person Zodiacs (for non-licence-holders); the latter cost €80/100 per half-day in low/high season.

Grimaud

pop 3847 / elevation 105m

Port Grimaud's popular medieval sibling is 3km inland. The typically Provençal hilltop village is most notable for the dramatic shell of **Château du Grimaud** that towers over it, built in the 11th century and fortified in the 15th.

Lower down the village, local lore comes to life in Grimaud's small but sweet **Musée des Arts et Traditions Populaires** (☎ 04 94 43 39 29; rte Nationale; admission free; ⏱ 2.30-6pm Mon-Sat May-Sep, 2-5.30pm Mon-Sat Oct-Apr), based in an ancient oil mill.

Guided tours of the village (1¼ hours) depart from place de l'Église at 10.30am every Thursday. The **tourist office** (☎ 04 94 55 43 83; www.grimaud-provence.com; 1 blvd des Aliziers; ⏱ 9am-12.30pm & 3-7pm Mon-Sat) also has a couple of brochures outlining short village walks: highlights include the restored **Moulin St-Roch** (medieval windmill; admission free; ⏱ 9am-1pm & 2.30-7.15pm Mon & Wed-Fri) and the **Pont des Fées** (Fairy Bridge); it's actually a 15th-century aqueduct!

Grimaud's **market** springs up on Thursday morning in the place Vieille.

South of the village, along the D61 towards St-Tropez, the fruity aroma of local wine can be enjoyed at **Les Vignerons de Grimaud** (☎ 04 94 43 20 14; fax 04 94 43 30 00; 36 av des Oliviers; ☺ 8.30am-12.30pm & 2-6.15pm Mon-Sat), a cooperative where you can stock up on Côtes de Provence wine for as little as €2 a litre (even less for non-AOC table wine).

In summer there are six to eight daily buses between St-Tropez and St-Raphaël (€8.90, 1¼ hours minutes) via Grimaud or Port Grimaud (€3.20, 20 minutes).

NORTHERN VAR

What a difference a few miles can make! The northern half of the Var *département* (generally agreed to be everything above the noisy A8 *autoroute*) is vastly different from its coastal counterpart: in this rural hinterland there's not a grain of sand or oiled body to be seen. Instead, peaceful hilltop villages drowse beneath the midday sun, creating a glorious vision of unspoilt Provence.

Draguignan is the sore thumb in this romantic area, a gritty, hard-nosed town, where the French army maintains its largest military base. From here, the vast Plateau de Canjuers sprawls for some 30km north to the foot of the Gorges du Verdon (see p186).

East of Draguignan, the green Pays Dracénois is pierced by the perched villages of Fayence and Bargemon, where the Beckhams reputedly have their Riviera hideaway. West of Draguignan, numerous little places deal in black truffles and terracotta tiles. Regional wines can be tried and tasted in and around medieval Les Arcs-sur-Argens, to the south.

DRAGUIGNAN

pop 34,814 / elevation 187m

France's 'Capital d'Artillerie' is the hard nut at the centre of chocolate-box Provence, and perhaps not to everyone's taste. However, you'll almost certainly pass through it when travelling round the Pays Dracénois, and it could just provide a welcome bite of reality.

Collect a free town map from the **tourist office** (☎ 04 98 10 51 05; www.ot-draguignan.fr; 2 blvd Lazare Carnot; ☺ 9am-7pm Mon-Sat, 9am-1pm Sun). **Le Comité Départemental du Tourisme** (☎ 04 94 50 55 65; www.tourismevar.com in French; 1 blvd Foch) is the tourist office for Var department.

Sights

The **Musée de l'Artillerie** (Artillery Museum; ☎ 04 98 10 83 85; admission free; quartier Bonaparte; ☺ 9am-noon & 1.30-5.30pm Sun-Wed) is inside the artillery school, and contains quite a collection of old guns, cannons and munitions. In Draguignan's **American cemetery**, a monument pays homage to the heavy combat that occurred around Draguignan during WWII – 9000 American and British soldiers were parachuted in on 15 August 1944.

Traditional Provençal costumes, musical instruments and other ethnographic finds are displayed in the **Musée des Traditions Provençales** (Museum of Provençal Traditions; ☎ 04 94 47 05 72; 15 rue Roumanille; adult/child €3.50/1.50; ☺ 9am-noon & 2-6pm Tue-Sat, 2-6pm Sun).

In the last tiny patch of Draguignan's old town, the 18m **tour d'horloge** (clock tower), topped with an ornate campanile, is worth a gander. The **market** (place du Marché) is on Wednesday and Saturday mornings.

Sleeping & Eating

Camping de la Foux (☎ 04 94 68 18 27; quartier de la Foux; adult/tent & car €4/4; ☺ Apr-Oct; ☒) Three kilometres southeast of the centre along a quiet country lane, this site also rents bungalows and caravans. Its restaurant opens in July and August only.

The most atmospheric places to stay and eat are around Draguignan; ask at the tourist office, and see p295.

Getting There & Around

From the **bus station** (☎ 04 94 68 15 34; blvd des Martyrs de la Résistance), **Estérel Cars** (☎ 04 94 52 00 50) runs 12 daily buses to/from St-Raphaël (€5.70, 1¼ hours). There are less frequent services to Grasse, Marseille and Toulon. Draguignan is also served by regular daily buses to and from Les Arcs-sur-Argens, which has the closest train station (see p298).

Hire wheels to explore the Pays Dracénois from **Holiday Bikes** (☎ 04 98 10 63 08; draguignan@holiday-bikes.com; 834 rte de Draguignan). A mountain bike/50cc scooter/125cc motorbike costs €14/39/58 per day.

AROUND DRAGUIGNAN
Pays Dracénois

East of Draguignan (along the D562, then the D225 and D25 north) is dinky **Callas** (population 1400), where the 1928 oil mill **Moulin de Callas** (☎ 04 94 39 03 20; www.moulindecallas.com;

(☾ 10am-noon & 3-7pm Mon-Sat) still turns at the southern foot of the village. Buy olive oil here from €14 a litre, then make your way towards the central square for a stunning panorama of the red-rock Massif de l'Estérel.

Bargemon (population 1228, elevation 480m), 6km north, hit the headlines when the Beckhams bought a pad here in 2004. It has plenty of medieval streets and ramparts to stroll, and a Thursday **market**. Its small **tourist office** (☎ 04 94 47 81 73; www.ot-bargemon .fr; av Pasteur; ☾ 10.15am-1pm & 3-6pm Mon-Fri, 10am-noon Sat) has information on the entire area.

Medieval **Fayence** (population 3502, elevation 350m) is a picturesque stepping stone between Pays Dracénois and the Cannes area, with wonderful views from the weathered **bell tower**: check out the handpainted tiles that explain the panorama. The **tourist office** (☎ 04 94 76 20 08; ot.fayence@wanadoo.fr; place Léon Roux) has details on available accommodation options.

Haut-Var

The rich soil of the Haut-Var region, west of Draguignan, hides earthy black truffles, snouted out from November to March. Other gastronomic delights await in the sleepy villages, although you'll need your own transport to reach them.

CHÂTEAUDOUBLE
pop 390

Sample and buy freshly ripened *chèvre* (goats' cheese) at the **Bastide de Fonteye** (☎ 04 94 70 90 00; cfleury@libertysurf.fr; ☾ 9am-1pm & 3-7pm Apr-Sep), a goat farm at the junction of the D955 and perilously narrow D51, which leads into the actual village.

In the village itself, **Restaurant du Château** (☎ 04 94 70 90 05; place Vieille; B&B €55, lunch/dinner menu €34/42), actually inside the former chateau, offers fine rustic dining and a couple of *chambres d'hôtes* (B&Bs) guaranteed to charm your socks off. Tables must be reserved in advance.

TOURTOUR
pop 470 / elevation 650m

Tourtour really titillates the tastebuds. In its restored 17th-century **moulin à huile** (oil mill; ☎ 04 94 70 54 74) you can buy oil and, from around 15 December (after the harvest), watch olives being pressed. Each year the mill squashes between 18,000kg

and 25,000kg of olives, producing 4000L to 5000L of oil. At other times, the vaulted stone building hosts art exhibitions. **Guided tours** (€1.80; by appointment only) of the mill and village are run by the **tourist office** (☎ /fax 04 94 70 59 47; www.tourisme-tourtour.com; montée de St-Dénis; ☾ 9am-noon & 2.30-6pm).

Le Relais de St-Dénis (☎ 04 94 70 54 06; place des Ormeaux; menus €14/19.50), at the entrance to the village, is a highly recommended place to eat. It's rustic, cooks up wholly regional products and is bursting with character.

AUPS
pop 1900 / elevation 505m

In the truffle season (November to March), those alien-looking nuggets of black fungus can be viewed at the Thursday morning **truffle market**, held on the central square. Truffle hunts and demonstrations of pig-snouting techniques lure a crowd on the fourth Sunday in January, when Aups throws its **Journée de la Truffe** (Day of the Truffle).

SALERNES & AROUND
pop 3343

Some 9km south of Aups along the wiggly D31 is **Salernes**, where handmade terracotta tiles, known as *terres cuites* (literally 'baked earth'), have been manufactured since the 18th century. Ask at the **tourist office** (☎ 04 94 70 69 02; www.ville-salernes.fr in French; place Gabriel Péri; ☾ 9.30am-12.30pm & 2.30-6.30pm Tue-Sat) for a copy of the free *Artisans Terres de Salernes* guide (www.terresdesalernes.asso.fr in French), which includes a list of 21 Salernais potters and tilemakers who open their workshop doors to visitors (many close in August). New for 2005 is the **Terra Rossa Maison de la Céramique de Salernes**, a museum tracing the town's ceramic history. The tourist office also has information on walking and mountain-biking trails around Salernes; hire wheels for €15 a day from **Papou Cycles & Chasse** (☎ 04 94 67 59 29; 2 rue Édouard Basset).

Cotignac (population 2040, elevation 230m), 11km southwest of Salernes, with its lively **market** (☾ 8am-1pm Fri, Jun-Sep); and hilltop **Entrecasteaux** (population 868), a classified historical monument with a 17th-century chateau, are other pretty Varois villages worth a mooch. **Château de Bernes** (☎ 04 94 60 43 53; www.chateauberne.com; chemin de Berne), a wine-growing estate 2km north of Lorgues, offers all kinds of entertainment between

April and December, including wine tasting, mushroom days, truffle-hunting demos and wonderful jazz and creole picnics.

Le Thoronet & La Celle

The third in a trio of great Cistercian abbeys, **Abbaye de Thoronet** (☎ 04 94 60 43 90; www .monum.fr; adult/under 18 yrs €6.10/4.10; ⓨ 10am-6.30pm Mon-Sat, 10am-noon & 2pm-6.50pm Sun Apr-Sep, 10am-1pm & 2-5pm Mon-Sat, 10am-noon & 2-5pm Sun Oct-Mar), 12km southwest of Lorgues, is truly remarkable for its ultra-austere architecture: pure proportions, perfectly dressed stone and the subtle fall of light and shadow are where its beauty lies. The chapter house, where the monks met to discuss community problems, is noticeably more ornate as the only secular room in the complex. It was built between 1160 and 1190, and some early Gothic influences are visible in the pointed arches, which rest on two columns. Musical soirees are held in summer. Thoronet's sister abbeys are Silvacane (p180) and Sénanque (p172), constructed in the 12th and 13th centuries.

About 15km southwest of Thoronet is **Abbaye de la Celle** (☎ 04 94 59 10 05), a 12th-century Benedictine abbey in the tiny village of La Celle, 2km south of Brignoles. It was a convent from 1225 until its eventual closure in 1657. The church continues to serve the village community today and the abbey cloister can be visited. Restoration work was taking place at the time of writing: phone first for opening times and prices. The adjoining convent houses the **Maison des Vins Coteaux Varois** (☎ 04 94 69 33 18; cotvarois@aol.com), where you can taste and buy Coteaux Varois AOC wines.

Hostellerie de l'Abbaye de la Celle (☎ 04 98 05 14 14; www.abbaye-celle.com; d from €200; P ⌘ ⌘) is a fabulous four-star hotel and restaurant run by top chefs Bruno Clément and Alain Ducasse. It has 11 country-style rooms, including the Rolle room (adapted for visitors with disabilities) and the Cedar Tree room, with a legged bathtub and dashing Salernes tiles on the bathroom walls. For day trips, the restaurant can prepare you a gourmet picnic hamper (€29 per person).

Les Arcs-sur-Argens

pop 5515

Les Arcs (11km south of Draguignan) is a perfectly restored old town perched on a hillock, with a bacchanalian House of

---

AUTHOR'S CHOICE

Chez Bruno (☎ 04 94 85 93 93; fax 04 94 85 93 99; rte de Vidauban; menus €55 & €100; ⓨ closed Sun evening & Mon) France's most famous truffle restaurant can be found in a country house a couple of kilometres east of the tiny backwater of Lorgues, on the D562 towards Les Arcs. In his Michelin-starred restaurant, chef Clément Bruno cooks almost exclusively with those knobbly, pungent delicacies: he gets through an incredible 1000kg of the world's most expensive foodstuff every year.

Wines where you can taste, learn about and buy Côtes de Provence wines.

The **tourist office** (☎ /fax 04 94 73 37 30; off.tour isme.arcssurargens@wanadoo.fr; place du Général de Gaulle; ⓨ 9am-noon & 2-6pm Mon-Sat, 9-11.30am Sun) is at the foot of the medieval village. Lordly lodgings can be found in the 11th-century castle crowning the village, which shelters the luxurious **Le Logis du Guetteur** (☎ 04 94 99 51 10; fax 04 94 99 51 29; place du Château; high season d/ste €140/169; ⓨ closed mid-Jan-Feb; P ⌘ ⌘).

WINE TASTING

The **Maison des Vins Côtes de Provence** (House of Wines; ☎ 04 94 99 50 20; www.caveaucp.fr; ⓨ 10am-8pm Jul & Aug, to 7pm May, Jun & Sep, to 6pm Apr & Oct, closed Sun Oct-Mar), 2.5km south of the village on the westbound N7, is the obvious place to start. Sixteen different Côtes de Provence wines are selected for tasting each week (look for the list that tells you the ideal dish to eat with each wine, be it steamed fish with bananas or blood sausage with apple sauce) and over 600 different wines are for sale at producers' prices (from €2.70). To experience the pleasure of wining *and* dining, there's an upmarket restaurant, **Le Bacchus Gourmand** (☎ 04 94 47 48 47; menu €35), inside the House of Wines.

A prestigious *cru classé* wine, produced since the 14th century, can be tasted and bought at **Château Ste-Roseline** (☎ 04 94 99 50 30; www.sainte-roseline.com; ⓨ 9am-6pm), nestled among vineyards 4.5km east of Les Arcs-sur-Argens (on the D91 towards La Motte). A lovely 1975 mosaic by Marc Chagall illuminates the estate's 13th-century Romanesque **Chapelle de Ste-Roseline** (ⓨ 2.30-6pm Tue-Sun), which contains the corpse of St

ST-TROPEZ TO TOULON

Roseline. Roseline was born at the chateau in Les Arcs in 1263 and became a Carthusian nun. She experienced numerous visions during her lifetime and was said to be able to curtail demons. Upon her death in 1329, her eyes were taken out and separately preserved. Chapelle de Ste-Roseline hosts piano recitals and musical concerts in July and August; tickets cost from €25.

La Motte, the first village in Provence to be liberated after the August 1944 Allied landings, is 3km further east along the D91. For the ultimate Provençal feast, head east out of La Motte along the D47 to **Domaine de la Maurette** (☎ 04 94 45 92 82; fax 04 94 45 01 11; rte de Callas; menus from €18), on the intersection of the D47 and the D25. On this wine estate you can taste and buy wine, and dine in its *ferme auberge*, a roadside inn where the atmosphere of chattering people dining on wholesome, home-made food is nothing short of electric.

GETTING THERE & AROUND

From Les Arcs-Draguignan train station, turn left out of the exit, then right at the end of the street. It's a 2km walk straight up this road (av Jean Jaurès) to the town centre.

Les Arcs is on the rail line between St-Raphaël and Toulon and is well served by coastal trains to Nice (€14, 1½ hours) and Marseille (€17.40, 1¼ hours). Les Arcs also serves as the train station for Draguignan. **Les Rapides Varois** (☎ 04 94 47 05 05) runs buses every 30 minutes between Les Arcs train station and Draguignan (€2.90, 20 minutes).

MASSIF DES MAURES

Wild boar still roam the forests of the Massif des Maures, whose hidden towns and villages are little oases of peace. Traditional industries – chestnut harvests, cork production, pipe-making – are their lifeblood, a pleasant surprise in the tourist-economied south of France.

There are superb walking and cycling opportunities, particularly as much of the area is inaccessible by car. The GR9 long-distance trail penetrates the massif at its northern edge, near **Carnoules** (population 2622), wending its way past **Notre Dame des Anges** (780m) and La Sauvette to the medieval village of La Garde Freinet.

The D14 runs through Collobrières, the largest town in the massif and chestnut capital of the universe. This road is particularly popular with cyclists (drivers, take note and slow down!) and is graced with fine panoramas. Similarly dramatic is the D39 from Collobrières, which winds and soars up to Notre Dame des Anges before plunging down to Gonfaron. The parallel N98, which skims through vineyards and cork-oak-tree plantations, runs from St-Tropez to Bormes-les-Mimosas and on to Hyères.

The Corniche des Maures is the southernmost extent of the area, where pine trees give way to buckets and spades at Le Lavandou and smaller beach resorts to the east.

Due to fire risks, forest roads are sometimes closed in summer, particularly when winds are high.

COLLOBRIÈRES

pop 1710 / elevation 150m

Hidden deep in the forest 24km west of Grimaud, the leafy village of Collobrières is the self-proclaimed 'capital' of the Maures. Nut-lovers will be in seventh heaven: the town is famous throughout France for its chestnut produce. Food and drink made from the nuts is sold in summer in front of the tourist office, along with souvenirs made from cork-oak, another local industry. Market day is Thursday (July and August) and Sunday (year-round).

Information

The wonderful staff in the **tourist office** (☎ 04 94 48 08 00; www.collotour.com in French; blvd Charles Caminat; ⏱ 10am-12.30pm & 2-6.30pm Mon-Sat Jul & Aug, 10am-noon & 2-6pm Tue-Sat Sep-Jun) take accommodation bookings and have details on joining in the October chestnut harvest and participating in guided forest walks (€7). Three short walking trails – including a 200m trail to a *châtaigneraie* (chestnut grove) – are mapped out on the noticeboard outside.

Sights

Over the 11th-century bridge, the **Confiserie Azuréenne** (☎ 04 94 48 07 20) sells a nutty array of products. Sample *glaces aux marrons glacés* (chestnut ice creams), *crème de marrons* (chestnut cream), *marrons au sirop* (chestnuts in syrup), or a shot of *liqueur de châtaignes* (chestnut liqueur). Opposite the shop is a small **Musée de la Fabrique** (admission free; ⊗ 9.30am-1pm & 2-7pm or 8pm) that explains the art of making *marrons glacés* (candied chestnuts).

Festivals & Events

Collobrières marks its annual **Grande Fête des Fontaines** in August by cooking up a monstrous-sized aïoli and making the place de la Libération fountain spout rosé wine! It celebrates a **Fête de la Châtaigne** (Chestnut Festival) on the last three Sundays in October, with craft and home-produce markets, street entertainments and the warming smell of roasted chestnuts drifting over the proceedings. In April the **Fête de la Transhumance** celebrates the seasonal moving of shepherds' flocks.

Sleeping & Eating

Bar-Hôtel-Restaurant des Maures (☎ 04 94 48 07 10; fax 04 94 48 02 73; 19 blvd Lazare Carnot; d €20, half-/full board per person €25/33) Grab one of the rooms at the back of this central hotel, which overlook the river and *pétanque* court. Its family-friendly, waterside restaurant is good for cheap, filling *menus*, and the downstairs bar sells chestnut ice cream for €3 a bowl.

La Bastide de la Cabrière (☎ 04 94 48 04 31; www .provenceweb.fr/83/cabriere; rte de Gonfaron; d €75-125; P) This welcoming five-roomed *chambre d'hôte*, 6km north of town along the relentlessly winding D39, prepares delicious, seasonal home-grown meals (€35). You can also buy goats' cheese, fruit wine and jams to take away.

Ferme de Peïgros (☎ 04 94 48 03 83; fermede peigros@wanadoo.fr; Col de Babaou) Goats and chestnuts are the mainstay of this farm restaurant, 1.8km along a gravel track signposted from the top of the Babaou mountain pass (8km from Collobrières). At different times of year, its menu includes farm-killed goat or poultry, boar, cepes, *chèvres* and sometimes farm-made chestnut ice cream; credit cards and cheques are not accepted. If you can't bear to leave, ask about their farmhouse accommodation.

CHARTREUSE DE LA VERNE

Majestic, 12th- to 13th-century **Monastère de la Verne** (☎ 04 94 43 45 51; adult/8-14 yrs €5/3; ⊗ 11am-5pm or 6pm Wed-Mon, closed Jan) is in a dramatic forest setting 12km southeast of Collobrières. The Carthusian monastery was founded in 1170, possibly on the site of

---

A MENHIR DETOUR

With your walking boots firmly laced, set off from the old bridge in Collobrières, walking uphill into town along rue Camille Desmoulins, rue Blanqui and rue Galilée. Follow the signs for the camp site and ruined 15th-century Église St Pons, which will lead you onto the GR90.

It's a steep climb out of town and into the woods, composed of oak trees (including cork oak), pine, heathers and ferns, then the path ascends more gradually to about 450m above sea level, before levelling off as it reaches Plateau Lambert.

The trail comes out onto a forest road; follow it leftwards for 150m and it will lead you to the *garde forestière* Ferme Lambert. Ask permission from the forest ranger before crossing the field to see the two biggest **menhirs** in the Var region, now heritage-listed monuments. Each one is over 3m high, and they were raised sometime between 3000 BC and 2000 BC. Another super sight is the **Châtaignier de Madame**, the biggest chestnut tree in Provence, with a mighty 10.4m circumference.

The walking detour should take you around four hours there and back again.

---

a temple to the goddess Laverna, protector of the bandits who hung out in the Maures. The Huguenots destroyed most of the original charterhouse in 1577. Since 1982 the solitary complex has been home to 15 nuns, of the Sisters of Bethlehem.

One of the old monks' cells has been fully restored, complete with a small formal garden, workshop and covered corridor, where the monk would pray as he paced. Other interesting features include the use of serpentine, a stripy green stone, as decoration; it's particularly noticeable in the door arches and vaulted ceiling of the 17th-century church. Various walking trails lead from the monastery into its forested surroundings.

Smoking and revealing clothes are forbidden in the monastery; nor can you steal the nuns' chestnuts from the trees outside. From Collobrières, follow rte de Grimaud (D14) east for 6km, then turn right (south) onto the narrow D214. Follow this road for a further 6km to the monastery; the final section of the single-track road is unpaved.

LA GARDE FREINET

pop 1656 / elevation 365m

A stark, rocky spur supports the 13th-century **ruins of Fort Freinet** (450m), from where there are fantastic panoramic views over the red rooftops of La Garde Freinet, a dinky medieval town best explored outside high season.

The **tourist office** (☎ 04 94 43 67 41; www .lagardefreinet-tourisme.com; Chapelle St-Jean, place de la Mairie; ☒ 9.30am-12.30pm & 3.30-6.30pm Mon-Sat year-round, plus 9.30am-12.30pm Sun Easter-Oct) has details on walking, wine tasting and *chambres d'hôtes* in the massif. Village traditions and customs unfold in the adjoining **Conservatoire du Patrimoine et du Traditions du Freinet** (☎ 04 94 43 08 57; fax 04 94 43 08 69; Chapelle St-Jean, place de la Mairie; adult/under 12 yrs €1.50/free; ☒ 10am-12.30pm & 3-6pm Tue-Sat).

Markets fill the old town squares on Wednesday and Sunday mornings.

Festivals & Events

Below the ruined fort is a large stone cross where pilgrims pay their respects on 1 May each year during the town's *bravades*. The relics of St Clément, the village's patron saint, are paraded there, accompanied by the blasting of blunderbusses. The cross is a 20-minute uphill walk from the village centre, signposted from place Neuve.

La Garde Freinet celebrates its traditional **Fête de la Transhumance**, which marks the seasonal moving of the flocks, in mid-June, and hosts a **Fête de la Châtaigne** (Chestnut Fair) in mid-October.

Sleeping & Eating

Hôtel La Claire Fontaine (☎ 04 94 43 63 76; fax 04 94 55 23 54; 4 place Vieille; d from €40) Out of a trio of mid-range places to stay, this is the best value. Half the rooms overlook a buzzing pedestrianised street, filled with bars and restaurants that can be noisy on summer weekends: ask for a back room if you value your sleep.

Auberge La Sarrazine (☎ 04 94 55 59 60; www .lasarrazine.fr; rte Nationale; d from €85, menu €30; ☒ restaurant closed Wed; ☒) More upmarket than the Claire Fontaine, La Sarrazine's bedrooms strike just the right balance between tradition and comfort. Sample Provençal fare in its rustic restaurant, in front of an open fire (winter) or on a flowery patio (summer).

COGOLIN

pop 9181

Industrious Cogolin, 15km south of La Garde Freinet, has a worldwide reputation for clarinet and saxophone reeds! It's also a centre for wooden pipes, cork products and *tapis de Cogolin* (carpets), woven in the village since the 1920s when Armenian refugees settled here.

Several pipemakers on av Georges Clémenceau welcome visitors, including M Courrieu at **Les Pipes de Cogolin** (☎ 04 94 54 63 82; www.courrieupipes.fr in French; 58 av Georges Clémenceau). The **tourist office** (☎ 04 94 55 01 50; www.cogolin-provence.com; place de la République; ☒ 9am-1pm & 2-7pm Mon-Sat) has a complete list of artisans and also arranges visits.

Provence's first screen hero, Raimu (see p50), is honoured at the **Musée Espace Raimu** (☎ 04 94 54 18 00; www.musee-raimu.com in French; 18 av Georges Clémenceau; adult/11-18 yrs €3.50/1.75; ☒ 10am-noon & 3-6pm low season, 10am-noon & 4-7pm high season, closed Sun morning), a museum established by the comic actor's granddaughter in the basement of the arts cinema.

The sugary *tarte Tropézienne* was created here in 1955 at the Micka patisserie **La Tarte Tropézienne** (☎ 04 94 54 42 59; www.tarte-tropez ienne.com; 2 rue Beausoleil).

Cogolin's sandy beach and pleasure port is 5km northeast.

Bicycles can be hired from **Cycles Évasion** (☎ 04 94 54 71 13; www.cycles-evasion.com; 61 av Georges Clémenceau) for €12/70 per day/week.

LA MÔLE & AROUND

Tiny La Môle (population 803), 9km southwest from Cogolin along the vineyard-laden N98, is recognised for three things: Antoine de Saint-Exupéry, author of *Le Petit Prince*, visited his grandparents here as a boy – their chateau features in the book; a fabulous **bakery** (south side of the N98, towards Cogolin) selling nut and olive breads; and the **Auberge de La Môle** (☎ 04 94 49 57 01; place de l'Église; menus €25 & €50), a former petrol station complete with old pump stuck on 333, which fills up with eager diners, serving themselves from huge terrines of pâté and jars of pickles. Credit cards are not accepted. Sample local wine here or at one of the many chateaux along the westbound N98.

From La Môle, narrow rte du Canadel (D27) dives to the coast. All is green serenity until you hit **Pachacaïd** (☎ 04 94 55 70

VILLAGE DES TORTUES

About 20km north of Collobrières on the northern tip of the massif is a tortoise village, where one of France's rarest and most endangered species can be viewed in close quarters. The Hermann tortoise *(Testudo hermanni)*, once common along the Mediterranean coastal strip, is today found only in the Massif des Maures and Corsica. Forest fires in 1990 destroyed 2500 sq km of forest in the massif, reducing the tortoise population further still.

The Station d'Observation et de Protection des Tortues des Maures (SOPTOM; Maures Tortoise Observation and Protection Station) was set up in 1985 by French film-maker Bernaud Devaux and an English biologist to ensure the Hermann's survival.

A well-documented trail (captions in English) leads visitors around the centre: from the tortoise clinic, where wounded tortoises are treated and then released into the Maures; to the quarantine quarter and reproduction enclosures; and to the tropical conservatory, egg hatcheries and nurseries, where the young tortoises (a delicacy for preying magpies, rats, foxes and wild boars) spend the first three of their 60 to 100 years. There's also a great palaeontology trail, where vicious-looking models of the tortoise's ancestors lurk among the bushes.

In summer the best time to see the tortoises is in the morning and late afternoon (they tend to shelter from the heat during the day). Watch tortoises hatch from mid-May to the end of June; from November through to early March they hibernate.

The **Village des Tortues** (☎ 04 94 78 26 41; www.tortues.com; adult/3-16 yrs €8/6; ☼ 9am-7pm Mar-Nov), about 6km east of Gonfaron, is only accessible by private transport.

80; www.pachacaid.com; rte du Canadel; 4-person mobile homes low/high season per week €230/730), a whopping camp site full of wildly holidaying families, and next-door **Niagara Parc Nautique** (☎ 04 94 55 70 80; www.parcniagara.com; rte du Canadel adult/5-13 yrs Jun & Sep €11/9, Jul & Aug €12.50/10.50; ☼ 10.30am-7pm Jun-Sep), a water park with toboggan slide and aquatic climbing wall.

FORÊT DU DOM & BORMES-LES-MIMOSAS

Vineyards melt into a rich patchwork of cork-oak, pine and chestnut trees as the N98 continues its path west into the Forêt du Dom, 12km west of La Môle.

From the top of the **Col de Gratteloup** (199m), the steep D41, a popular cycling route, climbs north over the **Col de Babaou** (415m) towards Collobrières. Southbound, the D41 wiggles its way across the **Col de Caguo-Ven** (237m), from where there are good views of **Bormes-les-Mimosas** (population 6399, elevation 180m). This green-fingered 12th-century village is famous for its floral displays.

The Bormes-les-Mimosas **tourist office** (☎ 04 94 01 38 38; www.bormeslesmimosas.com; 1 place Gambetta; ☼ 9am-12.30pm & 3-6.30pm Apr-Sep, Mon-Sat only Oct-Mar) takes bookings for a pleasant 1½-hour guided **stroll** (adult/under 12 yrs €5/free) round town, and for the 2½-hour **nature walk** (adult/under 12 yrs €7/free; ☼ 3pm Wed Apr, Jul & Aug) led by forest wardens in the Forêt du Dom.

CORNICHE DES MAURES

From La Môle, the breathtaking 267m **Col du Canadel** (the D27) offers unbeatable views of the Massif des Maures, the coastline and its offshore islands before plummeting to the Corniche des Maures, a 26km coastal road (D559) stretching southwest from La Croix-Valmer to Le Lavandou. The shoreline is trimmed with sandy beaches ideal for swimming, sunbathing and windsurfing.

In **Cavalaire-sur-Mer**, you'll find the largest **tourist office** (☎ 04 94 01 92 10; http://golfe -infos.com/cavalaire; promenade de la Mer; ☼ 9am-7pm mid-Jun–mid-Sep, 9am-12.30pm & 2-6pm Mon-Fri, 9am-12.30pm Sat mid-Sep–mid-Jun) on the Corniche des Maures. In season, boats sail from this busy seaside resort to the Îles d'Hyères.

Domaine du Rayol

From Le Rayol, a narrow road runs south towards the beautiful **Domaine du Rayol** (☎ 04 98 04 44 00; www.domainedurayol.org; av des Belges; adult/8-16 yrs €6.50/3.50; ☼ 9.30am-12.30pm & 2.30-6.30pm Tue-Sat Apr-Sep, 9.30am-12.30pm & 2-5.30pm Tue-Sat Feb, Mar, Oct & Nov), a 20-hectare botanical garden rescued from abandonment in 1989 and stuffed with plants from around the world. The flowers are at their most colourful in April and May, but it's always worth a visit.

In summer there's a brilliant **Sentier Marin** (Marine Trail; adult/8-18 yrs €15/12; ☼ Sun-Fri Jul & Aug), where you can observe underwater flora and fauna with an experienced guide. The price includes entrance to the gardens, and your wet suit, flippers, mask and snorkel. Advance bookings essential.

In July and August the estate hosts open-air musical soirees (adult/eight to 18 years €23/17) at 9pm on Monday; again, book to ensure a place.

Beaches

Continuing west, seaside resorts include the tiny hamlets of **Le Rayol**, **Pramousquier**, **Cavalière** and **Aiguebelle**. With the exception of busy **Plage de Cavalière**, a popular family destination, the beaches along this stretch are quiet, sandy and usually tucked in pretty coves. Tiny **Plage du Royal** and **Plage de l'Escale** are particularly enchanting: they're backed by pine trees and have a restaurant on the sand.

Cycling

From Cavalière a silky-smooth cycling track wends 4.5km west along the coast to **St-Clair**, the easternmost suburb of Le Lavandou.

Sleeping & Eating

Le Bailli de Suffren Hôtel (☎ 04 98 04 47 00; www .lebaillidesuffren.com; av des Américains, Le Rayol; d low/mid-/high season from €154/218/283; ✖ ⚓) An oh-my-gosh gasp of a place, nestled in an inlet right on the shore. Rooms have rich red terracotta floors, quilted Provençal bedspreads on the romantic four-posters, and spectacular sea views. The hotel has its own private slice of beach, and there are two restaurants, for al fresco lunches and sophisticated evening dinners.

Les Roches (☎ 04 94 71 05 07; www.hotellesroches .com; 1 av des Trois Dauphins, Aiguebelle; d mid-/high sea-son from €190/220, half-board for 2 people high season from €514; ✖ ⚓) The stuff of dreams: Humphrey Bogart, Jean Cocteau and Winston Church-ill all stayed at this fabulous four-star hotel and restaurant, perched on a cliff looking out to sea.

LE LAVANDOU

pop 5508

Once a fishing village, Le Lavandou (from the Provençal 'Lou Lavandou', meaning washhouse) is now another capital-lettered BEACH RESORT, thanks to its 12km sandy beach, endless stretch of bars and restau-rants, cheap-and-cheerful accommodation, and proximity to the idyllic Îles d'Hyères.

It's dominated by concrete blocks to the southwest, but the northeastern old town is beautifully intact. Dramatist Bertolt Bre-cht and composer Kurt Weill wrote parts of *The Threepenny Opera* while they were holidaying here in 1928.

Le Lavandou sits northeast of **Cap de Bré-gançon**, a rocky cape embraced by a lovely sandy beach in **Cabasson**, on its western side, and crowned with the 16th- to 18th-century **Fort de Brégançon**. Since 1968 the heavily guarded fortress (good views from Cabasson beach) has served as the summer residence for the president of France.

Orientation & Information

Quai Gabriel Péri and its continuation, quai Baptistin Pins, runs northeast along the beachfront. The port (Gare Maritime), quai des Îles d'Or, sits at its easternmost end, opposite the old town.

The bus station is nothing more than a shelter on either side of the D559. From there, walk one block south then turn left (east) onto av des Martyrs de la Résistance to get to the centre. Its continuation, av du Général de Gaulle, traverses the old town.

The **tourist office** (☎ 04 94 00 40 50; www.lelav andou.com; quai Gabriel Péri; ☽ 9am-12.30pm & 3-7pm) is opposite the port.

Boat Excursions

All boats depart from Le Lavandou's port (quai des Îles d'Or). Tickets are sold at the ticket office 30 minutes before departure. **Vedettes Îles d'Or et Le Corsaire** (☎ 04 94 71 01 02; www.vedettesilesdor.fr; 15 quai Gabriel Péri) runs various trips, including **glass-bottomed boat trips** (adult/4-12 yrs €11.50/9) that depart every 40 minutes between 9.40am and 4.40pm daily all summer. Destinations include Île du Le-vant (adult/four to 12 years €22/17.60, 30 minutes, six times daily in July and August, four or five daily April to June and Septem-ber, twice daily rest of the year); Porquer-olles (€27.70/21.30, 50 minutes, once daily in July and August, and one a day Mon-day, Wednesday and Saturday from April to June and in September, out of season reserve tickets in advance); and Port-Cros (€22/17.60, 40 minutes, seven times daily in July and August, four times daily April to June and September, and twice daily the rest of the year). La Croisiè Bleue (a combined ticket for all three islands) costs

€41.40/33.20. Boats also sail to St-Tropez (€41.40/33.20, two hours, Tuesday and Saturday from June to September; book places in advance).

Festivals & Events
The popular **Fête du Soleil et des Fleurs** (Festival of Sun and Flowers) occurs in mid-March: floats filled with huge figures made of flowers parade through town.

Sleeping
There's a cluster of camp sites along rte Benat, 2km south of the centre in the suburb of La Favière; ask the tourist office for details.

Hôtel La Lune (☎ 04 94 71 04 20; www.hotel-la-lune.com; 10 av Général de Gaulle; d with sea views high season from €70; ⚡) From the outside, you may think the blue balconies are an eyesore, but you'll change your mind when you're gazing at the Med from one. Rooms are of the bland, identikit variety, but within seashell-hurling distance of the golden shore.

Hôtel de l'Îlot Fleuri (☎ 04 94 71 14 82; lilotfleuri@9online.fr; rue Cazin; d with sea views high season from €58; ☾ Apr–mid-Nov; ⚡) At the back, the two-star 'Flowery Islet' has leaf-topped balconies with sea views. To snag one, ask for a 1st-floor room. It also has secure, free parking, something of a novelty on the Côte d'Azur!

Hôtel l'Oustaou (☎ 04 94 71 12 18; www.lavandou-hotel-oustaou.com in French; 20 av Général de Gaulle; d/tr with sea views high season from €55/68) This family-run place has the friendliest staff in Le Lavandou. There's a touch of the 1980s about the rooms, but when you're a block from the beach, who cares? Some four- and five-person rooms are available too.

Hôtel Le Rabelais (☎ 04 94 71 00 56; www.le-rabelais.fr; 2 rue Rabelais; d with/without sea views high season €90/82; ☾ mid-Jan–mid-Dec; ⚡) A rambling building overlooking the port on quai Baptistin Pins. Its pretty-in-pink façade shields a flowery garden, and breakfast is served overlooking the ocean. Rooms on the street side don't have air-con.

Eating
There are plenty of touristy restaurants on the waterfront, but the best eating places are the terraces in the old town.

Chez Mimi (☎ 04 94 71 00 85; 11 quai Gabriel Péri; ☾ mid-Jan–mid-Nov) Overlooking the *pétanque* pitch from its portside perch, this is an ideal spot to breakfast in the early-morning sun or sip an evening aperitif.

La Pignato (☎ 04 94 71 13 02; 13 rue Abbé Hélin; menus €16.50 & €19.50) On a relaxed pedestrianised street, they've been dishing up *cuisine Provençale* here for almost 30 years. Try anchovy toasts followed by rabbit in mustard sauce.

La Favouille (☎ 04 94 71 34 29; 9 rue Abbé Hélin; menus €16 & €22; ☾ Easter-Oct) Occupying a small square near La Pignato, this restaurant is just as satisfying as La Pignato. There's a long list of regional aperitifs, including orange wine, and the service is impeccable. Note the sloping tables!

La Galiote (☎ 04 94 71 08 26; 15 rue Patron Ravello; menus €16 & 20; ☾ Feb-Nov) A third good choice in the old town, this is a larger and more impersonal place, but the food is just as tasty, with a highly satisfying, seafood-encrusted paella. Fussy eaters in the family will cheer at the pizza and pasta menu.

Getting There & Away
Le Lavandou is on the main bus route (up to seven daily) between St-Tropez (€9.70, one hour) and Toulon (€10.60, 1½ hours). Buses follow the coastal road, also stopping in Le Rayol, Bormes-les-Mimosas, La Londe and Hyères.

Getting Around
Hire wheels from **Holiday Bikes** (☎ 04 94 15 19 99; lavandou@holiday-bikes.com; av Vincent Auriol), with daily rates for Rollerblades/mountain bikes/50cc scooters starting at €9/14/42. At the port, **Star Bike** (☎ 04 94 01 03 82; fax 04 94 01 03 82; quai Baptistin Pins) rents road bikes with/without gears for €10/7 a day.

ÎLES D'HYÈRES & ÎLES DU FUN

Legend says that the gods turned a group of swimming princesses into the Îles d'Hyères, and they do have a magical look when viewed from the sea. Their mica-rich rock, which glitters and gleams in the sunlight, gives them their other name, the Îles d'Or (Islands of Gold).

At 7km long and 3km wide, Porquerolles is the largest island; Port-Cros, in the middle, is a national park, while its eastern sister, Île du Levant, is a nudist colony.

Wild camping is forbidden throughout the archipelago, as are cars.

Bendor and Embiez, known as the Îles du Fun, are more sub-Disney than the stuff of myth, but make for a tongue-in-cheek day trip. They lie west of the Îles d'Hyères, off Toulon's shores.

ÎLE DE PORQUEROLLES
pop 350
Despite its huge influx of visitors each year, Porquerolles is surprisingly unspoiled: 10 sq km of its sandy white beaches, pine woods and maquis are protected by the Parc National de Port-Cros. A wide variety of indigenous and tropical flora thrive, including the requien larkspur, which grows nowhere else in the world. In winter blossoming mimosas splash the green island with colour. April and May are the best months to spot some of its 114 bird species.

Pottering around the island's walking trails, then lazing on the beach with a picnic lunch, is a delicious way to spend a day. Avoid July and August, when the owners of Porquerolles' numerous *résidences secon-*

daires return to the island, increasing the population six-fold. Smoking is forbidden outside the village.

Orientation & Information
Boats dock at the port on the island's northern coast. Walk 200m to the tourist office at the end of the jetty, then bear right along rue de la Ferme to place d'Armes, the central village square.

The **tourist office** (☎ 04 94 58 33 76; www.porque rolles.com; ⊗ 9am-5.30pm Apr-Nov, 9am-1pm Fri-Wed Dec-Mar) sells island maps (€0.50) showing the *pistes cyclables* (cycling paths) and *sentiers pédestres* (footpaths), and the plastic *Guide Sous-Marin des Espèces Méditerranéenes* to help snorkellers identify underwater flora (€15).

Société Marseillaise de Crédit (☎ 04 94 58 30 54; 3 rue de la Ferme) has an ATM and currency exchange. The **post office** (☎ 04 94 58 30 99) is adjacent to Église Ste-Anne on place d'Armes.

Sights & Activities
Central **place d'Armes** is dominated by a giant, tree-shaded *pétanque* pitch. In summer

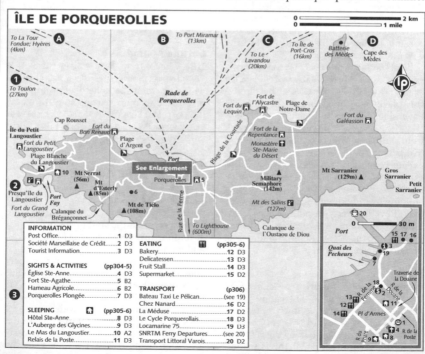

ÎLE DE PORQUEROLLES

INFORMATION	
Post Office...................................1 D3	
Société Marseillaise de Crédit.....2 D3	
Tourist Information......................3 D3	

SIGHTS & ACTIVITIES	(pp304-5)
Église Ste-Anne..........................4 D3	
Fort Ste-Agathe...........................5 B2	
Hameau Agricole..........................6 B2	
Porquerolles Plongée...................7 D3	

SLEEPING	(pp305-6)
Hôtel Ste-Anne............................8 D3	
L'Auberge des Glycines.................9 D3	
Le Mas du Langoustier...............10 A2	
Relais de la Poste......................11 D3	

EATING	(pp305-6)
Bakery......................................12 D3	
Delicatessen..............................13 D3	
Fruit Stall.................................14 D3	
Supermarket..............................15 D2	

TRANSPORT	(p306)
Bateau Taxi Le Pélican.........(see 19)	
Chez Nanard.............................16 D2	
La Méduse................................17 D2	
Le Cycle Porquerollais...............18 D3	
Locamarine 75...........................19 D3	
SNRTM Ferry Departures.......(see 20)	
Transport Littoral Varois............20 D2	

music concerts are held in **Église Ste-Anne**, on the south of the square. Festivities fill the church and the square on 25 July, when islanders celebrate their patron saint's day.

From place d'Armes, head south along chemin Ste-Agathe to the 16th-century **Fort Ste-Agathe** (☎ 04 94 12 30 40; adult/5-17 yrs €3/1.50; ☺ 10am-12.30pm & 1.30-5.30pm May-Sep), the only fortification open to visitors. It contains historical and natural-history exhibitions, and the ticket includes access to the tower, with its eye-popping island panorama. Much of the building dates from between 1812 and 1814, when Napoleon had it rebuilt after the British destroyed it in 1739.

From place d'Armes, walk or cycle south along rue de la Ferme and turn right at the crossroads. The **Hameau Agricole**, home to the **Conservatoire Botanique National Méditerranéen**, is 700m along this trail. An open-air exhibition documents the history of the island flora, and a botanical trail leads visitors through gardens featuring typical plants: 20 types of almond trees, 150 fig types, 83 lauriers rose types and numerous olive trees.

Two kilometres further along rue de la Ferme, on the tip of the cape, is the island's 82m-tall **lighthouse** (☎ 04 94 58 30 78; admission free; ☺ 11am-noon & 2-4pm Apr-Sep). Climb its winding stairs if the weather's clear for a stunning panorama from the top. A military semaphore (142m) northeast of here marks the highest point of the island; it cannot be visited.

Porquerolles' vineyards cover a square kilometre of the western part of the island, and are tended by three wine producers. Each offers *dégustation* (wine-tasting) sessions of their predominantly rosé wines; the tourist office has a list.

BEACHES

Porquerolles' northern coast is laced with beautiful sandy beaches, including **Plage de la Courtade**, signposted 800m east from the port (follow the track uphill behind the tourist office). **Plage de Notre-Dame**, Porquerolles' largest and most beautiful beach, is 2.5km further east along the same track. **Plage d'Argent**, 2km west of the village, is popular with families because of its summer beachside café-restaurant and lifeguards. It's also the shortest walk from the port; follow rue de la Ferme, then turn right and follow the signs.

More secluded is **Plage Blanche du Langoustier**, a former lobster farm 4.5km from the village on the northern shores of the Presqu'île du Langoustier. It's called 'white' beach in contrast to the black sand that darkens the peninsula's southern shores around Port Fay – the legacy of a 19th-century soda-processing plant, which produced potash and soda from sulphuric acid and sea salt between 1828 and 1876.

Cliffs line the island's more dangerous southern coast where swimming and diving is restricted to **Calanque du Brégançonnet** to the east and **Calanque de l'Oustaou de Diou** to the west. Both are accessible by bicycle or foot.

Porquerolles Plongée (☎ 04 98 04 62 22; www.porquerolles-plongee.com), at the port, organises diving courses and expeditions (first-time/night dive €43/38 including equipment). The company has a catamaran, on which you can breakfast while speeding round Porquerolles and Port-Cros.

Sleeping & Eating

Porquerolles is expensive. It has no camp site and wild camping is forbidden. Hotels generally only accept guests on a half-board basis in July and August, and charge single-person supplements into the bargain. Ask the tourist office for a list of self-catering apartments to rent on a weekly basis. Place d'Armes is surrounded by bistros and cafés.

L'Auberge des Glycines (☎ 04 94 58 30 36; www.aubergedesglycines.net; place d'Armes; half-board per person low/mid-/high season from €69/99/149, under 12 yrs free; ❄) This is an absolutely charming place with comfortable rooms and a pretty garden. Its recommended restaurant specialises in *cuisine Porquerollaise* (Porquerollais *menu* €21.90) – lots of fresh fish dishes.

Hôtel Ste-Anne (☎ 04 94 04 63 00; www.sainteanne.com; place d'Armes; s/d half-board high season €205/215; ❄) Superior rooms cost a few euros more, but are worth it for the extra space. The hotel lends *boules* to guests keen to have a spin on the *pétanque* pitch in front. Prices drop considerably outside July and August.

Relais de la Poste (☎ 04 94 04 62 62; www.lerelaisdelaposte.com; place d'Armes; d from €80) This two-star place is the cheapest on the island. Room 6 is a favourite for its large terrace and views of the harbour. Other attractions include the billiard table in the bar and its resident champion, Tony!

AN ISLAND ROMANCE

Three toasters and a bath-towel set just weren't enough. In 1911 newly married Mrs Fournier received the perfect wedding present from hubby François: the island of Porquerolles!

Le Mas du Langoustier (☎ 04 94 58 30 09; www .langoustier.com; d with half-board per person low/high season from €180/214; ✖) For guests thinking of dropping in by helicopter, this is *the* choice. The hotel has its own vineyards and offers stunning views from its southwestern seaside perch. As you would expect, everything from bedrooms to the two restaurants (one for guests only) is impeccable.

Back to reality…place d'Armes is armed with fruit stalls, a delicatessen and bakery, enabling you to build a perfect picnic, and there's a small supermarket at the port.

Getting There & Away

Regular boats operated by **Transport Littoral Varois** (TLV; www.tlv-tvm.com) link La Tour Fondue near Hyères (see p311) with Porquerolles year-round. June to September there's one boat daily to and from Toulon; four weekly boats to and from St-Tropez; and one a day from Wednesday to Saturday (daily in July and August) to and from Le Lavandou (see Boat Excursions in those sections).

June to September **SNRTM** (☎ 04 94 05 21 14) operates two or three boats daily from Port Miramar, south of La Londe, to Porquerolles (adult/four to 10 years €19.50/13 return). The same company operates boats from La Croix-Valmer and Cavalaire-sur-Mer in July and August.

Getting Around

The two options are feet or bicycle wheels (motorised vehicles are forbidden). There are no fewer than 10 bicycle-rental outlets in the village, including **La Méduse** (☎ 04 94 58 34 27; ✖ 7am-6pm or 7pm Mar-Sep) and **Chez Nanard** (☎ 04 94 58 34 89; ✖ 7am-6pm or 7pm Mar-Sep) at the port. Both charge €12.50/9 per day for an adult/child's bike. Energetic parents can hire covered *remorques* (buggies) to pedal kids around the island for €12.50 per day. In the village, **Le Cycle Porquerollais** (☎ 04 94 58 30 32; www.cycle-porquerollais.com; 1 rue de la Ferme;

✖ year-round) has all types of two-wheel contraptions, including tandems costing €19/28 per half-/full day.

BOAT

Opposite the tourist office at the port, **Locamarine 75** (☎ 04 94 58 35 84; www.locamarine75 .com) hires speedboats (6cv without a licence) for €70/85 per half-/full day for up to five people.

Bateau Taxi Le Pélican (☎ 04 94 58 31 19; www .locamarine75.com) operates a 24-hour boat taxi service.

TAXI

The luggage-laden can hail an **electric taxi** (☎ 06 81 67 77 12; www.locavelo.fr) to bear the load between port and hotel.

ÎLE DE PORT-CROS

pop 30

France's smallest national park, the **Parc National de Port-Cros**, was created in 1963 to protect at least one small part of the Côte d'Azur's natural beauty from overdevelopment. The park encompasses the 7-sq-km island of Port-Cros and a 13-sq-km zone of water around it. Until the end of the 19th century, the islanders' vineyards and olive groves ensured their self-sufficiency. Today, tourism is their sustenance.

The island can be visited all year, but walkers must stick to the 30km of marked trails. Fishing, fires, camping, dogs, motorised vehicles and bicycles are not allowed, and smoking is forbidden outside the portside village.

Port-Cros has a rich variety of insects, butterflies and birds, but is primarily a marine reserve. Keeping the water around it clean is one of the national park's biggest problems.

Parc National de Port-Cros also manages its westerly neighbour **Île de Bagaud**, the fourth of the Îles d'Hyères. Its 40 hectares of dense vegetation are used for scientific research and are off-limits to tourists.

Orientation & Information

Boats dock at the port in the village on the island's northwestern shores.

The **Maison du Parc** (☎ 04 94 01 40 72; fax 04 94 01 40 71; ✖ 10.30am-5.30pm May-Oct, for 30min after boats dock Nov-Apr), at the port, has information on walking, diving and snorkelling.

ST-TROPEZ TO TOULON

Sights & Activities

The ray-shaped, glass-bottomed **Aquascope** (☎ 04 94 05 92 22; adult/4-12 yrs €15/10; every 40min) allows passengers a 360° view of the sea-life round Port-Cros on a 30-minute ride.

Plage de la Palud, on the island's northern shores, is a 30-minute walk from the **Fort du Moulin**. From the beach, a 35-minute **sentier sous-marin** (underwater trail; ☼ mid-Jun–mid-Sep) allows snorkellers to discover the park's marine flora and fauna, which include 500 algae species and 180 types of fish; the Maison du Parc has details.

Miniscule **Îlot de la Gabinière**, an islet off Port-Cros' southern shore, is popular with experienced divers. **CIP Lavandou** (☎ 04 94 71 54 57; www.cip-lavandou.com), a diving school in Le Lavandou, arranges trips to the island with two dives for €60.

Hire banana-yellow **canoes** (1/4/8hr €15/40/65) from Hostellerie Provençale (see right).

WALKING

From the portside post office, a track leads inland, from where 30km of footpaths crisscross the island. The 15th-century Fort du Moulin is the starting point for a circular, 1½-hour **sentier des plantes** (botany trail) to Plage de la Palud; it returns along an inland route. This trail also takes in imposing 16th-century **Fort de L'Estissac** (admission free; ☼ 10.30am-5.30pm Jun-Sep), which hosts summer exhibitions. Climb the tower for a panoramic view of Port-Cros and the neighbouring islands.

The more demanding **sentier des crêtes** (crests trail; three hours) explores the southwestern corner of the island, and the slightly easier **sentier des Port-Man** (Port-Man trail; four hours) takes walkers to Port-Cros' northeastern tip.

Sleeping & Eating

Accommodation is limited and needs to be booked months in advance. At the port there is a handful of self-catering studios to rent in the **Maison du Port**; the neighbouring Maison du Parc (see opposite) has details. Five restaurants offering sea-inspired cuisine surround the port.

Hostellerie Provençale (☎ 04 94 05 90 43; www .hostellerie-provencale.com; d per person with half-board

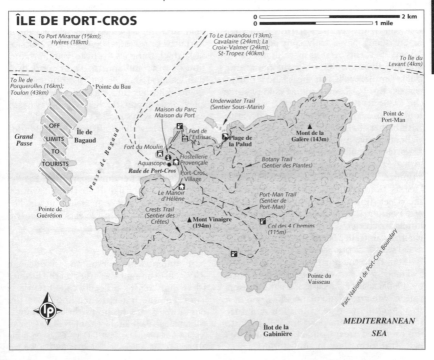

ÎLE DE PORT-CROS

To Port Miramar (15km); Hyères (18km)
To Le Lavandou (13km); Cavalaire (24km); La Croix-Valmer (24km); St-Tropez (40km)
To Île du Levant (4km)
To Île de Porquerolles (16km); Toulon (43km)
Pointe du Bau
GRAND PASSE
OFF LIMITS TO TOURISTS
Île de Bagaud
Passe de Bagaud
Maison du Parc; Maison du Port
Underwater Trail (Sentier Sous-Marin)
Point de Port-Man
Fort de l'Estissac
Fort du Moulin
Plage de la Palud
Mont de la Galère (143m)
Aquascope
Rade de Port-Cros
Hostellerie Provençale
Port-Cros Village
Botany Trail (Sentier des Plantes)
Le Manoir d'Hélène
Port-Man Trail (Sentier de Port-Man)
Crests Trail (Sentier des Crêtes)
Pointe de Guérétion
Mont Vinaigre (194m)
Col des 4 Chemins (115m)
Parc National de Port-Cros Boundary
Pointe du Vaisseau
Îlot de la Gabinière
MEDITERRANEAN SEA
0 — 2 km
0 — 1 mile

low/high season €80/95; ☺ Mar–mid-Nov; ⌗) On the opposite side of the port to the Maison du Parc, there are five comfortable doubles here with big sunny windows. The hostellerie's restaurant and cocktail bar are eye-openers, with deftly arranged food mountains and drinks served in weird holders.

Le Manoir d'Hélène (☎ 04 94 05 90 52; fax 04 94 05 90 89; s/d/ste from €130/229/259; ☺ mid-Apr–Sep; ⌗ ⌗) This atmospheric 23-room manor, at an aloof distance above the port, is the exclusive option. It's set in a sweet-smelling eucalyptus grove, and has a dinky outdoor pool and upmarket restaurant.

Getting There & Away
Le Lavandou (see p302) is the main stepping stone to Port-Cros. There are also frequent boats year-round from Hyères (see p315).

From June to September boats sail several times weekly from Toulon (see p315) and St-Tropez (see p287). There are also crossings in July and August from Port Miramar, La Croix-Valmer and Cavalaire-sur-Mer.

ÎLE DU LEVANT
pop 186

Oddball Île du Levant, a narrow 8km strip of an island, has a truly split personality. Ninety percent of it is a military camp and strictly off limits, while the remaining pocket of **Héliopolis** (on the island's northeastern tip) has been a nudist colony since the 1930s. Its tiny population increases tenfold in summer, when the village is overrun with bathers baring all.

Boats arrive at and depart from **Port de l'Ayguade**. A small **tourist information hut** (☎ 04 94 05 93 52; www.iledulevant.info) operates here in summer. The central square, place du Village, is 1km uphill along rte de l'Ayguade, the street running along Héliopolis' southern boundary. The post office, cafés and hotels are clustered around this square. The island's camp site, **Colombero** (☎ 04 94 05 90 29; rte de l'Ayguade; camping per person €8; ☺ Easter-Sep), is 150m from the port.

The eastern part of the colony is covered by the **Domaine des Arbousiers**, a nature reservation with rare island plants like *Eryngium tricuspidatum* (a type of thistle). A nature trail leads east from place du Village, into the protected area. Contact the tourist office for information on guided tours.

Baring all is not obligatory – except on sandy **Plage Les Grottes**, the main nudist beach east of Port de L'Ayguade. From the port, walk in the direction of Plage de Sable Levant along **sentier Georges Rousseau**, a rocky coastal path. Bold signs reading '*Nudisme Intégral Obligatoire*' mark the moment you are required to strip.

Getting There & Away
Île du Levant is 10 minutes by boat from Port-Cros. There are regular boats year-round from Le Lavandou (see p302) and Hyères (see p311), and in July and August from Port Miramar (La Londe), La Croix-Valmer and Cavalaire-sur-Mer.

ÎLE DE BENDOR
A place of exile during the 17th century, the desolate, pinprick islet of Bendor was subsequently abandoned for 250 years. Then in 1951 along came Paul Ricard, a pastis millionaire, who transformed it into one of the most sanitised spots on the south coast.

Bendor is now a leisure centre dominated by larger-than-life Ricard creations, including the **Espace Culturel Paul Ricard** (☎ 04 94 29 44 34; admission free), where art exhibitions are held, and the **Exposition Universelle des Vins et Spiritueux** (admission free; ☺ 10am-noon & 2-6pm Tue-Sun), which unravels the history and production of wine and spirits. It's the port itself that's surreal, though, with its shrunken toytown buildings and meticulously planned alleys and squares. Its shallow-sloping **beach**, with lifeguards, is perfect for tiny kids.

Bendor lies 300m offshore from Bandol, 19km east of Toulon.

Getting There & Away
Boats to Île de Bendor depart from Bandol (see p317) every half-hour (less in winter) between 7am and 2am year-round. The journey (adult/four to 12 years €7/5 return) takes seven minutes.

ÎLES DES EMBIEZ
Not content with owning one island, Paul Ricard also bought the largest of the Embiez islets in 1958; it's officially called Île de la Tour Fondue but is better known as Îles des Embiez. It's home to the **Institut Océanographique Paul Ricard** (☎ 04 94 34 02 49; www .institut-paul-ricard.org; adult/4-11 yrs €4/2; ☺ 10am-12.30pm & 1.30-6.30pm Jul & Aug, to 5.30pm Sep-Jun,

closed Sat morning Sep-Apr & Wed & Sun morning Nov-Mar), where over 100 Mediterranean species can be viewed in the 27 seawater aquariums and marine museum.

The rest of Ricard's 95-hectare island is occupied by a vast pleasure port, patches of pine forest, maquis scrub and vineyards, apartment blocks and a couple of posh hotels.

The Embiez archipelago is less than 1km off the Presqu'île du Cap Sicié, between Sanary-sur-Mer and Toulon.

Getting There & Away

Boats to the island leave year-round from the small port at **Le Brusc**, a beach resort adjoining Six-Fours-les-Plages, 5km south of Sanary-sur-Mer. In summer boats run about every 40 minutes, less frequently at other times. The journey (adult/three to 10 years €7/5 return) takes 10 minutes.

June to September there are also boats to the island from Bandol (€7/5 return) and Sanary-sur-Mer (see p317).

TOULON & AROUND

Relatively unspoilt coastline becomes increasingly urban as you head west to Toulon and Marseille. A final pocket of blue and green surrounds **La Londe** (population 8840), midway between Le Lavandou and Hyères. Explore its olive groves, vineyards and flower gardens on guided walks organised by the **tourist office** (☎ 04 94 01 53 10; www.ot-lalondelesmaures.fr; av Albert Roux).

Two kilometres east, 450 species of tropical birds fly around the **Jardin d'Oiseaux Tropicaux** (☎ 04 94 35 02 15; www.jotropico.com; rte de Valcros; adult/3-12 yrs €7/5; ☒ 9am-7pm Jun-Sep, 2-6pm Oct & Feb-May, reduced days/hr Nov-Jan), signposted off the N98 or via bus No 103 (Toulon to Le Lavandou).

Port Miramar, 3km south, is a landing stage for seasonal boats to/from Porquerolles and Port-Cros. From the small port, follow signs to **L'Argentière** and further east to Fort de Brégançon. This scenic lane, dubbed the **rte des Vins de la Londe** (the wine trail of La Londe), goes past dozens of wine-tasting chateaux.

HYÈRES

pop 51,417

With its age-old palm trees, colonial air and intact Vieille Ville (old town), Hyères

GETTING AWAY FROM IT ALL

It's a strange truth in Hyères that the higher you climb, the quieter it gets. Tone your calf muscles, choose the steepest streets, and you'll leave the crowds behind. Bonuses include magnificent views over the Vieille Ville and a healthy glow.

retains a lot of the charm that made it the Côte d'Azur's first resort. Tolstoy came to town in 1860 to take a winter 'cure'; Robert Louis Stevenson worked on *Kidnapped* (1886) here, claiming it was the only place he'd ever been happy; and Queen Victoria herself breezed through in 1892.

La Capte, 4km south of Hyères centre, comprises two narrow sand bars supporting saltpans (Les Salins des Presquiers) and a lake (Étang des Presquiers). Pink flamingos add a splash of colour to the otherwise barren landscape. The spectacular western sand bar road – the rte du Sel (Salt Rd) – is only accessible in summer. Buses use the eastern bar road – the D42. The northern section of the latter is lined with a smooth, two-lane cycling track that runs for 2km from the beach resort of **L'Ayguade** to the roundabout in front of Toulon-Hyères airport.

At the foot of La Capte sits beach-lined **Presqu'île de Giens**, which briefly became an island in the huge storms of 1811. One person's storm is another person's diving opportunity: the Presqu'île de Giens and Îles d'Hyères are excellent dive sites, with atmospheric shipwrecks sunk around the coast, including the boats the *Donator* and the *Grec*. A baptism dive costs around €50: contact **Sub-Plongée** (☎ 04 94 58 25 30 10; www.sub-plongee.com; 9 route de Giens, allée du Pousset) for further details.

French poet and 1960 Nobel Literature prize-winner, St-John Perse (1887–1975), is buried in the tiny cemetery off rte Madrague, on the peninsula's northwestern shores.

Orientation

Hyères' medieval Vieille Ville is perched on a hillside north of the new town. The nearest beach is La Capte. The pleasure port, Port d'Hyères, from where boats to Le Levant and Port-Cros depart, is on La Capte's eastern shore. Boats to Porquerolles use La Tour Fondue – the port on the southeastern corner of Presqu'île de Giens.

The train station, on place de l'Europe, is 1.5km south of the old town centre. Walk northeast from the station on av Edith Cavelland to place du 11 Novembre, then north along palm-tree-lined av Gambetta, the main street into the new town; or catch the bus (see p312).

Information

Cyber L'Arène (rue Pierre Moulis; Internet access per 30min €2.50; 🕙 10am-10pm)

Post Office (av Joseph Clotis)

Tourist Office (☎ 04 94 01 84 50; www.ot-hyeres.fr; 3 av Ambroise Thomas; 🕙 9am-6pm high season)

Sights & Activities

A wonderful jumble of second-hand furniture, floor tiles, clothes, olives and lavender-spiced marmalade fills **place Georges Clémenceau** at the Saturday morning market. The 13th-century **Porte Massillon**, on the western side of the square, is the main entrance to the Vieille Ville. West along cobbled rue Massillon is beautiful arcaded **rue des Porches**.

Returning to the market square, head north to the 13th-century **Église St-Louis**, a fine example of sober, Romanesque-style architecture. Weave your way uphill to rue Bourgneuf, then walk west along its continuation, rue St-Esprit, to the limestone arch of **Porte Barruc**. From here, steps pass an iron gate to the rambling hillside grove

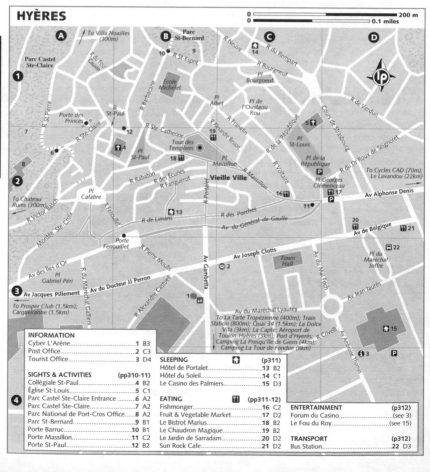

HYÈRES

of **Parc St-Bernard**. Remnants of the 12th-century defensive city wall and Château St-Bernard are visible. Below the walls stands the Villa Noailles.

Heading back downhill along rue Barbacane, you come to 12th-century **Porte St-Paul**, the first city gate to be built. It frames the **Collégiale St-Paul** (10am-noon Wed-Sat year-round, plus Mon & Wed-Sat 3-6.30pm Apr-Oct), comprising two churches dating from the 12th and 14th centuries joined together perpendicularly. The Gothic section houses a vast collection of predominantly 18th-century, ex-votive paintings.

West of Porte St-Paul, rue St-Paul and rue Ste-Claire lead to the **Parc Castel Ste-Claire**, a 17th-century convent converted into a private residence. The American writer Edith Wharton lived here from 1927. Today it houses the administrative headquarters of the **Parc National de Port-Cros** (04 94 12 82 30; www.portcrosparcnational.fr; 50 rue Ste-Claire). You can stroll freely through the grounds.

VILLA NOAILLES
The imposing **Villa Noailles** (04 94 01 84 30; fax 04 94 01 84 31; during visiting exhibitions, plus guided tours on request Wed-Mon mid-Jun–mid-Sep) was designed by Robert Mallet-Stevens in 1923 for Vicomte Charles de Noailles, a devoted patron of modern art. The architect's mission: to build a winter residence 'interesting to inhabit'. The result: a cubist maze of concrete and glass, set within a Mediterranean park and featuring a cubist garden designed by Gabriel Guévrékian in 1925.

BOAT EXCURSIONS
Boats operated by **Transport Littoral Varois** (TLV; www.tlv-tvm.com) sail from Hyères to the three Îles d'Hyères year-round.

Gare Maritime de La Tour Fondue (04 94 58 21 81) on the Presqu'île de Giens is the departure point for **glass-bottomed boat rides** (04 94 58 95 14; adult/4-10 yrs €11.50/9; up to 5 sailings Sun-Fri May-Sep) that do a nonstop circuit to Porquerolles and back.

It's also the departure point for **Porquerolles trips** (adult/4-10 yrs return €15/13.50; 20min; every 30min 7.30am-6.30 or 7pm May-Sep, 6-10 daily crossings Oct-Apr), and **Porquerolles/Port-Cros two-island tours** (adult/4-10 yrs €26/13 return; Mon-Fri Jul & Aug) – the Porquerolles–Port-Cros connection leaves at 1.30pm, the Port-Cros–Porquerolles connection at 4.45pm.

Port d'Hyères (Port de la Gavine; 04 94 57 44 07) on La Capte is the departure point for **Port-Cros trips** (adult/4-10 yrs return €22/11; 1hr; at least once daily year-round; up to 4 daily high season), **Île du Levant trips** (adult/4-10 yrs return €22/11; 1½hr; at least one return sailing daily year-round) and **Île du Levant/Port-Cros two-island tours** (adult/4-10 yrs return €25/13; daily Jul & Aug) – the Port-Cros–Levant connection leaves at noon or 3.15pm, returning from Levant to Hyères 5pm.

Motorists must pay €3/6 per half-/full day to park at either port.

Sleeping
BUDGET
Camping is the only pauper's choice. Ask at the tourist office for a full list of the nine sites on Presqu'île de Giens.

Camping La Presqu'île de Giens (04 94 58 22 86; www.camping-giens.com; 153 rte de la Madrague; camping for 2 people, tent & car low/high season €12.80/17.60, 4-person mobile homes low/high season per week €205/630; Apr-Sep) A three-star camping ground with dozens of facilities, including kids' playground. Its smaller sister site, Camping La Tour de Fondue, almost spitting distance from the Gare Maritime de la Tour de Fondue, charges the same rates.

MID-RANGE & TOP END
Hôtel du Soleil (04 94 65 16 26; www.hoteldusoleil .com; rue du Rempart; high season s/d/tr/q €51/67/95/111) Teetering at the top of a vertical medieval street (read: not for the unfit), this two-star, ivy-clad place is Hyères' loveliest hotel. Glowingly recommended.

Hôtel de Portalet (04 94 65 39 40; hoteldu portalet@aol.com; 4 rue de Limans; s/d €45/49) Also in the Vieille Ville, but at the bottom of the hill, the Portalet is comfortably snug. Rooms are large, airy and have appealing furnishings.

Le Casino des Palmiers (04 94 12 80 80; fax 04 94 12 80 94; 1 av Ambroise Thomas; d high season from €110;) The plush, glass-topped casino contains 15 rooms (one adapted for disabled visitors) for those who like to wake to the sound of the roulette wheel. Top-notch, four-star accommodation with all mod cons and a hint of nostalgia for the resort's golden age.

Eating
Rue de Limans, rue Portalet and rue Massillon in the lower part of the old town are lined with touristy places to eat. Place Massillon is one big terrace restaurant in summer.

Le Bistrot Marius (☎ 04 94 35 88 38; fax 04 94 12 78 77; 1 place Massillon; menus €17, €25 & €30; ☺ closed Mon & Tue Sep-Jun) A rather smart restaurant, with a reputation for its fish dishes. In fine weather there are outdoor tables in the shadow of the impressive Tour des Templiers.

Le Chaudron Magique (☎ 04 94 35 38 45; 8 place Massillon; ☺ closed Tue lunch & Mon) Also in the heart of the old town, the Magic Cauldron invites you to lunch on a hearty plate of *aïoli Provençal complet* (a mound of boiled vegetables, potatoes and egg, with shellfish and a bowl of garlicky aïoli) or a well-grilled fish of the day (€17).

Le Jardin de Sarradam (☎ 04 94 65 97 53; 35 av de Bélgique; lunch/dinner menu €15/18.50, tajines from €16; ☺ closed Sun dinner & Mon low season) Mediterranean and oriental cuisine are served in a beautiful, flowerpot-filled garden. For a real Arabian Nights feel, round off your meal with syrupy mint tea poured from a silver pot. Vegetarians can escape the ubiquitous pizzas/omelettes and feed on couscous with seasonal vegetables.

Picnics can be built from produce sold at the Saturday-morning **fruit and vegetable market** (place Georges Clémenceau). In the old town there are a couple of fabulous **fishmongers** (rue Massillon; ☺ morning only) where you buy the catch of the day. Delicious cakes, biscuits and bread are baked several times daily at **La Tarte Tropézienne** (53 av Gambetta).

Entertainment

La Dolce Vita (☎ 04 94 58 16 24; rte de Giens; ☺ to 5am Fri & Sat, to 5am Wed-Sun high season) Out of town on the way to La Capte, this place has a wild atmosphere, cracking DJs and a tribe of regulars.

Le Fou du Roy (☎ 04 94 12 80 84; fax 04 94 65 01 99; 1 av Ambroise Thomas; ☺ to 5am Fri & Sat) This nightclub inside the casino is quite a dressy affair; music is latest dance chart hits, mixed with bits of house and funk.

Prosper Club (☎ /fax 04 94 58 54 40; www.leprosper club.com; blvd Jules Arpinetti, Carqueiranne; ☺ Wed-Sat from 11pm) The Prosper Club is in Carqueiranne, a suburb of Hyères, and lures in an older crowd (mid-20s to mid-40s) with an eclectic selection of tunes.

Getting There & Away

AIR

Towards La Capte, **Aéroport de Toulon-Hyères** (Toulon-Hyères airport; ☎ 04 94 00 83 83; http://aero port.var.cci.fr; aeroport@var.cci.fr) is 3km south of Hyères centre.

BUS

From the **bus station** (place du Maréchal Joffre), **Sodetrav** (☎ 04 94 12 55 12) operates at least seven buses daily to and from Toulon (€4.40, one hour), Le Lavandou (€5.90, 30 minutes) and St-Tropez (€13.60, 1¼ hours). Nice–Toulon buses run by **Phocéens Cars** (☎ 04 93 85 66 61) stop in Hyères.

TRAIN

From the Hyères **train station** (place de l'Europe), there are around eight local trains per day to/from Toulon (€3.50, 20 minutes). The Marseille–Hyères train (€12, 1¼ hours, four daily) stops at Cassis, La Ciotat, Bandol, Ollioules-Sanary and Toulon.

Getting Around

TO/FROM THE AIRPORT

Sodetrav runs a regular shuttle bus from Toulon-Hyères airport to Hyères bus station (€4.50, 10 minutes). During the summer there are also regular daily services from the airport to Toulon and St-Tropez; buses coincide with flight arrivals and departures.

BICYCLE & ROLLERBLADE

You can rent mountain bikes at **Cycles CAD** (☎ 04 94 65 07 69; fax 04 94 35 33 19; 59 av Alphonse Denis) for €11/19/61 per day/weekend/week.

Quai 34 (☎ 04 94 38 54 06; fax 04 94 57 55 55; 3579 rte de l'Almanarre), on the road out of town past the train station, is the place to hire Rollerblades (per day €14).

AUTHOR'S CHOICE

L'Oursinade (☎ 04 94 21 77 06; Les Oursinières; menu €35) The indisputable highlight of Cap de Carqueiranne, and perhaps one of the gastronomic wonders of the Var, is lunch overlooking the sea at L'Oursinade. Tucked away on a cliff in Les Oursinières (by car follow the signs), this hidden spot only serves seafood and is famed for its fabulous Toulonnais bouillabaisse (€38; order 48 hours in advance), which has potatoes in it as well as a shoal of fish. The terrace, where meals are served, is set in a cool grove of trees and looks down onto pounding waves and the huge blue sea.

BUS
Buses, all costing €1.30, link Hyères bus station with the train station (five minutes), Port d'Hyères (15 minutes), La Capte (20 minutes), Giens (30 minutes) and La Tour Fondue (35 minutes). Buses run almost every 30 minutes between 6.25am and 10pm.

For Tour Fondue (boats to Porquerolles), get off at the Tour Fondue stop. For Port d'Hyères (boats to Îles du Levant and Port-Cros), get off at Le Port stop, av de la Méditerranée.

CAP DE CARQUEIRANNE
Immediately west of Hyères, pretty little Cap de Carqueiranne is a partly forested stretch of headland, crisscrossed by tiny lanes. The coastal path that edges its way from the town of Carqueiranne is a particularly scenic means of exploring the cape.

Romantic images are conjured up by the **Site Archaéologique d'Olbia** (☎ /fax 04 94 57 98 28; www.monum.fr; adult/under 18 yrs €4/free; ☼ 9.30am-12.30pm & 3-7pm Jul-Sep, 9.30am-12.30pm & 2.30-7pm Tue, Thu & Fri, 3-6pm Sat Apr & Jun-Sep), the remnants of a sea port founded by the Greeks in the 4th century BC; there are Roman remains there too. The site is in **L'Almanarre**, at the Presqu'île de Giens' northwesternmost tip.

In **La Garonne** the **Musée de la Mine** (☎ 04 94 08 32 46; www.mine-capgaronne.fr; chemin du Bau Rouge; adult/student/6-18 yrs €6.20/3.80/3.80; ☼ 2-6pm school holidays, 2-5pm Jul & Aug, 2-5pm Wed, Sat & Sun rest of year), with its distinctive redbrick chimneys, is a disused copper mine where the cape's mineral traditions are delved into.

In **Les Oursinières**, a delightful little harbour on the cape's southwestern shore, **Centre de Plongée** (☎ 04 94 08 38 09) runs dives.

Local bus No 9 links Toulon with Les Oursinières (€1.30, hourly 6.45am to 6pm). There's also a two-way cycling track between Toulon and the cape.

TOULON
pop 160,639
The French navy's largest base, Toulon, provokes the kind of reaction that a tramp might get in St-Tropez. It certainly doesn't fit in with the beaches-and-bronzed-bodies image of the Côte d'Azur, but there's a lot to be said for its down-to-earth feel. As in every large port, there's a bustling quarter near the water, with heaps of bars, where lo-cals and sailors spill out every door. An atmospheric food market materialises down the whole length of cours Lafayette from Tuesday to Saturday, and a hectic flea market fills place du Théâtre on Fridays.

Named after Télo, a Celtic-Ligurian goddess of springs, Toulon's watery origins can still be seen in its many fountains. Toulon only became part of France in 1481, when Provence was annexed; the city grew in importance after Henri IV established its arsenal. In the 17th century the port was enlarged by Vauban. The young Napoleon Bonaparte first made a name for himself here in 1793 during a siege in which the English, who had taken over Toulon, were expelled.

Toulon's funniest contemporary product is the great Provençal actor Raimu (see p50). A statue of the lovable comic stands in the old town on place des Trois Dauphins.

Orientation
Toulon is built around a *rade*, a sheltered bay lined with quays. To the west is the naval base, and east, the ferry terminal, where boats set sail for Corsica. The city is at its liveliest along quai de la Sinse and quai Constradt – from where ferries depart for the Îles d'Hyères – and in the pedestrianised old city. Northwest of the old city is the train station.

Separating the old city from the northern section is a multi-lane, multi-named thoroughfare (av du Maréchal Leclerc and blvd de Strasbourg as it runs through the centre).

Information
Commercial banks line blvd de Strasbourg.
Cyberspace (☎ 04 98 00 69 11; www.multimania .com/espacecyber; 61 rue Marquetas; Internet access per hr €6; ☼ 10am-1pm & 2.30-10pm Mon-Fri, 10am-10pm Sat & Sun)
Hôpital Font-Pré (☎ 04 94 61 60 03, 04 94 61 60 83; 1208 av Colonel Picot)
Post Office (rue Dr Jean Bertholet) Cyberposte available.
Tourist Office (☎ 04 94 18 53 00; www.toulon tourisme.com; place Raimu; ☼ 9am-6pm Mon & Wed-Sat, 10am-6pm Tue, 10am-noon Sun) Guided city tours (adult/12-18 yrs €3/2) twice a week.

Dangers & Annoyances
Women on their own should avoid some of the old city streets at night, particularly around seedy rue Chevalier Paul and the western end of rue Pierre Sémard.

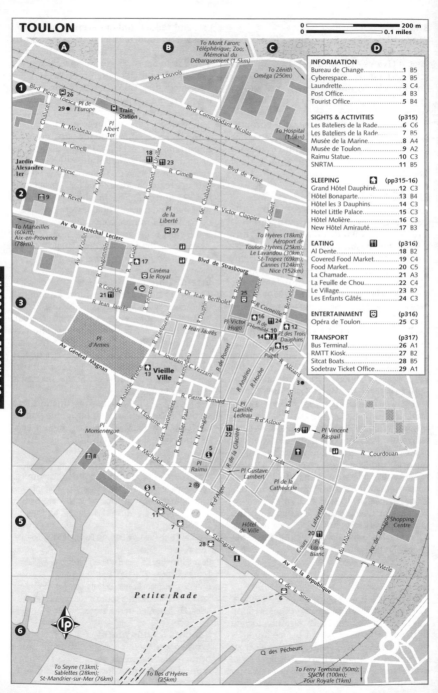

TOULON

0 _____ 200 m
0 _____ 0.1 miles

To Mont Faron;
Téléphérique; Zoo;
Mémorial du
Débarquement (1.5km)

To Zénith
Oméga (250m)

To Hospital
(1.5km)

To Hyères (18km);
Aéroport de
Toulon-Hyères (25km);
Le Lavandou (30km);
St-Tropez (69km);
Cannes (124km);
Nice (152km)

To Marseilles
(60km);
Aix-en-Provence
(78km)

To Seyne (13km);
Sablettes (28km);
St-Mandrier-sur-Mer (76km)

To Îles d'Hyères
(25km)

To Ferry Terminal (50m);
SNCM (100m);
Tour Royale (1km)

Blvd Louvois
Blvd Commandant Nicolas
Blvd Pierre Toesca Pl de l'Europe
R Chalucet
R Mirabeau
Pl Albert 1er
R Gimelli
Jardin Alexandre 1er
R Peiresc
R Revel
Av Vauban
R Gimelli
R Dumont d'Urville
R de Chabannes
R Victor Clappier
Blvd de Tessé
Colbert
Pl de la Liberté
Av Hyères
Av du Maréchal Leclerc
Av Y Toulin
R Dugommier
Av Y Toulin
R Guiol
Cinéma le Royal
Blvd de Strasbourg
R Comédie
R Ferrero
R Dr Jean Bertholet
Racine
R Molière
Berthelot
R Jean Jaurès
R Pastoureau
R Dauphin
R Corneille
Pl Victor Hugo
R de l'Humilité
Pl des Trois Dauphins
Av Général Magnan
Pl d'Armes
R Jean Jaurès
R L Jourdan
R C Vezzani
R de Pomet
Puget
Pl Puget
Vieille Ville
R Anatole France
R l'Equerre
R des Savonnières
R Chevalier Paul
R N Laugier
R Pierre Semard
R Lamalgué
R Andrieu
R Hoche
R Alézard
R Baudin
Pl Vincent Raspail
R Courdouan
Pl Camille Ledeau
R d'Astour
R Zola
Pl Monsenergue
R Micholet
R de la Glacière
Pl Raimu
Pl Gustave Lambert
Pl de la Cathédrale
R Cronstadt
R d'Alger
Q Stalingrad
Hôtel de Ville
Cours Lafayette
Av de Bazeille
Shopping Centre
Pl Louis Blanc
R du Mûrier
R Merle
Q de la Sinse
Av de la République
Q des Pêcheurs

Petite Rade

Sights & Activities

MONT FARON

Overlooking the old city from the northern side is Mont Faron (584m), from where you can see Toulon's red-roofed houses and the epic port in its true magnificence. Not far from the hill's summit rises the **Mémorial du Débarquement** (☎ 04 94 88 08 09; adult/8-16 yrs €3.80/1.55; ☉ 9.45am-12.45pm & 1.45-5pm in summer, shorter hr winter), which commemorates the Allied landings that took place along the coast here in August 1944. Historical displays and a film form part of this fascinating museum.

The Med's only **cable car** (téléphérique; ☎ 04 94 92 68 25; adult/4-10 yrs €5.80/4; ☉ 9.30am-7.45pm summer, closed windy days) climbs the mountain from blvd Amiral Vence. Kids will love the **Zoo du Mont Faron** (☎ 04 94 88 07 89; adult/4-10 yrs €7/5; ☉ 10am-6pm, closed rainy days), a wildcat breeding centre: combination zoo/cable-car tickets cost adult/four to 10 years €10/6.50.

To get to the cable car, take bus No 40 from place de la Liberté to the *téléphérique* stop. The tourist office has mountains of information on walking and mountain-bike trails on Mont Faron.

BOAT EXCURSIONS

SNRTM (☎ 04 94 62 41 11; fax 04 94 09 30 34; quai Cronstadt) is one of several companies running one-hour **excursions** (adult/4-10 yrs €8.50/5.50) around the bay and Port Militaire, with a French-only commentary on events that took place here during WWII.

In July and August **Les Bateliers de la Rade** (☎ 04 94 46 24 65; fax 04 94 31 21 36; quai de la Sinse) runs a daily boat trip to Porquerolles (adult/four to 10 years €20/11) and a weekdays-only circuit of Porquerolles, Levant and Port-Cros (€30/16).

Sitcat boats (☎ 04 94 46 35 46), run by the local transport company RMTT, link quai Cronstadt with the towns on the peninsula across the harbour, including La Seyne, St-Mandrier-sur-Mer and Sablettes. Tickets for the 20-minute journey cost €1.70 at the portside **ticket office** (☉ 7.30am-6.30pm Mon, Tue, Thu & Fri, 7.30am-12.15pm & 1.45-6.30pm Wed & Sat). Boats run from around 6am to 8pm.

TOUR ROYALE & MUSÉE DE LA MARINE

The sturdy **Tour Royale** (Royal Tower; ☎ 04 94 02 02 01; ☉ 10am-6.30pm Apr–mid-Sep, 10am-noon & 2-6pm Wed-Mon mid-Sep–Mar) is on the Pointe de la Mître in the suburb of Le Mourillon, just south of Toulon centre and the ferry terminal (walk or take the slightly tacky tourist train from the port). It was constructed under Louis XII at the start of the 16th century, and has served as a prison in the past. Views of the bay, Toulon and Mont Faron from the top of the tower are quite breathtaking.

The **Musée de la Marine** (Marine Museum; ☎ 04 94 02 02 01; place Monsenergue; combined ticket to Royal Tower & Musée de la Marine adult/under 18 yrs €4.60/free) is in Toulon's lovely 18th-century arsenal building (beware of wandering accidentally into the next-door military base!). This seafaring museum, which contains some marvellous models of old sailing ships, is open the same hours as the Royal Tower.

MUSÉE DE TOULON

Musée de Toulon (Toulon Museum; ☎ 04 94 36 81 00; 113 blvd Maréchal Leclerc), in a Renaissance-style building, houses an unexceptional **Musée d'Art** (Art Museum; admission free; ☉ 1-7pm Tue-Sun) and a moth-eaten **Musée d'Histoire Naturelle** (Natural History Museum; admission free; ☉ 9.30am-noon & 2-6pm Mon-Fri, 1-6pm Sat & Sun).

Festivals & Events

For 55 years Toulon has held an **International Festival of Music** (mainly classical) in various locations around town, including the Théâtre Municipal on place Victor Hugo, from June to early July.

Sleeping

BUDGET

There are plenty of cheap options in the old city, though some (particularly those at the western end of rue Jean Jaurès) are rumoured to double as brothels.

Hôtel des 3 Dauphins (☎ 04 94 92 65 79; fax 04 94 09 09 17; 9 place des Trois Dauphins; d with washbasin/ shower/shower & toilet €30/37/40) Peering down on Raimu's statue in the old town, the Three Dolphins is as smart as you get for a one-star joint in Toulon. White paintwork and azure tiles give it a cool continental feel, and washbasins and showers are hidden behind cunning curtains. Reception is at the Hotel Little Palace opposite.

Hôtel Molière (☎ 04 94 92 78 35; hotel.moliere@ tiscali.fr; 12 rue Molière; s/d with washbasin from €19/25, with shower €24/29, with shower & toilet €35/41) Right in the heart of things, balconies look out onto the opera house and its bustling square. Rooms are simple but pleasant; the only drawback is a neighbouring nightclub, noisy at the weekend. Use of the hallway shower costs €3.

MID-RANGE

Hotel Little Palace (☎ 04 94 92 26 62; www.hotel-little palace.com; 6 & 8 rue Berthelot; s/d/tr/ste €45/50/60/70) Bright Mediterranean orange colours give the smallish rooms a strangely warm feeling, offset by heavenly electric fans. There's a singularly cheerful receptionist, and the hotel itself overlooks one of Toulon's prettiest squares.

Hôtel Bonaparte (☎ 04 94 93 07 51; 16 rue Anatole; s/d/ste €45/50/80; 🖳) Completely overhauled in 2003, the Bonaparte is shining new. It's well placed for the port and Musée de la Marine and, although it has no private parking, the huge place d'Armes car park is just opposite. Bedrooms are a deep and cosy yellow, and staff are sweet and cheerful.

Grand Hôtel Dauphiné (☎ 04 94 92 20 28; www .grandhoteldauphine.com; 10 rue Berthelot; s/d from €48/54; P 🖳) Rooms are large and comfy, and people guard your car for you as you sleep. The hotel's situated on a pedestrianised street in the old town, so there's no problem with screeching traffic noise. There's wheelchair access.

New Hôtel Amirauté (☎ 04 94 22 19 67; www.new -hotel.com; 4 rue A Guiol; s/d €77/83; 🖳) A middle-of-the-road, could-be-anywhere-in-the-world type of place. Fancy door handles and strangely shaped bedheads relieve the business-style blandness, and rooms contain safes for the security conscious. Also has wheelchair access.

Eating

Restaurants, terraces and bars with occasional live music are abundant along the quays. Another buzzing eating area is place Victor Hugo and neighbouring place Puget.

BUDGET & MID-RANGE

There are lots of cheap eateries in the dilapidated streets around rue Chevalier Paul. Buy food outside at Toulon's open-air morning **food market** (cours Lafayette; 🕑 Tue-Sun) or inside at its **covered food market** (place Vincent Raspail; 🕑 Tue-Sun).

Les Enfants Gâtés (The Spoilt Children; ☎ 04 94 09 14 67; 7 rue Corneille; starters/mains €9/15; 🕑 lunch Mon-Fri low season, lunch & dinner Mon-Fri high season) This refreshingly contemporary literary café is run by a young and cheery crowd. Its regulars pile in for Provençal dishes and basil-rich Italian suppers.

La Feuille de Chou (☎ 04 94 62 09 26; 15 rue de la Glacière; plat du jour €9, menu €17; 🕑 lunch Mon-Sat, dinner Sat) A simple but absolutely charming bistro complete with peaceful terrace on olive tree-bespeckled place Eugène Baboulene. Tables are set a discrete distance apart, encouraging you to relax and linger over its traditional dishes. Get there at noon on the dot, or you may not get a table.

Al Dente (☎ /fax 04 94 93 02 50; 30 rue Gimelli; menus €10.80/18.40; 🕑 closed lunch Sun) Named in honour of the way pasta should be cooked, this is a cool and elegant tummy-filling option near the train station. It serves meat dishes, salads and fresh pasta, and if they don't satisfy your appetite, its giant puddings will.

Le Village (☎ 04 94 22 03 03; 10 rue Dumont d'Urville; menus €12/19; 🕑 closed Sun & lunch Sat; 🖳) Deciphering the squiggly menu here is an art! Traditional seafood, lasagnes and big fat cakes are in there somewhere. Occasional live jazz creates a mellow atmosphere.

TOP END

La Chamade (☎ 04 94 92 28 58; 25 rue Comédie; 2-course menu €23; 🕑 closed several weeks in Aug) An upmarket restaurant where you can dine on temptations such as foie gras pan-fried in three types of vinegar, roasted pigeon or chocolate soup with caramelised fruits and hot pistachio gateau. Reservations are definitely required.

Entertainment

As France's largest military port, Toulon is filled with unsalubrious drunken-sailor bars: non-navy types take their dancing shoes to Hyères (see p312).

Operas and ballets are staged at the newly cleaned **Opéra de Toulon** (☎ 04 94 93 03 76; operadetoulon@wanadoo.fr; place Victor Hugo), with tickets from €15 to €50.

Toulon's prime venue for rock, pop and other big-band concerts is **Zénith Oméga** (☎ 04 94 22 66 77; zenith.omega@wanadoo.fr; blvd du Commandant Nicolas).

Pick up a free copy of the chunky directory *Terre de Festivals* from the tourist office, for all entertainment in the region.

Getting There & Away
AIR
Aéroport de Toulon-Hyères (Toulon-Hyères airport; ☎ 04 94 00 83 83; www.toulon-hyeres.aeroport.fr) is 25km east of the city.

BOAT
Buy ferry tickets to Corsica and Sardinia from the **SNCM office** (☎ 08 91 70 18 01; 49 av de l'Infanterie de Marine; ☽ 8.30am-noon & 2-5.45pm Mon-Fri, from 11.30am Sat); see p355 for more details.

For information about boats to the Îles d'Hyères, see p315.

BUS
From the Toulon **bus terminal** (place de l'Europe), to the right as you exit the train station, **Sodetrav** (☎ 04 94 28 93 40; 4 blvd Pierre Toesca) is the main coastal bus operator.

Bus Nos 29, 39 and 103 go to Hyères (€4.40, 40 minutes), continuing east along the coast to Le Lavandou (€10.60, 1¼ hours) and other towns, before arriving in St-Tropez (€16.60, 2¼ hours, seven daily).

Phocéens Cars (☎ 04 93 85 66 61) operates buses to and from Nice (adult/senior €23/15, 2½ hours, two per day Monday to Saturday), via Hyères and Cannes.

TRAIN
From the **train station** (place de l'Europe) there are frequent connections to numerous coastal cities, including Marseille (€9.70, one hour), St-Raphaël (€13, 50 minutes), Cannes (€17, 1¼ hours), Nice (€20, 2½ hours), Antibes (€19, 1½ hours), Monaco (€22, 2½ hours) and Menton (€22, 2½ hours).

Getting Around
TO/FROM THE AIRPORT
There are shuttle buses run by **Sodetrav** (☎ 04 94 18 93 40; www.sodetrav.fr) from Toulon-Hyères airport to Toulon train station (€9.60, 40 minutes), via Hyères (€4.40, 10 minutes). Buses coincide with flight arrivals and departures. Buy tickets in advance (€15.50 return to Toulon) or on the bus.

BUS
Local buses are run by **RMTT** (☎ 04 94 03 87 03; www.rmtt.fr), which has an **information kiosk** (place de la Liberté; ☽ 7.30am-noon & 1.30-6.30pm Mon-Fri) at the main local bus hub. A single ticket/10-ticket carnet costs €1.40/8.80.

Buses run until around 9pm, although a few night buses exist (€3.90). Sunday service is limited.

TOWARDS MARSEILLE
Before you hit sizzling, sizeable Marseille, catch your breath in some of the smaller towns on the way: Sanary-sur-Mer, as serene as its name suggests; Bandol, best known for its wines; and the inland Circuit du Castellet, strictly for wannabe racers!

Sanary-sur-Mer
pop 17,177
The sugary pink-and-white houses in this quiet seaside resort, 15km west of Toulon, give it a settled, mumsy feel. It was home to novelist Aldous Huxley (1894–1963) in the early 1930s, his biographer Sybille Bedford in the late 1930s, and to a host of German refugees very soon after. Thomas Mann and his brother Heinrich sought refuge here, as did the German painter Feuchtwanger.

Sanary's sandy but shallow beaches get packed in summer. From the small and busy port, **Croix du Sud III** (☎ 04 94 07 69 89; www.croixdusud.com; 5 place du Coquillon) runs boat excursions west towards Cassis and its *calanques* (literally 'rocky inlets'; adult/three to 10 years €20/10 for 10 *calanques*, three hours) at 2.30pm Monday to Saturday; around the Baies du Soleil (€12/6, 1½ hours) on Sunday afternoon; and to the Île des Embiez (€9/5, 15 minutes), departing three times per day from Monday to Saturday in summer.

Fourteen kilometres north inland, **Ollioules** (population 12,336) is known for its October **Fête de l'Olivier** (Olive-tree Festival). The **tourist office** (☎ 04 94 63 11 74; office -tourisme@ollioules.com; 116 rue Philippe de Hauteclocque) has details.

In Sanary **Hôtel de la Tour** (☎ 04 94 74 10 10; www.sanary-hoteldelatour.com; quai du Général de Gaulle; s/d with breakfast from €63/77; ☒) is a particularly welcoming spot. It's wrapped around a 12th-century tower – hence its name – and has great views over the port.

Bandol
pop 7975
Bandol, 8km west of Sanary, attracted ailing foreigners like DH Lawrence and Katherine Mansfield in the 1900s. Now wine-lovers and windsurfers pour to its sandy shores.

Bandol's terraced vineyards stretch 15km northwest of town (as far as St-Anne du Castellet) and are managed by 50 wine producers. Their produce, most famously the matchless reds, have been sold under their own coveted AOC since 1941. For a list of wine cellars, contact the **tourist office** (☎ 04 94 29 41 35; www.bandol.fr; allées Vivien; ☺ 9am-7pm Jul & Aug, 9am-noon & 2-6pm Mon-Fri, 9am-noon Sat Sep-Jun). Wine growers celebrate the year's new wine production each year in early December with a **Fête du Millésime** (Vintage Festival).

From Bandol port from June to September, **Atlantide I** (☎ 04 94 32 51 41; www.atlantide1 .com; quai d'Honneur) runs boat excursions to Île des Embiez (adult/four to 12 years €9/5), Porquerolles (€32/16) and around the *calanques* (six/10/14 *calanques* €16/20/24). You can also sail around the port in a **glass-bottomed boat** (☎ 06 03 44 59 63; adult/3-10 yrs €11/6; 35min) from Easter to September. Boats sail year round to Île de Bendor (see p308).

Les Lecques
The seaside resort of Les Lecques, 17km west of Bandol, is unstartling apart from the remnants of two Roman villas displayed in the **Musée de Tauroentum** (☎ 04 94 26 30 46; 131 rte de la Madrague; adult/7-13 yrs €3/1; ☺ 3-7pm Wed-Mon Jun-Sep, 2-5pm Sat & Sun Oct-May); be warned, parking here is difficult. The museum is arranged around three restored mosaics dating from around AD 1. Archaeologists believe that the Roman town after which the museum is named would have stood somewhere between here and **St-Cyr-sur-Mer**, 2km inland. For more information contact the **tourist office** (☎ 04 94 26 73 73; www.saintcyr surmer.com; place de l'Appel du 18 Juin; ☺ 9am-7pm Mon-Sat, 10am-1pm & 4-7pm Sun Jul & Aug, 9am-6pm Mon-Sat Sep & Jun, 9am-6pm Mon-Fri, 9am-noon & 2-6pm Sat Oct-May) in Les Lecques.

Circuit du Castellet
The calm and tranquillity that caresses the northern Bandol vineyards around the perched village of **Le Castellet** (population 3839, elevation 252m) is smashed with racy aplomb at the Circuit du Castellet, a couple of kilometres out of town. The motorsports racetrack was built by industrialist Paul Ricard in 1970 and sold to Formula One racing magnate Bernie Ecclestone in 1999.

Monaco

The tiny principality of Monaco is the world's second-smallest country – after the Vatican. Its territory, surrounded by France, covers just 1.95 sq km.

Somerset Maugham dubbed Monaco 'a sunny place for shady people', and it still functions as a tax haven for astronomical earners. With absolutely no natural resources to rely on, the principality has made pampering the super-rich its speciality.

Since 1949 Monaco has been ruled by Prince Rainier III, whose sweeping constitutional powers make him much more then a mere figurehead. The 'builder prince' expanded the size of his principality by 20% in the late 1960s, by reclaiming land from the sea to create the industrial quarter of Fontvieille. By 2004 he had doubled the size of the harbour with an incredible floating dike.

Since the death in 1982 of the much-loved Princess Grace (best remembered from her Hollywood days as the actress Grace Kelly), the tabloids have slavered over the far-from-fairy-tale love lives of the couple's children, Caroline, Stephanie and Albert.

Glamorous Monte Carlo – Monaco's capital – is famed for its casino and its role as host to the annual Formula One (F1) Monaco Grand Prix, which sees drivers tear round a track that winds through the town and around the port. Unsurpassable views of the race, the principality and its legendary skyscraper skyline can be had from the Musée Océanographique's terrace or the Trophée des Alps in La Turbie, France.

By law, it's forbidden to walk around town barechested, barefooted or bikini-clad, or to Rollerblade (the prince doesn't like it).

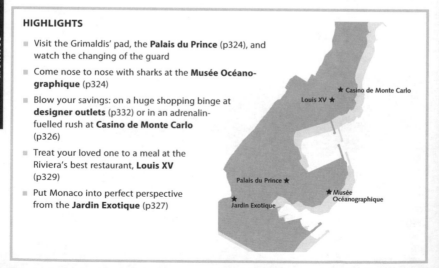

HIGHLIGHTS

- Visit the Grimaldis' pad, the **Palais du Prince** (p324), and watch the changing of the guard
- Come nose to nose with sharks at the **Musée Océanographique** (p324)
- Blow your savings: on a huge shopping binge at **designer outlets** (p332) or in an adrenalin-fuelled rush at **Casino de Monte Carlo** (p326)
- Treat your loved one to a meal at the Riviera's best restaurant, **Louis XV** (p329)
- Put Monaco into perfect perspective from the **Jardin Exotique** (p327)

Casino de Monte Carlo

Louis XV

Palais du Prince

Musée Océanographique

Jardin Exotique

HISTORY

Monaco's early Greek and Roman history is buried under a million tonnes of concrete: since the 13th century, the history of Monaco has really been the history of the Grimaldi family. Their rule began in 1297, when François 'the Spiteful' disguised himself as a monk and begged for shelter at the door of Le Rocher fortress. When pitying soldiers let him in, François promptly stabbed them, then opened the gates to his followers, an event commemorated on the Grimaldi coat-of-arms.

Monégasque independence was first recognised in 1489 by Charles VIII, king of France. The tide turned when Monaco was seized by France during the French Revolution, and the royal family were imprisoned. On release, they were forced to sell their remaining possessions to survive, and the palace was turned into a warehouse.

The Grimaldi family was restored to the throne under the 1814 Treaty of Paris, but their bad luck continued. Monaco lost its territories Menton and Roquebrune in 1848, along with the huge income they generated through oranges and lemons, and became the poorest country in Europe. In 1860 Monégasque independence was recognised for a second time by France, and a monetary agreement in 1865 sealed the deal on future cooperation between the two countries. In the same year, the far-sighted Charles III built the casino, giving a mighty boost to Monaco's luck.

Monaco's current economic status is a strange one. Although not a member of the European Union, because of its continuing special relationship with France, Monaco does participate in the EU customs territory and uses the euro as its currency.

ORIENTATION

Monaco consists of five principal areas: Monaco Ville (where the Palais du Prince stands), a 60m outcrop of rock on the southern side of the Port de Monaco; Monte Carlo, famous for its casino and Grand Prix, north of the port; La Condamine, the flat area around the port; Fontvieille, the industrial area southwest of Monaco Ville; and Larvotto, the beach area east of Monte Carlo. The French town of Beausoleil is three streets up the hill from Monte Carlo, while Moneghetti borders Cap d'Ail's western fringe.

THE MONÉGASQUES

Citizens of Monaco (Monégasques), of whom there are only about 7000, do not pay any taxes. They have their own flag (red and white), national anthem and national holiday (19 November).

The traditional dialect is Monégasque (broadly speaking, a mixture of French and Italian), which is taught in schools alongside French, Monaco's official language. Many of the street signs are bilingual.

Monaco is not quite an absolute monarchy: the ruling prince is assisted by a national council with 18 democratically elected members. Only Monégasques aged 21 or over can vote; elections are held every five years.

INFORMATION
Bookshops

Le Khédive (☎ 93 90 29 33; 9 blvd Albert 1er; 🕑 6.30am-8pm) Newsagent with unsurpassable choice of foreign-language newspapers and magazines.
Scruples (☎ 93 50 43 52; 9 rue Princesse Caroline; 🕑 9am-12.30pm & 2.30-7pm Mon-Fri, 10am-12.30pm & 2.30-6.30pm Sat) Monaco's English-language bookshop.

Emergency

Ambulance & Fire Brigade (☎ 18)
Police (☎ 17)
Police Station (& Lost Property ☎ 93 15 30 18; 3 rue Louis Notari)

Internet Access

Stars 'n' Bars (see p330; per 30min €6)

Laundry

Lave Azur (23 blvd du Général Leclerc; per 7kg wash €5; 🕑 9am-7pm)

Libraries

Princess Grace Irish Library (☎ 93 50 12 25; www .monaco.mc/pglib; 9 rue Princesse Marie de Lorraine; 🕑 9am-6.30pm Mon-Fri) Centre for Irish cultural studies, built around Princess Grace's own library.

Media

Radio Monte Carlo (RMC; www.radiomontecarlo.net) French- and Italian-language broadcasts on 98.8MHz FM in Monaco.
Riviera Radio (www.rivieraradio.mc) English-language, with hourly BBC news summaries, broadcasting on 106.3MHz FM.

MONACO

MONACO

A **B** **C** **D**

MONACO *(vertical side tab)*

FRANCE
(Beausoleil)

Monte
Carlo

R. de Rochevville
Blvd Princesse Charlotte
Av. de la Costa
44
24
Train
Station
17
Blvd de Suisse
Av. Président JF
94
Q. des États-Unis
Pl. Ste-
Dévote
La Condamine
Pedestrian
Tunnel
95
Blvd Rainier III
R. Louise Aureglia
R. Grimaldi
78
84
62
66
58
R. Princesse Caroline
39
R. Suffren Reymond
75
R. Grimaldi
Blvd Albert Ier
77
Moneghetti
91
Blvd de Belgique
Rte de la Moyenne Corniche (N7)
Av. Hector Otto
Blvd du Jardin Exotique
90
11
54
6
13
82
60
88
61
92
56
53
43
79
93
51
Rampe
Major
Av. du Pont
Av. de la
R. des
Remparts
R. Baisse
31
N7
Pl. d'Armes
38
40
33
Pl. du Palais
21
Centre
Commercial
de Fontvielle
34
22
36
To Nice
(16km)
Jardin
Exotique
14
26
30
97
Pointe
Ste-Barbe
Port de
Fontvieille
Blvd Charles III
Av. de Fontvieille
Blvd Rainier III
Corniche
Inférieure
Av. Pasteur
Blvd Charles III
R. du Gabian
Av. Prince Héréditaire Albert
Av. des Papalins
Q. Jean-Charles-Rey
Roseraie
Princesse
Grace
Parc
Fontvieille
Stade
Louis II
Av. des
Castelans
Fontvieille
MONACO
FRANCE
N98
Espace
Fontvieille
87

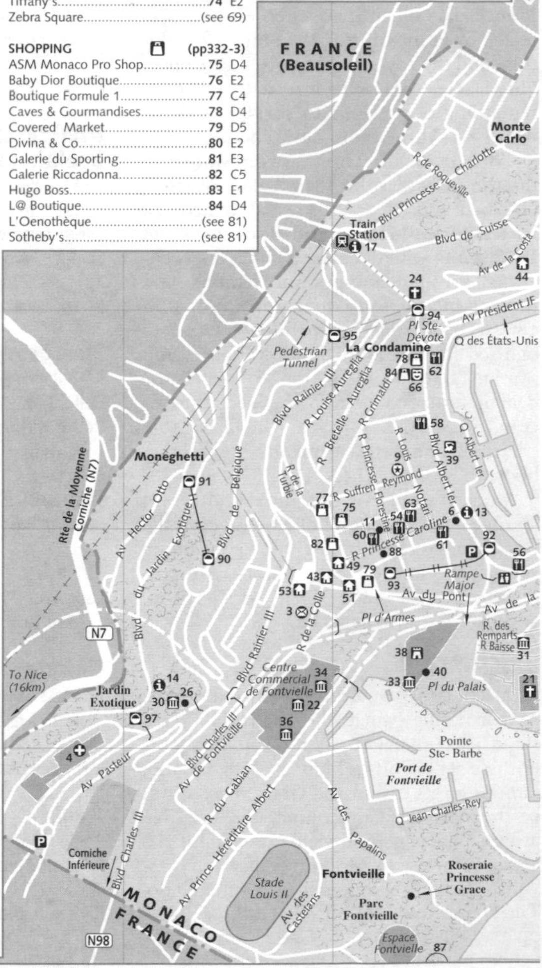

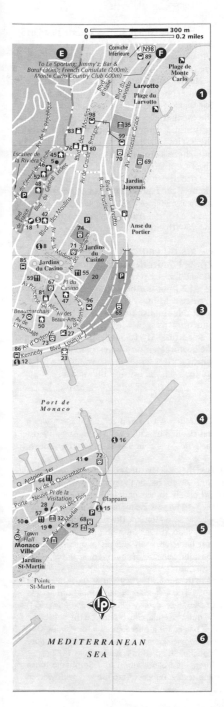

Medical Services
Centre Hospitalier Princesse Grace (emergencies ☎ 97 98 97 69, switchboard ☎ 97 98 99 00; av Pasteur)

Money
Monaco uses the euro, although the Monégasque version of the currency is a rarity. There are numerous banks near the casino in Monte Carlo.
Amex (☎ 97 70 77 59; 35 blvd Princesse Charlotte; 9.30am-noon & 2-5.30pm Mon-Sat) Cashes travellers cheques.

Post
Monégasque stamps are only valid for letters sent within Monaco (use a French stamp to send a postcard). Postal rates are the same as those in France.
Branch Post Office (☎ 93 30 34 10; place de la Mairie; 8am-7pm Mon-Fri, 8am-noon Sat) Near the Palais du Prince. Contains a small **philatelic counter** (☎ 93 15 41 18; www.oetp-monaco.com).
Main Post Office (☎ 97 97 25 25; Palais de la Scala, Monte Carlo; 8am-7pm Mon-Fri, 8am-noon Sat) Inside Galerie Charles Despaux, near the casino.

Telephone
Telephone numbers in Monaco have eight digits and no area code.

Calls between Monaco and France are treated as international calls. When calling Monaco from the rest of France or abroad, dial ☎ 00 followed by Monaco's country code, 377. To call France from Monaco, dial ☎ 00 and France's country code, 33.

Monaco's public telephones accept Monégasque or French phonecards.

Tourist Information
National Tourist Office (☎ 92 16 61 16; www .monaco-tourisme.com; 2a blvd des Moulins; 9am-7pm Mon-Sat, 10am-noon Sun)
Summer tourist information kiosks (8am-8pm Jun-Sep) Outside the Jardin Exotique; in the Parking des Pêcheurs car park; on quai des États-Unis overlooking the port; on blvd Albert 1er; on the new harbour extension; and at the train station.

SIGHTS
Monaco Ville
Monaco Ville (also known as Le Rocher), which thrusts skywards on a pistol-shaped rock, is the best place to start your visit. The most alluring sights – the palace, the twisting old town, gardens and museums – are

here; plus the superb state-wide views help you get your bearings.

The 16th-century red-brick Rampe Major provides a steep pedestrian link from the port area of La Condamine to the palace. Bus Nos 1 and 2 run from the tourist office (via the place d'Armes) up to Le Rocher, stopping at place de la Visitation.

MUSÉE OCÉANOGRAPHIQUE & AROUND

Monaco's world-renowned **Musée Océanographique** (Oceanographic Museum; ☎ 93 15 36 00; www .oceano.mc; av St-Martin; adult/student/6-18 yrs €11/6/6; ⊙ 9.30am-7.30pm Jul & Aug, 9.30am-7pm Apr-Jun, 10am-6pm Jan-Mar & Oct-Dec) is a stunner. Its centrepiece is the 7.5m-long coral reef, with vivid tropical fish on one side and deep-sea predators (including white- and black-tipped reef sharks) on the other. Ninety smaller tanks contain a dazzling 450 Mediterranean and tropical species, sustained by 250,000L of freshly pumped sea water per day.

The interior of the purpose-built museum, founded in 1910 by Prince Albert I (1848–1922), features fanciful seabird-covered chandeliers, mosaic floors, and oak doorframes carved into marine shapes. The Whale Room, filled with cetacean skeletons and pickled embryos, is also worth a squint.

The steep-sided, statue-studded **Jardins St-Martin** (⊙ 7am-6pm Oct-Mar, to 8pm Apr-Sep), which run round the coast outside the museum, are perfect for a post-aquarium stroll.

Monte Carlo Story (☎ 93 25 32 33; setav_mc@ monaco.377.com; adult/student/6-14 yrs €6.50/5/3; ⊙ 2-5pm Jan-Jun, Sep & Oct, 2-6pm Jul & Aug), reached via the escalator in front of the Musée Océanographique, shows a 35-minute film about the Grimaldi dynasty. Undeniably tacky, but there's an interesting display of old cinema posters.

Directly opposite the museum entrance is the **Azur Express** (☎ 92 05 64 38; av St-Martin; adult/under 5 €6/free; ⊙ 10am-5pm Sep-Jun, to 6pm Jul & Aug), a tourist train offering 30-minute city tours with English commentary.

PALAIS DU PRINCE

Prince Rainier III and his **palace** (☎ 93 25 18 31; place du Palais) are protected by an elite company of 112 guards, the Carabiniers du Prince (Prince's Military Police). In summer they resemble English bobbies with bleached hats and uniforms; in winter they adopt moody black attire. At 11.55am daily the **changing of the guard** ceremony takes place, when a gigantic scrum scrambles to watch the pristine soldiers parade outside the palace.

THE GRIMALDI DYNASTY

The House of Grimaldi has ruled 'The Rock' with a golden fist on and off since 1297, when François Grimaldi sneaked through the city gates and claimed it as his own. The dynasty almost died in 1731 when Antoine I failed to produce a male heir. His daughter stepped in as queen, retaining her Grimaldi name.

Two centuries on, Prince Charles III (1818–89) gave the poverty-stricken state independence, followed in 1865 by the million-dollar-generating casino. His successor, the seafaring Prince Albert I (1848–1922), preferred marine biology and devoted his life to oceanographic research.

Despite its 'neutrality' in WWII, Prince Louis II (1870–1949) was a supporter of the Vichy government, and turned a blind eye to Jewish 'disappearances' in Monaco. The principality's annual revenues rose from three million francs in 1941 to 80 million in 1943 through money-laundering on the Nazis' behalf. This foreign policy caused a rift between Louis and his grandson Rainier III (1923–), who particularly detested Louis II's pro-Hitler Minister of State, Émile Roblôt, and demanded his dismissal (Louis refused).

Rainier III, Monaco's longest-ruling monarch, came to the throne in 1949 and won the heart of a nation with his fairy-tale marriage to Grace Kelly in 1956. The legendary Philadelphia-born actress had made 11 films in the 1950s, including Hitchcock's Dial M for Murder (1954), Rear Window (1954) and To Catch a Thief (1955), in which she starred as the quintessential cool blonde on the coast. The movie took Kelly to Cannes, then to the Monégasque palace for a photo shoot with Rainier. One year later Monaco's prince charming wed Hollywood's movie queen. The princess made no more films and devoted herself to duties as Princess of Monaco. She died in a car crash in 1982.

The soap-opera lives of the couple's three children – Caroline, Albert and Stephanie, born 1957, 1958 and 1965 respectively – take centre stage today. Princess Caroline was widowed in

If the Grimaldi standard is flying from the palace tower, it means Prince Rainier is at home. Who knows, you might bump into him on an audioguided tour of the grandiose **state apartments** (adult/8-14 yrs €6/3; 9.30am-6pm Jun-Sep, 10am-5pm Oct); in summer be prepared to queue for up to 45 minutes to get in.

Far more personal than the formal apartments is the **Musée des Souvenirs Napoléoniens et Archives Historiques du Palais** (Museum of Napoleonic Souvenirs & the Palace's Historic Archives; adult/ 8-14 yrs €4/2; 9.30am-6.30pm Jun-Sep, 10am-5pm Oct–mid-Nov, 10.30am-12.30pm & 2-5pm mid-Dec–May) in the palace's southern wing. Its princely collections of bric-a-brac (medals, coins, uniforms, swords), and items including Napoleon's socks, are fascinating.

A combined ticket for the apartments and museum costs €8/4.

CATHÉDRALE DE MONACO
This Romanesque-Byzantine **cathedral** (93 30 87 70; www.cathedrale.mc; 4 rue Colonel Bellando de Castro), built in 1875, receives a flood of visitors despite its ugliness; they're drawn by the flower-covered grave of Princess Grace (1929–82). The burial spots of other royal dead folk receive barely a glance in the sprint round the choir stall to the princess's headstone, simply inscribed *Gratia Patricia, Principis Rainerii III Uxor.*

From September to June Sunday Mass at 10am is sung by **Les Petits Chanteurs de Monaco** (93 15 80 88), Monaco's boys' choir. Organ recitals are at held at 6pm on alternate Saturdays from July to September.

OTHER MUSEUMS
Life-sized wax figures pose in 24 tableaux snapshotting Grimaldi history at the **Musée de Cires** (Wax Museum; 93 30 39 05; 27 rue Basse; adult/8-14 yrs €3.80/2; 10am-6pm); their costumes were donated by the royal family.

Religious artworks by some big-hitters, including Rubens, Zurbaran and Ribera, are displayed in the enchanting **Musée de la Chapelle de la Visitation** (93 50 07 00; place de la Visitation; adult/6-14 yrs €3/1.50; 12.30-4pm Tue, 10am-4pm Wed-Sun), in a 17th-century baroque chapel.

Monte Carlo
The **Jardins du Casino** form the district's green hub, and are wonderfully pleasant to sit and stroll in. Changing art exhibitions in the central strip add intrigue. For further brushes with nature, follow the coastal path (two to three hours) from Monte Carlo to Roquebrune-Cap Martin.

1990 when her second husband (her marriage to the first was annulled), and father of her three children, was killed in a speedboat accident. In 1999, on her 42nd birthday, she secretly wed Prince Ernst of Hanover, a cousin to Britain's Queen Elizabeth: only eight guests attended the civil ceremony. In August 2004 Caroline won a 10-year battle against the paparazzi, when the European Court of Human Rights found that, unless there's a proper story behind those long-lens photos of toe-sucking celebs, publishing them is not on. The ruling could have far-reaching effects on newspapers and magazines across Europe.

The heir to the throne and 'world's most eligible bachelor', 46-year-old Albert, has a reputation as an international playboy and athlete. Linked to endless strings of beautiful women, Albert also set up Monaco's bobsleigh team in 1986, competing in five Olympic Games. He has managed to avoid much of the publicity received by his wild-child sisters, but the eyes of the press are now turning on him: Rainier III is a frail 81, and was hospitalised three times in 2004, meaning that a reluctant Albert may soon end up on the throne.

The youngest of the trio, Princess Stephanie, has been shocking Monégasques and keeping the tabloids in business for over 20 years. After a series of shady boyfriends, she wed her bodyguard in 1995, but divorced him a year later after he was snapped frolicking with a Belgian stripper. Her second marriage, to circus acrobat Adan Peres, lasted a mere 10 months; within a couple of weeks, a casino croupier was rumoured to be her latest lover. During the 1980s and early 1990s the entrepreneurial princess launched her own swimwear label (Pool Position), and released a flurry of pop songs, including 'Ouragan' (Hurricane) and 'I am Waiting for You'.

The Rose Ball (in May), the Summer Ball, the fundraising *Gala de la Croix Rouge* (Red Cross Ball) and the Gala Ball are Monaco's key society events of the year. They afford a rare glimpse of the House of Grimaldi in the world's spotlight. Tickets cost around €1000.

CASINO DE MONTE CARLO

The drama of watching poker-faced people risk all in Monte Carlo's marble-and-gold **casino** (☎ 92 96 20 00; www.casino-monte-carlo.com; place du Casino; ☼ from noon Jul & Aug, from 2pm Mon-Fri & noon Sat & Sun Sep-Jun) makes the stiff admission fees, stakes and obligatory cloakroom 'tips' almost bearable. The **Salon Ordinaire** (€10/22/42/57 per day/week/month/season) has European roulette (minimum stake €5) and trente et quarante (minimum stake €20); and the **Salons Privés** (per day €20; ☼ from 4pm) offer baccarat, craps, English roulette and chemin de fer.

To enter the casino, you must be 18 or over, have a passport handy for ID, and be dressed relatively smartly (no shorts, trainers etc). A jacket and tie are required to enter the Salons Privés and the Salon Ordinaire in the evening. The one-armed bandits, to the right as you enter, do not command a fee or dress code.

MUSÉE NATIONAL

More innocent pleasures are to be found in Monaco's **Musée National** (National Museum; ☎ 93 30 91 26; www.monte-carlo.mc/musee-national; 17 av Princesse Grace; adult/6-14 yrs €6/3.50; ☼ 10am-6.30pm Easter-Sep, 10am-12.15pm & 2.30-6.30pm Sep-Easter), a sumptuous Garnier-designed villa containing a huge doll collection. Magical mechanical toys, including an illusionist who makes his own head disappear, are demonstrated in the afternoons at half-past the hour.

JARDIN JAPONAIS & GRIMALDI FORUM

Sandwiched between the built-up quarters of Monte Carlo, Larvotto and the Mediterranean, the **Jardin Japonais** (Japanese garden; av Princesse Grace; ☼ 9am-dusk) is intended as a piece of paradise. It was blessed by a Shinto high priest; quiet contemplation and meditation is encouraged in the Zen garden.

The nearby **Grimaldi Forum** (☎ 99 99 30 00; www.grimaldiforum.mc; 10 av Princesse Grace), Monaco's congress and conference centre, hosts occasional contemporary art exhibitions – always eclectic and well worth seeing. All the more astonishing is the gigantic glass edifice itself, two-thirds of which is submerged in the sea.

Fontvieille

Adjoining Cap d'Ail in neighbouring France, Fontvieille – built on 30 hectares of land reclaimed from the sea between 1966 and 1973 – covers the southernmost part of Monaco. From here a 3.5km-long coastal path leads southwest to Cap d'Ail. The lush gardens of **Parc Fontvieille** are equally pleasant for a summer stroll; over 4000 rose bushes and a small swan-filled lake adorn the **Roseraie Princesse Grace** (Princess Grace Rose Garden), planted in her memory in 1984.

LOSER RISKS ALL

The beautiful *belle époque* décor of Monte Carlo Casino – Europe's oldest – is as extravagant as those who play in it. It went up in several phases, the earliest being the Salon de l'Europe, built in 1865 and splendidly lit with eight 150kg crystal chandeliers from 1898. The second phase saw French architect Charles Garnier, who'd just completed the Paris opera house, move to Monte Carlo to create the luxurious fresco-adorned Salle Garnier in 1878. The main entrance hall, with its 28 marble columns and flurry of gamblers and voyeurs, opened the same year. The third part, the Salle Empire, was completed in 1910.

Monaco's Prince Charles III, who saw the casino as the solution to the principality's financial troubles, was nevertheless concerned about the malign effect of gambling on his subjects. He therefore made it illegal for his family, or any Monégasque, to set foot in the precincts! Money-losing was for rich foreigners only…Monte Carlo Casino remains in the hands of its founding owners, the Société des Bains de Mer (SBM; Sea Bathing Society), established in 1863. Original shareholders included Charles III, who held a 10% stake. The state remains the leading shareholder today.

In 1875, when the then-future Edward VII and Queen Alexandra visited, around 150,000 players per day were frequenting the casino. Shotgun suicides, hot on the heels of a heavy loss at the gaming tables, were common well into the 1920s. When Charles Deville Wells broke the bank in 1891 – the first and last to do so – gaming tables were draped in black for three days.

Despite an initial drop in revenue in 1933 after roulette was legalised in neighbouring France, Monte Carlo Casino continues to rake it in. The SBM is Monaco's largest corporation, owning all the principality's upmarket hotels and restaurants.

Contemporary sculptures, including works by César and Arman, line the length of the park's **Chemin des Sculptures**. Museum-wise, Fontvieille is Monaco's collector's corner.

COLLECTION DE VOITURES ANCIENNES

More than 100 immaculate vehicles are on display in Prince Rainier III's **Collection de Voitures Anciennes** (Collection of Classic Cars; ☎ 92 05 28 56; www.palais.mc; Centre Commercial de Fontvieille; adult/8-14 yrs €6/3; ◷ 10am-6pm). Highlights include a Rolls Royce Silver Cloud, his wedding present from local shopkeepers; a black London cab (Austin 1952) especially fitted out for Grace Kelly; and the first F1 racing car to win the Monaco Grand Prix – the Bugatti 1929.

MUSÉE NAVAL

An impressive collection of 200-plus model ships, many constructed by the Grimaldi princes, is displayed in Monaco's **Musée Naval** (Naval Museum; ☎ 92 05 28 48; www.naval-museum.mc in French; Centre Commercial de Fontvieille; adult/8-14 yrs €4/2.50; ◷ 10am-6pm). Pieces include an imperial gondola built for Napoleon to admire; a 17th-century sailing ship; and a miniature of the *Missouri*, where the armistice with Japan was signed in 1945.

MUSÉE DES TIMBRES ET DES MONNAIES

Prince Rainier also has a **Musée des Timbres et des Monnaies** (Museum of Stamps & Coins; ☎ 93 15 41 50; fax 93 15 41 45; Centre Commercial de Fontvieille; adult/12-14 yrs €3/2; ◷ 10am-6pm Jul-Sep, 10am-5pm Oct-Jun), containing just what its name promises: Monégasque stamps dating from 1885, and numismatic wonders dating from 1640.

Moneghetti

The largest succulent and cactus collection in the world tumbles down the slopes of the wonderful **Jardin Exotique** (☎ 93 15 29 80; www.monte-carlo.mc/jardinexotique; 62 blvd du Jardin Exotique; adult/6-18 yrs €6.70/3.40; ◷ 9am-7pm mid-May–mid-Sep, 9am-6pm or dusk mid-Sep–mid-May). Seven thousand varieties, from small *echinocereus* to 10m-tall African candelabras, are linked by winding paths and wooden bridges, with spectacular views. Keep a firm hold of toddlers – there are some holey fences and unthinkable drops.

Your ticket also gets you a guided tour (35 minutes) round the **Grottes de l'Observatoire** (Observatory Caves; ◷ access with tour only, hourly 10am-5 or 6pm). This prehistoric complex comprises a fantastical cave network stuffed with sta-

lactites and stalagmites, 279 steps down inside the hillside; strangely, it's the only cave in Europe where the temperature rises as you descend. Prehistoric rock scratchings found here are among the oldest of their kind in the world. Admission to the **Musée d'Anthropologie Préhistorique** (Museum of Prehistoric Anthropology; ☎ 93 15 80 06), with displays of human artefacts, is also included; it closes 15 minutes before the gardens.

From the tourist office, take bus No 2 to the Jardin Exotique terminus.

ACTIVITIES
Boats & Beaches

Palatial pleasure crafts containing cinemas, saunas and helicopter pads dominate the **Port de Monaco** (La Condamine); the website www.powerandmotoryacht.com/megayachts has a list of the world's top 100 private yachts – see how many you can spot here. At the eastern end of quai Antoine 1er is the exclusive members-only **Yacht Club de Monaco** (☎ 93 10 63 00; www.yacht-club-monaco.mc; 16 quai Antoine 1er).

Lesser mortals can sail the waters in a glass-bottomed catamaran operated by the

MONACO

Compagnie de Navigation et de Tourisme (☎ 92 16 15 15; www.aquavision-monaco.com; quai des États-Unis), at the eastern end of the quay. Boat excursions (55 minutes) depart three or four times daily from June to September (on reservation in May and October). Tickets are €11/8 per adult/three to 18 years.

The nearest fine-shingle beaches, **Plage du Larvotto** and **Plage de Monte Carlo**, are a couple of kilometres east of Monte Carlo in Larvotto. Both have private, paying sections where you can hire cushioned sun-lounges and parasols for around €8/10 per half-/full day. One section of Plage du Larvotto, **Handiplage**, is kitted out for disabled travellers. Take bus No 4 from the train station or bus No 6 from the port to Le Sporting stop.

Pools & Spas

Beautiful swimmers frequent **Stade Nautique Rainier III** (☎ 93 30 64 83; quai Albert 1er; adult/over 60/3-11 yrs €4.30/2.70/2.40; ☀ 9am-6pm May, Jun, Sep & Oct, 9am-8pm Jul & Aug), the Olympic-sized outdoor pool at the port. If exercise is too taxing, hire a comfortable mattress and/or parasol (€3.70 each).

Casino owners SBM run the prestigious **Les Thermes Marins de Monte-Carlo** (☎ 92 16 49 46; www.montecarloresort.com; 2 av de Monte Carlo), which has a heated sea-water pool and solarium, and offers spa treatments, shiatsu massages, reflexology sessions, skin peels and lord-knows-what-else. Three-day slimming, well-being and cellulite-attack packages cost from €823 per person, including accommodation.

FESTIVALS & EVENTS

Poor old Ste Dévote, martyred in Corsica in AD 312, was thrown into a boat and left to drift to sea. Miraculously, a dove flew from the dead woman's mouth and blew the boat safely to Monaco, where the inhabitants snapped her up as their patron saint. The **Fête de la Ste-Dévote** on 27 January celebrates her feast day, with a traditional Mass celebrated in Monégasque in the **Église Ste-Dévote** (☎ 93 50 52 60; fax 97 70 83 07; place Ste-Dévote). In the evening a torchlight procession, blessing and symbolic boat-burning take place in front of the church.

Lively dancers in traditional Monégasque folk costume (long, frilly skirts and red-and-white patterned garments) leap around the **Saint-Jean Bonfires**, on place du Palais on 23 June and on place des Moulins on 24 June.

AUTHOR'S CHOICE

Hôtel Boeri (☎ 04 93 78 38 10; fax 04 93 41 90 95; 29 blvd du Général Leclerc; s/d with bath from €62/68) An appealing 30-room option, with totally charming staff and a small garden. The mirrored, plant-filled public spaces give it a terrarium feel, and some rooms have flower-adorned balconies with sea views.

Early August brings a glittering **International Fireworks Festival** to the port area, while a carnival spirit fills the streets during the **Fête Nationale Monégasque** – Monaco's national holiday – on 19 November.

SLEEPING
Budget & Mid-Range

Monaco's one true budget option, the **Centre de la Jeunesse Princesse Stéphanie**, was flattened during works to relocate the station; it will be rebuilt and opened in 2008. Most of Monaco's accommodation options sport four stars; for cheaper hotels, head for Beausoleil (over the 'border' in France). Rates rocket out of control at Easter, New Year and during the Grand Prix, when many places demand a minimum three-night stay.

BEAUSOLEIL

Blvd du Général Leclerc is the street to head for in Beausoleil, in France (the even-numbered side is in Monaco and is called blvd de France). Remember to call the country code for France (☎ 00 33) if dialling these numbers from Monaco.

Hôtel Olympia (☎ 04 93 78 12 70; www.olympiahotel .tk; 17bis blvd du Général Leclerc; d with shower from €120; ☒) This family-run place has less character than the Boeri, but is equally friendly. The newly renovated rooms are soundproofed and bathrooms are tasteful marble affairs. A lift (elevator) and availability of larger rooms enable wheelchair access.

Hôtel Cosmopolite (☎ 04 93 78 36 00; hotel.cosmo politesoleil@wanadoo.fr; 19 blvd du Général Leclerc; s/d with shower from €59/68; ☒) Businesslike but rather bland.

Hôtel Diana (☎ 04 93 78 47 58; www.monte-carlo .mc/hotel-diana-beausoleil; 17 blvd du Général Leclerc; s/d with washbasin €35/35, s/d with shower & toilet €46/50) The cheapest accommodation within hand-bag-hurling distance of Monaco. Use of the communal bathroom costs €8 a throw.

MONACO

Hôtel Ambassador (☎ 97 97 96 96; www.ambassador
monaco.com; 10 av Prince Pierre; s/d/tr €140/170/200; ⊠)
With three stars, the Ambassador is known
for its graceful interior and Liberty-style
restaurant serving inspired Italian cuisine.
Breakfast included.

Hôtel de France (☎ 93 30 24 64; hotel-france@monte
-carlo.mc; 6 rue de la Turbie; s/d with bathroom €71/90)
This renovated pad with welcoming recep-
tion desk and bright, comfortable rooms is
a cut above. Breakfast included.

Hôtel Helvetia (☎ 93 30 21 71; hotel-helvetia@monte
-carlo.mc; 1bis rue Grimaldi; s/d from €60/80) A dual entrance means you can spit yourself out on
rue Grimaldi or rue de la Turbie, depending
on where you're going, and the civilised tearoom is open all day. Wheelchair access.

Hôtel Alexandra (☎ 93 50 63 13; www.monaco
-hotel.com/montecarlo/alexandra; 35 blvd Princesse Charlotte; s/d/tr €115/140/170; ⊠) The Alexandra is
on an offputtingly busy intersection, but
inside all is calm and light. Rooms are clean
and soundproofed, although the furnishings feel oddly flimsy.

Tulip Inn Monaco Terminus (☎ 92 05 63 00; www
.terminus.monte-carlo.mc; 9 av Prince Pierre; s/d/tr/q
€150/190/230/270; ⊠) By the old railway station
(hence the 'Terminus'), this is part of the
Tulip Inn international hotel chain. Rooms
are elegant, and there's a decent 2nd-floor
restaurant serving Provençal specialities. A
buffet breakfast is included.

Hôtel Le Versailles (☎ 93 50 79 34; hotelversailles
monaco@hotmail.com; 4-6 av Prince Pierre; s/d from €60/80;
⊠) Right next to the central place d'Armes,
this traditional little hotel offers good-value
rooms. There's a restaurant serving French
and Italian food on the ground floor.

Top End

Hôtel de Paris (☎ 92 16 30 00; hp@sbm.mc; place du
Casino; d from €570; P ⊠ ⊠) This magnificent,
belle époque pad was Monte Carlo's first hotel,
and the place where writer Colette spent her
last years. It was built between 1859 and 1864
on the magical place du Casino, and hosts a
gastronomic temple, Louis XV (see the boxed
text right). Guests receive an SBM Gold Card
on arrival, a fairy wand granting free access
to the casino, Monte-Carlo Beach Club and
Les Thermes Marins, and various discounts.

Hôtel Hermitage (☎ 92 16 40 00; hh@sbm.mc;
square Beaumarchais; d €480) Also owned by SBM,
this luxurious four-star place has an Italian-

inspired façade, pink-marbled restaurant
and full complement of Rolls and Beam-
ers parked outside. It was also the literary
James Bond's hotel of choice.

Hôtel Balmoral (☎ 93 50 62 37; www.hotel-balmoral
.mc; av de la Costa; d €200) Set coolly apart from
the clamour of the casino, the Balmoral,
run by the same family since 1896, has fine
views over the port. The hotel often has
special Internet deals.

EATING
Restaurants

Brasseries that don't break the bank abound
on the pedestrianised rue Princesse Caroline, near the port.

Huit & Demi (☎ 93 50 97 02; 4 rue Langlé; pizza
€10.50-12.50, pasta €11.50-13.50, meat dishes €16-20;
closed Sat lunch & Sun) A chic, clean-cut place
with an industrial interior and fabulous pavement terrace that fills a whole pedestrianised
street off rue Princesse Caroline. Delicious
Italian fare includes fresh, home-made pasta
and a scrummy mixed seafood grill.

Planet-Pasta (☎ 93 50 80 14; 6 rue Imberty; pasta
€10) Overlooking a beautiful little green
square, this bistro is absolutely packed at
lunch time; get there early. It dishes up filling bowls of fusilli, spaghetti, penne, fagio-
lini et al to the hungry crowds.

AUTHOR'S CHOICE

Louis XV (☎ 92 16 29 76; place du Casino;
menus from €150; closed Tue year-round, Wed
out of season & Dec) Reputed to be the best
restaurant on the Riviera, Louis XV, run by
the busy Alain Ducasse, is the height of
sophisticated dining. Set jewel-like inside
the opulent Hôtel de Paris, the dining room,
which looks as though it's been teleported
from 17th-century Versailles, sparkles with
gold. It has a charmingly intimate atmosphere (settings are kept to a mere 50), and
would make the perfect place to dine while
gazing into your loved one's eyes.

Head chef Franck Cerutti uses seasonal
ingredients in his themed French menus,
with dashes of Italy, Bavaria, Scotland and
the Far East to keep things peppy. The restaurant contains the world's largest wine
cellar: 250,000 bottles of wine (many price-
less) stashed in a rock cave. Reservations are
essential, as are jacket and tie for fellas.

MONACO

Bilig Café (☎ 97 77 08 70; 11bis rue Princesse Caroline; dish of the day €11; ☺ closed Sun) Cheap eats, an informal atmosphere and the opportunity to try Monégasque specialities are the attractions at this central spot.

Stars 'n' Bars (☎ 97 97 95 95; www.starsnbars.com; 6 quai Antoine 1er; mains around €15; ☺ closed Mon out of season; ✕) This American bar and restaurant sports one of Monaco's sexiest portside terraces, and is plastered inside with sporting memorabilia. TexMex platters, burgers and wedges of Mom's apple pie are served from 11am to midnight. There's a cyber-caff and supervised children's room, and a midnight-blue nightclub (over-21s only) sometimes patronised by young celebs.

Le Dauphin Vert (☎ 93 30 86 30; 20 rue Princesse Caroline; mains €15; ☺ closed Sun) A notable standout, rustling up salads, pizzas, seafood and meat, as well as fancier dishes for finer palates. It has a small **terrace** (☎ 93 30 73 55) on quai Albert 1er, which sells drinks and snackettes.

Le Bistroquet (☎ 93 50 65 03; www.monte-carlo.mc/bistroquet; 11 galerie Charles III; mains €19-28; ☺ til 5am) The huge, shady terrace is a big draw on summer afternoons, as are the solid portions of regional cuisine. At the weekend, late-night samba sessions and befeathered dancing-girls are for extroverts only.

Bar & Boeuf (☎ 92 16 60 60; b.b@sbm.mc; Le Sporting, 26 av Princesse Grace; full meal around €150; ☺ dinner, closed mid-Sep–mid-May) Crowds of style-setters hobnob within the minimalist wood-and-glass interior designed by Philippe Starck; the hypnotic sea view adds to the feeling of space. A venture of French chef Alain Ducasse, the Bar & Boeuf specialises in just that –*bar* (sea perch) and *boeuf* (beef).

Cafés & Fast Food

Casino supermarket (17 blvd Albert 1er; ☺ 8.30am-midnight Mon-Sat summer, 8.30am-10pm Mon-Sat winter) Contains a Pizza System counter for slices to munch on the move.

Häagen-Dazs (place du Casino) The company runs a great little ice-cream outlet and *salon de thé* (tearoom) in a pavilion in the Jardins du Casino, and another inside the Galerie du Sporting. Prices are steep, though: one/two scoops cost €3.80/6.10 to eat in.

Café de Paris (☎ 92 16 21 24; place du Casino; starters €15, mains €25-50) This café has been in business since 1882, and is *the* place to people-watch in Monte Carlo. Cheese-on-toast on its legendary terrace costs €12.50…make it last!

Café Grand Prix (☎ 93 25 56 90; reservation@café grandprix.com; 1 quai Antoine 1er), This portside pad throbs with drivers' girlfriends and support teams during the Grand Prix.

Carlino's (☎ 97 97 88 88; www.mchoc.com; place de la Visitation) Wash down creamy patisserie creations with a cocktail, or one of dozens of different teas, at this classy chocolatier and *salon de thé*.

ENTERTAINMENT

To find out what's on, turn to *l'essentiel*, a weekly listings magazine covering Monaco (free at the tourist office), or check out www.monaco-spectacle.com (with online booking service). Alternatively, head for the individual box offices of the venues listed in this section, or **FNAC** (☎ 93 10 81 81; www.fnac.com; Centre Commercial Le Métropole, 17 av des Spélugues; ☺ 10am-7.30pm Mon-Sat), which also sells tickets.

Nightclubs & Bars

Pure hedonism and a total disregard for cost are essential ingredients for Monaco's nightlife. Most clubs open from 11pm til dawn; admission is around €16, although women often get in for free.

Sass Café (☎ 93 25 52 00; 11 av Princesse Grace) Hipper-than-hip lounge lizards gather here to dine and jive to live jazz.

Zebra Square (☎ 99 99 25 50; 10 av Princesse Grace) On the top floor of the Grimaldi Forum, this is Monaco's other super-chic drink 'n' dine hang-out. Take one look at its stunning waterside terrace and you'll see why.

Jimmy'z (☎ 92 16 36 36; 26 av Princesse Grace) Inside Le Sporting complex, this is the most famous nightclub in town, complete with Cuban smoking room, top DJs, models and celebrities a-go-go. Drinks cost around €30; make sure your wallet is healthy and turn up fashionably late!

The Living Room (☎ 93 50 80 31; www.mcpam.com; 7 av des Spélugues) This hybrid piano-bar/disco/nightclub has a tough door policy. Dress up nice and be as famous as possible.

Tiffany's (☎ 93 50 53 13; 3 av des Spélugues; ☺ closed Mon & Tue Oct-Apr) Adjoining the Metropole shopping centre, Tiffany's is a popular disco; glittery showgirls turn up on Sunday.

Live Music & Ballet

Le Sporting (☎ 92 16 36 36; www.sportingmontecarlo.com; 26 av Princesse Grace) is Monaco's prime pop-concert and cabaret-show venue. Tickets, around €48/80 with a drink/dinner for concerts and €40/80 for cabarets, are sold at the Café de Paris and FNAC (see opposite).

Performances by the Monte Carlo Philharmonic Orchestra (1863) are held in the **Auditorium Rainier III** inside the **Centre de Congrès Auditorium** (☎ 93 10 85 00; www.opmc.mc; blvd Louis II). Tickets cost €8 to €40. In July and August its venue shifts to the star-topped **Cour d'Honneur** (Courtyard of Honour) at the Palais du Prince. Tickets (€18 to €75), sold

at the **Atrium du Casino** (☎ 92 16 22 99; place du Casino; ☻ 10am-5.30pm Tue-Sun), inside the casino, are like gold dust.

The ballet and orchestra also perform in the **Salles des Princes** at the **Grimaldi Forum** (☎ 99 99 30 00; www.grimaldiforum.mc; 10 av Princesse Grace) – see p326.

The **Salle Garnier** (1892), adjoining Monte Carlo Casino, is the permanent home of the Monte Carlo opera and ballet companies. It's an absolutely sumptuous confection of

---

THE FORMULA ONE GRAND PRIX

If there's one trophy a Formula One driver would like to have on the mantelpiece, it would have to be from the most glamorous race of the season, the Monaco Grand Prix. This race has everything. Its spectators are the most sensational: the merely wealthy survey the spectacle from the Hôtel Hermitage, the really rich watch from their luxury yachts moored in the harbour, while the Grimaldis see the start and finish from the royal box at the port. Then there's the setting: the cars scream around the very centre of the city, racing uphill from the start/finish line to place du Casino, then downhill around a tight hairpin and two sharp rights to hurtle through a tunnel and run along the harbourside to a chicane and more tight corners before the start/finish. To top it all off there's the race's history: it was first run in 1929, and the winners' list features a roll-call of racing greats right down to Michael Schumacher's five victories between 1994 and 2001, although recently he's not been so lucky at Monaco.

But despite its reputation, the Monaco Grand Prix is not really one of the great races. The track is simply too tight and winding for modern Grand Prix cars, and overtaking is virtually impossible. The Brazilian triple world champion Nelson Piquet famously described racing at Monaco as like 'riding a bicycle around your living room'. Piquet clearly rides a much faster bicycle than most of us; Monaco may be the slowest race on the calendar, but the lap record is still over 160km/h and at the fastest point on the circuit they reach 280km/h. Even the corner in the gloom of the tunnel is taken at 250km/h (over 150 m/h).

Over the years the race has featured some unexpected surprises. In 1955 Alberto Ascari's Lancia was about to take the lead from Englishman Stirling Moss' silver Mercedes when the Italian arrived at the chicane travelling too fast, shot through the straw bales (this was more than 20 years before modern Armco barriers arrived on the scene) and plunged straight into the harbour. Seconds later the twice-world champion bobbed to the surface with only minor injuries. Remarkably the feat was repeated 10 years later at exactly the same spot. That time it was Australian driver Paul Hawkins who drove into the harbour in his Lotus. If spinning into the harbour was still possible the unlucky driver probably wouldn't have to walk too far to find some dry clothes – typically 10 to 12 (of the 20 to 24) Grand Prix drivers actually live in Monaco.

The track may be slow and overtaking may be difficult, but the circuit has still seen some great races, particularly in 1961 when Stirling Moss (the greatest driver never to win a world championship) held off the might of Ferrari in his under-powered Lotus. I've been to the Monaco Grand Prix just once, but fortuitously I also chose a classic year. In 1970 Austrian driver Jochen Rindt overtook Australian Jack Brabham on the final corner of the race. Later in the year Rindt was killed at the Italian Grand Prix at Monza, but no-one was able to surpass his points total and he became Formula One's only posthumous world champion.

The 78-lap race takes place on a Sunday afternoon in late May, the conclusion of several days of practice, qualifying and supporting races. Tickets are available from the **Automobile Club de Monaco** (☎ 93 15 26 24; www.acm.mc; 23 blvd Albert 1er). Prices range from around €50 for general admission to €300 and up for grandstand seats. Monaco residents with terrace views often rent out spaces during the Grand Prix week and some restaurants overlooking the circuit book lunch with a view.

Tony Wheeler

neoclassical splendour, but is expected to remain closed for renovation until late 2005.

A jacket and tie for men is obligatory at all performances (except Le Sporting pop concerts).

Cinemas

Cinéma Le Sporting (French number ☎ 08 36 68 00 72; www.cinemasporting.com; place du Casino; adult/ student, senior or under 20 €9/5.50) shows original-language films daily. Weekday matinee screenings are cheaper.

The New Open-Air Cinema (Cinéma d'Été; ☎ 93 25 86 80; Terrasses du Parking-des-Pêcheurs), the largest outdoor screen in Europe, shows films in English at 9.30pm from July to mid-September: for the programme, see the *cinéma d'été* link on www.cinemasporting.com.

Theatre

The interior of the **Théâtre Princesse Grace** (☎ 93 25 32 27; www.tpgmonaco.com; 12 rue d'Ostende) was designed by Grace Kelly. Tickets vary according to the performance, but cost roughly adult/under 21 years €40/20.

The charming **Théâtre du Fort Antoine** (☎ 93 15 80 00; av de la Quarantaine) is an open-air theatre in an early-18th-century fortress. Free plays and musical concerts are staged in July and August – ask the tourist office for details.

Sport

FOOTBALL

Football team AS Monaco play at **Stade Louis II** (Louis II Stadium; ☎ 92 05 40 11; stadlouis2@gouv.mc; 3 av des Castelans) in Fontvieille; tickets are sold from the **ticket office** (☎ 92 05 74 73; ☿ 9am-7pm) inside. Forty-five minute **guided tours** (adult/under 12 yrs €4/2; ☿ twice daily Mon, Tue, Thu & Fri) of the stadium are available in English.

See opposite for footy-related gifts.

MOTOR SPORT

The legendary **Monte Carlo Rally** kicks off in January. This high-octane three-day race is a series of timed stages, starting and finishing at Port de Monaco and ripping through Haute-Provence in between. The traditional night stage and the concentration run, where drivers set off from various European cities to meet in Monte Carlo (like Disney's on-screen VW Beetle Herbie in the 1970s), were scrapped in 1997. The scent of singed tyres also fills the air at the **Monaco Formula One Grand Prix**, held in May: see p331. More information about both races can be found at www.acm .mc. See opposite for F1-related gifts.

SHOPPING

Essential reading for fashion aficionados is the annual 150-page *Monaco Shopping* guide, free from the tourist office. Designer clothes are Monégasques' chief weapon: tool up at a dizzying array of big-name couturiers.

Antiques

Auction house **Sotheby's** (place du Casino) keeps a clutch of antique galleries company in the Galerie du Sporting shopping centre.

Clothes

This area, with its array of luxury shops, is known as the 'Golden Circle'. Kick-start your spree on the av des Beaux Arts, on the western side of the casino gardens, where you can swirl through Cartier, Chanel, Christian-Dior, Céline, Louis Vuitton, Yves St-Laurent and Swiss watch-maker Piaget in one fell swoop. Bow down at the altar of Italian fashion house Prada, inside Hôtel Hermitage.

Av de Monte Carlo, just downhill from place du Casino, is a short-but-chic street where Gucci, Valentino, Hermès, Lalique and Prada display their tantalising wares.

Blvd des Moulins in Larvotto is another quality clothing extravaganza. Costume jeweller **Divina & Co** (☎ 93 50 52 47; divina@monaco-center.com) sells a fantastic array of fantasy gems and accessories at No 36. One for the chaps, **Hugo Boss** (☎ 93 25 25 02) struts his stuff down the road at No 39. A few doors along at No 31, indoctrinate your kids (from one month to 12 years) into the world of fashion at the **Baby Dior Boutique** (☎ 93 25 72 12).

Food & Wine

Gourmands should try upmarket grocer **Caves & Gourmandises** (☎ 97 70 54 94; 25 blvd Albert 1er).

L'Oenothèque (Galerie du Sporting) is an opulent wine and champagne cellar.

MONACO MARKET

Surely one dines out in five-star luxury every night of the week? If not, Monaco's **covered market** (place d'Armes, La Condamine; ☿ 6am-1pm) is a colourful riot of vegetables, herbs, fruit and flowers...and a prime people-watching spot.

SPORTY SHOPPING

On rue Grimaldi, football and F1 fans can bring their heroes closer through commerce. The **ASM Monaco Pro Shop** (☎ 97 77 74 74; 16 rue Grimaldi) peddles red-and-white products to footy-team followers, from shorts and shirts to ashtrays and champagne flutes.

Petrol-heads should drop into **Boutique Formule 1** (☎ 93 15 92 44; 15 rue Grimaldi), stuffed to the rafters with posters, watches, cigarette lighters, toilet seats etc by Porsche Design and Ferrari. Alternatively, buy the official Automobile Club de Monaco T-shirt at **L@ Boutique** (☎ 97 70 45 35; laboutique@acm .mc; 46 rue Grimaldi).

Furniture
Galerie Riccadonna (7 rue Grimaldi) sells fabulously funky, one-off pieces of designer furniture.

GETTING THERE & AWAY
There are no border formalities upon entering Monaco from France.

Air
The nearest airport is Nice-Côte d'Azur: see p351 for travelling to Nice.

Monaco's helicopter companies are **Héli Air Monaco** (☎ 92 05 00 50; www.heliairmonaco.com) and **Monacair** (☎ 97 97 39 01; www.monacair.mc), based at **Héliport de Monaco** (☎ 92 05 00 10; av des Ligures). They can whirl you anywhere along the coast, including to and from Nice airport (around €70 one way, excluding airport taxes; at least 20 flights per day during summer).

Bus
For airport buses, see Getting Around, right.

Bus No 100 runs along the Corniche Inférieure (see p228) between Nice and Menton, stopping in Monaco. However, the train is much cheaper and faster.

Car & Motorcycle
The Corniche Moyenne (N7) links Monaco to the A8. For Italy, look for signs indicating Gênes (Genova in Italian).

Train
Monaco train station is at the northern end of blvd Rainier III; enter via the tunnels and escalators from av Prince Pierre or the northern end of rue Grimaldi.

Trains to and from Monaco are run by France's **SNCF** (in France ☎ 08 92 35 35 35; www.sncf .fr). Taking the train along the coast is highly recommended – there's a frequent service, and the sea and the mountains are a magnificent sight. Trains run east to Menton (€1.80, 15 minutes) and Ventimiglia (Vintimille in French; €3.10, 25 minutes), in Italy. For trains to Nice (€3.10, 20 minutes) and onward connections to other towns, see p225.

GETTING AROUND
To/From the Airport
Nice-based **Rapides Côte d'Azur** (☎ 04 93 85 64 44; www.rca.tm.fr) operates daily buses between Monaco and Nice-Côte d'Azur airport (€14.40 one way, 45 minutes). Buses leave at 40 minutes past the hour from Terminal 2, 45 minutes past from Terminal 1, and 55 minutes past from the Casino stop.

Bicycle
MBK (☎ 93 50 10 80; 7 rue de Millo; ☿ 8am-noon & 2-7pm Mon-Fri, 8am-noon Sat) rents road/mountain bikes from €8/12 per day, as well as 50cc/80cc scooters costing from €25/35 per 24 hours.

Bus
Monaco's urban bus system has six lines. Line No 2 links Monaco Ville with Monte Carlo and then loops back to the Jardin Exotique. Line No 4 links the train station with the tourist office, the casino and Larvotto beach. A one-way ticket/one-day pass costs €1.40/3.40. Alternatively, buy a four-/eight-ride magnetic card (€3.40/5.45) from the bus driver or from vending machines at most bus stops. An eight-ride card taking in Monaco and Beausoleil costs €6. Buses run from 7.30am to 9pm.

The local bus company, **Compagnie des Autobus de Monaco** (CAM; ☎ 97 70 22 22; www .cam.mc; 3 av Président JF Kennedy; ☿ 8.30am-noon & 2-5.35pm Mon-Thu, 8.30am-noon & 2-5pm Fri), has its office on the port's northern side.

Lift (Elevator)
One of Monaco's most unusual features is the system of escalators and public lifts (marked on the free maps from the tourist office) linking the steep streets. Most operate 24 hours; some run from 6am to midnight or 1am.

Taxi
Order a taxi on ☎ 93 15 01 01 (24 hours).

MONACO

Directory

CONTENTS

ACCOMMODATION

Accommodation is notorious for being France's most expensive, but with a bit of planning and consideration of all the options, it is not unaffordable.

Budget options in this guide command around €25/35 a night for a double hotel room with shared/private shower and toilet. Mid-range options cover the €50 to €70 price range; and top end entails anything upwards of €80. With the exception of *chambre d'hôte* (B&B) accommodation, rates don't include breakfast.

In July and August don't even contemplate the coast unless you have a reservation or are prepared to pay a fortune for the few rooms available. The exception is rock-bottom budget accommodation, especially in Nice, which rarely gets booked up weeks in advance – but is full most days by noon. Tourist offices can tell you where rooms are available. Some mid-range hotels only accept reservations accompanied by a credit card number. Most budget joints demand payment upon arrival.

Local authorities impose a tourist tax *(taxe de séjour)* on each visitor in their jurisdiction, usually only enforced in the high season (Easter to September). At this time prices charged are €0.20 to €1.50 per person higher than posted rates.

Camping

The region has camp sites galore, most open March or April to September or October.

Stars reflect facilities and amenities. Separate tariffs are charged for people, tents or caravans, and vehicles. Many places have *forfaits* (fixed-price deals) for two people with tent and car. Camp-site receptions are often closed during the day; the best time to call is early morning or evening.

Camping à la ferme (camping on the farm) is coordinated by Gîtes de France (see p336).

Wild camping *(camping sauvage)* is illegal but tolerated in some places. Some hostels (like the Relais International de la Jeunesse on Cap d'Antibes) allow travellers to pitch in the back garden.

Chambres & Maisons d'Hôtes

A *chambre d'hôte* is a B&B, the most upmarket of which occasionally tag themselves as *maisons d'hôtes*. Breakfast is included in the price, and many places serve dinner for €15 to €30 more. Many are in beautiful chateaux, farmhouses or *moulins* (mills) and are highly sought-after.

Tourist offices have lists of *chambres d'hôtes;* some are listed in the annual catalogues published by Gîtes de France (see p336) and there are many more in Editions Rivages' *Maisons d'Hôtes de Charme* (€22;

www.guidesdecharme.com), an excellent national guide – with its entire contents online – which lists upmarket B&Bs.

Avignon & Provence (www.avignon-et-provence.com) is an exceptional online accommodation guide.

Chateaux

There are several wine-growing estates *(domaines viticoles)* – invariably arranged around a gorgeous chateau – in the Côtes de Provence wine region where you can stay. In addition to a comfortable bed, hearty breakfast and, upon request, an evening meal of fabulous proportions, many let you taste wine and tour their vineyards. Maison des Vins in Les Arcs-sur-Argens (p297) has a list.

Should you wish to buy a chateau or *domaine viticole* of your own, contact **Le Bureau Viticole** (☎ 04 90 92 48 74; www.bureauviticole.fr; 10 blvd Mirabeau, 13210 St-Rémy de Provence), a specialist estate agent run by upmarket real-estate agent **Émile Garcin** (www.emilegarcin.fr), with offices in St-Rémy de Provence, Mougins and Ménerbes.

The Riveria's *belle époque* follies, celebrity real estate and various other properties of dreamy proportions are handled by **John Taylor** (www.john-taylor.fr).

Hostels

There are hostels along the coast at Cap d'Antibes (p260), Cap d'Ail (p232), Cassis (p91), Cannes (p249), Fréjus-St-Raphaël (p275), Le Trayas (p273), Marseille (p79), Menton (p238), Nice (p219), Saignon near Apt (p180) and Stes-Maries de la Mer (p116); in the mountains at La Foux d'Allos (p119), La Palud-sur-Verdon (p188) and Manosque (p183); and towards the west in Aix-en-Provence (p99), Arles (p112), Nîmes (p160) and Fontaine de Vaucluse (p150).

Expect to pay €10 per night, plus €3/3.50/9 for sheets/breakfast/dinner. Not all hostels have kitchen facilities. Most don't accept telephone reservations.

Affiliates of the **Fédération Unie des Auberges de Jeunesse** (FUAJ; www.fuaj.org) and the **Ligue Française pour les Auberges de Jeunesse** (LFAJ; www.auberges-de-jeunesse.com) require an HI card.

Hotels

Hotels have one to four stars and charge €6 (budget and mid-range) to €25 (top end) per person for breakfast. Rooms with bathtubs cost more than rooms with showers. Beds usually tout neck-aching, hot-dog-shaped bolsters – find regular pillows *(oreillers)* hidden in a cupboard in the room.

PRACTICALITIES

- France uses the metric system for weights and measures.

- Plugs have two round pins (bring an international adapter) and the electric current is 220V at 50Hz AC.

- Videos in France work on the PAL system.

- Pick up regional news, views, chat and gossip with the Monte Carlo-based, English-language Riviera Radio (106.3MHz FM in Monaco, 106.5MHz FM in France; www.rivieraradio.mc); and the BBC World Service with Radio France Internationale (RFI; 100.5MHz FM and 100.9MHz FM; www.rfi.fr).

- French radio stations include Radio Provence (103.6MHz and 102.9MHz FM), Radio Vaucluse (100.4MHz FM), Radio Lubéron (88.6MHz FM) and Cannes Radio (91.5MHz FM).

- Read regional news in French in *Nice Matin* (www.nicematin.fr) and *La Provence* (www.laprovence-presse.fr); and in English in the *Riviera Reporter* (www.riviera-reporter.com) and *Riviera Times* (www.rivieratimes.com).

- Glossy English-French mags worth a beach-read include the quarterly, 250-plus-page *Nice Riviera Magazine* (€6), a mainly fashion-driven magazine with sleeping and eating reviews, a strong arts section, social diary and plenty of gossip; and *Côte Magazine* (€2.30), great for uncovering the season's hottest dining and partying spots.

- Switch on the box with private French TV stations TF1 and M6; or state-run France 2, France 3 and 5 (Arte after 7pm).

In many hotels single rooms don't exist as such; rather, doubles are flogged as singles. Triples and quads often have two double beds. Out of season, most hotels close for at least two weeks for their *congé annuel* (annual closure). Ski resort hotels in Haute-Provence only open for the winter ski season and a couple of months in summer for walkers.

Budget hotels tend to charge the same rates year-round. Move into the mid-range price bracket and there are three sets of seasonally adjusted prices – low-season (October/November to February/March), mid-season (March to May and September/October) and high season (June to September). Certain festivals (Festival d'Avignon, p129; the Nîmes *férias*, p160) bump up prices beyond belief. Reliable bets in the mid-range price range are hotels affiliated to **Logis de France** (www.logisdefrance.com).

Many four-star hotels languish in traditional properties: farmhouses, monasteries *(monastères)*, oil mills *(moulins à huile)*, priories *(prieurés)* or restored Cistercian abbeys *(abbayes)*. Lakes, rose gardens and olive groves pepper the vast grounds of these exclusive estates where a night's sleep costs anything upwards of €150. **Châteaux & Hotels de France** (www.chateauxhotels.com) and **Relais & Châteaux** (www.relaischateaux.fr) are two umbrella organisations under which these exclusive and expensive hotels often fall.

Refuges & Gîtes d'Étapes

This accommodation studs the Parc National de Mercantour and Haute-Provence where undeveloped rural areas still exist.

Gîtes d'étapes (basic dorm rooms) tend to be in towns and villages popular with walkers and climbers; *refuges* (simple mountain shelters) are in isolated wildernesses, often accessible only on foot.

Both are basic and equipped with bunks, mattresses and blankets, but not sheets. Nightly rates start at €10 per person. Cooked meals are occasionally available.

To reserve a *refuge* bed contact the **Club Alpin Français des Alpes-Maritimes** (Map pp212-14; ☎ 04 93 62 59 99; http://cafnice.org in French; 14 av Mirabeau, F-06000 Nice).

Rental Accommodation

Tourist offices have lists of self-catering studios, apartments and villas to rent on a short- (one week) or long-term (several

months) basis. The most sought-after properties are booked a year in advance.

Many extra-charming *gîtes ruraux* (self-catering accommodation) – a century-old *mas* (Provençal farmhouse) in an olive grove or cherry tree orchard, say, or converted farm stables surrounded by a menagerie of farmyard animals – are represented by **Gîtes de France** (www.gites-de-france.com), an organisation that liaises between owners and renters. Amenities range from basic bathroom facilities and a simple kitchenette (with oven, hot plates and fridge) to a bathroom, fully equipped kitchen, washing machine, TV, telephone, garden and pool. Linen is never provided, but can be rented. *Gîtes panda* are in regional and national parks.

Bookings can be made online or through a Gîtes de France office:

Alpes de Haute-Provence (☎ 04 92 31 30 40; www .gites-de-france-04.fr in French; rond-point du 11 Novembre, BP 201, 04000 Digne-les-Bains)

Alpes-Maritimes (Map pp212-14; ☎ 04 92 15 21 30; www.guideriviera.com/gites06; 55-57 promenade des Anglais, BP 1602, 06011 Nice)

Bouches du Rhône (☎ 04 90 59 49 39; www.visit provence.com; Domaine du Vergon, 13370 Mallemort)

Var (☎ 04 94 50 93 93; www.gites-de-france-var.fr in French; rond-point du 4 Decembre 1974, BP 215, 83006 Draguignan)

Vaucluse (Map pp128-9; ☎ 04 90 85 45 00; www .gites-de-france-vaucluse.asso.fr in French; place Campana, BP 164, 84008 Avignon)

ACTIVITIES

The wealth of outdoor activities on offer in the region is tremendous; see p37.

BUSINESS HOURS

On Sunday, a bakery is usually about all that opens (morning only) and public transport services are less frequent. In villages, shops (including bakeries) close for a long lunch between 2pm and 4pm. Hotels, restaurants, cinemas, cultural institutions and shops close for their *congé annuel* in winter.

Some hotels, museums and *chambres d'hôtes* only open *Pâques à la Tous-saint* (Easter to All Saints' Day, 1 November). Many places to eat and/or drink in Nice and Marseille brandish 'open nonstop' signs. Far from meaning they open 24 hours, it simply means the place doesn't close for lunch.

Standard hours for commercial banks, museums, pharmacies, post offices, shops, restaurants and supermarkets are listed on the Quick Reference page on the inside back cover. Places to eat close for two consecutive days a week, often Sunday, Monday and/or Tuesday. Opening hours for bars, pubs and clubs fluctuate wildly.

CHILDREN
Practicalities
Most car-rental firms hire children's car seats for around €30 per rental, but the concept of organising a car seat in a taxi is an alien one.

Many hotels can provide cots (free) or an extra bed (€15 to €40), but families travelling with younger children will find *chambre d'hôte* (p334) accommodation more hospitable. Pick one that serves evening meals too, allowing you to feast in peace while the kids sleep upstairs with a baby monitor (bring your own). For kiddie-dining practicalities see p61.

Cobbled streets, ultra-narrow pavements in old towns and bumper-to-bumper parked cars can make strolling with a pushchair something of an obstacle course. Supermarkets and pharmacies sell disposable nappies (diapers) and high-factor sun protection creams.

Tourist offices maintain lists of baby sitters and crèches. For region-specific information read *Le Curieux, Monaco/French Riviera for Families* by Helen Misseri and Elisabeth Moati, a bilingual French-English book written by two mothers living on the coast. Lonely Planet's *Travel with Children* is a general resource.

Sights & Activities
Kids are well-catered for: a huge amusement park in Biot (p262), giant waterslides at the Niagara Parc Nautique near La Môle (p301), and tortoises at the Village des Tortues in the Massif des Maures (p301) are but some of the ways to win the heart of a howling child. Museum-wise, try Monaco's Musée Océanographique (p324) and the Grande Expo du Pont du Gard (p163) with its kid-friendly Ludo centre.

Horse riding in the Camargue (p107), canoeing beneath the Pont du Gard (p163), cycling around the island of Porquerolles (there are pedal-powered chariots for kids too small to pedal themselves; p306), snorkelling off Port-Cros' shores (p307),

Rollerblading in Nice and Marseille (p78) or skiing in Haute-Provence (p198) are outdoor highlights. The Parc National du Mercantour (p197) and Office National des Forêts (ONF) organise nature walks for children.

CLIMATE CHARTS
Mistral aside (p32), the region enjoys a temperate climate with mild winters. For climatic considerations see p9.

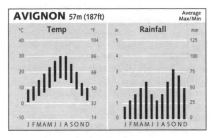

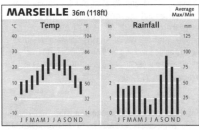

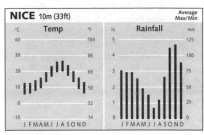

COURSES
Cookery courses are big; see p62.

Language
There are dozens of French language schools; tourist offices have lists.

Alliance Française Marseille (off Map pp72-3; ☎ 04 96 10 24 60; www.alliancefrmarseille.org; 310 rue Paradis, 13008 Marseille) Two-/four-week courses with 20 hours tuition per week (€260/520) plus one week of sailing/diving (€100/190).

Alliance Française Nice (Map pp212-14; ☎ 04 93 62 67 66; www.alliance-francaise-nice.com; 2 rue de Paris, 06000 Nice) Extensive/intensive courses (two/four hours' tuition per day), evening classes, private lessons and speciality courses (literature, business etc).

Association de Langue Française d'Avignon (☎ 04 90 85 86 24; www.alfavignon.com; 4 impasse Romagnoli, 84000 Avignon) Two-week course with 15 hours tuition/week (€460) and B&B accommodation (€107/week).

Centre Méditerranéen d'Études Françaises (☎ 04 93 78 21 59; www.monte-carlo.mc/centremed; chemin des Oliviers, 06320 Cap-Ail) School dating to 1952 with open-air amphitheatre designed by Cocteau; two-week courses €400/880 with no accommodation/half-board in a hotel.

Crea Langues (☎ 04 92 77 74 58; www.crealangues .com; Monastère de Segres, 04360 Moustiers-Ste-Marie) Language training in a cloistered monastery, with hiking/canyoning/cycling options (€90-135); one-/two-week course €665/995 plus €283/610 for full-board monastery accommodation.

International House (☎ 04 93 62 60 62; www.ih-nice .com; 62 rue Gioffredo, 06000 Nice) Two-week course with 50 lessons (45 minutes) for €500, plus €61 enrolment fee.

Université Paul Cézanne d'Aix Marseille III (Université d'Aix Marseille III; ☎ 04 42 21 70 90; www .univ.u-3mrs.fr/cgi-bin/WebObjects/SiteAix in French; 23 rue Gaston de Saporta, 13625 Aix-en-Provence) Four-week intensive course (€950) at the university's Institute of French Studies for Foreign Students.

Arts & Crafts

Hôtel Les Ateliers de l'Image (Map p152; ☎ 04 90 92 51 50; www.hotelphoto.com; 36 blvd Victor Hugo, 13210 St-Rémy de Provence) English-French photography workshops.

Usine Mathieu Okhra (☎ 04 90 05 66 69; www.okhra .com in French; 84220 Roussillon) Imaginative paper dying, wall-mural painting and wood-craft workshops using traditional techniques and natural dyes and pigments, extracted from the village's ochre earth (€100/85/70 for the 1st/2nd/3rd day).

CUSTOMS

Goods brought in and exported within the EU incur no additional taxes, provided duty has been paid somewhere within the EU and the goods are for personal consumption. There is no more duty-free shopping within the EU either; you have to be leaving Europe to benefit.

Coming from non-EU countries, duty-free allowances for adults are 200 cigarettes, 50 cigars, 1L of spirits, 2L of wine, 50g of perfume, 250ml of toilet water and other goods up to €183. Anything over these limits must be declared and paid for.

DANGERS & ANNOYANCES

Beaches

Larger beaches on the Côte d'Azur have a *poste de secours* (safety post) during the beach season, staffed by lifeguards. In water-sport areas a section of the sea is always sectioned off for swimmers. Note the colour of the flag flying before diving in: green means it is safe to swim; yellow means bathing is risky; red means that swimming is forbidden; and purple means the water is polluted.

Extreme Weather

During the balmy days of June and the steamy days of July/August, it is hard to believe that the region can be freezing cold when the mistral (p32) strikes.

Thunderstorms in the mountains and hot southern plains can be sudden, violent and dangerous. Check the weather report before embarking on a long walk; even then, be prepared for a sudden change in the weather. Storms are common in August and September.

Forest Fires

Forest fires are common in July and August when the sun is hot and the land is dry. Such fires spread incredibly quickly – between 20m and 30m per minute. Between 1 July and the second Sunday in September, forest authorities close high-risk areas. Never walk in a closed zone. Tourist offices can tell you if a walking path is closed. If you come across a fire, call the **fire brigade** (☎ 18).

Forests are crisscrossed with road tracks enabling fire crews to penetrate quickly. These roads, signposted DFCI (*défense forestière contre l'incendie*), are closed to private vehicles but you can follow them on foot.

Lighting a campfire is forbidden. Barbecues, even in private gardens, are forbidden in many areas in July and August.

Poisonous Mushrooms

Wild-mushroom picking is a national pastime. Pick by all means, but don't eat anything until it has been positively identified as safe by a pharmacist. Most pharmacies in the region offer a mushroom-identification service.

Rivers & Lakes

Major rivers are connected to hydroelectric power stations operated by the national electricity company, Electricité de France (EDF). Water levels rise dramatically if the EDF opens a dam. White-water sports on the Verdon River downstream of the Chaudanne Dam are forbidden when the water flow is less than 5 cubic metres/sec. For information on water levels and dam releases call ☎ 04 92 83 62 68.

Swimming is prohibited in lakes that are artificial and have steep, unstable banks (ie Lac de Ste-Croix, southwest of the Gorges du Verdon; and Lac de Castillon and the adjoining Lac de Chaudanne, northeast of the gorges). Sailing, windsurfing and canoeing are restricted to flagged areas.

Theft

Theft – from backpacks, pockets, cars, trains, laundrettes, beaches – is a problem, particularly along the Côte d'Azur. Keep an eagle eye on your bags, especially at train and bus stations, on overnight train rides, in tourist offices and on beaches.

Always keep your money, credit cards, tickets, passport, driving licence and other important documents in a money belt worn inside your trousers or skirt. Keep enough money for the day in a separate wallet. Theft from hotel rooms is less common but it's still not a great idea to leave your life's belongings in your room. In hostels lock your non-valuables in a locker provided and cart your valuables along. Upmarket hotels have safes (coffres).

When swimming at the beach or taking a dip in the pool, have members of your party take turns sitting with packs and clothes. On the Prado beaches in Marseille, keeping your valuables in one of the free (staffed) lockers provided is a good idea.

Motorists in Marseille should always keep their doors locked when stopped at red traffic lights; it is not unheard of for aspiring bandits to open the door to your car, ask you what the time is and, at the same time, scan you and your car for valuables.

DISABLED TRAVELLERS

The region is gradually becoming more user-friendly for handicapés (people with disabilities), but kerb ramps remain rare, older public facilities and budget hotels lack lifts, and the cobblestone streets typical to hilltop villages are a nightmare to navigate in a fauteuil rouant (wheelchair).

But all is not lost. Many two- or three-star hotels are equipped with lifts. On the coast there are beaches – flagged handiplages on city maps – with wheelchair access in Cannes, Marseille, Nice, Hyères, Ste-Maxime and Monaco.

International airports offer assistance to travellers with disabilities. TGV and regular trains are also accessible for passengers in wheelchairs; call the **SNCF Accessibilité Service** (☎ 0 800 154 753) for information. Its brochure (with one page in English), Le Mémento du Voyageur à Mobilité Réduite, is a useful guide.

DISCOUNT CARDS
Billets Jumelés

Many museums and monuments sell billets jumelés (combination tickets), which cover admission to more than one sight and offer a considerable saving. Some cities have museum passes that cut sightseeing costs further.

Carte Musées Côte d'Azur

The Carte Musées Côte d'Azur (French Riviera Museum Pass) gives card-holders unlimited admission to 65 museums along the coast. A one-/three-day pass costs €10/17 (no reduced rates) and a seven-day pass valid for seven days within a 15-day period is €27. Passes are sold at museums, tourist offices and FNAC stores.

Hostel Card

You need an annual Hostelling International (HI) card to stay at official youth hostels, although some let you in with a one-night stamp (€1.50). HI cards costing €10.70/15.25 for those under/over 26 are sold at HI-affiliated hostels and national **Youth Hostelling Associations** (YHA; www.iyhf.org).

Seniors Card

Those aged over 60 or 65 are entitled to discounts on public transport, museum admission fees, public theatres and so on. The Société Nationale des Chemins de Fer (SNCF) issues the Carte Senior (€45) to those aged over 60, which gives reductions of 25% to 50% on train tickets, valid for one year.

Student, Youth & Teacher Cards

An International Student Identity Card (ISIC) costs €10 and pays for itself through half-price admissions and discounted air and ferry tickets etc. Many stockists stipulate a maximum age, usually 24 or 25.

If you're under 26 but not a student you can buy an International Youth Travel Card (IYTC; €12), which entitles you to much the same discounts as an ISIC.

Teachers, professional artists, museum conservators and journalists are admitted to some museums free. Bring proof of affiliation, for example, an International Teacher Identity Card (ITIC; €17) or official press card.

All three cards are administered by the **International Student Travel Confederation** (www .istc.org) and issued by student travel agencies and online at www.carteisic.com. Within the region try branches of **OTU Voyages** (www .otu.fr in French) in **Aix-en-Provence** (☎ 04 42 27 76 85; av Jules Ferry) or **Nice** (off Map pp212-14; ☎ 04 93 96 85 43; 80 blvd Éduard Herriot).

EMBASSIES & CONSULATES
French Embassies & Consulates

See www.france.diplomatie.fr for a complete listing of French diplomatic and consular representatives abroad.

Australia Canberra (☎ 02-6216 0100; www.ambafrance -au.org; 6 Perth Ave, Yarralumla, ACT 2600) Sydney Consulate (☎ 02-9261 5779; www.consulfrance-sydney.org; 20th fl, St Martin's Tower, 31 Market St, NSW 2000)
Belgium Brussels (☎ 02 54 887 11; www.ambafrance -be.org; 65 rue Ducale, 1000) Brussels Consulate (☎ 02 22 985 00; www.consulfrance-bruxelles.org in French; 12a place de Louvain, 1000)
Canada Ottawa (☎ 613-789 1795; www.ambafrance -ca.org; 42 Sussex Drive, Ottawa, Ont K1M 2C9) Toronto Consulate (☎ 416-925 8041; www.consulfrance-toronto .org; 130 Bloor West, Suite 400, Ont M5S 1N5)
Germany Berlin (☎ 030-590 039 000; www.botschaft -frankreich.de in German & French; Parizer Platz 5, 10117) Munich Consulate (☎ 089-419 41 10; Möhlstrasse 5, 81675)
Ireland Dublin (☎ 01-217 5000; www.ambafrance -ie.org; 36 Ailesbury Rd, Ballsbridge, 4)
Italy Rome (☎ 066 86 011; www.ambafrance-it.org; Piazza Farnese 67, 00186)
Netherlands The Hague (☎ 0703-12 58 00; www .ambafrance-nl.org in Dutch & French; Smidsplein 1, 2514 BT) Amsterdam Consulate (☎ 0205-30 69 69; www .consulfrance-amsterdam.org in Dutch & French; Vijzel- gracht 2, 1017 HR)
New Zealand Wellington (☎ 04-384 2555; www.amba france-nz.org; Rural Bank Building, 34-42 Manners St)
South Africa Pretoria (☎ 012-425 1600; www.amba france-rsa.org; 250 Melk Street, New Muckleneuk, 0181)

Spain Madrid (☎ 91 423 89 00; Calle de Salustiano, Olozaga 9, 28001) Barcelona Consulate (☎ 93 270 30 00; www.consulfrance-barcelone.org in French; Ronda Universitat 22, 08007)
Switzerland Berne (☎ 031 359 21 11; Schosshaldenstrasse 46, 3006) Geneva Consulate (☎ 022 319 00 00; www.consul france-geneve.org in French; 11 rue Imbert Galloix, 1205)
UK London (☎ 020-7073 1000; www.ambafrance-uk.org; 58 Knightsbridge, SW1X 7JT) London Consulate (☎ 020- 7073 1200; 21 Cromwell Rd, London SW7 2EN) Visa Section (☎ 020-7838 2051; 6A Cromwell Place, London SW7 2EW)
USA Washington (☎ 202-944 6000; 4101 Reservoir Rd NW, DC 20007) New York Consulate (☎ 212-606 3600/89; www.consulfrance-newyork.org; 934 Fifth Ave, NY 10021) San Francisco Consulate (☎ 415-397 4330; www.consul france-sanfrancisco.org; 540 Bush St, CA 94108)

Monégasque Embassies

Diplomatic missions abroad include:
Belgium (☎ 02-217 9140; 118-126 blvd Adolphe May, B-1000 Brussels)
Spain (☎ 91 319 93 17; Calle Miguel Angel 19, ES-28010 Madrid)
Switzerland (☎ 022 708 01 01; 4 cours des Bastions, CH-1205 Geneva)
USA (☎ 212-286 0500; www.monaco-consulate.com; 565 Fifth Ave, 23rd Floor, New York NY 10017)

Consulates in Provence & Monaco

Foreign embassies are in Paris but most countries have a consulate in Nice, Marseille and/or Monaco:
Belgium Marseille (☎ 04 96 10 11 16; 75 cours Pierre Puget) Nice (Map pp212-14; ☎ 04 93 87 79 56; 5 rue Gabriel Fauré) Monaco (☎ 377-93 50 59 89; 13 av des Castelans)
Canada Nice (Map pp212-14; ☎ 04 93 92 93 22; 10 rue Lamartine) Monaco (Map pp322-3; ☎ 377-97 70 62 42; Palaid de la Scala, Bureau No 1178, 1 av Henri Dunant)
France Monaco (off Map pp322-3; ☎ 377-92 16 54 60; www.consulatfrance.mc in French; 1 rue du Ténao)
Germany Marseille (☎ 04 91 16 75 20; 338 av du Prado) Nice (off Map pp212-14; ☎ 04 93 83 55 25; Le Mino- taure, 34 av Henri Matisse) Monaco (☎ 377-97 97 49 65; spaethe@monaco377.com; 13 blvd Princesse Charlotte)
Ireland Cap d'Antibes (☎ 04 93 61 50 63; 152 blvd John Fitzgerald Kennedy)
Italy Marseille (☎ 04 91 18 49 18; 56 rue d'Alger) Nice (☎ 04 93 14 40 96; 74 blvd Gambetta) Monaco (☎ 377- 93 50 22 71; 17 av de l'Annonciade)
Monaco Marseille (☎ 04 91 33 30 21; 3 pl aux Huiles) Nice (Map pp212-14; ☎ 04 93 80 00 22; 12 montée Désambrois)
Netherlands Marseille (☎ 04 91 25 66 64; 139 av de Toulon) Nice (☎ 04 93 87 52 94; 14 rue Rossini) Monaco (☎ 377-92 05 15 02; 24 av de Fontvieille)
Switzerland Marseille (☎ 04 96 10 14 10; 7 rue d'Arcole)

UK Marseille (off Map pp72-3; ☎ 04 91 15 72 10; 24 av du Prado) Monaco (Map pp322-3; ☎ 377-93 50 99 54; 33 blvd Princesse Charlotte)
US Marseille (Map pp72-3; ☎ 08 10 26 46 26, 04 91 54 92 00; www.amb-usa.fr; place Varian Fry) Nice (Map pp212-14; ☎ 04 93 88 89 55; 7 av Gustave V)

FESTIVALS & EVENTS

Provence boasts a spicier-than-spicy cultural calendar. Many festivals celebrate a historical or folklore tradition, or a performing art. For those celebrating the region's most beloved pastimes – food and wine – see p59.

Destination-specific festivals are listed in the relevant regional chapters. For a complete listing, pick up *Terre de Festivals*, a meaty 200-page festival-listing guide available for free at most tourist offices, or read it online at www.viafrance.com/paca.

Regional festivals:

May & June
Les Musicales du Lubéron (Lubéron; May–Jul) Three-month bonanza of classical music concerts in churches and abbeys in Cavaillon, Ménerbes and other villages.
May Day (region-wide; 1 May) Workers' day is celebrated with trade union parades and diverse protests. People give each other *muguet* (lilies of the valley) for good luck. No one works (except waiters and *muguet* sellers).
Fête de la Musique (region-wide; 21 Jun; www.fete delamusique.culture.fr) Bands, orchestras, crooners, buskers and spectators take to the streets for France's national celebration of music.

July
National Day (region-wide; 14 Jul) Fireworks, parades and all-round hoo-ha to mark the storming of the Bastille in 1789, symbol of the French Revolution.

December
Christmas (region-wide; 25 Dec) Most villages celebrate Noël with midnight Mass, traditional chants in Provençal and a ceremony in which shepherds offer a new-born lamb. Séguret (p142) still celebrates Christmas with Mass and a living crèche.

FOOD

For the full low-down on gastronomic Provence see p54.

In the Eating listings in this guide, we indicate the price of a *menu* (two- or three-course meal at a set price); ordering á la carte is generally more expensive.

Budget restaurants serve simple, generally unadventurous meals for €10 or so and set

menus for €8 to €12. Mid-range places, of which there are plenty, cook up seasonal specialities accompanied by bags of atmosphere, with *menus* costing €15 to €25 (less at lunch time). More formal service, creative cuisine, an unusual and stylish décor, and *menus* costing anything upwards of €30 are distinguishing features of top-end eating spots.

GAY & LESBIAN TRAVELLERS

There are large gay and lesbian communities in Aix-en-Provence, Nice, Cannes and Marseille, the latter being host to the colourful **Gay Pride march** (www.marseillepride.org in French) in late June or early July and the week-long **Universités Euroméditerranéennes des Homosexualités** (www.france.qrd.org/assocs/ueh/), a Euro-Mediterranean gay and lesbian summer school held in July. Smaller gay groups along the Riviera join forces for the annual **Gay Pride Côte d'Azur** (www.gaypride.fr.st in French), held most years in Cannes.

The lesbian scene is less public than its gay counterpart. The region's most active gay and lesbian groups are in Marseille: they include **Act Up Marseille** (☎ 04 91 34 04 14; fax 04 91 34 06 28; 1 rue Roussel Doria, 4e); and lesbian group **Centre Évolutif Lilith** (CEL; ☎ 04 91 05 81 41; http://celmrs.free.fr in French; 17 allées Léon Gambetta).

The hub of gay nightlife is in Cannes (p252) and Nice (p224), with Juan-les-Pins (p256) following closely behind.

HOLIDAYS
French Public Holidays

Museums and shops (but not cinemas, restaurants or bakeries) and most business shut on the following *jours fériés* (public holidays). When one falls on a Thursday, many make a *pont* (bridge, ie with the weekend), meaning they don't work the Friday either.
New Year's Day (Jour de l'An) 1 January
Easter Sunday & Monday (Pâques & lundi de Pâques) Late March/April
May Day (Fête du Travail) 1 May
Victoire 1945 8 May – celebrates the Allied victory in Europe that ended WWII
Ascension Thursday (L'Ascension) May – celebrated on the 40th day after Easter
Pentecost/Whit Sunday & Whit Monday (Pentecôte & lundi de Pentecôte) Mid-May to mid-June – celebrated on the seventh Sunday after Easter
Bastille Day/National Day (Fête Nationale) 14 July
Assumption Day (L'Assomption) 15 August
All Saints' Day (La Toussaint) 1 November

Remembrance Day (L'onze Novembre) 11 November – celebrates the WWI armistice
Christmas (Noël) 25 December

Monégasque Public Holidays

Monaco shares the same holidays with France *except* those on 8 May, 14 July and 11 November. Additional public holidays:
Feast of Ste-Dévote 27 January – patron saint of Monaco
Corpus Christi June – three weeks after Ascension
Fête Nationale (National Day) 19 November
Immaculate Conception 8 December

School Holidays

Travelling to/from and around the region can be hell during the following French *vacances scolaires* (school holidays), especially in July/August when French families hit the coast for their annual summer holiday; Saturday is a horrendous day to travel.
Christmas–New Year Schools nationwide are closed 20 December to 4 January.
February–March The 'Feb' holidays last from about 7 February to 5 March; pupils in each of three zones are off for overlapping 15-day periods.
Easter The month-long spring break, which begins around Easter, also means pupils have overlapping 15-day holidays.
Summer The nationwide summer holiday lasts from the tail end of June until very early September.

INSURANCE

A travel insurance policy to cover theft, loss and medical problems is recommended. Some policies exclude dangerous activities like scuba diving, motorcycling and trekking up very high mountains.

You may prefer a policy that pays doctors or hospitals directly rather than you having to pay on the spot and claim later. If you have to claim later ensure you keep all documentation. Check that the policy covers ambulances or an emergency flight home. Paying for your airline ticket with a credit card often provides limited travel accident insurance. Ask your credit card company what it's prepared to cover.

See p362 for health insurance and p359 for car insurance.

INTERNET ACCESS

France's postal service, La Poste, operates Internet stations known as **Cyberposte** (www
.cyberposte.com in French) at many post offices across the region. A Carte Cyberposte – a rechargeable chip card – costs an initial

€7.60, including one hour's online access, then €4.60 per hour. Private mail boxes that can receive messages can be set up at any Cyberposte station. Alternatively, set up your own Web-based account for free with Hotmail or Yahoo. French accents in email addresses can safely be ignored. Addresses in France are sometimes preceded by *mél*, short for *message électronique*. Commercial Internet cafés (listed under Information in the town and city sections of the regional chapters) charge €3 to €5 an hour.

If you plan to take along your laptop or palmtop computer, note that the 220V power supply in France may vary from that at home. Invest in a universal AC adapter for your appliance. You'll also need an adapter between your telephone plug and the standard T-shaped French receptacle. If you do not go with a global Internet service provider (such as AOL), make sure your ISP has a dial-up number in France. Local ISPs **Free** (www.free.fr in French), **Tiscali** (www.tiscali.fr in French) and **Wanadoo** (www.wanadoo.fr in French) offer cheap or free short-term membership.

Most mid-range hotels are quite Internet savvy, although telephones hard-wired into the wall remain a common problem; if this is the case, ask the receptionist if you can plug directly into the hotel's fax line. On newer SNCF trains an 'office space' next to the luggage compartments between carriages – complete with desk and plug to hook your laptop into the electricity supply – is provided for passengers.

For WiFi users, things are improving rapidly: dozens of hotels, airports and café's in the region already tout wireless access points and many more are on their way. For an up-to-date list of regional WiFi zones, see www.wifinder.com. For useful travel-related websites, turn to p10.

LEGAL MATTERS
Police

French police have wide powers of search and seizure, and can ask you to prove your identity at any time. Foreigners must be able to prove their legal status in France (eg passport, visa, residency permit) without delay.

Verbally (and of course physically) abusing a police officer can carry a hefty fine, even imprisonment. You can refuse to sign a police statement, and you have the right to ask for a copy.

LEGAL AGES

Driving: 18

Buying alcohol: 16

Age of majority: 18

Age of consent: 15

Age considered minor under anti- child-pornography and child-prostitution laws: 18

Voting: 18

People who are arrested are considered innocent until proven guilty, but can be held in custody until trial. The website www.service-public.fr has information about legal rights.

French police are ultrastrict about security. Do not leave baggage unattended at airports or train stations: suspicious objects will be summarily blown up.

Drugs & Alcohol

Contrary to popular belief, French law does not officially distinguish between 'hard' and 'soft' drugs. The penalty for any personal use of *stupéfiants* (including cannabis, am-

phetamines, ecstasy and heroine) can be a one-year jail sentence and a €3750 fine. Importing, possessing, selling or buying drugs can get you up to 10 years in prison and a fine of €7,500,000.

Being drunk in public places is theoretically punishable with a €150 fine.

LOCAL GOVERNMENT

Provence-Alpes-Côte d'Azur is one of 22 French *régions* (administrative regions). It has an elected *conseil régional* (regional council) based in Marseille.

The *région* is split into six *départements* (departments). This guidebook covers five of them: Alpes de Haute-Provence (04), Alpes-Maritimes (06), Bouches du Rhône (13), Var (83) and Vaucluse (84). The town of Nîmes on the western bank of the River Rhône falls into the Gard *département* in the neighbouring Languedoc-Roussillon *région*. *Départements* are known by their two-digit code (listed above), included in postcodes. France (including Corsica) has 96 *départements*.

Each of the *départements* has a *préfet* (prefect) – based in a *préfecture* (prefecture) – who

ADMINISTRATIVE REGIONS & DEPARTMENTS

0 — 50 km
0 — 30 miles

RHÔNE-ALPES `26`

`05`

`07`

ITALY

`84`

LANGUEDOC-ROUSSILLON

`84`

Digne-les-Bains

`04`

`06`

`30`

Avignon

P R O V E N C E - A L P E S

Nice

MONACO

`13`

CÔTE D'AZUR

`83`

Marseille

Toulon

MEDITERRANEAN SEA

DEPARTMENTS
04 Alpes de Haute-Provence
05 Hautes-Alpes
06 Alpes-Maritimes
07 Ardèche
13 Bouches du Rhône
26 Drôme
30 Gard
83 Var
84 Vaucluse

— · — International Boundary
——— Régional Boundary
– – – Départemental Boundary

represents the national government, and an elected *conseil général* (general council). There is a *préfecture* located in Digne-les-Bains (04), Nice (06), Marseille (13), Toulon (83) and Avignon (84).

MAPS

Quality regional maps are widely available outside France. **Michelin** (www.viamichelin.com) and **IGN** (www.ign.fr in French) both have online boutiques where you can purchase maps. Michelin's yellow-jacketed map *Provence and the Côte d'Azur* No 245 covers the area included in this guide at a scale of 1:200,000.

Within the region you can find city maps at *maisons de la presse* (newsagencies) in most towns and cities, at *papeteries* (stationery shops), tourist offices, travel bookshops, and also at many of the mainstream bookshops. Kümmerly + Frey, with its orange-jacketed *Blay-Foldex Plans-Guides* series, and Éditions Grafocarte, with its blue-jacketed *Plan Guide Bleu & Orange,* are the main city-map publishers. A city map typically costs around €4. The free street *plans* (maps) distributed by tourist offices range from the superb to the useless.

For walking and cycling maps see p38 and p43.

MONEY

The euro (€) – Europe's common currency in circulation in 12 Euroland countries since 1 January 2002 – is the only legal tender in France and Monaco.

One euro is divided into 100 cents, also called centimes in France. Coins come in one, two, five, 10, 20 and 50 cents and €1 and €2; the latter has a brass centre and silvery edges and the €1 has the reverse (silvery centre, brass edges). Euro banknotes, adorned with fictitious bridges (which bear a striking resemblance to the Pont du Gard) are issued in denominations of €5, €10, €20, €50, €100, €200 and the often-unwelcome €500.

Exchange rates are given on the inside back cover of this book. For information on costs see p9.

ATMs

ATMs – *distributeurs automatiques de billets* or *points d'argent* – invariably provide the easiest means of getting cash. Most spit out euro banknotes at a superior exchange rate through Visa or MasterCard and there

are plenty of ATMs in the region linked to the international Cirrus and Maestro networks. If you remember your PIN code as a string of letters, translate it into numbers; French keypads don't show letters.

Credit Cards

This is the cheapest way to pay for things and to get cash advances. Visa (Carte Bleue in France) is the most widely accepted, followed by MasterCard (Access or Eurocard). Amex cards are not very useful except at upmarket establishments, but they do allow you to get cash at certain ATMs and at Amex offices. Travelling with two different credit cards (stashed in different wallets) is safer than taking one.

To report a lost or stolen credit card:

Visa (Carte Bleue; ☎ 0 800 902 033)
MasterCard, Eurocard & Access (Eurocard France; ☎ 0 800 901 387)
Diners Club (☎ 0 810 314 159)
Amex (☎ 01 47 77 72 00)

Tipping

French law requires that restaurant, café and hotel bills include a service charge (usually 10% to 15%), so a tip is neither necessary nor expected. However, most people – dire service apart – do usually leave a euro or two in restaurants.

Travellers Cheques

Most banks cash travellers cheques issued by Amex (in US dollars or euros) and by Visa (in euros) for a charge of around €5 per transaction or a percentage fee.

Amex offices (which also cash Amex travellers cheques):

Aix-en-Provence (L'Agence; Map p96; ☎ 04 42 26 84 77; 15 cours Mirabeau)
Cannes (Map p248; ☎ 04 93 38 15 87; 8 rue des Belges)
Marseille (Canebière Change; Map pp80-1; ☎ 04 91 13 71 26; 39 La Canebière)
Nice (☎ 04 93 16 53 53; 11 promenade des Anglais)
Monaco (☎ 377-97 70 77 59; 35 blvd Princesse Charlotte)

Rates vary, so it pays to compare. France's central bank, Banque de France, can offer the best rate, but branches only exchange foreign currency for two or three hours weekday mornings, making it a pain in the neck to catch them open. Commercial banks and post offices open longer weekday hours (some even open Saturday) and can charge up to €10 per foreign currency transaction. Exchange offices *(bureaux de change)*, however, are generally quickest, easiest, open the longest hours and give the best exchange rate.

POST

Postal services are fast (next-day delivery for most domestic letters), reliable and expensive. Post offices are signposted **La Poste** (www.laposte.fr in French). For a pretty postage stamp *(un timbre)* rather than the uninspiring blue sticker *(une vignette)* that comes out of post office coin-operated machines, go to a window marked *toutes opérations* (all services). Tobacconists and shops selling postcards sell stamps too. French stamps can be used in Monaco, but Monégasque stamps are only valid in Monaco.

From France and Monaco, domestic letters up to 20g cost €0.50. Postcards and letters up to 20g cost €0.50 within the EU, €0.75 to most of the rest of Europe and Africa, and €0.90 to the USA, Canada and Australasia.

SHOPPING

For olive oil–shopping tips and tricks see p55.

Many edible products typical to Provence – *marrons au sirop* (chestnuts in syrup) from the Massif des Maures, *calissons* (sweets frosted with icing sugar) from Aix-en-Provence and rice from the Camargue – are easy to transport home. But most glass-jar products sold at markets are homemade and rarely contain preservatives. Lavender marmalade from Carpentras market, for example, lasts one month after being opened, while onion chutney from the Lubéron – mind-blowingly delicious as it is – will not survive outside a fridge. The same goes for bread, cheese and fresh truffles. But not for wine.

Less-tasty treats worth a shopping spree include perfumes from Grasse; leather sandals from St-Tropez; colourful wicker baskets and carnations from Antibes; glassware from Biot; Picasso-inspired ceramics from Vallauris; faïence from Moustiers-Ste-Marie; pipes and carpets from Cogolin; soap and *santons* ('little saints'; p102) from Marseille or Salon de Provence; *courgourdons* (traditional ornaments made from dyed and hollowed marrows/squash) from Nice; lavender oil, pottery, sundials and wrought-iron pieces from the Lubéron;

colourful Provençal fabrics from practically anywhere in the region; antiques from L'Isle-sur-la-Sorgue; terracotta and ceramic tiles from Salernes; gallery art from St-Paul de Vence and Mougins; and the latest haute-couture designs from Monaco.

Bargaining

Market shopping is one of the region's greatest joys; market days are listed at the start of each regional chapter. Little bargaining goes on although it's always worth a try.

SOLO TRAVELLERS

Male or female, travelling solo in the region poses few problems bar the fact a sizeable chunk of hotels don't have single rooms, or charge the same price for a so-called 'single' as a double. Dining alone in restaurants or sipping coffee in cafés is quite common, although lone women might well attract unwanted attention in busier spots on the coast. See p349 for more information.

TELEPHONE

France and Monaco have separate telephone systems.

French telephone numbers have 10 digits and need no area code; those starting with the digits 06 are mobile-phone numbers. To call anywhere in Provence and the Côte d'Azur from Monaco and abroad, dial your country's international access code, followed by 33 (France's country code) and the 10-digit number, dropping the initial 0. To call abroad from Provence, dial 00 (France's international access code), followed by the country code, area code (dropping the initial 0 if necessary) and local number.

Telephone numbers in Monaco have eight digits and likewise need no area code. To call Monaco from France and abroad, dial the international access code, followed by 377 (Monaco's country code) and the eight-digit number. To call abroad (including France) from Monaco, dial 00, followed by the country code, area code (dropping the initial zero if necessary) and local number.

Mobile Phones

France uses GSM 900/1800 – compatible with the rest of Europe and Australia but not with the North American GSM 1900 or the totally different system in Japan. Mobile phones cannot be rented in the

DIRECTORY

region, but assuming your phone is GSM 900/1800–compatible you can buy a SIM card package from mobile-phone providers **Bouygues** (www.bouygues.fr); **Orange** (www.orange.fr), France Télécom's mobile arm; or **SFR** (www .sfr.fr). Card packages, sold at phone shops and branches of FNAC in Avignon, Nice, Nîmes and Marseille, enable you to have your own French mobile telephone number and make and receive calls at local rates.

Phonecards

Almost all public telephones are card-operated. Magnetic chip–driven phone-cards come in unit denominations of 25, 50 or 120 and are sold at post offices, *tabacs* (tobacconists) and anywhere touting a blue sticker reading '*télécartes en vente ici*'.

In addition, France Télécom offers a rash of customised *tickets de téléphone,* designed to meet different national and/or international dialling needs. Its Ticket International, for example, costs €7.50/15 and – if used exclusively during reduced-tariff periods – covers 180/363 minutes of international calls to Europe or the USA and Canada. Cards can be used from private and public phones; to use one, dial ☎ 3089 followed by the code written on the reverse side of the card, '#' and the subscriber's number.

For help in English on other France Télécom services dial ☎ 0 800 364 775.

Telephone Rates

The cheapest time to call home is during reduced-tariff periods – weekdays from 7pm to 8am (until 1pm to the USA and Canada), weekends and public holidays. Updated tariffs are published on France Télécom's website at www.francetelecom.com.

A phone call to most of Europe, the USA and Canada costs €0.12 to connect and €0.22 per minute or €0.12 at reduced-

tariff times. To telephone Australia, New Zealand or Japan costs €0.12 plus €0.49 per minute (reduced tariff €0.34 per minute).

Local calls cost €0.091 for the first minute, then €0.033 per minute during peak periods (weekdays 8am to 7pm) and €0.018 per minute at off-peak times (weekdays 7pm to 8am and at any time over the weekend). National calls are billed at €0.11 for the initial 39 seconds, then €0.091 per minute (€0.061 in reduced-rate periods).

Calling a mobile phone from a fixed line is expensive: €0.21 to €0.24 for the initial 30 seconds, plus €0.21 to €0.25 per minute during peak periods (8am to 9.30pm Monday to Friday and 8am to noon Saturday) or €0.10 to €0.13 at other times.

Mobile-phone calls made within France from France Télécom's Orange network with its pay-as-you-go Mobicarte cards (sold at phone shops and FNAC outlets for various denominations starting at €10) cost €0.45 per minute. Sending an SMS is €0.15 per message and WAP costs €0.25 per minute.

TIME

French and Monégasque time is GMT/UTC plus one hour, except during daylight-saving time (from the last Sunday in March to the last Sunday in October) when it is GMT/UTC plus two hours. The UK and France are always one hour apart – when it's 6pm in London, it's 7pm in Nice. New York is six hours behind Nice.

France uses the 24-hour clock and writes time like this: 15h30 (ie 3.30pm). Time has no meaning for many people in Provence.

TOILETS

Public toilets, signposted *toilettes* or WC, are surprisingly few and far between, which means you can be left feeling really rather desperate. Towns that have public toilets generally tout them near the *mairie* (town hall) or in the port area. Many have coin-operated, self-flushing toilet booths – highly disconcerting should the automatic mechanism fail with you inside. They can usually be found in car parks and public squares; they cost €0.20 to enter. Some places sport flushless, kerbside *urinoirs* (urinals) reeking with generations of urine. Failing that, there's always McDonald's.

Restaurants, cafés and bars are often woefully underequipped with such ameni-

---

PHONEBOOK

International reverse-charge (collect) call ☎ 00-33 plus relevant country code (11 instead of 1 for the USA and Canada) and telephone number

Directory Inquiries ☎ 12

International Directory Inquiries ☎ 00-3312 plus relevant country code (11 instead of 1 for the USA and Canada)

ties, so start queuing ahead of time. Bashful males be warned: some toilets are almost unisex; the urinals and washbasins are in a common area through which all and sundry pass to get to the toilet stalls. Older establishments often sport Turkish-style *toilettes à la turque* – a squat toilet with a high-pressure flushing mechanism that can soak your feet if you don't step back in time.

TOURIST INFORMATION
Local Tourist Offices

Almost every city, town and village has an *office du tourisme* (tourist office run by some unit of local government) or *syndicat d'initiative* (tourist office run by an organisation of local merchants). Both are excellent resources and can always provide a local map and information on accommodation.

Regional tourist information is handled by five *comités départementaux du tourisme* (departmental tourist offices):

Alpes de Haute-Provence (☎ 04 92 31 57 29; www .alpes-haute-provence.com; Maison des Alpes de Haute-Provence, 19 rue du Docteur Honnorat, Digne-les-Bains)
Alpes-Maritimes (Map pp212-14; ☎ 04 93 21 80 95; www.guideriviera.com; 55 promenade des Anglais, 06011 Nice)
Bouches du Rhône (Comité Départemental du Tourisme; Map pp72-3; ☎ 04 91 13 84 13; www.visitprovence.com; Le Montesquieu, 13 rue Roux de Brignoles,13006 Marseille)
Var (☎ 04 94 50 55 50; www.tourismevar.com in French; 1 blvd Maréchal Foch, BP 99, 83003 Draguignan)
Vaucluse (Map pp128-9; ☎ 04 90 80 47 00; www. provenceguide.com; 12 rue Collège de la Croix, BP 147, 84008 Avignon)

For tourist information on the principality of Monaco, contact its national tourist office in Monte Carlo (see p323).

French Tourist Offices Abroad

French tourist offices abroad (www.france guide.com), called *maisons de la France:*
Australia Sydney (☎ 02-9231 5244; info.au@franceguide .com; Level 20, 25 Bligh St, NSW 2000)
Belgium Brussels (☎ 09 02 880 25; info.be@franceguide .com; 21 av de la Toison d'Or, 1050)
Canada Montreal (☎ 514-288 2026; canada@franceguide .com; Suite 490, 1981 McGill College Ave, Que H3A 2W9
Germany Frankfurt (☎ 019-057 00 25; info.de@ franceguide.com; Zeppelinallee 37, D-60325)
Ireland Dublin (☎ 01560 235 235; info.ie@franceguide .com; 10 Suffolk St, 2)

Italy Milan (☎ 166 11 62 16; info.it@franceguide.com; Via Larga 7, 20122)
Netherlands Amsterdam (☎ 0900-112 23 32; www.frans verkeersbureau.nl; Prinsengracht 670, 1017 KX)
Spain (☎ 807 11 71 81) Madrid (info.es@franceguide .com; Plaza de España 18, 28008) Barcelona (Gran Via Corts Catalanes 656, 08010)
Switzerland Geneva (☎ 090 090 06 99; info.gva@ franceguide.com; 2 rue Thalberg, 1201)
UK London (☎ 090-6824 4123; info.uk@franceguide.com; 178 Piccadilly, W1V 9AL)
USA New York (☎ 410-286 8310; www.francetourism .com; 444 Madison Ave, NY 10022) Los Angeles (☎ 310-271 6665; info.losangeles@franceguide.com; 9454 Wilshire Blvd, Suite 715, Beverly Hills, CA 90212-2967)

Monégasque Tourist Offices Abroad

Monaco has its own string of tourist offices (www.monaco-tourisme.com):
France (☎ 01 42 96 12 23; dtcparis@monaco-congres .com; 9 rue de la Paix, F-75002 Paris)
Germany (☎ 211-323 78 43; monaoc-duesseldorf@t-on line.de; WZ Center, Königsallee 27-31, D-40212 Düsseldorf)
Italy (☎ 02 8645 8480; principato.monaco@monaco .inet.it; Via Dante 12, I-20121 Milan)
UK (☎ 020-7352 9962, 050 000 61 14; www.monaco .co.uk; The Chambers, Chelsea Harbour, London SW10 0XF)
USA (☎ 800-753 9696, 212-286 3330; www.visitmonaco .com; 565 Fifth Ave, New York NY 10017)

TOURS

Dozens of enticing half- and full-day tours available through tourist offices and reception desks at bigger hotels are peppered throughout the regional chapters of this guide.

Most organised tours are activity-driven, focusing on the great outdoors; see p44 for outdoor-activity tours from abroad. But there are some lovely ones focusing on art, craft, food and wine, too:
Arblaster & Clarke (☎ 01730-893344; www.arblaster andclarke.com; Farnham Rd, West Liss, Hants GU33 6JQ, UK) Food and wine tour specialists offer a four-night 'Gourmet Provence' tour, with four-star chateau accommodation, a couple of meals in two star Michelin restaurants, cookery demonstrations etc (UK £1599 per person, including airfare); wine tours too.
Inn Travel (☎ 01653-629001; www.inntravel.co.uk; Hovingham, York YO62 4JZ, UK) Gastronomy weekends (two nights from UK £389), weekends of indulgence (three nights from UK £568, including airfare) and other short breaks, as well as riding holidays, six-day or more discovery journeys and cycling tours (seven nights from UK £537/739 self-drive/by air); accommodation in family-run hotels, inns and chateaux.

La Provence Verte (☎ 04 94 72 04 21; www.la-provence-verte.net; Maison du Tourisme, Carrefour de l'Europe, F-83170 Brignoles) Three-day gastronomy and food 'weekends' (€240); three-day 'patrimony' sightseeing trips (€130) and plenty of outdoor thrills and spills.

Martin Randall Travel (☎ 020-8742 3355; www.martinrandall.com; 10 Barley Mow Passage, London W4 4PH, UK) A fabulous wealth of art and architecture tours led by art historians or experts in their fields. Tours in 2004–05 included a seven-day 'art on the Cote d'Azur' trip costing UK £1900 with flights from the UK, and a six-day 'Aix musical festival: Music in Provence' tour for UK £1630, including flights and three opera tickets.

Service Loisirs Accueil Bouches du Rhône (Map pp72-3; ☎ 04 90 59 49 36; www.visitprovence.com; 13 rue Roux de Brignoles, F-13006 Marseille) Wealth of imaginative packages offered by the Bouches du Rhône tourist board: two-day impressionist-painting courses (€250), two-day chocolate courses (€130), seven days 'discovering Provence' (€550), four-day 'pottery in Aubagne' workshops (€250) and mountains of outdoor activity-driven ideas.

VISAS

Up-to-date visa regulations are posted on the Foreign Affairs Ministry website at www.diplomatie.gouv.fr.

EU nationals and citizens of Switzerland, Iceland and Norway only need a passport or national identity card to enter, and stay in, France.

As tourists, citizens of Australia, the US, Canada, New Zealand, Japan and Israel don't need a visa for stays of up to three months.

As a practical matter, if you don't need a visa to visit France, no one is likely to kick you out after three months. The unspoken policy seems to be that you can stay and spend your money in France as long as you don't try to work, apply for social services or commit a crime. Staying longer than three months is nonetheless illegal, and without a *carte de séjour* (residence permit) you can face real problems renting an apartment, opening a bank account and so on.

Tourist Visa

Those not exempt need a tourist visa, also known as a **Schengen visa** (www.eurovisa.com) after the Schengen agreement that abolished passport controls between Austria, Belgium, Denmark, Finland, France, Germany, Greece, Iceland, Italy, Luxembourg, the Netherlands, Norway, Portugal, Spain and Sweden. A Schengen visa allows unlimited travel throughout this zone for 90 days.

Applications are made with the consulate of the country you are entering first, or that will be your main destination. Among other things, you will need medical insurance and proof of sufficient funds to support yourself.

If you enter France overland, it is unlikely that your visa will be checked at the border, but major problems can arise later on if you don't have one.

Tourist visas *cannot* be extended except in emergencies (such as medical problems); you'll need to leave and reapply from outside France when your visa expires.

Long-Stay & Student Visa

This is the first step if you want to work or study in France, or stay for more than three months. Long-stay and student visas will allow you to enter France and apply for a *carte de séjour*. Contact the French embassy or consulate nearest your residence, and begin your application well in advance as it can take months. Tourist visas cannot be changed into student visas after arrival. However, short-term visas are available for students sitting university-entry exams in France.

Working-Holiday Visa

Citizens of Australia, Canada, Japan and New Zealand aged between 18 and 29 years (inclusive) are eligible for a one-year, multiple-entry working-holiday visa, allowing you to travel around France and work at the same time.

You have to apply to the embassy or consulate in your home country, and you must have a return ticket home, insurance and sufficient money to fund the start of your stay. Apply early as quotas do apply.

Once you have found a job in France, you have to apply for a temporary work permit *(autorisation provisoire de travail)*, valid for the duration of the employment position offered. The permit can be renewed under the same conditions up to the limit of the authorised length of stay.

Carte de Séjour

Once issued with a long-stay visa, you can apply for a *carte de séjour*, and are usually required to do so within eight days of arrival in France. Make sure you have all the necessary documents *before* you arrive.

EU passport-holders and citizens of Switzerland, Iceland and Norway no longer need a *carte de séjour* to reside (or work) in France. Other foreign nationals must contact the local *préfecture* or *commissariat* (police station) for their permit. Students of all nationalities need a *carte de séjour*.

WOMEN TRAVELLERS

French men have clearly given little thought to the concept of *harcèlement sexuel* (sexual harassment). Most still believe that staring suavely at a passing woman is paying her a compliment. Women need not walk around the region in fear, however. Suave stares are about as adventurous as most French men get, with women rarely being physically assaulted on the street or touched up in bars at night.

Unfortunately, it's not French men that women travellers have to concern themselves with. While women attract little unwanted attention in rural Provence, on the coast it's a different ball game. In the dizzying heat of the high season, the Côte d'Azur is rampant with men and women of *all* nationalities out on the pull. Apply the usual 'women traveller' rules and the chances are you'll emerge from the circus unscathed. Remain conscious of your surroundings, avoid going to bars and clubs alone at night and be aware of potentially dangerous situations: deserted streets, lonely beaches, dark corners of large train stations, and on night buses in certain districts of Marseille and Nice.

Topless sunbathing is not generally interpreted as deliberately provocative.

Organisations

SOS Viol is a voluntary women's group that staffs the national **rape-crisis hotline** (☎ 0 800 059 595). Its centre in Marseille is spearheaded by **SOS Femmes** (Map pp72-3; ☎ 04 91 24 61 50; www.sosfemmes.com; 14 blvd Théodore Thurner) and in Nice by **Femmes Battues** (☎ 04 93 52 17 81; accueilfemmesbattues@hotmail.com; 81 rue de France, bureau 312).

WORK

EU nationals have an automatic right to work in France. Non-EU citizens need to apply for a work permit, for which they first need a *carte de séjour* or working-holiday visa (see p348), as well as a written promise of employment. Permits can be refused on the grounds of high local unemployment. That said, work 'in the black' (ie without documents) is possible in the Côte d'Azur's tourist industry and during Provence's grape harvest.

France's national employment service, the **Agence National pour L'Emploi** (ANPE; www .anpe.fr in French), advertises jobs in the region on its website.

Agricultural Work

To pick up a job in a field, ask around in areas where harvesting is taking place; Provence sees a succession of apple, strawberry, cherry, peach, pear and pumpkin harvests from mid-May to September.

The annual grape harvest happens from about mid-September to mid- or late October. The sun-soaked fruits of the Côtes de Provence vineyards are ready for harvest before those of the more northern Châteauneuf du Pape vineyards. Harvesting is increasingly being done by machine, although mechanical picking is forbidden in some places (such as Châteauneuf du Pape). Once the harvest starts, it lasts just a couple of weeks. The start date is announced up to one week in advance.

Food for *vendangeurs* (grape pickers) is usually supplied but accommodation is often not (that is why most pickers live locally). Tourist offices in the region have a list of local producers who might need an extra pair of hands, as do the different *maisons des vins* (wine houses).

Au Pair

Under the au pair system, single young people (aged 18 to about 27) who are studying in France live with a French family and receive lodging, full board and a bit of pocket money in exchange for taking care of the kids, babysitting, doing light housework and perhaps teaching English to the children.

Many families want au pairs who are native English speakers, but knowing at least some French may be a prerequisite. **Association Familles & Jeunesse** (☎ 04 93 82 28 22; www .afj-aupair.org/apfrance.htm; 4 rue Masséna, 06000 Nice) is one of dozens of au pair agencies on the Côte d'Azur that arrange placements. Online, there's an agency directory at www .europa-pages.com/au_pair.

Beach Hawkers & Street Performers

Selling goods and services on the beach is one way to make a few euros, though you've got to sell an awful lot of *beignets* (doughnuts) or wrap a lot of hair with coloured beads to make a living.

One good place street musicians, actors and jugglers might try to busk is in Avignon during its July theatre festival.

Crewing on a Yacht

Working on a yacht looks glamorous but the reality is far from cushy. Cannes, Antibes or any other yacht-filled port on the Côte d'Azur are the places to look for work. In Antibes, **International Crew Recruitment** (☎ 04 93 34 27 71; 16b av du 24 Août) might be able to assist.

Yacht owners often take on newcomers for a trial period of day crewing before hiring them for the full charter season. By late September long-haul crews are in demand for winter voyages to the West Indies.

Environmental Work

Each summer the Village des Tortues (p301), in the Massif des Maures, offers a limited number of placements to students aged 17 and over. The centre allows its students to spend 15 days to a month working at the village, March to November. Free board and lodging is included.

Ski Resorts

The region's ski resorts – Isola 2000, Pra-Loup and La Foux d'Allos among them – are small and offer few work opportunities. If you contact the ski resort months in advance you might be able to pick up some hospitality work in a hotel or restaurant.

Transport

GETTING THERE & AWAY

See also p347 for information on tours to Provence and the Côte d'Azur.

AIR
Airports

A popular tourist destination, Provence has two major airports: Marseille and Nice (although most long-haul destinations still require you to change planes in Paris, London or some other European capital). Some international flights use Nîmes, St-Tropez-La Môle and Toulon. Domestic flights use tiny Avignon, and charters and private planes use Cannes.

Avignon (code AVN; www.avignon.aeroport.fr)
Cannes (code CEQ; www.cannes.aeroport.fr)
Marseille-Provence (code MRS; www.marseille .aeroport.fr)
Nice-Côte d'Azur (code NCE; www.nice.aeroport.fr)
Nîmes-Arles-Camargue (code FNI; www.nimes.cci.fr)
St-Tropez-La Môle (code LTT; www.st-tropez-airport.com)
Toulon-Hyères (code TLN; http://aeroport.var.cci.fr)

For details on travelling between airports and city centres, see the Getting Around sections in the relevant chapters.

Airlines

The following airlines fly to and from Provence and the Côte d'Azur:

Air Algérie (code AH; Marseille ☎ 04 95 09 31 10, Nice ☎ 04 93 21 48 20; www.airalgerie.dz; hub Algiers)
Air France (code AF; ☎ 08 20 82 08 20; www.airfrance .com; hub Paris)
Alitalia (code AZ; ☎ 08 20 31 53 15; www.alitalia.it; hub Rome)
bmibaby (code CWW; ☎ 08 90 71 00 81; www.bmibaby .com; hub East Midlands)
British Airways (code BA; ☎ 08 25 82 54 00; www .britishairways.com; hub Heathrow)
Corse Méditerranée (code CCM; ☎ 08 20 82 08 20; www.ccm-airlines.com; hub Paris)
easyJet (code U2; ☎ 08 25 08 25 08; www.easyjet.com; hub Luton)
Royal Air Maroc (code AT; Marseille ☎ 04 42 14 24 79, Nice ☎ 04 93 21 48 80; www.royalairmaroc.com; hub Casablanca)
Ryanair (code FR; ☎ 08 92 55 56 66; www.ryanair.com; hub Dublin)
Tunis Air (code TU; ☎ 08 20 04 40 44; www.tunisair .com.tn; hub Tunis)
VirginExpress (code TV; ☎ 08 00 52 85 28; www .virgin-express.com; hub Brussels)

Tickets

Air travel is a competitive business, and fares fluctuate wildly according to time of year and general availability: shop around!

The Internet makes researching airfares easy. Most airlines have websites listing special offers, and there are some good online ticket agencies which will compare prices for you (eg www.travelocity.co.uk and www.deckchair.com). However, using face-to-face methods like travel agencies can furnish details not available on the Internet, like which airlines have the best

---

THINGS CHANGE...

The information in this chapter is particularly vulnerable to change. Check directly with the airline or a travel agent to make sure you understand how a fare (and ticket you may buy) works and be aware of the security requirements for international travel. Shop carefully. The details given in this chapter should be regarded as pointers and are not a substitute for your own careful, up-to-date research.

DEPARTURE TAX

International airport departure taxes are included in the price of your ticket.

---

facilities for children or which travel insurance is most suitable.

Look out for the cheap 'no-frills' flights that service Marseille, Nice, Nîmes and Toulon (see right and opposite).

Africa

Marseille is a hub for flights to and from North Africa.

Air Algérie operates flights to Algeria. From Marseille there are up to five daily to Algiers and Constantine, five per week to Annaba and Oran, and flights at least weekly to Batna, Bejaia and Tlemcen. From Nice there are weekly flights to Algiers and Constantine.

Royal Air Maroc and Air France codeshare on flights to and from Morocco. From Marseille there are twice-daily flights to Casablanca and weekly flights to Oudja. There are daily flights to Casablanca from Nice.

Tunis Air flies to and from Tunis (up to four times daily) and Monastir (weekly) from both Nice and Marseille. Air France also flies to both cities.

Australia & New Zealand

Airlines such as Thai Airways International, Malaysia Airlines, Qantas Airways and Singapore Airlines have frequent promotional fares. High-season full-price return fares to Paris cost around A$3000 from Melbourne or Sydney, and around NZ$3500 from Auckland. The following are major agencies for cheap fares:

Flight Centre Australia (☎ 133 133; www.flightcentre.com.au); New Zealand (☎ 0800 243 544; www.flightcentre.co.nz)
STA Travel Australia (☎ 1300 733 035; www.statravel.com.au); New Zealand (☎ 0508 782 872; www.statravel.co.nz)

Canada

Airlines flying from Canada to France include British Airways, Air France and Air Canada. Flights leave from all major cities including Montreal, Ottawa, Toronto and Vancouver. A Toronto–Paris round trip costs around C$1200 in high season.

For online bookings try www.expedia.ca and www.travelocity.ca.

Continental Europe

There are flights two or three times daily between Nice/Marseille and most other European cities, cheapest in early spring and late autumn.

There are also a handful of interesting no-frills routes: easyJet offers year-round daily flights between Geneva/Amsterdam and Nice. Fares vary enormously depending on travel dates and special offers (from €40 to €180 at the time of research).

VirginExpress flies between Nice and Brussels up to four times daily, from where onward connections abound. Again, prices vary hugely.

Across Continental Europe there are many agencies with ties to **STA Travel** (www.statravel.com) where cheap tickets can be purchased.

UK & Ireland

No-frills airlines have slashed fares between the UK and southern France. Internet bookings are the norm; telephone bookings cost marginally more. Tickets are nonrefundable, but can be changed for a fee.

There are easyJet flights from Nice to Belfast, Bristol, Liverpool, London Gatwick, London Stansted, Luton and Newcastle, and from Marseille to London Gatwick. One-way fares cost anything between UK£30 and UK£135 including airport taxes.

There are bmibaby flights between Nice and Nottingham (around UK£60).

Dublin-based Ryanair operates low-fare flights between Nîmes-Arles-Camargue airport and London Luton, as well as between Nîmes and London Stansted, and Nîmes and Liverpool.

Both Nice and Marseille are served by daily British Airways and Air France flights from London (Gatwick or Heathrow).

Discount air travel is big business in London. Travel-agency ads appear in the travel pages of the weekend broadsheet newspapers, in *Time Out* and in the *Evening Standard*. Some recommended travel agencies and online ticket sites:

Cheap Flights (www.cheapflights.co.uk)
Flightbookers (☎ 0870 010 7000; www.ebookers.com)
STA Travel (☎ 0870 160 0599; www.statravel.co.uk)
Caters especially for travellers under the age of 26.

USA

Any journey to Provence from the North American continent entails a change in

Paris, London or another European transport hub. A New York–Paris round trip can cost anything from US$400/900 in low/high season with Air France or British Airways.

Discount travel agents are known as consolidators in the USA; track them down through the *Yellow Pages* or the major daily newspapers. The *New York Times*, the *Los Angeles Times*, the *Chicago Tribune* and the *San Francisco Examiner* all have weekly travel sections where you'll find a number of ads.

Travel agencies recommended for online bookings:

Expedia (☎ 1 800 397 3342; www.expedia.com)
STA Travel (☎ 1 800 781 4040; www.sta.com)
Travelocity (☎ 1 888 709 5983; www.travelocity.com)

Within France
Air France is the leading carrier on domestic routes, linking Bordeaux, Brest, Clermont-Ferrand, Lille, Lyon, Metz-Nancy, Mulhouse, Nantes, Strasbourg and Toulouse with Avignon, Nice, Nîmes, Marseille and Toulon.

No-frills airline easyJet has lots of cheap fares from Paris Orly to Marseille and Nice (sometimes as low as €30).

Corsica is served by regular CCM Airlines flights, run in conjunction with Air France, from Nice and Marseille to Ajaccio, Bastia, Calvi and Figari.

Some good online agencies:

Degriftour (☎ 08 92 70 50 00; www.degriftour.fr)
Nouvelles Frontières (☎ 08 25 00 07 47; www.nouvelles-frontieres.fr)

LAND
Continental Europe
BUS
Eurolines (www.eurolines.com) is an association of companies forming Europe's largest international bus network. It links Provençal cities such as Nice, Marseille and Avignon with points all over Western and central Europe, Scandinavia and Morocco. Most buses operate daily in summer and several times a week in winter; advance ticket purchases are necessary. Some of Eurolines' representatives in Europe:

Bohemia Euroexpress International (Prague; ☎ 224 218 680; www.bei.cz)
Bus Éireann (Dublin; ☎ 83 66 111; www.buseireann.ie)
Deutsche Touring (Frankfurt; ☎ 069-790 350; www.deutsche-touring.de)
Eurolines Austria (☎ 01-798 29 00; www.eurolines.at)
Eurolines France (☎ 08-92 89 90 91; www.eurolines.fr)

Eurolines Italy SRL (☎ 39 055 35 71 10; www.eurolines.it)
Eurolines Nederland (☎ 020-560 87 88; www.eurolines.nl)
Eurolines Scandinavia (☎ 07 010 00 10; www.eurolines.dk)
Eurolines Spain (☎ 915 06 32 55; www.eurolines.es)

The **Eurolines Pass** (15-/30-/60-day pass Jun–mid-Sep €195/290/333, under 26 & over 60 €165/235/259, cheaper mid-Sep–Jun) allows unlimited travel to 35 cities across Europe. Children aged four to 12 get up to 80% off the adult fare.

Travelling from Nice, Cannes or Toulon, sample return fares include Amsterdam (€165), Rome (€98) and Florence (€75).

Intercars (www.intercars.fr) links France with cities in southern and central France. In Provence it has a number of **bus-station offices** (Nice ☎ 04 93 80 08 70; nice@intercars.fr; Aix-en-Provence ☎ 04 91 50 57 55; Marseille ☎ 04 91 50 08 66; marseille@intercars.fr; Nîmes ☎ 04 66 29 84 22; nimes@intercars.fr). Sample return fares from Nice include Budapest (€159, 21 hours) and Warsaw (€176, 29 hours). Discounts are available for children, and those aged under 26 and over 60 (approximately 5% to 10% off a full adult fare).

Linebús (Avignon ☎ 04 90 86 88 67; Nîmes ☎ 04 66 29 50 62; Barcelona ☎ 932 65 07 00; Lisbon ☎ 021-357 17 45) links Avignon and Nîmes with Barcelona (7½ hours), Lisbon (24 hours) and other cities in Spain and Portugal.

TRAIN
Paris has connections to cities all over Europe. Within the region, Nice is the major hub, sitting on the busy Barcelona–Rome train line. Day and overnight trains run in both directions. A single 1st-/2nd-class fare from Nice to Rome costs around €86/60 (plus €24 for a couchette) for the 10-hour journey. There are also direct train services between Nice and Milan (€52/38, 4½ hours).

Book tickets and get information from Rail Europe (see the boxed text, p354) up to two months ahead. Direct bookings through Société Nationale des Chemins de Fer (p354) are also possible.

The *Thomas Cook European Timetable*, updated monthly, is the train traveller's bible. It's available from www.thomascook publishing.com.

For transporting your car by train to Avignon and St-Raphaël, see p355. Two months' advance booking is generally required.

UK

BUS

Eurolines UK (☎ 0870 514 3219; www.nationalexpress .com/eurolines) runs from London's Victoria coach station via the Dover–Calais channel crossing to Aix-en-Provence, Avignon, Marseille, Nice and Toulon. All direct return fares are around UK£100.

CAR & MOTORCYCLE

High-speed shuttle trains operated by **Eurotunnel** (UK ☎ 0870-535 3535, France ☎ 03 21 00 61 00; www.eurotunnel.com) whisk cars, motorcycles, bicycles and coaches from Folkestone via the Channel Tunnel to Coquelles, 5km southwest of Calais. Journey time is 35 minutes. Trains run 24 hours a day, every day of the year, with up to five departures an hour. A high-season return fare for a car and passengers costs around UK£500, but there are numerous promotional fares.

TRAIN

The high-speed passenger service **Eurostar** (UK ☎ 0870 518 6186, France ☎ 08 92 35 35 39; www .eurostar.com) takes three hours from London to Paris, and six hours direct to sunny Avignon (not including the one-hour time dif-ference). You can also catch the Eurostar to Lille or Paris, from where there are numerous southbound trains (see below).

An average 2nd-class return ticket from London to Avignon, Marseille, Nice, Toulon or St-Raphaël costs UK£150, but keep your eyes peeled for special offers. Student travel agencies often have youth fares not directly available from Eurostar.

Within France

BUS

French transport policy is completely biased in favour of its state-owned rail system: inter-regional bus services are an alien concept. Take a train.

CAR & MOTORCYCLE

For detailed information on driving, see p358.

TRAIN

France's efficient national rail network is run by the state-owned **Société Nationale des Chemins de Fer** (SNCF; ☎ 08 92 35 35 35; www.sncf.fr). The network is very Paris-centric, with key lines radiating from the capital like the spokes of a wheel.

TRAIN PASSES & DISCOUNT FARES

The following passes are sold at student travel agencies, major train stations within Europe, and the SNCF subsidiary **Rail Europe** (www.raileurope.com; Canada ☎ 1 800 361 7245, UK ☎ 0870 5848 848, USA ☎ 1 800 438 7245).

SNCF Discount Fares & Passes

Children aged under four travel free; those aged four to 11 travel for half price. Discounted fares (25% reduction) automatically apply to travellers aged 12 to 25, those aged over 60, one to four adults travelling with a child aged four to 11, two people on a return journey together, or anyone taking a return journey of at least 200km and spending a Saturday night away.

Purchasing a one-year travel pass can yield a 50% discount (25% if the cheapest seats are sold out): a **Carte 12-25** for travellers aged 12 to 25 costs €49; the **Carte Enfant Plus** for one to four adults travelling with a child aged four to 11 costs €65; and a **Carte Sénior** for those aged over 60 costs €50.

The **France Railpass** entitles nonresidents of France to unlimited travel on SNCF trains for four days over a one-month period (1st/2nd class US$252/218). Cheaper youth and senior versions exist.

European Train Passes

If you're planning an extensive European journey, consider buying a **Eurail** (US ☎ 1 888 667 9734; www.eurail.com) pass, available to non-European residents, or a **Euro Domino** or **InterRail** (www .interrailnet.com) pass, available to European residents. All are valid on the national train network and allow unlimited travel for varying periods of time.

SNCF's pride and joy is the **Train à Grande Vitesse** (TGV; www.tgv.com) high-speed train service. TGV Sud-Est links Paris with Dijon and Lyon, from where the TGV Rhône-Alpes continues southeast to Valence. Here, the TGV Méditerranée zips at 310km/h to Avignon where the superfast track splits: east to Marseille and west to Nîmes. Avignon and Aix-en-Provence have out-of-town TGV train stations, separate from the town-centre stations used by regional trains. Sample 1st-/2nd-class single TGV fares between Paris and Provence destinations include: Avignon (€110/80, 3½ hours), Marseille (€120/80, three hours), Nice (€160/120, seven hours) and Orange (€120/80, 4½ hours).

The SNCF also operates cheaper, slower rail services. Both *grande ligne* (main line) trains and those operated by **Transport Express Régional** (TER; ☎ 08 36 67 68 69; www.ter-sncf .com) link smaller cities and towns with the TGV network. Many towns not on the SNCF network are linked with nearby railheads by buses.

Under Motorail's Auto Train scheme you can travel with your car on a train. Cars are loaded on the train one hour before departure and unloaded 30 minutes after arrival. This service is available at Avignon, St-Raphaël, Marseille and Nice train stations. Information in the UK is available from Rail Europe (see the boxed text, opposite). In France, ticketing is handled by SNCF.

Generally, bicycles are transported free of charge *if* they are packed down into a special 120cm x 90cm transit bag (available from bike shops). Some main-line trains (flagged with a bicycle symbol on timetables) don't make this requirement. On night trains and certain TGV Sud-Est and TGV Méditerranée routes, bikes can only be transported in a four- to six-bicycle wagon which must be reserved in advance (€10). See the multilingual SNCF brochure *Guide Train & Vélo* (free), available at train stations.

RIVER

Provence is well connected with waterways thanks to the Rhône. The most popular canal route to Provence is via the Canal du Midi, a 240km waterway that runs from Toulouse to the Bassin de Thau between Agde and Sète, from where you continue northeast to Aigues-Mortes in the Camargue. From Toulouse the Canal du Midi is connected with the Gardonne River leading west to the Atlantic Ocean at Bordeaux. See p357 for details on self-cruising boat rental agencies.

SEA

Provence has ferry links with Corsica, Italy and North Africa; boats sail to and from Nice, Toulon and Marseille.

Algeria

Travel in Algeria is considered dangerous for foreign tourists because of ongoing political troubles.

Algérie Ferries (www.algerieferries.com) operates ferries between Marseille and Algiers, Bejaia, Annaba, Skikda and Oran (20 hours). A single/return fare on any of these routes costs €162/300 for a *fauteuil* (armchair seat), and €250/450 in a four-bunk cabin. Children aged two to 12 and students get discounts. Transporting a car one-way/ return costs a hefty €475/760. Add another €5/7/9 in port taxes each way per armchair passenger/cabin passenger/vehicle.

Tickets are sold in Marseille by **Algérie Ferries** (☎ 04 91 90 64 70; 29 blvd des Dames), and in Algeria at **Algerian ports** (Algiers ☎ 021-747828; quai d'Ajaccio; Bejaia ☎ 034-202766; Annaba ☎ 021-423050).

Corsica

Corsica Ferries (☎ 08 25 09 50 95; www.corsicaferries .com) sails from Nice to Ajaccio (4½ hours), Bastia (five hours) and Calvi (three hours); and from Toulon to Ajaccio (six hours) and Bastia (eight hours). The basic single fare for a low-/high-season *fauteuil* is €29.50/45.50 (four to 12 years €14.50/30.50). Transporting a small car in low/high season costs €40/110. For port taxes see the following SNCM section. There are ticket offices at the **French ports** (Nice ☎ 04 92 00 42 93; Toulon ☎ 04 94 41 11 89) and the **Corsican ports** (Ajaccio ☎ 04 95 50 78 82; Bastia ☎ 04 95 32 95 95; Calvi ☎ 04 95 65 43 21).

Nearly all ferries between Provence (Marseille, Nice and Toulon) and Corsica (Ajaccio, Bastia, Calvi, Île-Rousse, Porto Vechio and Propriano) are handled by **Société Nationale Maritime Corse Méditerranée** (SNCM; ☎ 08 91 70 18 01; www.sncm.fr). Ferries run year-round from Nice and Marseille, and from April to October from Toulon.

Between Nice and the Corsican ports, a one-way passage in a *fauteuil* costs low/ high season €35/48 (ages four to 12 €18/22), and it's €40/58 (four to 12 years €12/24) to or from Marseille or Toulon. A small car costs between €40 and €108, depending on the season and port you depart from. Motorcycles under 100cc/bicycles cost €21/10. Add an additional €7.70 to €10.60 per passenger for port taxes, plus €6.50 to €9.30 per vehicle, depending on the port.

SNCM also operates a 70km/h express Navire à Grande Vitesse (NGV) from Nice to Calvi (2¾ hours) and Bastia (3½ hours), and from Toulon to Ajaccio (6½ hours). Fares command a €5 supplement in addition to the basic fares listed above for regular ferries. NGVs cannot sail in bad weather.

In July and August advance reservations are essential. Tickets in Corsica are sold from the **SNCM offices** (Ajaccio ☎ 04 95 29 66 69/63; 3 quai l'Herminier; Bastia ☎ 04 95 54 66 99/60; New Port; Calvi ☎ 04 95 65 01 38, 04 95 65 17 77; quai Landry). In France, contact the SNCM offices in Nice, Marseille or Toulon (see relevant chapters for details).

Italy

SNCM (p355) runs two or three car ferries weekly from Marseille or Toulon to Porto Torres on the Italian island of Sardinia (Sardaigne in French). Sailing time is 17 hours.

A one-way passage in a *fauteuil* costs €64/74 in low/high season (four to 12 years €37/43). There are discounts for passengers aged 12 to 25, InterRail Pass holders and those aged over 60. Transporting a car costs an extra €59/104. Port taxes are an additional €2/2.85 per passenger departing from Marseille/Toulon, plus €2.93/4.09 per vehicle.

Tickets and information are available from SNCM offices in Provence. In Sardinia, tickets are sold by SNCF agent **Paglietti Petertours** (☎ 079-51 44 77; Corso Vittorio Emanuele 19) in Porto Torres.

Tunisia

SNCM (see p355) and Tunisian **CTN** (Compagnie Tunisienne de Navigation; ☎ 216-135 33 31; 122 rue de Yougoslavie, Tunis) together operate car ferries between Marseille/Toulon and Tunis (20 to 22 hours). A one-way *fauteuil* costs €144 (two to 16 years €72) year-round. If you're taking a vehicle (€344), it's vital to book ahead. Taxes from either port are €8/5 per passenger/vehicle.

UK & Ireland

There are no direct ferries to Provence, but you can take a ferry year-round from Dover to Calais or from Folkestone to Boulogne (the shortest and cheapest crossings). Longer channel crossings include Newhaven–Dieppe, Poole–Cherbourg, and Portsmouth–Cherbourg/Le Havre/Ouistreham/St-Malo. Fares vary crazily according to demand. Some companies and their routes:

Brittany Ferries (www.brittany-ferries.co.uk; France ☎ 08 25 82 88 28; Ireland ☎ 021-427 7801; UK ☎ 08703 665 333) Poole–Cherbourg (4½ hours), Portsmouth–Caen (5¾ hours), Portsmouth–Cherbourg (six hours), Portsmouth–St-Malo (10½ hours), Plymouth–Roscoff (six hours), Cork–Roscoff (14 hours).

Condor Ferries (www.condorferries.co.uk; St-Malo ☎ 02 99 20 03 00; UK ☎ 084-5345 2000) Weymouth/Poole–St-Malo with change of vessel in Guernsey (5½ hours), Poole–Cherbourg (4½ hours).

Hoverspeed (www.hoverspeed.co.uk; France ☎ 08 20 00 35 55; UK ☎ 0870 240 8070) Nippy SeaCat catamarans: Dover–Calais (one hour), Newhaven–Dieppe SuperSeaCats (two hours).

Irish Ferries (www.irishferries.ie; Cherbourg ☎ 02 33 23 44 44; Ireland ☎ 01-661 0715; Roscoff ☎ 02 98 61 17 17; UK ☎ 099-0171 717) Rosslare–Roscoff (15 hours), Rosslare–Cherbourg (17 hours).

P&O Portsmouth (www.poportsmouth.com; France ☎ 08 25 01 30 13; UK ☎ 0870 520 20 20) Portsmouth–Le Havre (six to 8¼ hours), Portsmouth–Cherbourg (5½ to 7½ hours).

P&O Stena Line (www.posl.com; France ☎ 08 20 010 020; UK reservations ☎ 0870 600 0600, info ☎ 0870 600 0611) Dover–Calais (1½ hours), Portsmouth–Le Havre (seven hours), Portsmouth–Cherbourg (six hours).

SeaFrance (www.seafrance.com; Calais ☎ 08 03 04 40 45 office hr, ☎ 03 21 46 80 00 weekends & evenings; UK ☎ 0870 5711 711) Dover–Calais.

GETTING AROUND

AIR

There are no scheduled, interregional plane flights within Provence, but increasing numbers of high-flyers are taking to the air by helicopter. A handy online source of helicopter information is **Héli Riviera** (www.heliriviera.com).

BICYCLE

Provence – particularly the Lubéron – is an eminently cyclable region, thanks to its extensive network of inland back roads with relatively light traffic. They're an ideal way to view Provence's celebrated lavender fields, vineyards and olive groves. On the coast there are several excellent cycle paths; see individual chapters for information. Cycling in national parks in Provence (Mercantour and Port-Cros) is forbidden.

By law your bicycle must have two functioning brakes, a bell, a red reflector on the back and yellow reflectors on the pedals. After sunset and when visibility is poor, cyclists must turn on a white light in front and a red one in the rear. Cyclists must ride in single file when being overtaken.

Bicycles are forbidden on most buses, but can be taken on local TER trains in the Provence-Alpes-Côte d'Azur region, except at peak times. For transporting bikes on national train routes, see p353.

BOAT
Canal Boat
One of the most relaxing ways to see the region is to rent a houseboat and cruise along the Camargue's canals and rivers. Boats usually accommodate two to 12 passengers and can be rented on a weekly basis. Anyone over 18 can pilot a river boat without a licence: learning the ropes takes about half an hour. The speed limit is 6km/h on canals and 10km/h on rivers.

The following companies rent boats in Provence. Prices are for July and August; rates drop by around a third in low season.

Crown Blue Line Camargue (☎ 04 66 87 22 66; www.crownblueline.com; 2 quai du Canal, F-30800 St-Gilles) Rates around €2470 per week for a six-berth boat.

Rive de France (☎ 04 66 53 81 21; www.rive-de-france .tm.fr; Péniche St-Louis, rte de Grau de Roi, F-30220 Aigues-Mortes) Rates around €1750 per week for a six-berth boat.

Ferry
A plethora of boats ply the waters from the shores of the Côte d'Azur to its various offshore islands. Daily ferries sail as follows (for schedules and prices, see the individual chapters).

- Île du Levant (Îles d'Hyères) to and from Le Lavandou and Hyères (year-round), Port Miramar, La Croix-Valmer and Cavalaire-sur-Mer (July and August)
- Île de Bendor to and from Bandol (year-round)
- Île des Embiez to and from Le Brusc (year-round) and Sanary-sur-Mer (June to September)

- Îles du Frioul to and from Marseille (year-round)
- Îles de Lérins to and from Cannes (year-round), Juan-les-Pins (May to October) and Vallauris/Golfe-Juan (May to October)
- Porquerolles (Îles d'Hyères) to and from Le Lavandou and Hyères (year-round), Ste-Maxime and St-Tropez (April to September), Port Miramar, La Croix Valmer, Cavalaire and Toulon (July and August)
- Port-Cros (Îles d'Hyères) to and from Le Lavandou or Hyères (year-round), Ste-Maxime or St-Tropez (April to September), Port Miramar, La Croix-Valmer, Cavalaire-sur-Mer and Toulon (July and August)

From St-Tropez there are additional boat services to and from St-Raphaël (April to October), Port Grimaud and Ste-Maxime (April to October).

Yacht
One of Europe's largest *ports de plaisance* (pleasure ports) is Port Vauban in Antibes.

Yachts with or without a crew can be hired at most marinas along the coast, including the less-pompous sailing centres at Ste-Maxime and Le Lavandou. A complete list of yacht-rental places is included in the free booklet *Nautisme: Côte d'Azur Riviera* published by the Comité Régional du Tourisme Riviera Côte d'Azur (available from tourist offices).

For up-to-date marina or harbour master information, contact the **Fédération Française des Ports de Plaisance** (FFPP; ☎ 01 43 35 26 26; www .ffports-plaisance.com).

BUS
Services and routes are extremely limited in rural areas. Bus services are more efficient between towns served by only a few trains (or none at all); for example, there are several daily trains between Marseille and Aix-en-Provence, but buses speed between the two towns approximately every 30 minutes.

Autocars (regional buses) are operated by a muddling host of different bus companies, which usually have an office at the *gare routière* (bus station) in the cities they serve. One company generally sells tickets for all the buses operating from the same station.

CAR & MOTORCYCLE

Having your own wheels is vital to discover the region's least touched backwaters. Numerous treasures tucked in Haute-Provence's nooks and crannies are impossible to uncover by public transport. Except in the traffic-plagued high season, it's easy to drive on the Côte d'Azur.

Car drivers are required by French law to carry a national ID card or passport; a valid *permis de conduire* (driving permit or licence); car-ownership papers, known as a *carte grise* (grey card); and proof of insurance, called a *carte verte* (green card). If you're stopped by the police and don't have one or more of these documents, you risk a hefty on-the-spot fine.

Autoroutes are the fastest roads (in this region, the A8 *autoroute* runs from near Aix-en-Provence to Ventimiglia). *Routes nationales* are wide, well-signposted highways, *routes départementales* are local roads, and *chemins communaux* are narrow rural roads. Tolls are charged on almost all *autoroutes;* for sample costs and distances between towns and cities in the region, see the table below. *Autoroutes* in southern France are managed by the **Autoroutes du Sud de la France** (☎ 04 90 32 90 05; www.asf.fr) and the **Société des Autoroutes Estérel Côte d'Azur-Provence-Alpes** (☎ 08 36 69 36 36; www.escota.com). The national **Association des Sociétés Françaises d'Autoroutes** (www.autoroutes.fr) has an excellent website with masses of traffic-related information.

Bring Your Own Vehicle

If you bring your own vehicle to France, you'll need registration papers, unlimited third-party liability insurance and a valid driving licence. In the UK, contact the **RAC** (☎ 0906 470 1470; www.rac.co.uk) or the **AA** (☎ 0870 600 0371; www.theaa.com) for more advice. In other countries, contact your appropriate automobile association.

Vehicles entering France must display a sticker identifying their country of registration. A right-hand drive vehicle brought from the UK or Ireland has to have deflectors fitted to the headlights to avoid dazzling oncoming traffic. A reflective warning triangle, to be used in the event of breakdown, must be carried in your car.

Road Distances (km) & Road Tolls (euro)

Key: km (€)

	Aix/Marseille	Avignon	Cannes	Nice	Nîmes	Menton	Monaco	Orange	Toulon
Avignon	98 / 4.40								
Cannes	166 / 11.50	226 / 15.90							
Nice	205 / 14	262 / 18.40	34 / 2.50						
Nîmes	123 / 4.80	50 / 1.50	250 / 16.30	279 / 18.80					
Menton	236 / 17	287 / 21.40	66 / 5.50	30 / 1.80	315 / 21.80				
Monaco	228 / 17.30	285 / 21.70	58 / 5.80	20 / 2.10	310 / 22.10	12 / 1.10			
Orange	115 / 7.70	29 / 1.10	243 / 17.40	274 / 19.90	56 / 2.60	304 / 22.90	302 / 23.20		
Toulon	65 / 4.40	160 / 10.70	120 / 7.30	143 / 9.80	185 / 8.10	180 / 12.80	170 / 13.10	177 / 12.20	
Bordeaux	648 / 46.20	573 / 37.60	775 / 52.40	804 / 54.90	532 / 35.50	836 / 57.90	834 / 58.20	584 / 39.20	712 / 44.20
Calais	1071 / 77	982 / 70.40	1204 / 75.10	1232 / 77.60	1011 / 60.70	1259 / 80.60	1255 / 80.90	955 / 57.30	1133 / 66.90
Lyons	328 / 19.30	231 / 16.50	448 / 31.10	473 / 33.60	253 / 16.70	504 / 36.60	502 / 36.90	202 / 13.30	380 / 22.90
Paris	781 / 56.10	692 / 41.60	911 / 57.60	941 / 60.10	720 / 43.20	966 / 63.10	965 / 63.40	615 / 39.80	842 / 49.40
Toulouse	407 / 25.40	331 / 22.10	534 / 36.90	562 / 39.40	291 / 20	595 / 42.40	586 / 42.70	342 / 23.70	470 / 28.70

TRANSPORT

Driving Licence

You are not required to have an international driving licence in France; your domestic licence alone will do.

Fuel & Spare Parts

Be warned that many service stations close on Saturday afternoon and Sunday. Some petrol pumps stay open after hours, but you have to pay by credit card. Fuel is most expensive at *autoroute* service stations and cheapest at supermarkets.

There are Peugeot, Renault and Citroën garages everywhere, but if you've brought your own non-French car to France, you may have trouble with repairs in more remote areas.

Hire

Try to prebook your vehicle, which always works out cheaper. If you've left it too late, national French firms like ADA or National-Citer tend to be better value than international companies.

ADA (☎ 08 25 16 91 69; www.ada-sa.fr in French)

Auto Europe (☎ 1 888 223 5555; www.autoeurope.com) US-based hire company.

Avis (☎ 08 20 05 05 05; www.avis.com)

Budget (☎ 08 25 00 35 64 www.budget.com)

Easycar (UK ☎ 0906 33 33 33 3; www.easycar.com)

Europcar (☎ 08 25 35 93 59; www.europcar.com)

Hertz (☎ 01 41 91 95 25; www.hertz.com)

Holiday Autos (☎ 0870 530 0400; www.holidayautos.co.uk) UK-based online hire company.

National-Citer (☎ 08 25 16 12 12. www.citer.com in French)

Whoever you rent from, be sure that you understand what your liabilities are and what's included in the price (injury insurance, tax, collision damage waiver etc), and how many 'free' kilometres you'll get. *Kilométrage illimité* (unlimited mileage) means you can drive to your heart's content.

Most rental companies require the driver to be over 21 years and have had a driving licence for at least one year. You'll probably be asked to leave a signed credit-card slip without a sum written on it as a *caution* (deposit). Make sure it's destroyed when you return the car.

Insurance

Unlimited third-party liability insurance is mandatory for all automobiles. If you rent a car, this will be included in the package; however, collision damage waivers (CDW) vary greatly between rental companies. When comparing rates, the most important thing to check is the *franchise* (excess/deductible), which is usually €500 for a small car. If you're in an accident where you are at fault, or the car is stolen or damaged by an unknown party, this is the amount you are liable for before the policy kicks in. Some US credit-card companies (such as Amex) have built-in CDW, although you may have to pay up, then reclaim the money when you get home.

Road Conditions

If you're planning to drive along the coast in July or August, be prepared to take hours to move a few kilometres. For traffic reports in English, tune into 107.7MHz FM, which gives updates every 30 minutes in summer.

Road Rules

Drive on the right side of the road and overtake on the left. Under the *priorité à droite* rule, any car entering an intersection (including a T-junction) from a road on your right has right of way, unless the intersection is marked '*vous n'avez pas la priorité*' (you do not have right of way) or '*cédez le passage*' (give way). North American drivers should remember that turning right on a red light is illegal in France.

All passengers, including those in the back seat, must wear seatbelts. Babies under nine months of age must be carried in a rear-facing baby seat (which cannot be placed on the front passenger seat of the car if the car has airbags) or carrycot. Children aged between nine months and three years must be seated in a baby seat. Children aged between three and 10 years must be seated in a booster seat.

Using a mobile phone while driving can incur a fine of €22 to €150 and two points on your licence. Mobile phones may only be used with a hands-free kit or speakerphone.

It was compulsory in France for the first time in winter 2004–05 for motorists to have their headlights turned on night and day. A decision is expected to be made in 2005, following the trial period, as to whether this will become law.

Helmets are compulsory for anyone riding a two-wheeled vehicle with a motor. Bikes of more than 125cc must have their headlights on during the day.

In forested areas such as the Massif des Maures, Massif de l'Estérel and Haute-Provence, unpaved tracks signposted DFCI (*défense forestière contre l'incendie*) are for fire crews to gain quick entry in the event of a fire: they are strictly off limits to private vehicles.

ALCOHOL
It is illegal to drive with a blood-alcohol concentration (BAC) of over 0.05% (0.5g per litre of blood) – the equivalent of two glasses of wine. The police conduct frequent random Breathalyser tests.

SPEED LIMITS
Unless otherwise signposted, a speed limit of 50km/h applies in *all* areas designated as built up, no matter how rural they may appear to be. On intercity roads, you must slow to 50km/h the moment you pass a white sign with red borders on which a place name is written in black or blue letters. This remains in force until you pass an identical sign – but with a red diagonal bar across the name – on the other side of town.

Outside built-up areas, speed limits are 90km/h (80km/h in the rain) on undivided N and D highways, 110km/h (100km/h in the rain) on dual carriageways (divided highways) or short sections of highway with a divider strip, and 130km/h (110km/h in the rain, 60km/h in icy conditions) on *autoroutes*.

TRAIN
The SNCF's regional rail network in Provence, served by **TER** (www.ter-sncf.com/paca), is comfortable and efficient. It comprises two routes: one that follows the coast (disappearing inland for the stretch between Hyères and St-Raphaël) and another that traverses the interior, running from Marseille through Aix-en-Provence, Manosque and Sisteron before leaving the region northwards. There's also a narrow-gauge railway linking Nice with Digne-les-Bains

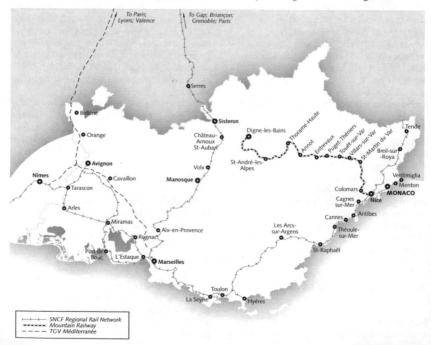

SNCF Regional Rail Network
Mountain Railway
TGV Méditerranée

in Haute-Provence (see Along the Mountain Railway, p194).

Indispensable for anyone doing a lot of train travel, the *Guide Régional des Transports* is a free booklet of interregional rail and SNCF bus schedules available at larger train stations.

It's important that you time-stamp your ticket in a *composteur* (an orange post at the entrance to the platform) before boarding or you risk a stiff fine.

Reservations

Reservations are not mandatory on most regional trains. However, in summer it's advisable to buy your ticket for any straight-through trains well in advance.

Train Passes

Two regional passes are available to travellers of all ages, from July to September.

Carte Isabelle (€11) One-day pass allowing unlimited train travel along the coast between Théoule-sur-Mer and Ventimiglia, and inland between Nice and Tende. Cannot be used on TGVs. Allows you to sit in 1st class for no extra.

Côte Bleue (€5) Weekend pass giving unlimited 2nd-class travel between Marseille and Miramas.

For countrywide SNCF discounts and rail passes, see the boxed text on p354.

Health

Travel health depends on your predeparture preparations, your daily health care while travelling and how you handle any medical problem that does develop. Provence and the Côte d'Azur are healthy places to travel. Your main risks are likely to be sunburn, foot blisters, insect bites and mild stomach problems from eating and drinking too much.

BEFORE YOU GO

Prevention is the key to staying healthy while abroad. A little planning before departure, particularly for pre-existing illnesses, will save trouble later. See your dentist before a long trip, carry a spare pair of contact lenses and glasses, and take your optical prescription with you. Bring medications in their original, clearly labelled, containers. A signed and dated letter from your physician describing your medical conditions and medications, including generic names, is also a good idea. If carrying syringes or needles, be sure to have a physician's letter documenting their medical necessity.

INSURANCE

If you're an EU citizen or from Switzerland, Iceland, Norway or Liechtenstein, the European Health Insurance Card will cover you for emergency health care or in the case of accident while in the region. It will not cover you for nonemergencies or emergency repatriation. This card is being phased in from mid-2004 and will be fully operational by the end of 2005. Old documentation (such as the previously used E111) will be available in the interim. Every family member will need a separate card. In the UK, application forms are available from post offices or can be downloaded from the Department of Health website (www.dh.gov.uk).

Citizens of other countries should find out if there is a reciprocal arrangement for free medical care between their country and the country visited. If you do need health insurance, strongly consider a policy that covers you for the worst possible scenario, such as an accident requiring an emergency flight home. Find out in advance if your insurance plan will make payments directly to providers or reimburse you later for overseas health expenditures.

RECOMMENDED VACCINATIONS

No vaccinations are required to travel to Provence and the Côte d'Azur. However, the World Health Organization (WHO) recommends that all travellers should be covered for diphtheria, tetanus, measles, mumps, rubella and polio, regardless of their destination.

IN TRANSIT

DEEP VEIN THROMBOSIS (DVT)

Blood clots may form in the legs during plane flights, chiefly because of prolonged immobility. The longer the flight, the greater the risk. The chief symptom of DVT is swelling or pain of the foot, ankle or calf, usually but not always on just one side. When a blood clot travels to the lungs, it may cause chest pain and breathing difficulties. Travellers with any of these symptoms should immediately seek medical attention.

To prevent the development of DVT on long flights you should walk about the cabin, contract the leg muscles while sitting, drink plenty of fluids and avoid alcohol and tobacco.

JET LAG
To avoid jet lag (common when crossing more than five time zones) try drinking plenty of nonalcoholic fluids and eating light meals. Upon arrival, get exposure to natural sunlight and readjust your schedule (for meals, sleep and so on) as soon as possible.

IN PROVENCE & THE CÔTE D'AZUR

AVAILABILITY & COST OF HEALTH CARE
Excellent health care is readily available and for minor illnesses pharmacists can give valuable advice and sell over-the-counter medications. They can also advise when more specialised help is required and point you in the right direction. The standard of dental care is usually good, however, it is sensible to have a dental check-up before a long trip.

When you ring ☎ 15, the 24-hour dispatchers of the Service d'Aide Médicale d'Urgence (SAMU; Emergency Medical Aid Service) take details of your problem and send out a private ambulance with a driver or, if necessary, a mobile intensive-care unit. For less serious problems SAMU can dispatch a doctor for a house call. If you prefer to be taken to a particular hospital, mention this to the ambulance crew, as the usual procedure is to take you to the nearest one. In emergency cases (those requiring intensive-care units), billing will be taken care of later. Otherwise, you need to pay in cash at the time.

If your problem is not sufficiently serious to call SAMU, but you still need to consult a doctor at night, call the 24-hour doctor service, operational in most towns in the region. Telephone numbers are listed in the relevant town sections under Medical Services, or see the Quick Reference page on the inside back cover.

DIARRHOEA
If you develop diarrhoea, be sure to drink plenty of fluids, preferably an oral rehydration solution (eg Dioralyte). If diarrhoea is bloody, persists for more than 72 hours

or is accompanied by fever, shaking, chills or severe abdominal pain you should seek medical attention.

ENVIRONMENTAL HAZARDS
Hay Fever
Those who suffer from hay fever can look forward to sneezing their way around rural Provence in May and June when the pollen count is at its highest.

Heat Exhaustion
Heat exhaustion occurs following excessive fluid loss with inadequate replacement of fluids and salt. Symptoms include headache, dizziness and tiredness. Dehydration is already happening by the time you feel thirsty – aim to drink sufficient water to produce pale, diluted urine. To treat heat exhaustion, replace lost fluids by drinking water and/or fruit juice, and cool the body with cold water and fans.

Hypothermia
Proper preparation will reduce the risks of getting hypothermia. Even on a hot day in the mountains the weather can change rapidly; carry waterproof garments and warm layers, and inform others of your route.

Acute hypothermia follows a sudden drop in temperature over a short time. Chronic hypothermia is caused by a gradual loss of temperature over hours.

Hypothermia starts with shivering, loss of judgment and clumsiness. Unless rewarming occurs, the sufferer deteriorates into apathy, confusion and coma. Prevent further heat loss by seeking shelter, warm dry clothing, hot sweet drinks and shared bodily warmth.

Insect Bites & Stings
Mosquitoes are found in most parts of Europe. They may not carry malaria but can cause irritation and infected bites. Use a DEET-based insect repellent.

Sand flies are found around the Mediterranean beaches. They usually cause only a nasty itchy bite but can carry a rare skin disorder called cutaneous leishmaniasis.

SEXUAL HEALTH
Emergency contraception is available with a doctor's prescription in the region. Condoms are readily available. When buying condoms, look for a European CE mark,

which means they have been rigorously tested, and then keep them in a cool dry place or they may crack and perish.

TRAVELLING WITH CHILDREN

All travellers with children should know how to treat minor ailments and when to seek medical treatment. Make sure the children are up to date with routine vaccinations, and discuss possible travel vaccines well before departure as some vaccines are not suitable for children under a year.

If your child has vomiting or diarrhoea, lost fluids and salts must be replaced. It may be helpful to take rehydration powders for reconstituting with boiled water.

WOMEN'S HEALTH

Emotional stress, exhaustion and travelling through different time zones can all contribute to an upset in the menstrual pattern. If using oral contraceptives, remember some antibiotics, diarrhoea and vomiting can stop the pill from working and lead to the risk of pregnancy – remember to take condoms with you just in case. Time zones, gastrointestinal upsets and antibiotics do not affect injectable contraception.

Travelling during pregnancy is usually possible but always consult your doctor before planning your trip. The most risky times for travel are during the first 12 weeks of pregnancy and after 30 weeks.

HEALTH

Language

CONTENTS

Arming yourself with some French will broaden your travel experience, endear you to the locals and, in rural Haute-Provence (where tourism hasn't yet developed enough to persuade people in service industries to speak English), ensure an easier ride around the region. On the coast, practically everyone you are likely to meet speaks basic English (and, in many cases, a rash of other European languages).

Standard French is taught and spoken in Provence. However, travellers accustomed to schoolbook French, or the unaccented, strait-laced French spoken in cities and larger towns, will find the flamboyant French spoken in Provence's rural heart (and by the majority of people in Marseille) somewhat bewildering. Here, words are caressed by the heavy southern accent and end with a flourish, vowels are sung, and the traditional rolling 'r' is turned into a mighty long trill. The word *douze* (the number 12), for example, becomes 'douz-eh' with an emphasised 'e', and *pain* (bread) becomes 'peng'. Once your ears become accustomed to the local lilt you'll soon start picking up the beat.

PROVENÇAL

Despite the bilingual signs that visitors see when they enter most towns and villages, the region's mother tongue – Provençal – is scarcely heard on the street or in the home. Just a handful of older people in rural Provence *(Prouvènço)* keep alive the rich lyrics and poetic language of their ancestors.

Provençal *(prouvençau* in Provençal) is a dialect of *langue d'oc* (Occitan), the traditional language of southern France. Its grammar is closer to Catalan and Spanish than to French. In the grand age of courtly love between the 12th and 14th centuries, Provençal was the literary language of France and northern Spain and even used as far afield as Italy. Medieval troubadours and poets created melodies and elegant poems motivated by the ideal of courtly love, and Provençal blossomed.

The 19th century witnessed a revival of Provençal after its rapid displacement by *langue d'oïl*, the language of northern France that originated from the vernacular Latin spoken by the Gallo-Romans and which gave birth to modern French *(francés* in Provençal). The revival was spearheaded by Frédéric Mistral (1830–1914), a poet from Vaucluse, whose works in Provençal won him the 1904 Nobel Prize for Literature.

FRENCH

PRONUNCIATION

Most of letters in the French alphabet are pronounced more or less the same as their English counterparts; a few that may cause confusion are listed below.

c	before **e** and **I**, as the 's' in 'sit'
	before **a**, **o** and **u** it's pronounced as English 'k'
ç	always as the 's' in 'sit'
h	always silent
j	as the 's' in 'leisure'; written 'zh' in the pronunciation guides'
r	from the back of the throat while constricting the muscles to restrict the flow of air

n, m where a syllable ends in a single **n** or **m**, these letters are not pronounced, but the preceding vowel is given a nasal pronunciation. Note that in the pronunciation guides, 'un' and 'on' are nasal sounds.

s often not pronounced in plurals or at the end of words

BE POLITE!

While the French rightly or wrongly have a reputation for assuming that all humans should speak French – until WWI it was the international language of culture and diplomacy – you'll find that any attempt you make to communicate in French will be very much appreciated.

What is often perceived as arrogance is often just a subtle objection to the assumption by many travellers that they should be able to speak English anywhere, and in any situation, and be understood. You can easily avoid the angst by approaching people politely, and addressing them in French. Even if the only sentence you can muster is *Pardon, madame/monsieur/mademoiselle, parlez-vous anglais?* (Excuse me, madam/sir/miss, do you speak English?), you're sure to be more warmly received than if you blindly address a stranger in English.

An important distinction is made in French between *tu* and *vous*, which both mean 'you'; *tu* is only used when addressing people you know well, children or animals. If you're addressing any adult who isn't a personal friend, *vous* should be used unless the person invites you to use *tu*. In general, younger people insist less on this distinction between polite and informal, and you will find that in many cases they use *tu* from the beginning of an acquaintance.

GENDER

All nouns in French are either masculine or feminine and adjectives reflect the gender of the noun they modify. The feminine form of many nouns and adjectives is indicated by a silent **e** added to the masculine form, as in *ami* and *amie* (the masculine and feminine for 'friend').

In the following phrases both masculine and feminine forms have been indicated where necessary. The masculine form comes first and is separated from the feminine by a slash. The gender of a noun is often indicated by a preceding article: 'the/a/some,' *le/un/du* (m), *la/une/de la* (f); or one of the possessive adjectives, 'my/your/his/her,' *mon/ton/son* (m), *ma/ta/sa* (f). With French, unlike English, the possessive adjective agrees in number and gender with the thing in question: 'his/her mother' is *sa mère*.

ACCOMMODATION

I'm looking for a ...
Je cherche ...   zher shersh ...
  camping ground
  un camping   un kom·peeng
  guesthouse
  une pension (de famille)   ewn pon·syon (der fa·mee·yer)
  hotel
  un hôtel   un o·tel
  youth hostel
  une auberge de jeunesse   ewn o·berzh der zher·nes

Where is a cheap hotel?
  Où est-ce qu'on peut trouver un hôtel pas cher?
  oo es·kon per troo·vay un o·tel pa shair
What is the address?
  Quelle est l'adresse?
  kel e la·dres
Could you write the address, please?
  Est-ce que vous pourriez écrire l'adresse, s'il vous plaît?
  e·sker voo poo·ryay e·kreer la·dres seel voo play
Do you have any rooms available?
  Est-ce que vous avez des chambres libres?
  e·sker voo·za·vay day shom·brer lee·brer

I'd like (a) ...
Je voudrais ...   zher voo·dray ...
  single room
  une chambre à un lit
    ewn shom·brer a un lee
  double-bed room
  une chambre avec un grand lit
  ewn shom·brer a·vek un gron lee
  twin room with two beds
  une chambre avec des lits jumeaux
  ewn shom·brer a·vek day lee zhew·mo
  room with a bathroom
  une chambre avec une salle de bains
  ewn shom·brer a·vek ewn sal der bun
  to share a dorm
  me coucher dans un dortoir
  me koo·sher don zun dor·twa

How much is it ...? *Quel est le prix ...?* kel e ler pree ...
| **per night** | *par nuit* | par nwee |
| **per person** | *par personne* | par per·son |

May I see it?
Est-ce que je peux voir   es·ker zher per vwa
la chambre?   la shom·brer
Where is the bathroom?
Où est la salle de bains?   oo e la sal der bun
Where is the toilet?
Où sont les toilettes?   oo·son lay twa·let
I'm leaving today.
Je pars aujourd'hui.   zher par o·zhoor·dwee
We're leaving today.
On part aujourd'hui.   on par o·zhoor·dwee

CONVERSATION & ESSENTIALS

Hello.	*Bonjour.*	bon·zhoor
Goodbye.	*Au revoir.*	o·rer·vwa
Yes.	*Oui.*	wee
No.	*Non.*	no
Please.	*S'il vous plaît.*	seel voo play
Thank you.	*Merci.*	mair·see
You're welcome.	*Je vous en prie.*	zher voo·zon pree
	De rien. (inf)	der ree·en
Excuse me.	*Excusez-moi.*	ek·skew·zay·mwa
Sorry. (forgive me)	*Pardon.*	par·don

What's your name?
Comment vous appelez-vous? (pol)
ko·mon voo·za·pay·lay voo
Comment tu t'appelles? (inf)
ko·mon tew ta·pel
My name is ...
Je m'appelle ...
zher ma·pel ...
Where are you from?
De quel pays êtes-vous? (pol)
der kel pay·ee et·voo
De quel pays es-tu? (inf)
der kel pay·ee e·tew
I'm from ...
Je viens de ...
zher vyen der ...
I like .../I don't like ...
J'aime .../Je n'aime pas ...
zhem .../zher nem pa ...
Just a minute.
Une minute.
ewn mee·newt

DIRECTIONS

Where is ...?
Où est ...?   oo e ...
Go straight ahead.
Continuez tout droit.   kon·teen·way too drwa
Turn left.
Tournez à gauche.   toor·nay a gosh
Turn right.
Tournez à droite.   toor·nay a drwat

at the corner/at traffic lights
au coin/aux feux   o kwun/o fer

behind	*derrière*	dair·ryair
in front of	*devant*	der·von
far (from)	*loin (de)*	lwun (der)
near (to)	*près (de)*	pray (der)
opposite	*en face de*	on fas der

SIGNS

Entrée	Entrance
Sortie	Exit
Renseignements	Information
Ouvert	Open
Fermé	Closed
Interdit	Prohibited
(Commissariat de)	Police Station
Police	
Toilettes/WC	Toilets
Hommes	Men
Femmes	Women

---

beach	*la plage*	la plazh
bridge	*le pont*	ler pon
castle	*le château*	ler sha·to
cathedral	*la cathédrale*	la ka·tay·dral
church	*l'église*	lay·gleez
island	*l'île*	leel
lake	*le lac*	ler lak
main square	*la place centrale*	la plas son·tral
museum	*le musée*	ler mew·zay
old city (town)	*la vieille ville*	la vyay veel
ruins	*les ruines*	lay rween
sea	*la mer*	la mair
square	*la place*	la plas
tourist office	*l'office de*	lo·fees der
	tourisme	too·rees·mer

HEALTH

I'm ill.
Je suis malade.   zher swee ma·lad
It hurts here.
J'ai une douleur ici.   zhay ewn doo·ler ee·see

I'm ...	*Je suis ...*	zher swee ...
asthmatic	*asthmatique*	(z)as·ma·teek
diabetic	*diabétique*	dee·a·be·teek
epileptic	*épileptique*	(z)e·pee·lep·teek

I'm allergic	*Je suis*	zher swee
to ...	*allergique ...*	za·lair·zheek ...
antibiotics	*aux antibiotiques*	o zon·tee·byo·teek
bees	*aux abeilles*	o za·bay·yer

nuts	*aux noix*	o nwa
peanuts	*aux cacahuètes*	o ka·ka·wet
penicillin	*à la pénicilline*	a la pay·nee· see·leen

antiseptic	*l'antiseptique*	lon·tee·sep·teek
condoms	*des préservatifs*	day pray·zair·va·teef
contraceptive	*le contraceptif*	ler kon·tra·sep·teef
diarrhoea	*la diarrhée*	la dee·ya·ray
medicine	*le médicament*	ler me·dee·ka·mon
nausea	*la nausée*	la no·zay
sunblock cream	*la crème solaire*	la krem so·lair
tampons	*des tampons hygiéniques*	day tom·pon ee·zhen·eek

EMERGENCIES

Help!
Au secours! o skoor

There's been an accident!
Il y a eu un accident! eel ya ew un ak·see·don

I'm lost.
Je me suis égaré/e. (m/f) zhe me swee·zay·ga·ray

Leave me alone!
Fichez-moi la paix! fee·shay·mwa la pay

Call ...!	*Appelez ...!*	a·play ...
a doctor	*un médecin*	un med·sun
the police	*la police*	la po·lees

LANGUAGE DIFFICULTIES

Do you speak English?
Parlez-vous anglais?
par·lay·voo ong·lay

Does anyone here speak English?
Y a-t-il quelqu'un qui parle anglais?
ya·teel kel·kung kee par long·glay

How do you say ... in French?
Comment est-ce qu'on dit ... en français?
ko·mon es·kon dee ... on fron·say

What does ... mean?
Que veut dire ...?
ker ver deer ...

I understand.
Je comprends.
zher kom·pron

I don't understand.
Je ne comprends pas.
zher ner kom·pron pa

Could you write it down, please?
Est-ce que vous pourriez l'écrire, s'il vous plaît?
es·ker voo poo·ryay le·kreer seel voo play

Can you show me (on the map)?
Pouvez-vous m'indiquer (sur la carte)?
poo·vay·voo mun·dee·kay (sewr la kart)

NUMBERS

0	*zero*	ze·ro
1	*un*	un
2	*deux*	der
3	*trois*	twa
4	*quatre*	ka·trer
5	*cinq*	sungk
6	*six*	sees
7	*sept*	set
8	*huit*	weet
9	*neuf*	nerf
10	*dix*	dees
11	*onze*	onz
12	*douze*	dooz
13	*treize*	trez
14	*quatorze*	ka·torz
15	*quinze*	kunz
16	*seize*	sez
17	*dix sept*	dee·set
18	*dix-huit*	dee·zweet
19	*dix-neuf*	deez·nerf
20	*vingt*	vung
21	*vingt et un*	vung tay un
22	*vingt-deux*	vung·der
30	*trente*	tront
40	*quarante*	ka·ront
50	*cinquante*	sung·kont
60	*soixante*	swa·sont
70	*soixante-dix*	swa·son·dees
80	*quatre-vingts*	ka·trer·vung
90	*quatre-vingt-dix*	ka·trer·vung·dees
100	*cent*	son
1000	*mille*	meel

PAPERWORK

name	*nom*	nom
nationality	*nationalité*	na·syo·na·lee·tay
date/place	*date/place*	dat/plas
of birth	*de naissance*	der nay·sons
sex/gender	*sexe*	seks
passport	*passeport*	pas·por
visa	*visa*	vee·za

QUESTION WORDS

Who?	*Qui?*	kee
What?	*Quoi?*	kwa
What is it?	*Qu'est-ce que c'est?*	kes·ker say
When?	*Quand?*	kon
Where?	*Où?*	oo
Which?	*Quel/Quelle?*	kel
Why?	*Pourquoi?*	poor·kwa
How?	*Comment?*	ko·mon
How much?	*Combien?*	kom·byun

SHOPPING & SERVICES

I'd like to buy ...
Je voudrais acheter ...   zher voo-dray zash-tay ...
I'm looking for ...
Je cherche ...   zhe shersh ...
How much is it?
C'est combien?   say kom-byun
I don't like it.
Cela ne me plaît pas.   ser-la ner mer play pa
May I look at it?
Est-ce que je peux le voir?   es-ker zher per ler vwar
I'm just looking.
Je regarde.   zher rer-gard
It's cheap.
Ce n'est pas cher.   ser nay pa shair
It's too expensive.
C'est trop cher.   say tro shair
I'll take it.
Je le prends.   zher ler pron

Can I pay by ...?
Est-ce que je peux payer avec ...?
es-ker zher per pay-yay a-vek ...
credit card
ma carte de crédit   ma kart der kre-dee
travellers cheques
des chèques de voyage   day shek der vwa-yazh

more	plus	plew
less	moins	mwa
smaller	plus petit	plew per-tee
bigger	plus grand	plew gron

a bank	une banque	ewn bonk
the ... embassy	l'ambassade de ...	lam-ba-sahd der ...
the hospital	l'hôpital	lo-pee-tal
the market	le marché	ler mar-shay
the police	la police	la po-lees
the post office	le bureau de poste	ler bew-ro der post
a public phone	une cabine téléphonique	ewn ka-been te-le-fo-neek
a public toilet	les toilettes	lay twa-let

TIME & DATES

What time is it? Quelle heure est-il? kel er e til
It's (8) o'clock. Il est (huit) heures. il e (weet) er
It's half past ... Il est (...) heures et il e (...) er e
demie. der-mee
It's quarter to ... Il est (...) heures il e (...) er
moins le quart. mwun ler kar

in the morning	du matin	dew ma-tun
in the afternoon	de l'après-midi	der la-pray-mee-dee
in the evening	du soir	dew swar

today	aujourd'hui	o-zhoor-dwee
tomorrow	demain	der-mun
yesterday	hier	yair

Monday	lundi	lun-dee
Tuesday	mardi	mar-dee
Wednesday	mercredi	mair-krer-dee
Thursday	jeudi	zher-dee
Friday	vendredi	von-drer-dee
Saturday	samedi	sam-dee
Sunday	dimanche	dee-monsh

January	janvier	zhon-vyay
February	février	fev-ryay
March	mars	mars
April	avril	a-vreel
May	mai	may
June	juin	zhwun
July	juillet	zhwee-yay
August	août	oot
September	septembre	sep-tom-brer
October	octobre	ok-to-brer
November	novembre	no-vom-brer
December	décembre	day-som-brer

TRANSPORT
Public Transport

What time does À quelle heure a kel er
... leave/arrive? part/arrive ...? par/a-reev ...
boat le bateau ler ba-to
bus le bus ler bews
plane l'avion la-vyon
train le train ler trun

I'd like a ... Je voudrais zher voo-dray
ticket. un billet ... un bee-yay ...
one-way simple sum-pler
return aller-retour a-lay rer-toor
1st class de première classe der prem-yair klas
2nd class de deuxième classe der der-zyem klas

I want to go to ...
Je voudrais aller à ...   zher voo-dray a-lay a ...
The train has been delayed.
Le train est en retard.   ler trun et on rer-tar

the first	le premier (m)	ler prer-myay
	la première (f)	la prer-myair
the last	le dernier (m)	ler dair-nyay
	la dernière (f)	la dair-nyair
platform	le numéro	ler new-may-ro
number	de quai	der kay
ticket office	le guichet	ler gee-shay
timetable	l'horaire	lo-rair
train station	la gare	la gar

LANGUAGE

Private Transport

I'd like to hire a/an...	Je voudrais louer ...	zher voo-dray loo-way ...
bicycle	un vélo	un vay-lo
car	une voiture	ewn vwa-tewr
4WD	un quatre-quatre	un kat-kat
motorbike	une moto	ewn mo-to

Is this the road to ...?
C'est la route pour ...?   say la root poor ...
Where's a service station?
Où est-ce qu'il y a   oo es-keel ya
une station-service?   ewn sta-syon-ser-vees
Please fill it up.
Le plein, s'il vous plaît.   ler plun seel voo play
I'd like ... litres.
Je voudrais ... litres.   zher voo-dray ... lee-trer

petrol/gas	essence	ay-sons
unleaded	sans plomb	son plom
leaded	au plomb	o plom
diesel	diesel	dyay-zel

ROAD SIGNS

Cédez la Priorité	Give Way
Danger	Danger
Défense de Stationner	No Parking
Entrée	Entrance
Interdiction de Doubler	No Overtaking
Péage	Toll
Ralentissez	Slow Down
Sens Interdit	No Entry
Sens Unique	One Way
Sortie	Exit

(How long) Can I park here?
(Combien de temps) Est-ce que je peux stationner ici?
(kom-byun der tom) es-ker zher per sta-syo-nay ee-see
I've run out of petrol.
Je suis en panne d'essence.
zher swee zon pan day-sons
I need a mechanic.
J'ai besoin d'un mécanicien.
zhay ber-zwun dun me-ka-nee-syun
The car/motorbike has broken down (at ...)
La voiture/moto est tombée en panne (à ...)
la vwa-tewr/mo-to ay tom-bay on pan (a ...)
The car/motorbike won't start.
La voiture/moto ne veut pas démarrer.
la vwa-tewr/mo-to ner ver pa day-ma-ray
I had an accident.
J'ai eu un accident.
zhay ew un ak-see-don

I have a flat tyre.
Mon pneu est à plat.
mom pner ay ta pla

TRAVEL WITH CHILDREN

Is there a/an ...?
Y a-t-il ...?   ya teel ...
I need a/an ...
J'ai besoin ...   zhay ber-zwun ...

baby change room
d'un endroit pour   dun on-drwa poor
changer le bébé   shon-zhay ler be-be
car baby seat
d'un siège-enfant   dun syezh-on-fon
child-minding service
d'une garderie   dewn gar-dree
children's menu
d'un menu pour enfant   dun mer-new poor on-fon
disposable nappies/diapers
de couches-culottes   der koosh-kew-lot
formula
de lait maternisé   de lay ma-ter-nee-zay
(English-speaking) babysitter
d'une babysitter (qui   dewn ba-bee-see-ter (kee
parle anglais)   parl ong-glay)
highchair
d'une chaise haute   dewn shay zot
potty
d'un pot de bébé   dun po der be-be
pusher/stroller
d'une poussette   dewn poo-set

Do you mind if I breastfeed here?
Cela vous dérange si j'allaite mon bébé ici?
ser-la voo day-ron-zhe see zha-lay-ter mon bay-bay ee-see
Are children allowed?
Les enfants sont permis?
lay zon-fon son pair-mee

Also available from Lonely Planet:
French Phrasebook

Glossary

Word gender is indicated as (m) masculine, (f) feminine;
(pl) indicates plural

abbaye (f) – abbey
anse (f) – cove
AOC – *appellation d'origine contrôlée;* wines and olive oils
that have met stringent government regulations governing
where, how and under what conditions the grapes or olives
are grown and the wines and olive oils are fermented and
bottled
arène (f) – amphitheatre
arrondissement (m) – one of several districts into which
large cities, such as Marseille, are split
atelier (m) – artisan's workshop
auberge (f) – inn
auberge de jeunesse (f) – youth hostel
autoroute (f) – motorway, highway

baie (f) – bay
bastide (f) – country house
billetterie (f) – ticket office or counter
borie (f) – primitive beehive-shaped dwelling, built from
dry limestone around 3500 BC
boulangerie (f) – bread shop, bakery
bureau de location (m) – ticket office

CAF – Club Alpin Français
calanque (f) – rocky inlet
carnet (m) – a book of five or 10 bus, tram or metro
tickets sold at a reduced rate
cave (f) – wine or cheese cellar
centre (de) hospitalier (m) – hospital
chambre d'hôte (f) – bed and breakfast accommodation, usually in a private home
charcuterie (f) – pork butcher's shop and delicatessen;
also cold meat
chateau (m) – castle or stately home
chèvre (m) – goat
col (m) – mountain pass
comité départemental du tourisme (m) – departmental tourist office
commissariat de police (m) – police station
conseil général (m) – general council
corniche (f) – coastal or cliff road
corrida (f) – bullfight
cour (f) – courtyard
cour d'honneur (f) – courtyard of honour
course Camarguaise (f) – Camargue-style bullfight
cueillette des olives (f) – olive harvest

dégustation (f) – the fine art of tasting wine, cheese,
olive oil or seafood
département (m) – administrative area (department)
DFCI – *défense forestière contre l'incendie;* fire road (public
access forbidden)
digue (f) – dike
domaine (m) – a wine-producing estate

eau potable (f) – drinking water
église (f) – church
épicerie (f) – grocery shop
étang (m) – lagoon, pond or lake

faïence (f) – earthenware
farandole (f) – a Provençal dance dating to the Middle
Ages, particularly popular in Arles today
féria (f) – bullfighting festival
ferme auberge (f) – family-run inn attached to a farm
or chateau; farmhouse restaurant
fête (f) – party or festival
flamant rose (m) – pink flamingo
formule (f) – fixed main course plus starter or dessert
fromagerie (f) – cheese shop

galets (m) – large smooth stones covering Châteauneuf
du Pape vineyards
gardian (m) – Camargue horseman
gare (f) – train station
gare maritime (m) – ferry terminal
gare routière (m) – bus station
garrigue (f) – ground cover of aromatic plants; see also
maquis
gitan (m) – Roma; Gypsy
gîte d'étape (m) – hikers accommodation, often found
in the mountains or rural areas
gîte rural (m) – country cottage
golfe (m) – gulf
grand cru (m) – wine of recognised superior quality;
literally 'great growth'
grotte (f) – cave

halles (f pl) – covered market; central food market
hôtel de ville (m) – town hall
hôtel particulier (m) – private mansion

jardin (botanique) (m) – (botanic) garden
joute nautiques (f) – nautical jousting tournament

lavoir (m) – communal wash house

mairie (f) – town hall
maison de la France (f) – French tourist office abroad
maison de la presse (f) – newsagent
manade (f) – bull farm
maquis (m) – aromatic Provençal scrub, see also *garrigue*; name given to the French Resistance movement
marais (m) – marsh or swamp
marais salant (m) – saltpan
marché paysan (m) – farmers market
marché Provençal (m) – open air market
mas (m) – Provençal farmhouse
menu (m) – meal at a fixed price with two or more courses
mistral (m) – incessant north wind
monastère (m) – monastery
Monégasque – native of Monaco
moulin à huile (m) – oil mill
musée (m) – museum

navette (f) – shuttle bus, train or boat
novillada (f) – fight between bulls less than four years old

office du tourisme, office de tourisme (m) – tourist office (run by a unit of local government)
ONF – Office National des Forêts; National Forests Office

papeterie (f) – stationery shop
parapente (f) – paragliding
parc national (m) – national park
parc naturel régional (m) – regional nature park
pétanque (f) – a Provençal game, not unlike lawn bowls
phare (m) – lighthouse
pic (m) – mountain peak
pied noir (m) – Algerian-born citizen
place (f) – square
plage (f) – beach
plan (m) – city map
plat du jour (m) – dish of the day
plongée (f) – dive
pont (m) – bridge
porte (f) – gate or door, old-town entrance
préfecture (f) – main town of a *département*
préfet (m) – prefect; regional representative of national government, based in a *préfecture*
presqu'île (f) – peninsula

prieuré (m) – priory
produits du terroir (m) – local food products

quai (m) – quay or railway platform
quartier (m) – quarter or district

rade (f) – gulf or harbour
refuge (m) – hikers shelter (mountain hut)
région (m) – administrative region
rollers (m) – Rollerblades
rond-point (m) – roundabout

salin (m) – salt marsh
santon (m) – traditional Provençal figurine
savon (f) – soap
savonnerie (f) – soap factory
sentier (m) – trail, footpath
sentier de grande randonnée (m) – long-distance path with alphanumeric name beginning with 'GR'
sentier littoral (m) – coastal path
sentier sous-marin (m) – underwater trail
SNCF – Société Nationale des Chemins de Fer; state-owned railway company
SNCM – Société Nationale Maritime Corse-Méditerranée; state-owned ferry company linking Corsica and mainland France
stade (m) – stadium
SRV – *sur rendez-vous;* by appointment only
syndicat d'initiative (m) – tourist office (run by an organisation of local merchants)

tabac (m) – tobacconist (also sells newspapers, bus tickets etc)
taureau (m) – bull
TGV – *train à grande vitesse*; high-speed train or bullet train
théâtre antique (m) – Roman theatre
tour d'horloge (f) – clock tower
trottinette (f) – microscooter

vendange (f) – grape harvest
vieille ville (f) – old town
vieux port (m) – old port
vigneron (m) – wine grower
vin de garde (m) – a wine best drunk after several years in storage
VTT (m) – *vélo tout terrain*; mountain bike

Behind the Scenes

THIS BOOK

This 4th edition of *Provence & the Côte d'Azur* was coordinated by Nicola Williams, who also wrote the introductory, Directory, Marseille Area, The Camargue, Avignon Area and The Lubéron chapters. Co-author Fran Parnell wrote the Haute-Provence, Nice to Menton, Cannes Area, St-Tropez to Toulon, Monaco and Transport chapters. Tony Wheeler wrote the boxed text 'The Fomula One Grand Prix'. Dr Caroline Evans contributed to the Health chapter. The 1st edition of *Provence & the Côte d'Azur* was written by Nicola Williams in 1999; she also updated the 2nd and 3rd editions.

THANKS FROM THE AUTHORS
NICOLA WILLIAMS

Far too many people to mention in this short paragraph passed on hot tips, revealed their favourite eating places/romantic hideaways and so on. An extra-special thank you to Christine Juillan at the Maison du Parc Régional de Camargue for her help (and excellent directions to Chez Marc et Mireille); Martine Louberel in Eyragues for a fabulous kid-friendly *gîte;* Martine di Gicco from Apt tourist office; the press and marketing department at Avignon tourist office; Marie Scherre in Le Barroux for an insightful lama tour; Tony Wheeler at LP for travelling with this guide and mailing feedback at breakneck speed; and co-author Fran for stepping in to save the day.

At home, oodles of *bisous* to the girls for running the crèche (thanks Mummy and Michelle!); Christa, Karl Otto, Peter and Marianne – ditto; Chiara, David, Martha and Vicky for coming along; and to the sweetest of sweet travelling companions, Matthias, Niko and Mischa Lüfkens.

FRAN PARNELL

Thanks to everyone who helped me in Provence. Especially sweet were the hotel staff at Toulon, the old lady who told me all about boar-hunting in the Maures, and Brigitte at Nice bus station. Gratitude to Marielle T for putting me up. I'm also indebted to helpful park and tourist offices across the region, in particular: the wolf experts at St-Étienne de Tinée; the kindly souls at Toulon and Collobrières; Patricia Mertzig at Menton; Deborah at Monaco; Frédérique at St-Tropez, all patient enough to answer endless questions in the height of the summer season; and to Ingrid Picquet at the wonderful Château de la Napoule.

Thanks to Nicola Williams for providing a fun and informative text to work from; to Sam Trafford for her virtual gin and editing expertise; and to Mark Griffiths for his carto communications.

Love to Mum and Dad (your phone calls kept me sane!) and to Billy (sorry for being a bat).

CREDITS

Provence & the Côte d'Azur 4 was commissioned in Lonely Planet's London office by Sam Trafford. The editing of this book was coordinated by Andrea Dobbin, with assistance from Kate James, Charlotte Orr, Helen Yeates, Sasha Baskett and Craig Kilburn. Cartography was coordinated by Celia Wood. Chris Love and Charles Rawlings-Way managed the project through production. The cover was designed by Maria Vallianos, and Wendy Wright

---

THE LONELY PLANET STORY

The story begins with a classic travel adventure: Tony and Maureen Wheeler's 1972 journey across Europe and Asia to Australia. There was no useful information about the overland trail then, so Tony and Maureen published the first Lonely Planet guidebook to meet a growing need.

From a kitchen table, Lonely Planet has grown to become the largest independent travel publisher in the world, with offices in Melbourne (Australia), Oakland (USA) and London (UK). Today Lonely Planet guidebooks cover the globe. There is an ever-growing list of books and information in a variety of media. Some things haven't changed. The main aim is still to make it possible for adventurous travellers to get out there – to explore and better understand the world.

At Lonely Planet we believe travellers can make a positive contribution to the countries they visit – if they respect their host communities and spend their money wisely. Every year 5% of company profit is donated to charities around the world.

prepared the artwork. The book was laid out by Sonya Brooke and David Kemp. Adriana Mammarella and Sally Darmody oversaw layout. The managing editors were Bruce Evans and Yvonne Byron; the managing cartographer was Alison Lyall. The language chapter was compiled by Quentin Frayne. Thanks also to Carol Chandler and Graham Imeson from Print Production. Many thanks and best wishes to Lisa Steer-Guérard.

THANKS from Lonely Planet

Many thanks to the following travellers who used the last edition and wrote to us with helpful hints, useful advice and interesting anecdotes.

C Cao, Romelle Castle, Kam Champaneri, Mike Clark, Alys & Jo Cummings, Mark Deverill, Laura & Ami Diner, Hans Engh, Gordon Fear, Tony Feeney, Robert Feldman, Lotta Fredstam, Christopher Gabel, Alyson & David Hilbourne, Andrew Killoran, Kathleen & Richard Kimball, Philip Littler, Sarah McDougall, Michael Moloff, Peter Monk, AP Moore, Rory Murray, Matt Newman, Jenny & John Pryce-Davies, Sophie Raniwala, Peter Rasmussen, Peter Rombach, Jon Sadler, Barb Satink, Diana Self, Ritva Siikala, Marianne & Kjetil Spernes, Barry Thompson, Lillian Todorov, Clare Tomlinson, Astrid Van Dijk, Mary Viola, Anna Watson, JM Whale, Amanda Wilkinson, Jo Wort, Matt Wort

SEND US YOUR FEEDBACK

We love to hear from travellers – your comments keep us on our toes and help make our books better. Our well-travelled team reads every word on what you loved or loathed about this book. Although we cannot reply individually to postal submissions, we always guarantee that your feedback goes straight to the appropriate authors, in time for the next edition. Each person who sends us information is thanked in the next edition – and the most useful submissions are rewarded with a free book.

To send us your updates – and find out about Lonely Planet events, newsletters and travel news – visit our award-winning website: **www.lonelyplanet.com/feedback**.

Note: We may edit, reproduce and incorporate your comments in Lonely Planet products such as guidebooks, websites and digital products, so let us know if you don't want your comments reproduced or your name acknowledged. For a copy of our privacy policy visit www.lonelyplanet.com/privacy.

Index

000 Map pages
000 Location of colour photographs

000 Map pages
000 Location of colour photographs

MAP LEGEND

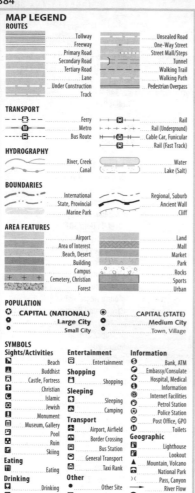

ROUTES

Tollway	Unsealed Road
Freeway	One-Way Street
Primary Road	Street Mall/Steps
Secondary Road	Tunnel
Tertiary Road	Walking Trail
Lane	Walking Path
Under Construction	Pedestrian Overpass
Track	

TRANSPORT

Ferry	Rail
Metro	Rail (Underground)
Bus Route	Cable Car, Funicular
	Rail (Fast Track)

HYDROGRAPHY

River, Creek	Water
Canal	Lake (Salt)

BOUNDARIES

International	Regional, Suburb
State, Provincial	Ancient Wall
Marine Park	Cliff

AREA FEATURES

Airport	Land
Area of Interest	Mall
Beach, Desert	Market
Building	Park
Campus	Rocks
Cemetery, Christian	Sports
Forest	Urban

POPULATION

○ **CAPITAL (NATIONAL)**	◉ **CAPITAL (STATE)**
● **Large City**	● **Medium City**
● Small City	○ Town, Village

SYMBOLS

Sights/Activities

Beach	
Buddhist	
Castle, Fortress	
Christian	
Islamic	
Jewish	
Monument	
Museum, Gallery	
Pool	
Ruin	
Skiing	

Eating

Eating	

Drinking

Drinking	
Café	

Entertainment

Entertainment	

Shopping

Shopping	

Sleeping

Sleeping	
Camping	

Transport

Airport, Airfield	
Border Crossing	
Bus Station	
General Transport	
Taxi Rank	

Other

Other Site	
Parking Area	

Information

Bank, ATM	
Embassy/Consulate	
Hospital, Medical	
Information	
Internet Facilities	
Petrol Station	
Police Station	
Post Office, GPO	
Toilets	

Geographic

Lighthouse	
Lookout	
Mountain, Volcano	
National Park	
Pass, Canyon	
River Flow	
Waterfall	

LONELY PLANET OFFICES

Australia
Head Office
Locked Bag 1, Footscray, Victoria 3011
☎ 03 8379 8000, fax 03 8379 8111
talk2us@lonelyplanet.com.au

USA
150 Linden St, Oakland, CA 94607
☎ 510 893 8555, toll free 800 275 8555
fax 510 893 8572, info@lonelyplanet.com

UK
72-82 Rosebery Ave,
Clerkenwell, London EC1R 4RW
☎ 020 7841 9000, fax 020 7841 9001
go@lonelyplanet.co.uk

Published by Lonely Planet Publications Pty Ltd
ABN 36 005 607 983

4th Edition – April 2005

First Published – June 1999